Managerial Economics

Managerial Economics

VANITA AGARWAL

Lakshmibai College
University of Delhi

Pearson

Assistant Editor–Acquisition: Debapriya Mukherjee
Associate Editor–Production: Ruchi Sachdev

ISBN: 978-81-317-7562-2

First Impression, 2013
Tenth Impression, 2024
Eleventh Impression, 2025

Published by Pearson India Education Services Pvt. Ltd, CIN: U72200TN2005PTC057128

Head Office: 1st Floor, Berger Tower, Plot No. C-001A/2, Sector 16B, Noida – 201 301,Uttar Pradesh, India.

Registered Office: Featherlite, 'The Address' 5th Floor, Survey No 203/10B, 200 Ft MMRD Road, Zamin Pallavaram, Chennai - 600044
Website: in.pearson.com; Email:companysecretary.india@pearson.com

Compositor: White Lotus Infotech Pvt. Ltd
Digitally printed in India by Trinity Academy for Corporate Training Ltd, New Delhi in the year of 2025.

To my parents

Contents

Preface xv
About the Author xvii

1 An Introduction to Managerial Economics: Nature and Scope **1**

Introduction 1
What Is Managerial Economics? 1
Differences Between Microeconomics and Macroeconomics, and Their Relation to Managerial Economics 3
Need to Study Managerial Economics 4
Applications of Managerial Economics 5
Managerial Economics and Business Economics: Ambiguity in the Use of the Two Terms 6
Summary • *Review Questions* • *Answers*

2 Objectives of a Business Firm, Decision Rules and the Process of Optimization **10**

Introduction 10
Objectives of a Business Firm 10
Profit Objective 11
Profit Theories 12
Profit Maximization: An Algebraic Explanation 13
Other Economic Objectives of a Firm 16
Non-economic Objectives 18
Profit: A Control Mechanism 18
Decision Rules 19
Process of Optimization 20
Summary • *Review Questions* • *Answers*

3 Demand, Elasticity of Demand and Elasticity of Supply **24**

Introduction 24
Demand 25
Supply 34
Equilibrium 38
Elasticity of Demand 40
Revenue Concepts 47
Income Elasticity of Demand 51
Cross Price Elasticity of Demand 53
Advertising Elasticity 54

Elasticity of Price Expectations 56
Elasticity of Supply 57
Summary • Review Questions • Answers

4 Demand Forecasting 68
Introduction 68
What Is Demand Forecasting? 68
Methods of Forecasting Demand 70
Conclusion 73
Summary • Review Questions • Answers

5 Cardinal Utility Approach 76
Introduction 76
Marshall's Utility Analysis 76
What Is Utility? 76
Concept of Cardinal and Ordinal Utilities 77
Cardinal Utility Approach 77
Law of Diminishing Marginal Utility 78
Law of Equi-marginal Utility 83
Limitations of the Cardinal Utility Approach 83
Summary • Review Questions • Answers

6 Ordinal Utility Approach: Indifference Curve Theory and Its Applications 88
Introduction 89
Assumptions of the Indifference Curve Theory 89
An Indifference Curve 90
Characteristics of an Indifference Curve 91
Exceptions: Complements and Substitutes 93
Budget Line of the Consumer 95
Shifts in the Budget Line 96
Consumer's Equilibrium 98
Changes in the Income Level: Income Consumption Curve 99
Changes in the Price Level: Price Consumption Curve 100
Price Effect: Substitution Effect and Income Effect 103
Derivation of the Demand Curve 105
Consumer Surplus 107
Limitations of the Indifference Curve Theory 108
A Comparison of Cardinal and Ordinal Utility Approaches 109
Applications of Indifference Curve Theory 110
Summary • Review Questions • Answers

7 Revealed Preference Theory **117**

Introduction 117
What Is Revealed Preference Theory? 117
Assumptions of Revealed Preference Theory 118
A Derivation of Demand Curve 119
An Evaluation of Revealed Preference Theory 120
Summary • *Review Questions* • *Answers*

8 Production Function **124**

Introduction 124
Basic Concepts 125
Production Function 126
Production: Short Run 127
Production: Long Run 129
Isoquants 130
Characteristics of Isoquants 131
Exceptions: Complements and Substitutes 132
Isocost Line 134
Equilibrium of the Producer 135
Expansion Path 138
Elasticity of Substitution 138
Economic Region of Production and Ridge Lines 139
Law of Returns to Scale 140
Summary • *Review Questions* • *Answers*

9 Cost Function **149**

Introduction 149
Some Basic Cost Concepts 149
Cost Function 151
Traditional Theory of Costs 151
Long-run Cost Analysis 156
Economies and Diseconomies of Scale 158
Break-even Analysis 161
Summary • *Review Questions* • *Answers*

10 Perfect Competition **169**

Introduction 169
Types of Market Structures and Pricing Decisions 169
Characteristics of Perfect Competition 170
Firm's Revenue Curves Under Perfect Competition 171
Short-run Equilibrium of a Firm 172

Long-run Equilibrium of a Firm 175
Applications of Perfect Competition 176
Summary • Review Questions • Answers

11 Monopoly and Monopolistic Competition **181**
Introduction 181
Monopoly 181
Types of Monopoly 182
Firm's Revenue Curves Under Monopoly 182
Short Equilibrium of a Firm 185
Long-run Equilibrium of a Firm 187
Price Discrimination 188
Control of Monopoly 191
Monopolistic Competition 192
Equilibrium of a Firm 193
Short-run Equilibrium of a Firm 194
Long-run Equilibrium of a Firm 196
Excess Capacity 196
Selling Costs 198
Summary • Review Questions • Answers

12 Oligopoly and Strategies of Pricing **204**
Introduction 204
Causes of Oligopoly 204
Characteristics of Oligopoly 205
Models of Non-Collusive Oligopoly 206
Sweezy's Kinked Demand Curve Model 208
Models of Collusive Oligopoly 210
Price Leadership 211
Games Theory and Prisoner's Dilemma 212
Summary • Review Questions • Answers

13 Capital Budgeting and the Decision to Invest **219**
Introduction 219
What Is Capital Budgeting? 219
Significance of Capital Budgeting 220
Steps in Capital Budgeting 220
Determination of the Optimum Level of Capital 221
Decision to Invest Under Certainty 223
Sources and the Cost of Capital 225
Decision to Invest Under Risk and Uncertainty 226
Summary • Review Questions • Answers

14 Theories of Distribution 234

Introduction 234
Wages 235
Wage Determination Under Perfect Competition 236
Supply of Labour 241
Rent 242
Ricardian Theory of Rent 242
Modern Theory of Rent 243
Profit 245
Risk Theory 246
Uncertainty Theory 247
Innovation Theory 247
Interest 248
Classical Theory 248
Neo-classical Theory 249
Keynesian Theory 252
Summary • Review Questions • Answers

15 General Equilibrium and Welfare Economics 261

Introduction 261
General Equilibrium of Production and Exchange 261
Welfare Economics 267
Utility Possibility Frontier 267
Social Welfare Function 269
Summary • Review Questions • Answers

16 National Income 273

Introduction 273
National Income Aggregates 273
Measurement of National Income 277
Problems in the Measurement of National Income, Especially in Underdeveloped Countries 280
Summary • Review Questions • Answers

17 Classical Model of Income Determination 287

Introduction 287
Background of Macroeconomics 287
Need to Study Macroeconomics 289
Concepts in Macroeconomics 290
Say's Law 294
Output and Employment in Classical Model 295
A Criticism of Classical Model 300
Summary • Review Questions • Answers

18 Keynesian Model of Income Determination in a Two-sector Economy, Shifts in Aggregate Demand and Multiplier **305**

Introduction 305
Aggregate Demand in a Two-sector Economy 306
Consumption 306
Saving as a Counterpart of the Consumption Function 309
Determination of Equilibrium Income or Output in a Two-sector Economy 312
Shifts in Aggregate Demand and Multiplier 317
Uses and Limitations of Multiplier 321
Applicability of Multiplier to LDCs 322
Multiplier and Paradox of Thrift 323
Summary • Review Questions • Answers

19 Keynesian Model of Income Determination in Three-sector and Four-sector Economies **336**

Introduction 336
Determination of Equilibrium Income or Output in a Three-sector Economy 337
First Model of Income Determination (Introducing Government Expenditure and Tax) 338
Second Model of Income Determination (Introducing Government Transfer Payments) 342
Third Model of Income Determination (Including Government Expenditures, Transfer Payments and Introducing Tax as a Function of the Income Level) 344
Multipliers in a Three-sector Economy–Fiscal Multipliers 345
Determination of Equilibrium Income or Output in a Four-sector Economy 348
Equilibrium Income and Output 350
Introduction of Government Transfer Payments in a Four-sector Model 351
Multiplier in a Four-sector Economy–Foreign Trade Multiplier 354
Summary • Review Questions • Answers

20 *IS–LM* Model for a Two-sector Economy **366**

Introduction 366
IS–LM Model in a Two-sector Economy 366
Goods Market Equilibrium in a Two-sector Economy: *IS* Curve 367
Money Market Equilibrium in a Two-sector Economy: *LM* Curve 369
Equilibrium in Two Markets: Goods Market and Money Market 372
Equilibrium in the Two Markets (Goods Market and Money Market): An Algebraic Explanation 375
Disequilibrium to Equilibrium: The Process of Adjustment 377
A Shift in *IS–LM* Curves 378
Summary • Review Questions • Answers

21 Theories of Investment Spending **391**

Introduction 391
Basic Concepts 392
Decision to Invest 394
Marginal Efficiency of Capital 397
Marginal Efficiency of Investment 400
Changes in the Rate of Interest, MEC and Capital Accumulation 402
Theories of Investment 405
Summary • Review Questions • Answers

22 Economic Growth, Business Cycles and Stabilization Policy **413**

Introduction 413
Economic Growth 414
Factors Determining Economic Growth 414
Theories of Economic Growth 415
Business Cycles and Stabilization 421
Summary • Review Questions • Answers

23 Theory of International Trade, Trade Policy and Foreign Exchange **436**

Introduction 437
Classical Approach 437
Heckscher–Ohlin Theory of Trade 441
Terms of Trade 445
Trade Policy 447
Foreign Exchange Market 448
Exchange Rate Systems 450
Exchange Rate Determination 451
Fixed Versus Flexible Exchange Rate 458
Summary • Review Questions • Answers

24 Balance of Payments and the International Monetary System **466**

Introduction 466
Meaning and Structure of Balance of Payments 467
Double Entry Bookkeeping 471
Disequilibrium in the Balance of Payments 473
Kinds of Disequilibria in the Balance of Payments 474
Process of Adjustment in the Balance of Payments 476
Performance of Indian Economy in the External Sector 482
International Monetary System 484
Summary • Review Questions • Answers

25 Monetary Policy and Fiscal Policy **492**

Introduction 492
Monetary Policy 493
Instruments of Monetary Policy 493
Limitations of Monetary Policy 503
Fiscal Policy 504
Instruments of Fiscal Policy 504
Full Employment Budget Surplus 506
Limitations of Fiscal Policy 509
Crowding Out and Its Importance 510
Banking Sector 512

Summary • Review Questions • Answers

Glossary 528
Index 537

Preface

It is increasingly being recognized that teaching economics helps business students better appreciate and envisage the economic forces that shape decisions in the real business world besides developing and strengthening the overall analytical talent of students.

Now business schools, both at undergraduate and postgraduate levels, worldwide and in India ensure that students undertake suitable courses in economics. Managerial economics mainly introduces topics in microeconomics and macroeconomics to students to enable them to apply the same to business decisions. The purpose of teaching managerial economics is to equip them with the ability to deliberate logically and critically the challenging process of framing business strategies later on in their careers.

The purpose of this book is not only to make the study of microeconomics and macroeconomics simple for business students but also to enable them to apply it to every day business situations. To achieve that, various tools have been used in the book.

- **Topics chosen for discussion:** They cover various aspects of microeconomics and macroeconomics which are of relevance at the undergraduate level.
- **Learning objectives:** At the beginning of each chapter, the learning objectives are mentioned which give to students as to what aspects of the subject the chapter focuses on.
- **Boxes:** In every chapter, there are some boxes which contain interesting features and supplementary material relevant to the chapter for some additional information.
- **Definitions of important concepts**: In every chapter, definitions are given in marginalia making it simpler for students to review and learn these important concepts.
- **RECAP at the end of every section**: At the end of each section in every chapter, a recap has been given, the purpose of which is to assist the student in recapitulating and reviewing the text discussed in every section.
- **Chapter summary**: Each chapter has a brief summary of the entire chapter which is especially useful during examinations for a quick recollection of the chapter.
- **Review questions**: At the end of every chapter, there are review questions, categorized under true or false, short and long answer questions which aim at checking the understanding of students with regard to the chapter.
- **Numerical illustrations:** Some of the chapters, wherever required, contain numerical illustrations which improve the student's understanding of the text.
- **Diagrams:** Generous use of diagrams to illustrate the text and assist in clarifying the concepts discussed.
- **Unsolved numericals:** By attempting to find a solution to the unsolved numericals, the student can check his understanding of the mathematical problems.
- **Relevance to the Indian conditions**: References to the Indian conditions are given in the chapters wherever considered relevant for better insight.
- **Glossary:** Key terms have been included and defined in the Glossary.
- **Index:** A list of key words is included in the index.

I sincerely hope that this book will prove handy and helpful to both students and teachers. I would at all times welcome any observations and suggestions for further improvement of the book.

ACKNOWLEDGEMENTS

A textbook is not a solitary venture of its author but it is rather a collaborative project of a team of dedicated and competent people. The team of editors who worked on this edition helped tremendously in bringing this venture to fruition in a very professional manner. I extend special thanks to them for their superb work. For their efforts, care and expertise, I thank Dhiraj Pandey, Debapriya Mukherjee and Ruchi Sachdev.

I am also grateful for the contributions and inputs of the reviewers and colleagues who offered very useful comments during the various stages of preparation of the drafts of the book. Last and yet most important, I thank my husband, Pradeep, and children, Tanay and Prakriti, for their continuous encouragement, patience and support.

Vanita Agarwal

About the Author

Vanita Agarwal is currently Associate Professor of Economics at Lakshmibai College, University of Delhi. She teaches economics at undergraduate level and has a teaching experience of more than 26 years.

Dr Vanita Agarwal is an alumna of Miranda House, University of Delhi. She obtained her post-graduate degree of MA (Economics) from the prestigious Delhi School of Economics, University of Delhi and completed her Ph.D. from the Department of Commerce, Delhi School of Economics. Besides her teaching and research assignments at the University of Delhi, she has also written books on macroeconomics.

An Introduction to Managerial Economics: Nature and Scope

1

After studying this chapter, you should be able to understand:

- ✓ *The economic problem of scarcity arises because the limited resources have to be utilized to satisfy the unlimited human wants.*
- ✓ *Managerial economics is a discipline, which requires the application of economics in the complex business decision-making process to formulate and achieve the rational managerial objectives.*
- ✓ *Microeconomics is a branch of economics, which analyses the market behaviour and the decision-making process of an individual consumer and a firm.*
- ✓ *Macroeconomic is the study of how the national economy as a whole grows and the changes which occur over time.*
- ✓ *Managerial economics can be thought of as applied microeconomics though, to some extent, macroeconomics is also relevant at some stages.*
- ✓ *Business economics is concerned with economic issues and problems related to business organization, management and strategy.*

INTRODUCTION

In this chapter, we aim to make readers understand as to what the managerial economics is. Then, we move on to analyse the differences between microeconomics and macroeconomics, and their relation to managerial economics. We also examine the need to study the managerial economics and its relationship to business economics.

WHAT IS MANAGERIAL ECONOMICS?

Economics is concerned with the optimum utilization of the resources of the economy to satisfy the human wants. While wants are unlimited, the natural resources such as land, labour and capital are limited. The crux of the country's economic problem is that the limited resources have to be utilized to satisfy the unlimited wants of the human beings. This gives rise to the *economic problem of the scarcity*. Hence, given the limited resources, a choice has to be made at every stage. The three *economic problems*: what to produce, how to produce and for whom to produce have to be tackled by every economist of a nation. The knowledge of the economics is the crucial one in finding out a viable solution to those problems addressed above.

> Managerial economics is that discipline which requires the application of economics in the complex business decision-making process to formulate and achieve the rational managerial objectives.

As far as the problem of *what to produce* is concerned, it involves various decisions. Firstly, the decision as to 'which goods are to be produced' has to be made; once that decision has been made, it has to be decided as to 'what quantities of those goods should be produced'. For example, the problem may relate to whether to produce more of capital goods or more of consumer goods depending on the objectives of the economy. Once this choice has been made, the next question would arise as to, for example, in the context of consumer goods, whether to produce more of necessities or luxuries. To resolve these issues, it is imperative for a manager to have knowledge of the objectives of a business firm, the decision rules and the optimization process. Also a manager should be able to conduct an analysis of demand and forecast the demand. He should also be in a position to understand the behaviour of a consumer.

The second basic economic problem of *how to produce* involves the selection of the technique of the production. A technique of production relates to the combination, which is used to produce a good. The technique may be labour-intensive using more labour or it may be capital-intensive using more capital. It is important to note that more advanced techniques are generally more productive, but they are more capital intensive. While making the decision on how to produce a good, it is imperative that the manager should utilize the scarce resources in an efficient manner using the labour-intensive techniques in an economy where labour is in abundance, and the capital-intensive techniques in an economy where capital is in abundance. Hence, the choice relating to the technique of production is a crucial decision which the manager has to make. For this, it is necessary that he is able to evaluate the process of production and the attached costs and then to make the relevant decisions. Also he should be able to make the decisions relating to investment and capital budgeting.

The third basic economic problem of *for whom to produce* relates to the distribution of the national product amongst the members of the society. This problem occurs because on one hand, the wants are unlimited and on the other hand, the resources are scarce. Therefore, the crucial decision has to be made as to the distribution of the national products. In a free enterprise economy, the decision as to how much of the national output each one gets will be determined according to the ability to pay. This will depend on the remuneration that these factors will earn from their ownership of the different factors that they own. The owner of labour will earn the wages, the owner of land will earn the rent, the owner of capital will earn the interest and the entrepreneur will earn the profits. Hence to understand the distribution of the national product, the manager should be able to understand as to how the wages, rent, interest and profit are determined. The knowledge of the market structures, general equilibrium analysis and welfare economics will guide him as to the role he can play in the welfare of the society. It is also necessary for him to understand the role of the government and as to how it is able to influence the economy through taxes, subsidies and various government expenditures.

These all constitute a part of microeconomics. But to get the complete understanding, it is equally important for a manager to have some knowledge of the economy's total output, employment and price level. Knowledge about national income and its determination will help the managements apply the macroeconomics in evolving their strategic business policies and decisions.

The manager should have a thorough knowledge about the theories of economic growth if he has to play an important role in the growth and development of the economy.

A manager deals not only with the economy of the country, but also with the other economies of the world. For this, he should have a thorough knowledge of the international scenario relating to the theory of international trade, trade policy, foreign exchange, balance of payments and the international monetary system.

RECAP

- The limited resources in an economy have to be utilized to satisfy the unlimited wants of the human beings.
- Managerial economics is that discipline which requires application of economics in the complex business decision-making process to formulate and achieve the rational managerial objectives.

DIFFERENCES BETWEEN MICROECONOMICS AND MACROECONOMICS, AND THEIR RELATION TO MANAGERIAL ECONOMICS

The study of economics can be classified into two distinct types: microeconomics and macroeconomics.

Microeconomics focuses on the demand, supply and equilibrium and also the determination of price and output in individual market.

Macroeconomics analyses the big or the macropicture of the economy of a country. Hence, the basic concerns of the macroeconomics are to measure to how the economy works, as to how the economy is performing and how to improve the performance of the economy. Macroeconomics is very complex and influenced by many factors. These factors can be analysed through the various economic indicators which tell us about the overall health of an economy. Thus, macroeconomics deals with the larger issues such as price stability or inflation and full employment or unemployment.

> Microeconomics is a branch of economics, which analyses the market behaviour and decision-making process of the individual consumer and firm and also the interactions among the individual buyers and sellers.
>
> Macroeconomics is the study of how the national economy as a whole grows and how the changes occur over time.

Microeconomics and macroeconomics are both intertwined. By improving their knowledge of certain phenomena, economists can help individuals and nations in making more efficient decisions in allocating the resources. On one hand, it is important to note that what microeconomics takes as given, the total output, the total employment and the total expenditure on the goods and services; macroeconomics takes it as one of its most important variables. On the other hand, what macroeconomics takes as given, the distribution of the total output, the total employment and the total expenditure between the goods and services of the different firms and the different industries; microeconomics takes it as a variable to be determined.

Although a distinction has often been made between microeconomics and macroeconomics, strictly speaking there is only one 'economics'. While the foundation of the microeconomics lies in the macroeconomics, the foundation of the macroeconomics lies in the microeconomics. Thus, an analysis of an economy cannot be conducted in two separate watertight compartments of macroeconomics and microeconomics.

As already discussed, since our resources are limited in comparison with our wants and needs, both individuals and nations will have to make decisions as to the goods and services they can purchase and the ones they have to forgo.

Managerial economics can be thought of as applied microeconomics though, to some extent, macroeconomics is also relevant at some stages.

So due to the problem of the scarcity, individuals and economists have to make the decisions in the allocation of their resources. Economics seeks to study as to why we make these decisions and how we can allocate our resources most efficiently. Managerial economics involves the organization and allocation of a firm's limited resources to achieve its objectives. Managerial economics is the application of economics to business decisions to achieve the firm's desired objectives using its limited resources.

It focuses on those topics of microeconomics, which are of more interest and important to the managers in their day-to-day decision making. If applied rationally, the principles, relating to, for example, the behaviour of the firms and consumers in the economy, can be of immense help to the manager in making his decisions and in achieving the objectives of the firm.

The principles of managerial economics can be used by the firm in many ways. It can help the firm in an efficient allocation of resources. In case there is a change in the price of a factor, say capital, the firm can make use of the principles of managerial economics to decide whether to substitute by other inputs, for example the cheaper factor labour in the production of a good.

Economics is a tool in the hands of the manager which helps in sharpening his skills and in making the efficient decisions.

RECAP

- Microeconomics is a branch of economics, which analyses the market behaviour and decision-making process of the individual consumer and firm, and also the interactions among the individual buyer and seller.
- Macroeconomics is the study of how the national economy as a whole grows and how the changes occur over time.
- Managerial economics can be thought of as applied microeconomics though macroeconomics is also relevant at some stages.

NEED TO STUDY MANAGERIAL ECONOMICS

It was not long ago that the business scenario was dominated by a few business houses that were in complete control of the industrial sector in India. The impact could be seen even in the other sectors of the economy like finance.

Once the economy started growing and the complexities of the business increased, it became necessary to apply the economics with its different theories, concepts and tools to solve the diverse economic problems faced by the firm. It was then realized that the knowledge of economics would be more appropriate in solving these problems relating to the consumer, the market and the various aspects. It was felt that a manager should be equipped with the tools of economics if he wants to be successful. Hence, it was realized that the knowledge of the economics is increasingly relevant for a manager. It was obvious that a professionally trained manager could perform better than one who lacked the necessary knowledge.

RECAP

- It was realized that the knowledge of the economics is increasingly relevant for a manager.
- It was obvious that a professionally trained manager could certainly perform better than one who lacked the necessary knowledge.

BOX 1.1

How high can the management price a new model of a smart phone before it turns out to be too expensive to sell? How should the management decide if the business can afford to offer its workers a raise or just an increased bonus? How will companies that sell cars to individuals be impacted if the government decides to raise the interest rates?

These are the types of questions a student of business and managerial economics will need to answer. Students learn how to use the concepts of the economics to study and analyse the businesses. As such, the study of the subject facilitates bridging the economic theory and economics in practice.

APPLICATIONS OF MANAGERIAL ECONOMICS

Managerial economics can be applied by a firm in making its business decisions. These decisions include:

(i) **Decision Regarding the Price:** When a firm is planning on its production, it has to determine the price of the product. This will depend on the structure of the market. If there exists perfect competition, then the firm will be just a price taker. However, if there is a monopoly, then the firm will have some controls over the price. Hence, the determination of the price involves an understanding of the different market structures.

(ii) **Forecasting and Estimation of the Demand for the Product:** The firm will have to forecast and estimate the demand for the product to be able to decide on the level of output of the product. The managers will have to foresee and provide for the future increases in the demand for the product. This involves an understanding of the nature of the demand and the ability to forecast the demand.

(iii) **Choice Relating to the Technique of Production:** The manager will have to make the crucial decision as to whether to use a labour-intensive technology or a capital-intensive technology. The decision will, to some extent, depend on which factor of production is more readily available and is in abundance in the economy. This involves an understanding of the cost and production analysis.

(iv) **Advertising Expenditures:** Under imperfect competition, often, to sell its product, a firm may have to resort to advertising. It will have to decide on the amount of expenditure to incur on advertising, the medium of information to be used: television, newspapers and other such decisions. This involves an understanding of the optimum advertising expenditure under the monopoly, monopolistic competition and oligopoly.

(v) **Decisions Relating to Investment:** In the long-run, a firm has to decide on expanding the production of the product. Hence, it has to incur the capital expenditure. This involves an understanding of the theory of capital budgeting.

RECAP

- Managerial economics can be applied by a firm in making its business decisions such as the price, forecasting and estimation of the demand for the product.

MANAGERIAL ECONOMICS AND BUSINESS ECONOMICS: AMBIGUITY IN THE USE OF THE TWO TERMS

> Managerial economics is concerned with the application of economic theory and economic analysis to the task of arriving at rational managerial decisions.
>
> Business economics, in a wider context, is concerned with the economic issues and problems related to the business organization, management and strategy.

It is sometimes referred to as business economics and is a branch of economics that makes use of microeconomic analysis in decision-making process in businesses or other management organizations.

The term 'business economics' is used in many ways and is quite often used as managerial economics. The website (http://www.mbe-du.org/) of the Delhi University's prestigious 'Master in Business Economics' course states that 'Business Economics deals with the behavioural analysis of firms, markets and industries and determination of costs and prices'. There may be relative differences in the usage of 'managerial economics' and 'economics for business' with the former used more narrowly. An emerging view is that the business economics is wider in its scope than the managerial economics. Economics for business relates and applies the major principles of economics to the real world of business. Managerial economics is the application of economic tools and methods in the managerial decision-making process (Figure 1.1).

Managerial decisions in any business area would include:

(i) Assessment and evaluation of investible funds
(ii) Selection of business area
(iii) Choice of product to deal with
(iv) Determination of optimum level of output
(v) Determination of price of product
(vi) Determination of input-combination, mix and technology
(vii) Publicity and sales promotion

As almost any business decision can be analysed with the managerial economics techniques, the need to compartmentalize the business economics and the managerial economics would, perhaps, be an exercise in futility. At universities and business schools, the subject is approached more as an integration subject. That is, it integrates many concepts from a wide variety of related courses. In many countries, a

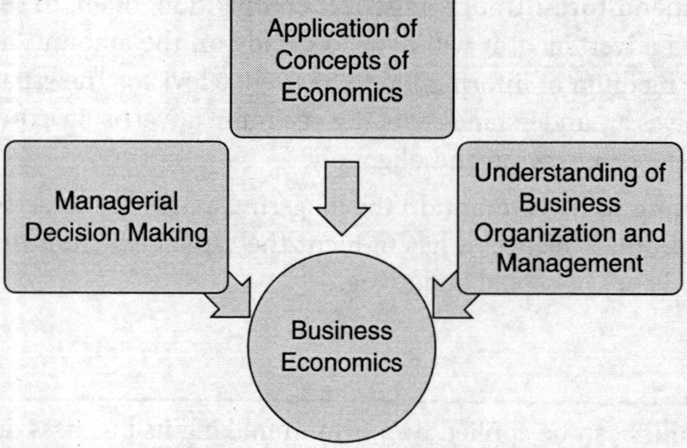

Figure 1.1 Dynamics of Business Economics

degree in 'Business Economics' would cover the managerial economics, financial economics, business forecasting, game theory and industrial economics. Universities across the world offer courses in business economics giving diverse interpretations as far as the meaning and the curriculum of the subject are concerned.

RECAP

- Business economics is concerned with the economic issues and the problems related to the business organization, management and strategy.

SUMMARY

WHAT IS MANAGERIAL ECONOMICS?

1. The crux of the problem is that the limited resources in an economy have to be utilized to satisfy the unlimited wants of the human beings. This gives rise to the economic problem of scarcity.
2. Managerial economics is that discipline which requires application of economics in the complex business decision-making process to formulate and achieve the rational managerial objectives.
3. The three economic problems, what to produce, how to produce and for whom to produce, have to be tackled by every economy.
4. As far as the problem of what to produce is concerned, it involves the decision as to which goods are to be produced and as to what quantities of those goods should be produced.
5. The second basic economic problem of how to produce involves the selection of the technique of the production.
6. The third basic economic problem of for whom to produce relates to the distribution of the national product between the members of the society.

DIFFERENCES BETWEEN MICROECONOMICS AND MACROECONOMICS, AND THEIR RELATION TO MANAGERIAL ECONOMICS

1. Microeconomics is a branch of economics, which analyses the market behaviour and the decision-making process of the individual consumer and firm and also the interactions between the individual buyer and seller.
2. Microeconomics focuses on the demand, supply and equilibrium and the price and output determination in the individual market.
3. Macroeconomics is the study of how the national economy as a whole grows and the changes which occur over time.
4. Macroeconomics deals with the big issues such as price stability or inflation and full employment or unemployment.
5. Although a distinction has often been made between microeconomics and macroeconomics, strictly speaking there is only one 'economics'.
6. Managerial economics can be thought of as applied microeconomics though, to some extent, macroeconomics is also relevant at some stages.
7. Economics is a tool, in the hands of the manager, which helps in sharpening his skills and in making the efficient decisions.

NEED TO STUDY MANAGERIAL ECONOMICS

1. It was not long ago that the business scenario was dominated by a few business houses that were in complete control of the industrial sector in India.

2. Once the economy started growing and the complexities of business increased, it was realized that economics is increasingly relevant for a manager.

APPLICATIONS OF MANAGERIAL ECONOMICS

1. Managerial economics can be applied by a firm in making its business decisions. These decisions include: decision regarding the price, forecasting and estimation of the demand for the product, choice relating to the technique of production, advertising expenditures and the decision relating to the investment.

MANAGERIAL ECONOMICS AND BUSINESS ECONOMICS: AMBIGUITY IN THE USE OF THE TWO TERMS

1. Managerial economics is concerned with the application of the economic theory and the economic analysis to the task of arriving at rational managerial decisions.
2. Business economics, in a wider context, is concerned with the economic issues and the problems related to the business organization, management and strategy.

REVIEW QUESTIONS

TRUE OR FALSE QUESTIONS

1. In an economy, the unlimited resources have to be utilized to satisfy the limited wants of the human beings.
2. Managerial economics requires the application of economics in making the complex business decisions.
3. The three economic problems, what to produce, how to produce and for whom to produce, have to be tackled by every individual.
4. The problem of what to produce involves the decision as to which goods are to be produced and as to what quantities of those goods should be produced.
5. The second basic economic problem of how to produce relates to the distribution of the national products between the members of the society.

SHORT ANSWER QUESTIONS

1. Define the managerial economics.
2. What are the differences between microeconomics and macroeconomics?
3. What is the purpose of studying the managerial economics?
4. How does a firm make use of the managerial economics to
   (a) decide on the price of the product.
   (b) estimate the demand for the product.
5. How does a firm make use of the managerial economics to
   (a) choose the technique of the production.
   (b) determine its advertising expenditures.

LONG ANSWER QUESTIONS

1. What is the managerial economics? Discuss.
2. 'The three economic problems, what to produce, how to produce and for whom to produce, have to be tackled by every economy.' Comment.
3. How are microeconomics and macroeconomics related to the managerial economics? Analyse.
4. What are the crucial business decisions that a firm has to make? How can a firm apply the managerial economics in making these decisions? Discuss.
5. To resolve the three basic economic problems of what, how and for whom to produce, what are the areas of micro- and macro-economics that a manager should be familiar with?

ANSWERS

TRUE OR FALSE QUESTIONS

1. **False.** Limited resources have to be utilized to satisfy the unlimited wants of the human beings.
2. **True.** Managerial economics is that discipline which requires application of the economics in the complex business decision-making process to formulate and achieve the rational managerial objectives.
3. **False.** The three economic problems, what to produce, how to produce and for whom to produce, have to be tackled by every economy.
4. **True.** This is the first basic economic problem, which every economy has to solve.
5. **False.** The second basic economic problem of how to produce involves the selection of the technique of production.

Objectives of a Business Firm, Decision Rules and the Process of Optimization

2

After studying this chapter, you should be able to understand:

- ✓ *In traditional economic theory, the firm's objective is to maximize the profits.*
- ✓ *In modern economic theory, there are a variety of objectives before a firm.*
- ✓ *For profit maximization, marginal cost (MC) should equal marginal revenue (MR) and MR should be falling while the MC is rising.*
- ✓ *A firm may pursue many goals simultaneously with the primary goal being that of maximization of profits.*
- ✓ *The problem occurs when the interest of the manager may be at variance from that of the stockholder.*
- ✓ *By keeping employees and consumers happy, the firm nowadays has to fulfill the social responsibilities.*
- ✓ *Optimization is the process, where the best feasible solution is determined to a problem.*

INTRODUCTION

In Chapter 1, we have explained that managerial economics requires the application of economics to the firm's decision-making process to enable it to allocate the firm's scarce economic resources so that it can achieve the managerial objectives. An optimal decision is one which enables the firm to achieve these objectives making them as close as possible to the desired objectives.

This chapter focuses on some of these objectives of the firm.

OBJECTIVES OF A BUSINESS FIRM

In traditional economic theory, it was assumed that the firm's objective was to maximize the profits. Whether it was a perfect competition, a monopoly, a monopolistic competition or an oligopoly—in all the market structures—the firm's sole objective was to maximize the profits.

Modern economic theory believes that there are a variety of objectives of a firm. These include maximization of the sales revenue, the market shares, the growth rate of the firm and manager's utility function providing a complete line of products, preventing entry and avoiding the risk. A firm can choose its objectives from them. The firm can aim at pursuing more than one objective.

We analyse some of these objectives focusing on the primary objective in the conventional theory, which is profit maximization.

RECAP

- In traditional economic theory, it was assumed that the firm's objective was to maximize the profits.
- Modern economic theory believes that there are a variety of objectives of a firm.

PROFIT OBJECTIVE

As already mentioned, the objective of the profit maximization is the most important objective that a firm aims to achieve.

Nature and Measurement of Profit

In the literal sense, labour earns wages, land earns rent, capital earns interest and an entrepreneur earns profit. In terms of a layman, profit is that income which the investor earns. In terms of an accountant, profit is the difference between revenue and costs (including the manufacturing and overhead expenses). Hence, accounting profit is the difference between revenue and explicit costs incurred.

In economics, profit has different connotations. The accountant's concept of cost is calculated on a historical basis. The economist is more concerned about future costs or, in other words, opportunity costs or alternative costs. Opportunity cost is the price that a firm must pay to a factor to prevent it from moving to the next best alternative use of the factor. Pure profit or economic profit is the return that the firm earns over and above the opportunity costs.

Economic profit is the difference between total revenue (*TR*) and total costs (*TC*) where costs include both the explicit and the implicit costs. Explicit costs are the costs which arise when a firm transacts with other parties from whom it purchases its raw materials and other services. These costs include labour costs, insurance costs, costs of raw materials, electricity and others. Implicit costs are the costs which are related to the use of the resources owned by the firm and are an indication of the fact that these resources could have an alternative use. These include the wages of the entrepreneur, which could also be earned with an alternative firm; the interest that is earned on the owned capital, which could also have been earned in an alternative investment and the rent that is earned on the owned land and buildings, which again could have been earned by renting them out to another firm.

$$\text{Accounting Profit} = TR - \text{Explicit Cost}$$

$$\text{Economic Profit} = TR - TC$$

where

$$TC = \text{Explicit Cost} + \text{Implicit Cost}$$

thus

$$\text{Economic Profit} = \text{Accounting Profit} - \text{Implicit Cost}$$

Economic profit may be positive, negative or even zero. Here, it is important to note that under the perfect competition economic profit relates only to the short-run.

In the process of measuring the profit, a firm may face two problems:

(i) Which concept of profit should be applied: accounting profit or economic profit?

(ii) What are the cost components, which should be included in the implicit and explicit costs?

As far as the concept of profit is concerned, it will be determined by the purpose for which the profit is being measured. If the purpose relates to depicting the firm's progress to the shareholders and the creditors and also for calculating the firm's tax liability, then the concept of accounting profit is appropriate. However, if the firm's accurate performance is to be judged, then it is the concept of economic profit which needs to be applied. It is a reflection of the true profitability of the firm.

Once the decision regarding which concept of profit should be considered has been made, the next decision relates to the cost components to be included in the profit. Here, problems occur in measuring the depreciation, capital gains and losses, and also current and historical costs.

RECAP

- In traditional economic theory, it was assumed that the firm's objective was to maximize the profits.
- Modern economic theory believes that there are a variety of objectives before a firm.
- Profit maximization is the most important objective that a firm aims to achieve.
- Accounting profit is the difference between revenue and explicit costs incurred.
- Opportunity cost is the price that a firm must pay to a factor to prevent it from moving to the next best alternative use of the factor.
- Economic profit is the difference between *TR* and *TC*s, where costs include both the explicit cost and the implicit cost.
- Under the perfect competition, economic profit relates only to the short-run.

PROFIT THEORIES

Many theories of profit have emerged. These are as follows:

(i) **Clark's Theory:** J. B. Clark had presented the dynamic theory where profits occur only in a dynamic economy. In a static economy, there would be no profits. In a dynamic economy, there are changes like an increase in the population and thus a change in the wants of the consumer, growth of capital and technology. A successful entrepreneur is able to increase the sales and also able to bring about the expansion in his business thus making the pure profits. However, this profit will disappear in the long-run. But in a dynamic economy where the change is a continuous process, profits keep occurring.

(ii) **Walker's Theory:** According to F. A. Walker, an entrepreneur, who possesses the extraordinary abilities, earns rent on these abilities when he uses the abilities in a business. This rent is the profit earned by him. Like rent, which is the difference between the returns on the less and the more fertile land, profit is the difference between the earnings of the less and the more competent entrepreneur. Walker also believed that there existed only the perfect competition where each firm possesses the same managerial skills and thus earns only the normal profit.

(iii) **Schumpeter's Theory:** J. A. Schumpeter had presented a theory where profits occur on innovations in the manufacturing sector or even in the technique of supplying the goods. They may occur, for example, when a new product or a new quality of the product is launched or alternatively a new technique of production is introduced. However, overtime these profits may get wiped out.

(iv) **Knight's Theory:** According to Frank H. Knight, profit is a return on bearing the uncertainty. Risks are of two types: insurable risks which can be calculated and thus insured against, for example, risks due to accidents and fire; *uninsurable* risks which cannot be calculated and thus cannot be insured against, for example, uncertainties regarding the competitor's reaction. It is here that the entrepreneur's ability to make the right decision earns him a profit.

(v) **Hawley's Theory:** F. B. Hawley had presented a theory where profit is a return on bearing the risk. One who takes a risk earns a reward in the form of a profit. He would not be willing to take a risk when he does not get a return.

RECAP

- Many theories of profit have emerged, such as Clark's theory, Walker's theory and so on.

PROFIT MAXIMIZATION: AN ALGEBRAIC EXPLANATION

As already discussed, according to the conventional economic theory, a firm's aim is to maximize its profit. It is in equilibrium when it maximizes the profits. Here, we examine the profit maximizing output decision of a firm. This analysis will hold irrespective of whether the firm is operating under conditions of perfect competition or in a situation where there is some control over price.

The firm's economic profit is the difference between *TR* and *TC*.

$$\Pi = TR - TC$$

where Π is total economic profit, which a firm attempts to maximize while making its decision about the output level and the price of the product. *TR* is total revenue, which is the revenue earned from the sale of the output. It is calculated as price multiplied by the quantity sold or $TR = P \times Q$. *TC* is total cost, which is the total of all costs involved in producing a given output level. It is calculated as the sum of total fixed cost and total variable cost or *TC* is total fixed cost + Total variable cost.

For the profit maximization, two conditions need to be satisfied at the equilibrium point:

(i) **First-Order or Necessary Condition:** It is necessary that *MC* equals *MR*.

(ii) **Second-Order or Sufficient Condition:** The *MR* should be falling while the *MC* should be rising.

Here *MC* is marginal cost which is the addition to the *TC* as the output level is raised by one more unit. It is calculated as

$$\frac{\partial(TC)}{\partial Q}$$

MR is Marginal revenue which is the addition to the *TR*, when an additional unit of the output is sold. It is calculated as

$$\frac{\partial(TR)}{\partial Q}$$

Profit maximization requires that as far as the profit function, $\Pi = TR - TC$, is concerned.

(i) The first derivative is equal to zero.

(ii) The second derivative is < 0 or negative.

Now, $$\Pi = TR - TC.$$

$$\frac{\partial \Pi}{\partial Q} = \frac{\partial (TR)}{\partial Q} - \frac{\partial (TC)}{\partial Q} = 0$$

$$\frac{\partial (TR)}{\partial Q} = \frac{\partial (TC)}{\partial Q}$$

Slope of TR = Slope of TC.

Thus, $MR = MC$. This proves that MC equals MR. Now the second-order condition requires that

$$\frac{\partial^2 \Pi}{\partial Q^2} = \frac{\partial^2 (TR)}{\partial Q^2} - \frac{\partial^2 (TC)}{\partial Q^2} < 0$$

Or $$\frac{\partial^2 (TR)}{\partial Q^2} - \frac{\partial^2 (TC)}{\partial Q^2} < 0$$

Thus, slope of MR < Slope of MC. This proves that MR should be falling while the MC should be rising.

Profit Maximization: A Graphical Explanation

Total Approach

Figure 2.1 illustrates as to how a firm maximizes profits using the total approach. The figure depicts the *TC*, *TR* and *Π* curves. The *TC* curve is an inverse S-shaped curve beginning at the level of the fixed cost. The *TR* curve is through the origin. *Π* curve is the profit curve showing the total profit that a firm makes. A firm chooses that level of output at which the difference between the *TR* and *TC* curves, in other words, the profit level is the greatest.

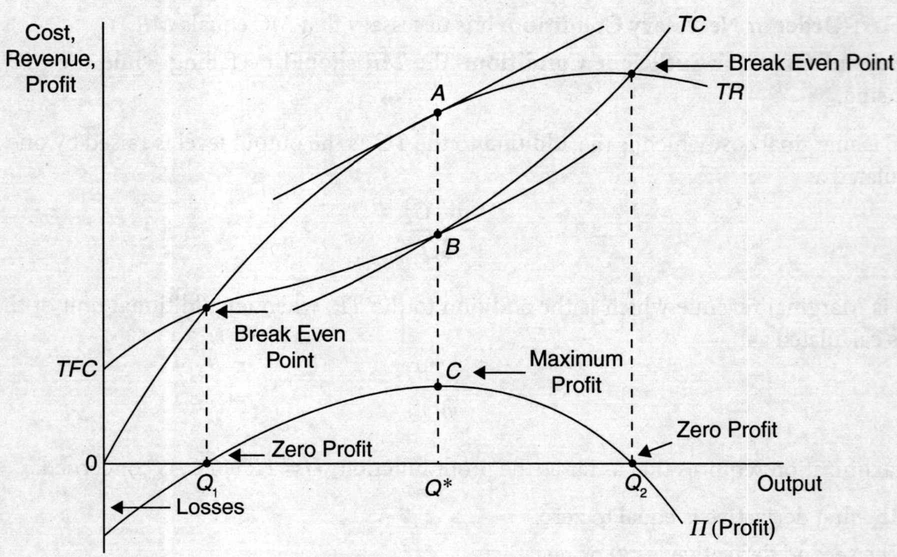

Figure 2.1 Profit Maximization: The Total Approach

In the figure,

(i) Between the origin and the output level OQ_1, the TC curve is above the TR curve. Hence, there occurs negative profit or losses as shown by the profit curve.

(ii) The firm will make zero profits at the output level of OQ_1 and OQ_2. These are called the *Break Even Points*. Here, there is no difference between TR and TC curves or, in other words, the vertical distance between the two curves is zero. The profit curve also shows zero profit at the output level of OQ_1 and OQ_2.

Break Even Points are those points at which the firm will make zero profits.

(iii) The firm will maximize the profits at the output level of OQ^*. The vertical distance between TR and TC curves, AB is the maximum. At the output level OQ^*, the slope of the TR curve (which measures the addition to the TR when an additional unit of the output is sold), the firm's MR, is equal to the slope of the TC curve (which measures the addition to the TC as the output level is raised by one more unit), the firm's MC. The profit curve also shows the highest level of profit at OQ^* level of output, CQ^*.

(iv) Between the output level OQ^* and OQ_2, the TC curve is rising more rapidly than the TR curve. Thus, the profit curve is declining.

(v) Beyond the output level OQ_2, the TC curve is again above the TR curve. Hence, there occurs negative profit as shown by the profit curve.

Marginal Approach

Figure 2.2 illustrates as to how a firm maximizes the profits using the marginal principle or the per-unit curves. The figure depicts the MC and MR curves. The MC curve is U-shaped while the MR curve is downward sloping. A firm chooses that level of output at which

(i) $MR = MC$.

(ii) Slope of MR < Slope of MC or in other words, the MC curve cuts the MR curve from below.

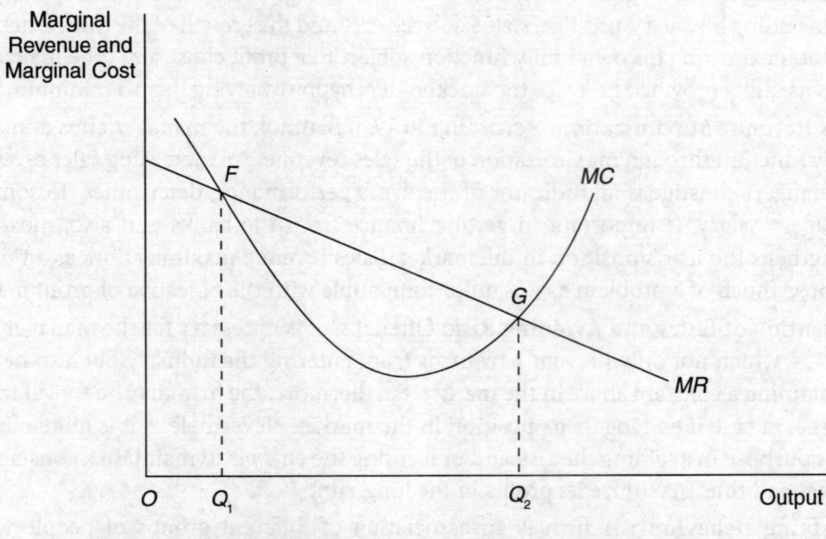

Figure 2.2 Profit Maximization: The Marginal Approach

The figure shows that

(i) The firm will maximize the profits by producing that level of output at which *MR* is equal to *MC*. This occurs at two points, *F* and *G*. But it is only at point *G* that the second condition, the *MC* curve cuts the *MR* curve from below is also satisfied. Point *G* corresponds to OQ_2 level of output. At point *F*, the *MC* curve cuts the *MR* curve from above and thus at OQ_1 level of output the firm is not maximizing the profits.

(ii) For output levels less than OQ_2, *MR* is greater than *MC*. Hence, the addition to the *TR* is more than the addition to the *TC*. Since the firm will be adding more to *TR* than to *TC*, its profit will increase. Thus, the firm must increase its output.

(iii) For output levels greater than OQ_2, *MR* is less than *MC*. Hence, the addition to the *TR* is less than the addition to the *TC*. Since the firm will be adding more to *TC* than to *TR*, its profit will decrease. Thus, the firm must decrease its output.

RECAP

- For profit maximization at the equilibrium point, two conditions need to be satisfied: *MC* equals *MR* and *MR* should be falling while the *MC* should be rising.

OTHER ECONOMIC OBJECTIVES OF A FIRM

In a modern corporation, the stockholders often employ managers to look after the firm's operations. The managers get a salary for this purpose. *The problem occurs when the interest of the manager may be at variance from that of the stockholder.* The goal of the two may be different and this, in fact, may be an important determinant of the managerial behaviour and the goals he sets out to achieve. Some of these alternative goals are as follows:

(i) **Maximizing the Manager's Utility Function:** The manager's utility function depends on many factors including his salary, prestige, status, job security and the growth of the firm. Often the manager aims at maximizing his own utility function subject to a profit constraint. The manager can maximize his utility provided he keeps the stockholders happy by giving them a minimum level of profit.

(ii) **Sales Revenue Maximization:** According to W. J. Baumol, the manager aims at maximizing his utility function through maximization of the sales revenue. An increasing sales revenue increases the manger's prestige is an indicator of the firm's performance, determines (to some extent) the manager's salary, is important in getting finance from the banks and also, most importantly, strengthens the firm's position in the market. Sales revenue maximization, as an objective, may not pose much of a problem as it is quite compatible with the objective of profit maximization.

(iii) **Prevention of Entry and Avoiding Risk:** Often it seems necessary for the manager to pursue the policies, which not only prevent new firms from entering the industry but also help the firm in maintaining a constant share in the market. Furthermore, the firm may be forced to avoid taking any risk in case it endangers its position in the market. Nevertheless, it is quite obvious that the firm's purpose in avoiding the risk and preventing the entry is to maintain a constant share in the market and thus maximize its profits in the long-run.

(iv) **Satisfying Behaviour:** A firm is an association of different groups of people who form the stockholders, managers, employees and others. The firm attempts at keeping all of them happy by following a satisfying behaviour. The stockholders are given satisfactory profits, the managers are provided a satisfactory remuneration and the employees are provided a satisfactory salary and a good working environment. Thus, here again the objective of profit maximization does not seem to conflict with the satisfying behaviour of the firm.

(v) **Long-run Survival:** Often it is important for a firm to be able to continue to exist in the industry in the long-run. Thus, while aiming at a secure profit level, the firm may attempt to keep its position secure in the industry in the long-run.

(vi) **Maintaining Liquidity:** A firm may attempt to maintain a situation, where there is enough liquidity to ensure a sound financial position for the firm.

It appears that although firms may have a variety of objectives from which they can choose but, in fact, their choice is really limited. A manager who does not aim at long-run profit maximization may be replaced with another manager. Shareholders may withdraw their capital from a firm, which is paying them less than average earnings and may invest them elsewhere. Alternately, it is quite possible that the firm may not be able to survive. Hence, a firm may pursue many goals simultaneously with the primary goal being that of maximization of the profits as shown in Figure 2.3.

Often the rewards paid out to the business executives may be linked to profits and may be paid in terms of stocks of companies. This strategy may prove an incentive to managers to take the goal of profit maximization more seriously. Even the prices of the stocks of a firm may fall in case its profitability is low. In addition, it is important for a manager to remember that in case his performance, as far as profits are concerned, in the given situation is poor then it will affect his future job prospects. Lastly, it is obvious that a firm which does not earn enough profits will not be able to withstand competition and survive in the industry.

Many economists are of the belief that the assumption of a firm aiming at profit maximization helps in analysing and solving the several problems.

RECAP

- The problem occurs in that the interest of the manager may be at variance from that of the stockholder.

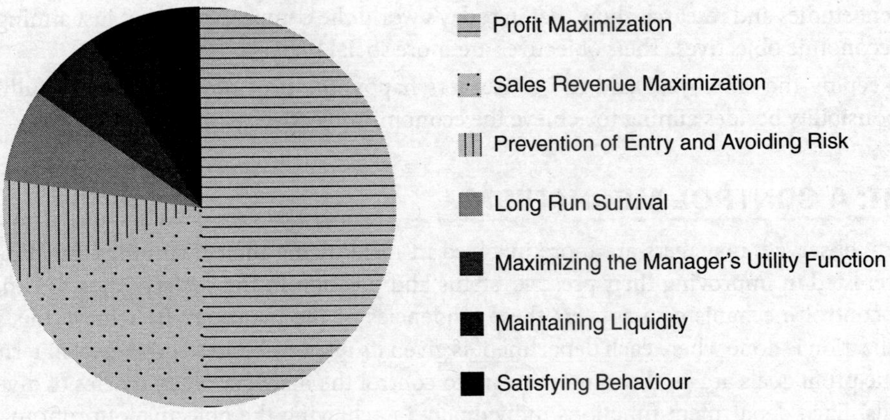

Figure 2.3 Economic Objectives of a Firm

BOX 2.1

The Director of finance in a company may be required to invest in plant and machinery. This may be essential for the future growth plans of the company. However, the dilemma that the Director may face is that the depreciation charges against the plant and machinery may have to be deducted from the current profits which may reduce the profits of the company thus reflecting on the performance of the Director.

- Some of the alternative goals a manager pursues are maximizing the manager's utility function, sales revenue maximization, prevention of entry and avoiding the risk, satisfying behaviour, long-run survival and others.

NON-ECONOMIC OBJECTIVES

Recent studies and research show that in today's world the companies are not just aiming to achieve the economic objectives. Their objectives are more social than economic. They may aim at providing a good working environment for their employees because they realize that happy employees are more efficient and therefore more productive and also will remain for a longer time with the company, thus reducing the turnover of the labour. Again offering good products and services to the consumers will keep them happy and satisfied and thus the company will survive competition and remain in business longer. Organizing a place for themselves in the society by acting as good citizens and supporting charitable and other such organizations will lead to goodwill in the society and will ultimately boost the firm's sales.

These objectives are not only compatible with the objective of profit maximization, but also ultimately support the sales and thus the profits. By keeping the employees and the consumers happy, the firm nowadays has to fulfill its social responsibility besides aiming to achieve the economic objectives. They, in fact, are said to aim at 'adequate' or a reasonable level of profits.

RECAP

- Recent studies and research show that in today's world the companies are not just aiming to achieve the economic objectives. Their objectives are more social than economic.
- By keeping the employees and the consumers happy, the firm nowadays has to fulfill its social responsibility besides aiming to achieve the economic objectives.

PROFIT: A CONTROL MECHANISM

As already observed, managers are more involved in maximizing their own utility function. They are more interested in improving their prestige, status and position in the society. Thus, it is necessary to devise a control mechanism to subvert these tendencies of the manager. To achieve this managerial decentralization is done where each department is given its responsibilities and targets in terms of profit. Hence, the profit goals are used as a mechanism to control the managerial tendencies of diverting from their goals. Each department functions individually in achieving the objective of profit maximization and yet continues to be a part of the organization.

RECAP

- Managerial decentralization is done where each department is given its responsibilities and targets in terms of profit.

DECISION RULES

To achieve the various objectives that a firm aims at, a manager has to take the decisions from time to time. This involves the knowledge of the tools, which assist the manager in making these crucial decisions. These decision rules include:

Marginal Principle

The marginal unit refers to the change in the total quantity due to a per-unit change in the factor that influences it.

As already discussed before, in the *cost analysis*, an important concept is *MC*. Marginal cost is the addition to the *TC* as the output level is raised by one more unit. We can write

$$MC = TC_N - TC_{N-1}$$

where *N* is the number of units of a commodity. It is also calculated as

$$\frac{\partial(TC)}{\partial Q}$$

In the *revenue analysis*, an important concept is *MR*. Marginal revenue is the addition to the TR when an additional unit of the output is sold. We can write

$$MR = TR_N - TR_{N-1}$$

where *N* is the number of units of a commodity. It is also calculated as

$$\frac{\partial(TR)}{\partial Q}$$

The decision rule for a firm aiming at profit maximization is

(i) A firm chooses that level of output at which $MR = MC$.
(ii) Slope of $MR <$ Slope of MC or in other words, the *MC* curve cuts the *MR* curve from below.

The marginal principle is also used in other analysis like the maximization of the utility of a consumer and minimization of the firm's cost.

Opportunity Cost Principle

In any economy, the resources are limited while the demands and expectations are unlimited. These scarce resources can be put to many alternative uses. Opportunity cost is the price that a firm must pay to a factor to prevent it from moving to the next best alternative use of the factor. Thus, the opportunity cost of using a resource is what the resource could earn in its next best alternative use. For example, the opportunity cost to a firm in the use of an input is what that input could earn in its next best alternative use. This is true whether the input is owned or hired by the firm.

In making its decisions whether to continue using the input, a firm must include in the cost of the input the opportunity cost that the input could have earned in its next best alternative employment.

Incremental Principle

Often in the real world, it is difficult to implement the marginal principle. It may be difficult to obtain the per-unit estimates of the demand and the cost. Hence, in making a business decision, the incremental principle may be used.

The incremental principle involves the concept of incremental cost and incremental revenue. Incremental cost is the change in the *TC* related to a decision, for example, the entry into a new line of business. Incremental revenue is the change in the *TR* related to a decision, for example, the extra revenue generated by the entry into the new line of business. If incremental revenue is greater than the incremental cost, then a new project should be undertaken. It is important to note that only those costs and revenues should be considered that will change with the undertaking of the new business project. Hence, it is obvious that the sunk costs should not be considered in the decision.

If incremental cost is taken on a per-unit basis, it turns out to be *MC*.

RECAP

- The decision rules for a manager include marginal principle, opportunity cost principle and the incremental principle.

PROCESS OF OPTIMIZATION

Optimization is the process, where the best feasible solution is determined to a problem. Often, there exist many alternative lines of action to a problem. The best possible solution is one which is in synchronization with the objectives of the entity.

Two steps are involved in an optimization process:

(i) The economic relationships involved should be expressed in the form of equations, tables and graphs which can be analysed easily.

(ii) The different mathematical techniques used for optimization include linear programming, game theory and differential calculus. Linear programming is used when the optimization problem takes a linear form like linear equations and linear inequalities. Game theory technique is used when there exists interdependence in the decisions of the different players in the market. Differential calculus plays an important role in finding a solution to the business problem. For example, in the marginal analysis, calculus is used.

Till now, we have focused on an unconstrained optimization process, where there are no limitations on the firm, for example, in the form of inputs and finance. However, in the real world, there may be many constraints which a manager has to contend with. Constrained optimization occurs when the maximization or the minimization of the function is done under some constraints, for example, those related to inputs. The techniques used here are called constrained optimization techniques, for example, linear programming.

> Optimization is the process, where the best feasible solution is determined to a problem.

RECAP

- Optimization is the process where the best feasible solution is determined to a problem.

SUMMARY

OBJECTIVES OF A BUSINESS FIRM

1. In traditional economic theory, it was assumed that the firm's objective was to maximize the profits.
2. Modern economic theory believes that there are a variety of objectives before a firm.
3. These include maximization of the sales revenue, maximization of the market share, and maximization of the growth rate of the firm and others.

PROFIT OBJECTIVE

1. The objective of the profit maximization is the most important objective that a firm aims to achieve.

Nature and Measurement of Profit

1. In the literal sense, while labour earns wages, land earns rent, capital earns interest and an entrepreneur earns profit.
2. Accounting profit is the difference between revenue and explicit costs incurred.
3. The economist is more concerned about the future costs, or in other words, opportunity costs or alternative costs.
4. Opportunity cost is the price that a firm must pay to a factor to prevent it from moving to the next best alternative use of the factor.
5. Economic profit is the difference between *TR* and *TC*s, where costs include both the explicit cost and the implicit cost.
6. Explicit costs are the costs which arise when a firm transacts with other parties from whom it purchases its raw materials and other services.
7. Implicit costs are the cost which are related to the use of the resources owned by the firm and are an indication of the fact that these resources could have an alternative use.
8. Economic profit may be positive, negative or even zero.
9. Under the perfect competition, economic profit relates only to the short-run.
10. If the firm's accurate performance is to be judged, then it is the concept of economic profit which needs to be applied.

Profit Theories

1. According to Clark's theory, profits occur only in a dynamic economy.
2. According to Walker's theory, an entrepreneur who possesses the extraordinary abilities earns a rent on these abilities when he uses them in a business. This rent is the profit earned by him.
3. J. A. Schumpeter had presented a theory, where profits occur on innovations in the manufacturing sector or even in the technique of supplying the goods.
4. According to Frank H. Knight, profit is a return on bearing the uncertainty.
5. F. B. Hawley had presented a theory, where profit is a return on bearing the risk.

Profit Maximization: An Algebraic Explanation

1. The firm's economic profit is the difference between *TR* and *TC*, $\Pi = TR - TC$.
2. Profit maximization requires that as far as the profit function, $\Pi = TR - TC$, is concerned, the first derivative is equal to zero and the second derivative is < 0 or negative.

Profit Maximization: A Graphical Explanation

Total Approach

1. A firm chooses that level of output at which the difference between the *TR* and *TC* curves, in other words the profit level is the greatest.
2. Break even points are those points at which the firm will make the zero profits.

Marginal Approach

A firm chooses that level of output at which $MR = MC$ and the *MC* curve cuts the *MR* curve from below.

OTHER ECONOMIC OBJECTIVES OF A FIRM

1. The problem occurs in that the interest of the manager may be at variance from that of the stockholder. The goal of the two may be different and this, in fact, may be an important determinant of the managerial behaviour and the goals he sets out to achieve.
2. Some of these alternatives goals are: maximizing the manager's utility function, sales revenue maximization, prevention of entry and avoiding the risk, satisfying the behaviour, long-run survival and others. Hence, a firm may pursue many goals simultaneously with the primary goal being that of maximization of profits.

NON-ECONOMIC OBJECTIVES

1. Recent studies and research shows that in today's world the companies are not just aiming to achieve the economic objectives. Their objectives are more social than economic.
2. By keeping the employees and the consumers happy, the firm nowadays has to fulfill its social responsibility besides aiming to achieve the economic objectives.
3. They, in fact, are said to aim at 'adequate' or a reasonable level of profits.

Profit: A Control Mechanism

1. It is necessary to devise a control mechanism to subvert these tendencies of the manager, where they are concerned with maximizing their own utility function.
2. To achieve this managerial decentralization is done, where each department is given its responsibilities and its targets in terms of profit.
3. Each department functions individually in achieving the objective of profit maximization and yet continues to be a part of the organization.

DECISION RULES

1. To achieve the various objectives that a firm aims at, a manager has to take decisions from time to time.
2. The decision rules include: marginal principle where the marginal unit refers to the change in the total quantity due to a per-unit change in the factor that influences it; opportunity cost principle where in making its decisions whether to continue using the input, a firm must include in the cost of the input the opportunity cost that the input could have earned in its next best alternative employment; incremental principle where if the incremental revenue is greater than the incremental cost, then a new project should be undertaken.

PROCESS OF OPTIMIZATION

1. Optimization is the process, where the best feasible solution is determined to a problem.
2. In an optimization, the economic relationships involved should be expressed in the form of equations, tables and graphs, which can be analysed easily.
3. The different mathematical techniques used for optimization include: linear programming, game theory and differential calculus.
4. Constrained optimization occurs when the maximization or the minimization of the function is done under some constraints.

REVIEW QUESTIONS

TRUE OR FALSE QUESTIONS

1. Traditional economic theory believes that there are a variety of objectives before a firm.
2. Opportunity cost is the price that a firm must pay to a factor to prevent it from moving to the next best alternative use of the factor.
3. Economic profit is the difference between *TR* and *TC*s.
4. J. A. Schumpeter had presented a theory, where profits occur only in a dynamic economy.
5. By keeping the employees and the consumers happy, the firm nowadays has to fulfill the social responsibility.

SHORT ANSWER QUESTIONS

1. What are the objectives of a business firm?
2. Differentiate between accounting profit and economic profit.
3. How does a firm maximize the profits? Give an algebraic explanation.
4. What are the non-economic objectives of a firm? Discuss.
5. What is the optimization process? Explain.

LONG ANSWER QUESTIONS

1. What are profits? How can they be measured?
2. Discuss the different theories of profit.
3. How does a firm maximize the profits? Give a graphical explanation.
4. Besides profit maximization, what are the other economic objectives of a firm?
5. 'To achieve the various objectives that a firm aims at, a manager has to take decisions from time to time'. What are these decision rules?

ANSWERS

TRUE OR FALSE QUESTIONS

1. **False.** In traditional economic theory, it was assumed that the firm's objective was to maximize the profits.
2. **True.** Opportunity costs are also called future costs or alternative costs.
3. **True.** Here costs include both the explicit cost and the implicit cost.
4. **False.** J. A. Schumpeter had presented a theory, where profits occur on innovations in the manufacturing sector or even in the technique of supplying the goods.
5. **True.** By keeping the employees and the consumers happy, the firm nowadays has to fulfill the social responsibility besides aiming to achieve the economic objectives.

Demand, Elasticity of Demand and Elasticity of Supply

3

After studying this chapter, you should be able to understand:

- ✓ *Quantity demanded of a good is the amount of that good demanded at a particular price over a certain time.*
- ✓ *According to the law of demand, there exists a negative relationship between the quantity demanded of a good and the price of the good.*
- ✓ *A change in demand or a change in the quantity demanded of the good is a movement, which occurs along the demand curve and is caused by a change in the price of the good, ceteris paribus.*
- ✓ *A shift in the demand curve is caused by a change in any of the factors, which influence the demand other than the price of the good itself. It is important to note that there is a shift of the demand curve.*
- ✓ *According to the law of the supply, other things remaining the same, the quantity supplied of a good increases when the price of the good increases and decreases when price decreases.*
- ✓ *Graphically, equilibrium occurs at the point of the intersection of the market demand and the supply curves of the good.*
- ✓ *Price elasticity of the demand is a measure of the responsiveness of the quantity demanded of a good to a change in the price of the good.*
- ✓ *Income elasticity of demand is a measure of the responsiveness of the quantity demanded of a good to a change in the income of the consumer, ceteris paribus.*
- ✓ *Cross price elasticity of the demand is a measure of the responsiveness of the quantity demanded of a particular good to a change in the price of another good, ceteris paribus.*
- ✓ *Advertisement elasticity is a measure of the responsiveness of the quantity demanded of a particular good to a change in advertising, ceteris paribus.*
- ✓ *The elasticity of price expectations is a measure of the responsiveness of the expected change in the future prices to the change in the current prices of a good.*
- ✓ *Elasticity of supply is a measure of the responsiveness of the quantity supplied of a good to a change in the price of the good.*

INTRODUCTION

The price of a good or service is the rate at which it is exchanged for anything else. This price is determined by the interaction of the demand and the supply. While the demand is determined by the needs and wants of the human beings, the supply is determined by the scarce resources available in the economy. To analyse the changes in price, it is necessary to analyse the demand and the supply.

DEMAND

What Is Demand?

In economics, demand means the wants for goods which are backed up by the sufficient money to be able to pay for the goods which are demanded. Thus, the quantity demanded of a good is the amount of that good demanded at a particular price over a certain time.

There are four characteristics of the demand:

> Quantity demanded of a good is the amount of that good demanded at a particular price over a certain time.

(i) Demand for a good or service always exists at a particular price.

(ii) Demand is always with reference to a certain time. Thus, the demand for good or service is a flow concept.

(iii) The demand for a good depends on the utility of the good. Only those goods, which give the consumers a utility, are demanded by the consumers.

(iv) Demand for a good should always be backed up by the ability to buy the good, or in other words, purchasing power. Willingness alone is not sufficient for a good to be demanded.

> Individual demand is the quantity of a good that an individual is willing to purchase at a certain price over a given time.

It is important to distinguish between the individual demand and the market demand. Individual demand is the quantity of a good that an individual is willing to purchase at a certain price over a given time. Market demand is the total quantity of a good that is demanded by all the individuals in the market at a certain price over a given time. Hence, it is the aggregate demand by all the consumers of the product.

Demand Function

The demand for a good by an individual depends on many factors. These include the own price (price of the good itself), price of other related goods (substitutes and complements), income of the consumer, tastes and preferences of the consumer, income and wealth distribution and others.

The demand function for a good can be expressed as:

$$Dd_x = f(P_x, P_o, Y, T)$$

where Dd_x is demand for good *x*, P_x is price of good *x*, P_o is price of other goods, *Y* is income of the consumer and *T* is tastes and preferences of the consumer.

To analyse the demand function, we examine the relationship of demand to one factor at a time, using the Latin phrase, *ceteris paribus*, which means 'other things remaining the same'.

Demand and Price of Good *x*: Law of Demand

$$Dd_x = f(P_x)$$

The above function shows that there exists a relationship between the demand for a good and the price of the good, *ceteris paribus*. This relationship is called the law of demand. According to this law, other things remaining the same, an individual demands more of the good (and service) at a lower price than at a higher price. Hence, there exists a negative relationship between the quantity demanded of a good

According to the law of the demand, there exists a negative relationship between the quantity demanded of a good and the price of the good, assuming that the price of the other goods, income of the consumer and tastes and preferences of the consumer remain the same.

and the price of the good, assuming that the price of the other goods, income of the consumer and tastes and preferences of the consumer remain the same.

Demand Schedule

A demand schedule depicts the quantity of the good which is demanded at each price, assuming that the price of the other goods, income of the consumer and tastes and preferences of the consumer remain the same (*ceteris paribus* assumption).

Illustration 1: Suppose an individual's demand function for good x is $Dd_x = 10 - P_x$. Determine the individual's demand schedule and the demand curve.

Individual's Demand Schedule

By substitution of different prices of good x into this equation, we can obtain the individual's demand schedule as in Table 3.1.

Table 3.1 Individual's Demand Schedule: $Dd_x = 10 - P_x$

P_x	Dd_x	Points on Demand Curve in Figure 3.1
8	2	A
7	3	B
6	4	C
5	5	D
4	6	E

The demand schedule of an individual shows the alternative quantities of the good x demanded by the individual at different prices, *ceteris paribus.*

Individual's Demand Curve

By plotting the different pairs of values on a graph and then by joining the points so obtained, we can get the individual's demand curve for good x as in Figure 3.1.

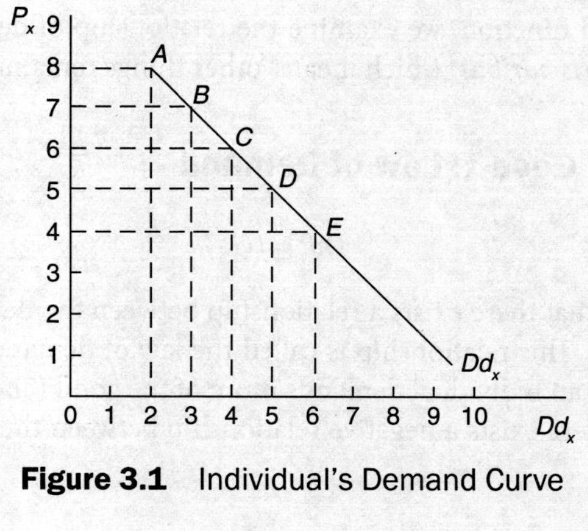

Figure 3.1 Individual's Demand Curve

The demand curve is a graphical representation of the demand schedule.

Thus, the demand curve is a graphical representation of the demand schedule. It is downward sloping showing the inverse relationship between the price and the quantity demanded of a good. The demand curve in Figure 3.1 depicts that at a particular point in time if the price of good x is ₹8 the individual's demand for the good is two units over time (for example, for a month or for an year). This is represented by point A on the demand curve. If the price of good x falls to ₹7, the individual's demand for the good increases to three units represented by point B on the demand curve.

If the price of good x further falls to ₹4, the individual's demand for the good increases to six units represented by point E on the demand curve.

Market Demand

The market demand schedule shows the alternative quantities of the good x demanded per time period by all the individuals in a market at different prices, *ceteris paribus*.

Thus, the market demand for good x will depend on P_x, price of good x; P_o, price of the other goods; Y, income of the consumers; T, tastes and preferences of the consumers; the number of consumers of good x in the market and the distribution of income.

Illustration 2: There are two individual's in the market with identical demand schedules for good x, $Dd_x = 10 - P_x$. Determine the market demand schedule and the market demand curve.

Table 3.2 and Figure 3.2 show the construction of the market demand schedule and market demand curve for the five individual's in the market.

Table 3.2 Market Demand Schedule: A Construction

P_x	Dd_{1x}	Dd_{2x}	DD_x
8	2	2	4
7	3	3	6
6	4	4	8
5	5	5	10
4	6	6	12

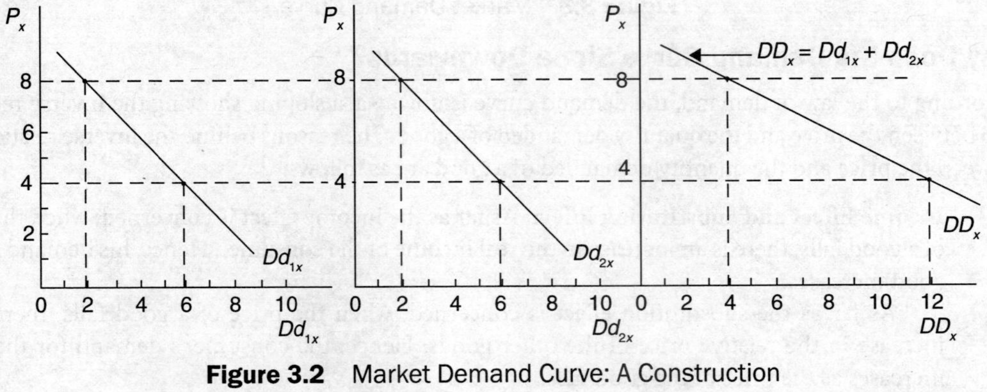

Figure 3.2 Market Demand Curve: A Construction

Illustration 3: There are 1000 individuals in the market with the identical demand schedules for good x, $Dd_x = 10 - P_x$. Determine the market demand schedule and the market demand curve.

Market demand curve for good x (if there are 1000 individuals in the market who are identical):

Individual demand schedule: $Dd_x = 10 - P_x$

Market demand schedule: $DD_x = 1000\ (Dd_x)$

$$= 1000\ (10 - P_x)$$

$$= 10{,}000 - 1000\ P_x$$

Table 3.3 and Figure 3.3 depict the market demand schedule and market demand curve, respectively, for the 1000 individuals in the market.

Table 3.3 Market Demand Schedule

P_x	Dd_x	Points on Demand Curve in Figure 3.3
1	9000	A
2	8000	B
3	7000	C
4	6000	D

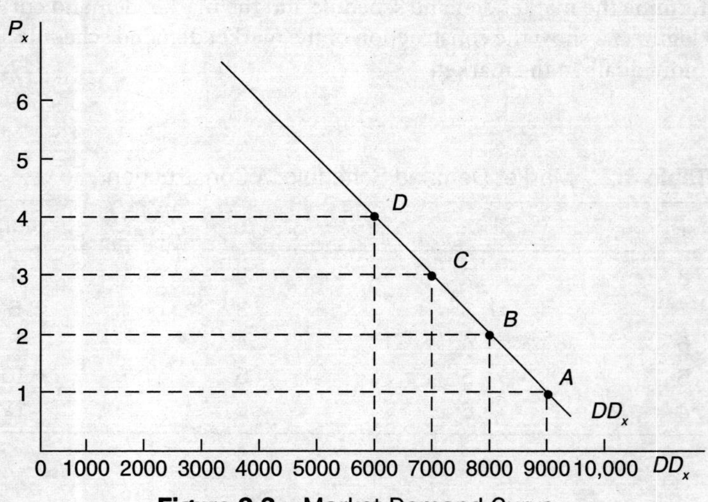

Figure 3.3 Market Demand Curve

Why Does the Demand Curve Slope Downwards?

According to the law of demand, the demand curve is downward sloping showing the inverse relationship between the price and the quantity demanded of a good. The reasons behind the inverse relationship between the price and the quantity demanded of a good are as follows:

(i) **Income Effect and Substitution Effect:** As far as the income effect is concerned, when the price of a good falls, there is an increase in the real income of the consumer. Hence, his demand for the good increases.

As far as the substitution effect is concerned, when the price of a good falls, there is an increase in the relative price of the other goods. Hence, the consumer's demand for the good increases as the price of the good falls.

(ii) **Law of Diminishing Marginal Utility:** According to the law of diminishing marginal utility as a consumer consumes additional units of a good, the additional utility that he gets from consuming the good goes on decreasing. Thus, he is willing to pay a lower price for the additional units of the good. Hence, the demand curve is downward sloping.

(iii) **Effect of Price on Demand:** When the price of a good increases, the consumer uses the good for the most essential purposes. Thus, at high prices, the demand for the commodity is low. However, when the price of a good decreases, the consumer uses the good for the less essential purposes. Thus, at low prices, the demand for the commodity is high, for example, water and electricity.

It is important to note that it is not necessary that the law of demand will apply in all cases. Though the law applies in the case of normal goods, exceptions may exist. For example, in the case of Giffen goods (named after Sir Robert Giffen), which are inferior goods, the demand curve slopes upwards. In addition, if the price of a good is rising and, in the future also, the consumer expects the price to increase, then in that case he will buy more of the good at higher prices.

Demand for Good *x* and Price of Other Goods

$$Dd_x = f(P_o)$$

The above function shows that there exists a relationship between the demand for a good and the price of other goods, for example, good *z*, *ceteris paribus*. As far as the other goods are concerned, there can be two cases.

When Goods x and z Are Complements

Goods are complements when they are used jointly in satisfying a want, for example, printer and print cartridge and coffee and sugar. Hence, they are consumed together and their consumption increases or decreases simultaneously. When the price of good *z* (for example, sugar) increases, the demand for good *x* (coffee) will decrease.

Figure 3.4 depicts the effect of a change in the price of the complementary good *z* on the demand for the good *x*. Figure 3.4(a) shows an increase in the price of good *z* from P_z to P'_z (for example, sugar), *ceteris paribus*. This is shown by an upward movement along the demand curve DD_z. Since

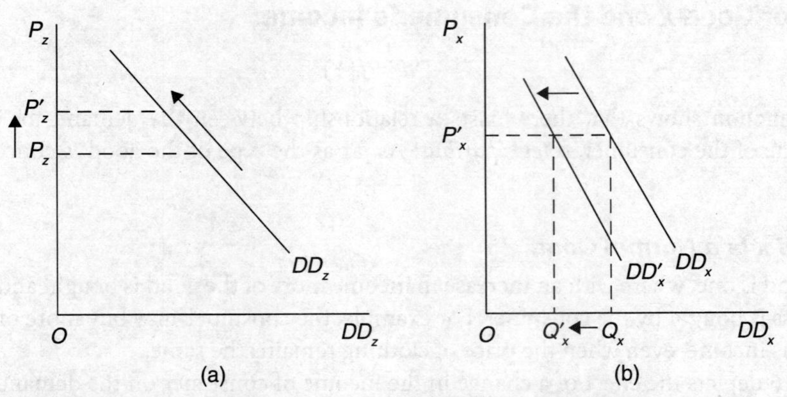

Figure 3.4 Effect of a Change in the Price of the Complementary Good *z* on the Demand for the Good *x*

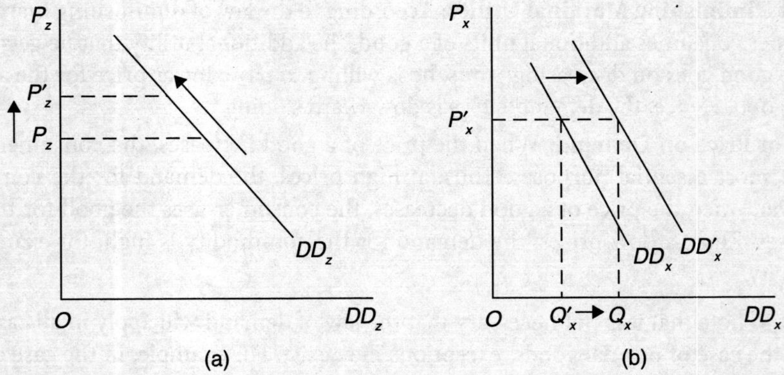

Figure 3.5 Effect of a Change in the Price of the Substitute Good z on the Demand for the Good x

good x and z are complements, in Figure 3.4(b), there will occur a downward shift of the demand curve for good x (coffee) from DD_x to DD'_x. At the price P'_x, the consumer's demand for good x will decrease from Q_x to Q'_x.

When Goods x and z Are Substitutes

Goods are substitutes when they can replace each other in consumption, for example, tea and coffee, butter and margarine. As far as consumption is concerned, they serve the same purpose. When the price of good z (for example, tea) increases, the demand for good x (coffee) will increase.

Figure 3.5 depicts the effect of a change in the price of the substitute good z on the demand for the good x. Figure 3.5(a) shows an increase in the price of good z from P_z to P'_z (for example, tea), *ceteris paribus*. This is shown by an upward movement along the demand curve DD_z. Since goods x and z are substitutes, in Figure 3.5(b), there will occur an outward shift of the demand curve for good x (coffee) from DD_x to DD'_x. At the price P'_x, the consumer's demand for good x will increase from Q_x to Q'_x.

Demand for Good *x* and the Consumer's Income

$$Dd_x = f(Y)$$

The above function shows that there exists a relationship between the demand for a good and the money income of the consumer, *ceteris paribus*. As far as the type of the good is concerned, there can be two cases.

When Good x Is a Normal Good

A normal good is one, where with an increase in income more of the good is bought and with a decrease in income less is bought by the consumer. For example, the consumer may buy more of clothes with an increase in his income, even when the price of clothing remains the same.

Figure 3.6 depicts the effect of a change in the income of consumer on the demand for the good x, *ceteris paribus*. Figure 3.6(a) shows an upward shift of the demand curve from Dd_x to Dd'_x. Since x is a normal good at the price P_x, the consumer's demand for good x will increase from Q_x to Q'_x.

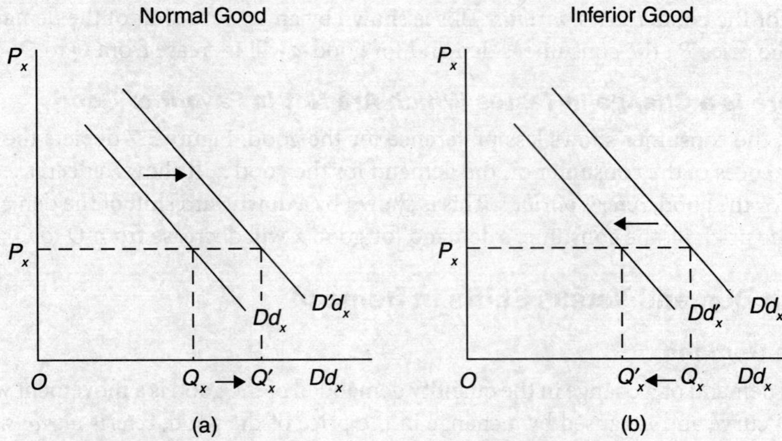

Figure 3.6 Effect of a Change in Income of the Consumer on the Demand for Good x

When Good x Is an Inferior Good

An inferior good is one, where with an increase in income less of the good is bought and with a decrease in income more of the good is bought by the consumer. In Figure 3.6(b), there is a downward shift of the demand curve from Dd_x to Dd'_x. Since *x* is an inferior good, at the price P_x, the consumer's demand for good *x* will decrease from Q_x to Q'_x.

Demand, and Tastes and Preferences of the Consumer

$$Dd_x = f(T)$$

The above function shows that there exists a relationship between the demand for a good and the tastes of the consumer, *ceteris paribus*. As far as the tastes are concerned, there can be two cases:

When Tastes Change in Favour of Good x

In this case, the consumer shows more preference for the good. Figure 3.7 depicts the effect of a change in the preferences of the consumer on the demand for the good *x*. It shows an increase in the consumer's

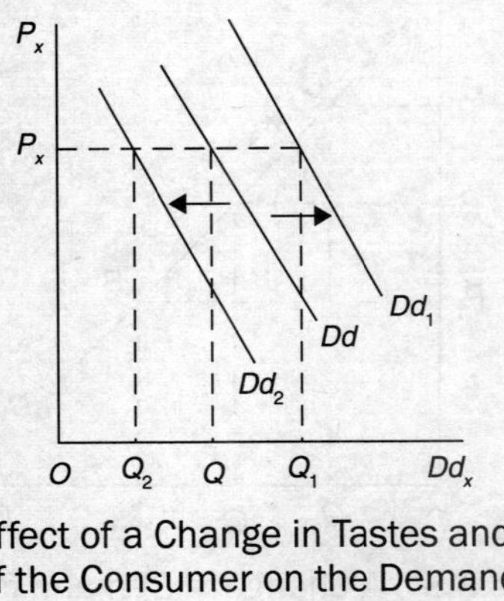

Figure 3.7 Effect of a Change in Tastes and Preferences of the Consumer on the Demand for Good x

preference for the good, *ceteris paribus*. This is shown by an upward shift of the demand curve from *Dd* to Dd_1. At the price P_x, the consumer's demand for good *x* will increase from *Q* to Q_1.

When There Is a Change in Tastes Which Are Not in Favour of Good x

In this case, the consumer shows less preference for the good. Figure 3.7 depicts the effect of a change in the preferences of the consumer on the demand for the good *x*. It shows a decrease in the consumer's preference for the good, *ceteris paribus*. This is shown by a downward shift of the demand curve from *Dd* to Dd_2. At the price P_x, the consumer's demand for good *x* will decrease from *Q* to Q_2.

Change in Demand Versus Shifts in Demand

Change in Demand

A change in demand or a change in the quantity demanded of the good is a movement which occurs along the demand curve and is caused by a change in the price of the good, *ceteris paribus*. It is important to note that there is only a movement along the demand curve. The change in demand can be of two types:

(i) **Expansion of Demand:** An expansion or extension of demand is a rise in the demand for the good as a result of a fall in the price of the good.

Figure 3.8 depicts the effect of a change in demand. Initially, the consumer is on the demand curve Dd_x at point *A* demanding *OQ* units of good *x* at price *OP*. With a fall in the price of the good to OP_1, the consumer is at point *B* increasing the quantity demanded of the good to OQ_1. This is called an expansion of demand.

(ii) **Contraction of Demand:** A contraction of demand is a fall in the demand for the good as a result of a rise in the price of the good.

In Figure 3.8, initially the consumer is on the demand curve Dd_x at point *A* demanding *OQ* units of good *x* at price *OP*. With an increase in the price of the good to OP_2, the consumer is at point *C* decreasing the quantity demanded of the good to OQ_2. This is called a contraction of demand.

Shifts In Demand

A shift in the demand curve is caused by a change in any of the factors, which influence the demand other than the price of the good itself. These factors include the price of other goods, P_o, income of the

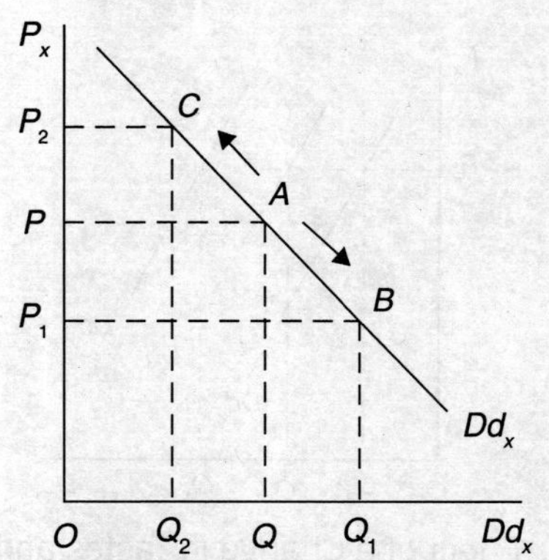

Figure 3.8 A Change in Demand for Good x

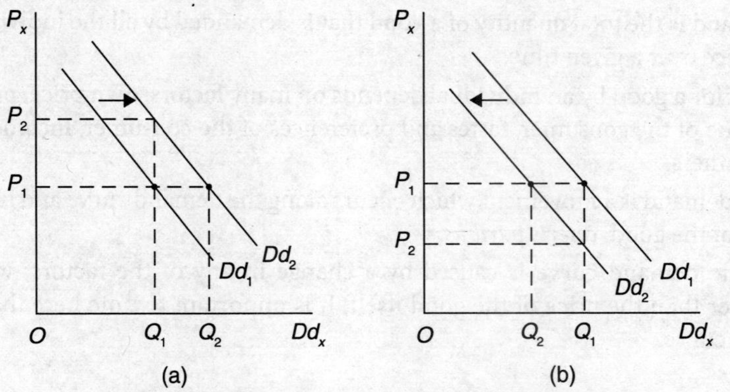

Figure 3.9 Shifts in Demand for Good *x*

consumer, *Y* and the tastes and preferences of the consumer, *T*. It is important to note here that there is a shift of the demand curve. The shift in demand can be of two types:

(i) **Increase in Demand:** An increase in demand is an increase in the demand for the good as a result of a change in any of the factors which influence the demand other than the price of the good itself, for example, an increase in the price of the substitute good or a rise in the consumer's income.

Figure 3.9(a) shows an increase in demand. Initially, the consumer is on the demand curve Dd_1 consuming OQ_1 units of the good at the price P_1. An increase in demand leads to an upward movement in the demand curve from Dd_1 to Dd_2. An increase in demand implies that

— the same quantity of the good OQ_1 is now demanded at a higher price P_2 or

— at the same price P_1 a larger quantity of the good is demanded, which has increased from OQ_1 to OQ_2.

(ii) **Decrease in Demand:** A decrease in demand is a decrease in the demand for the good as a result of a change in any of the factors which influence demand other than the price of the good itself, for example, a decrease in the price of the substitute good or a decrease in the consumer's income.

Figure 3.9(b) shows a decrease in demand. Initially, the consumer is on the demand curve Dd_1 consuming OQ_1 units of the good at the price P_1. A decrease in demand leads to a downward movement in the demand curve from Dd_1 to Dd_2. A decrease in demand implies that

— the same quantity of the good OQ_1 is now demanded at a lower price P_2 or

— at the same price P_1 a smaller quantity of the good is demanded, which has decreased from OQ_1 to OQ_2.

RECAP

- The quantity demanded of a good is the amount of that good demanded at a particular price over a certain time.
- Individual demand is the quantity of a good that an individual is willing to purchase at certain price over a given time.

- Market demand is the total quantity of a good that is demanded by all the individuals in the market at certain price over a given time.
- The demand for a good by an individual depends on many factors: own price, price of other related goods, income of the consumer, tastes and preferences of the consumer, income and wealth distribution and others.
- A change in demand is a movement which occurs along the demand curve and is caused by a change in the price of the good, *ceteris paribus*.
- A shift in the demand curve is caused by a change in any of the factors, which influence the demand other than the price of the good itself. It is important to note here that there is a shift of the demand curve.

SUPPLY

What Is Supply?

The supply of a good is the total amount of a good, which the producer is willing to produce and supply at a particular price over a certain time.

While understanding the demand, we focused on consumers. To understand the supply, we now examine the producer. The supply of a good is the total amount of a good, which the producer is willing to produce and supply at a particular price over a certain time.

Law of the Supply

$$Ss_x = f(P_x)$$

According to the law of supply, other things remaining the same, the quantity supplied of a good increases when the price of the good increases and decreases when the price decreases.

The above function shows that there exists a relationship between the supply of a good and the price of the good, *ceteris paribus*. This relationship is called the law of supply. According to the law of supply, other things remaining the same, the quantity supplied of a good increases when the price of the good increases and decreases when the price decreases. Hence, there exists a direct and positive relationship between the quantity supplied of a good and the price of the good, assuming that the other things remain the same.

Supply Function

The supply of a good depends on many factors. These include the own price (price of the good itself), price of the other related goods, changes in technology, price of the inputs or the factors of production, government policies and taxes and others.

The supply function of a good can be expressed as

$$Ss_x = f(P_x, P_o, P_I, T, G_T)$$

where Ss_x is supply of good x, P_x is price of good x, P_I is price of the inputs or the factors of production, P_o is price of other related goods, T is changes in technology and G_T is government policies and taxes.

Supply Schedule and Supply Curve

A supply schedule depicts the quantity of the good, which is supplied at each price, assuming that other things remain the same (*ceteris paribus* assumption).

Illustration 4: Suppose the supply function of a single producer for good x is $Ss_x = -20 + 20\ P_x$. Determine the supply schedule and the supply curve.

Single Producer Supply Schedule

By substitution of different prices of good x into this equation, we can obtain the supply schedule as in Table 3.4.

Table 3.4 Single Supply Schedule: $Ss_x = -20 + 20\ P_x$

P_x	Ss_x	Points on Supply Curve in Figure 3.10
6	100	A
5	80	B
4	60	C
3	40	D
2	20	E

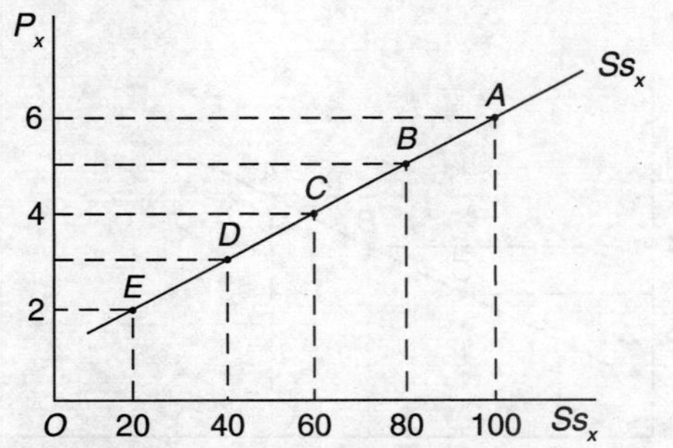

Figure 3.10 Single Producer's Supply Curve

The supply schedule shows the different quantities of the good x supplied by the producer at different prices, *ceteris paribus*.

By plotting the different pairs of values on a graph and then by joining the points so obtained, we can get the supply curve for good x as in Figure 3.10.

Thus, the supply curve is a graphical representation of the supply schedule. It is upward sloping showing the positive relationship between the price and the quantity supplied of a good.

> The supply curve is a graphical representation of the supply schedule. It is upward sloping. showing the positive relationship between the price and the quantity supplied of a good.

Market Supply Schedule

The market supply schedule shows the different quantities of good x supplied, per time period, by all the producers of good x in the market at different prices, *ceteris paribus*. Hence, it is the aggregate of the supply of the entire producers of good x in the market. The market supply of a good depends on all the factors, which determine the single producer's supply curve and also on the number of producers of good x.

Illustration 5: There are 100 identical producers in the market with identical supply schedules for good *x*, $Ss_x = -20 + 20\ P_x$. Determine the market supply schedule and market supply curve.

Single producer's supply schedule: $Ss_x = -20 + 20\ P_x$.

Market supply curve for good *x* (if there are 100 producers in the market who are identical)

$$SS_x = 100\ (Ss_x) = -2000 + 2000\ P_x.$$

We can obtain the market supply schedule in Table 3.5 and the market supply curve in Figure 3.11.

Table 3.5 Market Supply Schedule

P_x	SS_x	Points on Supply Curve in Figure 3.11
5	8000	A
4	6000	B
3	4000	C
2	2000	D

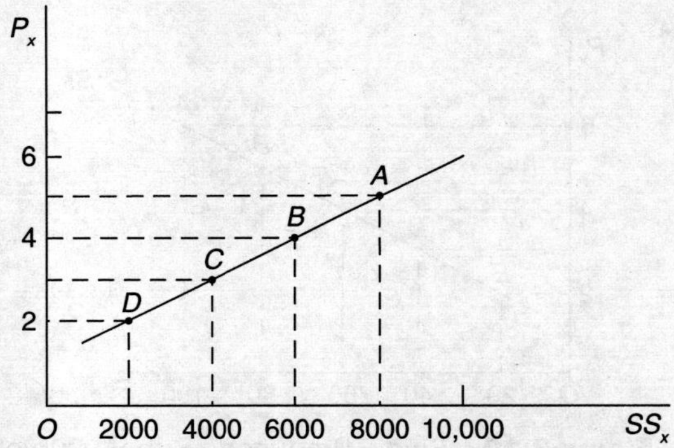

Figure 3.11 Market Supply Curve

Why Does the Supply Curve Slope Upwards?

The reasons behind the positive relationship between the price and the quantity supplied of a good are as follows:

(i) An increase in production and thus an increased supply can only occur at a higher price because of the law of diminishing returns.

(ii) By selling at a higher price, the producer is able to make greater profits. Thus with an increase in price, he increases the quantity supplied.

Change in Supply Versus Shifts in Supply

Change in Supply

A change in supply or a change in the quantity supplied of the good is a movement, which occurs along the supply curve and is caused by a change in the price of the good, *ceteris paribus*. It is important to note that there is only a movement along the supply curve. The change in supply can be of two types:

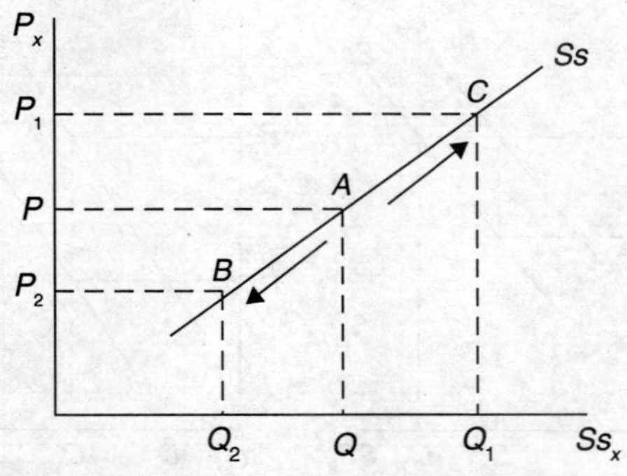

Figure 3.12 A Change in Supply of Good *x*

(i) **Expansion of Supply:** An expansion or extension of supply is a rise in the supply of the good as a result of an increase in the price of the good.

A change in supply or a change in the quantity supplied of the good is a movement, which occurs along the supply curve and is caused by a change in the price of the good, *ceteris paribus*.

Figure 3.12 depicts the effect of a change in supply. Initially, the producer is on the supply curve *Ss* at point *A* supplying *OQ* units of good *x* at price *OP*. An increase in the price of the good to OP_1 leads to an increase in the quantity supplied of the good to OQ_1. This is called an expansion of supply.

(ii) **Contraction of Supply:** A contraction of supply is a decrease in the supply of the good as a result of a fall in the price of the good.

In Figure 3.12, initially the consumer is on the supply curve *Ss* at point *A* supplying *OQ* units of good *x* at price *OP*. A fall in the price of the good to OP_2 leads to a decrease in the quantity supplied of the good to OQ_2. This is called a contraction of demand.

Shifts in Supply

A shift in supply curve is caused by a change in any of the factors, which influence the supply other than the price of the good itself. These factors include changes in technology and in government policies. It is important to note here that there is shift of the supply curve. The shift in supply can be of two types.

A shift in supply curve is caused by a change in any of the factors, which influence supply other than the price of the good itself. It is important to note here that there is shift of the supply curve.

(i) **Increase in Supply:** An increase in supply is an increase in the supply of the good as a result of a change in any of the factors, which influence the supply other than the price of the good itself.

Figure 3.13(a) shows an increase in supply. Initially, the producer is on the supply curve Ss_1 supplying OQ_1 units of the good at the price P_1. An increase in supply leads to an outward movement in the supply curve from Ss_1 to Ss_2. An increase in supply implies that

— the same quantity of the good OQ_1 is now supplied at a lower price P_2 or

— at the same price P_1, a larger quantity of the good is supplied which increases from OQ_1 to OQ_2.

(ii) **Decrease in Supply:** A decrease in supply is a decrease in the supply of the good as a result of a change in any of the factors, which influence the supply other than the price of the good itself.

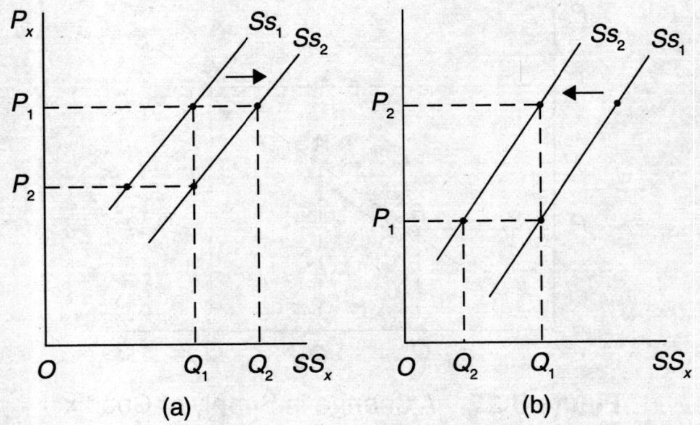

Figure 3.13 Shifts in Supply of Good x

Figure 3.13(b) shows a decrease in supply. Initially, the producer is on the supply curve Ss_1 supplying OQ_1 units of the good at the price P_1. A decrease in supply leads to an inward movement in the supply curve from Ss_1 to Ss_2. A decrease in supply implies that

— the same quantity of the good OQ_1 is now supplied at a higher price P_2 or

— at the same price P_1, a smaller quantity of the good is supplied, which decreases from OQ_1 to OQ_2.

RECAP

- The supply of a good is the total amount of a good which the producer is willing to produce and supply at a particular price over a certain time.
- According to the law of supply, other things remaining the same, the quantity supplied of a good increases when the price of the good increases and decreases when the price decreases.
- A supply schedule depicts the quantity of the good which is supplied at each price, assuming that other things remain the same (*ceteris paribus* assumption).
- The supply curve is upward sloping showing the positive relationship between the price and the quantity supplied of a good.
- The market supply schedule shows the different quantities of good *x* supplied, per time period, by all the producers of good *x* in the market at different prices, *ceteris paribus*.

EQUILIBRIUM

Equilibrium occurs when the quantity demanded of a good in the market over a certain time is equal to the quantity supplied of the good over the same time.

Equilibrium occurs when the quantity demanded of a good in the market over a certain time is equal to the quantity supplied of the good over the same time. Graphically, equilibrium occurs at the point of intersection of the market demand and the supply curves of the good. The equilibrium price is that price at which the equilibrium exists. The equilibrium quantity is that quantity at which the equilibrium exists.

Illustration 6: There are 1000 individuals in the market with identical demand schedules for good *x*, $Dd_x = 10 - P_x$ and 100 identical producers in the market with the identical supply schedules for good *x*, $Ss_x = -20 + 20\,P_x$. Determine the equilibrium price and equilibrium quantity for good *x*.

Market demand schedule:

$$DD_x = 1000\,(Dd_x)$$
$$= 1000\,(10 - P_x)$$
$$= 10{,}000 - 1000\,P_x$$

Market supply curve for good x: $SS_x = 100\,(Ss_x) = -2000 + 2000\,P_x$.

Table 3.6 depicts the market demand and supply schedules while Figure 3.14 shows the equilibrium.

Table 3.6 Market Demand and Supply Schedules

P_x	DD_x	SS_x
5	5000	8000
4	6000	6000
3	7000	4000
2	8000	2000

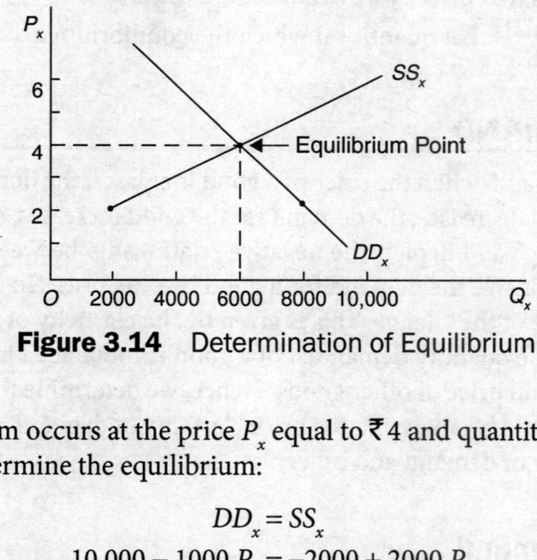

Figure 3.14 Determination of Equilibrium

Graphically, equilibrium occurs at the price P_x equal to ₹4 and quantity Q_x equal to 6000. Mathematically to determine the equilibrium:

$$DD_x = SS_x$$
$$10{,}000 - 1000\,P_x = -2000 + 2000\,P_x$$
$$3000\,P_x = 12{,}000$$
$$P_x = ₹4$$

Substituting the equilibrium price into the demand or supply equations:

$$DD_x = 10{,}000 - 1000\,P_x$$
$$= 10{,}000 - 1000\,(4)$$
$$= 6000$$

Or

$$SS_x = -2000 + 2000\,P_x$$
$$= -2000 + 2000\,(4)$$
$$= 6000$$

BOX 3.1

Alfred Marshall was a prominent figure in British economics from 1890 till his death in 1924. He specialized in microeconomics. One of the most important books written by him was the *Principles of Economics*, where Marshall laid emphasis on the fact that the output and the price of a good are determined by both the demand and the supply of the good. Marshall was responsible for bringing out the concept of price elasticity of demand to show the sensitivity of demand to the changes in the price of the good. He also introduced the concept of the consumer's surplus. The credit goes to Marshall for introducing the three periods in time, the market period, short period and the long period.

RECAP

- Graphically, equilibrium occurs at the point of intersection of market demand and supply curves of the good.
- The equilibrium price is that price at which the equilibrium exists.
- The equilibrium quantity is that quantity at which the equilibrium exists.

ELASTICITY OF DEMAND

According to the law of demand, when the price of a good increases, the demand for the good decreases, and when the price of a good decreases, the demand for the good increases, *ceteris paribus*. While the law shows the direction of change and depicts the negative relationship between price and quantity, it does not indicate as to how responsive the demand for a good is to its price. In other words, it does not give the magnitude or the degree of the change. This is given by the elasticity of demand.

As already discussed, the quantity demanded of a good is influenced by many factors, for example, price of the good, income, and price of other goods. Hence, we determine the magnitude of the relationship of these factors to demand by analysing the price elasticity of demand, income elasticity of demand, and the cross price elasticity of demand and others.

Price Elasticity of Demand

What Is Price Elasticity of Demand?

The concept was first discussed by Alfred Marshall. Price elasticity of demand is a measure of the responsiveness of the quantity demanded of a good to a change in the price of the good. Price elasticity of demand can be defined as the ratio of the percentage change in the quantity demanded of a good, per unit of time, to the percentage change in the price of the good.

$$E_p = \frac{\text{Percentage change in the quantity demanded of a good}}{\text{Percentage change in the price of the good}}$$

$$= \text{Change in quantity demanded} - \text{Change in price}$$

$$= \frac{\Delta Q}{Q} - \frac{\Delta P}{P}$$

$$E_P = \frac{\Delta Q}{\Delta P} \times \frac{P}{Q}$$

where E_P is price elasticity of demand, Q is original quantity demanded, P is original price, ΔQ is change in quantity demanded and ΔP is change in price.

(It is important to note that the coefficient of price elasticity of demand, E_P, is negative since there is an inverse relationship between the price and the quantity demanded.)

Factors Influencing the Price Elasticity of Demand

Price elasticity of demand depends on certain following factors:

(i) **Nature of the Good**: Goods can be grouped into necessities, comforts and luxuries. Necessities such as bread, milk and clothes are goods, which are necessary for the survival. Their demand elasticity is low. Comforts are goods, whose demand is more elastic as compared with the luxuries. Luxuries such as LCD and fancy cars are goods, whose demand is highly elastic. An increase in the price of luxuries leads to a decrease in demand while a decrease in the price leads to an increase in demand.

(ii) **Availability of Substitutes for the Good:** The elasticity of demand will be higher, the more is the availability of close substitutes for the good. For example, tea and coffee are close substitutes and thus have a high elasticity of demand. An increase in the price of coffee implies that tea is relatively less expensive. Hence, there is an increase in demand for the relatively less expensive tea. For goods such as sugar and salt, in general, the elasticity of demand will be lower since they do not have any close substitutes.

In addition, the elasticity of demand may be much larger for, the different brands of soap, for example, than for soap itself. This is because each brand of soap is a close substitute of the other brand.

(iii) **Variety of Uses of the Good:** At a lower price, a good will be used for many purposes, for example, there are many uses of electricity. Thus, if a good has a large number of uses then its elasticity is high for a fall in price as it can be used for the less important tasks. However, at a higher price, the good will be used only to satisfy the more essential demands.

(iv) **Fraction of the Income Spent on the Good:** If a consumer spends a small fraction of his income on buying a good, then its elasticity will be low, for example, salt, pens and pencils. If the price of any of these goods increases, there will be almost no change in demand since the expenditure on them forms a very small part of the total expenses by a consumer.

On the other hand, if a consumer spends a large proportion of his income on buying a good, for example, LCD and cars, then an increase in its price may lead to a decrease in demand depicting a high elasticity for the good.

(v) **Possibility of Postponement of Consumption:** Goods, where the consumption can be postponed, will have a high elasticity of demand. An increase in the price of durable goods such as televisions will lead to a postponement of demand by the consumers and thus the demand will fall.

(vi) **Price of the Good:** If the price is high, then the demand for the good is elastic and if the price is low then the demand is inelastic.

All these factors play an important role in determining the elasticity of the demand.

Measurement of Price Elasticity of Demand

The following are different methods of measuring the price elasticity of the demand.

Percentage Method

According to this method, the price elasticity of demand is the ratio of the percentage change in the quantity demanded of a good, per unit of time, to the percentage change in the price of the good.

$$E_P = \frac{\text{Percentage change in the quantity demanded of a good}}{\text{Percentage change in the price of the good}}$$

$$= \text{Change in quantity demanded} - \text{Change in price}$$

$$= \frac{\Delta Q}{Q} - \frac{\Delta P}{P}$$

$$E_P = \frac{\Delta Q}{\Delta P} \times \frac{P}{Q}$$

where E_P is price elasticity of demand, Q is original quantity demanded, P is original price, ΔQ is change in quantity demanded and ΔP is change in price.

The coefficient of elasticity of demand can take a value between zero and infinity.

(i) **Demand Is Perfectly Inelastic, $E_P = 0$:** In such a situation, the ratio of percentage change in the quantity demanded to the percentage change in the price of the good is zero. This implies that whatever is the price of the good the quantity demanded remains the same. The demand curve is shown in Figure 3.15(a) as a straight line parallel to the *y* axis. *Example:* Medicines.

(ii) **Demand Is Relatively Inelastic, $E_P < 1$:** In such a situation, the ratio of percentage change in the quantity demanded to the percentage change in the price of the good is < 1. This implies that the percentage change in the quantity demanded is less than the percentage change in the price of the good. The demand curve is shown in Figure 3.15(b). A decrease in the price of the good from P_1 to P_2 leads to an increase in the quantity demanded from OQ_1 to OQ_2. The decrease in the price, ΔP is larger than the increase in the quantity demanded, ΔQ. *Example:* Necessities.

(iii) **Demand Has a Unitary Elasticity, $E_P = 1$:** In such a situation, the ratio of percentage change in the quantity demanded equals the percentage change in the price of the good. The demand curve is shown in Figure 3.15(c) as a rectangular hyperbola. A decrease in the price of the good from P_1 to P_2 leads to an increase in the quantity demanded from OQ_1 to OQ_2. The decrease in the price, ΔP is equal to the increase in the quantity demanded, ΔQ. *Example:* Normal goods.

(iv) **Demand Is Elastic, $E_P > 1$:** In such a situation, the ratio of percentage change in the quantity demanded to the percentage change in the price of the good is >1. This implies that the percentage change in the quantity demanded is more than the percentage change in the price of the good. The demand curve shown in Figure 3.15(d) is relatively flatter. A decrease in the price of the good from P_1 to P_2 leads to an increase in the quantity demanded from OQ_1 to OQ_2. The decrease in the price, ΔP is less than the increase in the quantity demanded, ΔQ. *Example:* Luxuries.

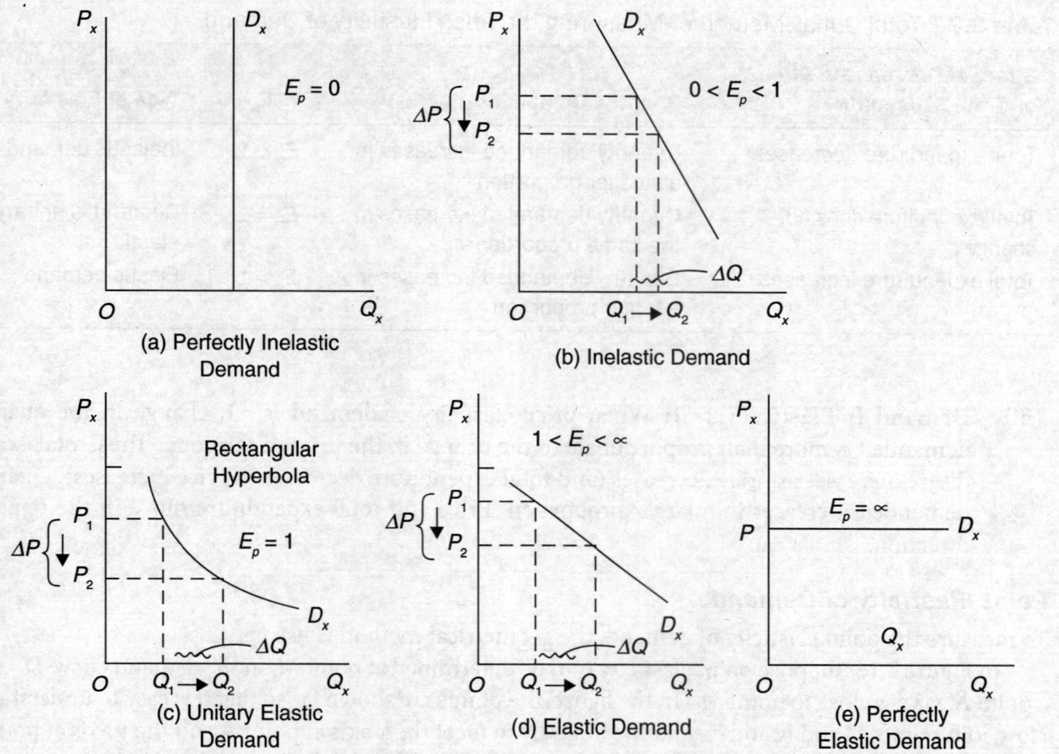

Figure 3.15 Percentage Method of Measuring the Price Elasticity of the Demand

(v) **Demand Is Perfectly Elastic, $E_p = \infty$:** In such a situation, any price change, which may be very small, leads to an infinite change in the quantity demanded of good *x*. The demand curve is shown in Figure 3.15(e) as a straight line parallel to the *x* axis. Such a situation exists under the perfect competition.

Outlay Method

This is also known as the total expenditure method or the total revenue method. Here, the total outlay of the consumer, on the good, is compared before and after the price change. Given that total outlay is measured by quantity multiplied by the price of the good, there can be three situations:

(i) **Demand Is Relatively Inelastic, $E_p < 1$:** When price elasticity of demand is < 1, change in the quantity demanded is less than proportionate to the change in the price of the good. Thus, total expenditure decreases as price decreases (and total expenditure increases as price increases). Quantity demanded increases in a smaller proportion. Price and total expenditure move in the same direction.

(ii) **Demand Has a Unitary Elasticity, $E_p = 1$:** When price elasticity of demand is equal to one, change in the quantity demanded is in the same proportion to the change in the price of the good. Thus total expenditure does not change as price decreases (or as price increases). Quantity demanded increases in the same proportion.

Table 3.7 Total Outlay Method of Measuring the Price Elasticity of Demand

Effect of Decrease in Price on Total Expenditure	Quantity Demanded	E_P	Type of Elasticity
Total expenditure decreases	Quantity demanded increases in a smaller proportion	$E_P < 1$	Inelastic demand
Total expenditure does not change	Quantity demanded increases in the same proportion	$E_P = 1$	Demand is unitary elastic
Total expenditure increases	Quantity demanded increases in a larger proportion	$E_P > 1$	Elastic demand

(iii) **Demand Is Elastic, $E_P > 1$:** When price elasticity of demand is >1, change in the quantity demanded is more than proportionate to the change in the price of the good. Thus, total expenditure increases as price decreases (and total expenditure decreases as price increases). Quantity demanded increases in a larger proportion. Price and total expenditure move in the opposite direction.

Point Elasticity of Demand

To measure the point elasticity of demand, the geometrical method is used.

In Figure 3.16, suppose point elasticity is to be determined at point *M* on the demand curve D_x. Take a point *N* as very close to point *M*. (In the figure, the points are shown far so that it is easy to understand.) Now, join points *M* and *N* and extend the line *MN* to meet the *x* axis at point *A* and the *y* axis at point *B*. To determine the elasticity, we use the formula in the percentage method:

$$E_P = \frac{\Delta Q}{\Delta P} \times \frac{P}{Q}$$

where $Q = OO_1$, $P = OP_1$, $\Delta Q = Q_1Q_2$ and $\Delta P = P_1P_2$.
By substituting in the formula, we get

$$E_P = \frac{Q_1Q_2}{P_1P_2} \times \frac{OP_1}{OQ_1}$$

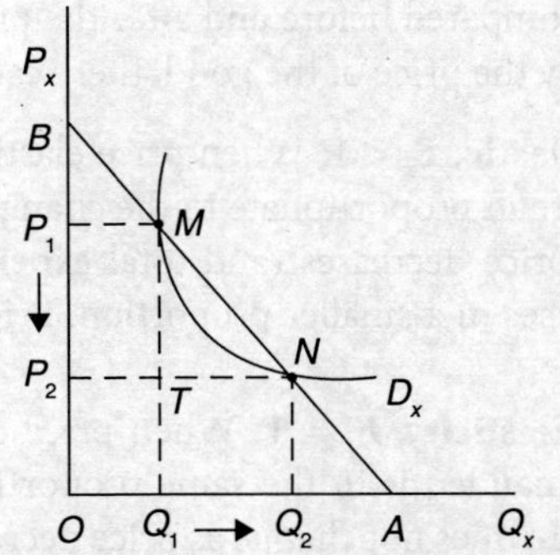

Figure 3.16 Point Elasticity of Demand

But in the figure

$$Q_1Q_2 = TN$$
$$P_1P_2 = MT$$
$$OP_1 = MQ_1$$

Thus, by substituting for these values, we have

$$E_P = \frac{TN}{MT} \times \frac{OP_1}{OQ_1}$$

Comparing triangles MTN and MQ_1A, we find them similar (since each corresponding angle is equal). Thus,

$$\frac{TN}{MT} = \frac{Q_1A}{MQ_1}$$

Thus, by substituting for these values, we have

$$E_P = \frac{Q_1A}{MQ_1} \times \frac{MQ_1}{OQ_1}$$

$$E_P = \frac{Q_1A}{OQ_1}$$

In addition, comparing triangles BP_1M and MQ_1A, we find them similar (since each corresponding angle is equal). Thus,

$$\frac{Q_1A}{P_1M} = \frac{MA}{BM}$$

Also $\quad P_1M = OQ_1$

Thus,

$$\frac{Q_1A}{OQ_1} = \frac{MA}{BM}$$

$$E_P = \frac{Q_1A}{OQ_1} = \frac{MA}{BM}$$

$$= \frac{Q_1A}{OQ_1} = \frac{\text{Lower segment}}{\text{Upper segment}}$$

If the demand curve is non-linear, then again the geometrical method can be used to measure the elasticity at a point on the demand curve by drawing a tangent at the point and then by applying the formula

$$E_P = \frac{\text{Lower segment}}{\text{Upper segment}}$$

Arc Elasticity

Under the point elasticity of demand, we measured the elasticity at a point on the demand curve, where the change in price is infinitesimally small. To measure arc elasticity, we take two finite points on a demand curve, which are close to each other as in Figure 3.17. Suppose arc elasticity is to be calculated on the demand curve D_x over the arc MN.

$$E_p = \frac{\Delta Q}{\Delta P} \times \frac{\frac{P_1 + P_2}{2}}{\frac{Q_1 + Q_2}{2}}$$

$$= \frac{\Delta Q}{\Delta P} \times \frac{(P_1 + P_2)}{(Q_1 + Q_2)}$$

In Figure 3.17

$$E_p = \frac{Q_2 - Q_1}{P_2 - P_1} \times \frac{(P_1 + P_2)}{(Q_1 + Q_2)}$$

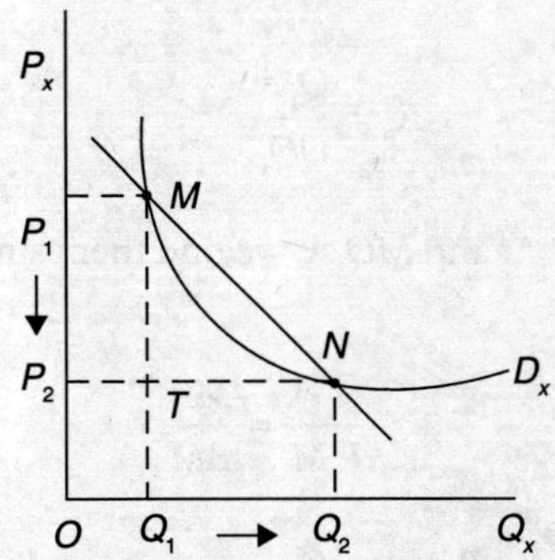

Figure 3.17 Arc Elasticity of Demand

Price Elasticity of Demand on a Linear Demand Curve

Along a linear demand curve, which is downward sloping, price elasticity varies at different points along the demand curve. In Figure 3.18 on the demand curve DD', we can calculate elasticity by the formula

$$E_p = \frac{\text{Lower segment}}{\text{Upper segment}}$$

(i) At point D on the y axis, $E_p = \frac{DD'}{0} = \infty$.

(ii) At point M, the midpoint on the demand curve DD' $E_p = \frac{MD'}{DM} = 1$.

(iii) At point D' on the x axis, $E_p = \frac{0}{DD'} = 0$.

Thus, as we move down a demand curve, the price elasticity goes on decreasing.

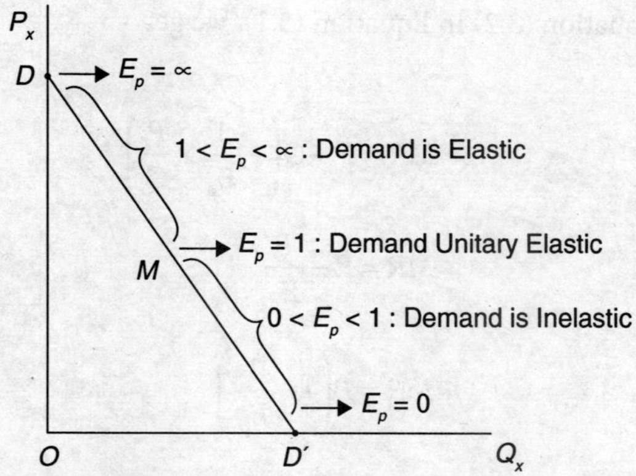

Figure 3.18 Price Elasticity of Demand on a Linear Demand Curve

REVENUE CONCEPTS

We can depict the relationship between average revenue, marginal revenue, total revenue and price elasticity as follows.

Average Revenue, Marginal Revenue and Their Relationship with Price Elasticity

We have

$$\text{TR} = P \times Q$$

$$MR = \frac{\partial TR}{\partial Q}$$

$$MR = \frac{\partial (P \times Q)}{\partial Q}$$

$$MR = P \times \frac{\partial Q}{\partial Q} + Q \times \frac{\partial P}{\partial Q}$$

$$MR = P + Q\frac{\partial P}{\partial Q} \tag{3.1}$$

But

$$E_p = -\frac{\Delta Q}{\Delta P} \times \frac{P}{Q}$$

Thus,

$$\frac{\partial P}{\partial Q} = -\frac{1}{E_p} \times \frac{P}{Q} \tag{3.2}$$

Substituting the value of Equation (3.2) in Equation (3.1), we get

$$MR = P + Q\left(-\frac{1}{E_P} \times \frac{P}{Q}\right)$$

$$MR = P - \frac{P}{E_P}$$

$$MR = P\left(1 - \frac{1}{E_P}\right)$$

But *P* and *AR* are the same.

Thus,

$$MR = AR\left(1 - \frac{1}{E_P}\right)$$

Or

$$MR = AR - \frac{AR}{E_P}$$

$$\frac{AR}{E_P} = AR - MR$$

$$E_P = \frac{AR}{AR - MR}$$

The formula shows the relationship between AR, MR and E_P. Table 3.8 shows the different values of AR and MR when E_P lies between zero and infinity.

Figure 3.19 graphically depicts the average revenue, marginal revenue and their relationship with price elasticity.

Table 3.8 Average Revenue, Marginal Revenue and Their Relationship with Price Elasticity

E_P	AR	MR
$E_P = \infty$	$AR = MR$	$MR = AR$
$E_P > 1$	$AR > 0$	$MR > 0$
$E_P = 1$	$AR > 0$	$MR = 0$
$E_P < 1$	$AR > 0$	$MR < 0$
$E_P = 0$	$AR = 0$	$MR < 0$

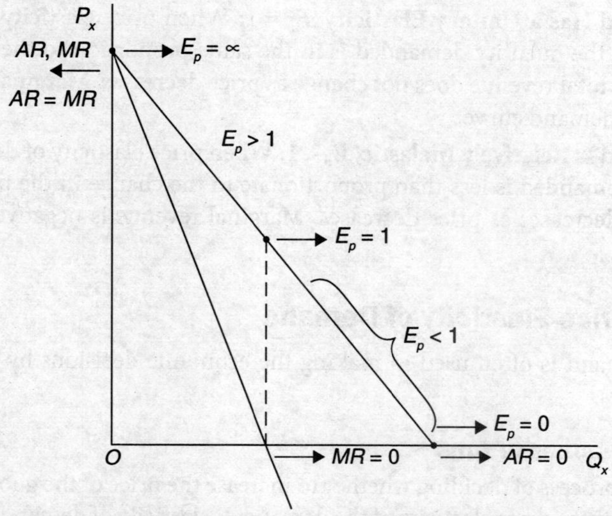

Figure 3.19 Average Revenue, Marginal Revenue and Their Relationship with Price Elasticity

Total Revenue and Its Relationship with Price Elasticity

The relationship between total revenue and price elasticity has been depicted in Figure 3.20.

(i) **When Demand Is Elastic, $E_p > 1$:** When price elasticity of demand is >1, change in the quantity demanded is more than proportionate to the change in the price of the good. Thus, total revenue increases as price decreases. Also, marginal revenue is positive. Thus, a firm will benefit if it reduces its price in this elastic range of the demand curve.

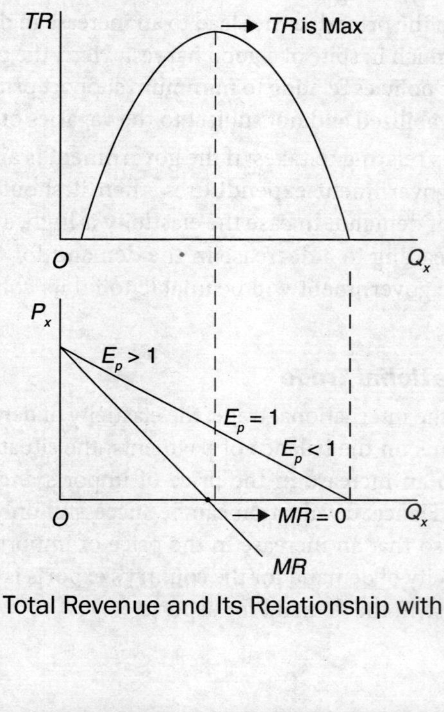

Figure 3.20 Total Revenue and Its Relationship with Price Elasticity

(ii) **When Demand Has a Unitary Elasticity, $E_p = 1$:** When price elasticity of demand is equal to one, change in the quantity demanded is in the same proportion to the change in the price of the good Thus, total revenue does not change as price decreases. Marginal revenue is zero in this portion of the demand curve.

(iii) **When Demand Is Relatively Inelastic, $E_p < 1$:** When price elasticity of demand is < 1, change in the quantity demanded is less than proportionate to the change in the price of the good. Thus, total revenue decreases as price decreases. Marginal revenue is negative in this portion of the demand curve.

Significance of Price Elasticity of Demand

Price elasticity of demand is often used in making the economic decisions by the business firms, the government and others.

Decisions by the Business Firms

When a firm is in the process of deciding whether to increase the price of the good that it is producing, it is important to consider the price elasticity of the demand. If elasticity of demand is high, then a decrease in price will lead to an increase in the sales of the good. Under the monopoly when a monopolist goes in for price discrimination of charging different prices in different markets, he determines the price in each market by taking into consideration the price elasticity of demand in each market.

Decisions by the Government

Important decisions have to be made by the government in its formulation of policies. These include the following:

(i) Fixation of minimum support prices for agriculture. The elasticity of demand for agricultural products including wheat, rice and vegetables is low since they are necessities. A good harvest leads to an increase in supply, and given the demand there occurs a fall in the price. Since the demand is inelastic, a fall in the price does not lead to an increase in demand. Hence, the farmer's income does not increase much in spite of a good harvest. Here, the government plays an important role in formulating the policies relating to minimum support price such that the prices of the agricultural products are stabilized and not subject to the vagaries of nature.

(ii) While formulating policies relating to taxes, if the government is aiming at maximizing its tax revenues to finance the government expenditures, then it should levy high taxes only on goods with low elasticity of demand. In case the elasticity is high, a tax will lead to an increase in the price of the good leading to a decrease in the demand for the good and thus a fall in the tax revenue. Then, the government will be unable to fill its coffers through the collection of taxes.

Decisions Relating to International Trade

In analysing the issues relating to the international trade, the elasticity of demand plays a very important role. If a country is facing problems on the balance of payments, the situation can be tackled through devaluation. Devaluation leads to an increase in the price of imports and a decrease in the price of exports of the devaluing country. Hence, devaluation can be successful only if the elasticity of demand for the country's imports is high so that an increase in the price of imports leads to a decrease in the demand for imports and the elasticity of demand for the country's exports is low so that a decrease in the price of exports leads to an increase in the demand for exports.

RECAP

- Price elasticity of demand can be defined as the ratio of the percentage change in the quantity demanded of a good, per unit of time, to the percentage change in the price of the good.
- Price elasticity of demand depends on certain factors: nature of the good, availability of substitutes for the goods, variety of uses of the good, the fraction of the income spent on the good, possibility of postponement of consumption and the price of the good.
- There are many ways by which price elasticity of demand can be measured: percentage method, outlay method, point elasticity of demand and arc elasticity.
- As we move down a demand curve, the elasticity goes on decreasing.

INCOME ELASTICITY OF DEMAND

What Is Income Elasticity of Demand?

An important determinant of demand is the consumer's income.

Income elasticity of demand is a measure of the responsiveness of the quantity demanded of a good to a change in the income of the consumer, *ceteris paribus*. Income elasticity of demand can be defined as the ratio of the percentage change in the quantity demanded of a good, per unit of time, to the percentage change in the income of the consumer.

Income elasticity of demand is a measure of the responsiveness of the quantity demanded of a good to a change in the income of the consumer, *ceteris paribus*.

$$E_Y = \frac{\text{Percentage change in quantity demanded of a good}}{\text{Percentage change in income}}$$

$$= \frac{\text{Change in quantity demanded}}{\text{Change in income}}$$

$$= \frac{\frac{\Delta Q}{Q}}{\frac{\Delta Y}{Y}}$$

$$= \frac{\Delta Q}{\Delta Y} \times \frac{Y}{Q}$$

where E_Y is income elasticity of the demand, Q is quantity demanded, Y is income, ΔQ is change in quantity demanded and ΔY is change in income.

Different Types of Income Elasticity of Demand

The coefficient of income elasticity can take a value, which may be positive or even negative as shown in Table 3.9.

(i) **Income Elasticity of Demand Is High: $E_Y > 1$:** In such a situation, the ratio of percentage change in the quantity demanded to the percentage change in the income is >1. This implies that the percentage change in the quantity demanded is more than the percentage change in the income.

Table 3.9 Types of Income Elasticity of Demand

Nature of the Good	Coefficient of Income Elasticity	Effect of Increase in Income on Quantity Demanded of the Good
Luxuries	$E_Y > 1$	Increases more than proportionately
Comforts	$E_Y = 1$	Increases proportionately
Necessities	$0 < E_Y < 1$	Increases less than proportionately
Inferior good	$E_Y < 0$	Decreases in absolute terms

When the consumer's income increases, the quantity demanded of the good increases more than proportionately. *Example:* Luxuries.

(ii) **Income Elasticity of Demand Is Equal to One or Unitary Income Elasticity: $E_Y = 1$:** In such a situation, the ratio of percentage change in the quantity demanded is equal to the percentage change in the income. When the consumer's income increases, the quantity demanded of the good increases proportionately. *Example:* Comforts.

(iii) **Income Elasticity of Demand Is Low: $0 < E_Y < 1$:** In such a situation, the ratio of percentage change in the quantity demanded to the percentage change in the income is < 1. This implies that the percentage change in the quantity demanded is less than the percentage change in the income. When the consumer's income increases, the quantity demanded of the good increases less than proportionately. Thus, here income elasticity is positive but < 1. *Example:* Necessities.

(iv) **Income Elasticity of Demand Is Zero: $E_Y = 0$:** In such a situation, there does not occur any change in the quantity demanded when there is a change in the income. It is very difficult to specify the type of good, which will have zero income elasticity.

(v) **Income Elasticity of Demand Is < 0 or Negative Income Elasticity: $E_Y < 0$:** In such a situation, an increase in the income leads to a decrease in the quantity demanded of the good. *Example:* Inferior goods.

Significance of Income Elasticity of Demand

(i) Income elasticity of demand helps classify goods into luxuries, comforts, necessities and inferior goods. This is of great use to a firm when it is making its decision as to which goods to produce.

(ii) Income elasticity of demand is very useful when forecasts of demand for the different goods are to be made. Thus, it helps the firm in planning its production strategies.

RECAP

- Income elasticity of demand is a measure of the responsiveness of the quantity demanded of a good to a change in the income of the consumer, *ceteris paribus*.
- The coefficient of income elasticity can take a value, which may be positive or even negative.
- Income elasticity of demand helps classify goods into luxuries, comforts, necessities and inferior goods.
- Income elasticity of demand is very useful when forecasts of demand for the different goods are to be made.

CROSS PRICE ELASTICITY OF DEMAND

What Is Cross Price Elasticity of Demand?

Besides the price and the consumer's income, there are many other factors which influence the demand for a good. An important determinant of demand is the price of the related goods.

Cross price elasticity of demand is a measure of the responsiveness of the quantity demanded of a particular good to a change in the price of another good, *ceteris paribus*. Cross price elasticity of demand can be defined as the ratio of the percentage change in the quantity demanded of good *x*, to the percentage change in the price of good *y*.

> Cross price elasticity of demand is a measure of the responsiveness of the quantity demanded of a particular good to a change in the price of another good, *ceteris paribus*.

$$E_{xy} = \frac{\text{Percentage change in quantity demanded of good } x}{\text{Percentage change in price of good } y}$$

$$= \frac{\text{Change in quantity demanded of good } x}{\text{Change in price of good } y}$$

$$= \frac{\frac{\Delta Q_x}{Q_x}}{\frac{\Delta P_y}{P_y}}$$

$$= \frac{\Delta Q_x}{\Delta P_y} \times \frac{P_y}{Q_x}$$

where E_{xy} is cross price elasticity of demand, Q_x is quantity demanded of good *x*, P_y is price of good *y*, ΔQ_x is change in quantity demanded of good *x* and ΔP_y is change in price of good *y*.

Different Types of Cross Price Elasticity of Demand

The coefficient of cross price elasticity can take a value, which may be between zero and infinity as depicted in Table 3.10.

(i) **Cross Elasticity of Demand Is > 0, $E_{xy} > 0$:** In such a situation, the two goods *x* and *y* are substitutes, for example, tea and coffee. An increase in the price of good *y* leads to an increase in the quantity demanded of good *x*.

Table 3.10 Types of Cross Price Elasticity of Demand

Nature of the Good	Coefficient of Cross Elasticity	Effect of Increase in the Price of Good *y* on Quantity Demanded of Good *x*
Substitutes	$E_{xy} > 0$	Increases
Unrelated goods	$E_{xy} = 0$	Does not change
Complements	$E_{xy} < 0$	Decreases

(ii) **Cross Elasticity of Demand Is Equal to Zero, $E_{xy} = 0$:** In such a situation, the two goods *x* and *y* are independent goods or goods which are not related to each other, for example, car and mobile phones. An increase in the price of good *y* does not lead to any change in the quantity demanded of good *x*.

(iii) **Cross Elasticity of Demand Is < 0, $E_{xy} < 0$:** In such a situation, the two goods *x* and *y* are complements, for example, coffee and sugar. An increase in the price of good *y* leads to a decrease in the quantity demanded of good *x*.

Significance of Cross Price Elasticity of Demand

Most often firms are interested in analysing the cross elasticity of demand for their goods with respect to other goods, especially the complementary and substitute goods. This is important so that the effect of any changes in the prices can be evaluated and taken into consideration when the firm is planning on its production and pricing strategies.

RECAP

- Cross price elasticity of demand is a measure of the responsiveness of the quantity demanded of a particular good to a change in the price of another good, *ceteris paribus*.
- The coefficient of cross price elasticity can take a value, which may be between zero and infinity.
- Cross elasticity of demand is important in that the effect of any changes in the prices of complementary and substitute goods can be evaluated and taken into consideration when the firm is planning on its production and pricing strategies.

ADVERTISING ELASTICITY

What Is Advertising Elasticity?

Nowadays, most firms spend on sales promotion activities, including advertising, to influence the sales of a good. It is important to note that although advertising does increase the sales, however, the degree to which it does so differs at different levels of the sales. Hence, it is of great importance to determine the optimum level of expenditure that should be incurred on advertising. This is even more important when a firm has to compete with other rival firms who are also involved in advertising their products.

> Advertisement elasticity is a measure of the responsiveness of the quantity demanded of a particular good to a change in advertising, *ceteris paribus*.

Advertisement elasticity is a measure of the responsiveness of the quantity demanded of a particular good to a change in advertising, *ceteris paribus*. Advertisement elasticity can be defined as the ratio of the percentage change in the quantity demanded of good or sales to the percentage change in advertising.

$$E_A = \frac{\text{Percentage change in quantity demanded}}{\text{Percentage change in advertising}}$$

$$= \frac{\dfrac{\text{Change in quantity demanded or sales}}{\text{Quantity demanded or sales}}}{\dfrac{\text{Change in advertising expenditure}}{\text{Initial advertising expenditure}}}$$

$$= \frac{\frac{\Delta Q}{Q}}{\frac{\Delta A}{A}}$$

$$= \frac{\Delta Q}{\Delta A} \times \frac{A}{Q}$$

where E_A is advertisement elasticity, Q is quantity demanded or sales, A is initial advertising expenditure, ΔQ is change in quantity demanded or sales and ΔA is change in advertising expenditure.

If a 10 per cent increase in advertising causes an increase in the sales by 4 per cent, *ceteris paribus*, the advertising elasticity is 0.4.

Factors Influencing Advertising Elasticity

Some of the factors which influence the advertising elasticity are as follows:

(i) **Advertisements by Other Competing Firms:** When firms are in a competitive situation, the effectiveness advertisement in influencing the sales of a firm will depend on the advertising expenditures of other firms.

(ii) **Sale of a Good:** When a new product is launched in a market E_A or the advertisement elasticity for the product may be >1. However, as the sales of the product go on increasing the advertisement elasticity may decrease once the consumers become aware of the product.

(iii) **Cumulative Effect of Advertising Expenditure:** In the initial stages of the product, the expenditure on advertising may be insufficient. Hence, the advertising elasticity may be low. However, as the advertising expenditure picks up the advertising elasticity may increase having a cumulative effect.

Types of Advertising Elasticity

The coefficient of advertising elasticity can take a value which may be between zero and infinity as depicted in Table 3.11.

(i) **Advertising Elasticity Is Equal to Zero, $E_A = 0$:** In such a situation, an increase in the advertising expenditure does not lead to an increase in sales.

(ii) **Advertising Elasticity Is > 0 But < 1, $1 < E_A > 0$:** In such a situation, an increase in the advertising expenditure leads to a less than proportionate increase in sales.

Table 3.11 Types of Advertising Elasticity

Coefficient of Advertising Elasticity	Effect of Increase in the Advertising Expenditure
$E_A = 0$	No increase in sales
$1 < E_A > 0$	Less than proportionate increase in sales
$E_A = 1$	A proportionate increase in sales
$E_A > 1$	More than proportionate increase in sales

(iii) **Advertising Elasticity Is Equal to Unity, $E_A = 1$:** In such a situation, an increase in the advertising expenditure leads to a proportionate increase in sales.

(iv) **Advertising Elasticity Is > 1, $E_A > 1$:** In such a situation, an increase in the advertising expenditure leads to a more than proportionate increase in sales.

RECAP

- Advertisement elasticity is a measure of the responsiveness of the quantity demanded of a particular good to a change in advertising, *ceteris paribus*.
- Some of the factors which influence the advertising elasticity are: advertisements by other competing firms, sales of a good and the cumulative effect of advertising expenditure.
- The coefficient of advertising elasticity can take a value, which may be between zero and infinity.

ELASTICITY OF PRICE EXPECTATIONS

The concept of elasticity of price expectations was devised by J. R. Hicks. The price expectations of people are influenced by many factors including past prices, current prices, current events on the economic scenario and political events.

The elasticity of price expectations is a measure of the responsiveness of the expected change in the future prices to the change in the current prices of a good.

The elasticity of price expectations is a measure of the responsiveness of the expected change in the future prices to the change in the current prices of a good. Elasticity of price expectations can be defined as the ratio of the relative change in expected future price of a good to the relative change in the current price of the good.

$$E_{PE} = \frac{\frac{\Delta P_F}{P_F}}{\frac{\Delta P_C}{P_C}}$$

$$= \frac{\Delta P_F}{\Delta P_C} \times \frac{P_C}{P_F}$$

where E_{PE} is elasticity of price expectations, P_F is expected future price of a good, P_C is current price of the good, ΔP_C is change in current price of the good and ΔP_F is change in expected future price of the good.

Types of Elasticity of Price Expectations

The coefficient of elasticity of price expectations can take a value, which may be < 0 or even greater than unity as depicted in Table 3.12.

(i) **Elasticity of Price Expectations Is > 1, $E_{PE} > 1$:** In such a situation, the consumers expect that the future prices will increase by a greater percentage than the current prices.

(ii) **Elasticity of Price Expectations Is Equal to One, $E_{PE} = 1$:** In such a situation, the consumers expect that the future prices will increase by the same percentage as the current prices.

(iii) **Elasticity of price expectations Is Smaller Than One, $E_{PE} < 1$:** In such a situation, the consumers expect that the future prices will increase by a lesser percentage than the current prices.

Table 3.12 Types of Elasticity of Price Expectations

Elasticity	Coefficient of Elasticity of Price Expectations	Effects of Change in Current Prices
High elasticity	$E_{PE} > 1$	Consumers expect that the future prices will increase by a greater percentage than the current prices
Unitary elasticity	$E_{PE} = 1$	Consumers expect that the future prices will increase by the same percentage as the current prices
Low elasticity	$E_{PE} < 1$	Consumers expect that the future prices will increase by a lesser percentage than the current prices
Zero elasticity	$E_{PE} = 0$	Consumers expect that the future prices will not be affected by the current prices
Negative elasticity	$E_{PE} < 0$	Consumers expect that the increase in the current prices will lead to a decrease in the future prices

(iv) **Elasticity of Price Expectations Is Equal to Zero, $E_{PE} = 0$:** In such a situation, the consumers expect that the future prices will not be affected by the current prices.

(v) **Elasticity of Price Expectations Is Smaller Than Zero, $E_{PE} < 0$:** In such a situation, the consumers expect that the increase in the current prices will lead to a decrease in the future prices.

The elasticity of price expectations is of great help to the firms when they are planning on the future prices of their goods.

RECAP

- The elasticity of price expectations is a measure of the responsiveness of the expected change in the future prices to the change in the current prices of a good.
- The coefficient of elasticity of price expectations can take a value, which may be < 0 or even greater than unity.

ELASTICITY OF SUPPLY

What Is Elasticity of Supply?

The concept was first discussed by Alfred Marshall. Elasticity of supply is a measure of the responsiveness of the quantity supplied of a good to a change in the price of the good. Elasticity of supply can be defined as the ratio of the percentage change in the quantity supplied of a good, per unit of time, to the percentage change in the price of the good.

Elasticity of supply is a measure of the responsiveness of the quantity supplied of a good to a change in the price of the good.

$$E_S = \frac{\text{Percentage change in the quantity supplied of a good}}{\text{Percentage change in the price of the good}}$$

$$= \frac{\text{Change in the quantity supplied}}{\text{Change in price}}$$

$$= \frac{\frac{\Delta Q_S}{Q_S}}{\frac{\Delta P}{P}}$$

$$= \frac{\Delta Q_S}{\Delta P} \times \frac{P}{Q_S}$$

where E_S is price elasticity of the supply, Q_S is quantity supplied, P is price, ΔQ_S is change in the quantity supplied and ΔP is change in the price.

(It is important to note that the coefficient of price elasticity of supply E_S is positive as there is a positive relationship between the price and the quantity supplied.)

Factors Influencing Elasticity of Supply

The factors on which the elasticity of supply depends are as follows:

(i) **Time Available:** If the time is very short, then in that case the supply of the good is inelastic as the factors of production are fixed. However, if the period is long enough, then the supply of a good is elastic as the factors of production are variable.

(ii) **Availability of the Factors of Production:** As already discussed, if the factors of production are available easily and at low prices, then the supply of the good will be elastic.

(iii) **Expectations Relating to the Future Prices:** If, in the future, firms expect an increase in the prices, they will shift their supplies from the present to the future. In other words, they will cut down the existing supplies of the good. The supply will become less elastic in the present.

Different Types of Elasticity of Supply

The coefficient of elasticity of supply can take a value between zero and infinity as depicted in Table 3.13.

(i) **Supply Is Perfectly Inelastic, $E_S = 0$:** In such a situation, the ratio of percentage change in the quantity supplied to the percentage change in the price of the good is zero. This implies that whatever is the price of the good the quantity supplied remains the same.

(ii) **Supply Is Relatively Inelastic, $0 < E_S < 1$:** In such a situation, the ratio of percentage change in the quantity supplied to the percentage change in the price of the good is < 1. This implies that the percentage change in the quantity supplied is less than the percentage change in the price of the good.

Table 3.13 Types of Elasticity of Supply

Change in Quantity Supplied to a Percentage Change in Price	E_S	Type of Elasticity
Quantity supplied remains the same	$E_S = 0$	Inelastic supply
Quantity supplied increases in a smaller proportion	$0 < E_S < 1$	Supply is inelastic
Quantity supplied increases in the same proportion	$E_S = 1$	Supply has unitary elasticity
Quantity supplied increases in a larger proportion	$E_S > 1$	Supply is elastic
Infinite change in the quantity supplied of the good	$E_S = \infty$	Supply is perfectly elastic

(iii) **Supply Has a Unitary Elasticity, $E_s = 1$:** In such a situation, the ratio of percentage change in the quantity supplied equals the percentage change in the price of the good.

(iv) **Supply Is Elastic, $E_s > 1$:** In such a situation, the ratio of percentage change in the quantity supplied to the percentage change in the price of the good is >1. This implies that the percentage change in the quantity supplied is more than the percentage change in the price of the good.

(v) **Supply Is Perfectly Elastic, $E_s = \infty$:** In such a situation, any price change, which may be very small, leads to an infinite change in the quantity supplied of the good.

RECAP

- Elasticity of supply is a measure of the responsiveness of the quantity supplied of a good to a change in the price of the good.
- The factors on which the elasticity of supply depends are: the time available, availability of the factors of production and expectations relating to the future prices.
- The coefficient of elasticity of supply can take a value between zero and infinity.

SUMMARY

INTRODUCTION

1. The price of a good or service is the rate at which it is exchanged for anything else.
2. This price is determined by the interaction of demand and supply.
3. While demand is determined by the human needs and wants, supply is determined by the scarce resources available in the economy.

DEMAND

What Is Demand?

1. The quantity demanded of a good is the amount of that good demanded at a particular price over a certain time.
2. There are four characteristics of demand: demand always exists at a particular price; demand is a flow concept; demand for a good depends on the utility of the good; demand for a good should always be backed by the purchasing power.
3. Individual demand is the quantity of a good that an individual is willing to purchase at certain price over a given time.
4. Market demand is the total quantity of a good that is demanded by all the individuals in the market at certain price over a given time.

Factors Influencing Demand and the Demand Function

1. The demand for a good by an individual depends on many factors: own price (price of the good itself), price of other related goods (substitutes and complements), income of the consumer, tastes and preferences of the consumer, income and wealth distribution and others.
2. The demand function for a good can be expressed as:

$$Dd_x = f(P_x, P_o, Y, T)$$

Demand and Price of Good *x*: Law of Demand

1. $Dd_x = f(P_x)$.
2. This relationship is called the law of demand.

3. According to this law, other things remaining the same, an individual demands more of the good (and service) at a lower price than at a higher price.
4. There exists a negative relationship between the quantity demanded of a good and the price of the good.

Demand Schedule

1. A demand schedule depicts the quantity of the good, which is demanded at each price, assuming that the price of the other goods, income of the consumer and tastes and preferences of the consumer remain the same (*ceteris paribus* assumption).
2. The demand schedule of an individual shows the alternative quantities of the good x demanded by the individual at different prices, *ceteris paribus*.

Individual's Demand Curve

1. By plotting the different pairs of values on a graph and then by joining the points so obtained, we can get the individual's demand curve for good x.
2. The demand curve is a graphical representation of the demand schedule.
3. It is downward sloping showing the inverse relationship between the price and the quantity demanded of a good.

Market Demand

1. The market demand schedule shows the alternative quantities of the good x demanded per time period by all the individuals in a market, at different prices, *ceteris paribus*.
2. The market demand for good x will depend on P_x, P_o, Y, T, the number of consumers of good x in the market and the distribution of income.

Why Does the Demand Curve Slope Downwards?

1. The reasons behind the inverse relationship between the price and the quantity demanded of a good are the income effect and substitution effect and the law of diminishing marginal utility.
2. It is not necessary that the law of demand will apply in all cases. For example, in the case of the Giffen goods, which are inferior goods, the demand curve slopes upwards. In addition, if the price of a good is rising and in the future also the consumer expects the price to increase, then in that case he will buy more of the good at higher prices.

Demand for Good *x* and Prices of Other Goods

1. $Dd_x = f(P_o)$.
2. The function shows that there exists a relationship between the demand for a good and the price of other goods, for example, good z, *ceteris paribus*.
3. When goods x and z are complements: When the price of good z (for example, sugar) increases, the demand for good x (coffee) will decrease.
4. When goods x and z are substitutes: When the price of good z (for example, tea) increases, the demand for good x (coffee) will increase.

Demand for Good *x* and the Consumer's Income

1. $Dd_x = f(Y)$.
2. The function shows that there exists a relationship between the demand for a good and the money income of the consumer, *ceteris paribus*.
3. When good x is a normal good: A normal good is one where with an increase in income more of the good is bought and with a decrease in income less is bought by the consumer.
4. When good x is an inferior good: An inferior good is one where with an increase in income less of the good is bought and with a decrease in income more of the good is bought by the consumer.

Demand, and Tastes and Preferences of the Consumer

1. $Dd_x = f(T)$.
2. The above function shows that there exists a relationship between the demand for a good and the tastes of the consumer, *ceteris paribus*.
3. When tastes change in favour of good *x*: In this case, the consumer shows more preference for the good.
4. When there is a change in tastes which are not in favour of good *x*: In this case, the consumer shows less preference for the good.

Change in Demand Versus Shifts in Demand

Change in Demand

1. A change in demand or a change in the quantity demanded of the good is a movement, which occurs along the demand curve and is caused by a change in the price of the good, *ceteris paribus*. It is important to note that there is only a movement along the demand curve.
2. An expansion or extension of demand is a rise in the demand for the good as a result of a fall in the price of the good.
3. A contraction of demand is a fall in the demand for the good as a result of a rise in the price of the good.

Shifts in Demand

1. A shift in the demand curve is caused by a change in any of the factors, which influence the demand other than the price of the good itself. These factors include the price of other goods, P_o, income of the consumer, *Y* and the tastes and preferences of the consumer, *T*. It is important to note here that there is a shift of the demand curve.
2. An increase in demand is an increase in the demand for the good as a result of a change in any of the factors, which influence the demand other than the price of the good itself, for example, an increase in the price of the substitute good or a rise in the consumer's income.
3. A decrease in demand is a decrease in the demand for the good as a result of a change in any of the factors, which influence the demand other than the price of the good itself, for example, a decrease in the price of the substitute good or a decrease in the consumer's income.

SUPPLY

What Is Supply?

The supply of a good is the total amount of a good, which the producer is willing to produce and supply at a particular price over a certain time.

Law of Supply

1. $Ss_x = f(P_x)$.
2. The above function shows that there exists a relationship between the supply of a good and the price of the good, *ceteris paribus*. This relationship is called the law of supply.
3. According to the law of supply, other things remaining the same, the quantity supplied of a good increases when the price of the good increases and decreases when the price decreases.

Factors Influencing Supply and the Supply Function

1. The supply of a good depends on many factors: own price (price of the good itself), price of the other related goods, changes in technology, price of the inputs or the factors of production, government policies and taxes and others.
2. The supply function of a good can be expressed as

$$Ss_x = f(P_x, P_o, P_I, T, G_T)$$

Supply Schedule and Supply Curve

1. A supply schedule depicts the quantity of the good, which is supplied at each price, assuming that other things remain the same (*ceteris paribus* assumption).
2. The supply curve is a graphical representation of the supply schedule. It is upward sloping showing the positive relationship between the price and the quantity supplied of a good.

Market Supply Schedule

1. The market supply schedule shows the different quantities of good *x* supplied, per time period, by all the producers of good *x* in the market, at different prices, *ceteris paribus*.
2. It is the aggregate of the supply of the entire producers of good *x* in the market.
3. The market supply of a good depends on all the factors, which determine the single producer's supply curve and also on the number of producers of good *x*.

Why Does the Supply Curve Slope Upwards?

1. There are reasons behind the positive relationship between the price and the quantity supplied of a good.
2. An increase in production and thus an increased supply can only occur at a higher price because of the law of the diminishing returns.
3. By selling at a higher price, the producer is able to make greater profits. Thus, with an increase in price, he increases the quantity supplied.

Change in Supply Versus Shifts in Supply

Change in Supply

1. A change in supply or a change in the quantity supplied of the good is a movement, which occurs along the supply curve and is caused by a change in the price of the good, *ceteris paribus*. It is important to note that there is only a movement along the supply curve.
2. An expansion or extension of supply is a rise in the supply of the good as a result of an increase in the price of the good.
3. A contraction of supply is a decrease in the supply of the good as a result of a fall in the price of the good.

Shifts in Supply

1. A shift in supply curve is caused by a change in any of the factors, which influence the supply other than the price of the good itself.
2. These factors include the changes in technology and in government policies. It is important to note here that there is a shift of the supply curve.
3. Increase in supply: An increase in supply is an increase in the supply of the good as a result of a change in any of the factors, which influence the supply other than the price of the good itself.
4. Decrease in supply: A decrease in supply is a decrease in the supply of the good as a result of a change in any of the factors, which influence the supply other than the price of the good itself.

EQUILIBRIUM

1. Equilibrium occurs when the quantity demanded of a good in the market over a certain time is equal to the quantity supplied of the good over the same time.
2. Graphically, equilibrium occurs at the point of intersection of market demand and supply curves of the good.
3. The equilibrium price is that price at which the equilibrium exists. The equilibrium quantity is that quantity at which the equilibrium exists.

ELASTICITY OF DEMAND

1. The law of demand does not indicate as to how responsive the demand for a good is to its price. This is given by the elasticity of demand.

2. The quantity demanded of a good is influenced by many factors, for example, price of the good, income and price of other goods. Hence, we are analysing the price elasticity of demand, income elasticity of demand and cross price elasticity of demand and others.

Price Elasticity of Demand

What Is Price Elasticity of Demand?

1. Price elasticity of demand is a measure of the responsiveness of the quantity demanded of a good to a change in the price of the good.
2. Price elasticity of demand can be defined as the ratio of the percentage change in the quantity demanded of a good, per unit of time, to the percentage change in the price of the good.
3. $E_p = -\frac{\Delta Q}{\Delta P} \times \frac{P}{Q}$

Factors Influencing the Price Elasticity of Demand

Price elasticity of demand depends on certain factors: nature of the good, availability of substitutes for the goods, variety of uses of the good, the fraction of the income spent on the good, possibility of postponement of consumption and the price of the good.

Measurement of Price Elasticity of Demand

1. **Percentage Method:** According to this method, the price elasticity of demand is the ratio of the percentage change in the quantity demanded of a good, per unit of time, to the percentage change in the price of the good.
$$E_p = -\frac{\Delta Q}{\Delta P} \times \frac{P}{Q}$$
2. **Coefficient of Elasticity of Demand Can Take a Value Between Zero and Infinity:** Demand is perfectly inelastic, $E_p = 0$; demand is relatively inelastic, $E_p < 1$; demand has a unitary elasticity, $E_p = 1$; demand is elastic, $E_p > 1$; demand is perfectly elastic, $E_p = \infty$.
3. **Outlay Method:** This is also known as the total expenditure method or the total revenue method. Here, the total outlay of the consumer, on the good, is compared before and after the price change.
4. Given that total outlay is measured by quantity multiplied by price of the good, there can be three situations: demand is relatively inelastic, $E_p < 1$; demand has a unitary elasticity, $E_p = 1$; demand is elastic, $E_p > 1$.
5. **Point Elasticity of Demand:** To measure the point elasticity of demand, the geometrical method is used.
$$E_p = \frac{\text{Lower segment}}{\text{Upper segment}}$$
6. **Arc Elasticity:**
$$E_p = \frac{\Delta Q}{\Delta P} \times \frac{(P_1 + P_2)}{(Q_1 + Q_2)}$$

Price Elasticity of Demand on a Linear Demand Curve

1. Along a linear demand curve, which is downward sloping, price elasticity varies at different points along the demand curve.
2. As we move down a demand curve, the elasticity goes on decreasing.

REVENUE CONCEPTS

Average revenue, total revenue and marginal revenue and their relationship with price elasticity.

$$E_p = \frac{AR}{AR - MR}$$

Significance of Price Elasticity of Demand

1. Price elasticity of demand is often used in making the economic decisions by the business firms, the government and others.

2. **Decisions by the Business Firms:** When a firm is in the process of deciding whether to increase the price of the good that it is producing, it is important to consider the price elasticity of demand.
3. **Decisions by the Government:** These include: fixation of minimum support prices for agriculture and formulation of policies relating to taxes.
4. **Decisions relating to International Trade:** If a country is facing problems on the balance of payments, the situation can be tackled through devaluation.

Income Elasticity of Demand

What Is Income Elasticity of Demand?

1. Income elasticity of demand is a measure of the responsiveness of the quantity demanded of a good to a change in the income of the consumer, *ceteris paribus.*
2. Income elasticity of demand can be defined as the ratio of the percentage change in the quantity demanded of a good, per unit of time, to the percentage change in the income of the consumer.

$$E_Y = \frac{\Delta Q}{\Delta Y} \times \frac{Y}{Q}$$

Different Types of Income Elasticity of Demand

The coefficient of income elasticity can take a value, which may be positive or even negative: income elasticity of demand is high: $E_Y > 1$; income elasticity of demand is equal to one or unitary income elasticity: $E_Y = 1$; income elasticity of demand is low: $0 < E_Y < 1$; income elasticity of demand is zero: $E_Y = 0$; income elasticity of demand is < 0 or negative income elasticity: $E_Y < 0$.

Significance of Income Elasticity of Demand

1. Income elasticity of demand helps classify goods into luxuries, comforts, necessities and inferior goods.
2. Income elasticity of demand is very useful when forecasts of demand for the different goods are to be made.

Cross Price Elasticity of Demand

What Is Cross Price Elasticity of Demand?

1. Cross price elasticity of demand is a measure of the responsiveness of the quantity demanded of a particular good to a change in the price of another good, *ceteris paribus.*
2. Cross price elasticity of demand can be defined as the ratio of the percentage change in the quantity demanded of good *x* to the percentage change in the price of good *y*.

$$E_{xy} = -\frac{\Delta Q_x}{\Delta P_y} \times \frac{P_y}{Q_x}$$

Different Types of Cross Price Elasticity of Demand

The coefficient of cross price elasticity can take a value, which may be between zero and infinity: $E_{xy} > 0$: In such a situation, the two goods *x* and *y* are substitutes; $E_{xy} = 0$: In such a situation, the two goods *x* and *y* are independent goods; $E_{xy} < 0$: In such a situation, the two goods *x* and *y* are complements.

Significance of Cross Price Elasticity of Demand

Most often firms are interested in analysing the cross elasticity of demand for their goods with respect to other goods, especially the complementary and substitute goods.

ADVERTISING ELASTICITY

What Is Advertising Elasticity?

1. Advertisement elasticity is a measure of the responsiveness of the quantity demanded of a particular good to a change in advertising, *ceteris paribus.*

2. Advertisement elasticity can be defined as the ratio of the percentage change in the quantity demanded of good or sales to the percentage change in advertising.

$$E_A = \frac{\Delta Q}{\Delta A} \times \frac{A}{Q}$$

Factors Influencing Advertising Elasticity

Some of the factors which influence the advertising elasticity are advertisements by other competing firms; the sales of a good and the cumulative effect of advertising expenditure.

Types of Advertising Elasticity

1. The coefficient of advertising elasticity can take a value, which may be between zero and infinity.
2. $E_A = 0$: In such a situation, an increase in the advertising expenditure does not lead to an increase in sales.
3. $1 < E_A > 0$: In such a situation, an increase in the advertising expenditure leads to a less than proportionate increase in sales.
4. $E_A = 1$: In such a situation, an increase in the advertising expenditure leads to a proportionate increase in sales.
5. $E_A > 1$: In such a situation, an increase in the advertising expenditure leads to a more than proportionate increase in sales.

ELASTICITY OF PRICE EXPECTATIONS

1. The elasticity of price expectations is a measure of the responsiveness of the expected change in the future prices to the change in the current prices of a good.
2. Elasticity of price expectations can be defined as the ratio of the relative change in expected future price of a good to the relative change in the current price of the good.

$$E_{PE} = \frac{\Delta P_F}{\Delta P_C} \times \frac{P_C}{P_F}$$

Types of Elasticity of Price Expectations

The coefficient of elasticity of price expectations can take a value, which may be < 0 or even greater than unity:

1. **$E_{PE} > 1$:** In such a situation, the consumers expect that the future prices will increase by a greater percentage than the current prices.
2. **$E_{PE} = 1$:** In such a situation, the consumers expect that the future prices will increase by the same percentage as the current prices.
3. **$E_{PE} < 1$:** In such a situation, the consumers expect that the future prices will increase by a lesser percentage than the current prices.
4. **$E_{PE} = 0$:** In such a situation, the consumers expect that the future prices will not be affected by the current prices.
5. **$E_{PE} < 0$:** In such a situation, the consumers expect that the increase in the current prices will lead to a decrease in the future prices.

ELASTICITY OF SUPPLY

What Is Elasticity of Supply?

1. Elasticity of supply is a measure of the responsiveness of the quantity supplied of a good to a change in the price of the good.
2. Elasticity of supply can be defined as the ratio of the percentage change in the quantity supplied of a good, per unit of time, to the percentage change in the price of the good.

$$E_S = \frac{\Delta Q_S}{\Delta P} \times \frac{P}{Q_S}$$

Factors Influencing Elasticity of Supply

The factors on which the elasticity of supply depends are: the time available; the availability of the factors of production and expectations relating to the future prices.

Different Types of Elasticity of Supply

The coefficient of elasticity of supply can take a value between zero and infinity.

1. **$E_S = 0$:** This implies that whatever is the price of the good the quantity supplied remains the same.
2. **$0 < E_S < 1$:** This implies that the percentage change in the quantity supplied is less than the percentage change in the price of the good.
3. **$E_S = 1$:** In such a situation, the ratio of percentage change in the quantity supplied equals the percentage change in the price of the good.
4. **$E_S > 1$:** This implies that the percentage change in the quantity supplied is more than the percentage change in the price of the good.
5. **Supply is Perfectly Elastic, $E_S = \infty$:** In such a situation, any price change, which may be very small, leads to an infinite change in the quantity supplied of good *x*.

REVIEW QUESTIONS

TRUE OR FALSE QUESTIONS

1. Individual demand is the total quantity of a good that is demanded by all the individuals in the market at a certain price over a given time.
2. A change in demand or a change in the quantity demanded of the good is a movement, which occurs along the demand curve.
3. As we move down a demand curve, the price elasticity goes on increasing.
4. Cross price elasticity of demand is a measure of the responsiveness of the quantity demanded of a good to a change in the income of the consumer, *ceteris paribus*.
5. Advertisement elasticity is a measure of the responsiveness of the quantity demanded of a particular good to a change in advertising, *ceteris paribus*.

SHORT ANSWER QUESTIONS

1. What is demand? What are its characteristics?
2. Why does the demand curve slope downwards?
3. Analyse the change in demand as compared with shifts in demand.
4. 'As we move down a linear demand curve, the price elasticity goes on decreasing'. Comment.
5. Discuss the significance of the price elasticity of demand.

LONG ANSWER QUESTIONS

1. What is supply? What are the factors which influence the supply? Analyse the supply function and the supply curve.
2. What is price elasticity of demand? How can it be measured?
3. What is advertising elasticity? Discuss.
4. What is elasticity of supply? Discuss.
5. What is income elasticity of demand? What are the different types of income elasticity?

ANSWERS

TRUE OR FALSE QUESTIONS

1. **False.** Market demand is the total quantity of a good that is demanded by all the individuals in the market at certain price over a given time.
2. **True.** A change in demand is caused by a change in the price of the good, *ceteris paribus*. It is important to note that there is only a movement along the demand curve.
3. **False.** As we move down a demand curve, the price elasticity goes on decreasing.
4. **False.** Income elasticity of demand is a measure of the responsiveness of the quantity demanded of a good to a change in the income of the consumer, *ceteris paribus*.
5. **True.** Advertisement elasticity can be defined as the ratio of the percentage change in the quantity demanded of good or sales to the percentage change in advertising.

Demand Forecasting

4

After studying this chapter, you should be able to understand:

- ✓ *Demand forecasting involves predicting the future demand for a good.*
- ✓ *Forecasts of demand are required not only by the established firms in the industry but also by the new entrants.*
- ✓ *The consumer survey method is a direct method of obtaining the relevant information relating to the future demand for the different goods.*
- ✓ *In direct interview method, a selected group of the users or the potential consumers are asked directly about their future plans for the good.*
- ✓ *In the complete enumeration method, all the consumers of the product are surveyed.*
- ✓ *In the sample survey method, only a few consumers are selected from the relevant market for the good.*
- ✓ *In the expert opinion method, the opinion of experts is taken to forecast the demand for the product.*
- ✓ *In the market experiments method, two experiments used are often controlled experiments and test marketing.*
- ✓ *In the time series analysis, the data used to predict the future demand for the good is primarily past data relating to the variable.*
- ✓ *In econometric methods, statistical methods and economic theory are used in conjunction to find a relationship between the economic variables.*
- ✓ *A technique of forecasting the demand should be chosen such that it applies to the data, which is available and is also convenient to handle.*

INTRODUCTION

The future is always unknown. Often when firms are planning on their production for the future, a major problem faced by them is how much of the good to produce. Once this major decision has been made, then only they can plan on the purchase of the inputs and the machinery, and acquire the necessary finance.

To solve this crucial problem, firms have to forecast the future demand for their goods.

WHAT IS DEMAND FORECASTING?

Demand forecasting involves predicting the future demand for a good. This is all the more important when there is a large-scale production of a good. Once the demand has been forecast, the manager will have to plan on the raw materials which will be required, and the labour and the machinery which will need to be installed. The necessary finance will also have to be obtained.

Forecasting of demand is one of the most important tasks that a manager has to perform. A good forecast reduces the uncertainties, which are involved in the production of a good. It simplifies the

BOX 4.1

While forecasting the demand, it is very important to prepare the data carefully. The usage of incorrect data may result in a forecasting, which is not of much use. There may occur errors even in entering the data. The strategic decisions made by using these forecasts may result in losses for the firm. Thus, the importance of data cannot be undermined.

planning process including the organization of production, advertising and related expenditures, and also in the organization of sales. Thus, it is of extreme importance for a firm to have a prior knowledge of the size of the market.

The demand forecast for a good may involve the forecast of the following:

(i) **Aggregate Demand for the Good:** This involves a forecasting of the total demand for the output of the good in the economy in the future. It depends on the level of the gross national product.

(ii) **Total Industry Demand for the Good:** This depends on the how some of the major sectors in the economy perform and also the overall economic activity.

(iii) **An Individual Firm's Demand for the Good:** This depends on the forecast of the aggregate industry demand for the good and the share of the firm in the industry's output of the good.

Forecasts of demand are required not only by the established firms in the industry but also by the new entrants. A new firm may be interested in the production of a good only if the demand forecasts for the good are large enough. Otherwise, it will not be in the interest of the firm to enter the industry. Even if a firm is planning for launching a new good, it will have to forecast the demand for the good before it commences the production of the good.

Demand forecasting involves predicting for the future demand for a good.

Demand forecasts can be the following:

(i) **Short-term forecasts** which may usually for a month or even for a year. They are generally made for the already established goods produced by a firm regarding the impact of the government policies and changes in the firm's own policies on the demand for the good.

(ii) **Long-term forecasts** which may usually for a year or more than a year. These may be for five years or even for 10 years. They are normally made for the new products launched by the firm. Since a large investment is involved in the launching of a new product, a firm will have to do a careful planning once the demand forecasts for the product have been made.

Whether it is the firm or the industry, demand forecasts play a crucial role. Whether the product is old or new, demand forecasts are necessary before the production can be commenced.

RECAP

- Demand forecasting involves predicting the future demand for a good.
- Forecasts of demand are required not only by the established firms in the industry but also by the new entrants.
- Demand forecasts can be short- and long-term forecasts.

METHODS OF FORECASTING DEMAND

To forecast the demand for a good, there are many methods. In choosing the appropriate method, the forecaster has to keep certain things in mind. These include the cost involved and the level of accuracy required. When the level of accuracy required is high, then more sophisticated and advanced methods are needed, which are relatively more expensive. The time limit is also important in which the forecast is to be prepared.

Consumer Survey Methods

This is a direct method of obtaining the relevant information relating to the future demand for the different goods. The forecasts are generally for the short term. Often when a firm is launching a new product or is making alterations in its existing product, it may conduct surveys. The surveys may be in the form of direct interviews of the consumer or it may through questionnaires, which have been mailed to the consumer making inquiries about their preferences and future plans, and spending on the goods. Surveys can be of three types:

(i) **Direct Interview:** In this method, a selected group of the users or the potential consumers are asked directly about their future plans for the good. This survey may be conducted in a number of cities. The consumers may be asked about their demand for the product at different prices and thus their willingness to buy the product at different prices may be taken into account.

(ii) **Complete Enumeration:** In this method, all the consumers of the product are surveyed regarding their preferences about the product and their future plans if there is an increase in the price of the product. The quantities specified by the different consumers are analysed and tabulated to arrive at the total demand for the good. Thus,

$$D = D_1 + D_2 + \cdots + D_N$$

or

$$D = \sum_{i=1}^{N} D_i$$

where D is total demand (forecast) for the good, D_1 is quantity demanded by Consumer 1, D_2 is quantity demanded by Consumer 2 and D_N is quantity demanded by Consumer N.

This method, where there is a complete enumeration, does not involve any value judgments and involves the recording and an analysis of the entire data. Its main drawback is that it cannot be used if there are too many consumers and also it is a time consuming and very expensive way of collecting the information.

(iii) **Sample Survey:** In this method, only a few consumers are selected from the relevant market for the good. The consumers may be selected on a random basis or through a sampling method. These consumers are then surveyed either through direct interview or mailed questionnaires. The questions which are asked from them may relate to their income, the demand and the price of the good, whose demand is being forecasted and the price of the other competing goods. The data, which is gathered, is classified, tabulated and then analysed to determine the demand of the consumers. The information so collected is then considered to be applicable to all the consumers of the product.

As compared with the complete enumeration method, this technique involving a sample survey is a less time consuming and less expensive way of collecting the information. Also, the data errors are fewer.

However, one has to be careful in selecting the sample. In case the size of the sample is too small, there are bound to be sampling errors. On the other hand, if there is a bias in the selection of the sample, the results of the survey will not be reliable. Thus, it is necessary that before a survey is conducted the sample should be selected such that its size is large enough to represent the entire population and also there should be a random selection to prevent any bias from entering.

One has to be careful that there is no response bias, where the respondents may not answer the questions in a correct manner. They may not be able to depict their preferences properly. Often, a consumer may not know about their responses to a proposed hike in the price of the good with certainty. Thus, his answers may not be very exact.

Expert Opinion Method

In this method, the opinion of experts is taken to forecast the demand for the product. The experts may be from the firm itself, for example, the sales managers who possess the sufficient knowledge about the market. Alternatively, the experts may be from outside the firm, for example, some marketing experts and consultant firms who are specially trained for such tasks. The different methods are mentioned below:

(i) **A Survey of the Sales Force:** A firm may sometimes seek the opinion of its sales representatives in assessing the future demand for the good. These executives are in close touch with the market and the conditions prevailing in the market. The information gathered from the various sales representatives is then compiled to arrive at the estimated of the demand.

This method is not only simpler but also less expensive than the other methods of collecting the information. Also, it motivates the sales representatives to achieve the targets, which they had predicted regarding the forecasts of demand. However, there are some problems here in that these representatives may often overstate or understate the forecast depending on the situation. Thus, it is necessary that some corrections are made to these forecasts before arriving at the total forecasts.

(ii) **Delphi Technique:** In this technique, the opinion of a group of experts is taken about the future demand for the product. Their divergent views are then put forward to them in the light of which they are then asked to revise their opinions. This process is repeated again till they arrive at a consensus, which then forms the final forecast of the demand for the good.

Empirical evidence shows that in the USA, this technique is widely used and is very successful. Also it is less expensive than the other techniques.

Market Experiments Method

It has been noticed quite often in the consumer surveys that the behaviour of the consumer may differ from what he actually conveys in a survey. Market experiments can overcome this problem to some extent. Two marketing experiments used often are as follows:

(i) **Controlled Experiments:** Here, a sample of consumers from the targeted group is requested to visit a particular shop of the firm, where the different brands of the good are on sale. The consumer is given relevant information about the different brands. From a fixed amount of money given to each consumer, they are asked to make their purchases of the good. Their preferences may be recorded in a questionnaire filled by them. It is possible that the experiment may be repeated after changing the price of the good. The firm may use this information to estimate the demand for the good.

As compared with the survey method, the controlled experiments method is better since the consumer has to make the actual decisions while in the survey method he is simply stating his intentions about the purchase of the good. However, the problem here is that there may be a bias involved in the selection of the sample of the consumers. Generally, the controlled experiments technique is used as a supplement to the other techniques.

(ii) **Test Marketing:** In this method, a test area is selected which represents the market, where the firm has to launch the new good. This test area may be in the form of a few towns or cities. The new good is introduced in the area and the response of the consumers is assessed. Different types of the models of the new good can be introduced in different areas. The responses in these different areas can be compared before taking a final decision regarding the forecasts of demand.

The major problem with test experiments is that they are very expensive and time consuming. Often, it is difficult to select an area as a representative of the potential market for the good to be launched. Also, once the good enters the market, the response of the consumers to the counter attacks by the competitors cannot be judged by test marketing method.

Time Series Analysis

In this method, in the forecasting of demand for a good, a pattern emerges over time. The data used to predict the future demand for the good is primarily past data relating to the variable. This is because the underlying assumption is that the past behaviour of the variable influences the future behaviour of the variable. However, there are some components, which may bring about a change in the variable under consideration. These components are:

(a) **Trends:** These bring about an increase or a decrease in the long-term values of the time series of a variable. For example, a change in tastes will influence the long-term demand for the good.

(b) **Seasonal Variations:** These occur due to changes in the seasons during the year, which bring about changes in the long-term values of the time series of a variable, for example, in the demand for a good. They generally occur consistently every year.

(c) **Cyclical Variations:** These involve substantial changes, which lead to expansion or contraction in the economic variable. They are generally for more than a year and do not occur consistently every year.

(d) **Random Fluctuations:** After taking into consideration the trend, seasonal and cyclical variations in the time series analysis of a particular variable, the remaining changes which occur can be attributed to random changes. These do not follow any set of patterns. Also, they cannot be predicted.

(e) **Econometric Methods:** Here, statistical methods and economic theory are used in conjunction to find a relationship between the economic variables. First using economic theory, a mathematical model relating the economic variables is arrived at. Then, with the help of the statistical methods, the estimates of the different parameters in the model are calculated and thus the demand forecasts are arrived at.

The advantage of the econometric method is that it helps in forecasting of an economic variable, for example, demand, and explaining it with the help of economic theory. It is of great help to the management in evaluating the impact of its different strategies on the variable, for example, in evaluating the changes in the price of a good on the demand for the good. Not only does the econometric method forecast the direction but also the change in the magnitude of the variable. With the use of the model, the different elasticities of demand including price elasticity and advertising elasticity can be measured and analysed.

CONCLUSION

There are many methods by which the forecasts of demand for a good can be done. The different methods have their own pros and cons. As to which method should be used differs from situation to situation. Most important is the purpose for which the forecasts are being made. An analyst has to be very careful in his choice of the technique. A technique of forecasting demand should be chosen such that it can be applied to the data, which is available and also convenient to handle. It should not be very expensive.

Whatever the techniques used, the judgment of the analyst is crucial at the different stages of forecasting. In the interpretation of the data and in using it for making the future projections, it is the analyst who has to make the judgment.

RECAP

- The consumer survey methods are a direct method of obtaining the relevant information relating to the future demand for the different goods.
- In the complete enumeration method, all the consumers of the product are surveyed regarding their preferences about the product and their future plans.
- In the sample survey method, only a few consumers are selected from the relevant market for the good.
- In the expert opinion method, the opinion of experts is taken to forecast the demand for the product. The experts may be from the firm or outside the firm.
- In the market experiments method, two experiments used often are controlled experiments and test marketing.
- In the method of the time series analysis, the data used to predict the future demand for the good is primarily past data relating to the variable.
- In econometric methods, statistical methods and economic theory are used in conjunction to find a relationship between the economic variables.
- There are many methods by which the forecasts of demand for a good can be done.
- A technique of forecasting demand should be chosen such that it can be applied to the data, which is available and also convenient to handle.

SUMMARY

INTRODUCTION

1. Often when firms are planning on their production for the future, a major problem faced by them is how much of the good to produce.
2. To solve this crucial problem, firms have to forecast the future demand for their good.

WHAT IS DEMAND FORECASTING?

1. Demand forecasting involves predicting of the future demand for a good.
2. Once the demand has been forecast, the manager will have to plan on the raw materials which will be required, and the labour and the machinery which will need to be installed. The necessary finance will have to be obtained.
3. A good forecast reduces the uncertainties, which are involved in the production of a good.
4. It is of extreme importance for a firm to have a prior knowledge of the size of the market.

5. The demand forecast for a good may involve the forecast of aggregate industry demand, total industry demand and the individual firm's demand for the good.
6. Forecasts of demand are required not only by the established firms in the industry but also by the new entrants.
7. Demand forecasts can be short-term forecasts, which are generally made for the already established goods regarding the impact of the government policies and changes in the firm's own policies on the demand for the good.
8. Long-term forecasts are normally made for the new products launched by the firm.
9. Whether the product is old or new, demand forecasts are necessary before the production can be commenced.

METHODS OF FORECASTING DEMAND

1. There are five methods of forecasting demand: the consumer survey methods, expert opinion method, market experiments method, time series analysis and econometric methods.
2. The consumer survey methods are direct methods of obtaining the relevant information relating to the future demand for the different goods.
3. The consumer surveys can be of three types.
4. In direct interview method, a selected group of the users or the potential consumers are asked directly about their future plans for the good.
5. In the complete enumeration method, all the consumers of the product are surveyed regarding their preferences about the product and their future plans if there is an increase in the price of the product.
6. In the sample survey method, only a few consumers are selected from the relevant market for the good. The data which is gathered is classified, tabulated and then analysed to determine the demand of the consumers.
7. In the expert opinion method, the opinion of experts is taken to forecast the demand for the product. The experts may be from the firm itself or from outside the firm. The different methods here include: a survey of the Sales Force and the Delphi Technique.
8. In the market experiments method, two experiments used often are: controlled experiments and test marketing.
9. In this method of the time series analysis, the data used to predict the future demand for the good is primarily past data relating to the variable. There are some components, which may bring about a change in the variable under consideration: These components are: trends, seasonal variations, cyclical variations and random fluctuations.
10. In econometric methods, statistical methods and economic theory are used in conjunction to find a relationship between the economic variables.
11. There are many methods by which the forecasts of demand for a good can be done.
12. A technique of forecasting demand should be chosen such that it can be applied to the data, which is available and is also convenient to handle.

REVIEW QUESTIONS

TRUE OR FALSE QUESTIONS

1. Demand forecasting involves predicting of the future demand for a good.
2. Forecasts of demand are required only by the established firms in the industry and not by the new entrants.
3. In complete enumeration method, a selected group of the users or the potential consumers are asked directly about their future plans for the good.
4. In the expert opinion method, the opinion of experts is taken to forecast the demand for the product.
5. In the time series analysis in the forecasting of demand for a good, a pattern emerges over time.

SHORT ANSWER QUESTIONS

1. What do you mean by the following:
   (a) Short-term forecasts
   (b) Long-term forecasts
2. What is the expert opinion method of forecasting demand?
3. What is the econometric method of forecasting demand?
4. What is the sample survey method? Discuss.
5. Discuss the complete enumeration method.

LONG ANSWER QUESTIONS

1. What is demand forecasting?
2. Discuss the consumer survey methods of forecasting demand.
3. Write short notes on the following methods of forecasting demand:
   (a) Market experiments method
   (b) Time series analysis
4. Write a short note on the methods of forecasting demand.
5. In your opinion, which is the best method for forecasting demand?

ANSWERS

TRUE OR FALSE QUESTIONS

1. **True.** Demand forecasting involves predicting of the future demand for a good. This is all the more important when there is large-scale production of a good.
2. **False.** Forecasts of demand are required not only by the established firms in the industry, but also by the new entrants.
3. **False.** In the direct interview method, a selected group of the users or the potential consumers are asked directly about their future plans for the good.
4. **True.** In the expert opinion method, the opinion of experts is taken to forecast the demand for the product. The experts may be from the firm itself or from outside the firm.
5. **True.** In the time series analysis in the forecasting of demand for a good, a pattern emerges over time. The data used to predict the future demand for the good is primarily past data relating to the variable.

5

Cardinal Utility Approach

After studying this chapter, you should be able to understand:

- ✓ *It was Alfred Marshall who first discussed the role played by the theory of utility in the theory of value.*
- ✓ *In Marshall's theory, the concept of utility is cardinal.*
- ✓ *The price that a consumer is willing to pay for a good is an indication of the utility of that good to the consumer.*
- ✓ *Total utility is the sum of the utility, which a consumer derives from the consumption of the different units of a good.*
- ✓ *Marginal utility of a good is the change in the total utility from consuming an additional unit of the good.*
- ✓ *According to the law of diminishing marginal utility as the quantity consumed of any one good increases, while the consumption of all other goods consumed remains constant, the marginal utility from the good must eventually decrease.*
- ✓ *The total utility for any unit of the good is the sum of the marginal utility till that unit.*
- ✓ *By using the law of diminishing marginal utility, Marshall derived the law of demand, which shows that there exists an inverse relationship between price and the quantity demanded of a good.*
- ✓ *The law of equi-marginal utility analyses the equilibrium of the consumer when he consumes more than one good.*

INTRODUCTION

According to the law of demand, there exists a negative relationship between the quantity demanded of a good and the price of the good. The law does not explain as to why this relationship holds. It does not explain as to why the consumer demands more of a good when the price falls. This aspect of the behaviour of the consumer is explained by three approaches: cardinal utility approach, ordinal utility approach and the revealed preference theory.

MARSHALL'S UTILITY ANALYSIS

H. H. Gossen, Leon Walras, Jevons and many others had analysed the utility theory. However, it was Alfred Marshall who first discussed the role played by the theory of utility in the theory of value.

WHAT IS UTILITY?

The utility of a good is the power of the good to satisfy a want. Thus, it is the satisfaction gained from the consumption of a good. Thus, if a person wants a good, it implies that the good has a certain amount of utility for that person.

Utility is a subjective concept. It is something, which exists entirely in the consumer's mind. It varies from person to person. Even for the same person, it may vary from time to time. For example, a glass of water may give an individual more utility on a hot summer afternoon than in the winters. Also, utility is ethically neutral in that it does not differentiate between bad and good. Alcohol and tobacco are both harmful but to one who drinks and smokes it may provide a utility.

The utility of a good is the power of the good to satisfy a want.

RECAP

- The utility of a good is the power of the good to satisfy a want.
- Utility is a subjective concept.
- Utility is ethically neutral in that it does not differentiate between bad and good.

CONCEPT OF CARDINAL AND ORDINAL UTILITIES

In Marshall's theory, the concept of utility is cardinal while the concept to be discussed in Chapter 6 is of ordinal utility. The concepts of cardinal and ordinal belong to the field of mathematics. One, two, three, four and the other such numbers are all cardinal numbers. Ordinal numbers are those which can be ranked or ordered. By how much the first number is greater than the second and the second by the third is not known. Ordinal utility, analysed by R. G. D. Allen and J. R. Hicks, does not assign any numbers to utility.

In simpler terms, cardinal utility implies that the utility can be measured in quantitative terms. One can say that a cup of tea gives two times more satisfaction as compared with a glass of milk. However, in terms of ordinal utility, one can just say that one prefers a cup of tea over a glass of milk. One cannot assign any numbers while expressing likes and dislikes.

According to the concept of cardinal utility, one can measure the utility in terms of utils. Professor Marshall was of the view that one can measure the utility in terms of price. The price that a consumer is willing to pay for a good is an indication of the utility of that good to the consumer. It was assumed that the utility of money does not change or remains constant.

RECAP

- In Marshall's theory, the concept of utility is cardinal.
- One can measure the utility in terms of utils.
- The price that a consumer is willing to pay for a good is an indication of the utility of that good to the consumer.

CARDINAL UTILITY APPROACH

Total Utility

Total utility is the sum of the utility, which a consumer derives from the consumption of the different units of a good. Suppose a consumer consumes five units of good x. He derives u_1, u_2, u_3, u_4 and u_5 from the successive units of the good. The total utility that the consumer derives from the consumption of the five units of good x is

$$U_x = u_1 + u_2 + u_3 + u_4 + u_5$$

Total utility is the sum of the utility, which a consumer derives from the consumption of the different units of a good.

If the consumer consumes n units of good x, then the total utility that the consumer derives from the consumption of n units of good x is

$$U_n = u_1 + u_2 + u_3 + u_4 + u_5 + \cdots + u_n$$

If the consumer consumes goods x, y and z, then the total utility that the consumer derives from the consumption of the goods is

$$U = U_x + U_y + U_z$$

where U is the total utility that the consumer derives from the consumption of goods x, y and z; U_x is the total utility that the consumer derives from the consumption of good x; U_y is the total utility that the consumer derives from the consumption of good y; and U_z is the total utility that the consumer derives from the consumption of good z.

Marginal Utility

Marginal utility of a good is the change in the total utility from consuming an additional unit of the good.

Marginal utility of a good is the change in the total utility from consuming an additional unit of the good. Hence,

$$MU = \frac{\Delta TU}{\Delta Q}$$

where MU is marginal utility, ΔTU is change in total utility and ΔQ is change in quantity.

Marginal utility can also be expressed in terms of total utility as

$$MU_n = TU_n - TU_{n-1}$$

where MU_n is marginal utility from the nth unit of the good, TU_n is total utility from n units of the good and TU_{n-1} is total utility from $(n - 1)$ units of the good.

RECAP

- Total utility is the sum of the utility which a consumer derives from the consumption of the different units of a good.
- Marginal utility of a good is the change in the total utility from consuming an additional unit of the good.

LAW OF DIMINISHING MARGINAL UTILITY

The law of diminishing marginal utility is based on certain assumptions:

(i) The units of the good, which are consumed, are homogenous.
(ii) The good is consumed within a short time without any gaps or any break in between.
(iii) The units of the good consumed are of a standard size and not very small or large.
(iv) The consumer's income does not change in the period under consideration.
(v) The consumer's tastes, preferences and habits do not change in the period under consideration.
(vi) The law does not hold good for the collection of say, antiques and rare stamps, since here the utility increases with the increase in the quantity of the good.

According to the law of diminishing marginal utility as the quantity consumed of any one good increases, while the consumption of all other goods consumed remains constant, the marginal utility from the good must eventually decrease. As more and more units of a good are consumed, the additional utility to the consumer from each successive unit of the good goes on decreasing, assuming that the consumption of all the other goods does not change. In other words, as additional units of the good are consumed, the total utility from the good increases at a decreasing rate and may become negative.

According to the law of diminishing marginal utility as the quantity consumed of any one good increases, while the consumption of all other goods consumed remains constant, the marginal utility from the good must eventually decrease.

Suppose that on a hot summer afternoon a person is very thirsty. The first glass of water that he drinks gives him the maximum utility. However, the second glass of water also gives him a utility but which is less than the first glass of water that he drinks. The third glass of water will give him even lesser utility. Thus, every additional glass of water that he drinks will give him a smaller amount of utility than the earlier glass. This will happen until he is fully satiated with the water, after which any additional glass of water may give him a disutility or a negative utility. This aspect of utility where it diminishes with the consumption of additional units of the good under consideration is called the law of diminishing marginal utility. The law is also known as the *law of satiable wants.*

To illustrate the law of diminishing marginal utility, we take a numerical example in Table 5.1, which is then depicted in a graph in Figure 5.1.

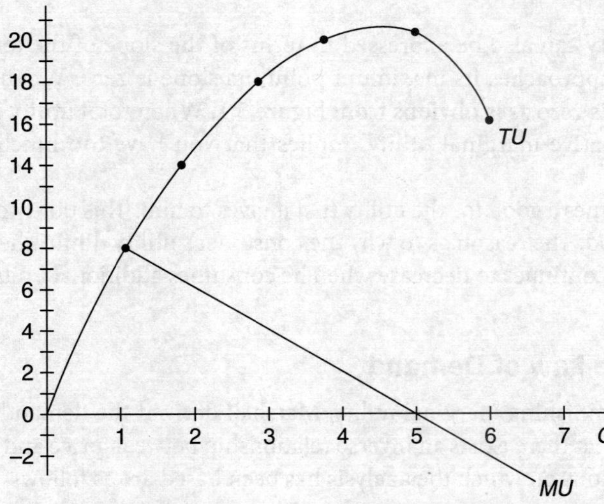

Figure 5.1 Total Utility and Marginal Utility

Table 5.1 shows that from the first unit of the good the consumer gets a total utility of eight units. When he consumes the second unit of the good, his total utility increases to 14 units and with the third unit it increases to 18. Thus, the total utility is increasing at a diminishing rate. With the consumption of the fourth unit of the good, his saturation point is reached at 20 units, which remain unchanged even when he consumes the fifth unit. As the sixth unit is consumed, his total utility starts decreasing. Thus, in Figure 5.1, the total utility curve increases at a decreasing rate, then reaches a maximum when five units of the good are consumed and then starts decreasing.

Table 5.1 Total Utility Schedule and Marginal Utility Schedule

Units Consumed	Total Utility	Marginal Utility
1	8	8
2	14	6
3	18	4
4	20	2
5	20	0
6	18	−2

As far as the marginal utility is concerned, it goes on decreasing with the consumption of every additional unit of the good and when the fifth unit is consumed it becomes zero at the point of saturation and thereafter if additional units are consumed it becomes negative causing disutility to the consumer. Thus, in Figure 5.1, the marginal utility curve slopes downwards showing that marginal utility decreases as additional units of the good are consumed. It reaches zero and intersects the *x* axis when five units of the good are consumed and the consumer is at the point of saturation. Thereafter, if additional units of the good are consumed, the marginal utility becomes negative. It is important to note that the total utility for any unit of the good is the sum of the marginal utility till that unit. Thus, for any quantity of a good, the area under the marginal utility curve would be the total utility for that quantity of the good.

The marginal utility can also be expressed in terms of the slope of the total utility curve. When the total utility curve approaches its maximum point, its slope is zero. When total utility is a maximum, marginal utility is zero as is obvious from Figure 5.1. When total utility is decreasing, marginal utility is negative. Negative marginal utility implies that you have too much of a good and would prefer lesser.

A consumer consumes a good for the utility that it gives to him. This utility depends on his intensity of the desire for the good. The reason as to why the consumer's utility diminishes is that the intensity of the desire for the good continues to decrease when he consumes additional units of the good.

A Derivation of the Law of Demand

By using the law of diminishing marginal utility, Marshall derived the demand curve, which is downward sloping showing that there exists an inverse relationship between price and the quantity demanded of a good. The assumptions on which the analysis has been based are as follows:

(i) The money income of the consumer is given. Hence, he can spend only a limited amount of money on the goods and services that he prefers.

(ii) The prices of all the related goods, complements and substitutes are given.

(iii) The consumer's tastes and preferences do not change in the period under consideration.

(iv) The consumer behaves in a rational manner. Given the price of the good and his money income, the consumer aims at maximizing his utility.

(v) Utility is assumed to be cardinal.

(vi) Utility is additive in that to arrive at total utility, the utility from different goods can be added together.

BOX 5.1

In the eighteenth century, the concept of cardinal utility gained popularity with the utilitarian economists. It was their belief that there should be a redistribution of wealth from those with higher levels of utility to those who have a lower level of utility from wealth. This was based on their belief of diminishing marginal utility of any good including wealth. However, those who opposed this belief argue that this redistribution is not practical and would also lead to a decrease in the total utility of wealth.

(vii) The utility derived from a good is independent of the utility from the consumption of another good. For example, the utility derived from good *x* depends on the consumption of good *x* only.

(viii) The marginal utility derived from a good diminishes. This is because the intensity of the desire for the good continues to decrease when he consumes additional units of the good.

(ix) Marshall expressed utility in terms of money. Hence, the consumer's willingness to pay for a good depends on the utility that he gets from the good.

(x) Since money is used to measure the utility, the marginal utility of money is assumed to be constant, whatever is the consumer's income. Since money is the measuring rod for utility, this assumption is required.

Given the above assumptions, one is now in a position to derive the law of demand. Table 5.2 depicts the behaviour of a consumer who consumes good *x*. The marginal utility from good *x* is expressed in terms of money. With each additional unit of good *x* that the consumer consumes, the marginal utility of good *x* decreases.

The marginal utility schedule derived in Table 5.2 is illustrated in Figure 5.2, which shows the marginal utility curve for good *x*.

Suppose the price of good *x* is ₹5 per unit. If the consumer purchases three units of good *x*, then the marginal utility from good *x* is greater than the per-unit price of good *x*. Thus, he will continue to purchase more units of good *x* until the marginal utility from the last unit purchased is equal to the price of good *x*. In other words, the consumer is in equilibrium when

$$MU_m = \frac{MU_x}{P_x},$$

where P_x is price per unit of good *x*, MU_x is marginal utility from good *x* and MU_m is marginal utility of money (which is assumed to be a constant).

Table 5.2 Marginal Utility Schedule

Units Consumed of Good *x*	Marginal Utility from Good *x* (in terms of money)
1	8
2	7
3	6
4	5
5	4
6	3

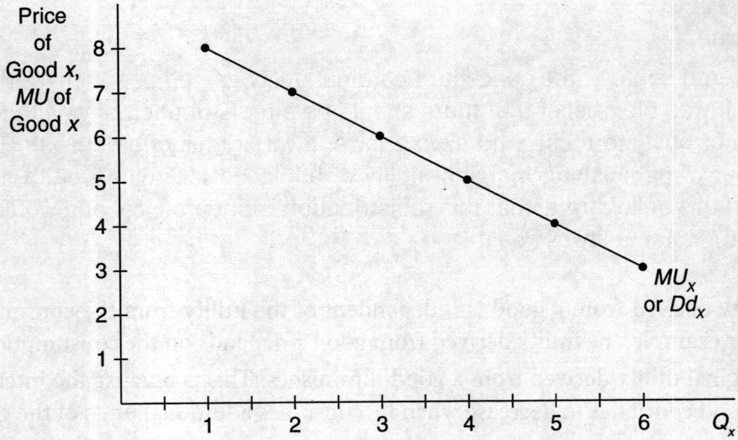

Figure 5.2 Derivation of the Demand Curve

When the price of good *x* is ₹5 per unit, the consumer will purchase four units of good *x* since then the marginal utility from good *x* is equal to the per-unit price of good *x*, which is equal to five. When the price of good *x* falls to ₹4 per unit, the consumer will purchase five units of good *x* since then the marginal utility from good *x* is equal to the per-unit price of good *x*, which is equal to four and when it falls further to ₹3 per unit, the consumer will purchase six units of good *x*. Thus, the consumer buys more units of good *x* only when the price of good *x* falls.

It is obvious from Figure 5.2 that when marginal utility of a good is measured in terms of money, the marginal utility curve can be interpreted as the demand curve for the good. The demand curve is downward sloping showing that with a decrease in price more units of good *x* are demanded.

According to the condition $MU_m = MU_x / P_x$, the consumer is in equilibrium when the ratio between the marginal utility of good *x* and the price of good *x* is equal to the marginal utility of money. Suppose that there is a decrease in the price of good *x*. Since the marginal utility of money is a constant, for the equilibrium to be re-established, it is necessary that the marginal utility of good *x* must also decrease. Marginal utility of good *x* will decrease only when the consumer demands more units of good *x*. Thus, a decrease in the price of good *x* leads to an increase in the demand for good *x*. Hence, the law of demand is proved.

RECAP

- According to the law of diminishing marginal utility as the quantity consumed of any one good increases, while the consumption of all other goods consumed remains constant, the marginal utility from the good must eventually decrease.
- The law of diminishing marginal utility is also known as the *law of satiable wants*.
- For any quantity of a good, the area under the marginal utility curve would be the total utility for that quantity of the good.
- The marginal utility can also be expressed in terms of the slope of the total utility curve.
- The reason as to why the consumer's utility diminishes is that the intensity of the desire for the good continues to decrease when he consumes additional units of the good.
- By using the law of diminishing marginal utility, Marshall derived the law of demand, which shows that there exists an inverse relationship between price and the quantity demanded of a good.

LAW OF EQUI-MARGINAL UTILITY

We have analysed the equilibrium of a consumer when he consumes only one good. But, in reality, a consumer consumes more than one good. The law of equi-marginal utility analyses the equilibrium of the consumer when he consumes more than one good.

Suppose that a consumer consumes two goods, x and y. The consumer is in equilibrium when

$$\frac{MU_x}{P_x} = \frac{MU_y}{P_y} = MU_m$$

where P_x is price per unit of good x, MU_x is marginal utility from good x, P_y is price per unit of good y, MU_y is marginal utility from good y and MU_m is marginal utility of money (which is assumed to be a constant).

Given his money income and the price of goods x and y, the consumer will be in equilibrium when he allocates his income between the two goods such that the ratios of the marginal utilities of the individual goods to their prices are equal. In other words, a rational consumer will so distribute his income such that the marginal utility from the last rupee spent on each good is the same.

> The law of equi-marginal utility analyses the equilibrium of the consumer when he consumes more than one good.

Suppose that a consumer consumes more than two goods, for example, $a, b, \ldots x$. Then, the consumer is in equilibrium when

$$\frac{MU_a}{P_a} = \frac{MU_b}{P_b} = \cdots = \frac{MU_x}{P_x} = MU_m$$

where P_a is price per unit of good a, MU_a is marginal utility from good a, P_b is price per unit of good b, MU_b is marginal utility from good b, P_x is price per unit of good x, MU_x is marginal utility from good x and MU_m is marginal utility of money.

RECAP

- The law of equi-marginal utility analyses the equilibrium of the consumer when he consumes more than one good.
- A rational consumer will so distribute his income such that the marginal utility from the last rupee spent on each good is the same.

LIMITATIONS OF THE CARDINAL UTILITY APPROACH

The cardinal utility approach suffers from many shortcomings:

(i) It was assumed that utility is cardinal. In reality, it is subjective and it is difficult to put a specific value on the utility that one gets from the consumption of a good. One can certainly compare the utilities from two goods but one cannot give a definite value to the utility derived from the two goods.

(ii) Utility is assumed to be additive and thus to arrive at total utility, the utility from different goods was added together. This is not true because utility is not cardinal and also because one derives different types of utility or satisfaction from different types of goods. One cannot add different types of utility or satisfaction from different goods.

(iii) The utility derived from the consumption of a good was assumed to be independent of the utility from the consumption of another good. However, this is not true as the different goods are interrelated and the utility from one good often depends upon the utility from another good.

(iv) The marginal utility of money was assumed to be constant. This is not true and it is often a subject of much debate as to whether the law of diminishing marginal utility applies to money.

(v) The utility analysis is unable to explain the existence of the Giffen goods.

(vi) The utility theory does not analyse the effect of a change in the price in terms of the income effect and the substitution effect.

RECAP

- In reality, utility is subjective and it is difficult to put a specific value on the utility that one gets from the consumption of a good.
- One cannot add different types of utility from different goods.
- Different goods are interrelated and the utility from one good often depends upon the utility from another good.
- The marginal utility of money is not constant.

SUMMARY

INTRODUCTION

1. The law of demand does not explain as to why there exists a negative relationship between the quantity demanded of a good and the price of the good.
2. This is explained by three approaches: cardinal utility approach, ordinal utility approach and the revealed preference theory.

MARSHALL'S UTILITY ANALYSIS

1. H. H. Gossen, Leon Walras, Jevons and many others had analysed the utility theory.
2. It was Alfred Marshall who first discussed the role played by the theory of utility in the theory of value.

WHAT IS UTILITY?

1. The utility of a good is the power of the good to satisfy a want.
2. Utility is a subjective concept.
3. Utility is ethically neutral in that it does not differentiate between bad and good.

CONCEPT OF CARDINAL AND ORDINAL UTILITY

1. The concepts of cardinal and ordinal belong to the field of mathematics.
2. Ordinal numbers are those which can be ranked or ordered.
3. Cardinal utility implies that the utility can be measured in quantitative terms.
4. According to the concept of cardinal utility, one can measure the utility in terms of utils.
5. Professor Marshall was of the view that one can measure the utility in terms of price.
6. The price that a consumer is willing to pay for a good is an indication of the utility of that good to the consumer.
7. It was assumed that the utility of money does not change or remains constant.

CARDINAL UTILITY APPROACH

Total Utility

1. Total utility is the sum of the utility which a consumer derives from the consumption of the different units of a good.
2. The total utility that the consumer derives from the consumption of five units of good *x* is

$$U_x = u_1 + u_2 + u_3 + u_4 + u_5.$$

3. If the consumer consumes *n* units of good *x*, then the total utility that the consumer derives from the consumption of *n* units of good *x* is

$$U_n = u_1 + u_2 + u_3 + u_4 + u_5 + \ldots + u_n.$$

4. If the consumer consumes goods *x*, *y* and *z*, then the total utility that the consumer derives from the consumption of the goods is

$$U = U_x + U_y + U_z.$$

Marginal Utility

1. Marginal utility of a good is the change in the total utility from consuming an additional unit of the good.

   Hence, $$MU = \frac{\Delta TU}{\Delta Q}.$$

2. Marginal utility can also be expressed in terms of total utility as

$$MU_n = TU_n - TU_{n-1}$$

LAW OF DIMINISHING MARGINAL UTILITY

1. The law of diminishing marginal utility is based on certain assumptions: units of the good which are consumed are homogenous; the good is consumed within a short time; the units of the good consumed are of a standard size and not too small or too large; consumer's income does not change in the period under consideration; consumer's tastes, preferences and habits do not change in the period under consideration and others.
2. According to the law of diminishing marginal utility as the quantity consumed of any one good increases, while the consumption of all other goods consumed remains constant, the marginal utility from the good must eventually decrease.
3. In other words, as additional units of the good are consumed, the total utility from the good increases at a decreasing rate and may become negative.
4. The aspect of utility, where it diminishes with the consumption of additional units of the good under consideration, is called the law of diminishing marginal utility. The law is also known as the *law of satiable wants*.
5. The marginal utility curve slopes downwards showing that the marginal utility decreases as additional units of the good are consumed.
6. It is important to note that the total utility for any unit of the good is the sum of the marginal utility till that unit.
7. For any quantity of a good, the area under the marginal utility curve would be the total utility for that quantity of the good.
8. The marginal utility can also be expressed in terms of the slope of the total utility curve.
9. When total utility is a maximum marginal utility is zero.
10. When total utility is decreasing, marginal utility is negative.
11. Negative marginal utility implies that you have too much of a good and would prefer lesser.
12. The reason as to why the consumer's utility diminishes is that the intensity of the desire for the good continues to decrease when he consumes additional units of the good.

A Derivation of the Law of Demand

1. By using the law of diminishing marginal utility, Marshall derived the law of demand.
2. The assumptions on which the analysis has been based are: money income of the consumer is given; prices of all the related goods, complements and substitutes are given; consumer's tastes and preferences do not change in the period under consideration; consumer behaves in a rational manner; utility is assumed to be cardinal; utility is additive; utility derived from a good is independent of the utility from the consumption of another good; marginal utility derived from a good diminishes; Marshall expressed utility in terms of money and the marginal utility of money is assumed to be constant.
3. When marginal utility of a good is measured in terms of money, the marginal utility curve can be interpreted as the demand curve for the good.
4. The demand curve is downward sloping showing that with a decrease in price more units of good x are demanded.

LAW OF EQUI-MARGINAL UTILITY

1. The law of equi-marginal utility analyses the equilibrium of the consumer when he consumes more than one good.
2. Suppose that a consumer consumes two goods, x and y. The consumer is in equilibrium when

$$\frac{MU_x}{P_x} = \frac{MU_y}{P_y} = MU_m$$

3. A rational consumer will so distribute his income such that the marginal utility from the last rupee spent on each good is the same.
4. If a consumer consumes more than two goods, for example $a, b, \ldots x$, then the consumer is in equilibrium when

$$\frac{MU_a}{P_a} = \frac{MU_b}{P_b} = \cdots = \frac{MU_x}{P_x} = MU_m$$

LIMITATIONS OF THE CARDINAL UTILITY APPROACH

1. It was assumed that utility is cardinal. In reality, it is subjective.
2. Utility is assumed to be additive. One cannot add different types of utility or satisfaction from different goods.
3. The utility derived from the consumption of a good was assumed to be independent of the utility from the consumption of another good. However, this is not true as the different goods are interrelated and the utility from one good often depends upon the utility from another good.
4. The marginal utility of money was assumed to be constant. This is not true. The utility analysis is unable to explain the existence of the Giffen goods.
5. The utility theory does not analyse the effect of a change in the price in terms of the income effect and the substitution effect.

REVIEW QUESTIONS

TRUE OR FALSE QUESTIONS

1. The utility of a good is the power of the good to satisfy a want.
2. Cardinal numbers are those which can be ranked or ordered.
3. The marginal utility curve slopes downwards.
4. For any quantity of a good, the area under the total utility curve would be the marginal utility for that quantity of the good.
5. The law of equi-marginal utility analyses the equilibrium of the consumer when he consumes one good.

SHORT ANSWER QUESTIONS

1. Differentiate between ordinal utility and cardinal utility.
2. What is total utility? Explain.
3. What is marginal utility? Explain.
4. What are the assumptions on which the law of diminishing marginal utility is based? Discuss.
5. What are limitations of the cardinal utility approach? Discuss.

LONG ANSWER QUESTIONS

1. Illustrate the law of diminishing marginal utility with a numerical example.
2. 'By using the law of diminishing marginal utility, Marshall derived the law of demand, which shows that there exists an inverse relationship between price and the quantity demanded of a good'. Comment.
3. 'The law of equi-marginal utility analyses the equilibrium of the consumer when he consumes more than one good'. Comment.
4. Write a short note on the cardinal utility approach.
5. With the help of a numerical example, analyse the relationship between total utility and marginal utility.

ANSWERS

TRUE OR FALSE QUESTIONS

1. **True.** It is the satisfaction gained from the consumption of a good. Thus, if a person wants a good, it implies that the good has a certain amount of utility for that person.
2. **False.** Ordinal numbers are those which can be ranked or ordered.
3. **True.** The marginal utility curve slopes downwards showing that marginal utility decreases as additional units of the good are consumed.
4. **False.** For any quantity of a good, the area under the marginal utility curve would be the total utility for that quantity of the good.
5. **False.** The law of equi-marginal utility analyses the equilibrium of the consumer when he consumes more than one good.

Ordinal Utility Approach: Indifference Curve Theory and Its Applications

6

After studying this chapter, you should be able to understand:

- ✓ An indifference curve depicts various combinations of two goods, which give the same level of satisfaction or utility to the consumer.
- ✓ A higher indifference curve depicts a larger amount of satisfaction than a lower one because it represents a greater quantity of good x or y or more of both x and y.
- ✓ An indifference curve is negatively sloped.
- ✓ An indifference curve is convex to the origin.
- ✓ Indifference curves cannot intersect.
- ✓ When goods x and y are perfect substitutes, the indifference curve is a downward sloping straight line and the MRS_{xy} is constant.
- ✓ When goods x and y are perfect complements, the indifference curves are L shaped and the MRS_{xy} is zero.
- ✓ A consumer aims at maximizing his utility by reaching the highest indifference curve that he can achieve.
- ✓ The budget line represents the various combinations of the amounts of the goods, which the consumer can purchase given his money income and the price of the goods.
- ✓ Shifts will take place in the budget line when there is a change in the consumer's money income, prices of the two goods x and y remaining unchanged.
- ✓ Shifts will also take place in the budget line when there is a change in the price of good x or good y or both, the money income of the consumer remaining unchanged.
- ✓ A consumer is in equilibrium when he is able to reach the highest indifference curve given the budget constraint.
- ✓ The income consumption curve is the locus of points representing the consumer's equilibrium when there is change in the money income of the consumer, ceteris paribus.
- ✓ The price consumption curve is the locus of points representing the consumer's equilibrium when there is a change in the price of a good assuming that there is no change in the money income of the consumer, price of the other good and the tastes and preferences of the consumer.
- ✓ The change in the demand for a good due to a change in its price, ceteris paribus, is called the price effect.
- ✓ The price effect can be split into two effects: substitution effect and income effect.
- ✓ By using the indifference curve analysis, Hicks derived the demand curve which is downward sloping showing that there exists an inverse relationship between price and quantity demanded of a good.
- ✓ While the movement of the substitution effect is always in the opposite direction, in the case of a normal good, the movement of the income effect is also in the opposite direction as the price change.
- ✓ The consumer surplus is a measure of the benefit, which accrues to a consumer when the price that he is willing to pay for a good is more than the price he actually pays for it.

INTRODUCTION

In Chapter 5, we had analysed the behaviour of the consumer and derived the law of demand by using the cardinal utility approach, where according to Professor Marshall utility can be measured. The present chapter focuses on the ordinal utility approach by R. G. D. Allen and J. R. Hicks according to which a consumer can only rank or order the utilities obtained from a good.

An indifference curve depicts the various combinations of two goods, which give the same level of satisfaction or utility to the consumer.

Hicks and Allen have analysed the consumer's behaviour through indifference curves. An indifference curve depicts the various combinations of two goods, which give the same level of satisfaction or utility to the consumer.

ASSUMPTIONS OF THE INDIFFERENCE CURVE THEORY

The indifference curve analysis is based on certain assumptions:

(i) Utility is assumed to be ordinal. Thus, a consumer can rank his preferences but cannot express the utility derived from any good in quantitative terms. He can give his scale of preferences between two goods, x and y, such that
- He prefers x to y.
- He prefers y to x.
- He is indifferent between x and y.

(ii) It is important to note that the scale of preferences of the consumer does not depend on his money income and the prices of the goods x and y.

(iii) It is assumed that the consumer is rational. He is assumed to have complete knowledge about the conditions prevailing in the market. Given his money income and the prices of the goods x and y, the consumer aims at maximizing his utility.

(iv) The tastes and habits of the consumer do not change.

(v) The marginal rate of substitution is diminishing. The marginal rate of substitution of good x for good y is the amount of y that the consumer is willing to give up in order to increase his consumption of good x by one unit, while total utility remains the same. The marginal rate of substitution of good x for good y is assumed to decrease as the quantity of good x with the consumer increases.

(vi) The preferences of the consumer are assumed to be transitive. If he is indifferent between goods a and b and between goods b and c, then he is indifferent between goods a and c. Similarly, if he prefers good a to good b and good b to good c, then he prefers good a to good c.

BOX 6.1

Francis Ysidro Edgeworth first developed the indifference curve theory in 1881 in his book *Mathematical Psychics: An Essay on the Application of Mathematics to the Moral Sciences*. The first author to actually draw these curves was Vilfredo Pareto in the book *Manual of Political Economy*. It is used widely not only in consumer theory but also in welfare economics.

(vii) As far as his choice of goods and services are concerned, the consumer is assumed to be consistent. This implies that if in one period the consumer shows a preference for good *a* as compared with good *b* then he will not prefer good *b* to good *a* in another period.

(viii) The consumer has not reached a situation of complete saturation in consuming a good. Hence, he will always prefer more of a good to less of a good.

RECAP

- Utility is assumed to be ordinal.
- It is assumed that the consumer is rational.
- The marginal rate of substitution is diminishing.
- The preferences of the consumer are assumed to be transitive.
- The consumer is assumed to be consistent.

AN INDIFFERENCE CURVE

An indifference curve depicts the various combinations of two goods, which give the same level of satisfaction or utility to the consumer. It is also called an equal utility curve or isoutility curve.

Table 6.1 shows an indifference schedule. *A, B, C, D* and *E* are the different combinations of the quantities of goods *x* and *y*, which give the same level of utility to the consumer. Thus, the consumer is indifferent between combinations *A, B, C, D* and *E*.

When Table 6.1 is plotted graphically, it yields a curve as in Figure 6.1. This curve is the indifference curve, IC_1 along which the combinations *A, B, C, D* and *E* yield the same level of utility to the consumer. Hence, the consumer is indifferent between these combinations of goods *x* and *y*.

In Figure 6.2, a set of indifference curves represents an indifference map. A higher indifference curve depicts a larger amount of satisfaction than a lower one because it represents a greater quantity of good *x* or *y* or more of both *x* and *y*. In the figure, all the combinations on indifference curve IC_3 represent the same level of utility and thus are preferred equally. But all combinations on IC_3 are preferred to the combinations on IC_1 and IC_2, which represent a lower level of utility than IC_3. Similarly, all combinations on IC_2 are preferred to the combinations on IC_1, which represent a lower level of utility than IC_2.

A set of indifference curves represents an indifference map.

Table 6.1 An Indifference Schedule

Combinations of Goods x and y	Quantity of Good x, Q_x	Quantity of Good y, Q_y
A	1	13
B	2	9
C	3	6
D	4	4
E	5	3

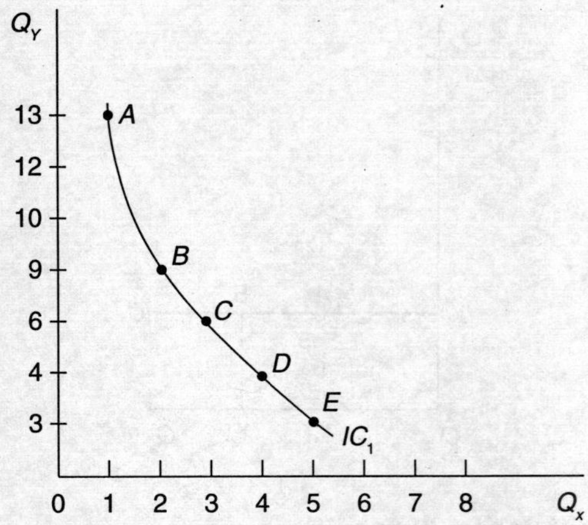

Figure 6.1 An Indifference Curve

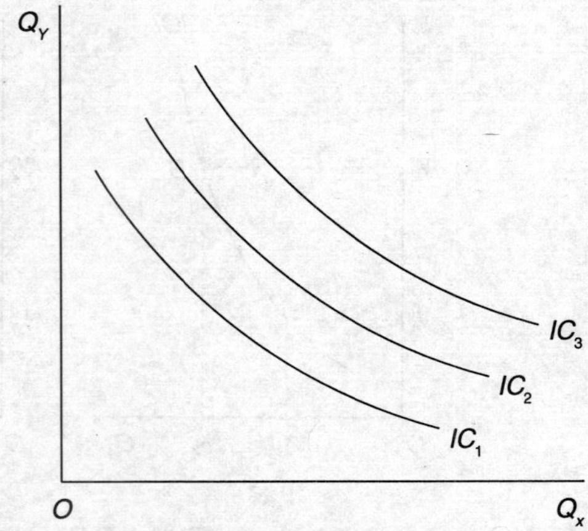

Figure 6.2 An Indifference Map

RECAP

- When an indifference schedule is plotted graphically, it yields the indifference curve.
- A set of indifference curves represents an indifference map.
- A higher indifference curve depicts a larger amount of satisfaction than a lower one because it represents a greater quantity of good *x* or *y* or more of both *x* and *y*.

CHARACTERISTICS OF AN INDIFFERENCE CURVE

An Indifference Curve Is Negatively Sloped

This is because if a consumer consumes more of good *x*, he will have to cut down on his consumption of good *y* (implying that the two goods can be substituted for each other) if he has to remain on the same indifference curve and his level of utility has to remain the same.

Figure 6.3 depicts inconsistent indifference curves. If an indifference curve does not slope downwards, then it can take any of the shapes as in Figure 6.3.

(i) In Figure 6.3(a), an indifference curve slopes upwards. This implies that the two combinations *A* and *B* give the same level of satisfaction to the consumer. However, this is not possible as combination *B* represents more of both *x* and *y* (x_2 and y_2) as compared with combination *A* (x_1 and y_1). Thus, *B* represents a higher level of utility than *A*. Combinations *A* and *B* cannot be on the same indifference curve. Hence, it is not possible for an indifference curve to slope upwards.

(ii) In Figure 6.3(b), an indifference curve is a straight line parallel to the *y* axis. This implies that the two combinations *A* and *B* give the same level of satisfaction to the consumer. However, this is not possible as combination *B* represents more of *y* and the same level of *x* (x_1 and y_2) as compared with combination *A* (x_1 and y_1). Thus, combination *B* represents a higher level of utility than *A*. Combinations *A* and *B* cannot be on the same indifference curve. Hence, it is not possible for an indifference curve to be parallel to the *y* axis.

(iii) In Figure 6.3(c), an indifference curve is a straight line parallel to the *x* axis. This implies that the two combinations *A* and *B* give the same level of satisfaction to the consumer. However,

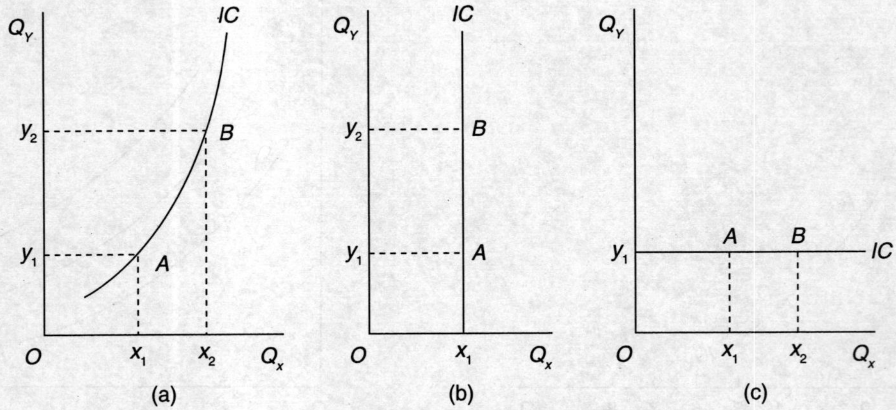

Figure 6.3 Inconsistent Indifference Curves

this is not possible as combination *B* represents more of *x* and the same level of *y* (x_2 and y_1) as compared with combination *A* (x_1 and y_1). Thus, *B* represents a higher level of utility than *A*. Combinations *A* and *B* cannot be on the same indifference curve. Hence, it is not possible for an indifference curve to be parallel to the *x* axis.

Indifference Curve Is Convex to the Origin

This is because the marginal rate of substitution is diminishing. As already discussed, the marginal rate of substitution of good *x* for good *y* is the amount of *y* that the consumer is willing to give up in order to increase his consumption of good *x* by one unit, while total utility remains the same. As the quantity of good *x* with the consumer increases and that of *y* decreases, the marginal rate of substitution of good *x* for good *y* decreases. A consumer is more and more unwilling to part with good *y* as the quantity of good *y* with the consumer decreases.

In Figure 6.1 (and Table 6.1), as the consumer moves down the indifference curve, IC_1, from combination *A* (1*x*, 13*y*) to *B* (2*x*, 9*y*) to acquire an additional unit of *x*, he is ready to give up four units of *y*, if he is to remain on the same indifference curve, IC_1. Thus, to remain at the same level of satisfaction, he has to decrease the consumption of *y* when he increases his consumption of *x*. Hence, his marginal rate of substitution of good *x* for good *y*, MRS_{xy}, when he moves from *A* to *B*, is 4:1.

As the consumer moves down the indifference curve, IC_1, from combination *B* (2*x*, 9*y*) to *C* (3*x*, 6*y*) to acquire an additional unit of *x*, he is ready to give up three units of *y*. Hence, his MRS_{xy} when he moves from *B* to *C* is 3:1.

Further as he moves down from combination *C* (3*x*, 6*y*) to *D* (4*x*, 4*y*) to acquire an additional unit of *x*, he is ready to give up two units of *y*. Hence, his MRS_{xy} when he moves from *C* to *D* is 2:1.

We have observed that as the consumer moves from *A* to *B* to *C* and so on his MRS_{xy} diminishes. It is because of this diminishing MRS_{xy} that the indifference curve is convex to the origin.

It is important to note that the MRS_{xy} equals the slope of the indifference curve at a point. Thus, it is the slope of the tangent at that point on the indifference curve. It can be written as:

$$MRS_{xy} = \text{Slope of the indifference curve} = \frac{\Delta y}{\Delta x}$$

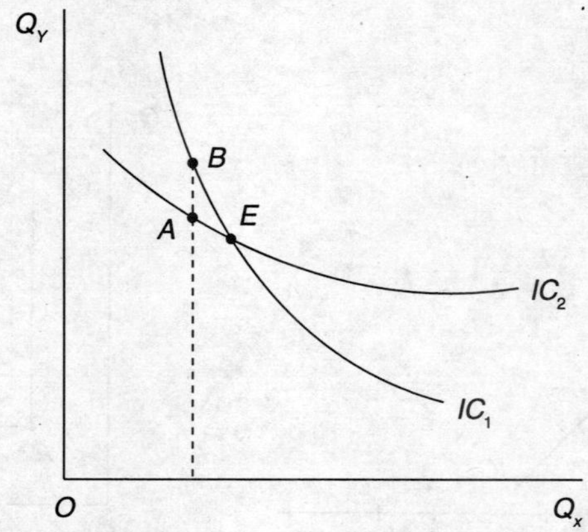

Figure 6.4 Indifference Curves Cannot Intersect

Indifference Curves Cannot Intersect

Figure 6.4 depicts two indifference curves IC_1 and IC_2, which intersect at point E.

Since combinations B and E lie on the same indifference curve IC_1, the consumer would be indifferent between the two combinations. Similarly, since combinations A and E lie on the same indifference curves IC_2, the consumer would be indifferent between the two combinations. But given the assumption of transitivity, the consumer would then be indifferent between combinations A and B. But combination B represents more of good y and the same amount of good x. Hence, a consumer will certainly prefer combination B to A. Since the result is contradictory, it is obvious that indifference curves cannot intersect.

RECAP

- An indifference curve is negatively sloped.
- An indifference curve is convex to the origin.
- Indifference curves cannot intersect.

EXCEPTIONS: COMPLEMENTS AND SUBSTITUTES

There are certain exceptional cases as far as the indifference curves are concerned:

(i) **Goods *x* and *y* Are Substitutes.** When goods x and y are perfect substitutes, the indifference curve is a downward sloping straight line as in Figure 6.5. Since the two goods are perfect substitutes, the MRS_{xy} is constant. For every additional unit of good x, the consumer is ready to give up an equal amount of good y.

(ii) **Goods *x* and *y* Are Complements.** When goods x and y are perfect complements, the indifference curves are L shaped as in Figure 6.6. Since the two goods are perfect complements, the MRS_{xy} is zero. Goods x and y are used jointly in a fixed proportion, for example, at points A and B, to satisfy the consumer. However, the consumer reaches a higher level of satisfaction on indifference curve IC_2 as compared with IC_1.

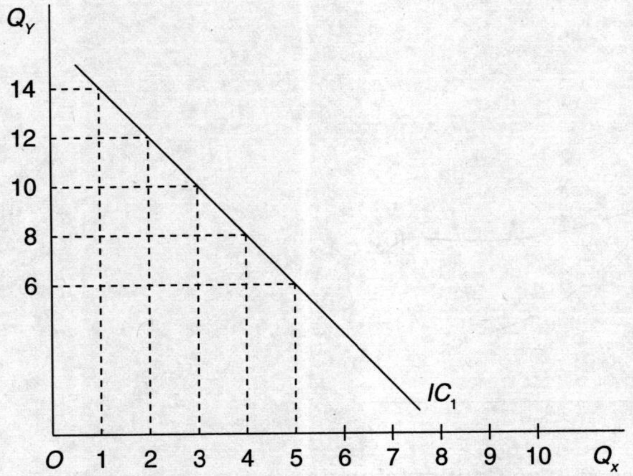

Figure 6.5 Indifference Curves: Goods *x* and *y* Are Perfect Substitutes

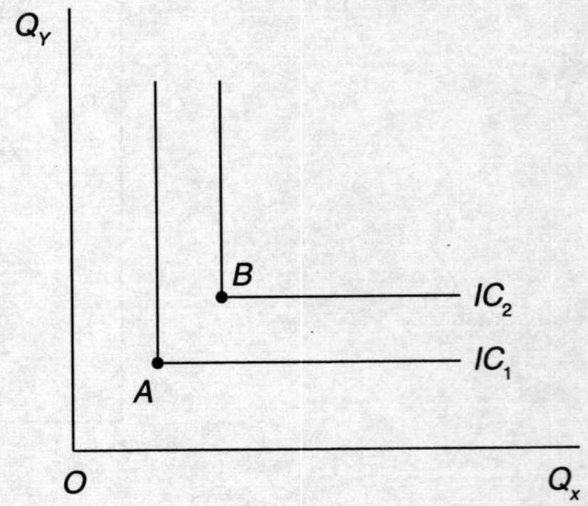

Figure 6.6 Indifference Curves: Goods *x* and *y* Are Perfect Complements

(iii) **A Commodity May Be Good, Bad or Neutral.** A consumer will always prefer more of a commodity (good), which is good in the literal sense (for example, fresh air in a garden) and less of that which is bad (pollution from a factory). In Figure 6.7(a), he will prefer to be on indifference curve IC_3 than on a lower indifference curve. The consumer prefers combination *B* on IC_3 than *A* on IC_2 because, although both the combinations represent the same amount of the bad commodity, *B* represents more of the good commodity as compared with *A*.

As far as a neutral good is concerned, it is a good which does not give the consumer any satisfaction. Thus, in Figure 6.7(b), he will prefer to be on indifference curve IC_3 than on a lower indifference curve. The consumer prefers combination *B* on IC_3 to *A* on IC_2 because, although both the combinations represent the same amount of the neutral commodity, *B* represents more of the good commodity as compared with *A*.

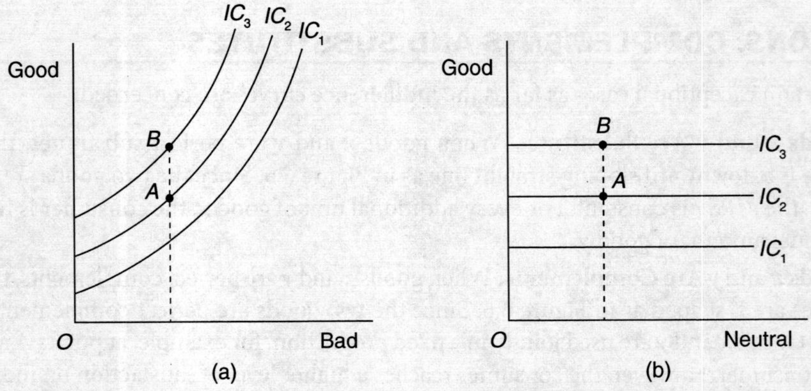

Figure 6.7 Indifference Curves for Good, Bad and Neutral Goods

RECAP

- When goods x and y are perfect substitutes the indifference curve is a downward sloping straight line and the MRS_{xy} is constant.
- When goods x and y are perfect complements, the indifference curves are L shaped and the MRS_{xy} is zero.
- A consumer will always prefer more of a commodity, which is good in the literal sense and less of that which is bad.
- As far as a neutral good is concerned, it is a good which does not give the consumer any satisfaction.

BUDGET LINE OF THE CONSUMER

A consumer aims at maximizing his utility by reaching the highest indifference curve that he can achieve. However, as to the level of the indifference curve, which he can achieve, depends on his money income and the prices of the goods.

The budget line represents the various combinations of the amounts of the goods, which the consumer can purchase given his money income and the price of the goods. It is also called the consumption possibility line or the price line.

> The budget line represents the various combinations of the amounts of the goods, which the consumer can purchase given his money income and the price of the goods.

Assume that there are only two goods, x and y, under consideration. The budget line can be expressed as:

$$M = P_x Q_x + P_y Q_y$$

where M is consumer's money income, P_x is per unit price of good x, Q_x is quantity of good x, P_y is per unit price of good y and Q_y is quantity of good y.

Figure 6.8 depicts the budget line of the consumer, AB, as a straight line intersecting the x axis and the y axis at points A and B, respectively. We can determine the intersection of the budget line

(i) **On the x axis (Point A):** Since Q_y is equal to zero,

$$Q_x = \frac{M}{P_x}$$

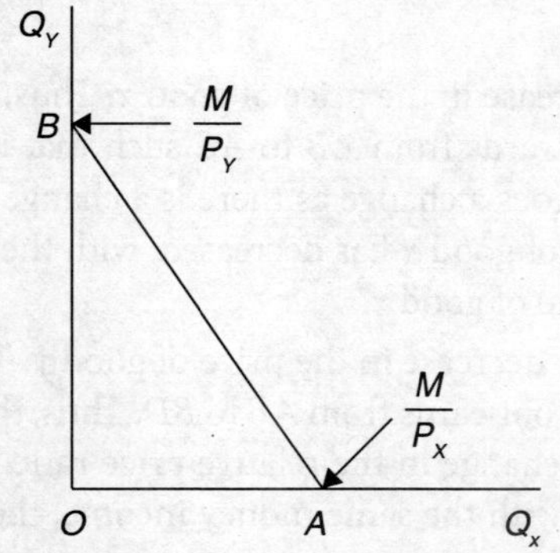

Figure 6.8 Budget Line of the Consumer

(ii) **On the *y* axis (Point *B*):** Since Q_x is equal to zero,

$$Q_y = \frac{M}{P_y}$$

Slope of the budget line,

$$AB = -\frac{OB}{OA} = -\frac{M/P_y}{M/P_x} = -\frac{P_x}{P_y}$$

The slope of the budget line is the price ratio of the two goods. The budget set is the right angled triangle *BOA*, which is formed by the budget line.

Since the consumer's savings are assumed to be zero, the consumer will spend all his income on goods *x* and *y* and he will choose a combination of *x* and *y* on the budget line.

RECAP

- A consumer aims at maximizing his utility by reaching the highest indifference curve that he can achieve.
- The budget line represents the various combinations of the amounts of the goods, which the consumer can purchase given his money income and the price of the goods.

SHIFTS IN THE BUDGET LINE

Shifts will take place in the budget line when there is

(i) A change in the consumer's money income, prices of the two goods *x* and *y* remaining unchanged. Suppose there is an increase in the consumer's money income. Thus, in Figure 6.9(a) there will be a parallel shift of the budget line outwards from *AB* to *CD*. The slope of the budget line remains unchanged at $-P_x/P_y$.

It is important to note that since the prices of the two goods *x* and *y* do not change while the money income of the consumer has increased he will be able to buy more of good *x* or good *y* or both.

(ii) A change in the price of good *x* or good *y* or both, the money income of the consumer remaining unchanged:

— Suppose there is a decrease in the price of good *x*. Thus, in Figure 6.9(b), there will be a shift of the budget line outwards from *AB* to *AC* such that it becomes flatter. Thus, the slope of the budget line undergoes a change as there is a change in the relative price ratio of the two goods. Since the price of good *x* has decreased, with the same money income, the consumer can now purchase more of good *x*.

— Suppose that there is a decrease in the price of good *y*. Thus, in Figure 6.9(c), there will be a shift of the budget line outwards from *AB* to *BD*. Thus, the slope of the budget line undergoes a change as there is a change in the relative price ratio of the two goods. Since the price of good *y* has decreased with the same money income, the consumer can now purchase more of good *y*.

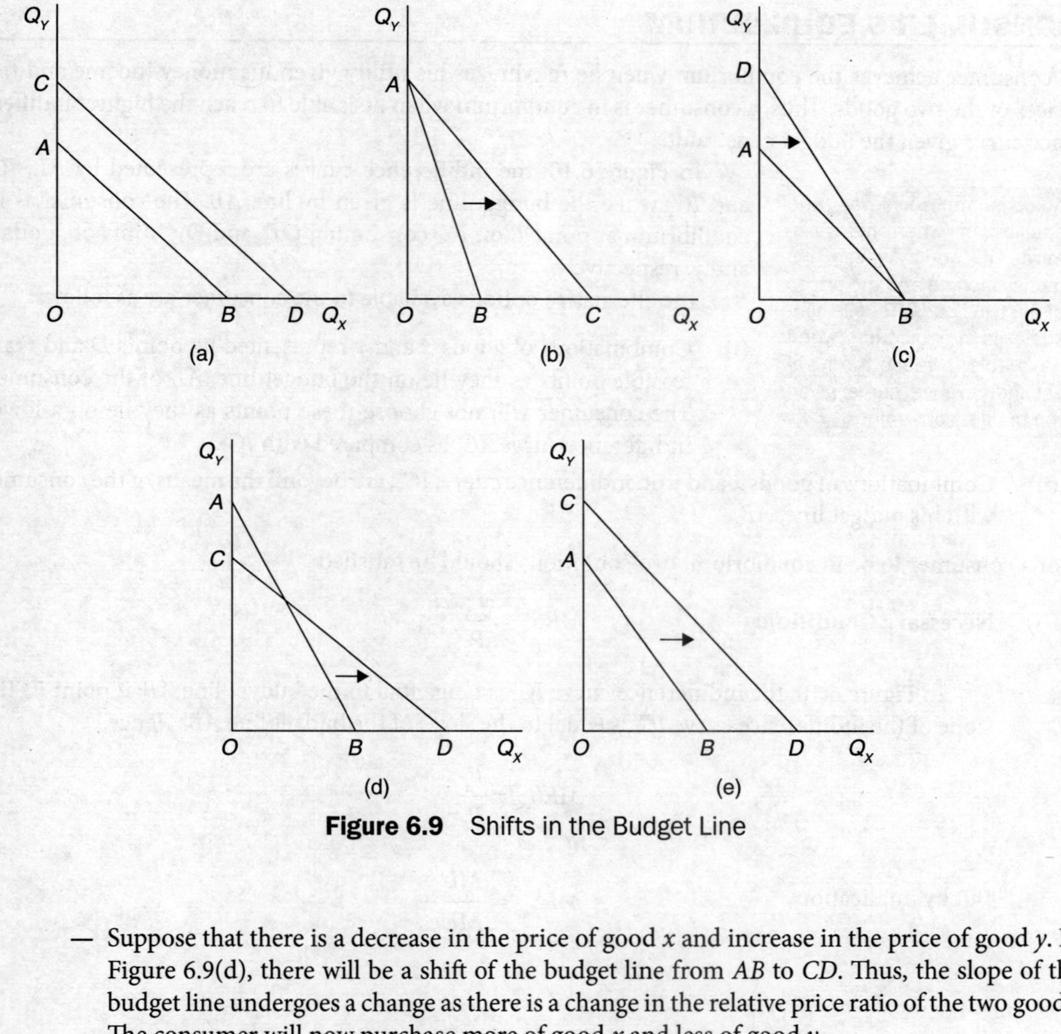

Figure 6.9 Shifts in the Budget Line

— Suppose that there is a decrease in the price of good *x* and increase in the price of good *y*. In Figure 6.9(d), there will be a shift of the budget line from *AB* to *CD*. Thus, the slope of the budget line undergoes a change as there is a change in the relative price ratio of the two goods. The consumer will now purchase more of good *x* and less of good *y*.

— Suppose that there is a decrease in the price of both goods, *x* and *y*, but the decrease in the price of good *x* is more than that of good *y*. In Figure 6.9(e), there will be a shift of the budget line from *AB* to *CD*. Thus, the slope of the budget line undergoes a change as there is a change in the relative price ratio of the two goods. The consumer will now purchase more of goods *x* and *y* but the demand for good *x* will be greater than that of good *y*.

RECAP

- Shifts will take place in the budget line when there is a change in the consumer's money income, prices of the two goods *x* and *y* remaining unchanged.
- Shifts will also take place in the budget line when there is a change in the price of good *x* or good *y* or both, the money income of the consumer remaining unchanged.

CONSUMER'S EQUILIBRIUM

A consumer achieves the equilibrium when he maximizes his utility given his money income and the prices of the two goods. Thus, a consumer is in equilibrium when he is able to reach the highest indifference curve given the budget constraint.

A consumer achieves the equilibrium when he maximizes his utility given his money income and the prices of the two goods. Thus, a consumer is in equilibrium when he is able to reach the highest indifference curve given the budget constraint.

In Figure 6.10, the indifference curves are represented by IC_1, IC_2 and IC_3 while the budget line is given by line *AB*. The consumer is in equilibrium at point *E* on IC_2 consuming *Ox** and *Oy** units of goods *x* and *y*, respectively.

The alternative options available to the consumer are as follows:

(i) Combinations of goods *x* and *y* represented by points *D* and *F* are feasible points as they lie on the budget line, *AB* of the consumer. The consumer will not choose these points as they lie on a lower indifference curve, IC_1 as compared with IC_2.

(ii) Combinations of goods *x* and *y* on indifference curve, IC_3, are beyond the means of the consumer with his budget line, *AB*.

For a consumer to be in equilibrium, two conditions should be satisfied:

(i) **Necessary Condition:** $MRS_{xy} = \frac{P_x}{P_y}$

In Figure 6.10, the indifference curve IC_2 is tangential to the budget line *AB* at point *E*. The slope of the indifference curve IC_2 is equal to the slope of the budget line *AB*. Hence,

$$MRS_{xy} = \frac{P_x}{P_y}$$

But by implication $MRS_{xy} = \frac{MU_x}{MU_y}$

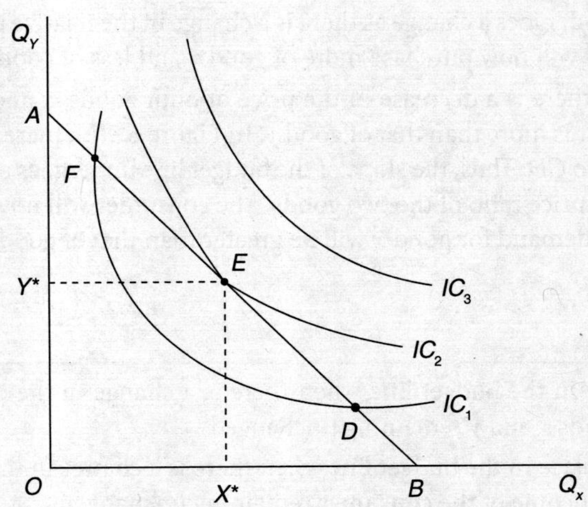

Figure 6.10 Consumer's Equilibrium

Thus,

$$MRS_{xy} = \frac{MU_x}{MU_y} = \frac{P_x}{P_y}$$

(ii) **Sufficient Condition:** At the point of tangency, the MRS_{xy} should be diminishing.

In Figure 6.10, at the point of equilibrium E, the indifference curve is convex to the origin. This is because the marginal rate of substitution is diminishing. Thus for equilibrium to be stable, the MRS_{xy} should de decreasing at the tangency point.

RECAP

- A consumer achieves equilibrium when he maximizes his utility given his money income and the prices of the two goods.
- A consumer is in equilibrium when he is able to reach the highest indifference curve given the budget constraint.
- For a consumer to be in equilibrium, two conditions should be satisfied:

  Necessary condition: $MRS_{xy} = \frac{P_x}{P_y}$

  Sufficient condition: At the point of tangency, the MRS_{xy} should be diminishing.

CHANGES IN THE INCOME LEVEL: INCOME CONSUMPTION CURVE

We now examine the effects of a change in the money income of the consumer, assuming that the price of the goods remains unchanged. The income consumption curve is the locus of points representing the consumer's equilibrium when there is a change in the money income of the consumer, *ceteris paribus*. The shape of the income consumption curve will depend on whether the good is a normal good or an inferior good.

> The income consumption curve is the locus of points representing the consumer's equilibrium when there is change in the money income of the consumer, *ceteris paribus*.

Normal Good

A normal good is one where with an increase in the income there is an increase in the consumption of the good. Hence, there is a positive relationship between changes in income and changes in consumption.

Figure 6.11(a) illustrates the income consumption curve in the case of a normal good, where both goods x and y are normal goods. Given his money income and the prices of the two goods, the initial equilibrium of the consumer exists at point E_1, where the indifference curve IC_1 is tangential to the budget line AB. The consumer is demanding Ox_1 units of good x and Oy_1 units of good y.

When there is an increase in the consumer's money income while the prices of the two goods do not change, there will be a parallel shift of the budget line outwards from AB to CD. The new equilibrium of the consumer will now exist at point E_2, where the indifference curve IC_2 is tangential to the budget line CD. The consumer is demanding Ox_2 units of good x and Oy_2 units of good y.

With a further increase in the consumer's money income, the prices of the two goods remaining unchanged, there will be a parallel shift of the budget line outwards from *CD* to *EF* with the equilibrium at point E_3, where the indifference curve IC_3 is tangential to the budget line *EF*. The consumer demands Ox_3 units of good *x* and Oy_3 units of good *y*.

Joining points like E_1, E_2 and E_3 representing the equilibrium of the consumer, we obtain the income consumption curve for a normal good. Since both goods *x* and *y* are normal goods, the income consumption curve is upward sloping. The movement from point E_1 to E_2 and then to E_3 representing the change in the consumption pattern of the consumer due to a change in money income is called the income effect, *ceteris paribus*. It is important to note that at each point on the income consumption curve, the slope of the indifference curve is equal to the slope of the budget line *AB*. Hence,

$$MRS_{xy} = \frac{P_x}{P_y}$$

Inferior Good

An inferior good is one where with an increase in the income there is a decrease in the consumption of the good. Hence, there is a negative relationship between changes in income and changes in consumption.

Figures 6.11(b) and (c) illustrate the income consumption curve in the case of an inferior good. In Figure 6.11(b), good *x* is an inferior good while *y* is a normal good. In Figure 6.11(c), good *y* is an inferior good while *x* is a normal good.

Given his money income and the prices of the two goods, the initial equilibrium of the consumer exists at point E_1, where the indifference curve IC_1 is tangential to the budget line *AB*. The consumer is demanding Ox_1 units of good *x* and Oy_1 units of good *y*.

When there is an increase in the consumer's money income while the prices of the two goods do not change, there will be a parallel shift of the budget line outwards from *AB* to *CD*. The new equilibrium of the consumer will now exist at point E_2, where the indifference curve IC_2 is tangential to the budget line *CD*. The consumer is demanding Ox_2 units of good *x* and Oy_2 units of good *y*.

With a further increase in the consumer's money income, the prices of the two goods remaining unchanged, there will be a parallel shift of the budget line outwards from *CD* to *EF* with the equilibrium at point E_3, where the indifference curve IC_3 is tangential to the budget line *EF*. The consumer demands Ox_3 units of good *x* and Oy_3 units of good *y*.

Joining points like E_1, E_2 and E_3 representing the equilibrium of the consumer, we obtain the income consumption curve for a normal good.

When good *x* is an inferior good while *y* is a normal good, the income consumption curve as in Figure 6.11(b) moves towards the *y* axis showing a decrease in the demand for good *x* as income increases. When good *y* is an inferior good while *x* is a normal good, the income consumption curve as in Figure 6.11(c) moves towards the *x* axis showing a decrease in the demand for good *y* as income increases.

CHANGES IN THE PRICE LEVEL: PRICE CONSUMPTION CURVE

While deriving the income consumption curve, we had allowed for a change in the money income of the consumer while the prices of the two goods remained unchanged.

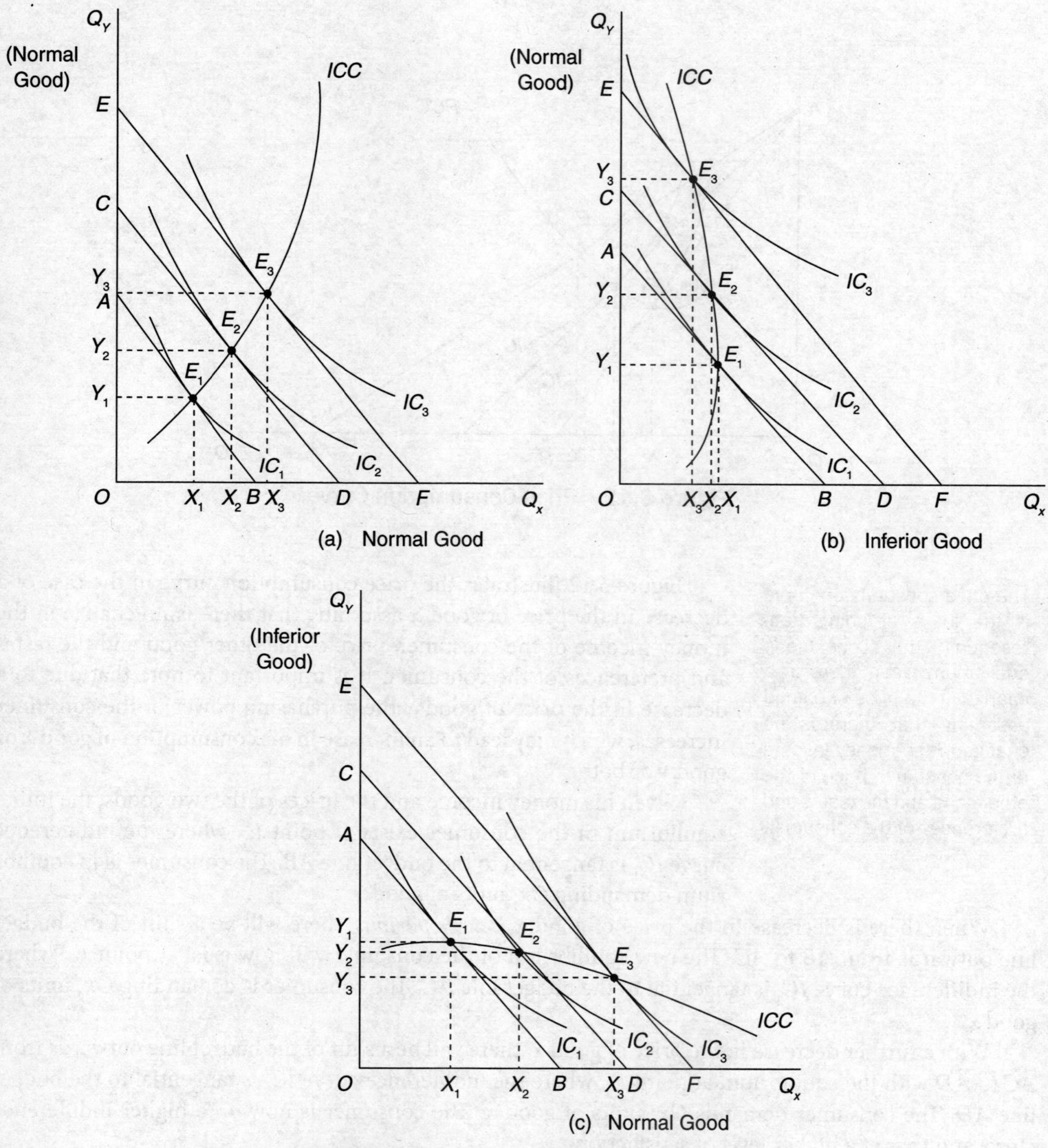

Figure 6.11 Income Consumption Curve

The price consumption curve is the locus of points representing the consumer's equilibrium when there is a change in the price of a good assuming that there is no change in the money income of the consumer, price of the other good and the tastes and preferences of the consumer.

The change in the demand for a good due to a change in its price is called the price effect. We now examine the effects of a change in the price of one of the goods, for example, good *x*, on the consumption pattern of the consumer.

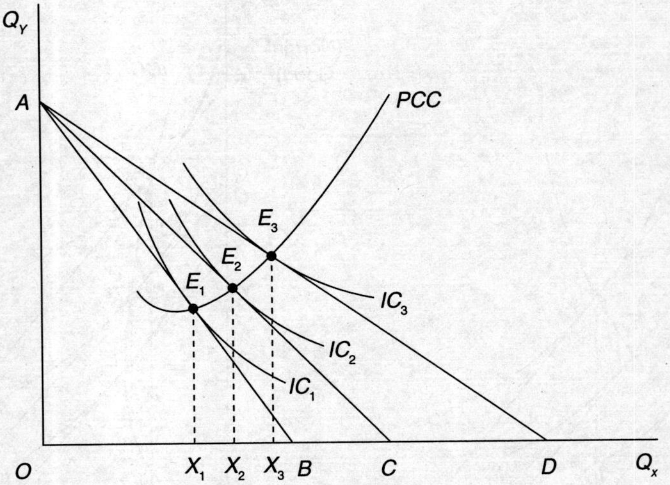

Figure 6.12 Price Consumption Curve

> The price consumption curve is the locus of points representing the consumer's equilibrium when there is a change in the price of a good assuming that there is no change in the money income of the consumer, price of the other good and the tastes and preferences of the consumer.

Figure 6.12 illustrates the price consumption curve in the case of a decrease in the price of good x assuming that there is no change in the money income of the consumer, price of the other good and the tastes and preferences of the consumer. It is important to note that due to a decrease in the price of good x the purchasing power of the consumer increases, which may lead to an increase in his consumption of good x or good y or both.

Given his money income and the prices of the two goods, the initial equilibrium of the consumer exists at point E_1, where the indifference curve IC_1 is tangential to the budget line AB. The consumer is in equilibrium demanding Ox_1 units of good x.

When there is decrease in the price of good x, *ceteris paribus*, there will be a shift of the budget line outwards from AB to AC. The new equilibrium of the consumer will now exist at point E_2, where the indifference curve IC_2 is tangential to the budget line AC. The consumer is demanding Ox_2 units of good x.

With a further decrease in the price of good x, there will be a shift of the budget line outwards from AC to AD with the equilibrium at point E_3, where the indifference curve IC_3 is tangential to the budget line AD. The consumer demands Ox_3 units of good x. The consumer is now on a higher indifference curve and thus at a higher level of satisfaction.

Joining points like E_1, E_2 and E_3 representing the equilibrium of the consumer, we obtain the price consumption curve of the consumer as a U-shaped curve for good x. The slope of the price consumption curve will depend on the price range. It is important to note that at each point on the price consumption curve the slope of the indifference curve is equal to the slope of the budget line AB. Hence,

$$MRS_{xy} = \frac{P_x}{P_y}$$

RECAP

- The price consumption curve is the locus of points representing the consumer's equilibrium when there is change in the price of a good assuming that there is no change in the money income of the consumer, price of the other good and the tastes and preferences of the consumer.

PRICE EFFECT: SUBSTITUTION EFFECT AND INCOME EFFECT

As already discussed, the change in the demand for a good due to a change in its price, *ceteris paribus*, is called the price effect. The price effect can be split into two effects, substitution effect and income effect. To analyse these effects, there are two approaches, Hicksian's approach and Slutsky's approach. In the present analysis, we will be concentrating on the Hicksian approach.

Figure 6.13 illustrates the price effect in the case of a decrease in the price of good x. Given his money income and the prices of the two goods, the initial equilibrium of the consumer exists at point E_1, where the indifference curve IC_1 is tangential to the budget line MB. The consumer is in equilibrium at point E_1 demanding Ox_1 units of good x and E_1x_1 units of good y.

When there is decrease in the price of good x, there will be a shift of the budget line from MB to MD. The new equilibrium of the consumer will now exist at point E_2, where the indifference curve IC_2 is tangential to the budget line MD. The consumer is demanding Ox_2 units of good x and E_2x_2 units of good y.

The consumer moves from equilibrium at point E_1 to E_2 due to a decrease in the price of good x. This movement is traced by the price consumption curve as in the figure. The increase in the quantity demanded of good x, shown by x_1x_2, due to a decrease in its price is called the price effect. We now analyse the price effect as split into the substitution effect and income effect.

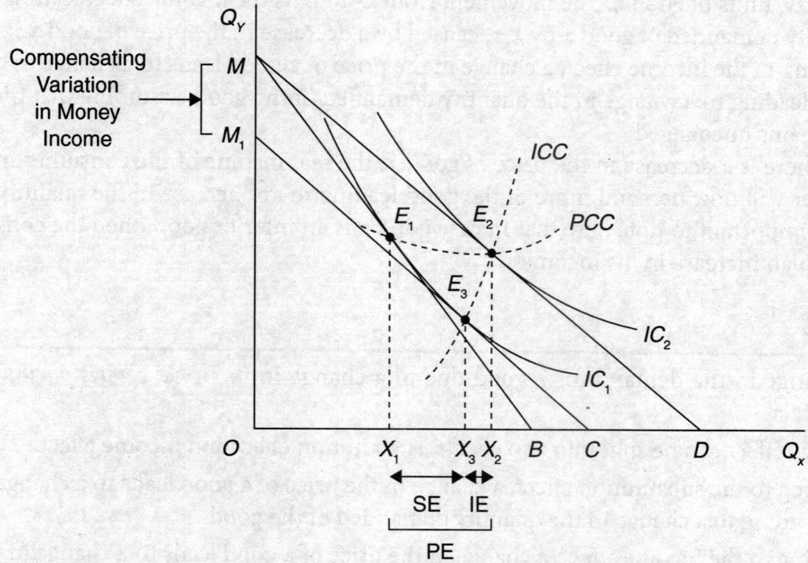

Figure 6.13 Price Effect: Substitution Effect and Income Effect

Substitution Effect

To analyse the substitution effect, the money income of the consumer is reduced by MM_1 such that the consumer is now on the budget line M_1C, which is

(i) parallel to the new budget line represented by *MD*.

(ii) tangent to the original indifference curve of the consumer IC_1.

MM_1 is called the compensating variation in income. The compensating variation in income is necessary to reduce the real income (equals the money income divided by the price of the good) of the consumer, which had gone up due to a decrease in the price of the good. Thus, after having eliminated the income effect of a decrease in the price of good *x*, the consumer is now on the original indifference curve IC_1 but with the new price ratio. He is in equilibrium at point E_3 consuming Ox_3 units of good *x*. The movement from E_1 to E_3 is the substitution effect leading to an increase in the quantity demanded of good *x* by x_1x_3 caused by a decrease in the price of good *x*.

According to the substitution effect, a change in the price of a good leads to a change in the relative prices leading to a change in the quantity demanded of the good.

When there is a decrease in the price of good *x*, the relative price ratio undergoes a change in that good *x* is relatively cheaper as compared with the other goods. Thus, the consumer will now substitute good *x* for the other goods. This will lead to an increase in the quantity demanded of good *x*. Hence, a decrease in the price of good *x* leads to an increase in the demand for good *x* implying that the substitution effect will always be negative, abiding by the law of demand.

Income Effect

To analyse the income effect, the money income of the consumer MM_1 is given back to him such that the consumer is now on the budget line *MD*, whose slope represents the new price ratio. Thus, the consumer is now on the indifference curve IC_2 but with the new price ratio. He is in equilibrium at point E_2 consuming Ox_2 units of good *x*. The movement from E_3 to E_2 is the income effect leading to an increase in the quantity demanded of good *x* by x_3x_2 caused by a decrease in the price of good *x*

According to the income effect, a change in the price of a good leads to a change in the consumer's real income leading to a change in the quantity demanded of the good, assuming that the relative price of goods remains unchanged.

When there is a decrease in the price of good *x*, the real income of the consumer increases. Thus, the consumer will now demand more of the good leading to an increase in the quantity demanded of good *x*. It is important to note here that in case good *x* is an inferior good, then the consumer will buy less of it with an increase in his income.

RECAP

- The change in the demand for a good due to a change in its price, *ceteris paribus*, is called the price effect.
- The price effect can be split into two effects, substitution effect and income effect.
- According to the substitution effect, a change in the price of a good leads to a change in the relative prices leading to a change in the quantity demanded of the good.
- According to the income effect, a change in the price of a good leads to a change in the consumer's real income leading to a change in the quantity demanded of the good, assuming that the relative price of goods remains unchanged.

DERIVATION OF THE DEMAND CURVE

Normal Good

By using the indifference curve analysis, Hicks derived the demand curve, which is downward sloping showing that there exists an inverse relationship between price and the quantity demanded of a good.

Figure 6.14 depicts the derivation of the demand curve for normal goods. Figure 6.14(a) shows the breakup of the price effect into the substitution effect and the income effect, which has already been explained earlier in Figure 6.13. While the movement of the substitution effect is always in the opposite direction, in the case of a normal good, the movement of the income effect is also in the opposite direction as the price change.

The initial price of good x is OP_1 as shown in Figure 6.14(b). It is represented by the budget line MB in Figure 6.14(a). The consumer is in equilibrium consuming Ox_1 units of good x as depicted in Figures 6.14(a) and (b).

With a decrease in the price of good x to OP_2, the budget line MB shifts outwards to MD. As we have already discussed, both the substitution effect and the income effect operate in such a manner that due to the fall in the price of good x more of good x is demanded by the consumer. Thus, due to the price effect, the consumer is in equilibrium consuming Ox_2 units of good x.

In Figure 6.14(b) by connecting points G (price OP_1 and quantity Ox_1) and H (price OP_2 and quantity Ox_2), the demand curve for a normal good has been derived as a downward sloping curve as per the law of demand.

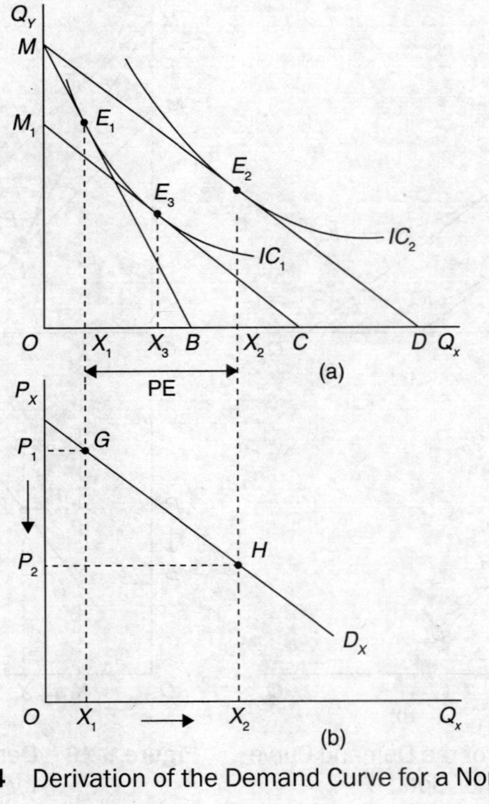

Figure 6.14 Derivation of the Demand Curve for a Normal Good

Inferior Good and Giffen Good

Figures 6.15 and 6.16 depict the derivation of the demand curve for inferior goods and Giffen goods, respectively. While the movement of the substitution effect is in the opposite direction, the movement of the income effect is in the same direction as the price change. Hence, for a decrease in the price of a good while the substitution effect will lead to an increase in the quantity demanded of the good, the income effect will lead to a decrease in the quantity demanded of the good. The ultimate result will depend on as to which effect is the stronger of the two effects:

(i) If the substitution effect is stronger than the income effect, then the demand curve will be downward sloping and inelastic as in the case of an inferior good as in Figure 6.15(b).

(ii) If the income effect is stronger than the substitution effect, then the demand curve will be upward sloping as in the case of a Giffen good as in Figure 6.16(b).

RECAP

- By using the indifference curve analysis, Hicks derived the demand curve which is downward sloping showing that there exists an inverse relationship between price and the quantity demanded of a good.

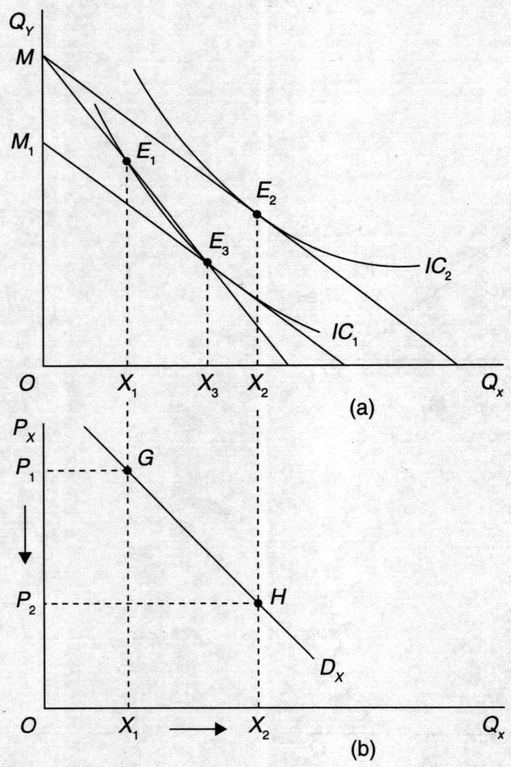

Figure 6.15 Derivation of the Demand Curve for an Inferior Good

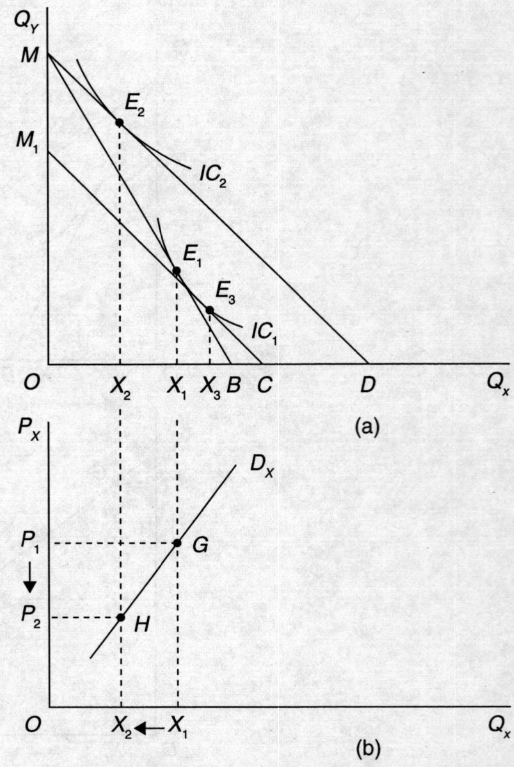

Figure 6.16 Derivation of the Demand Curve for a Giffen Good

- While the movement of the substitution effect is always in the opposite direction, in the case of a normal good, the movement of the income effect is also in the opposite direction as the price change.
- While the movement of the substitution effect is in the opposite direction, in the case of inferior goods and Giffen goods, the movement of the income effect is in the same direction as the price change.

CONSUMER SURPLUS

The consumer surplus is a measure of the benefit, which accrues to a consumer when the price that he is willing to pay for a good is more than the price he actually pays for it. Both, Marshall and Hicks, have examined the concept of the consumer surplus.

> The consumer surplus is a measure of the benefit, which accrues to a consumer when the price that he is willing to pay for a good is more than the price he actually pays for it.

Marshall's Consumer Surplus

Marshall's concept of the consumer's surplus is based on the law of diminishing marginal utility. For the initial units of a good, the marginal utility is high and thus the consumer is willing to pay a higher price (more than the market price) for the good under consideration. But as the number of units of the good increases, his marginal utility diminishes and so does his willingness to pay for the good. The consumer surplus is the excess over the market price that he is willing to pay minus the amount that he actually pays for the good.

Figure 6.17(a) depicts Marshall's consumer surplus. In the figure, D_x represents the demand curve of the consumer for good x while OP^* is the market price of good x.

Amount that the consumer is willing to pay for Ox units of good x = area under the demand curve $D_x = OREX$.

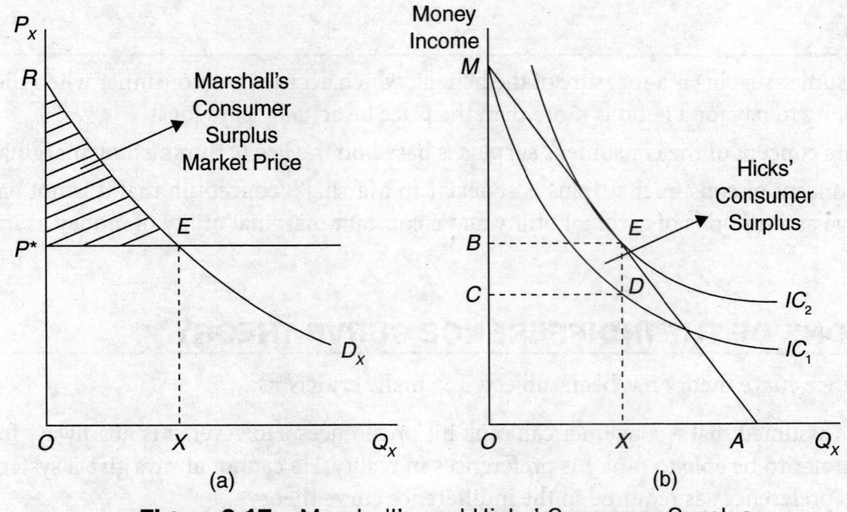

Figure 6.17 Marshall's and Hicks' Consumer Surplus

Amount that the consumer pays for Ox units of good $x = P_x \times Q_x$
$= OP^*OX$
$= OP^*EX$

Consumer surplus = Amount that the consumer is willing to pay for Ox units of good x
– Amount that the consumer pays for Ox units of good x

$= OREX - OP^* EX$
= Shaded area P^*RE

Thus, the consumer surplus is the triangular area between the demand curve and the market price of the good and the price line represented by the line P^*E.

Hicks' Consumer Surplus

Hicks' concept of consumer surplus is superior to Marshall's concept in that it is not based on the restrictive assumptions of cardinal utility and a constant marginal utility of money as in Marshall's analysis.

Figure 6.17(b) depicts Hicks' consumer surplus. In the figure, the consumer's money income is OM, which he spends on good x. Initially, the consumer may not be aware of the price of good x. Thus, he may choose point D on indifference curve IC_1, which implies that to buy Ox units of good x he is willing to give up MC amount of his money income. Suppose later the consumer is aware of the price of good x and thus of his budget line as MA. He will be in equilibrium at point E, where his budget line MA is tangential to the indifference curve IC_2. Thus, to buy Ox units of good x, he actually gives up MB amount of his money income

Consumer surplus = Amount that the consumer is willing to pay for Ox units of good x
– Amount that the consumer pays for Ox units of good x
$= MB - MC$
$= BC$

BC, the vertical distance between the two indifference curves, is the consumer surplus.

RECAP

- The consumer surplus is a measure of the benefit, which accrues to a consumer when the price that he is willing to pay for a good is more than the price he actually pays for it.
- Marshall's concept of the consumer's surplus is based on the law of diminishing marginal utility.
- Hicks' concept of consumer surplus is superior to Marshall's concept in that it is not based on the restrictive assumptions of cardinal utility and a constant marginal utility of money as in Marshall's analysis.

LIMITATIONS OF THE INDIFFERENCE CURVE THEORY

The indifference curve theory has been subjected to many criticisms:

(i) It was assumed that a consumer can rank his preferences. However, it is not always feasible for a consumer to be able to rank his preferences in reality. He cannot always give a systematic order of his preferences as required in the indifference curve theory.

(ii) The assumption that the consumer is rational has been criticized. It is not possible for the consumer to have complete knowledge about the conditions prevailing in the market. Also, his decisions may be influenced by habits and customs.

(iii) The indifference curve theory does not contribute anything new. It has just attempted to replace some of the concepts of the cardinal utility theory, for example, marginal utility by marginal rate of substitution.

(iv) The indifference curve theory is unable to analyse the consumer's behaviour in the face of risks and uncertainty.

(v) As far as empirical evidence is concerned to support the indifference curve theory, the data available is limited.

RECAP

- It is not always feasible for a consumer to be able to rank his preferences in reality.
- It is not possible for the consumer to have complete knowledge about the conditions prevailing in the market.
- The indifference curve theory does not contribute anything new.
- The indifference curve theory is unable to analyse the consumer's behaviour in the face of risks and uncertainty.
- To support the indifference curve theory the data available is limited.

A COMPARISON OF CARDINAL AND ORDINAL UTILITY APPROACHES

A comparison of the cardinal and ordinal utility approaches yields both similarities and differences between the two approaches.

As far as similarities are concerned, both approaches assume that the consumer is rational and aims at the maximization of his utility. In addition, the concept of diminishing marginal rate of substitution under the ordinal utility approach implies, to some extent, diminishing marginal utility as assumed under the cardinal utility approach.

As far as the differences between the two approaches are concerned, the ordinal utility approach is considered to be superior to the cardinal utility approach, in many respects:

(i) While the cardinal utility approach is restrictive in that it assumes that utility is cardinal or can be measured, according to the ordinal utility approach utility is ordinal or cannot be measured and can only be ranked. In addition, the ordinal utility approach does not assume that the marginal utility of money is constant as under the cardinal utility approach.

(ii) The concept of the consumer surplus is more realistically explained by Hicks compared with Marshall because it is not based on the assumption of cardinal utility and a constant marginal utility of money.

(iii) The cardinal utility approach ignores the interdependence between goods by assuming that the utility derived from a good is independent of the utility from the consumption of another good. The ordinal utility approach, in comparison, recognizes the interdependence between the goods, for example, substitutes through its analysis of the substitution effect.

(iv) In his indifference curve theory, Hicks splits up the price effect into the substitution effect and the income effect. Thus, using these effects he is able to analyse the demand for normal goods and differentiate them from the demand for inferior and Giffen goods. Because of its restrictive assumptions in his utility theory, Marshall does not, in any way, splits up the price effect.

RECAP

- Both approaches assume that the consumer is rational and aims at the maximization of his utility.
- While the cardinal utility approach assumes that utility is cardinal, according to the ordinal utility approach, utility is ordinal.
- The concept of the consumer surplus is more realistically explained by Hicks compared with Marshall.
- The cardinal utility approach ignores the interdependence between goods.

APPLICATIONS OF INDIFFERENCE CURVE THEORY

The indifference curve theory has been applied in many areas of economics including welfare economics and international trade. Some areas where it has been applied are:

(i) In making decisions relating to price subsidy as compared with a supplementary income. To give a financial relief to the poor in a price subsidy, the government may pay a part of the per unit price of a good and then the consumer can purchase any number of units of the good at the subsidized price. Alternatively, the government may grant a supplementary income in the form of cash to the consumer with which he can buy whatever good he desires. By using the indifference curve analysis, the government can compare the welfare effects of the two options.

(ii) In making decisions relating to food stamps as compared with cash grant. In 1960s, the government of the United States started many programmes to help the poor. One such programme was the Food Stamps Programme, where food stamps were given to the eligible families with which they could buy food items only. The alternative to the food stamps were a cash grant of an equivalent amount. The indifference curve is an effective technique to analyse the impact of a food stamp programme as compared with a cash subsidy by comparing the impact on the welfare of eligible families of the two types of subsidies.

(iii) Deriving the supply curve of labour by an individual worker. The supply of labour by an individual worker will depend on his choice between work and leisure. To earn an income, the individual has to forego on his leisure time and put in more hours of work. Thus, the individual's choice between income, on the one hand, and work and leisure, on the other hand, can be expressed in terms of indifference curves to depict the combinations of income, work and leisure which are available to him. The wage line shows as to the options which are available to him so that he can work and earn an income. By combining the indifference curve and the wage line, one can derive the wage offer curve and thus the supply curve of an individual worker.

RECAP

- The indifference curve theory has been applied in many areas of economics including welfare economics and international trade.

- In making decisions relating to price subsidy as compared with a supplementary income by using the indifference curve analysis, the government can compare the welfare effects of the two options.
- The indifference curve is an effective technique to analyse the impact of a food stamp programme as compared with a cash subsidy by comparing the impact on the welfare of eligible families of the two types of subsidies.
- By combining the indifference curve and the wage line, one can derive the wage offer curve and thus the supply curve of an individual worker.

SUMMARY

INTRODUCTION

1. The present chapter focuses on the ordinal utility approach by R. G. D. Allen and J. R. Hicks according to which a consumer can only rank or order the utilities obtained from a good.
2. Hicks and Allen have analysed the consumer's behaviour through indifference curves.
3. An indifference curve depicts the various combinations of two goods, which give the same level of satisfaction or utility to the consumer.

ASSUMPTIONS OF THE INDIFFERENCE CURVE THEORY

1. Utility is assumed to be ordinal. Thus, a consumer can rank his preferences but cannot express the utility derived from any good in quantitative terms.
2. It is important to note that the scale of preferences of the consumer does not depend on his money income and the prices of the goods x and y.
3. It is assumed that the consumer is rational. Given his money income and the prices of the goods x and y, the consumer aims at maximizing his utility.
4. The tastes and habits of the consumer do not change.
5. The marginal rate of substitution is diminishing. The marginal rate of substitution of good x for good y is the amount of y that the consumer is willing to give up in order to increase his consumption of good x by one unit, while total utility remains the same.
6. The preferences of the consumer are assumed to be transitive.
7. As far as his choice of goods and services are concerned, the consumer is assumed to be consistent.
8. The consumer has not reached a situation of complete saturation in consuming a good.

AN INDIFFERENCE CURVE

1. An indifference curve depicts the various combinations of two goods, which give the same level of satisfaction or utility to the consumer. It is also called an equal utility curve or isoutility curve.
2. An indifference schedule gives the different combinations of the quantities of goods x and y, which give the same level of utility to the consumer.
3. When an indifference schedule is plotted graphically, it yields an indifference curve.
4. A set of indifference curves represents an indifference map.
5. A higher indifference curve depicts a larger amount of satisfaction than a lower one because it represents a greater quantity of good x or y or more of both x and y.

CHARACTERISTICS OF AN INDIFFERENCE CURVE

1. An indifference curve is negatively sloped. This is because if a consumer consumes more of good x, he will have to cut down on his consumption of good y (implying that the two goods can be substituted for each other) if he has to remain on the same indifference curve and his level of utility has to remain the same.

2. An indifference curve is convex to the origin. This is because the marginal rate of substitution is diminishing;

$$MRS_{xy} = \text{Slope of the indifference curve} = \frac{\Delta y}{\Delta x}.$$

3. Indifference curves cannot intersect.

EXCEPTIONS: COMPLEMENTS AND SUBSTITUTES

1 Goods *x* and *y* are substitutes. When goods *x* and *y* are perfect substitutes, the indifference curve is a downward sloping straight line. The MRS_{xy} is constant and for every additional unit of good *x*, the consumer is ready to give up an equal amount of good *y*.

2 Goods *x* and *y* are complements. When goods *x* and *y* are perfect complements, the indifference curve is L shaped. Since the two goods are perfect complements, the MRS_{xy} is zero. Goods *x* and *y* are used jointly in a fixed proportion to satisfy the consumer.

3 A commodity may be good, bad or a neutral. A consumer will always prefer more of a commodity (good), which is good in the literal sense (for example, fresh air in a garden) and less of that which is bad (pollution from a factory). As far as a neutral good is concerned, it is a good which does not give the consumer any satisfaction.

BUDGET LINE OF THE CONSUMER

1. A consumer aims at maximizing his utility by reaching the highest indifference curve that he can achieve.
2. As to the level of the indifference curve, which he can achieve, depends on his money income and the prices of the goods.
3. The budget line represents the various combinations of the amounts of the goods, which the consumer can purchase given his money income and the price of the goods. It is also called the consumption possibility line or the price line.
4. Assume that there are only two goods, *x* and *y*, under consideration. The budget line can be expressed as

$$M = P_x Q_x + P_y Q_y.$$

5. The slope of the budget line is the price ratio of the two goods.
6. Slope of the budget line,

$$AB = -\frac{OB}{OA} = -\frac{M/P_y}{M/P_x} = -\frac{P_x}{P_y}$$

SHIFTS IN THE BUDGET LINE

Shifts will take place in the budget line when there is

1. A change in the consumer's money income, prices of the two goods *x* and *y* remaining unchanged. The slope of the budget line remains unchanged at $-P_x/P_y$. The consumer will be able to buy more of good *x* or good *y* or both.
2. A change in the price of good *x* or good *y* or both, the money income of the consumer remaining unchanged.
3. Suppose that there is a decrease in the price of good *x*. The slope of the budget line undergoes a change as there is a change in the relative price ratio of the two goods. Since the price of good *x* has decreased with the same money income, the consumer can now purchase more of good *x*.
4. Suppose that there is a decrease in the price of good *y*. The slope of the budget line undergoes a change as there is a change in the relative price ratio of the two goods. Since the price of good *y* has decreased with the same money income, the consumer can now purchase more of good *y*.
5. Suppose that there is a decrease in the price of good *x* and increase in the price of good *y*. The slope of the budget line undergoes a change as there is a change in the relative price ratio of the two goods. The consumer will now purchase more of good *x* and less of good *y*.

6. Suppose that there is a decrease in the price of both goods, x and y, but the decrease in the price of good x is more than that of good y. The slope of the budget line undergoes a change as there is a change in the relative price ratio of the two goods. The consumer will now purchase more of goods x and y but the demand for good x will be greater than that of good y.

CONSUMER'S EQUILIBRIUM

1. A consumer achieves equilibrium when he maximizes his utility given his money income and the prices of the two goods.
2. A consumer is in equilibrium when he is able to reach the highest indifference curve given the budget constraint.
3. For a consumer to be in equilibrium, two conditions should be satisfied:
   (a) Necessary condition: $MRS_{xy} = \frac{P_x}{P_y}$
   (b) Sufficient condition: At the point of tangency, the MRS_{xy} should be diminishing.

CHANGES IN THE INCOME LEVEL: INCOME CONSUMPTION CURVE

1. The income consumption curve is the locus of points representing the consumer's equilibrium when there is change in the money income of the consumer, *ceteris paribus*.
2. The shape of the income consumption curve will depend on whether the good is a normal good or an inferior good.
3. A normal good is one where with an increase in the income, there is an increase in the consumption of the good. Hence, there is a positive relationship between changes in income and changes in consumption. If both goods x and y are normal goods, the income consumption curve is upward sloping. It is important to note that at each point on the income consumption curve, the slope of the indifference curve is equal to the slope of the budget line AB. Hence,

$$MRS_{xy} = \frac{P_x}{P_y}$$

4. An inferior good is one where with an increase in the income, there is a decrease in the consumption of the good. Hence, there is a negative relationship between changes in income and changes in consumption. When good x is an inferior good while y is a normal good, the income consumption curve moves towards the y axis showing a decrease in the demand for good x as income increases. When good y is an inferior good while x is a normal good, the income consumption curve moves towards the x axis showing a decrease in the demand for good y as income increases.

CHANGES IN THE PRICE LEVEL: PRICE CONSUMPTION CURVE

1. The price consumption curve is the locus of points representing the consumer's equilibrium when there is a change in the price of a good assuming that there is no change in the money income of the consumer, price of the other good and the tastes and preferences of the consumer.
2. The change in the demand for a good due to a change in its price is called the price effect.
3. We can examine the effects of a change in the price of one of the goods, for example, good x, on the consumption pattern of the consumer.
4. The price consumption curve of the consumer is a U-shaped curve for good x.
5. It is important to note that at each point on the price consumption curve, the slope of the indifference curve is equal to the slope of the budget line AB. Hence,

$$MRS_{xy} = \frac{P_x}{P_y}$$

PRICE EFFECT: SUBSTITUTION EFFECT AND INCOME EFFECT

1. The change in the demand for a good due to a change in its price, *ceteris paribus*, is called the price effect.
2. The price effect can be split into two effects, substitution effect and income effect.

Substitution Effect

1. To analyse the substitution effect, the money income of the consumer is reduced by the compensating variation in income.
2. The compensating variation in income is necessary to reduce the real income (equals the money income divided by the price of the good) of the consumer, which had gone up due to a decrease in the price of the good.
3. According to the substitution effect, a change in the price of a good leads to a change in the relative prices leading to a change in the quantity demanded of the good.
4. The consumer will now substitute good x for the other goods. Hence, a decrease in the price of good x leads to an increase in the demand for good x implying that the substitution effect will always be negative, abiding by the law of demand.

Income Effect

1. According to the income effect, a change in the price of a good leads to a change in the consumer's real income leading to a change in the quantity demanded of the good, assuming that the relative price of goods remains unchanged.
2. When there is a decrease in the price of good x, the real income of the consumer increases. Thus, the consumer will now demand more of good x.
3. It is important to note here that in case good x is an inferior good, then the consumer will buy less of it with an increase in his income.

DERIVATION OF THE DEMAND CURVE

Normal Good

1. By using the indifference curve analysis, Hicks derived the demand curve, which is downward sloping showing that there exists an inverse relationship between price and the quantity demanded of a good.
2. While the movement of the substitution effect is always in the opposite direction, in the case of a normal good, the movement of the income effect is also in the opposite direction as the price change.
3. The demand curve for a normal good is a downward sloping curve as per the law of demand.

Inferior Good and Giffen Good

1. While the movement of the substitution effect is in the opposite direction, the movement of the income effect is in the same direction as the price change.
2. Hence, for a decrease in the price of a good while the substitution effect will lead to an increase in the quantity demanded of the good, the income effect will lead to a decrease in the quantity demanded of the good. The ultimate result will depend on as to which effect is the stronger of the two effects.
3. If the substitution effect is stronger than the income effect, then the demand curve will be downward sloping and inelastic.
4. If the income effect is stronger than the substitution effect, then the demand curve will be upward sloping.

CONSUMER SURPLUS

1. The consumer surplus is a measure of the benefit which accrues to a consumer when the price that he is willing to pay for a good is more than the price he actually pays for it.
2. Both, Marshall and Hicks, have examined the concept of the consumer surplus.

Marshall's Consumer Surplus

1. Marshall's concept of the consumer's surplus is based on the law of diminishing marginal utility.
2. The consumer surplus is the excess over the market price that he is willing to pay minus the amount that he actually pays for the good.
3. The consumer surplus is the triangular area between the demand curve and the market price of the good and the price line.

Hicks' Consumer Surplus

1. Hicks' concept of consumer surplus is superior to Marshall's concept in that it is not based on the restrictive assumptions of cardinal utility and a constant marginal utility of money as in Marshall's analysis.
2. Consumer surplus = Amount that the consumer is willing to pay for Ox units of good x – Amount that the consumer pays for Ox units of good x.
3. The vertical distance between the two indifference curves is the consumer surplus.

LIMITATIONS OF THE INDIFFERENCE CURVE THEORY

1. It was assumed that a consumer can rank his preferences. However, it is not always feasible for a consumer to be able to rank his preferences in reality.
2. The assumption that the consumer is rational has been criticized. It is not possible for the consumer to have complete knowledge about the conditions prevailing in the market.
3. The indifference curve theory does not contribute anything new. It has just attempted to replace some of the concepts of the cardinal utility theory, for example, marginal utility by marginal rate of substitution.
4. The indifference curve theory is unable to analyse the consumer's behaviour in the face of risks and uncertainty.
5. As far as empirical evidence is concerned to support the indifference curve theory, the data available is limited.

A COMPARISON OF CARDINAL AND ORDINAL UTILITY APPROACHES

1. As far as similarities are concerned, both approaches assume that the consumer is rational and aims at the maximization of his utility.
2. As far as the differences between the two approaches are concerned, the ordinal utility approach is considered to be superior to the cardinal utility approach, in many respects.
3. While the cardinal utility approach is restrictive in that it assumes that utility is cardinal or can be measured, according to the ordinal utility approach utility is ordinal or cannot be measured and can only be ranked.
4. The concept of the consumer surplus is more realistically explained by Hicks compared with Marshall.
5. The cardinal utility approach ignores the interdependence between goods. The ordinal utility approach, in comparison, recognizes the interdependence between the goods.
6. In his indifference curve theory, Hicks splits up the price effect into the substitution effect and the income effect. Thus, using these effects, he is able to analyse the demand for normal goods and differentiate them from the demand for inferior and Giffen goods.

APPLICATIONS OF INDIFFERENCE CURVE THEORY

1. In making decisions relating to price subsidy as compared with a supplementary income. By using the indifference curve analysis, the government can compare the welfare effects of the two options.
2. In making decisions relating to food stamps as compared with cash grant. The indifference curve is an effective technique to analyse the impact of a food stamp programme as compared with a cash subsidy by comparing the impact on the welfare of eligible families of the two types of subsidies.
3. Deriving the supply curve of labour by an individual worker. By combining the indifference curve and the wage line, one can derive the wage offer curve and thus the supply curve of an individual worker.

REVIEW QUESTIONS

TRUE OR FALSE QUESTIONS

1. An indifference curve depicts the various combinations of two goods, which give the same level of satisfaction or utility to the consumer.
2. An indifference curve is positively sloped.
3. An indifference curve is convex to the origin.
4. When goods x and y are perfect complements, the indifference curve is a downward sloping straight line and the MRS_{xy} is constant.
5. A consumer aims at minimizing his utility by reaching the highest indifference curve that he can achieve.

SHORT ANSWER QUESTIONS

1. What are the assumptions on which indifference curve theory is based?
2. What is an indifference schedule? How is it related to the indifference curve?
3. 'An indifference curve is convex to the origin'. Comment.
4. Write a short note on the budget line of the consumer.
5. Analyse the shifts in the budget line of the consumer.

LONG ANSWER QUESTIONS

1. What are the characteristics of an indifference curve? Discuss.
2. As far as the indifference curves are concerned, what are the exceptional cases?
3. Define the income consumption curve. Analyse the shape of the income consumption curve for a normal good and an inferior good.
4. 'The price effect can be split into two effects, substitution effect and income effect'. Comment.
5. By using the indifference curve analysis, derive the demand curve in the case of:
   (a) Normal good.
   (b) Inferior good and Giffen good.

ANSWERS

TRUE OR FALSE QUESTIONS

1. **True.** Hicks and Allen have analysed the consumer's behaviour through indifference curves.
2. **False.** An indifference curve is negatively sloped.
3. **True.** An indifference curve is convex to the origin. This is because the marginal rate of substitution is diminishing.
4. **False.** When goods x and y are perfect substitutes, the indifference curve is a downward sloping straight line and the MRS_{xy} is constant.
5. **False.** A consumer aims at maximizing his utility by reaching the highest indifference curve that he can achieve.

Revealed Preference Theory

7

After studying this chapter, you should be able to understand:

- ✓ *Revealed preference theory analyses the behaviour of the consumers from what is revealed by them in the market.*
- ✓ *It is a 'behaviourist–ordinalist' approach.*
- ✓ *The budget set includes all the combinations on and within the budget line from which a consumer can choose any combination of goods x and y.*
- ✓ *When a consumer chooses a combination in or on the budget set, he reveals his preference for that combination as compared with the other combinations.*
- ✓ *The cost difference variation in income is necessary to reduce the real income (equals the money income divided by the price of the good) of the consumer, which had gone up due to a decrease in the price of the good.*
- ✓ *When there is a decrease in the price of good x, due to the quasi-substitution effect and quasi-income effect, the consumer will demand more of the good leading to an increase in the quantity demanded of good x.*
- ✓ *The theory can explain the law of demand only in the case of normal goods and neither inferior nor Giffen goods.*

INTRODUCTION

In Chapters 5 and 6, we had discussed the theory of consumer behaviour in terms of the cardinal utility approach and the ordinal utility approach. The present chapter focuses on another approach to consumer behaviour, revealed preference theory, which analyses the behaviour of the consumers from what is revealed by them in the market. The theory has been developed further to derive the law of demand.

WHAT IS REVEALED PREFERENCE THEORY?

The revealed preference theory was presented by Professor Paul A. Samuelson in 1938. Since the theory is based on the consumer behaviour and is ordinal in its approach, it is a 'behaviourist–ordinalist' approach. The theory is not in any way based on the assumptions involved in the cardinal utility approach and the ordinal utility approach. A behaviourist approach is used to derive the law of demand as compared with the introspective approach used in the cardinal utility approach and the ordinal utility approach.

The revealed preference theory is a 'behaviourist–ordinalist' approach.

Figure 7.1 illustrates as to how a consumer reveals his preference for one combination as compared with another combination. There are two goods *x* and *y* and two combinations of the two goods *R* and *S*. Given the consumer's money income and the prices of the goods *x* and *y*, the consumer's budget line is represented by *MB*. The budget set is represented by triangle *MOB*, which

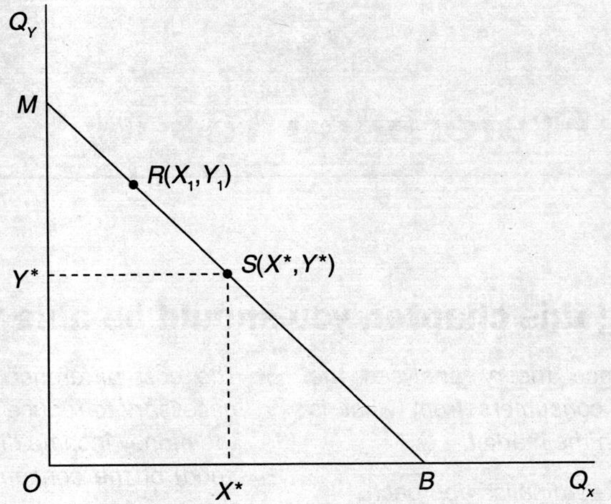

Figure 7.1 Revealed Preference

includes all the combinations on and within the budget line from which a consumer can choose any combination of goods *x* and *y*. The consumer cannot choose any combination, which lies outside the budget set.

> The budget set includes all the combinations on and within the budget line from which a consumer can choose any combination of goods *x* and *y*.

Suppose in the figure the consumer chooses the combination $S(x^*, y^*)$. This implies that he has revealed his choice for combination *S* as compared with, for example, combination $R(x, y)$ on the budget set *AOB*. Thus, the combination *S* represents the optimal bundle.

RECAP

- The revealed preference theory is a 'behaviourist–ordinalist' approach.
- The budget set includes all the combinations on and within the budget line from which a consumer can choose any combination of goods *x* and *y*.

ASSUMPTIONS OF REVEALED PREFERENCE THEORY

Given the consumer's money income and the prices of the goods *x* and *y*, the revealed preference theory is based on certain assumptions:

(i) It is assumed that the consumer is rational. He prefers more of a good to less of it.

(ii) The preferences of the consumer are assumed to be transitive. If he prefers combination *A* to combination *B* and combination *B* to combination C, then he prefers combination *A* to *C*.

(iii) As far as his choice of goods and services are concerned, the consumer is assumed to be consistent. This implies that if in one period the consumer reveals a preference for combination *A* as compared with combination *B*, then he will not reveal his preference for combination *B* as compared with combination *A* in another period.

(iv) When a consumer chooses a combination in or on the budget set, he reveals his preference for that combination as compared with the other combinations. This is because that combination must be giving him maximum satisfaction. He is not indifferent between any combinations. Hence, this implies that the consumer is capable of strongly ordering his preferences.

RECAP

- It is assumed that the consumer is rational.
- The preferences of the consumer are assumed to be transitive.
- As far as his choice of goods and services are concerned, the consumer is assumed to be consistent.
- When a consumer chooses a combination in or on the budget set, he reveals his preference for that combination as compared with the other combinations.

A DERIVATION OF DEMAND CURVE

Using the revealed preference theory, Samuelson derived the law of demand, which depicts the inverse relationship between the price and the quantity demanded of a good. It is assumed that the income elasticity of demand is greater than zero or positive. This condition is necessary for there to exist an inverse relationship between price and quantity demanded.

Figure 7.2 illustrates the derivation of the demand curve. Given the consumer's money income and the prices of the goods *x* and *y*, the consumer's budget line is represented by *MB*. The budget set is represented by triangle *MOB*. Suppose that the consumer chooses the combination *S*. Thus, he reveals his preference for combination *S* as compared with all other combinations on the budget set *MOB*. It is important to note that given that the consumer is rational he will choose a combination on the budget line *MB*. As to which combination he will choose will depend on his tastes and preferences. However, given that he is consistent in his preferences, once he chooses a particular combination, he will not choose any other alternative combination.

Suppose that there is a decrease in the price of good *x*. There will be a shift of the budget line from *MB* from *MD*. The consumer will now move to a combination like *T*, where he buys more of good *x*. This movement from combination *S* to *T* is the total effect of a price change and the increase in the quantity demanded of good *x* is equal to $x_1 x_2$.

The total effect can be split up into two effects.

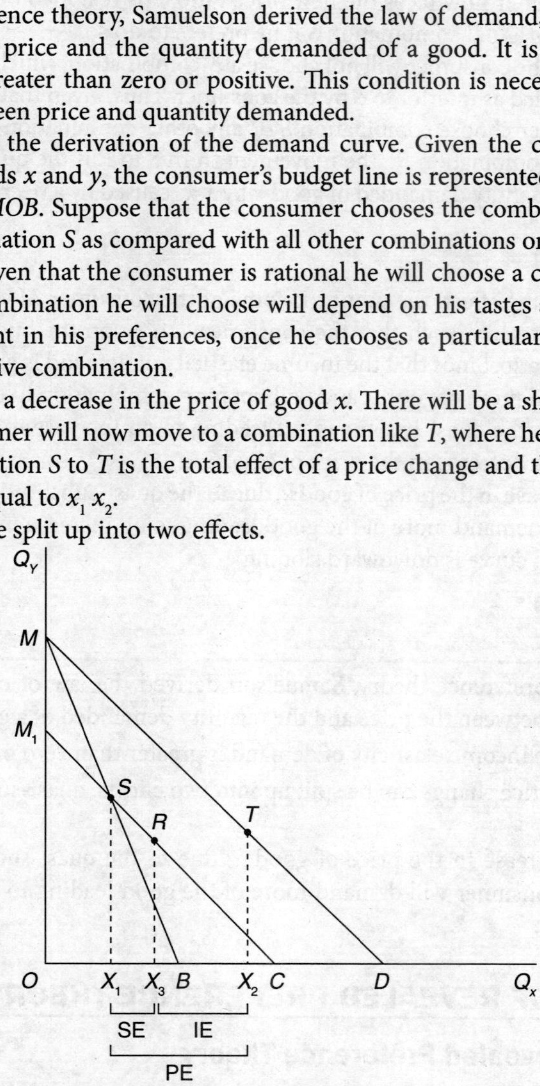

Figure 7.2 Price Effect: Quasi-substitution Effect and Quasi-income Effect

Quasi-substitution Effect

To analyse the quasi-substitution effect, the money income of the consumer is reduced by MM_1 such that the consumer is now on the budget line M_1C, which is

(i) parallel to the new budget line represented by *MD*.

(ii) passing through the combination *S*.

MM_1 is called the cost difference variation in income. The budget line M_1C is the cost difference line. The cost difference variation in income is necessary to reduce the real income (equals the money income divided by the price of the good) of the consumer, which had gone up due to a decrease in the price of the good. Thus, the consumer now faces the new price ratio. His real income is unchanged and is such that he can purchase the original combination *S* if he prefers to do so.

On budget line M_1C, the consumer will not choose any combination, which is to the left of *S* or on M_1S as they have all been revealed as inferior to *S* by the consumer. Thus, given that the consumer is consistent in his choices, he will either choose combination *S* or any other combination to the right of *R* or on *SC*. Suppose that he chooses combination *R*. The movement from *S* to *R* is the quasi-substitution effect leading to an increase in the quantity demanded of good *x* by x_1x_3 caused by a decrease in the price of good *x*.

Quasi-income Effect

To analyse the quasi-income effect, the money income of the consumer MM_1, cost difference variation in income, is given back to him such that the consumer is now on the budget line *MD*, whose slope represents the new price ratio. Since that the income elasticity of demand is greater than zero or positive, the consumer will demand more of good *x* and will opt for a combination like *T* on budget line *MD*. The movement from *R* to *T* is the quasi-income effect leading to an increase in the quantity demanded of good *x* by x_3x_2 caused by a decrease in the price of good *x*.

When there is a decrease in the price of good *x*, due to the quasi-substitution effect and quasi-income effect, the consumer will demand more of the good leading to an increase in the quantity demanded of good *x*. Thus, the demand curve is downward sloping.

RECAP

- Using the revealed preference theory, Samuelson derived the law of demand, which depicts the inverse relationship between the price and the quantity demanded of a good.
- It is assumed that the income elasticity of demand is greater than zero or positive.
- The total effect of a price change can be split up into two effects: quasi-substitution effect and quasi-income effect.
- When there is a decrease in the price of good *x*, due to the quasi-substitution effect and quasi-income effect, the consumer will demand more of the good leading to an increase in the quantity demanded of good *x*.

AN EVALUATION OF REVEALED PREFERENCE THEORY

Contributions of Revealed Preference Theory

The contributions of the theory are as follows:

(i) As compared with the cardinal utility and ordinal utility approaches, the revealed preference theory derives the demand curve without making use of the utility concept.

(ii) The theory does not assume that the consumer aims at utility maximization as in the other theories. Also the assumption of continuity as in the indifference curve analysis has been given up.
(iii) Unlike the cardinal utility and ordinal utility approaches, the revealed preference theory is based on a behaviourist approach, which can be empirically observed in the market.
(iv) The theory provides a simpler approach to understanding the theory of demand.
(v) The theory can be used to construct the index numbers of cost of living.

Limitations of Revealed Preference Theory

The limitations of the theory are as follows:

(i) The theory can explain the law of demand only in the case of normal goods and neither inferior nor Giffen goods.
(ii) The theory splits up the price effect into the quasi-substitution effect and quasi-income effect and not the pure substitution effect and pure income effect.
(iii) In the theory, it appears that as far as the behaviour of the consumer in the market is concerned, he is revealing his choice and not his preference for a combination.
(iv) The theory does not analyse as to how a consumer reaches equilibrium. It starts with a certain position of consumer equilibrium.

RECAP

- Revealed preference theory derives the demand curve without making use of the utility concept.
- Revealed preference theory is based on a behaviourist approach, which can be empirically observed in the market.
- The theory can explain the law of demand only in the case of normal goods and neither inferior nor Giffen goods.
- The theory splits up the price effect into the quasi-substitution effect and quasi-income effect and not the pure substitution effect and pure income effect.

SUMMARY

INTRODUCTION

1. The revealed preference theory analyses the behaviour of the consumers from what is revealed by them in the market.
2. The theory has been developed further to derive the law of demand.

WHAT IS REVEALED PREFERENCE THEORY?

1. The revealed preference theory was presented by Professor Paul A. Samuelson in 1938.
2. It is a 'behaviourist–ordinalist' approach.
3. A behaviourist approach is used to derive the law of demand as compared with the introspective approach used in the cardinal utility approach and the ordinal utility approach.
4. The budget set includes all the combinations on and within the budget line from which a consumer can choose any combination.
5. The consumer cannot choose any combination which lies outside the budget set.
6. The combination *S* represents the optimal bundle.

ASSUMPTIONS OF REVEALED PREFERENCE THEORY

1. It is assumed that the consumer is rational.
2. The preferences of the consumer are assumed to be transitive.
3. As far as his choice of goods and services are concerned, the consumer is assumed to be consistent.
4. The consumer is capable of strongly ordering his preferences.

A DERIVATION OF DEMAND CURVE

1. Using the revealed preference theory, Samuelson derived the law of demand, which depicts the inverse relationship between the price and the quantity demanded of a good.
2. It is assumed that the income elasticity of demand is greater than zero or positive.
3. It is important to note that given that the consumer is rational he will choose a combination on the budget line *MB*.
4. Given that he is consistent in his preferences, once he chooses a particular combination, he will not choose any other alternative combination.
5. The movement from combination *S* to *T* is the total effect of a price change and the increase in the quantity demanded of good *x* is equal to $x_1\, x_2$.
6. The total effect can be split up into two effects.
7. To analyse the quasi-substitution effect, the money income of the consumer is reduced by MM_1.
8. MM_1 is called the cost difference variation in income.
9. The budget line M_1C is the cost difference line.
10. The movement from *S* to *R* is the quasi-substitution effect leading to an increase in the quantity demanded of good *x* by x_1x_3 caused by a decrease in the price of good *x*.
11. To analyse the quasi-income effect, the money income of the consumer MM_1, cost difference variation in income, is given back to him such that the consumer is now on the budget line *MD*, whose slope represents the new price ratio.
12. The movement from *R* to *T* is the quasi-income effect leading to an increase in the quantity demanded of good *x* by x_3x_2 caused by a decrease in the price of good *x*.
13. When there is a decrease in the price of good *x*, due to the quasi-substitution effect and quasi-income effect, the consumer will demand more of the good leading to an increase in the quantity demanded of good *x*. Thus, the demand curve is downward sloping.

AN EVALUATION OF REVEALED PREFERENCE THEORY

Contributions of Revealed Preference Theory

1. As compared with the cardinal utility and ordinal utility approaches, the revealed preference theory derives the demand curve without making the use of the utility concept.
2. The theory does not assume that the consumer aims at utility maximization as in the other theories.
3. Unlike the cardinal utility and ordinal utility approaches, the revealed preference theory is based on a behaviourist approach, which can be empirically observed in the market.
4. The theory provides a simpler approach to understanding the theory of demand.
5. The theory can be used to construct the index numbers of cost of living.

Limitations of Revealed Preference Theory

The limitations of the theory are as follows:

1. The theory can explain the law of demand only in the case of normal goods and neither inferior nor Giffen goods.
2. The theory splits up the price effect into the quasi-substitution effect and quasi-income effect and not the pure substitution effect and pure income effect.

3. In the theory, it appears that as far as the behaviour of the consumer in the market is concerned, he is revealing his choice and not his preference for a combination.
4. The theory does not analyse as to how a consumer reaches equilibrium. It starts with a certain position of consumer equilibrium.

REVIEW QUESTIONS

TRUE OR FALSE QUESTIONS

1. The revealed preference theory is a 'behaviourist–ordinalist' approach.
2. The consumer can choose any combination, which lies outside the budget set.
3. The revealed preference theory derives the demand curve by making use of the utility concept.
4. The theory can explain the law of demand in the case of normal goods, inferior and Giffen goods.
5. The revealed preference theory is based on a behaviourist approach.

SHORT ANSWER QUESTIONS

1. What is the revealed preference theory?
2. What is the quasi-substitution effect? Discuss.
3. What is the quasi-income effect? Discuss.
4. What are the contributions of the revealed preference theory?
5. What are the limitations of the revealed preference theory?

LONG ANSWER QUESTIONS

1. What is the revealed preference theory? What are the assumptions on which the theory is based?
2. 'Using the revealed preference theory, Samuelson derived the law of demand'.
3. Evaluate the revealed preference theory by showing its contributions and limitations.
4. 'The total effect can be split up into two effects: quasi-substitution effect and quasi-income effect'. Comment.
5. Write a short note on the revealed preference theory.

ANSWERS

TRUE OR FALSE QUESTIONS

1. **True.** The revealed preference theory is based on consumer behaviour and is ordinal in its approach, it is a 'behaviourist–ordinalist' approach.
2. **False.** The consumer cannot choose any combination, which lies outside the budget set.
3. **False.** As compared with the cardinal utility and ordinal utility approaches, the revealed preference theory derives the demand curve without making the use of the utility concept.
4. **False.** The theory can explain the law of demand only in the case of normal goods and neither inferior nor Giffen goods.
5. **True.** Unlike the cardinal utility and ordinal utility approaches, the revealed preference theory is based on a behaviourist approach, which can be empirically observed in the market.

Production Function

8

After studying this chapter, you should be able to understand:

- ✓ The supply of a good is determined by, to a large extent, the cost of production of the good.
- ✓ Production is a process, where inputs are converted into an output.
- ✓ The production function is a technological relationship between the physical inputs and outputs in a particular time, given the technology.
- ✓ The law of variable proportions occurs in the short run where to increase production only one of the factors of production is increased while the others are kept fixed.
- ✓ The law of returns to scale occurs in the long run where to increase production all the factors of production are increased.
- ✓ An isoquant depicts the various combinations of two factors of production, for example, labour and capital, using which a firm can produce the same level of output.
- ✓ The marginal rate of technical substitution of labour for capital, $MRTS_{LK}$, is the quantity of capital that a firm is ready to give up for an additional unit of labour so that the level of output remains the same.
- ✓ A producer is in equilibrium when he is using the optimum (least cost) combination of the factors, labour and capital to achieve a given level of output.
- ✓ The expansion path is a locus of points of the producer's equilibrium represented by the points of tangency of successive isoquants with the corresponding isocost lines.
- ✓ Efficient range or the economic region of production is the range over which the marginal products of the factors, for example, labour and capital, are diminishing but greater than zero or positive.
- ✓ Ridge lines are the locus of points formed by the isoquants on which the marginal product of the factors is zero.
- ✓ The law which operates in the long run is the law of returns to scale.

INTRODUCTION

The price of a good is determined by its demand and supply. We had discussed the demand side of the market by studying the consumer behavior. We now shift our attention to the supply of a good in the market. As already mentioned in Chapter 3, the supply of a good is the total amount of a good, which the producer is willing to produce and supply at a particular price over a certain time.

The supply of a good is determined by, to a large extent, the cost of production of the good. The cost of production depends not only the techniques of production but also on the prices of the factors of production. The chapter analyses the techniques of production or the production function and also as to how a producer decides on the optimal level of output.

BASIC CONCEPTS

(i) **Production:** In the simplest terms, production is a process where inputs (factors of production) are converted into an output. Thus, through production, the resources of a society are converted into a good or a service. In other words, it is a process through which the consumer is able to avail of the goods and services.

> Production is a process where inputs (factors of production) are converted into an output.

(ii) **Input and Output:** An input is in the form of a service or a good that is used in the process of production. An output is a service or a good that results from the process of production. An input or a factor of production includes land, labour, capital and others.

> An input is in the form of a service or a good that is used in process of production.
>
> An output is a service or a good that results from the process of production.

(iii) **Fixed and Variable Factors:** Inputs or factors of production may be fixed or variable. A fixed factor is one where the supply is always inelastic in the short run. A variable factor is one where the supply is always elastic in the short run. It is important to note that this classification of inputs is valid only in the short run. In the long run, all inputs or factors of production are variable.

(iv) **Short Run and Long Run:** The short run is that time in which the supply of some of the factors of production is inelastic or fixed. The long run is that time in which the supply of most of the factors of production is elastic though the production technology is assumed to remain unchanged. Thus, both the fixed and variable factors can be changed in the long run. The very long run is that time in which the production technology can also undergo a change. The below mentioned figure depicts the time period, namely the short run and the long run.

> The short run is that time in which the supply of some of the factors of production is inelastic or fixed.
>
> The long run is that time in which the supply of most of the factors of production is elastic, though the production technology is assumed to remain unchanged.

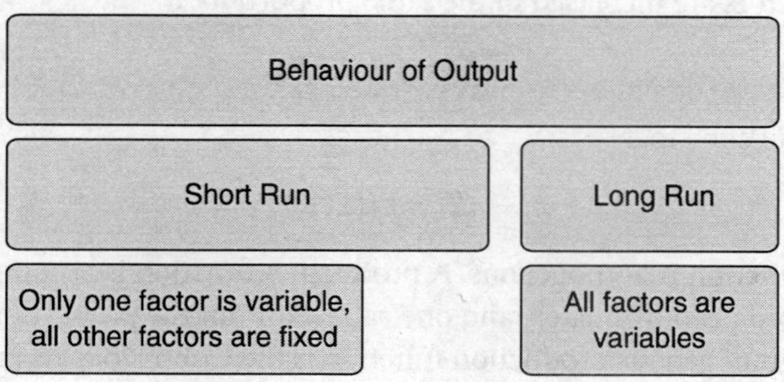

RECAP

- Production is a process where inputs (factors of production) are converted into an output.
- An input is in the form of a service or a good that is used in the process of production. An output is a service or a good that results from the process of production.
- The short run is that time in which the supply of some of the factors of production is inelastic or fixed.
- The long run is that time in which the supply of most of the factors of production is elastic, though the production technology is assumed to remain unchanged.

PRODUCTION FUNCTION

The production function is a technological relationship between the physical inputs and the physical output in a particular time, given the technology. The characteristics of a production function are as follows:

> The production function is a technological relationship between the physical inputs and outputs in a particular time given the technology.

(i) It depicts a technological relationship between the inputs and the outputs of a firm.
(ii) It relates to a time where the inputs and the outputs are flow concepts.
(iii) The state of technology is assumed to be given for that time.
(iv) Only the technically efficient combinations of the factors of production are included in the production process.
(v) The factors of production are used jointly to produce the output.

A general production function can be expressed as:

$$X = f(L, K, M, N, T)$$

where X is output, L is labour, K is capital, M is materials, N is land and T is technology.

For the sake of convenience, when there are only two factors of production, the production function is written as $X = f(L, K)$ *ceteris paribus.*

Cobb Douglas Production Function

The production function is written as

$$X = f(L, K)$$

Suppose that all the factors are increased in the same proportion 'n'. Thus,

$$X^* = f(nL, nK)$$

If 'n' can be factored out such that

$$X^* = nf(L, K)$$

then the production function is homogenous. A production function is homogenous if all the factors of production are increased proportionately and one can factor out the proportion (n).

An example of a homogenous production function is the Cobb Douglas production function

$$X = A\, L^{\alpha} K^{1-\alpha}$$

where X is output, A is a positive constant known as the efficiency parameter or in other words it shows the factor productivity, L is labour, K is capital, α is output elasticity of labour and $1 - \alpha$ is output elasticity of capital.

RECAP

- The production function is a technological relationship between the physical inputs and outputs in a particular time given the technology.

- For the sake of convenience, when there are only two factors of production, the production function is written as $Y = f(L, K)$ *ceteris paribus*.

PRODUCTION: SHORT RUN

Law of Variable Proportions

The law of variable proportions occurs in the short run when to increase production only one of the factors of production is increased while the others are kept fixed. The law of variable proportions is also known as the law of returns to a variable input or the law of diminishing returns.

Marshall had applied the law of diminishing returns only to agriculture. Later, it was called the law of variable proportions by economists like Stigler and Joan Robinson, who applied it to the other sectors in the economy also.

According to the law as more and more units of the variable factor are applied to a given amount of the fixed factors, the output will initially increase at an increasing rate, then at a constant rate and finally it will increase at a decreasing rate. Thus, when additional units of a variable factor are added to a given quantity of the fixed factors, the output of a good will, in the beginning, increase at an increasing rate, then it will increase at a constant rate and finally it will increase at a decreasing rate. Since the marginal increase, which occurs in the total output of the good, diminishes eventually it is also called the law of diminishing marginal returns.

The law of variable proportions is based on certain assumptions:

(i) The period under consideration is the short run.
(ii) There is only one variable input. All other inputs are fixed.
(iii) As far as the variable input is concerned, its units are all homogenous or are equally efficient in production.
(iv) There is a given time involved.
(v) The technology is assumed to be given.
(vi) The prices of the factors of production do not change in the time under consideration.

At this stage, it is important to understand some terms which will be used in our analysis.

(i) **Total Product:** The total product is the total output of a good, which is produced by a firm during a specific time. It can be increased by applying additional amounts of the variable factor.
(ii) **Marginal Product:** The marginal product is the change in the total product when additional amounts of the variable factor are employed.
(iii) **Average Product:** The average product is the total product divided by the amount of variable factor employed to produce the output.

Stages of Production

We are now in a position to analyse the three stages of production under the law of variable proportions. We assume that there are two factors of production, land which is fixed while labour which is variable. Thus, the short-run production function can be written as:

$$X = f(L, \overline{N})$$

A bar has been inserted over *N*, which indicates that land is fixed in the short run. In Figure 8.1, we analyse the total product, marginal product and average product of the variable factor labour in the three stages of production.

Stage 1

This is also called the stage of increasing returns to the factor. It starts from the origin and goes on till the point, where average product is a maximum. In this stage:

(i) Total product initially increases at an increasing rate and then once the point of inflexion, *P*, is reached, it increases at a decreasing rate.
(ii) Marginal product increases initially, reaches its maximum and then starts decreasing.
(iii) Average product increases all along till it reaches a maximum.

The reasons why marginal product and average product increase are because the fixed factor land is abundant and thus underutilized, and also when the employment of labour increases each unit of labour becomes more specialized.

Stage 2

This is also called the stage of decreasing (diminishing) returns to the factor. It starts from where Average Product is a maximum and goes on till the point at which Marginal Product becomes zero and total product is a maximum. In this stage:

(i) Total product increases at a decreasing rate and then reaches its maximum.
(ii) Marginal product is decreasing and becomes zero.
(iii) Average product is also decreasing but is positive.

All along this stage, average product is greater than the marginal product.

This is the stage, where a rational producer will operate because the efficiency of labour is the maximum in this stage. The reason why marginal product and average product decrease is that the labour to land ratio has reached beyond the optimal stage and thus the efficiency of labour begins to fall.

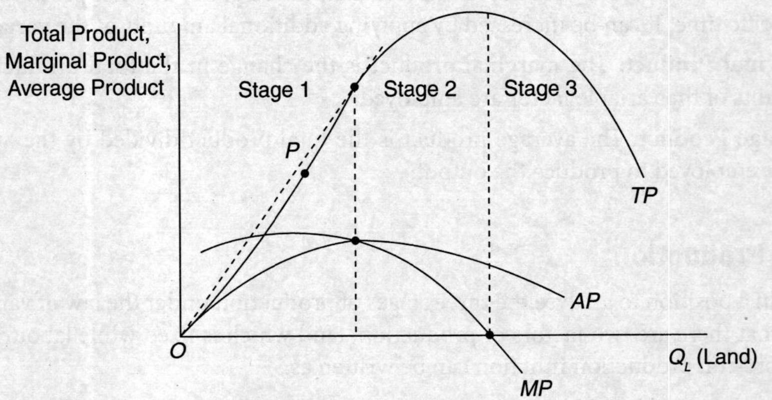

Figure 8.1 Law of Variable Proportions: Stages of Production

BOX 8.1

Economists such as James Stuart, Thomas Malthus and David Ricardo are responsible for the concept of diminishing returns. Some economists believed that diminishing returns occurred due to a worsening of the quality of the factors of production while there were others who tried to do away with this aspect of the problem by assuming that the units of the factor were identical or homogenous. Karl Marx also included it in his theory, which related to a fall in the profit rate.

Stage 3

This is also called the stage of negative returns to the factor. It starts from where total product after having reached its maximum starts decreasing. In this stage:

(i) Total product decreases.
(ii) Marginal product is negative.
(iii) Average product is also decreasing but is positive.

This is the stage, where a rational producer will never operate because the efficiency of labour and land are decreasing. Also, the specialization of labour has reached its limit and thus if more labour is employed, it will lead to inefficiencies.

As far as the applicability of the law of variable proportions is concerned, it has been found to be more relevant to agriculture, where nature plays a more important role as compared with the industry, where a major role is played by man-made factors. However, it plays an important role in all sectors in that it helps the firm in making rational decisions relating to the stage of production in which it should operate.

RECAP

- The law of variable proportions occurs in the short run when to increase production only one of the factors of production is increased while the others are kept fixed.
- According to the law as more and more units of the variable factor are applied to a given amount of the fixed factors, the output will initially increase at an increasing rate, then at a constant rate and finally it will increase at a decreasing rate.
- A rational producer will operate in stage 2 because the efficiency of labour is the maximum in this stage.

PRODUCTION: LONG RUN

In the earlier section, we had discussed the law of variable proportions which occur in the short run and where to increase production only one of the factors is increased while the others are kept fixed. In the present section, we focus on the law of returns to scale which occur in the long run and where to increase production all the factors of production are increased.

Suppose that the firm has two factors of production, capital and labour. The long-run production function can be written as:

$$X = f(L, K)$$

To represent the long-run production function, isoquants are used.

RECAP

- The law of returns to scale occurs in the long run where to increase production all the factors of production are increased.
- The long-run production function can be written as $X = f(L, K)$.

ISOQUANTS

In Chapter 6, we had analysed an indifference curve, which depicts the various combinations of two goods which give the same level of satisfaction or utility to the consumer. An isoquant is similar to an indifference curve.

An isoquant depicts the various combinations of two factors of production, for example, labour and capital, using which a firm can produce the same level of output. It is also called an isoproduct curve or an equal product curve. Similar to an indifference schedule, one can have an isoquant schedule. While constructing an isoquant, the following assumptions are made:

(i) There are only two factors of production.
(ii) Technology is given.
(iii) There is a continuity in the production function.

> An isoquant depicts the various combinations of two factors of production, for example, labour and capital using which a firm can produce the same level of output.

In Figure 8.2, a set of isoquants I_1, I_2 and I_3 represent an isoquant map. A higher isoquant I_3 (30 units) represents a larger amount of output than a lower one I_2 (20 units). A producer is indifferent among the different combinations of labour and capital, which lie on the same isoquant. Along an isoquant while the level of output is the same, the capital labour ratio differs.

RECAP

- An isoquant depicts the various combinations of two factors of production, for example, labour and capital, using which a firm can produce the same level of output.
- A producer is indifferent among the different combinations of labour and capital which lie on the same isoquant.
- Along an isoquant while the level of output is the same, the capital labour ratio differs.

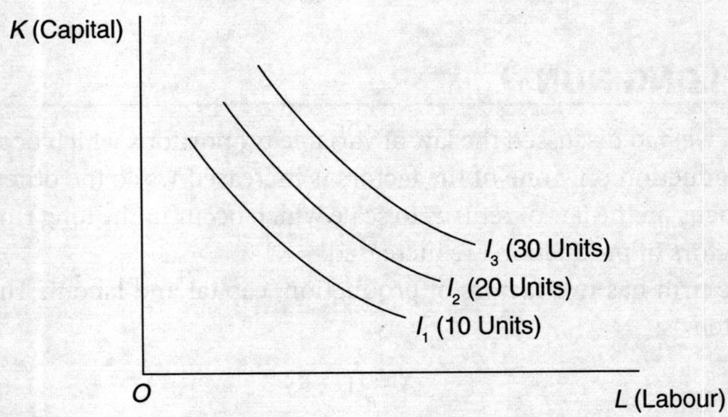

Figure 8.2 An Isoquant Map

CHARACTERISTICS OF ISOQUANTS

(i) An isoquant is negatively sloped or downward sloping (in the relevant range). This is because if a producer employs more of one factor he will have to cut down on the employment of the other factor if he has to remain on the same isoquant and his level of output has to remain the same. This implies that the two factors can be substituted for each other.

By analogy to the indifference curve analysis, one can prove that an isoquant does not slope upwards, is not a straight line parallel to the *Y* axis and is not a straight line parallel to the *X* axis. Thus, it slopes downward in the relevant range.

(ii) An isoquant is convex to the origin. This is because the marginal rate of technical substitution diminishes as we move down an isoquant.

The marginal rate of technical substitution is the slope of an isoquant. It shows the substitutability between the factors labour and capital. Thus,

$$MRTS_{LK} = \text{Slope of an isoquant} = \frac{\Delta K}{\Delta L}$$

The marginal rate of technical substitution of labour for capital, $MRTS_{LK}$, is the quantity of capital that a firm is ready to give up for an additional unit of labour so that the level of output remains the same. As the quantity of labour with the firm increases (and that of capital decreases), the marginal rate of technical substitution of labour for capital decreases.

A producer is more and more unwilling to part with capital as the quantity of capital with the firm decreases. The reason is that as the quantity of labour with the firm increases, there is a decrease in the marginal productivity of labour. Simultaneously, as the quantity of capital decreases, there is an increase in the marginal productivity of capital. Hence, to maintain the output constant, a smaller amount of capital is required to substitute every additional unit of labour. Thus, marginal rate of technical substitution diminishes.

We can express this analysis algebraically:

Loss in output as quantity of capital with the firm decreases
= Gain in output as quantity of labour with the firm increases

Or

$$-(MP_K)(\Delta K) = +(MP_L)(\Delta L)$$

$$MRTS_{LK} = \frac{\Delta K}{\Delta L} = \frac{MP_L}{MP_K}$$

The marginal rate of technical substitution is the ratio of the marginal products of the factors of production.

(iii) Isoquants cannot intersect each other. Figure 8.3 depicts two isoquants I_1 and I_2, which intersect at point *E*. Since point *E* lies on two isoquants, it implies that with the same combination of capital and labour, a firm can produce two different output levels. Since this is not possible, it is obvious that two isoquants cannot intersect each other.

RECAP

- An isoquant is negatively sloped or downward sloping (in the relevant range).
- An isoquant is convex to the origin.

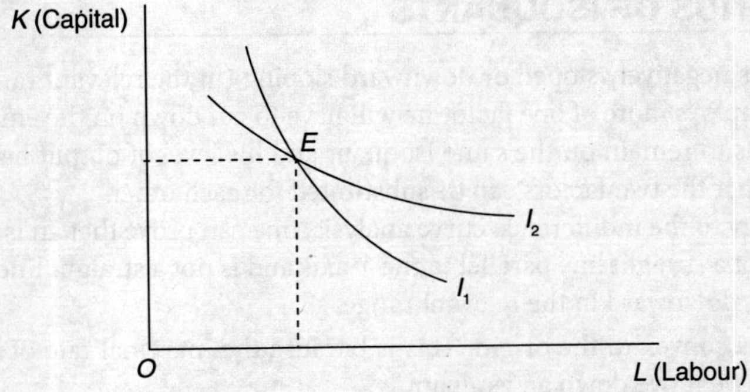

Figure 8.3 Isoquants Cannot Intersect

- The marginal rate of technical substitution of labour for capital, $MRTS_{LK}$, is the quantity of capital that a firm is ready to give up for an additional unit of labour so that the level of output remains the same.
- Isoquants cannot intersect each other.

EXCEPTIONS: COMPLEMENTS AND SUBSTITUTES

There are certain exceptional cases as far as isoquants are concerned:

(i) **Isoquants Are Linear:** When the factors of production, capital and labour, are perfect substitutes, the isoquant is a downward sloping straight line as in Figure 8.4. In other words, the isoquants are linear. Since the two factors are perfect substitutes, the $MRTS_{XY}$ is constant. For every additional unit of labour, the firm is ready to give up an equal amount of capital such that the level of output remains the same. Thus, to produce a good, a firm can use only capital or only labour or a combination of capital and labour.

(ii) **Isoquants Are L Shaped:** When the factors of production, capital and labour are perfect complements, the isoquant is L shaped as in Figure 8.5. Since the two factors are perfect complements, the MRS_{XY} is zero. Capital and labour are used jointly in a fixed proportion to produce a good, for example, at points *A* and *B*, which represent two different levels of output. If the quantity of capital is increased from OK_1 to OK_2, then the quantity of labour must be

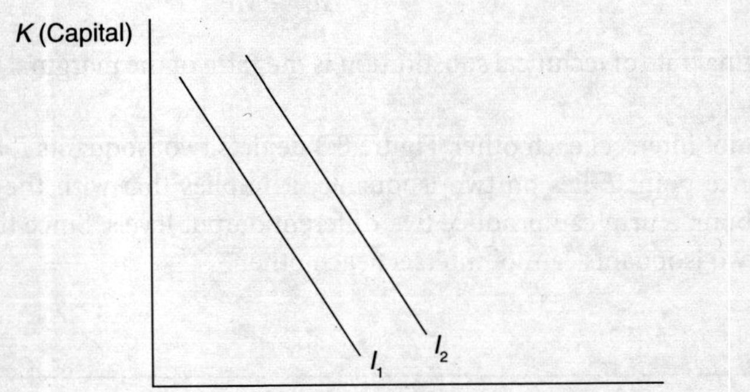

Figure 8.4 Isoquants are Linear

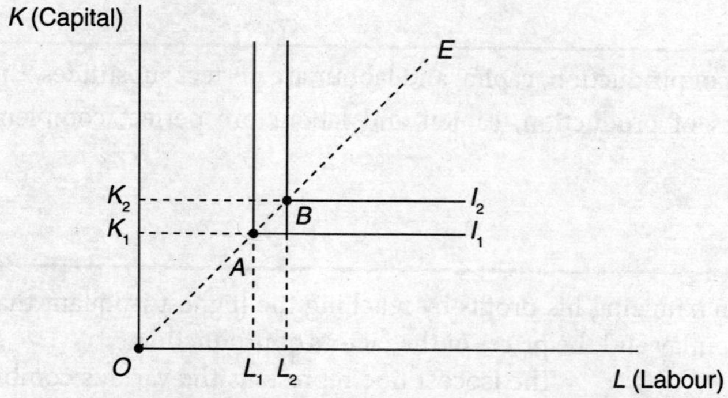

Figure 8.5 Isoquants are L shaped

increased from OL_1 to OL_2 to increase the level of output from I_1 to I_2. Thus, to increase the output, it is necessary that both the factors be increased proportionately. (The two factors cannot be substituted.) Production of the good will occur along the ray *OE*, which depicts the capital labour ratio. It is obvious from the ray that the technological relationship which exists between capital and labour involves a fixed proportion of the two factors or in other words that it is a fixed proportion production function.

(iii) **Isoquants Are Kinked:** In reality, there are many techniques to produce a given level of output with each technique employing a different combination of capital and labour. Figure 8.6 depicts an example in which to produce 10 units of good *x* four techniques are available, each using a different combination of capital and labour. Along the ray *OD*, the labour–capital ratio is 1:5, along the ray *OE*, the ratio is 2:4 and along *OF*, the ratio is 6:3 and along *OG*, it is 8:2. Joining *D, E, F,* and *G*, we can obtain a kinked isoquant as in Figure 8.6. It is only at combinations represented by the kinks *D, E, F,* and *G*, where it is technically possible to produce the output of 10 units of good *x*. Any other points on the isoquant, lying between the kinks *D* and *E*, *E* and *F*, *F* and *G*, are factor combinations which are not technically feasible.

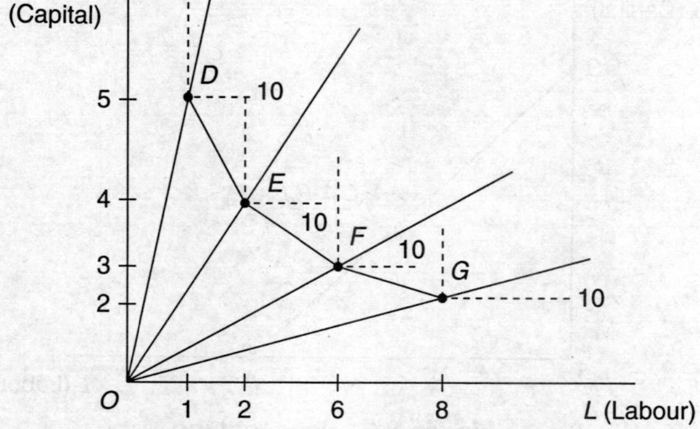

Figure 8.6 Isoquants Are Kinked

RECAP

- When the factors of production, capital and labour are perfect substitutes, the isoquant is linear.
- When the factors of production, capital and labour are perfect complements, the isoquant is L shaped.

ISOCOST LINE

A producer aims at maximizing his profits by reaching the highest isoquant that he can achieve. This depends on the total outlay and the prices of the factors of production.

The isocost line represents the various combinations of the factors, for example, labour and capital, which the firm can purchase given the total outlay and the prices of the factors of production. It is also called the outlay line or factor price line.

The isocost line represents the various combinations of the factors, for example, labour and capital, which the firm can purchase given the total outlay and the prices of the factors of production. It is also called the outlay line or factor price line.

Assume that there are only two factors, labour and capital. The isocost line can be expressed as

$$C = P_L L + P_K K$$

where C is cost or total outlay, P_L is price of labour, L is amount of labour employed, P_K is price of capital and K is amount of capital employed.

Figure 8.7 depicts the isocost line, AB, as a straight line intersecting the X axis and the Y axis at points A and B, respectively. We can determine the intersection of the isocost line.

(i) **On the X Axis (Point A):** Since K is equal to zero,

$$L = \frac{C}{P_L}$$

(ii) **On the Y Axis (Point B):** Since L is equal to zero,

$$K = \frac{C}{P_K}$$

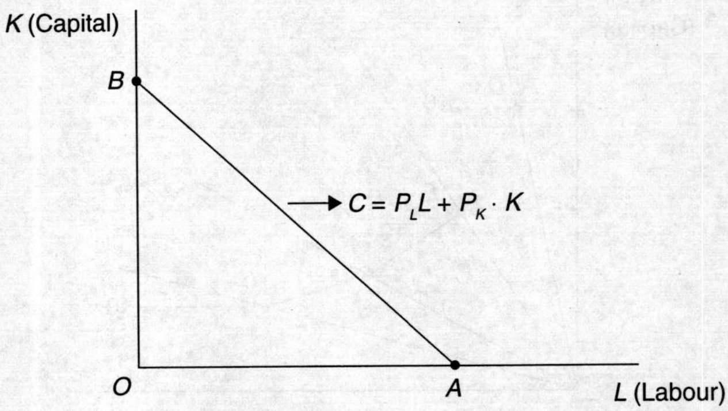

Figure 8.7 Isocost Line

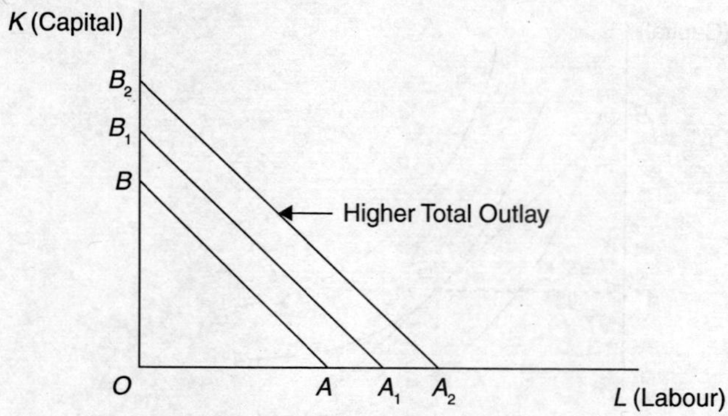

Figure 8.8 Isocost Lines

Slope of the isocost line,

$$AB = -\frac{OB}{OA} = \frac{C/P_L}{C/P_K} = -\frac{P_L}{P_K}$$

The slope of the isocost line is the price ratio of the two factors, labour and capital.

In Figure 8.8, a series of such isocost lines have been shown, where higher is the isocost line, greater is the total outlay or cost.

RECAP

- The isocost line represents the various combinations of the factors, for example, labour and capital, which the firm can purchase given the total outlay and the prices of the factors of production.
- The isocost line can be expressed as $C = P_L L + P_K K$.
- The slope of the isocost line is the price ratio of the two factors.
- Higher is the isocost line, greater is the total outlay or cost.

EQUILIBRIUM OF THE PRODUCER

A producer is in equilibrium when he is using the optimum (least cost) combination of the factors, labour and capital, to achieve a given level of output. There are two situations possible here.

> A producer is in equilibrium when he is using the optimum (least cost) combination of the factors, labour and capital, to achieve a given level of output.

Situation I: Maximization of Output Given the Cost

Given the cost, the producer aims at maximizing the output level. In Figure 8.9, the cost or the total outlay is given by the isocost line *AB* while the isoquants are I_1, I_2 and I_3. The producer is in equilibrium at point *E**, employing *OL** units of labour and *OK** units of capital, where he is able to achieve the maximum output, I_2 with the cost constraint represented by isocost line *AB*. Levels of output like I_3 are desirable but unattainable with the given outlay.

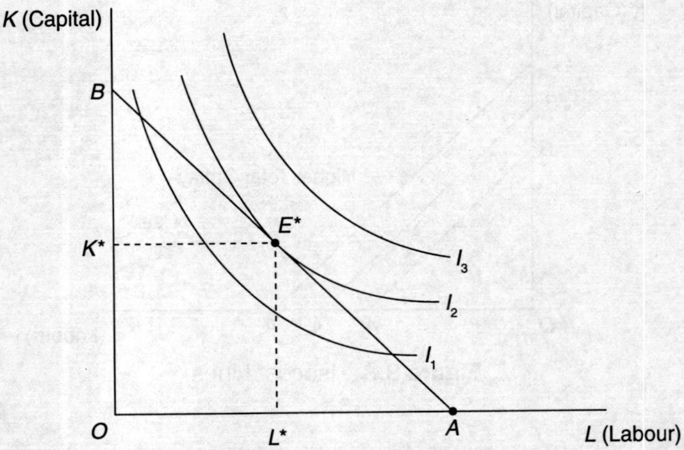

Figure 8.9 Producer's Equilibrium: Maximization of Output Given the Cost

At point E^*, the isoquant I_2 is tangential to the isocost line AB. Thus, the slope of the isoquant I_2 is equal to the slope of the isocost line AB. Hence,

$$MRTS_{LK} = \frac{P_L}{P_K}$$

But

$$MRTS_{LK} = \frac{\Delta K}{\Delta L} = \frac{MP_L}{MP_K}$$

Thus,

$$\frac{P_L}{P_K} = \frac{MP_L}{MP_K}$$

Or

$$\frac{MP_K}{P_K} = \frac{MP_L}{P_L}$$

The first-order condition for a producer to be in equilibrium is that he employs labour and capital such that the ratio of the marginal products of the factors of production is equal to the ratio of the factors prices.

The second order requires that the isoquant should be convex to the origin as in Figure 8.9 since marginal rate of technical substitution is diminishing.

Situation II: Minimization of Cost Given the Output

Given the output, the producer aims at minimizing the cost. In Figure 8.10, the output is given by the isoquant I_1 while the isocost lines are AB, A_1B_1 and A_2B_2. They are parallel to each other as the slope of the line P_L/P_K, the factor price ratio is constant.

A lower isocost line implies a lower total outlay.

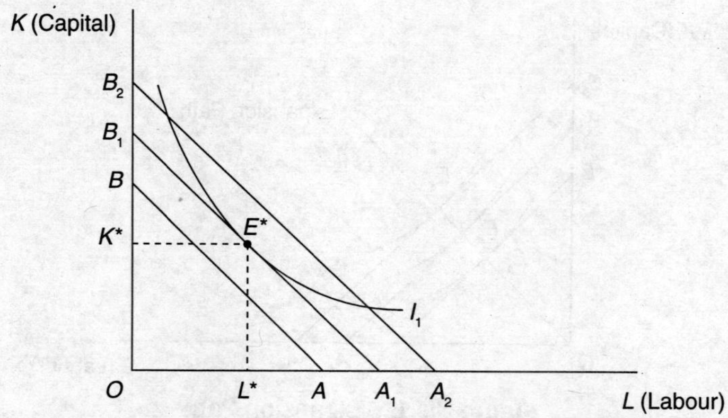

Figure 8.10 Producer's Equilibrium: Minimization of Cost Given the Output

The producer is in equilibrium at point E^*, employing OL^* units of labour and OK^* units of capital, where he is able to achieve the minimum cost represented by isocost line A_1B_1. It is the point of the least cost.

At point E^*, the isoquant I_1 is tangential to the isocost line A_1B_1. Thus, the slope of the isoquant I_1 is equal to the slope of the isocost line A_1B_1. Hence,

$$MRTS_{LK} = \frac{P_L}{P_K}$$

But

$$MRTS_{LK} = \frac{\Delta K}{\Delta L} = \frac{MP_L}{MP_K}$$

Thus,

$$\frac{P_L}{P_K} = \frac{MP_L}{MP_K}$$

Or

$$\frac{MP_K}{P_K} = \frac{MP_L}{P_L}.$$

The first-order condition for a producer to be in equilibrium is that he employs labour and capital such that the ratio of the marginal products of the factors of production is equal to the ratio of the factors prices.

The second order requires that the isoquant should be convex to the origin as in Figure 8.10 since marginal rate of technical substitution is diminishing.

RECAP

- A producer is in equilibrium when he is using the optimum (least cost) combination of the factors, labour and capital, to achieve a given level of output.
- The first-order condition for a producer to be in equilibrium is that he employs labour and capital such that the ratio of the marginal products of the factors of production is equal to the ratio of the factors prices.
- The second order requires that the isoquant should be convex to the origin.

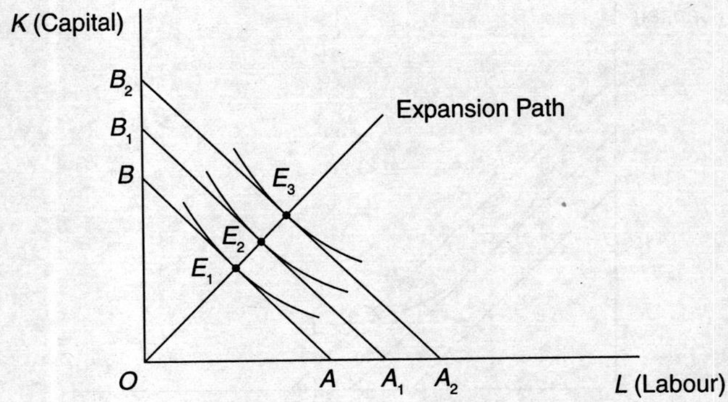

Figure 8.11 Expansion Path

EXPANSION PATH

We have observed that a rational producer aims at maximizing his profits by either maximizing his output given the cost or by minimizing the cost given the output. Thus, in the long run, a producer will choose a factor combination that is optimum. An optimum factor combination exists at the point of tangency of the isoquant and the isocost line. At this point, ratio of the marginal products of the factors of production is equal to the ratio of the factors prices.

> The expansion path is a locus of points of the producer's equilibrium represented by points of tangency of successive isoquants with the corresponding isocost lines.

In the long run, as firm increases its total outlay, there is a parallel shift outwards of the isocost lines. These isocost lines will be tangential to different isoquants representing different levels of output. Hence, there will be different points at which the producer is in equilibrium. The expansion path is a locus of points of the producer's equilibrium represented by points of tangency of successive isoquants with the corresponding isocost lines.

Figure 8.11 depicts an optimal expansion path along which the factor combinations are such that cost is a minimum, given the prices of the factors of production.

RECAP

- An optimum factor combination exists at the point of tangency of the isoquant and the isocost line. At this point, ratio of the marginal products of the factors of production is equal to the ratio of the factors prices.
- The expansion path is a locus of points of the producer's equilibrium represented by points of tangency of successive isoquants with the corresponding isocost lines.

ELASTICITY OF SUBSTITUTION

> Elasticity of substitution between two factors is a measure of the degree to which one factor can substitute the other.

Elasticity of substitution between two factors is a measure of the degree to which one factor can substitute the other. Thus, it is the proportionate change in the factor proportions or between the ratio of the two factors divided by the proportionate change in the marginal rate of technical substitution.

$$E_S = \frac{\text{Percentage change in } K/L}{\text{Percentage change in } MRTS_{LK}}$$

$$= \frac{\dfrac{\Delta(K/L)}{(K/L)}}{\dfrac{\Delta(MRTS_{LK})}{MRTS_{LK}}}$$

$$= \frac{\Delta(K/L)}{\Delta(MRTS_{LK})} \frac{MRTS_{LK}}{(K/L)}$$

RECAP

- Elasticity of substitution between two factors is a measure of the degree to which one factor can substitute the other.

ECONOMIC REGION OF PRODUCTION AND RIDGE LINES

In Figure 8.12, the isoquants are oval shaped. They can be divided into two ranges:

(i) Efficient range or the economic region of production is depicted by the convex part of the isoquant. It is the range over which the marginal products of the factors, for example, labour and capital, are diminishing but greater than zero or positive. The production techniques are efficient. In this range to produce the same output level if a firm increases the employment of a factor by one unit, it will have to give up some units of the other factor. It represents stage 2, which is the stage of decreasing (diminishing) returns to the factor. This is the stage, where a rational producer will operate because the efficiency of labour is the maximum in this stage.

(ii) Inefficient range of production or the uneconomic region of production is depicted by the non-convex part of the isoquant where to produce the same output level a firm uses increasing amounts of labour and capital. The production techniques are inefficient.

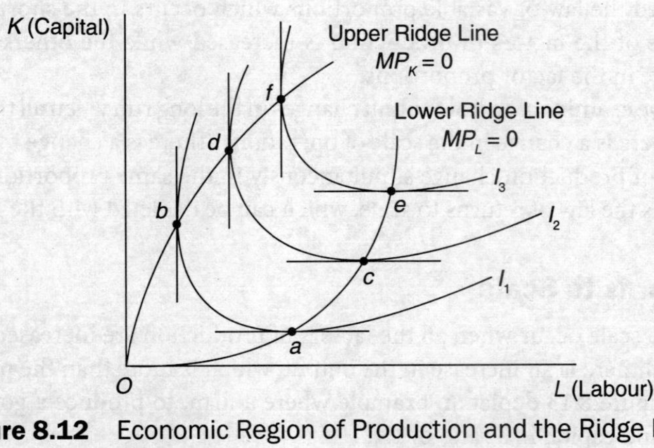

Figure 8.12 Economic Region of Production and the Ridge Lines

The efficient range is separated from the inefficient range by the ridge lines. Ridge lines are the locus of points formed by the isoquants on which the marginal product of the factors is zero. There are two ridge lines:

(i) Upper ridge line is formed by points like *b*, *d* and *f*. At these points and other such points, the marginal product of capital is zero (or $MP_K = 0$). This implies that capital has been utilized to its intensive margin. Thus,

$$MRTS_{LK} = \frac{MP_L}{MP_K} = \infty$$

(ii) Lower ridge line is formed by points like a, c and e. At these points and other such points, the marginal product of labour is zero or ($MP_L = 0$). This implies that the labour has been utilized to its intensive margin. Thus,

$$MRTS_{LK} = \frac{MP_L}{MP_K} = 0$$

RECAP

- Isoquants are oval shaped.
- Efficient range or the economic region of production is the range over which the marginal products of the factors are diminishing but positive.
- Inefficient range of production or the uneconomic region of production is depicted by the non-convex part of the isoquant.
- The efficient range is separated from the inefficient range by the ridge lines.
- Ridge lines are the locus of points formed by the isoquants on which the marginal product of the factors is zero.

LAW OF RETURNS TO SCALE

Economies and diseconomies of scale have been discussed in greater detail in Chapter 9.

We have analysed the law of variable proportions which occurs in the short run where to increase production only one of the factors of production is increased while the others are kept fixed. Hence, there occurs a change in the factor proportions.

In this section, we examine as to how output changes in the long run when all the factors of production are variable. Thus, there is a change in the scale of operations. There is a change in the scale of operations when all the factors of production change simultaneously in the same proportion. The law which operates in the long run is the law of returns to scale, which can be depicted with the help of isoquants.

Increasing Returns to Scale

Increasing returns to scale occur when all the factors of production are increased simultaneously in the same proportion and there is an increase in the output, which is more than the proportionate.

Table 8.1 and Figure 8.13 depict an example where a firm, to produce a good, uses two factors of production, labour and capital in a ratio of 1:1.

Table 8.1 Increasing Returns to Scale

Labour (Units)	Capital (Units)	Total Product (Units)
1	1	10
2	2	25

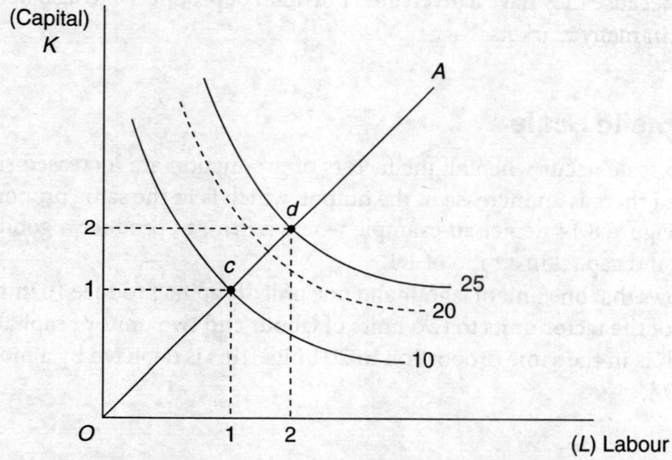

Figure 8.13 Increasing Returns to Scale

Figure 8.13 shows that one unit of labour and one unit of capital produce 10 units of the good. When there is a doubling of the factor units to two units of labour and two units of capital, there is an increase in the output, which is more than the proportionate to 25 units. This is depicted by a movement from point *c* to *d* along the ray *OA*.

Why Do Increasing Returns to Scale Occur?

A firm experiences increasing returns to scale because of economies of scale. When a firm increases its output by changing its scale of operations, the benefits that it experiences are called the economies of scale. They include the following:

(i) **Labour Economies:** When production is on a large scale, each laborer specializes and is involved in doing the work he is most suited for. Thus, his efficiency increases and there is an increase in the production.

(ii) **Technical Economies:** These include as follows:

— Economies of superior technology where due to its large size, a firm can purchase bigger and specialized machinery, which may be utilizing the latest technology and thus may be cost reducing.

— Economies of linked processes where due to an increase in its size, a firm can go for backward integration (manufacture its inputs) and forward integration (market its product).

— Economies in the use of its wastes to manufacture a byproduct.

(iii) **Marketing Economies:** A large firm is in a position to buy the raw materials and the factors of production at concessional rates because of its purchase in bulks. Similarly, as far as selling the product is concerned, it is able to reap the economies in its advertising, sales promotion and others.

(iv) **Financial Economies:** Because of its large asset base and credit worthiness in the market, a large firm can raise the finance more easily and at cheaper rates.

(v) **Risk-bearing Economies:** Large firms are better equipped to bear risks as compared with the small firms because they have a diversified portfolio of products and also because they are selling the product in many markets.

Constant Returns to Scale

Constant returns to scale occur when all the factors of production are increased simultaneously in the same proportion and there is an increase in the output, which is in the same proportion.

Table 8.2 and Figure 8.14 depict an example where a firm, to produce a good, uses two factors of production, labour and capital in a ratio of 1:1.

Figure 8.14 shows that one unit of labour and one unit of capital produce 10 units of the good. When there is a doubling of the factor units to two units of labour and two units of capital, there is an increase in the output, which is in the same proportion to 20 units. This is depicted by a movement from point *c* to *d* along the ray *OA*.

Table 8.2 Constant Returns to Scale

Labour (Units)	Capital (Units)	Total Product (Units)
1	1	10
2	2	20

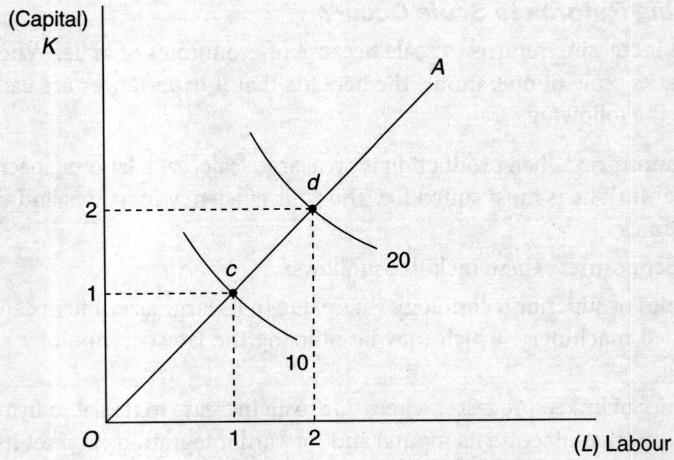

Figure 8.14 Constant Returns to Scale

Why Do Constant Returns to Scale Occur?

When the economies of scale have reached their limit while diseconomies of scale have not yet appeared, the returns to scale become a constant.

Decreasing Returns to Scale

Decreasing returns to scale occur when all the factors of production are increased simultaneously in the same proportion and there is an increase in the output, which is less than the proportionate.

Table 8.3 and Figure 8.15 depict an example where a firm, to produce a good, uses two factors of production, labour and capital in a ratio of 1:1.

Figure 8.15 shows that one unit of labour and one unit of capital produce 10 units of the good. When there is a doubling of the factor units to two units of labour and two units of capital, there is an increase in the output, which is less than the proportionate to 15 units. This is depicted by a movement from point *c* to *d* along the ray *OA*.

Why Do Decreasing Returns to Scale Occur?

A firm experiences decreasing returns to scale because of diseconomies of scale. When a firm increases its output beyond its optimum capacity by changing its scale of operations, the disadvantages that it experiences are called the diseconomies of scale. They include the following:

(i) **Managerial Diseconomies:** When production is on a large scale, it becomes difficult for the manager to coordinate the labour and also there is a problem of lack of control.

Table 8.3 Decreasing Returns to Scale

Labour (Units)	Capital (Units)	Total Product (Units)
1	1	10
2	2	15

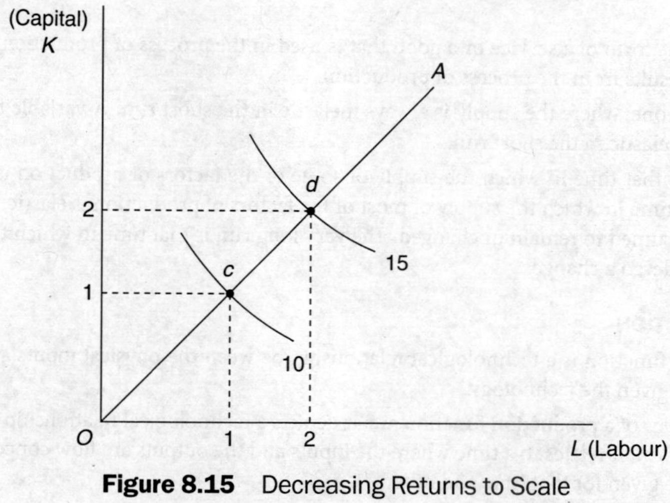

Figure 8.15 Decreasing Returns to Scale

(ii) **Technical Diseconomies:** These occur when a firm expands beyond its optimum limit due to increase in maintenance cost and other costs.

(iii) **Financial Diseconomies:** These occur when a firm raises finance beyond an optimum limit.

RECAP

- The law which operates in the long run is the law of returns to scale.
- Increasing returns to scale occur when all the factors of production are increased simultaneously in the same proportion and there is an increase in the output, which is more than the proportionate.
- Constant returns to scale occur when all the factors of production are increased simultaneously in the same proportion and there is an increase in the output, which is in the same proportion.
- Decreasing returns to scale occur when all the factors of production are increased simultaneously in the same proportion and there is an increase in the output, which is less than the proportionate.

SUMMARY

INTRODUCTION

1. We now shift our attention to the supply of a good in the market.
2. The supply of a good is determined by, to a large extent, the cost of production of the good.
3. The cost of production depends upon not only the techniques of production but also on the prices of the factors of production.
4. The chapter analyses the techniques of production or the production function and also as to how a producer decides on the optimal level of output.

BASIC CONCEPTS

1. In the simplest terms, production is a process, where inputs (factors of production) are converted into an output.
2. An input is in the form of a service or a good that is used in the process of production. An output is a service or a good that results from the process of production.
3. A fixed factor is one, where the supply is always inelastic in the short run. A variable factor is one, where the supply is always elastic in the short run.
4. The short run is that time in which the supply of some of the factors of production is inelastic or fixed. The long run is that time in which the supply of most of the factors of production is elastic, though the production technology is assumed to remain unchanged. The very long run is that time in which the production technology can also undergo a change.

PRODUCTION FUNCTION

1. The production function is a technological relationship between the physical inputs and physical output in a particular time, given the technology.
2. The characteristics of a production function are: it depicts a technological relationship between the inputs and the output of a firm; it relates to a time where the inputs and the outputs are flow concepts; state of technology is assumed to be given for that time and others.

3. A general production function can be expressed as: $X = f(L, K, M, N, T)$.
4. A production function is homogenous if all the factors of production are increased proportionately and one can factor out the proportion (n).
5. An example of a homogenous production function is the Cobb Douglas production function $X = A\, L^{\alpha}K^{1-\alpha}$.

PRODUCTION: SHORT RUN

Law of Variable Proportions

1. The law of variable proportions occurs in the short run when to increase production only one of the factors of production is increased while the others are kept fixed.
2. The law of variable proportions is also known as the law of returns to a variable input or the law of diminishing returns.
3. According to the law as more and more units of the variable factor are applied to a given amount of the fixed factors, the output will initially increase at an increasing rate, then at a constant rate and finally it will increase at a decreasing rate.
4. Since the marginal increase, which occurs in the total output of the good, diminishes eventually it is also called the law of diminishing marginal returns.
5. The law of variable proportions is based on certain assumptions: the period under consideration is the short run; there is only one variable input; a given time is involved and technology is assumed to be given.
6. The total product is the total output of a good, which is produced by a firm during a specific time.
7. The marginal product is the change in the total product when additional amounts of the variable factor are employed.
8. The average product is the total product divided by the amount of variable factor employed to produce the output.

Stages of Production

1. We assume that there are two factors of production, land which is fixed while labour which is variable.
2. The short-run production function can be written as: $X = f(L, \bar{N})$.
3. Stage 1 is also called the stage of increasing returns to the factor.
4. Stage 2 is also called the stage of decreasing (diminishing) returns to the factor. This is the stage, where a rational producer will operate because the efficiency of labour is the maximum in this stage.
5. Stage 3 is also called the stage of negative returns to the factor. This is the stage, where a rational producer will never operate because the efficiency of labour and land are decreasing.
6. As far as the applicability of the law of variable proportions is concerned, it has been found to be more relevant to agriculture.

PRODUCTION: LONG RUN

1. The law of returns to scale occurs in the long run where to increase production all the factors of production are increased.
2. The long-run production function can be written as $X = f(L, K)$.

ISOQUANTS

1. An isoquant depicts the various combinations of two factors of production, for example, labour and capital, using which a firm can produce the same level of output.
2. One can have an isoquant schedule.
3. While constructing an isoquant, the following assumptions are made: there are only two factors of production; technology is given and there is continuity in the production function.
4. A set of isoquants I_1, I_2 and I_3 represent an isoquant map.

5. A producer is indifferent among the different combinations of labour and capital which lie on the same isoquant.
6. Along an isoquant while the level of output is the same the capital labour ratio differs.

CHARACTERISTICS OF ISOQUANTS

1. An isoquant is negatively sloped or downward sloping (in the relevant range).
2. An isoquant is convex to the origin. This is because the marginal rate of technical substitution diminishes as we move down an isoquant.
3. $MRTS_{LK}$ = Slope of an isoquant $= \dfrac{\Delta K}{\Delta L}$.
4. The marginal rate of technical substitution of labour for capital, $MRTS_{LK}$, is the quantity of capital that a firm is ready to give up for an additional unit of labour so that the level of output remains the same.
5. As the quantity of labour with the firm increases and that of capital decreases, the marginal rate of technical substitution of labour for capital decreases.
6. The marginal rate of technical substitution is the ratio of the marginal products of the factors of production.
7. Isoquants cannot intersect each other.

EXCEPTIONS: COMPLEMENTS AND SUBSTITUTES

1. When the factors of production, capital and labour, are perfect substitutes, the isoquant is linear. Since the two factors are perfect substitutes, the $MRTS_{XY}$ is constant.
2. When the factors of production, capital and labour, are perfect complements, the isoquant is L shaped. Since the two factors are perfect complements, the MRS_{XY} is zero.
3. Isoquants can even be kinked.

ISOCOST LINE

1. The isocost line represents the various combinations of the factors, for example, labour and capital, which the firm can purchase given the total outlay and the prices of the factors of production.
2. The isocost line can be expressed as $C = P_L L + P_K K$.
3. The slope of the isocost line is the price ratio of the two factors, labour and capital. Slope of the isocost line, $= -\dfrac{P_L}{P_K}$.
4. Higher is the isocost line, greater is the total outlay or cost.

EQUILIBRIUM OF THE PRODUCER

1. A producer is in equilibrium when he is using the optimum (least cost) combination of the factors, labour and capital, to achieve a given level of output.
2. The first-order condition for a producer to be in equilibrium is that he employs labour and capital such that the ratio of the marginal products of the factors of production is equal to the ratio of the factors prices.
3. The second order requires that the isoquant should be convex to the origin.

EXPANSION PATH

1. An optimum factor combination exists at the point of tangency of the isoquant and the isocost line. At this point, ratio of the marginal products of the factors of production is equal to the ratio of the factors prices.
2. The expansion path is a locus of points of the producer's equilibrium represented by points of tangency of successive isoquants with the corresponding isocost lines.

ELASTICITY OF SUBSTITUTION

1. Elasticity of Substitution between two factors is a measure of the degree to which one factor can substitute the other.

2. It is the proportionate change in the factor proportions or between the ratio of the two factors divided by the proportionate change in the marginal rate of technical substitution.

ECONOMIC REGION OF PRODUCTION AND RIDGE LINES

1. Isoquants are oval shaped. They can be divided into two ranges.
2. Efficient range or the economic region of production is depicted by the convex part of the isoquant. It represents stage 2. This is the stage, where a rational producer will operate because the efficiency of labour is the maximum in this stage.
3. Inefficient range of production or the uneconomic region of production is depicted by the non-convex part of the isoquant.
4. The efficient range is separated from the inefficient range by the ridge lines.
5. Ridge lines are the locus of points formed by the isoquants on which the marginal product of the factors is zero. There are two ridge lines.
6. Along the upper ridge line, the marginal product of capital is zero (or $MP_K = 0$).
7. Along the lower ridge line, the marginal product of labour is zero or ($MP_L = 0$).

LAW OF RETURNS TO SCALE

1. The law which operates in the long run is the law of returns to scale, which can be depicted with the help of isoquants.
2. Increasing returns to scale occur when all the factors of production are increased simultaneously in the same proportion and there is an increase in the output, which is more than the proportionate.
3. A firm experiences increasing returns to scale because of economies of scale.
4. When a firm increases its output by changing its scale of operations, the benefits that it experiences are called the economies of scale. They include: labour economies, technical economies, marketing economies, financial economies and risk-bearing economies.
5. Constant returns to scale occur when all the factors of production are increased simultaneously in the same proportion and there is an increase in the output, which is in the same proportion.
6. When the economies of scale have reached their limit while diseconomies of scale have not yet appeared, the returns to scale become a constant.
7. Decreasing returns to scale occur when all the factors of production are increased simultaneously in the same proportion and there is an increase in the output, which is less than the proportionate.
8. A firm experiences decreasing returns to scale because of diseconomies of scale.
9. When a firm increases its output beyond its optimum capacity by changing its scale of operations, the disadvantages that it experiences are called the diseconomies of scale. They include: managerial diseconomies, technical diseconomies and financial diseconomies.

REVIEW QUESTIONS

TRUE OR FALSE QUESTIONS

1. An input is in the form of a service or a good that is used in the process of production.
2. The short run is that time in which the supply of most of the factors of production is elastic, though the production technology is assumed to remain unchanged.
3. When capital and labour are perfect complements, the isoquant is linear.
4. Ridge lines are the locus of points formed by the isoquants on which the marginal product of the factors is zero.
5. A firm experiences increasing returns to scale because of economies of scale.

SHORT ANSWER QUESTIONS

1. Write short notes on the following:
   (a) Production
   (b) Input and output
   (c) Fixed and variable factors
   (d) Short run and long run
2. Write a short note on the production function.
3. What is an isoquant?
4. What does the expansion path show? Analyse.
5. What is the economic region of production?

LONG ANSWER QUESTIONS

1. What are the three stages of production? Discuss.
2. What are characteristics of an isoquant? Discuss.
3. What is an isocost line? What does it show?
4. How does a producer reach equilibrium? Discuss.
5. Analyse increasing, constant and decreasing returns to scale.

ANSWERS

TRUE OR FALSE QUESTIONS

1. **True.** An input is in the form of a service or a good that is used in the process of production. An output is a service or a good that results from the process of production.
2. **False.** The long run is that time in which the supply of most of the factors of production is elastic, though the production technology is assumed to remain unchanged.
3. **False.** When the factors of production, capital and labour, are perfect complements, the isoquant is L shaped.
4. **True.** The efficient range is separated from the inefficient range by the ridge lines. Ridge lines are the locus of points formed by the isoquants on which the marginal product of the factors is zero. There are two ridge lines.
5. **True.** A firm experiences increasing returns to scale because of economies of scale. When a firm increases its output by changing its scale of operations, the benefits that it experiences are called the economies of scale.

Cost Function

9

After studying this chapter, you should be able to understand:

- ✓ *The cost function is a derived function since it is obtained from the production function.*
- ✓ *Total cost is the cost incurred to produce a given level of output in the short run by utilizing both the fixed and the variable factors.*
- ✓ *Marginal cost is the change in the total cost or the total variable cost due to a unit change in the level of output.*
- ✓ *The long-run cost curves are formed by the short-run cost curves.*
- ✓ *The long-run average cost curve is U shaped because of the law of returns to scale.*
- ✓ *A firm experiences increasing returns to scale because of economies of scale.*
- ✓ *A firm experiences decreasing returns to scale because of diseconomies of scale.*
- ✓ *While internal economies of scale cause the long-run average cost curve to fall, the internal diseconomies of scale cause the long-run average cost curve to rise.*
- ✓ *While external economies of scale cause the long-run average cost curve to shift downwards, the external diseconomies of scale cause the long-run average cost curve to shift upwards.*
- ✓ *The break-even level of output is that level of output at which a firm neither makes profits nor losses. It is the level of output at which total cost is equal to the total revenue.*

INTRODUCTION

In Chapter 8, we focused on the production function, which is a technological relationship between the physical inputs and outputs. The money value of these inputs is actually the cost of production. Thus, the cost of production depends not only upon the techniques of production but also upon the prices of the factors of production. This chapter analyses cost and shows its importance in business decisions.

SOME BASIC COST CONCEPTS

(i) **Actual Cost and Opportunity Cost:** Actual costs are the costs, which a firm incurs on raw materials, labour, machinery, advertising and other such expenses. Opportunity cost is the cost of the alternative option, which has been lost by putting the scarce resources in the present option. This cost arises because resources of the society are scarce.

> Actual costs are the costs, which a firm incurs on raw materials, labour, machinery, advertising and other such expenses.

(ii) **Variable Cost and Fixed Cost:** Variable cost is the cost, which varies with the level of output. It includes cost of raw material, labour, fuel and others. Fixed cost is the cost, which does not vary with the level of output. It includes cost of managerial and administrative staff, depreciation of building and machinery and others. It is also called the supplementary cost or overhead cost.

> Opportunity cost is the cost of the alternative option, which has been lost by putting the scarce resources in the present option. This cost arises because resources of the society are scarce.

> Variable cost is the cost, which varies with the level of output.
>
> Fixed cost is the cost, which does not vary with the level of output.

> Short-run costs are those incurred over the short run, which is that time in which the supply of some of the factors of production is inelastic or fixed.
>
> Long-run costs are those incurred over the long run, which is that time in which the supply of most of the factors of production is elastic.

(iii) **Explicit Cost and Implicit Cost:** Explicit costs are incurred by the firm when it buys or hires factors, which are required in the process of production. These factors are not owned by the firm. Such costs are depicted explicitly in the expenditure by the firm. They include, for example, wages and insurance. Implicit cost is incurred by the firm when it uses the factors, which are owned by the firm in the process of production. They include, for example, rent and interest on building and capital owned by the firm. They are also called the imputed cost. While calculating the total cost, both the explicit cost and the implicit cost are included.

(iv) **Private Cost and Social Cost:** Private cost is the monetary cost, which a firm incurs in the production of a good. Social cost is the real cost, which the society incurs in the production of a good, for example, pollution from a factory, which affects the health of people adversely.

(v) **Short-run Cost and Long-run Cost:** Short-run costs are those incurred over the short run, which is that time in which the supply of some of the factors of production is inelastic or fixed, for example, machinery. Long-run costs are those incurred over the long run, which is that time in which the supply of most of the factors of production is elastic. Thus, all the factors of production can be changed in the long run.

RECAP

- Opportunity cost is the cost of the alternative option, which has been lost by putting the scarce resources in the present option.
- Variable cost is the cost, which varies with the level of output.
- Fixed cost is the cost, which does not vary with the level of output.
- Short-run costs are those incurred over the short run, which is that time in which the supply of some of the factors of production is inelastic or fixed, for example, machinery.
- Long-run costs are those incurred over the long run, which is that time in which the supply of most of the factors of production is elastic. Thus, all the factors of production can be changed in the long run.

BOX 9.1

Economists often differentiate between accounting cost and economic cost. Accounting costs are incurred by the firm when it buys factors, which are required in the process of production. These factors are not owned by the firm. They are also called the explicit cost. Economic costs include both accounting costs and implicit costs. Accounting costs are often used in reporting and other such matters. Economic costs are used for decision-making purposes.

COST FUNCTION

The cost function is a derived function since it is obtained from the production function, which is a technological relationship between the physical inputs and physical outputs in a particular time, given the technology.

The element of time is very important in cost theory. As already discussed, short-run costs are those incurred over the time in which the supply of some of the factors of production are fixed. Long-run costs are those incurred over the time in which the supply of most of the factors of production can change.

A short-run cost function can be expressed as:

$$C = f(X, P_F, T, \bar{K})$$

where C is cost, X is output, P_F is price of factor, T is technology and $\bar{K}$ is fixed factor, capital.

A long-run cost function can be expressed as:

$$C = f(X, P_F, T)$$

RECAP

- The cost function is a derived function since it is obtained from the production function.
- The element of time is very important in cost theory.
- A short-run cost function can be expressed as $C = f(X, P_F, T, \bar{K})$.
- A long-run cost function can be expressed as $C = f(X, P_F, T)$.

TRADITIONAL THEORY OF COSTS

Short-run Cost Analysis

We have already observed above that short-run costs are those incurred over the time in which the supply of some of the factors of production is fixed. Thus, in the short run while some costs are fixed, others are variable.

Total Cost

Total cost is the cost incurred to produce a given level of output in the short run by utilizing both the fixed and the variable factors. It includes both the total fixed cost and the total variable cost.

$$\text{Total Cost} = \text{Total Fixed Cost} + \text{Total Variable Cost}$$

Total Fixed Cost

Total fixed cost includes those costs, which do not vary with the level of output. Whatever is the level of output, these costs have to be incurred. They include the cost of managerial and administrative staff, depreciation of building and machinery and others. In Figure 9.1, the total fixed cost curve is shown as a straight line, which is parallel to the X axis.

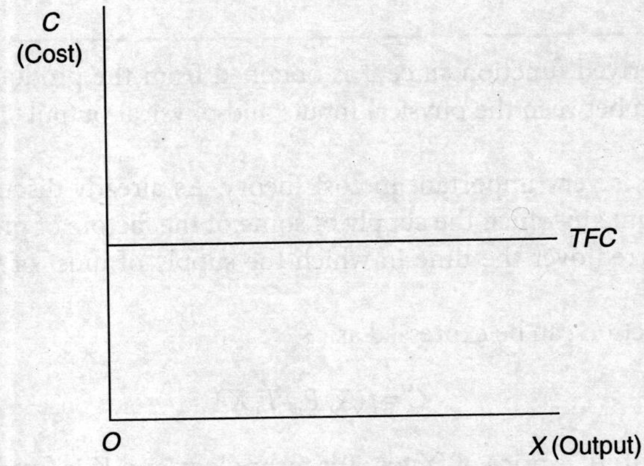

Figure 9.1 Total Fixed Cost

Total Variable Cost

Total variable cost is the cost, which varies with the level of output. It includes cost of raw material, labour, fuel and others. In Figure 9.2, the total variable cost curve is shown as inverse S-shaped curve. This is due to the law of diminishing returns:

(i) When the output is zero, the total variable cost is also zero.

(ii) As output increases, the total variable cost also increases. According to the law as more and more units of the variable factor are applied to a given amount of the fixed factors, the output will initially increase at an increasing rate. This implies that total variable costs will initially increase at a decreasing rate.

(iii) At the output level of X^* when additional units of the variable factor are added to a given quantity of the fixed factors, the output of a good will increase at a decreasing rate. This implies that total variable costs will increase at an increasing rate.

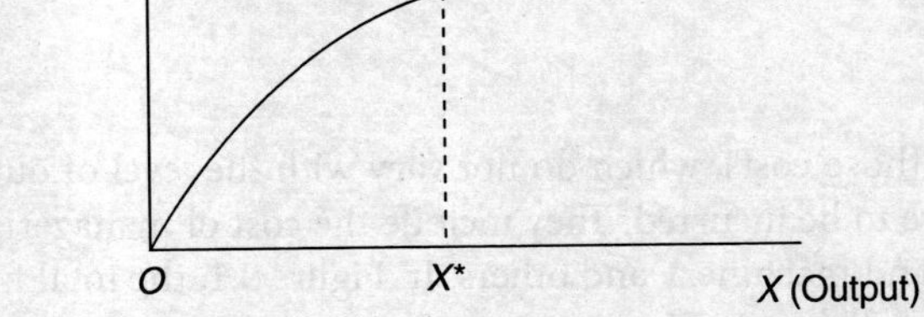

Figure 9.2 Total Variable Cost

Total Cost

Total cost is obtained by adding total fixed cost and total variable cost at the different levels of output. Thus, in Figure 9.3, the total cost curve is shown as a summation of the total fixed cost and total variable cost at the different levels of output. The total cost curve is also an inverse S-shaped curve like the total variable cost curve and is everywhere higher than the total variable cost curve by the same amount as the total fixed cost.

From the total cost curves explained above, we can now arrive at the per-unit cost curves.

Average Cost

Average cost can be obtained from the total cost.

$$\text{Total Cost} = \text{Total Fixed Cost} + \text{Total Variable Cost}$$

$$\text{Average Cost} = \frac{\text{Total Cost}}{\text{Output}} = \frac{\text{Total Fixed Cost}}{\text{Output}} + \frac{\text{Total Variable Cost}}{\text{Output}}$$

Thus,

$$\text{Average Cost} = \text{Average Fixed Cost} + \text{Average Variable Cost}$$

In Figure 9.4, the average cost curve is shown as U shaped. Initially, it falls, then reaches a minimum and starts rising.

Average Variable Cost

Average cost can be obtained from the total variable cost.

$$\text{Average Variable Cost} = \frac{\text{Total Variable Cost}}{\text{Output}}$$

In Figure 9.5, the average variable cost curve is shown as U shaped.

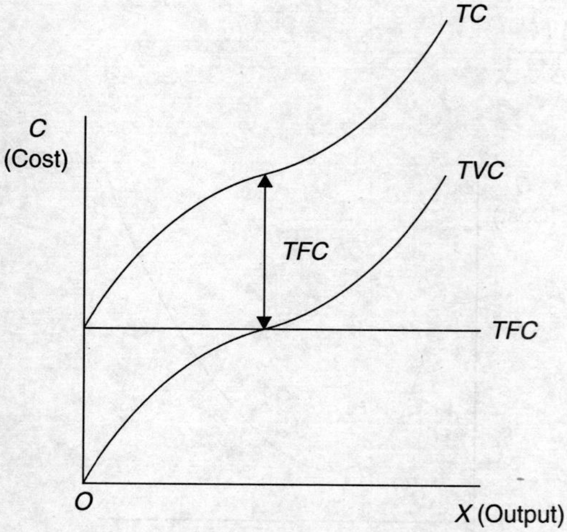

Figure 9.3 Total Cost

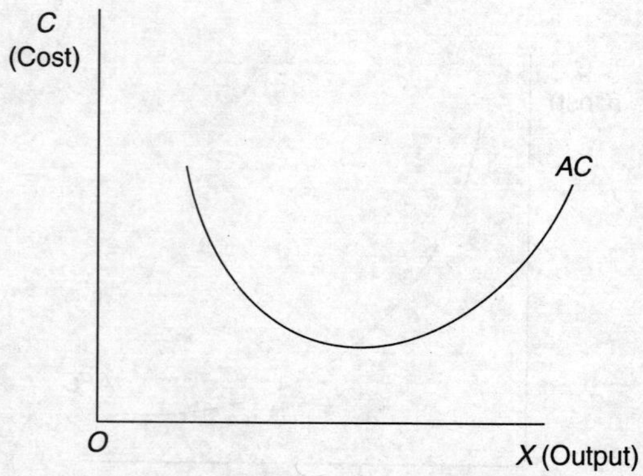

Figure 9.4 Average Cost Curve

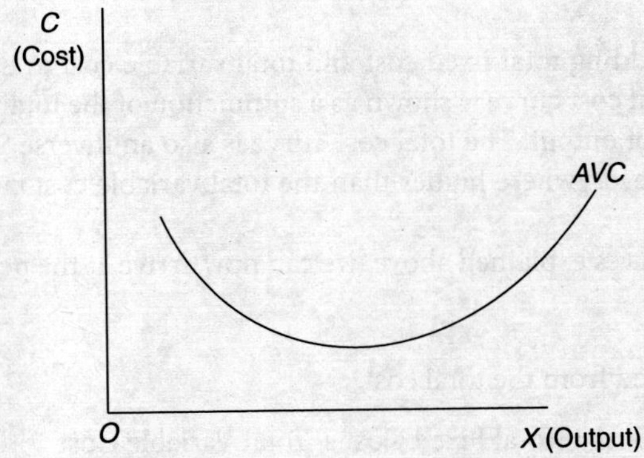

Figure 9.5 Average Variable Cost Curve

Average Fixed Cost

Average fixed cost can be obtained from the total fixed cost.

$$\text{Average Fixed Cost} = \frac{\text{Total Fixed Cost}}{\text{Output}}$$

In Figure 9.6, the average fixed cost curve is shown as a rectangular hyperbola because as the level of output increases, the fixed cost per unit decreases.

Marginal Cost

Marginal cost is the change in the total cost or total variable cost due to a unit change in the level of output. In Figure 9.7, the marginal cost curve is shown as U shaped. Initially, it falls as the variable factor is used more efficiently and then starts rising.

$$\text{Marginal Cost} = TC_N - TC_{N-1}$$

Alternatively, it can be written as:

$$\text{Marginal Cost} = \frac{\Delta TC}{\Delta X}$$

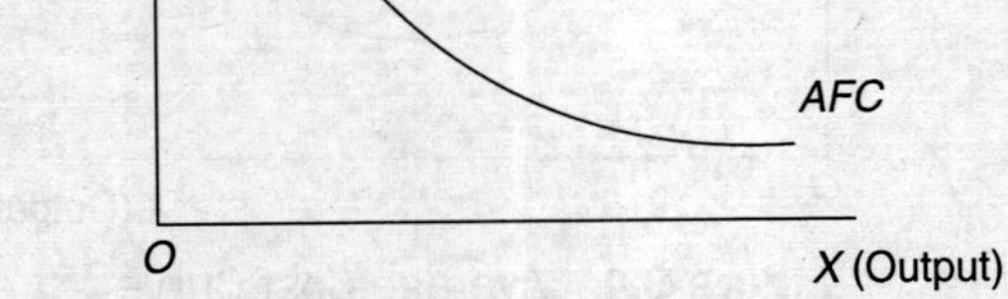

Figure 9.6 Average Fixed Cost Curve

Figure 9.7 Marginal Cost Curve

Some Relationships Between the Short-run Cost Curves

(i) **Relationship Between Total Fixed Cost and Average Fixed Cost:** At any point on the total fixed cost curve, the average fixed cost is the slope of the line, which joins the origin to that particular point on the total fixed cost curve.

(ii) **Relationship Between Total Variable Cost and Average Variable Cost:** At any point on the total variable cost curve, the average variable cost is the slope of the line, which joins the origin to that particular point on the total variable cost curve.

(iii) **Relationship Between Average Cost and Average Variable Cost:** In Figure 9.8, the average variable cost curve and average cost curve are both shown as U shaped due to the law of variable proportions. However, average variable cost curve reaches its minimum point before the average cost curve.

(iv) **Relationship Between Total Cost and Marginal Cost:** At any point on the total cost curve, the marginal cost curve is the slope of the total cost curve at that point.

(v) **Relationship Between Average Cost and Marginal Cost:** Both the average cost curve and the marginal cost çurve are U shaped. Figure 9.8 depicts that

- when average cost is falling, marginal cost is also falling and is below it.
- when average cost is rising, marginal cost is also rising and is above it.
- when average cost is at its minimum point, marginal cost is equal to average cost or the marginal cost curve intersects the average cost curve.

RECAP

- Total cost is obtained by adding total fixed cost and total variable cost at the different levels of output.
- Total fixed cost includes those costs, which do not vary with the level of output.
- Total variable cost is the cost, which varies with the level of output.
- Average Cost = Average Fixed Cost + Average Variable Cost
- Marginal cost is the change in the total cost or the total variable cost due to a unit change in the level of output.

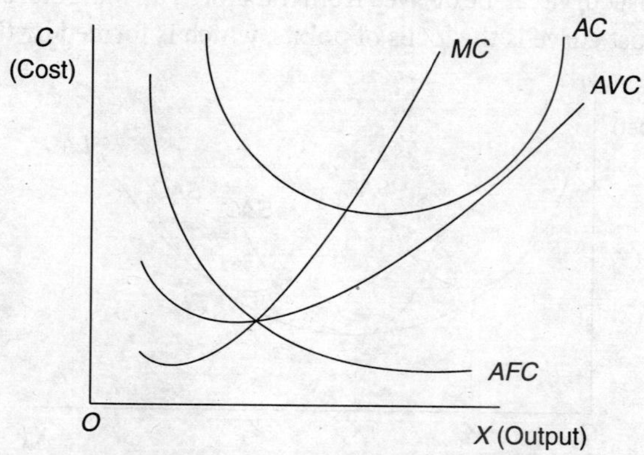

Figure 9.8 Short-run Cost Curves

LONG-RUN COST ANALYSIS

In the long run, the supply of most of the factors of production is elastic. No factors are fixed in the long run. Thus, all the factors of production can be changed in the long run. It is important to understand that the long-run cost curves are formed by the short-run cost curves.

Long-run Average Cost

The long-run average cost is the average per unit cost of production when all the factors of production are variable in the long run. The long-run average cost curve can be derived from the short-run average cost curves as it is tangent to the short-run average cost curves.

To start with it is assumed that given the technology, only three methods are available to the firm to produce the output. These three methods can be represented by three different plants each with a different scale of operations.

In Figure 9.9, SAC_1 is the short-run average cost of the small size of plant, SAC_2 is the short-run average cost of the medium size of plant, SAC_3 is the short-run average cost of the large size of plant. To produce an output of OX_1 per unit costs are lowest on plant SAC_1. Similarly, for an output of OX_2 per unit costs are lowest on plant SAC_2 and for an output of OX_3, they are lowest on plant SAC_3. If one examines the reality, there are infinite number of such plants each represented by an *SAC*. The long-run average cost curve is derived from the *SAC*'s as the minimum per-unit cost of producing each level of the output. It shows the least cost of producing each level of the output. The long-run average cost curve is called the envelope curve as it envelops the *SAC*'s.

The long-run average cost curve is U shaped because of the law of returns to scale:

(i) Initially, the long-run average costs fall as a firm experiences increasing returns to scale because of economies of scale.
(ii) When the economies of scale have reached their limit while diseconomies of scale have not yet appeared, the long-run average cost curve reaches its optimum plant producing the optimum output.
(iii) When a firm increases its output beyond its optimum capacity by changing its scale of operations, the disadvantages that it experiences are called the diseconomies of scale.

Long-run Marginal Cost

The long-run marginal cost curve can be derived from the short-run marginal cost curves as in Figure 9.10. The long-run marginal cost curve is the locus of points, which is formed by the point where the vertical

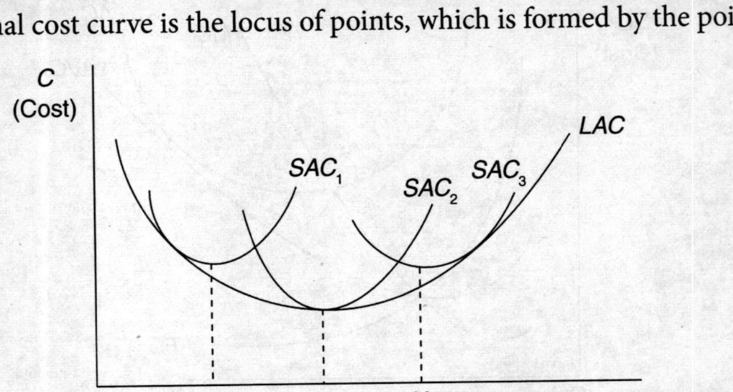

Figure 9.9 Long-run Average Cost Curve

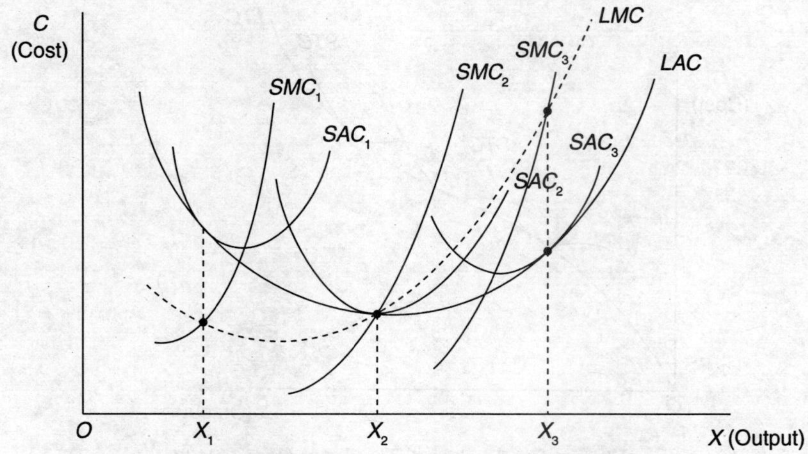

Figure 9.10 Long-Run Marginal Cost Curve

line, drawn from the point of tangency of the *SAC* with the long-run average cost curve, intersects the corresponding *SMC* curve. By joining all such points, one can draw the long-run marginal cost curve.

Relationship Between Long-run Average Cost and Long-run Marginal Cost

Figure 9.10 depicts that

(i) When long-run average cost is falling, long-run marginal cost is also falling and is below it.

(ii) When long-run average cost is rising, long-run marginal cost is also rising and is above it.

(iii) When long-run average cost is at its minimum point, long-run marginal cost is equal to long-run average cost, or the long-run marginal cost curve intersects the long-run average cost curve.

Also, at this point

Long-run Average Cost = Short-run Average Cost = Short-run Marginal Cost = Long-run Marginal Cost

Or

$$LAC = SAC = SMC = LMC$$

Long-run Total Cost

The long-run total cost curve is the minimum total cost of producing different levels of output from different plant sizes. In Figure 9.11, the long-run total cost curve is derived from the short-run total cost curves taking the point which represents the optimum size of the plant.

The short-run total cost curve begins from the level of the fixed costs while the long-run total cost curve begins from the origin since in the long run there are no fixed costs.

The long-run total cost curve is inverse S shaped because of the law of returns to scale.

RECAP

- The long-run cost curves are formed by the short-run cost curves.
- Long-run average cost curve can be derived from the short-run average cost curves.

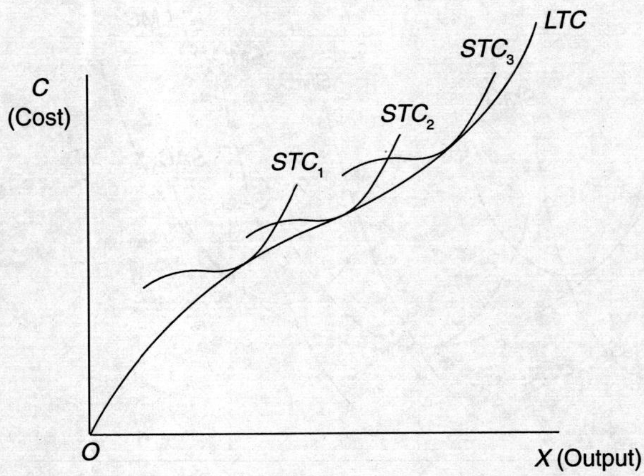

Figure 9.11 Long-Run Total Cost Curve

- The long-run average cost curve is U shaped because of the law of returns to scale.
- The long-run marginal cost curve can be derived from the short-run marginal cost curves.
- When long-run average cost is at its minimum point, long-run marginal cost is equal to long-run average cost. Also at this point, $LAC = SAC = SMC = LMC$.
- The long-run total cost curve is derived from the short-run total cost curves taking the point which represents the optimum size of the plant.

ECONOMIES AND DISECONOMIES OF SCALE

We have discussed the traditional theory of costs where the long-run average cost curve is U shaped because of the law of returns to scale.

Initially, the long-run average cost curve falls as a firm experiences increasing returns to scale because of economies of scale. However, when a firm increases its output beyond its optimum capacity, it experiences decreasing returns to scale because of diseconomies of scale.

Economies of Scale

> When a firm increases its output by changing its scale of operations, the benefits that it experiences are called the economies of scale.

When a firm increases its output by changing its scale of operations, the benefits that it experiences are called the economies of scale. A firm experiences increasing returns to scale because of economies of scale. The economies of scale are of two types:

Internal Economies

These economies are not dependent on the actions of other firms. An individual firm experiences them when it expands its production. It is due to these internal economies that the long-run average cost curve falls. They include:

(i) **Labour Economies:** When production is on a large scale, each labourer specializes and is involved in doing the work he is most suited for. Thus, his efficiency increases and there is an increase in the production.

(ii) **Technical Economies:** These arise when a firm grows in size. They include :

— **Economies of Superior Technology:** Due to its large size a firm can purchase bigger and specialized machinery, which may be utilizing the latest technology and thus may be cost reducing.

— **Economies of Linked Processes:** Due to an increase in its size a firm can go for backward integration (manufacture its inputs) and forward integration (market its product).

— **Economies of Increased Dimensions:** As the firm grows bigger in size, it can operate the different processes involved in production in its own premises, thus saving on time and cost.

— **Economies of Specialization:** A large firm can subdivide the production process leading to a greater specialization, which improves the productive efficiency of the firm.

— **Economies in the Use of its Wastes:** A large firm can utilize its wastes and manufacture its by-products.

(iii) **Marketing Economies:** A large firm is in a position to buy the raw materials and the factors of production at concessional rates because of its purchase in bulks. Similarly as far as selling the product is concerned, it is able reap economies in its advertising, sales promotion and others.

(iv) **Managerial Economies:** Unlike a small firm, a large firm is in a position to go in for a division in its diverse activities, for example, production manager, finance manager and others. This results in an expertise of different people in different areas leading to an increase in their efficiency.

(v) **Financial Economies:** Because of its large asset base and its credit worthiness in the market, a large firm can raise finance more easily and at cheaper rates.

(vi) **Risk-bearing Economies:** Large firms are better equipped to bear risks as compared with small firms because they have a diversified portfolio of products and also because they are selling the product in many markets.

External Economies

These economies occur because of the growth of the industry as a whole. They are generated from outside the firm and the benefit is shared by all the firms in the industry. It is due to these external economies that the long-run average cost curve shifts downwards. They include:

(i) **Economies of Information:** All the firms in a particular area can come together to share the information relating to labour, latest techniques of production and can even go in for research and development. All the information can be published in journals to benefit all the firms in the industry and thus improve their efficiency.

(ii) **Economies of Concentration:** When an industry comes up in an area, they all reap the advantages from localization like:

— availability of skilled labour.

— availability of cheap and easy finance.

— access to transport and communication facilities.

— access to adequate sources of power.

— access to marketing facilities because of concentration.

(iii) **Economies of Disintegration:** When the industry is concentrated in a particular area, firms can take advantage of the economies of disintegration. For example, all wastes from the different firms could be put to use by starting another firm in the area which utilizes the wastes.

Diseconomies of Scale

When a firm increases its output beyond its optimum capacity by changing its scale of operations, the disadvantages that it experiences are called the diseconomies of scale. A firm experiences decreasing returns to scale because of diseconomies of scale. The diseconomies of scale are of two types:

Internal Diseconomies

These diseconomies are not in any way dependent on the actions of other firms. It is due to these internal diseconomies that the firm's productive efficiency starts falling. They include:

(i) **Technical Diseconomies:** These diseconomies arise when a firm grows in size beyond its optimum capacity. They include increases in the costs of maintenance and in the occurrence of accidents.

(ii) **Managerial Diseconomies:** Beyond a limit, if there are too many managers at different levels, there may be problems relating to coordination and distortion of information. This may have an adverse affect on the decision-making ability of the managers. It may also lead to managerial problems and increase the inefficiencies in the firm.

(iii) **Financial Diseconomies:** We have observed that because of its large asset base and its credit worthiness in the market, a large firm can raise finance more easily and at cheaper rates. But if this raising of finance is indulged in beyond a limit, it may lead to problems relating to concentration of power and wealth and also in the repayments of the loan.

(iv) **Risk-bearing Diseconomies:** As already discussed, large firms are better equipped to bear risks as compared with small firms because they have a diversified portfolio of products. But if this diversification is done beyond the optimum limit, problems may occur and there may be a fear of loss in control by the management at the top.

External Diseconomies

These diseconomies occur because of the growth of the industry as a whole leading to an increase in the per-unit costs. They are generated from outside the firm and the disadvantages are faced by all the firms in the industry. It is due to these external diseconomies that the long-run average cost curve shifts upwards. They include:

(i) **Increase in the Price of the Factors of Production:** Due to the growth of the industry, there is an increase in the demand for the factors of production leading to an increase in their price. Thus, there in an increase in costs of production.

(ii) **Infrastructural Problems:** The expansion of the industry in a particular area puts pressures on the transport and communication facilities, power and other facilities, which are limited. This leads to bottlenecks and increases in the costs of production.

(iii) Problems relating to **disposal of too many wastes** in a particular area.

While internal economies of scale cause the long-run average cost curve to fall, the internal diseconomies of scale cause the long-run average cost curve to rise. While external economies of scale cause the long-run average cost curve to shift downwards, the external diseconomies of scale cause the long-run average cost curve to shift upwards.

RECAP

- A firm experiences increasing returns to scale because of economies of scale.
- It is due to the internal economies that the long-run average cost curve falls.

- It is due to the external economies that the long-run average cost curve shifts downwards.
- A firm experiences decreasing returns to scale because of diseconomies of scale.
- It is due to the external diseconomies that the long-run average cost curve shifts upwards.

BREAK-EVEN ANALYSIS

Break-even analysis is of immense help to business when they are making their decisions relating to output. It is also called the cost volume profit analysis or profit contribution analysis. It helps a firm in analysing the relationship between total revenue, total cost and total profit. With the help of this analytical tool, a firm is able to differentiate between the ranges of production, which are profitable from those which are not profitable. Thus, by using the break-even analysis, a firm is in a position to find out the level of output, where revenue and cost break even.

> The break-even level of output is that level of output at which a firm neither makes profits nor losses. It is the level of output at which total cost is equal to total revenue.

Break-even Analysis: Revenue and Cost Functions Are Linear

Figure 9.12 shows linear revenue and cost functions:

(i) The total revenue curve in the figure depicts the revenue, which a firm will earn at different levels of output, assuming that the price of the good is constant.

(ii) The total cost curve starts from point *F* on the *Y* axis depicting the linear relationship between cost and output.

(iii) The total fixed cost curve is a straight line starting from point *F* on the *Y* axis depicting a fixed cost of *OF*.

(iv) The total variable cost is the vertical distance between total cost curve and the total fixed cost curve. As the amount of output increases, the total variable cost increases.

It is obvious from the figure that

(i) Up to output *OX** of the good, the total cost is greater than the total revenue. Thus, the firm will incur losses.

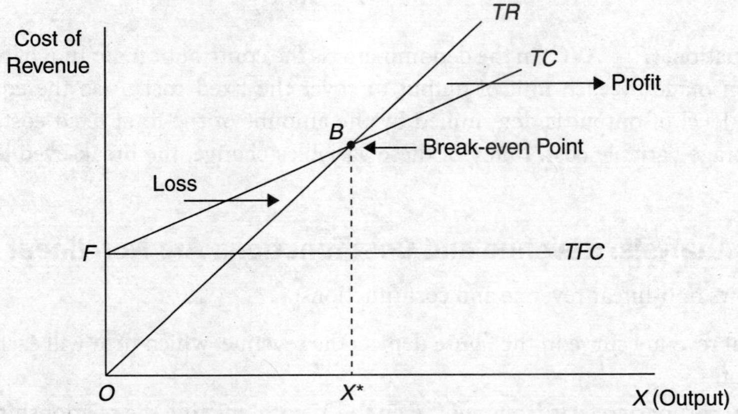

Figure 9.12 Break-even Analysis: Revenue and Cost Functions Are Linear

(ii) At the output OX^* of the good, total cost is equal to total revenue. Thus, the firm will break even making neither profits nor losses at point *B*, which is the break-even point. The break-even level of output is that level of output at which a firm neither makes profits nor losses. It is the level of output at which total cost is equal to total revenue.

(iii) Beyond the output OX^* of the good, the total cost is smaller than the total revenue. Thus, the firm will make profits.

Break-even analysis is useful when a firm is planning on its output for targeting a certain level of profits.

Algebraic Analysis

We can write

$$\Pi = TR - TC$$

where Π is profit, *TR* is total revenue and *TC* is total cost.

But $$TR = P_x \times Q_x$$

and $$TC = TVC + TFC$$

However, $$TVC = AVC \times Q_x$$

Thus, $$TC = AVC \times Q_x + TFC$$

where P_x is per-unit price of good *x*, Q_x is quantity of good *x*, *TVC* is the total variable cost and *AVC* is the average variable cost.

At the break-even level of output, the total cost is equal to the total revenue.

Assume that the break-even level of output is Q^*_x.

Thus,

$$TR = TC$$

$$P_x \times Q^*_x = AVC \times Q^*_x + TFC$$

$$P_x \times Q^*_x - AVC \times Q^*_x = TFC$$

$$Q^*_x (P_x - AVC) = TFC$$

$$Q^*_x = \frac{TFC}{(P_x - AVC)}$$

In the above equation, (P_x – AVC) in the denominator is the contribution per unit of output. It measures the contribution made by each unit of output to cover the fixed cost. Also the equation shows that the break-even level of output is determined by the amount of the total fixed cost, per-unit price of good *x* and average variable cost. If any of these variables change, the break-even level of output will also change.

Break-even Analysis: Revenue and Cost functions Are Non-linear

Figure 9.13 shows non-linear revenue and cost functions:

(i) The total revenue curve in the figure depicts the revenue, which firm will earn at different levels of output.

(ii) The total cost curve starts from point *F* on the *Y* axis depicting the relationship between cost and output.

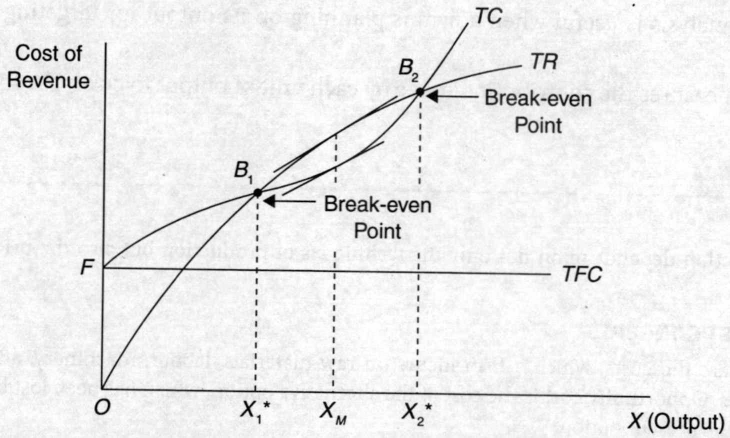

Figure 9.13 Break-even Analysis: Revenue and Cost Functions Are Non-linear

(iii) The total fixed cost curve is a straight line starting from point F on the Y axis depicting a fixed cost of OF.

(iv) The total variable cost is the vertical distance between total cost curve and the total fixed cost curve. As the amount of output increases, the total variable cost increases.

It is obvious from the figure that

(i) Up to output OX_1^* of the good, the total cost is greater than the total revenue. Thus, the firm will incur losses.

(ii) At the output OX_1^* of the good, total cost is equal to total revenue. Thus, the firm will break even making neither profits nor losses at point B_1. This is the break-even point. It represents the level of output at which total cost is equal to the total revenue.

(iii) Between the output OX_1^* and OX_2^* of the good, total cost is smaller than total revenue. Thus, the firm will make profits, which will be a maximum at the output level OX_M at which the distance between the total cost and total revenue curves is a maximum.

(iv) At the output OX_2^* of the good, total cost is equal to total revenue once again. Thus, the firm will break even making neither profits nor losses at point B_2. This is another break-even point at which total cost is equal to total revenue. The break-even point B_2 may not be of much relevance to a firm as it may be beyond the capacity of a firm to produce this output.

As already discussed, break-even analysis is useful when a firm is planning on its output for targeting a certain level of profits. However, a linear break-even analysis can be applied only when the selling price of a good and the average variable cost can be assumed to be constant. But, in spite of its limitations, break-even analysis plays a very crucial role in business decision making.

RECAP

- Break-even analysis is of immense help to business when they are making their decisions relating to output.
- The break-even level of output is that level of output at which a firm neither makes profits nor losses. It is the level of output at which the total cost is equal to the total revenue.

- Break-even analysis is useful when a firm is planning on its output for targeting a certain level of profits.
- $(P_x - AVC)$ measures the contribution made by each unit of output to cover the fixed cost.

SUMMARY

INTRODUCTION

The cost of production depends upon not only the techniques of production but also the prices of the factors of production.

SOME BASIC COST CONCEPTS

1. Actual costs are the costs, which a firm incurs on raw materials, labour, machinery, advertising and other such expenses. Opportunity cost is the cost of the alternative option, which has been lost by putting the scarce resources in the present option.
2. Variable cost is the cost, which varies with the level of output. It includes cost of raw material, labour, fuel and others. Fixed cost is the cost, which does not vary with the level of output.
3. Explicit costs are incurred by the firm when it buys or hires factors, which are required in the process of production. Implicit cost is incurred by the firm when it uses the factors, which are owned by the firm in the process of production.
4. Private cost is the monetary cost, which a firm incurs in the production of a good. Social cost is the real cost, which the society incurs in the production of a good, for example, pollution from a factory, which affects the health of the people adversely.
5. Short-run costs are those incurred over the short run, which is that time in which the supply of some of the factors of production is inelastic or fixed, for example, machinery. Long-run costs are those incurred over the long run, which is that time in which the supply of most of the factors of production is elastic. Thus, all the factors of production can be changed in the long run.

COST FUNCTION

1. The cost function is a derived function since it is obtained from the production function.
2. A short-run cost function can be expressed as $C = f(X, P_F, T, \bar{K})$.
3. A long-run cost function can be expressed as $C = f(X, P_F, T)$.

TRADITIONAL THEORY OF COSTS

Short-run Cost Analysis

1. In the short run, while some costs are fixed others are variable.
2. Total cost is the cost incurred to produce a given level of output in the short run by utilizing both the fixed and the variable factors.

   $$\text{Total Cost} = \text{Total Fixed Cost} + \text{Total Variable Cost}$$

3. Total fixed cost includes those cost, which does not vary with the level of output.
4. Total variable cost is cost, which varies with the level of output.
5. The total variable cost curve is shown as inverse S-shaped curve. This is due to the law of diminishing returns.
6. Total cost is obtained by adding total fixed cost and total variable cost at the different levels of output.
7. The total cost curve is also an inverse S-shaped curve like the total variable cost curve and is everywhere higher than the total variable cost curve by the same amount as the total fixed cost.
8. Average Cost = Average Fixed Cost + Average Variable Cost.

9. The average cost curve is shown as U shaped.
10. $\text{Average Variable Cost} = \dfrac{\text{Total Variable Cost.}}{\text{Output}}$
11. The average variable cost curve is shown as U shaped.
12. $\text{Average Fixed Cost} = \dfrac{\text{Total Fixed Cost.}}{\text{Output}}$
13. The average fixed cost curve is shown as a rectangular hyperbola because as the level of output increases, the fixed cost per unit decreases.
14. Marginal cost is the change in the total cost or total variable cost due to a unit change in the level of output.

$$\text{Marginal Cost} = \frac{\Delta TC}{\Delta X}$$

15. The marginal cost curve is shown as U shaped.

Some Relationships Between the Short-run Cost Curves

1. At any point on the total fixed cost curve, the average fixed cost is the slope of the line, which joins the origin to that particular point on the total fixed cost curve.
2. At any point on the total variable cost curve, the average variable cost is the slope of the line, which joins the origin to that particular point on the total variable cost curve.
3. The average variable cost curve and average cost curve are both U shaped due to the law of variable proportions. However, average variable cost curve reaches its minimum point before the average cost curve.
4. At any point on the total cost curve, the marginal cost curve is the slope of the total cost curve at that point.
5. Average cost curve and marginal cost curve are U shaped.
6. When average cost is falling, marginal cost is also falling and is below it.
7. When average cost is rising, marginal cost is also rising and is above it.
8. When average cost is at its minimum point, marginal cost is equal to average cost, or the marginal cost curve intersects the average cost curve.

LONG-RUN COST ANALYSIS

1. All the factors of production can be changed in the long run.
2. The long-run cost curves are formed by the short-run cost curves.

Long-run Average Cost

1. The long-run average cost is the average per-unit cost of production when all the factors of production are variable in the long run.
2. The long-run average cost curve can be derived from the short-run average cost curves as it is tangent to the short-run average cost curves.
3. The long-run average cost curve is derived from the *SAC*'s as the minimum per-unit cost of producing each level of the output.
4. It shows the least cost of producing each level of the output.
5. The long-run average cost curve is called the envelope curve as it envelops the *SAC*'s.
6. The long-run average cost curve is U shaped because of the law of returns to scale.
7. Initially, the long-run average costs fall as a firm experiences increasing returns to scale because of economies of scale.
8. When the economies of scale have reached their limit while diseconomies of scale have not yet appeared, the long-run average cost curve reaches its optimum plant producing the optimum output.

9. When a firm increases its output beyond its optimum capacity by changing its scale of operations, the disadvantages that it experiences are called the diseconomies of scale.

Long-run Marginal Cost

1. The long-run marginal cost curve can be derived from the short-run marginal cost curves.
2. When long-run average cost is falling, long-run marginal cost is also falling and is below it.
3. When long-run average cost is rising, long-run marginal cost is also rising and is above it.
4. When long-run average cost is at its minimum point, long-run marginal cost is equal to long-run average. At this point, $LAC = SAC = SMC = LMC$.

Long-run Total Cost

1. The long-run total cost curve is the minimum total cost of producing different levels of output from different plant sizes.
2. Long-run total cost curve is derived from the short-run total cost curves taking the point which represents the optimum size of the plant.
3. The long-run total cost curve is inverse S shaped because of the law of returns to scale.

ECONOMIES AND DISECONOMIES OF SCALE

Economies of Scale

1. When a firm increases its output by changing its scale of operations, the benefits that it experiences are called the economies of scale.
2. A firm experiences increasing returns to scale because of economies of scale.
3. The economies of scale are of two types: internal economies and external economies. These economies are not dependent on the actions of other firms. It is due to these internal economies that the long-run average cost curve falls.
4. Internal economies include: labour economies, technical economies, marketing economies, managerial economies, financial economies and risk-bearing economies.
5. External economies include: economies of information: economies of concentration, access to marketing facilities because of concentration and economies of disintegration.

Diseconomies of Scale

1. When a firm increases its output beyond its optimum capacity by changing its scale of operations, the disadvantages that it experiences are called the diseconomies of scale.
2. A firm experiences decreasing returns to scale because of diseconomies of scale.
3. The diseconomies of scale are of two types: internal diseconomies and external diseconomies.
4. It is due to these internal diseconomies that the firm's productive efficiency starts falling. They include: technical diseconomies, managerial diseconomies, financial diseconomies and risk-bearing diseconomies.
5. External diseconomies include: increase in the price of the factors of production, infrastructural problems and problems relating to disposal of too many wastes in a particular area.
6. While internal economies of scale cause the long-run average cost curve to fall, the internal diseconomies of scale cause the long-run average cost curve to rise.
7. While external economies of scale cause the long-run average cost curve to shift downwards, the external diseconomies of scale cause the long-run average cost curve to shift upwards.

BREAK-EVEN ANALYSIS

1. Break-even analysis is of immense help to business when they are making their decisions relating to output.
2. By using the break-even analysis, a firm is in a position to find out the level of output, where revenue and cost break even.

Break-even Analysis: Revenue and Cost Functions Are Linear

1. Figure 9.12 shows linear revenue and cost functions.
2. The total revenue curve in the figure depicts the revenue, which firm will earn at different levels of output, assuming that the price of the good is constant.
3. The total cost curve starts from point *F* on the *Y* axis depicting the linear relationship between cost and output.
4. The total fixed cost curve is a straight line starting from point F on the *Y* axis depicting a fixed cost of *OF*.
5. The total variable cost is the vertical distance between total cost curve and the total fixed cost curve. As the amount of output increases, the total variable cost increases.
6. At the output *OX** of the good, total cost is equal to total revenue. Thus, the firm will break even making neither profits nor losses at point *B*, which is the break-even point.
7. The break-even level of output is that level of output at which a firm neither makes profits nor losses. It is the level of output at which total cost is equal to total revenue.
8. Beyond the output *OX** of the good, total cost is smaller than total revenue. Thus, the firm will make losses.
9. $Q^*_x = \frac{TFC}{(P_x - AVC)}$.
10. In the above equation, $(P_x - AVC)$ in the denominator is the contribution per unit of output. It measures the contribution made by each unit of output to cover the fixed cost.
11. The equation shows that the break-even level of output is determined by the amount of the total fixed cost, per-unit price of good *x* and average variable cost. If any of these variables change, the break-even level of output will also change.

Break-even Analysis: Revenue and Cost Functions Are Non-linear

1. Figure 9.13 shows non-linear revenue and cost functions:
2. The total revenue curve in the figure depicts the revenue, which firm will earn at different levels of output.
3. The total cost curve starts from point *F* on the *Y* axis depicting the relationship between cost and output.
4. The total fixed cost curve is a straight line starting from point *F* on the *Y* axis depicting a fixed cost of *OF*.
5. The total variable cost is the vertical distance between total cost curve and the total fixed cost curve. As the amount of output increases, the total variable cost increases.
6. At the output OX_1* of the good, total cost is equal to total revenue. Thus, the firm will break even making neither profits nor losses at point B_1. This is the break-even point.
7. At the output OX_2* of the good, total cost is equal to total revenue once again. Thus, the firm will break even making neither profits nor losses at point B_2. This is another break-even point at which total cost is equal to total revenue.
8. The break-even point B_2 may not be of much relevance to a firm as it may be beyond the capacity of a firm to produce this output.
9. Break-even analysis is useful when a firm is planning on its output for targeting a certain level of profits.

REVIEW QUESTIONS

TRUE OR FALSE QUESTIONS

1. Fixed cost is the cost, which varies with the level of output.
2. Social cost is the real cost, which the society incurs in the production of a good.
3. When a firm increases its output by changing its scale of operations, the benefits that it experiences are called the economies of scale.
4. It is due to the internal economies that the long-run average cost curve rises.
5. It is due to these external economies that the long-run average cost curve shifts upwards.

SHORT ANSWER QUESTIONS

1. Write a short note on total cost.
2. Write a short note on average cost.
3. Analyse the relationships between the short-run cost curves.
4. 'The long-run marginal cost curve can be derived from the short-run marginal cost curves'. Discuss.
5. What is the relationship between long-run average cost and long-run marginal cost? Discuss.

LONG ANSWER QUESTIONS

1. 'The long-run average cost curve is called the envelope curve as it envelops the SAC's'. Comment.
2. What are economies of scale? Discuss.
3. What are diseconomies of scale? Discuss.
4. Analyse the break-even point when revenue and cost functions are linear.
5. Analyse the break-even point when revenue and cost functions are non-linear.

ANSWERS

TRUE OR FALSE QUESTIONS

1. **False.** Variable cost is the cost, which varies with the level of output.
2. **True.** Social cost is the real cost, which the society incurs in the production of a good, for example, pollution from a factory, which affects the health of people adversely.
3. **True.** When a firm increases its output by changing its scale of operations, the benefits that it experiences are called the economies of scale. A firm experiences increasing returns to scale because of economies of scale.
4. **False.** It is due to the internal economies that the long-run average cost curve falls.
5. **False.** It is due to these external economies that the long-run average cost curve shifts downwards.

Perfect Competition

10

After studying this chapter, you should be able to understand:

- ✓ *A market is a place, where the buyers and the sellers of a good are in close contact with each other, where the contact may be direct or indirect.*
- ✓ *Under perfect competition, the firm does not have any discretion in fixing the price of the good.*
- ✓ *A perfectly competitive firm is in equilibrium at the point, where MR = MC and also the marginal cost curve intersects the marginal revenue curve from below.*
- ✓ *A perfectly competitive firm is in the long-run equilibrium when it is earning normal profits.*
- ✓ *Minimum price policies aim at keeping the market price above the equilibrium price.*
- ✓ *Maximum price policies aim at keeping the market price below the equilibrium price.*

INTRODUCTION

We now examine the different market structures. Before we embark on a discussion of these different structures, we should be clear about the meaning of the term 'market'. A market is a place, where the buyers and the sellers of a good are in close contact with each other, the contact may be direct or indirect. It is the number of sellers and the number of buyers, which determine the price of a good in the market. The number of sellers of a good in the market determines the level of competition and thus the structure of the market.

TYPES OF MARKET STRUCTURES AND PRICING DECISIONS

The different types of market structures are as follows:

(i) **Perfect Competition:** There are a large number of buyers and sellers of the good. The price of a good is determined in the market by the demand and the supply. The firm does not have any discretion in fixing the price of the good.

(ii) **Monopoly:** There is a single seller of the good in the market with no close substitutes for the good. There is very little competition with the firm exercising a great deal of control over the price of the good.

(iii) **Monopolistic Competition:** There are a large number of firms, which are involved in the production of similar goods. Each firm has some discretion in fixing the price of its product.

(iv) **Oligopoly:** There are a few large firms selling similar or differentiated goods. There is intense competition between the firms and often they form cartels with the aim of controlling the markets. Each firm has a control over the price of the good it produces, especially if the good is differentiated.

RECAP

- Under perfect competition, the firm does not have any discretion in fixing the price of the good.
- Under monopoly, the firm exercises a great deal of control over the price of the good.
- Under monopolistic competition, each firm has some discretion in fixing the price of its product.
- Under oligopoly, each firm has a control over the price of the good it produces, especially, if the good is differentiated.

CHARACTERISTICS OF PERFECT COMPETITION

Perfect competition is a market structure, where there are a large number of buyers and sellers of a good for which there is no close substitute, with there being free entry and exit. Its characteristics are as follows:

(i) Large number of buyers and sellers of the good. There exist such a large number of buyers and sellers that no single buyer and no single seller can influence the price of the good. Each is a price taker.

(ii) Homogenous good. As far as the good is concerned, each and every unit of the good is similar to the other unit. For the buyer, each unit of the good is identical to the other unit irrespective of which firm has produced the good. Thus, no firm has any control over the price of the good.

(iii) Free entry and exit of firms. Firms are free to enter or exit the industry without there being any restrictions or barriers. Also, there is no cost involved as far as entry and exit are concerned.

(iv) Buyers and sellers have perfect knowledge about the conditions in the market. Buyers and sellers have a complete knowledge about the prices prevailing in the market. There are no uncertainties in the market about the future conditions.

(v) Factors of production are perfectly mobile. All factors of production including land, labour and capital are perfectly mobile from one place to another and from one occupation to another occupation. There are no legal restrictions or obstacles in the form of trade unions.

(vi) There is no government intervention. There is a *laissez-faire* policy followed by the government in the sense that there are no taxes, subsidies, duties, etc. imposed by the government.

(vii) There are no costs of transportation. Since it is necessary for a single price to exist in all markets, it is assumed that there no costs relating to transport.

(viii) The goal of the firm is to maximize the profits. Every firm in the market aims at maximizing its profits.

RECAP

- Perfect competition is a market structure, where there are a large number of buyers and sellers of a good for which there is no close substitute, with there being free entry and exit.
- Buyers and sellers have perfect knowledge about the conditions in the market.
- Factors of production are perfectly mobile.
- There is no government intervention.
- There are no costs of transportation.
- The goal of the firm is to maximize the profits.

BOX 10.1

A closer look at the real world shows that perfect competition is rarely found in practice. The closest one can come to it is agriculture sector, where there are so many farmers who are selling their output to the government at a fixed price that no single farmer can control the price.

FIRM'S REVENUE CURVES UNDER PERFECT COMPETITION

Total Revenue Curve

Total revenue can be defined as the total proceeds earned by a firm from the sale of a certain amount of the output.

Total revenue can be defined as the total proceeds earned by a firm from the sale of a certain amount of the output.

Thus,

$$TR = P \times X$$

where *TR* is total revenue, *P* is per-unit price of the good and *X* is quantity of the good or the output level.

Since, under perfect competition, a firm is a price taker, the total revenue curve will be a straight line through the origin as shown in Figure 10.1.

Average Revenue Curve

Average revenue can be defined as the average proceeds earned by a firm from the sale of a certain amount of the output.

Average revenue can be defined as the average proceeds earned by a firm from the sale of a certain amount of the output.

Thus,

$$AR = \frac{TR}{X}$$

$$AR = \frac{PX}{X}$$

$$AR = P$$

where *AR* is average revenue.

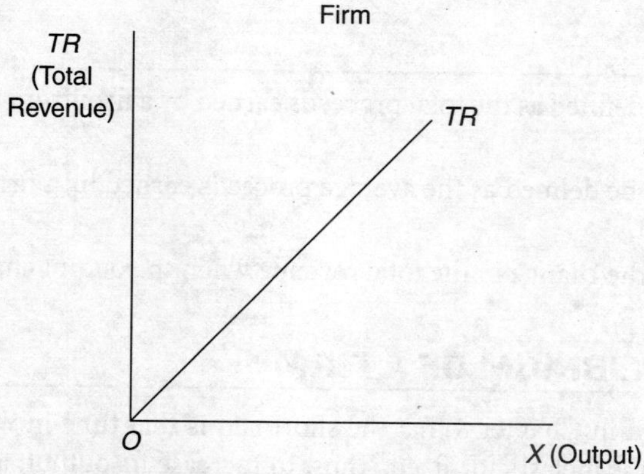

Figure 10.1 Total Revenue Curve

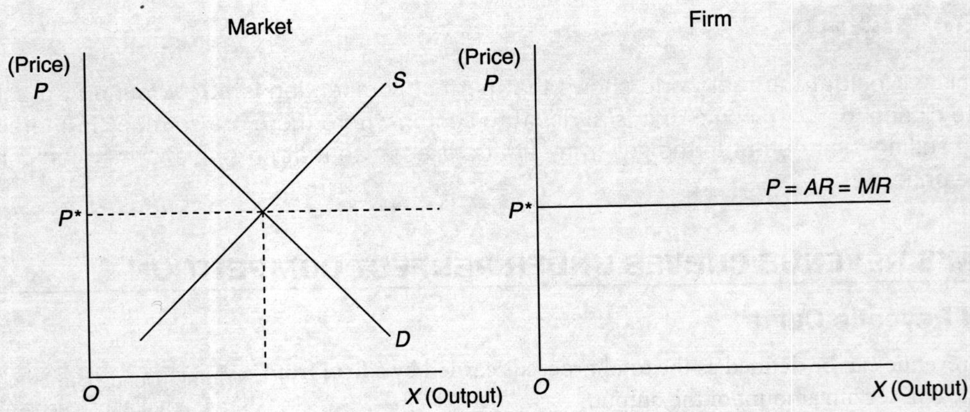

Figure 10.2 Average and Marginal Revenue Curves

Thus, the average revenue is the price of the good, which is determined by the market demand and supply of the good. The average revenue curve is also the demand curve for the good. It is shown as straight line parallel to the X axis in Figure 10.2 depicting that whatever are the quantities sold the price of the good will remain the same.

Marginal Revenue Curve

Marginal revenue is the change in the total revenue when the output changes by one unit. Thus,

$$MR = \frac{\partial TR}{\partial X}$$

Alternatively,

$$MR = TR_N - TR_{N-1}$$

> Marginal revenue is the change in the total revenue when the output changes by one unit.

In Figure 10.2, the marginal revenue curve is a shown as straight line parallel to the X. It is important to note that it coincides with the average revenue curve. Thus,

$$P = AR = MR$$

RECAP

- Total revenue can be defined as the total proceeds earned by a firm from the sale of a certain amount of the output.
- Average revenue can be defined as the average proceeds earned by a firm from the sale of a certain amount of the output.
- Marginal revenue is the change in the total revenue when the output changes by one unit.

SHORT-RUN EQUILIBRIUM OF A FIRM

We have already observed in Chapter 8 that the short run is that time in which the supply of some of the factors of production is inelastic or fixed. Thus, to increase its output, a firm can only increase the variable factors.

It is not possible for new firms to enter the industry nor is it possible for the existing firms to exit from the industry. Hence, the number of firms cannot change in the short run.

The objective of the firm is to maximize the profits.

(i) **Total Revenue – Total Cost Approach:** A firm is said to achieve the equilibrium when its profits are the maximum. Profits can be defined as the difference between total revenue and total cost. Thus,

$$\Pi = TR - TC.$$

In Figure 10.3, the total revenue curve is a straight line through the origin while the total cost curve is inverse S shaped due to the law of variable proportions. The profit curve is the difference between the total revenue and the total cost curves. Profits are a maximum at the output OX^* while at the outputs OX_1 and OX_2, the firm breaks even or makes zero profits.

(ii) **Marginal Approach:** We here use the per unit curves. We have

$$\Pi = TR - TC.$$

Profits will be a maximum when the first-order derivative is zero while the second-order derivative is less than zero or negative.

$$\Pi = TR - TC$$

$$\frac{\partial \Pi}{\partial X} = \frac{\partial TR}{\partial X} - \frac{\partial TC}{\partial X} = 0$$

Or

$$\frac{\partial TR}{\partial X} = \frac{\partial TC}{\partial X}$$

Or

$$MR = MC$$

But under perfect competition, $P = AR = MR.$

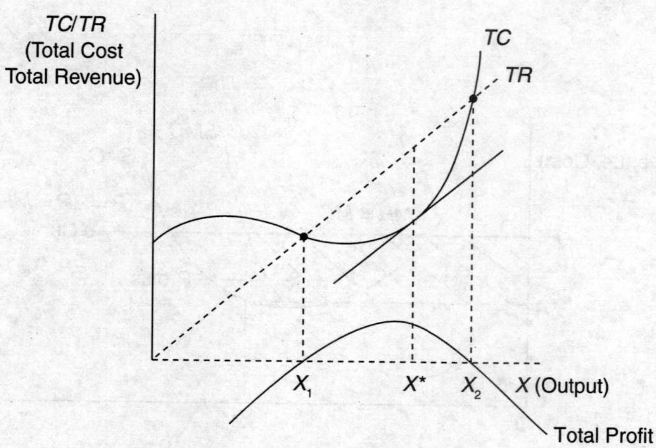

Figure 10.3 Total Revenue – Total Cost Approach

Thus,

$$P = MC$$

In addition,

$$\frac{\partial^2 \Pi}{\partial X^2} = \frac{\partial^2 TR}{\partial X^2} - \frac{\partial^2 TC}{\partial X^2} < 0$$

Or

$$\frac{\partial^2 TR}{\partial X^2} < \frac{\partial^2 TC}{\partial X^2}$$

Or

$$\text{Slope of } MR < \text{Slope of } MC$$

This implies that at the equilibrium point the marginal cost curve should intersect the marginal revenue curve from below as in Figure 10.4.

Firm's Equilibrium

The marginal approach to equilibrium for a perfectly competitive firm has been depicted diagrammatically in Figure 10.4:

(i) The firm's demand curve, *d*, is parallel to the *X* axis at a height equal to *OP**. It is also the firm's average and marginal revenue curve.

(ii) The short-run average cost curve of the firm is represented by the curve *SAC*. It is U shaped due to the law of variable proportions.

(iii) The short-run marginal cost curve of the firm is represented by the curve *SMC*. It is also U shaped due to the law of variable proportions. It cuts the short-run average revenue curve, *SAC* at its minimum point.

The firm is in equilibrium at point *E*, where *MR* = *MC* and also the marginal cost curve intersects the marginal revenue curve from below. The firm is in a position to earn supernormal profits equal to the rectangle *AP***EB*.

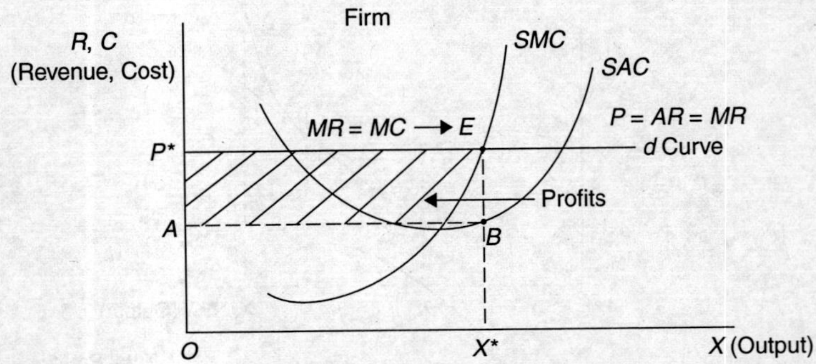

Figure 10.4 Perfectly Competitive Firm Making Supernormal Profits in the Short Run

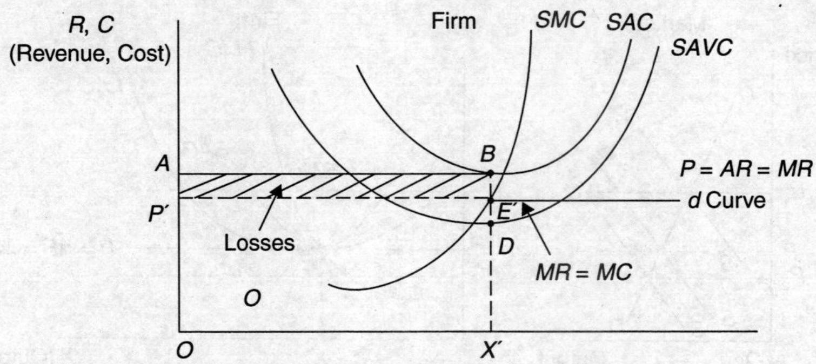

Figure 10.5 Perfectly Competitive Firm Incurring Losses in the Short Run

It is not necessary that a perfectly competitive firm will make super normal profits in the short run. Figure 10.5 depicts a firm, which is making losses in the short run. The firm's demand curve, *d*, is parallel to the *X* axis at a height equal to *OP′*. The firm is in equilibrium at point *E′*. The equilibrium price is *OP′* and the quantity is *OX′*. This market price covers only a part of the average fixed cost, completely. It does not cover the average fixed costs. Thus, the firm will incur losses equal to the rectangle *P′ABE′*. The firm will continue to produce as long as it covers the average variable cost.

RECAP

- There are two approaches to profit maximization:

  Total Revenue – Total Cost Approach and Marginal Approach.

- A perfectly competitive firm is in equilibrium at the point, where $MR = MC$ and also the marginal cost curve intersects the marginal revenue curve from below.
- It is not necessary that a firm will make super normal profits in the short run. A firm can incur losses also. The firm will continue to produce as long as it covers the average variable cost.

LONG-RUN EQUILIBRIUM OF A FIRM

A firm is in the long-run equilibrium when it is earning normal profits. This implies that to reach an equilibrium in the long-run a firm will have to make adjustments as depicted in Figures 10.6(a) and (b).

Figure 10.6(a) depicts the market demand and supply curves while in Figure 10.6(b) the firm's equilibrium has been shown.

(i) **Situation I:** In Figure 10.6(a) *DD′* and SS_1 intersect to determine the equilibrium price at P_1. In Figure 10.6(b), the firm is in short-run equilibrium at this price earning supernormal profits. Since, in the short run, there is free entry and exit, new firms are attracted to the industry because of these profits. There will be an increase in the market supply of the good and thus the market supply curve shifts rightwards to SS_2 resulting in a decrease in the equilibrium price to *OP*. At this price, the firm will reach long-run equilibrium at point *E* earning only normal profits as shown in Figure 10.6.

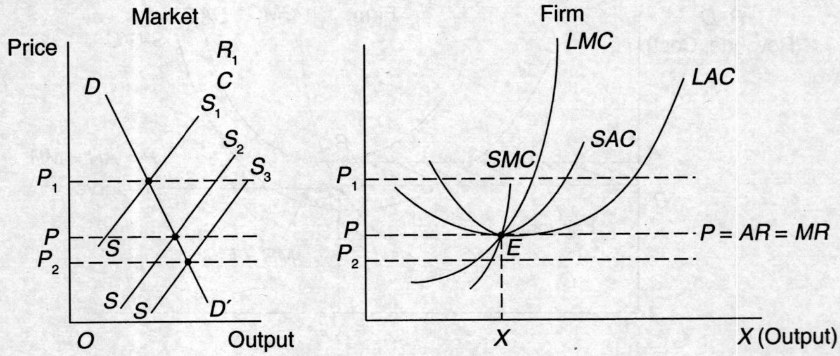

Figure 10.6 Long-run Equilibrium of the Firm

(ii) **Situation II:** In Figure 10.6(a), *DD′* and SS_3 intersect to determine the equilibrium price at P_2. In Figure 10.6(b), the firm is in short-run equilibrium at this price incurring losses. Since, in the short run, there is free entry and exit, the marginal firms will leave the industry. There will be a decrease in the market supply of the good and thus the market supply curve shifts leftwards to SS_2 resulting in an increase in the equilibrium price to *OP*. At this price, the firm reaches long-run equilibrium at point E earning only normal profits as shown in Figure 10.6.

At the price *OP*, the firm in the industry will be in long-run equilibrium earning normal profit. Thus, there is no incentive for new firms to enter the industry nor for existing firms to quit the industry. Both the individual firm and the industry are in long-run equilibrium.

RECAP

- A perfectly competitive firm is in the long-run equilibrium when it is earning normal profits.
- In the long run, there is no incentive for new firms to enter the industry nor for existing firms to quit the industry. Thus, both the individual firm and the industry are in long-run equilibrium.

APPLICATIONS OF PERFECT COMPETITION

The equilibrium price of a good is determined by the intersection of the market demand and market supply curves of the good. This can often be applied to analyse the effects of different government policies and is also often of use to the individual firm when they are involved in making the decisions. They include the following:

Price Controls

Often the government has to intervene in the market through controls on the price using tools like monetary policy and fiscal policy:

(i) Minimum price policies aim at keeping the market price above the equilibrium price. In Figure 10.7, the equilibrium is determined by the market demand and supply curves, *DD′* and *SS′*, respectively, at point E. The equilibrium price is *OP** while the equilibrium output is *OX**. Often, for example, in the case of some agricultural goods and also under the minimum wage laws, the government may fix a minimum price for the good at P_{Min}, which is above the equilibrium price *OP**. This will result in an excess supply of the good, which the government will have to purchase.

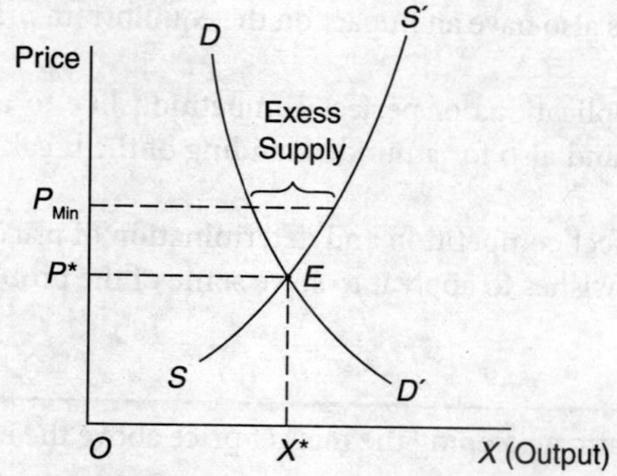

Figure 10.7 Minimum Price Policy

(ii) Maximum price policies aim at keeping the market price below the equilibrium price. In Figure 10.8, the equilibrium is determined by the market demand and supply curves, *DD′* and *SS′*, respectively, at point *E*. The equilibrium price is *OP** while the equilibrium output is *OX**. Often, for example, when the government wants to control the production of a good, the government may fix a maximum price for the good at P_{Max}, which is below the equilibrium price *OP**. This will result in an excess demand for the good, which, if not satisfied, may result in black marketing.

Impact of Taxes and Subsidies

Taxes, like excise tax, add to the costs leading to a leftwards (inwards) shift of the supply curve. Subsidies or negative tax leads to a rightwards (outwards) shift of the supply curve.

In Figure 10.9, the equilibrium is determined by the market demand and supply curves, *DD′* and *SS′*, respectively, at point *E*. The equilibrium price is *OP** while the equilibrium output is *OX**. An indirect tax on the good adds to the costs leading to a leftwards (inwards) shift of the supply curve to S_1S_1'. There occurs a change in the equilibrium price and the equilibrium output of the good. The price of the good increases from *OP** to OP_1 while the equilibrium output decreases from *OX** to OX_1.

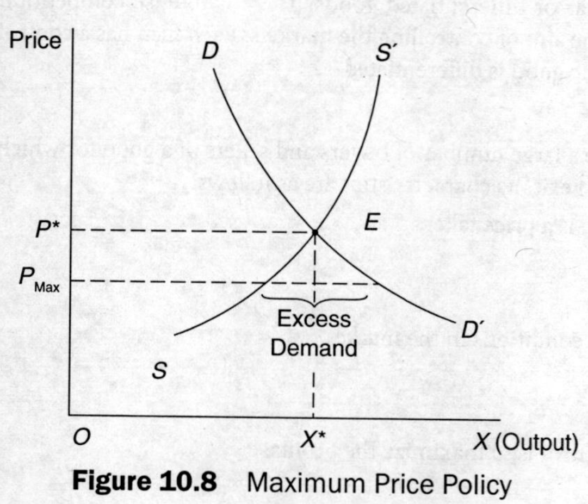

Figure 10.8 Maximum Price Policy

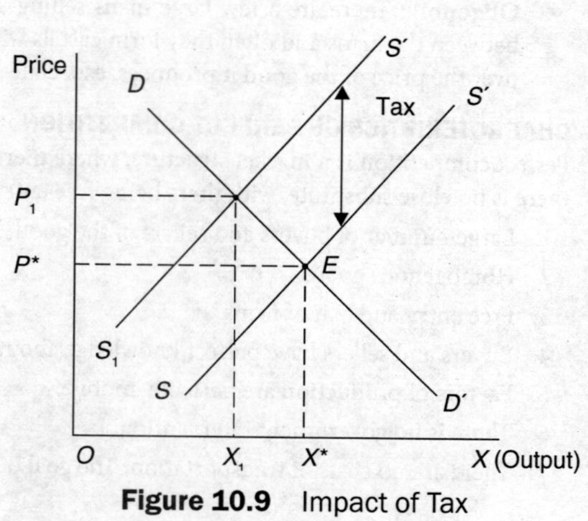

Figure 10.9 Impact of Tax

Subsidies or negative taxes also have an impact on the equilibrium price and the equilibrium output of the good.

There are many other applications of perfect competition like to analyse the stable equilibrium and the unstable equilibrium and also for an understanding of the break-even analysis, where the total approach can be used.

An understanding of perfect competition and determination of price in the short run and the long run is of immense help if one wishes to apply it to solve some of the problems one faces in reality.

RECAP

- Minimum price policies aim at keeping the market price above the equilibrium price.
- Maximum price policies aim at keeping the market price below the equilibrium price.
- Taxes, like excise tax, add to the costs leading to a leftwards (inwards) shift of the supply curve.

SUMMARY

INTRODUCTION

1. A market is a place, where the buyers and the sellers of a good are in close contact with each other where the contact may be direct or indirect.
2. It is the number of sellers and the number of buyers, which determine the price of a good in the market.
3. The number of sellers of a good in the market determines the level of competition and thus the structure of the market.

TYPES OF MARKET STRUCTURES AND PRICING DECISIONS

The different types of market structures are:

1. **Perfect Competition:** There are a large number of buyers and sellers of the good. The price of a good is determined in the market by the demand and the supply. The firm does not have any discretion in fixing the price of the good.
2. **Monopoly:** There is a single seller of the good in the market with no close substitutes for the good. There is very little competition with the firm exercising a great deal of control over the price of the good.
3. **Monopolistic Competition:** There are a large number of firms, which are involved in the production of similar goods. Each firm has some discretion in fixing the price of its product.
4. **Oligopoly:** There are a few large firms selling similar or differentiated goods. There is intense competition between the firms and often they form cartels with the aim of controlling the markets. Each firm has a control over the price of the good it produces, especially, if the good is differentiated.

CHARACTERISTICS OF PERFECT COMPETITION

Perfect competition is a market structure, where there are a large number of buyers and sellers of a good for which there is no close substitute, with there being free entry and exit. Its characteristics are as follows:

1. Large number of buyers and sellers of the good. Each is a price taker.
2. Homogenous good.
3. Free entry and exit of firms.
4. Buyers and sellers have perfect knowledge about the conditions in the market.
5. Factors of production are perfectly mobile.
6. There is no government intervention.
7. There are no costs of transportation. The goal of the firm is to maximize the profits.

A FIRM'S REVENUE CURVES UNDER PERFECT COMPETITION

1. Total revenue can be defined as the total proceeds earned by a firm from the sale of a certain amount of the output. Thus, $TR = P \times X$.
2. Average revenue can be defined as the average proceeds earned by a firm from the sale of a certain amount of the output. Thus, $AR = P$.
   The average revenue curve is also the demand curve for the good.
3. Marginal revenue is the change in the total revenue when the output changes by one unit. Thus $MR = \frac{\Delta TR}{\Delta X}$.

It is important to note that $P = AR = MR$.

SHORT-RUN EQUILIBRIUM OF A FIRM

1. The short run is that time in which the supply of some of the factors of production is inelastic or fixed. Thus, to increase its output, a firm can only increase the variable factors.
2. It is not possible for new firms to enter the industry nor is it possible for the existing firms to exit from the industry.
3. The objective of the firm is to maximize the profits. There are two approaches to profit maximization.
4. Under the Total Revenue – Total Cost Approach, profits can be defined as the difference between total revenue and total cost. Thus, $\Pi = TR - TC$.
   The profit curve is difference between the total revenue and total cost curves.
5. Under the marginal approach, per-unit curves are considered. At the equilibrium point $MR = MC$ and the marginal cost curve should intersect the marginal revenue curve from below.
6. The marginal approach to the firm's equilibrium for a perfectly competitive firm's has been depicted diagrammatically in Figure 10.4. The firm is in equilibrium at point *E*, where $MR = MC$ and also the marginal cost curve intersects the marginal revenue curve from below. The firm is in a position to earn supernormal profits equal to the rectangle AP^*EB.
7. It is not necessary that a firm will make super normal profits in the short run. A firm can incur losses also. The firm will continue to produce as long as it covers the average variable cost.

LONG-RUN EQUILIBRIUM OF A FIRM

1. A firm is in the long-run equilibrium when it is earning normal profits. This implies that to reach an equilibrium in the long run, a firm will have to make adjustments.
2. If the firm is in short-run equilibrium earning supernormal profits, new firms are attracted to the industry leading to an increase in the market supply of the good resulting in a decrease in the equilibrium price. At this price, the firm reaches long-run equilibrium earning only normal profits.
3. If the firm is in short-run equilibrium incurring losses, the marginal firms will leave the industry leading to a decrease in the market supply of the good resulting in an increase in the equilibrium price. At this price, the firm reaches long-run equilibrium earning only normal profits.
4. There is no incentive for new firms to enter the industry nor for existing firms to quit the industry. Both the individual firm and the industry are in long-run equilibrium.

APPLICATIONS OF PERFECT COMPETITION

1. Often, the government has to intervene in the market through controls on the price using tools like monetary policy and fiscal policy.
2. Minimum price policies aim at keeping the market price above the equilibrium price. This will result in an excess supply of the good, which the government will have to purchase.
3. Maximum price policies aim at keeping the market price below the equilibrium price. This will result in an excess demand for the good, which, if not satisfied, may result in black marketing.

4. Taxes, like excise tax, add to the costs leading to a leftwards (inwards) shift of the supply curve. Subsidies or negative tax leads to a rightwards (outwards) shift of the supply curve.
5. There are many other applications of perfect competition like to analyse the stable equilibrium and the unstable equilibrium and also for an understanding of the break-even analysis, where the total approach can be used.

REVIEW QUESTIONS

TRUE OR FALSE QUESTIONS

1. Under perfect competition, the firm exercises a great deal of control over the price of the good.
2. Under monopoly, there is a single seller of the good in the market with no close substitutes for the good.
3. There exists under perfect competition a free entry and exit of firms.
4. A firm is said to achieve the equilibrium when its profits are a minimum.
5. At the equilibrium point, the marginal revenue curve should intersect the marginal cost curve from below.

SHORT ANSWER QUESTIONS

1. Write short notes on the following market structures:
   (a) Perfect competition
   (b) Monopoly
   (c) Monopolistic competition
   (d) Oligopoly
2. 'The objective of the firm is to maximize the profits. There are two approaches to profit maximization.' Comment.
3. Show the short-run equilibrium of a firm when it is making super normal profits.
4. What are the minimum and maximum price policies?
5. What is the impact of taxes on the equilibrium price and output?

LONG ANSWER QUESTIONS

1. What are the characteristics of perfect competition? Discuss.
2. Analyse the firm's revenue curves under perfect competition.
3. Analyse the short-run equilibrium of the firm under perfect competition.
4. 'A perfectly competitive firm is in the long-run equilibrium when it is earning the normal profits'. Comment.
5. Discuss the applications of perfect competition in the context of
   (a) Price controls
   (b) Impact of taxes and subsidies

ANSWERS

TRUE OR FALSE QUESTIONS

1. **False.** Under monopoly, the firm exercises a great deal of control over the price of the good.
2. **True.** Under monopoly, there is a single seller of the good in the market with no close substitutes for the good. There is very little competition with the firm exercising a great deal of control over the price of the good.
3. **True.** Firms are free to enter or exit the industry without there being any restrictions or barriers. Also, there is no cost involved as far as entry and exit are concerned.
4. **False.** A firm is said to achieve the equilibrium when its profits are a maximum.
5. **False.** At the equilibrium point, the marginal cost curve should intersect the marginal revenue curve from below.

Monopoly and Monopolistic Competition

11

After studying this chapter, you should be able to understand:

- ✓ *Monopoly is a market structure, where there is a single seller of the good in the market with no close substitutes for the good.*
- ✓ *Under monopoly, the firm constitutes the industry. Hence, the demand curve of the firm is also the demand curve of the industry.*
- ✓ *The monopolist produces a larger output at a lower price and earns larger profits in the long run than it does in the short run.*
- ✓ *Price discrimination is a situation when different prices are charged from different consumers for the sale of the same good at the same point in time.*
- ✓ *Monopolistic competition is a market structure, where there are many firms in the market selling close substitutes (but not identical) of a good.*
- ✓ *Under monopolistic competition in the short run, the firm is earning supernormal profits.*
- ✓ *In the long run, the supernormal profits of each firm will be competed away till every firm faces a no-economic profit no-loss situation.*
- ✓ *Excess capacity is the difference between the ideal (the least cost) output and the profit-maximizing output of the firm.*
- ✓ *Selling costs are costs, which a firm incurs not only to change the position, but also to change the shape of the demand curve for the good.*
- ✓ *It is important for a firm to determine the optimum amount of selling costs that it should undertake such that its profits are maximized.*

INTRODUCTION

In Chapter 10, we had examined the perfectly competitive market structure. In this chapter, we focus on two other forms of market structures, monopoly and monopolistic competition.

MONOPOLY

Characteristics of Monopoly

Monopoly is a market structure, where there is a single seller of the good in the market with no close substitutes for the good. There is a very little competition, with the firm exercising a great deal of control over the price of the good. Also, there exist barriers to entry. Its characteristics are as follows:

> Monopoly is a market structure, where there is a single seller of the good in the market with no close substitutes for the good.

(i) **Single Seller of the Good:** There exists a single seller, who exercises control over the output of the whole industry. Thus, the firm constitutes the industry.

(ii) **No Goods Which Can Act as Substitutes:** As far as the good is concerned, the entire output of the good is produced by the monopoly firm. There are no goods, which can substitute for the good. Thus, the firm has control over the price of the good or is a price maker.

(iii) **Restrictions on Entry:** There exist barriers as far as entry is concerned, for example, patents. This is necessary for a monopoly firm to survive.

(iv) **Monopolist Has Perfect Knowledge:** The monopolist has perfect knowledge about the conditions in the market. There are no uncertainties in the market about the future conditions.

(v) **Goal of the Firm Is to Maximize the Profits:** The monopolist firm aims at maximizing its profits.

RECAP

- Monopoly is a market structure, where there is a single seller of the good in the market with no close substitutes for the good.
- The firm has control over the price of the good or is a price maker.
- The goal of the firm is to maximize the profits. The monopolist firm aims at maximizing its profits.

TYPES OF MONOPOLY

The different types of monopoly are as follows:

(i) **Natural Monopoly** where the monopoly exists due to the existence of natural factors, for example, the accessibility to some basic raw materials, which is required for the production of the good, climatic suitability for the good and economies of scale.

(ii) **Social Monopoly** where the monopoly is formed by the state or the government for the welfare of the people, for example, railways.

(iii) **Legal Monopoly** where the monopoly is created by legal barriers, for example, patents and copyrights. Often, a firm may discover a new method of producing a good and then may acquire exclusive rights for its production for a certain time.

(iv) **Fiscal Monopoly** where the monopoly is formed by the government, for example, the printing of currency and the minting of coins.

RECAP

- Natural monopoly exists due to the existence of natural factors.
- Social monopoly is formed by the state or the government for the welfare of the people.
- Legal monopoly is created by legal barriers, for example, patents and copyrights.
- Fiscal monopoly is the monopoly, which is formed by the government.

FIRM'S REVENUE CURVES UNDER MONOPOLY

Demand Curve

Under monopoly, there exists a single seller who exercises control over the output of the whole industry. Thus, the firm constitutes the industry. Hence, the demand curve of the firm is also the demand curve of the industry. Since the firm has control over the price of the good or is a price maker, the demand curve slopes downwards. It is important to note that though the firm is a price taker it can either fix the price or the output of the good, but not both. We assume a demand curve given by the equation

$$P = a - bX$$

where P is per-unit price of the good, a is intercept of the demand curve on the Y axis, b is slope of the demand curve and X is quantity of the good or the output level.

Total Revenue Curve

Total revenue can be defined as the total proceeds earned by a firm from the sale of a certain amount of the output. Thus,

$$TR = P \times X$$

Or

$$TR = (a - bX)X$$
$$TR = aX - bX^2$$

Under monopoly, the total revenue curve is an inverted U-shaped curve.

Average Revenue Curve

Average revenue can be defined as the average proceeds earned by a firm from the sale of a certain amount of the output. Thus,

$$AR = \frac{TR}{X}$$
$$AR = \frac{PX}{X}$$
$$AR = P$$
$$AR = a - bX$$

where AR is average revenue.

Thus, the average revenue is the price of the good. The average revenue curve is also the demand curve for the good.

Marginal Revenue Curve

Marginal revenue is the change in the total revenue when the output changes by one unit.

$$TR = aX - bX^2$$
$$MR = \frac{\partial TR}{\partial X}$$
$$MR = \frac{\partial(aX - bX^2)}{\partial X}$$
$$MR = a - 2bX$$

Alternatively, $$MR = TR_N - TR_{N-1}$$

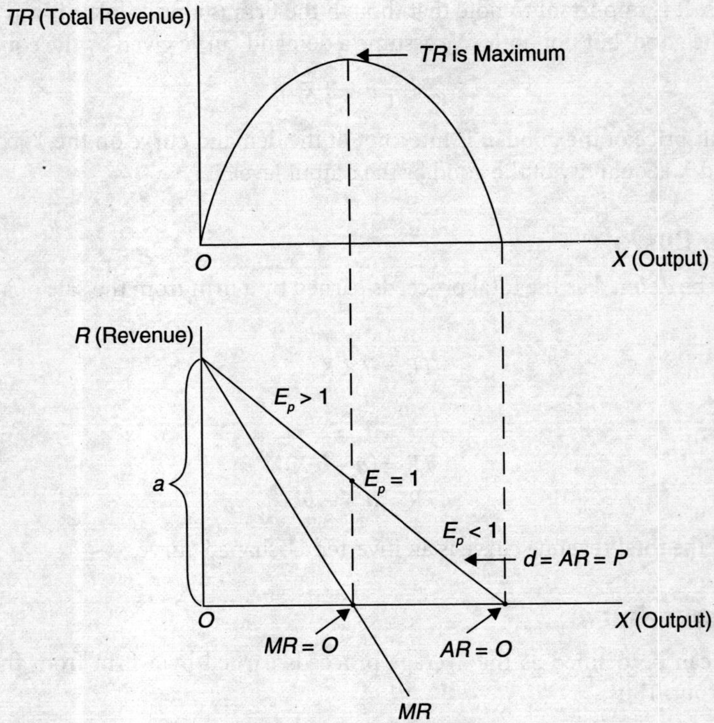

Figure 11.1 Demand Curve, Total Revenue Curve, Average Revenue Curve and Marginal Revenue Curve

In Figure 11.1, the marginal revenue curve is shown as a straight line, which begins from the same point on the *Y* axis as the *AR* curve.

Relationship Between Average Revenue, Marginal Revenue and Elasticity of Demand

We have observed that

$$TR = P \times X$$

$$MR = \frac{\partial TR}{\partial X}$$

$$MR = \frac{\partial (P \times X)}{\partial X}$$

Or

$$MR = P\frac{\partial X}{\partial X} + X\frac{\partial P}{\partial X}$$

$$MR = P + X\frac{\partial P}{\partial X}$$

But
$$E_P = \frac{-\partial X}{\partial P} \times \frac{P}{X}$$

Thus,
$$\frac{\partial P}{\partial X} = \frac{-1}{E_P} \times \frac{P}{X}$$

We can write
$$MR = P + X\left(\frac{-1}{E_P} \times \frac{P}{X}\right)$$

$$MR = P\left\{1 - \frac{1}{E_P}\right\}$$

It is obvious from the above equation that

(i) **If $E_P < 1$, Demand Is Relatively Inelastic:** When price elasticity of demand is < 1, change in the quantity demanded is less than proportionate to the change in the price of the good. Thus, total revenue decreases as price decreases. This implies that *MR* is negative.

(ii) **If $E_P = 1$, Demand Has a Unitary Elasticity:** When price elasticity of demand is equal to one, change in the quantity demanded is in the same proportion to the change in the price of the good. Thus, total revenue does not change as price decreases. This implies that *MR* is zero.

(iii) **If $E_P > 1$, Demand Is Elastic:** When price elasticity of demand is >1, change in the quantity demanded is more than proportionate to the change in the price of the good. Thus, total revenue increases as price decreases. This implies that *MR* is positive.

RECAP

- Under monopoly, there exists a single seller, who exercises control over the output of the whole industry.
- The demand curve of the firm is also the demand curve of the industry.
- Since the firm has control over the price of the good or is a price maker, the demand curve slopes downwards.
- The total revenue curve is an inverted U-shaped curve.
- The marginal revenue curve is shown as a straight line, which begins from the same point on the *Y* axis as the *AR* curve.

SHORT EQUILIBRIUM OF A FIRM

The objective of the monopoly firm is to maximize the profits:

(i) **Total Revenue – Total Cost Approach:** When the difference between total revenue and total cost is a maximum, profits are a maximum.

(ii) **Marginal Approach:** When marginal revenue is equal to marginal cost and the marginal cost curve intersects the marginal revenue curve from below, profits are a maximum.

The above two approaches have been discussed in detail in Chapter 10.

Firm's Equilibrium

The marginal approach to equilibrium for a monopoly firm has been depicted diagrammatically in Figure 11.2.

(i) The firm's demand curve, *d*, is downward sloping. It is also the firm's average revenue curve.

(ii) The short-run average cost curve of the firm is represented by the curve *SAC*. It is U shaped due to the law of variable proportions.

(iii) The short-run marginal cost curve of the firm is represented by the curve *SMC*. It is also U shaped due to the law of variable proportions. It cuts the short-run average revenue curve, *SAC* at its minimum point.

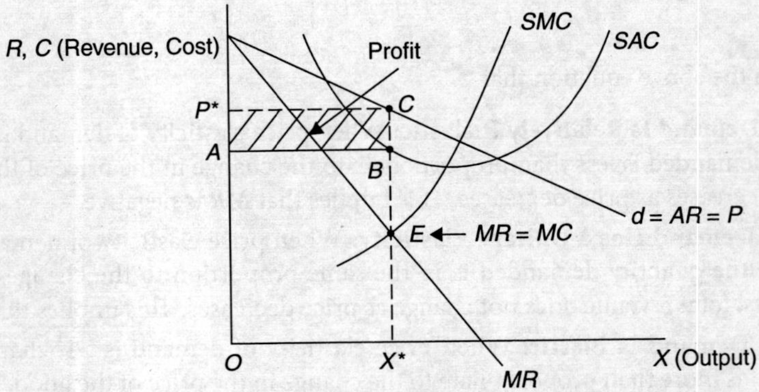

Figure 11.2 Monopoly Firm Making Supernormal Profits in the Short Run

The firm is in equilibrium at the point where marginal revenue equals marginal cost and also the marginal cost curve intersects the marginal revenue curve from below. The firm is in a position to earn supernormal profits equal to the rectangle *P*ABC*.

It is not necessary that a monopoly firm will make supernormal profits in the short run. Figure 11.3 depicts a firm, which is making losses in the short run. The firm is in equilibrium at point *E′*. The equilibrium price is *OP′* and the quantity is *OX′*. The price *OP′* does not cover the average fixed costs of production. Thus, the firm will incur losses equal to the rectangle *P′ABC*. The firm will continue to produce as long as it covers the average variable cost.

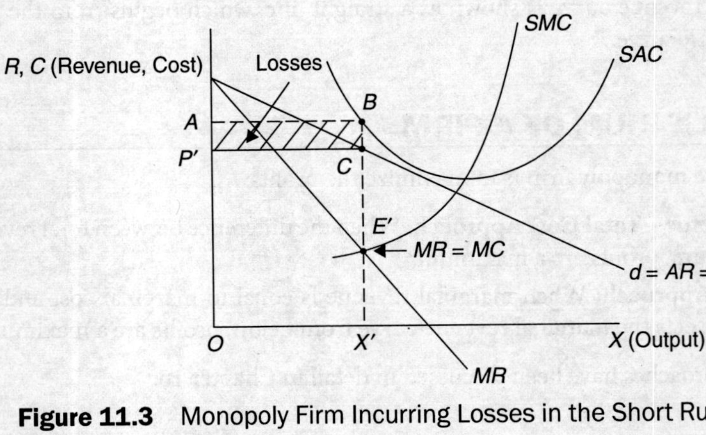

Figure 11.3 Monopoly Firm Incurring Losses in the Short Run

RECAP

- The firm is in equilibrium at the point, where marginal revenue equals marginal cost and also the marginal cost curve intersects the marginal revenue curve from below.
- The firm is in a position to earn supernormal profits equal to the rectangle.
- It is not necessary that a monopoly firm will make supernormal profits in the short run. It may make losses in the short run.

LONG-RUN EQUILIBRIUM OF A FIRM

The rules for profit maximization in the long run are the same as for the short run. However, in the long run, a monopolist is able to expand the firm's size so as to be able to increase its profit in the long run.

The marginal approach to equilibrium for a monopoly firm has been depicted diagrammatically in Figure 11.4.

(i) The firm's demand curve, *d*, is downward sloping. It is also the firm's average revenue curve.
(ii) The firm's marginal revenue curve is a straight line, which falls at a greater rate than the average revenue curve.
(iii) The short-run average cost curves of the firm are represented by the curves SAC_1 and SAC_2. They are U shaped due to the law of variable proportions.
(iv) The short-run marginal cost curves of the firm are represented by the curves SMC_1 and SMC_2. They are U shaped due to the law of variable proportions.
(v) The long-run average cost curve of the firm is represented by the curve *LAC*.
(vi) The long-run marginal cost curve of the firm is represented by the curve *LMC*.

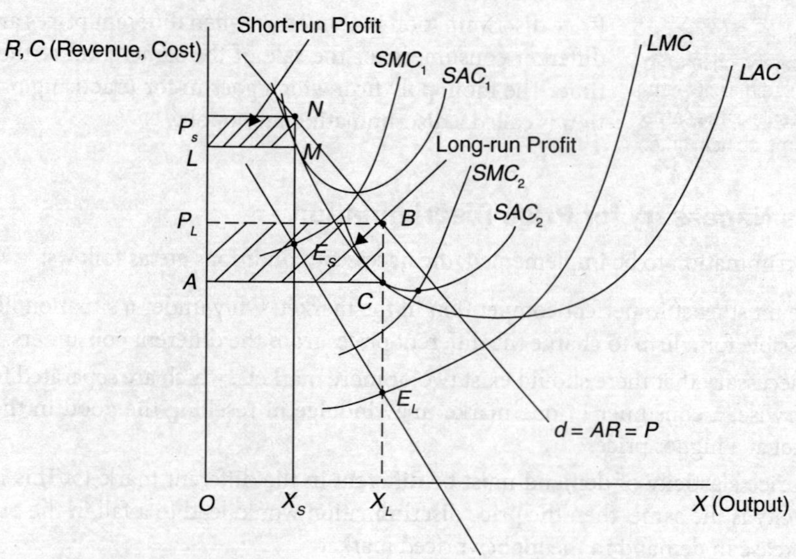

Figure 11.4 Monopoly Firm's Long-run Equilibrium

Firm's Equilibrium

The firm is in a short equilibrium at point E_S, where $MR = SMC_1$ and also the short-run marginal cost curve intersects the marginal revenue curve from below. The equilibrium price is OP_S while the equilibrium output is OX_S. The firm is earning supernormal profits equal to the rectangle P_SLMN.

The firm is in a long-run equilibrium at point E_L, where $MR = LMC$ and also the long-run marginal cost curve intersects the marginal revenue curve from below. The equilibrium price is OP_L while the equilibrium output is OX_L. The firm is earning supernormal profits equal to the rectangle P_LACB.

A comparison of the short- and long-run equilibrium of the monopolist depicts that:

(i) The long-run equilibrium output OX_L is larger than the short-run equilibrium output OX_S.
(ii) The long-run equilibrium price OP_L is lower than the short-run equilibrium price OP_S.
(iii) The long-run monopoly profit P_LACB is larger than the short monopoly profit P_SLMN.

Thus, the monopolist produces a larger output at a lower price and earns larger profits in the long run than it does in the short run.

RECAP

- In the long run, a monopolist is able to expand the firm's size so as to be able to increase its profit in the long run.
- The monopolist produces a larger output at a lower price and earns larger profits in the long run than it does in the short run.

PRICE DISCRIMINATION

Meaning of Price Discrimination

> Price discrimination is a situation when different prices are charged from different consumers for the sale of the same good at the same point in time.

Price discrimination is a situation when different prices are charged from different consumers for the sale of the same good at the same point in time. The monopoly firm which goes in for practising price discrimination is called a discriminating monopoly.

Conditions Necessary for Price Discrimination

For price discrimination to be implemented, the necessary conditions are as follows:

(i) There must exist imperfect competition in the market. Only under a situation like monopoly, it is possible for a firm to charge the different prices from the different consumers.
(ii) It is necessary that there should exist two or more markets, which are separated from each other. Otherwise, a consumer in one market may indulge in reselling the good in the higher-priced market at a higher price.
(iii) The price elasticity of demand must be different in the different markets. This is because if the elasticity is the same, then the price discrimination would lead to a fall in the profits by causing a decrease in demand in the higher-priced market.
(iv) The marginal revenue in each market should be greater than the marginal cost of the monopoly good.

Degrees of Price Discrimination

The degree of price discrimination is the limit to which a firm can make a division of the markets and extract the surplus from the consumers. There are three degrees of price discrimination.

First Degree Price Discrimination

Here, the monopolist charges the maximum price that each consumer is willing to pay for every unit of the good. Thus, he is able to extract the whole of the surplus from the consumer. The problem that may occur is that often the firm may not be aware of the maximum price that each consumer is willing to pay.

In Figure 11.5, if there had existed a simple monopoly, the monopolist would have charged a single price OP^* selling OX^* units of the good. Under first degree price discrimination, the monopolist will charge different prices OP_1, OP_2 and OP_3. The minimum price, which he would be ready to accept, would be OP_3 determined at the level, where the marginal cost curve intersects the demand curve.

Second Degree Price Discrimination

This is also called the block pricing method. Here, the monopolist divides the different markets into sub-markets or blocks charging a different price from each block. The basis on which the market is sub-divided is according to the quantity bought in each market. The price in each block is determined by what the marginal unit in that block is able to pay.

In Figure 11.6, the market has been sub-divided into three blocks. The monopolist charges the highest price OP_1 for OX_1 units—which forms the first block, price OP_2 for OX_2 units—which forms the second block, and price OP_3 for OX_3 units—which forms the third block. Thus, the monopolist is able to extract a considerable part of the consumer's surplus.

Third Degree Price Discrimination

Here, the monopolist divides the consumers of the good into different sub-markets or different groups and charges a different price from each one of them. The market may be divided on the basis of some geographical or demographic features. The important point to note here is that for third degree price discrimination to be possible, the price elasticity of demand should be different in each sub-market or group.

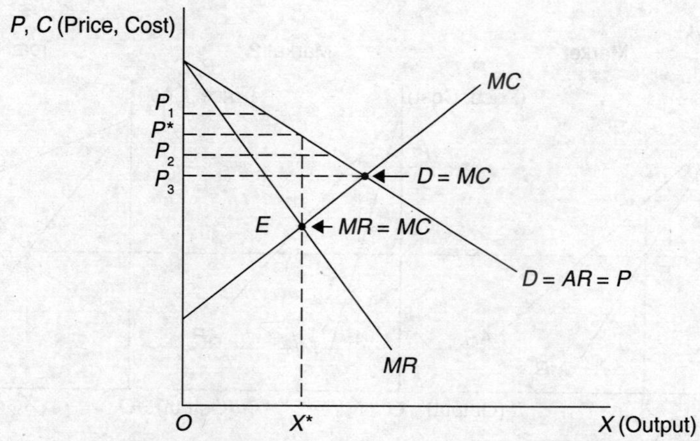

Figure 11.5 First Degree Price Discrimination

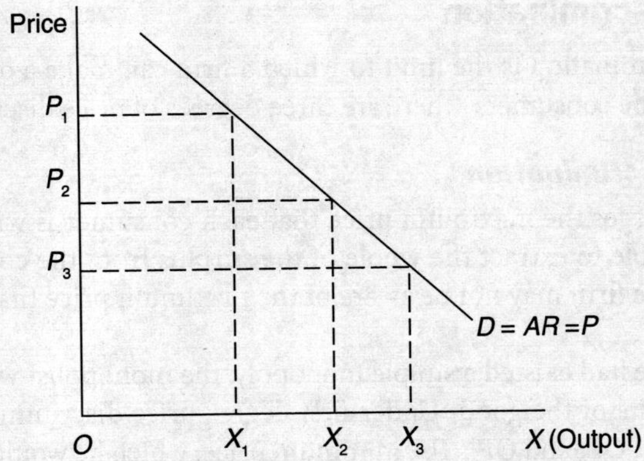

Figure 11.6 Second Degree Price Discrimination

Figure 11.7 shows a monopoly firm selling its output in two sub-markets, 1 and 2:

(i) In Figure 11.7(a), AR_1 and MR_1 are the average and marginal revenue curves, respectively, of Market 1.

(ii) In Figure 11.7(b), AR_2 and MR_2 are the average and marginal revenue curves, respectively, of Market 2.

(iii) In Figure 11.7(c), the total average revenue curve AR_T is the horizontal summations of AR_1 and AR_2 while the total marginal revenue curve MR_T is the horizontal summations of MR_1 and MR_2. MC, the firm's marginal cost curve, intersects the total marginal revenue curve MR_T at point E to determine the monopolist's equilibrium output at OX_T.

Since the monopolist aims at profit maximization, he will allocate the output in the two markets such that the equilibrium condition of equality between marginal revenue and marginal cost is satisfied in both the markets. A horizontal line is drawn from point E in Figure 11.7(c), parallel to the X axis, which intersects MR_1 at point E_1 and MR_2 at point E_2. Thus, the monopolist will maximize his profits in market 1 by selling an output of OX_1 at a price of OP_1 and in market 2 by selling an output of OX_2 at a price of OP_2. It is important to note that $OX_T = OX_1 + OX_2$.

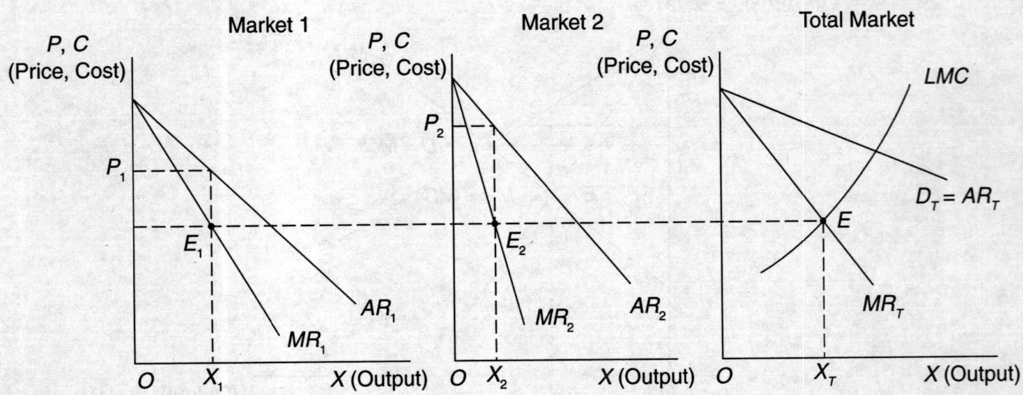

Figure 11.7 Third Degree Price Discrimination

RECAP

- Price discrimination is a situation when different prices are charged from different consumers for the sale of the same good at the same point in time.
- The degree of price discrimination is the limit to which a firm can make a division of the markets and extract the surplus from the consumers.
- Under first degree price discrimination, the monopolist charges the maximum price that each consumer is willing to pay for every unit of the good.
- Under second degree price discrimination, the monopolist divides the different markets into sub-markets or blocks charging a different price from each block.
- Under third degree price discrimination, the monopolist divides the consumers of the good into different sub-markets or different groups and charges a different price from each one of them.

CONTROL OF MONOPOLY

Monopoly is considered to be a social evil in that it exploits the consumer by charging a high price and in that it does not produce the optimum output. There are many ways in which monopoly can be regulated:

Imposition of a Lump Sum Tax

The government may levy a lump sum tax, for example, a profit tax on the monopolist. The impact of such a tax will be similar to the effect of an increase in the fixed costs.

In Figure 11.8, initially the monopolist is in equilibrium at point *E* producing an output of *OX** at price *OP**. With the imposition of a tax, the monopolist's average cost curve shifts up the amount of the tax from *AC* to *AC′*. While there is no change in the equilibrium, the firm's per-unit profit will decrease from *BC* to *B′C*. Thus, while the consumer is totally unaffected by the tax, there will be a decrease in the monopolist's profit.

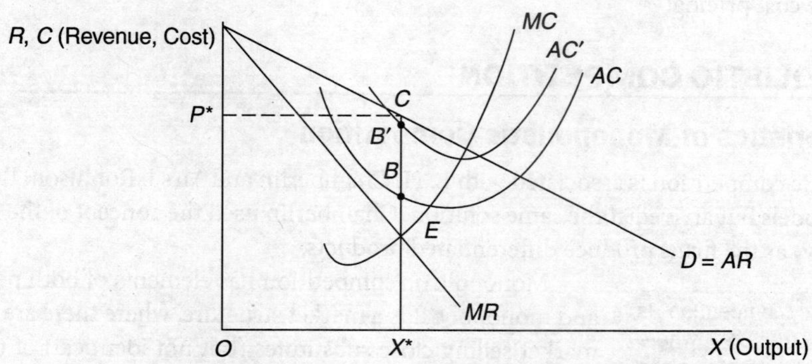

Figure 11.8 Imposition of a Lump Sum Tax

Marginal Cost Pricing and Average Cost Pricing

Most public utilities like railways and water supply are natural monopolies. Often the problem arises in fixing a price for these monopolies keeping in mind the welfare of the consumer.

In Figure 11.9, the monopolist who aims at profit maximization will be in equilibrium at point E, where marginal revenue equals marginal cost and the marginal cost curve cuts the marginal revenue curve from below. The equilibrium price is OP^* while the equilibrium output is OX^*.

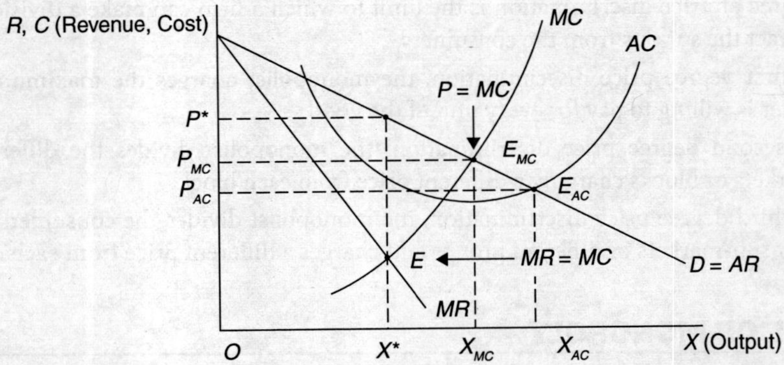

Figure 11.9 Marginal Cost Pricing and Average Cost Pricing

To regulate the monopolist, two following types of pricing policies are possible:

(i) **Marginal Cost Pricing:** The price is set where $P = MC$ at point E_{MC}. The equilibrium price is OP_{MC} while the equilibrium output is OX_{MC}.

(ii) **Average Cost Pricing:** The price is set where $P = AC$ at point E_{AC}. The equilibrium price is OP_{AC} while the equilibrium output is OX_{AC}.

RECAP

- The government may levy a lump sum tax, for example, a profit tax on the monopolist.
- To regulate the monopolist, two types of pricing policies are possible: marginal cost pricing and average cost pricing.

MONOPOLISTIC COMPETITION

Characteristics of Monopolistic Competition

Monopolistic competition is associated with E. H. Chamberlin and Mrs J. Robinson. Both had presented separate models but arrived at the same solution. Chamberlin used the concept of the 'group' (instead of the industry) as the firms produce differentiated products.

> Monopolistic competition is a market structure, where there are many firms in the market selling close substitutes for the good.

Monopolistic competition has elements of both perfect competition and monopoly. It is a market structure, where there are many firms in the market selling close substitutes (but not identical) of the good. It is one of the most prevalent forms of market structures that exist in the manufacturing sector in any economy, for example, in televisions, automobiles and soaps. Its characteristics are:

(i) In the 'group', there are a large number of buyers and sellers of the good. Each single seller has a limited influence over the price of the good.

(ii) There exists product differentiation. As far as the good is concerned, the goods produced by the group are close substitutes of each other.

BOX 11.1

E. H. Chamberlin and J. Robinson are associated with the monopolistic competition. In 1933, Chamberlin published the book, *Theory of Monopolistic Competition* and J. Robinson published *The Economics of Imperfect Competition*. This led to the monopolistic competition revolution. Also factors such as product differentiation, advertising and brand preference gained importance with the coming of monopolistic competition.

(iii) As far as the firms in the group are concerned, there exist free entry and exit.
(iv) All the firms in the group have identical cost and revenue curves.
(v) The goal of the firm is to maximize the profits.
(vi) Each firm acts independently of the other firm in the group.
(vii) Since the goods produced by the group are close substitutes of each other there exists non-price competition, for example, advertising, between the firms.

RECAP

- Monopolistic competition is associated with E. H. Chamberlin and Mrs J. Robinson.
- Monopolistic competition is a market structure, where there are many firms in the market selling close substitutes (but not identical) of the good.
- It is one of the most prevalent forms of market structures that exist in the manufacturing sector in any economy.

EQUILIBRIUM OF A FIRM

As already mentioned, the firm under monopolistic competition aims at maximizing the profits. The demand for the firm's product is influenced by three variables: price of the good, quality of the good when compared with other goods and the selling costs incurred by the firm. In our present analysis, since we are focusing on price as a variable, it is assumed that the firm does not incur any selling costs and also that the quality of the product remains the same.

Figure 11.10 depicts the demand curves of the firm and the group. Initially, the firm is in equilibrium at point E where the equilibrium price is OP^* and the equilibrium output is OX^*.

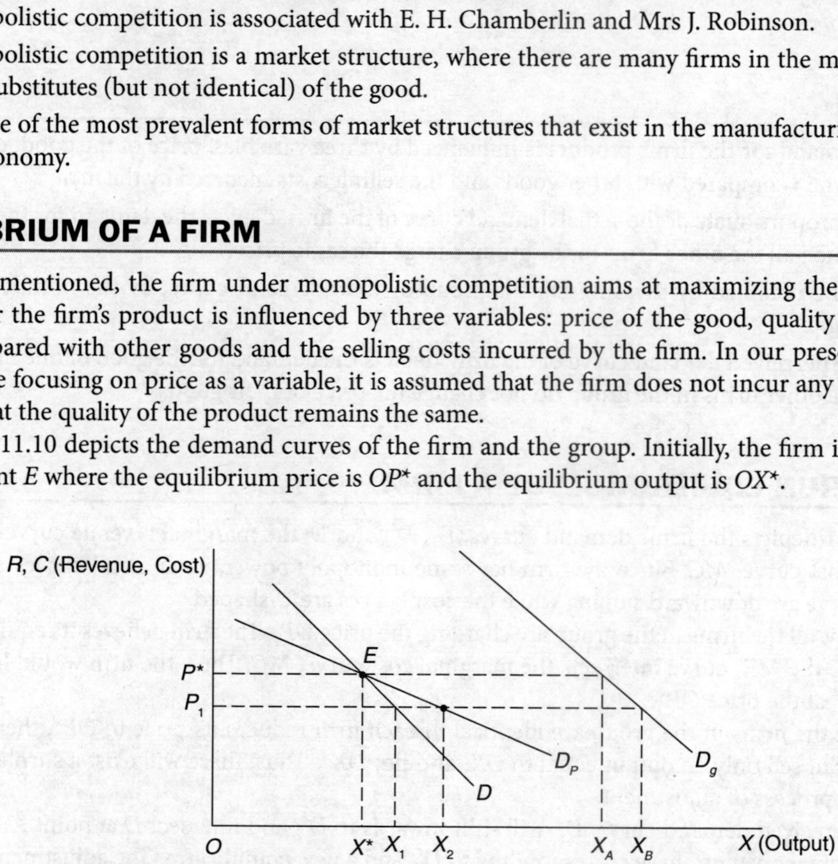

Figure 11.10 Demand Curves of the Firm and the Group

The proportionate demand curve of the firm depicts the demand for the good of one firm when all the other firms in the group charge the same price and also change the price of their goods simultaneously.

The perceived demand curve of the firm depicts the demand for the good of one firm assuming that the other firms in the group do not change the price of their goods.

D, the proportionate or the actual demand curve of the firm, depicts the demand for the good of one firm when all the other firms in the group charge the same price and also change the price of their good simultaneously. It can be obtained by dividing D_g, the group or total demand curve, by the number of firms in the group.

D_P, the perceived demand curve of the firm, depicts the demand for the good of one firm assuming that the other firms in the group do not change the price of their goods. D_P is more elastic than *D* because when only one firm in the group decreases its price, then the buyers may shift from other firms to this firm who reduces its price. Thus, the firm is able to capture the share of the other firms in the market. The individual firm may perceive its demand curve to be D_P because there are many firms in the group and may feel that its actions may not be noticed by the other firms.

In Figure 11.10, if just one firm alone decreases its price from OP^* to OP_1, then it can expect its sales to increase from OX^* to OX_2. However, if all the firms in the group decrease their price from OP^* to OP_1, then each firm's sales increase only from OX^* to OX_1. The sales of the group increase from OX_A to OX_B. It is important to note that $OX_1 - OX^*$ is simply $OX_B - OX_A$ divided by the total number of firms in the group.

RECAP

- The demand for the firm's product is influenced by three variables: price of the good, quality of the good when compared with other goods and the selling costs incurred by the firm.
- *D*, the proportionate or the actual demand curve of the firm, depicts the demand for the good of one firm when all the other firms in the group charge the same price.
- It can be obtained by dividing D_g, the group or total demand curve, by the number of firms in the group.
- D_P, the perceived demand curve of the firm, depicts the demand for the good of one firm assuming that the other firms in the group do not change the price of their goods.

SHORT-RUN EQUILIBRIUM OF A FIRM

Figure 11.11 depicts the firm's demand curves, D_P, D'_P and *D*; the marginal revenue curve MR_P and the marginal cost curve, *MC*. Since the firm has some monopoly power, its demand curves and marginal revenue curve are downward sloping while the cost curves are U shaped.

Initially, all the firms in the group are charging the price OP_1. The firm believes its equilibrium to be at E_P, where the MR_P curve intersects the marginal cost curve, *MC*. Thus, the firm would like to sell the output OX^* at the price OP^*.

But all the firms in the group are identical. If each firm reduces its price to OP^*, then in that case each firm can sell only an output equal to OX_1 and not OX^*. Thus, there will exist a surplus, which will initiate the process of adjustment.

The perceived demand curve, D_P, will shift inwards to D'_P and intersect *D* at point *A*. There will be a new marginal revenue curve corresponding to D'_P and a new equilibrium. The adjustment process will continue until the short-run equilibrium of a monopolistic firm is reached as in Figure 11.12.

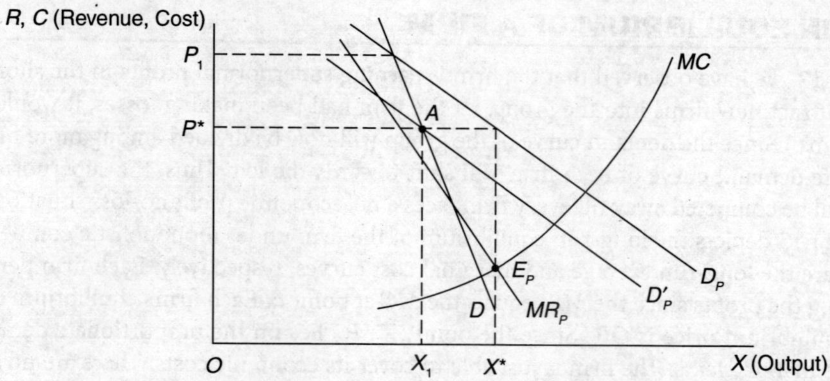

Figure 11.11 Adjustments of the Firm Under Monopolistic Competition in the Short Run

In Figure 11.12, each firm perceives that it is maximizing the profits since the MR_p equals the MC. Each firm's equilibrium output is OX_e while the equilibrium price is OP_e. Since the point (X_e, P_e) lies on the proportionate demand curve of the firm, it is obvious that the market clears. The firm is earning supernormal profits given by the shaded rectangle $P_e LMN$ in the figure. (The firm could have been making losses in the short run.) *SRAC* and *SRMC* are the short-run average and marginal cost curves, respectively.

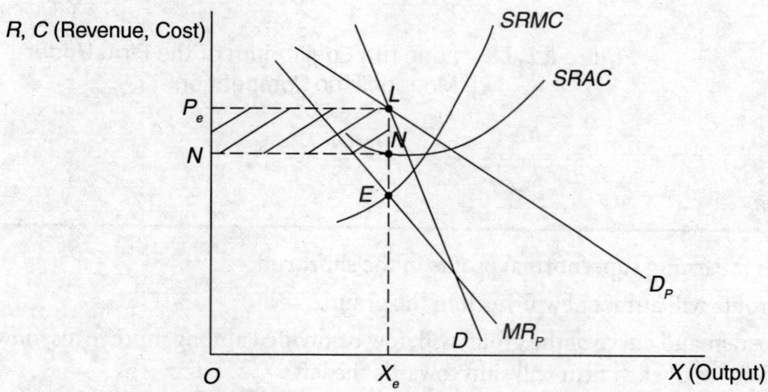

Figure 11.12 Short-Run Equilibrium of the Firm Under Monopolistic Competition

RECAP

- Since the firm has some monopoly power, its demand curves and marginal revenue curve are downward sloping while the cost curves are U shaped.
- Each firm perceives that it is maximizing the profits since the MR_p equals the MC.
- The firm is earning supernormal profits.

LONG-RUN EQUILIBRIUM OF A FIRM

In Figure 11.12, we have observed that the firm is earning supernormal profits in the short run. These profits will attract new firms into the group. (If the firm had been making losses, it would have led to an exit of firms.) Since the demand curve of the group will now be divided among more firms, now the proportionate demand curve of each firm will shift towards the left. Thus, the supernormal profits of each firm will be competed away till every firm faces a no-economic profit no-loss situation.

Figure 11.13 depicts the long-run equilibrium of the firm under monopolistic competition. *LRAC* and *LRMC* are the long-run average and marginal cost curves, respectively. Each firm perceives that it is maximizing the profits since the MR_P equals the MC at point *E*. Each firm's equilibrium output is OX_e while the equilibrium price is OP_e. Since the point (X_e, P_e) lies on the proportionate demand curve of the firm, the market clears. The firm is just able to cover its economic costs. There are no supernormal profits. Hence, there is no entry and no exit of firms.

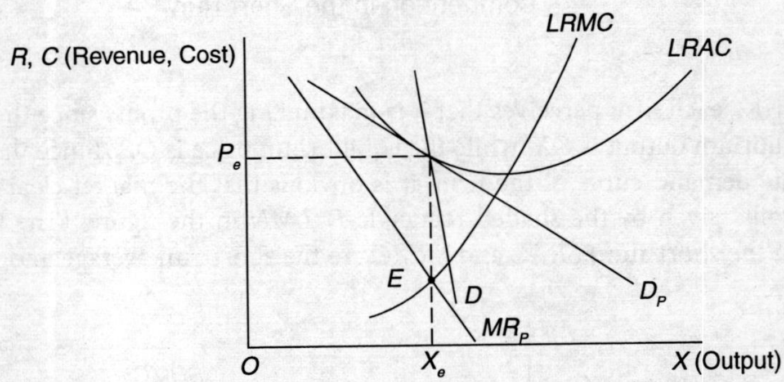

Figure 11.13 Long-run Equilibrium of the Firm Under Monopolistic Competition

RECAP

- The firm is earning supernormal profits in the short run.
- These profits will attract new firms into the group.
- Since the demand curve of the group will now be divided among more firms, now the proportionate demand curve of each firm will shift towards the left.
- The supernormal profits of each firm will be competed away till every firm faces a no-economic profit no-loss situation.

EXCESS CAPACITY

Figure 11.14 depicts the long-run equilibrium of the firm at the point of tangency of the perceived demand curve with the *LRAC* curve. But the demand curve under monopolistic competition is downward sloping because of product differentiation. This implies that at the point of tangency, the *LRAC* curve will also be downward sloping. Thus, the firm's equilibrium is not at the minimum point of the *LRAC* curve. Hence, the firm's equilibrium output OX_e is less than the least cost or the ideal output OX_I.

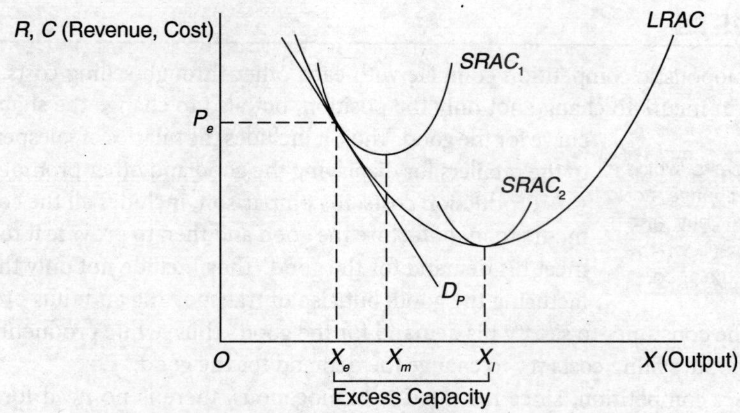

Figure 11.14 Excess Capacity of the Firm Under Monopolistic Competition

Under perfect competition in the long run, there does not exist any excess capacity as production takes place at the minimum point of the *LRAC* curve with the firm earning only normal profits.

> Excess capacity is the difference between the ideal output and the profit maximizing output of the firm.

In the long run, under monopolistic competition, there exists excess capacity equal to X_eX_I. Excess capacity is the difference between the ideal (the least cost) output and the profit-maximizing output of the firm. It can be split into two parts:

(i) X_eX_m, which exists because the plant $SRAC_1$ is not operated at its minimum point. $SRAC_1$ is the short-run average cost curve, which corresponds to the optimal plant for the firm's equilibrium output OX_e.

(ii) X_mX_I, which exists because the optimal plant $SRAC_2$ is not operated by the firm. $SRAC_2$ is the short-run average cost curve, which corresponds to the optimal plant for the firm's ideal output OX_I.

It is often argued that excess capacity leads to a waste of the society scarce resources and is thus a social loss. However, Chamberlin has put forward the view that the product differentiation under monopolistic competition provides a variety in life. The price, that people may be willing to pay for this variety in their life, may be the excess capacity, which exists under monopolistic competition in the long run.

RECAP

- The firm's equilibrium is not at the minimum point of the *LRAC* curve.
- In the long run, under monopolistic competition, there exists excess capacity.
- Excess capacity is the difference between the ideal (the least cost) output and the profit-maximizing output of the firm. It can be split into two parts.
- It is often argued that excess capacity leads to a waste of the society scarce resources and is thus a social loss.
- Chamberlin has put forward the view that the product differentiation under monopolistic competition provides a variety in life.

SELLING COSTS

Firms under monopolistic competition compete with each other through selling costs. Selling costs are costs, which a firm incurs to change not only the position, but also to change the shape of the demand curve for the good. Thus, it includes the salaries of salespersons, allowances to the retailers for displaying the good and other promotional activities.

> Selling costs are costs, which a firm incurs to change not only the position, but also to change the shape of the demand curve for the good.

Production costs, in comparison, includes all the costs, which a firm incurs to manufacture the good and then to provide it to the consumer to meet his demand for the good. They include not only the costs of manufacturing the good, but also of transporting and thus providing the good in the hands of the consumer to satisfy his demand for the good. Thus, while production costs meet the demand for the good, selling costs try to change the demand for the good.

Under perfect competition, since the good is homogenous, there is no need for any competitive advertising. The individual firm can sell any amount of the good at the given price. Under monopoly also since there are no close substitutes for the good, the monopoly firm may not go in for competitive advertising, but it may advertise to promote its product.

It is under monopolistic competition (and also under other forms of imperfect competition like differentiated oligopoly) that firms indulge in competitive advertising to promote the sale of their good. While the price and the design of the good remain the same, the competition between firms to increase the demand for the good is through advertisements. For example, the basic chemical formula used in all toothpastes is the same but one particular brand may try to promote itself emphasizing its special qualities. Such advertisements shift the demand curve for a particular brand outwards to the right implying that at a given price a greater quantity of the good is demanded.

It is important to note that selling costs are subject to initially increasing returns and then diminishing returns. Thus, it is important for a firm to determine the optimum amount of selling costs that it should undertake such that its profits are maximized.

Figure 11.15 analyses the optimum level of advertising expenditure for a firm under monopolistic competition which aims at profit maximization. In the figure, *ASC* is average selling cost curve, *APC* is average production cost curve, *AC* is *ASC* + *APC* which is average cost curve and *MC* is marginal cost curve.

The vertical distance between *APC* and *AC* is *ASC*.

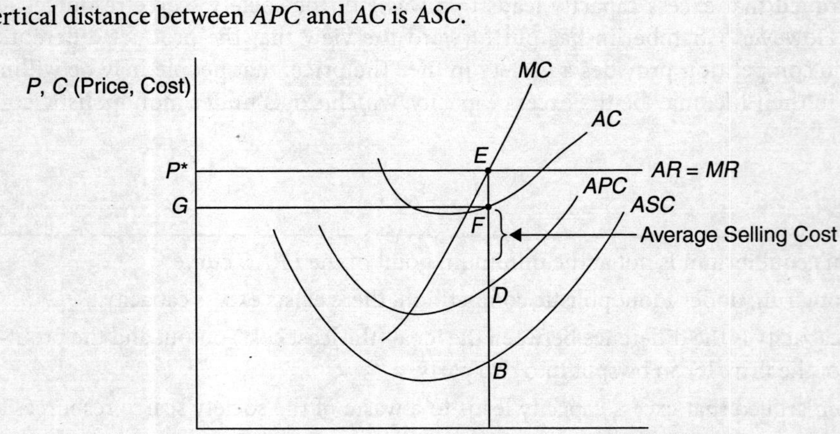

Figure 11.15 Optimum Level of Advertising Expenditure for a Firm Under Monopolistic Competition

The firm fixes the price of the good at OP^* and also does not change the nature of the good. The firm is in equilibrium at point E where the $AR = MR$ curve intersects the MC curve. The equilibrium price is OP^* while the equilibrium output is OX^*. The firm's profits are equal to the rectangle GP^*EF, while the average selling costs are equal to X^*B. Thus, the optimum advertising expenditure incurred by the firm when it is producing OX^* units of the output is equal to OX^* multiplied by X^*B.

RECAP

- Selling costs are costs, which a firm incurs to change not only the position, but also to change the shape of the demand curve for the good.
- Production costs includes all the costs, which a firm incurs to manufacture the good and then to provide it to the consumer to meet his demand for the good.
- While production costs meet the demand for the good, selling costs try to change the demand for the good.
- It is under monopolistic competition that firms indulge in competitive advertising to promote the sale of their good.
- Advertisements shift the demand curve for particular brand outwards to the right implying that at a given price a greater quantity of the good is demanded.
- It is important for a firm to determine the optimum amount of selling costs that it should undertake such that its profits are maximized.

SUMMARY

INTRODUCTION

We focus on two other forms of market structures, monopoly and monopolistic competition.

MONOPOLY

Characteristics of Monopoly

1. There exists a single seller, who exercises control over the output of the whole industry. Thus, the firm constitutes the industry.
2. As far as the good is concerned, the entire output of the good is produced by the monopoly firm. Thus, the firm has control over the price of the good or is a price maker.
3. There exist barriers as far as entry is concerned, for example, patents.
4. The monopolist has perfect knowledge about the conditions in the market.
5. The goal of the firm is to maximize the profits.

TYPES OF MONOPOLY

1. Natural monopoly, where the monopoly exists due to the existence of natural factors, for example, the accessibility to some basic raw materials, which is required for the production of the good, climatic suitability for the good and economies of scale.
2. Social monopoly, where the monopoly is formed by the state or the government for the welfare of the people, for example, railways.
3. Legal monopoly, where the monopoly is created by legal barriers, for example, patents and copyrights.
4. Fiscal monopoly, where the monopoly is formed by the government, for example, the printing of currency and the minting of coins.

FIRM'S REVENUE CURVES UNDER MONOPOLY

1. The demand curve of the firm is also the demand curve of the industry. It slopes downwards. We assume a demand curve given by the equation
$$P = a - b\,X$$
2. Total revenue can be defined as the total proceeds earned by a firm from the sale of a certain amount of the output. Thus,
$$TR = a\,X - b\,X^2$$
Under monopoly, the total revenue curve is an inverted U-shaped curve.
3. Average revenue can be defined as the average proceeds earned by a firm from the sale of a certain amount of the output. Thus,
$$AR = a - b\,X$$
4. Marginal revenue is the change in the total revenue when the output changes by one unit. Thus,
$$MR = a - 2\,b\,X$$
5. Relationship between *AR*, *MR* and elasticity of demand:
$$MR = P\left\{1 - \frac{1}{E_P}\right\}$$

SHORT EQUILIBRIUM OF A FIRM

1. The objective of the monopoly firm is to maximize the profits.
2. When the difference between total revenue and total cost is a maximum, profits are a maximum.
3. When marginal revenue is equal to marginal cost and the marginal cost curve intersects the marginal revenue curve from below, profits are a maximum.
4. In Figure 11.2, the firm is in equilibrium at point *E*, where $MR = MC$. It earns supernormal profits.
5. It is not necessary that a monopoly firm will make supernormal profits in the short run. The firm may also incur the losses.

LONG-RUN EQUILIBRIUM OF A FIRM

1. The rules for profit maximization are the same as for the short run. However, in the long run, a monopolist is able to expand the firm's size so as to be able to increase its profit in the long run.
2. The firm is in a short equilibrium at point E_S, where $MR = SMC_1$ and also the short-run marginal cost curve intersects the marginal revenue curve from below. The firm is earning supernormal profits.
3. The firm is in a long-run equilibrium at point E_L, where $MR = LMC$ and also the long-run marginal cost curve intersects the marginal revenue curve from below. The firm is earning supernormal profits.
4. The monopolist produces a larger output at a lower price and earns larger profits in the long run than it does in the short run.

PRICE DISCRIMINATION

1. Price discrimination is a situation when different prices are charged from different consumers for the sale of the same good at the same point in time.
2. The monopoly firm which goes in for practising price discrimination is called a discriminating monopoly.
3. For price discrimination to be implemented, the necessary conditions are: there must exist imperfect competition in the market; it is necessary that there should exist two or more markets, which are separated from each other; the price elasticity of demand must be different in the different markets; the marginal revenue in each market should be greater than the marginal cost of the monopoly good.
4. The degree of price discrimination is the limit to which a firm can make a division of the markets and extract the surplus from the consumers.
5. There are three degrees of price discrimination.

6. Under first degree price discrimination, the monopolist charges the maximum price that each consumer is willing to pay for every unit of the good. Thus, he is able to extract the whole of the surplus from the consumer. The problem here is that often the firm may not be aware of the maximum price that each consumer is willing to pay.
7. Under second degree price discrimination or the block pricing method, the monopolist divides the different markets into sub-markets or a block charging a different price from each block. The basis on which the market is sub-divided is according to the quantity bought in each market. The price in each block is determined by what the marginal unit in that block is able to pay. Thus, the monopolist is able to extract a considerable part of the consumer's surplus.
8. Under third degree price discrimination, the monopolist divides the consumers of its good into different sub-markets or different groups and charges a different price from each one of them. The market may be divided on the basis of some geographical or demographic features. The important point to note here is that for third degree price discrimination to be possible the price elasticity of demand should be different in each sub-market or group.

CONTROL OF MONOPOLY

1. Monopoly is considered to be a social evil in that it exploits the consumer by charging a high price and in that it does not produce the optimum output.
2. There are many ways in which monopoly can be regulated.
3. The government may levy a lump sum tax, for example, a profit tax on the monopolist. While the consumer is totally unaffected by the tax, there will be a decrease in the monopolist's profit.
4. Most public utilities such as railways and water supply are natural monopolies. Often the problem arises in fixing a price for these monopolies keeping in mind the welfare of the consumer.
5. To regulate the monopolist, two types of pricing policies are possible.
6. Under the policy of marginal cost pricing, the price is set where $P = MC$.
7. Under the policy of average cost pricing, the price is set where $P = AC$.

MONOPOLISTIC COMPETITION

Characteristics of Monopolistic Competition

1. Monopolistic competition is associated with E. H. Chamberlin and Mrs J. Robinson.
2. Chamberlin used the concept of the 'group' (instead of the industry) as the firms produce differentiated products.
3. Monopolistic competition is a market structure, where there are many firms in the market selling close substitutes (but not identical) of the good.
4. It is one of the most prevalent forms of market structures that exist in the manufacturing sector in any economy.
5. Its characteristics are: In the 'group', there are a large number of buyers and sellers of the good; there exists product differentiation; there exist free entry and exit; all the firms in the group have identical cost and revenue curves; goal of the firm is to maximize the profits; each firm acts independently of the other firm in the group; there exists non-price competition, for example, advertising between the firms.

EQUILIBRIUM OF A FIRM

1. The demand for the firm's product is influenced by three variables: price of the good, quality of the good when compared with other goods and the selling costs incurred by the firm.
2. In our present analysis, we are focusing on price as a variable.
3. D, the proportionate or the actual demand curve of the firm, depicts the demand for the good of one firm when all the other firms in the group charge the same price and also all the firms in the group change the price of their good simultaneously.
4. It can be obtained by dividing D_g, the group or total demand curve by the number of firms in the group.
5. D_p, the perceived demand curve of the firm, depicts the demand for the good of one firm assuming that the other firms in the group do not change the price of their good.
6. D_p is more elastic than D.

SHORT-RUN EQUILIBRIUM OF A FIRM

1. Since the firm has some monopoly power, its demand curves and marginal revenue curve are downward sloping while the cost curves are U shaped.
2. Each firm perceives that it is maximizing the profits since the MR_p equals the MC.
3. The firm is earning supernormal profits. (The firm could have been making losses in the short run.)

LONG-RUN EQUILIBRIUM OF A FIRM

1. The firm is earning supernormal profits in the short run.
2. These profits will attract new firms into the group.
3. Since the demand curve of the group will now be divided among more firms, now the proportionate demand curve of each firm will shift towards the left.
4. The supernormal profits of each firm will be competed away till every firm faces a no-economic profit no-loss situation.

EXCESS CAPACITY

1. The firm's equilibrium is not at the minimum point of the *LRAC* curve.
2. Hence, the firm's equilibrium output is less than the least cost or the ideal output OX_r.
3. In the long run, under monopolistic competition, there exists excess capacity.
4. Excess capacity is the difference between the ideal (the least cost) output and the profit-maximizing output of the firm. It can be split into two parts.
5. It is often argued that excess capacity leads to a waste of the society scarce resources and is thus a social loss.
6. Chamberlin has put forward the view that the product differentiation under monopolistic competition provides a variety in life.
7. The price that people may be willing to pay for this variety may be the excess capacity, which exists under monopolistic competition in the long run.

SELLING COSTS

1. Selling costs are the costs, which a firm incurs to change not only the position, but also to change the shape of the demand curve for the good.
2. Production costs include all the costs, which a firm incurs to manufacture the good and then to provide it to the consumer to meet his demand for the good.
3. While production costs meet the demand for the good, selling costs try to change the demand for the good.
4. It is under monopolistic competition that firms indulge in competitive advertising to promote the sale of their good.
5. Advertisements shift the demand curve for particular brand outwards to the right implying that at a given price a greater quantity of the good is demanded.
6. Selling costs are subject to initially increasing returns and then diminishing returns.
7. It is important for a firm to determine the amount of selling costs that it should undertake such that its profits are maximized.

REVIEW QUESTIONS

TRUE OR FALSE QUESTIONS

1. Monopoly is a market structure, where there is a single seller of the good in the market with no close substitutes for the good.
2. If $E_p < 1$, demand is elastic and MR is positive.

3. Under monopolistic competition in the short run, the firm may earn supernormal profits.
4. The proportionate demand curve of the firm depicts the demand for the good of one firm assuming that the other firms in the group do not change the price of their good.
5. In the long run a firm under monopolistic competition faces a no-economic profit no-loss situation.

SHORT ANSWER QUESTIONS

1. What are the characteristics of monopoly?
2. What are the different types of monopoly? Discuss.
3. Does there exist a relationship between *AR*, *MR* and elasticity of demand? Explain.
4. What are the characteristics of monopolistic competition? Discuss.
5. Write short notes on the
   (a) Proportionate demand curve
   (b) Perceived demand curve

LONG ANSWER QUESTIONS

1. Analyse the firm's revenue curves under monopoly.
2. 'The monopolist produces a larger output at a lower price and earns larger profits in the long run than it does in the short run.' Comment.
3. What are the different degrees of price discrimination? Discuss.
4. (a) Does a firm under monopolistic competition make profits in the long run?
   (b) What is excess capacity? Does it lead to wastage of the economy's scarce resources?
5. What are selling costs? How can a firm under monopolistic competition determine the optimum amount of selling costs that it should undertake such that its profits are maximized?

ANSWERS

TRUE OR FALSE QUESTIONS

1. **True.** Monopoly is a market structure, where there is a single seller of the good in the market with no close substitutes for the good. There is a very little competition with the firm exercising a great deal of control over the price of the good.
2. **False.** If $E_p < 1$, demand is relatively inelastic. Total revenue decreases as price decreases. This implies that *MR* is negative.
3. **True.** Under the monopolistic competition in the short run, the firm may earn supernormal profits. On the other hand, the firm could be making losses in the short run.
4. **False.** The perceived demand curve of the firm depicts the demand for the good of one firm assuming that the other firms in the group do not change the price of their good.
5. **True.** In the long run, a firm under the monopolistic competition, the supernormal profits earned in the short run by each firm will be competed away till every firm faces a no-economic profit no-loss situation.

Oligopoly and Strategies of Pricing

12

After studying this chapter, you should be able to understand:

- ✓ *Oligopoly is a market structure, where there are a few sellers of the product, which may be homogenous or differentiated.*
- ✓ *Since there are only a few firms in the industry, the actions of one firm influence other firms in the industry. Thus, there exists a mutual interdependence between the firms.*
- ✓ *There is no set pattern in an oligopoly. There exist many models each based on a different set of behavioural assumptions.*
- ✓ *Under non-collusive oligopoly, there are no implicit or explicit agreements relating to the price or to the sharing of the market.*
- ✓ *Cournot equilibrium exists at the point, where the two reaction curves intersect.*
- ✓ *The kinked demand curve model attempts at explaining as to why prices are rigid in spite of moderate changes in demand and cost under conditions of oligopoly.*
- ✓ *Under collusive oligopoly, firms cooperate and work together to determine the output and the price levels in a particular market. The purpose of the collusion is to reduce the competition between the firms and to increase the profits.*
- ✓ *Price leadership is an oligopoly model, where one firm sets the price while the other firms in the industry follow the firm.*
- ✓ *Game theory is a mathematical technique, which helps in examining the interdependence among the oligopoly firms and also the uncertainty involved in their decision making.*

INTRODUCTION

In the earlier chapters, we have examined some of the market structures like perfect competition, monopoly and monopolistic competition. In this chapter, we examine oligopoly. Oligopoly is a market structure, where there are a few sellers of the product, which may be homogenous or differentiated. Duopoly is a situation, where there are just two sellers of the product.

> Oligopoly is a market structure, where there are a few sellers of the product, which may be homogenous or differentiated. Duopoly is a situation, where there are just two sellers of the product.

Oligopoly may be a pure oligopoly when the product is homogenous or it may be a differentiated oligopoly when the product is differentiated.

CAUSES OF OLIGOPOLY

Like monopolistic competition, oligopoly is also a quite prevalent form of market structure in the manufacturing sector in an economy. It arises due to many following reasons:

(i) **Product Differentiation:** Often consumers may have a preference for a particular variety of a good produced by a firm. In that case, the firm may be in a position to control a large part of the sales of the good, thus providing a barrier to entry to the other firms, which would like to enter the industry.

(ii) **Large Capital Investment:** Some industries which are capital intensive involve huge investments, for example, iron and steel and shipbuilding. Since not everyone who is interested in setting up a factory can afford such investments, this again acts as a barrier to entry.

(iii) **Absolute Cost Advantages:** In case the existing firms in the industry have cost advantages, for example, in purchasing raw materials and in the techniques of production, a new firm will not find it easy to enter and operate in the industry.

(iv) **Mergers Between Firms:** Firms in an industry may often reduce the competition among themselves by merging with each other. New entrants to the industry may feel discouraged by the presence of such mergers.

(v) **Economies of Large Scale:** When a firm goes in for large scale production and reaps the benefit of the economies of scale, the smaller firms in the industry, which cannot join the rat race, may opt out of the industry.

It is because of all these factors that oligopoly may emerge in an industry.

RECAP

- The firm may be in a position to control a large part of the sales of the good, thus providing a barrier to entry.
- Some industries which are capital intensive involve huge investments, for example, iron and steel and shipbuilding.
- In case the existing firms in the industry have cost advantages, a new firm will not find it easy to enter and operate in the industry.
- Firms in an industry may often reduce the competition among themselves by merging with each other.
- When a firm goes in for large-scale production and reaps the benefit of the economies of scale, the smaller firms in the industry, which cannot join the rat race, may opt out of the industry.

CHARACTERISTICS OF OLIGOPOLY

Oligopoly is characterized by the following:

(i) A few dominant firms which produce a major part of the total industry output.

(ii) Since there are only a few firms in the industry, the actions of one firm influence the other firm in the industry. The output and price decisions made by one firm in the industry have a significant impact on the profits of the other firm in the industry. Thus, there exists a mutual interdependence between the firms, which provides them with an incentive to go in for a non-price competition in their objective of profit maximization.

(iii) The barrier to entry reduces the threat of entry into the industry, thus enabling the firms to maximize their profits in the long run.

Thus, we find that in an oligopoly since there are a very few firms in the industry they are mutually interdependent. The price and output decision of one firm affect the other firms in the industry. This leads to a reaction from the other firms. Different firms may react in different ways depending on their circumstances. It is because of this very fact that there is no set pattern in an oligopoly. Thus, we cannot define and construct a demand curve for an oligopolist as in the other market structures. Hence, there does not exist a general theory of oligopoly. There exist many models each based on a different set of behavioural assumptions. We here attempt an analysis of some of these models.

RECAP

- A few dominant firms produce a major part of the total industry output.
- Since there are only a few firms in the industry, the actions of one firm influence the other firm in the industry. Thus, there exists mutual interdependence between the firms.
- The barrier to entry reduces the threat of entry into the industry, thus enabling the firms to maximize their profits in the long run.
- There is no set pattern in an oligopoly. There exist many models each based on a different set of behavioural assumptions.

MODELS OF NON-COLLUSIVE OLIGOPOLY

Under non-collusive oligopoly, there are no implicit or explicit agreements relating to price or to the sharing of the market.

Cournot Duopoly Model

The model was developed by the French economist Augustin Cournot in 1838. The assumptions in the model are as follows:

(i) There are only two firms, Firm A and Firm B, in the industry selling spring water, which is assumed to be a homogenous good.

(ii) There are constant costs of production.

(iii) The firms sell their good in a market, where the demand curve is linear.

(iv) The behavioural assumption made in this model is that each firm in its attempt at profit maximization assumes that the other firm will keep its output constant.

Figure 12.1 depicts the Cournot Duopoly model. There are many situations depending on what Firm A assumes about Firm B's output:

(i) If Firm A assumes that Firm B will produce nothing, then Firm A's demand curve will be D_A (0) and will also be the market demand curve. D_A (0) is the demand curve of Firm A assuming that firm B produces a zero output. The figure also depicts the corresponding marginal revenue curve of Firm A as MR_A (0). MR_A (0) intersects the MC_A at point E_1 to determine Firm A's profit-maximizing output at 50 units. Thus, when Firm B produces a zero output, Firm A's output is 50. In Figure 12.2, this data can be plotted to arrive at the coordinate (0, 50).

(ii) If Firm A assumes that Firm B will produce 50 units, then Firm A's demand curve will be D_A (50). D_A (50) is the demand curve of Firm A assuming that firm B produces 50 units of the output. The figure depicts the corresponding marginal revenue curve of Firm A as MR_A (50). MR_A (50)

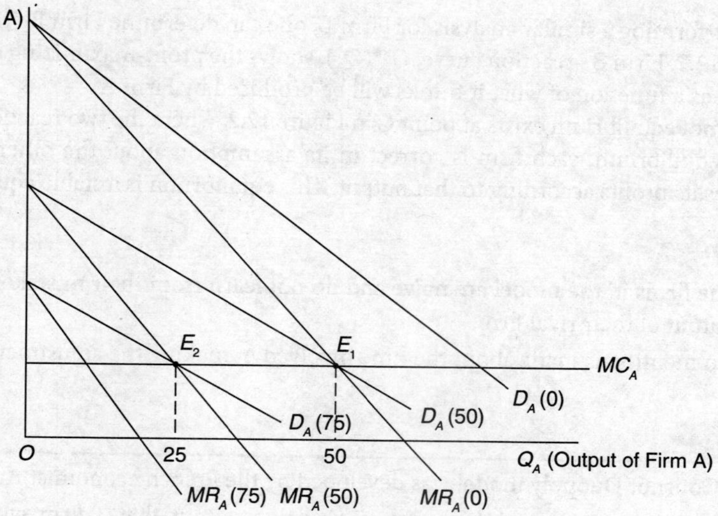

Figure 12.1 Cournot Duopoly Model

intersects the MC_A at point E_2 to determine Firm A's profit-maximizing output at 25 units. Thus, when Firm B produces 50 units of the output, Firm A's output is 25. Again in Figure 12.2, this can be plotted to arrive at the coordinate (50, 25).

By repeating this exercise with different levels of output and then by plotting them in Figure 12.2, one can arrive at Firm A's reaction curve. A reaction curve shows the profit-maximizing output that a firm will produce expressed as a function of what it thinks will be produced by the other firm. Firm A's reaction curve, $Q_A^*(Q_B)$ shows the profit-maximizing output that it will produce expressed as a function of what it thinks will be produced by Firm B.

A reaction curve shows the profit maximizing output that a firm will produce expressed as a function of what it thinks will be produced by the other firm.

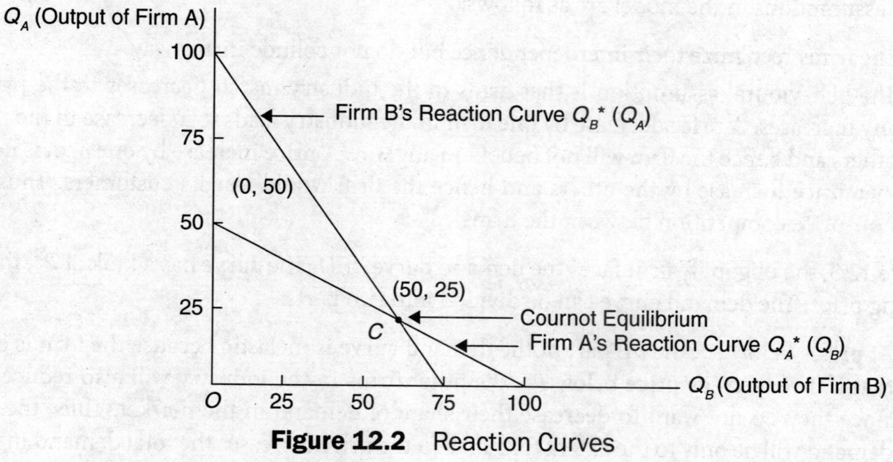

Figure 12.2 Reaction Curves

By performing a similar analysis for Firm B, one can determine Firm B's reaction curve, $Q_B{}^*(Q_A)$, as in Figure 12.2. Firm B's reaction curve, $Q_B{}^*(Q_A)$, shows the profit-maximizing output that it will produce expressed as a function of what it thinks will be produced by Firm A.

Cournot equilibrium exists at point *C* in Figure 12.2, where the two reaction curves intersect. At the Cournot equilibrium, each firm is correct in its assumption about the other firm's output and thus it maximizes its profits according to that output. This equilibrium is a stable equilibrium.

Criticism

(i) The firms in the model are naïve and do not learn from their mistakes about the past pattern of output of their rival firm.

(ii) No mention is made about the time involved in making the adjustments.

RECAP

- The Cournot Duopoly model was developed by the French economist Augustin Cournot.
- A reaction curve shows the profit-maximizing output that a firm will produce expressed as a function of what it thinks will be produced by the other firm.
- Cournot equilibrium exists at the point, where the two reaction curves intersect.
- At the Cournot equilibrium, each firm is correct in its assumption about the other firm's output and thus it maximizes its profits in according to that output.

SWEEZY'S KINKED DEMAND CURVE MODEL

The kinked demand curve model was developed by Paul Sweezy in 1939. The model attempts at explaining as to why prices are rigid or sticky in spite of moderate changes in demand and cost under conditions of oligopoly. The argument, which is generally given, is that in such market structures where there are only a few firms which are interdependent on each other if a firm reduces its price other firms in the industry will also match the decrease in price. Hence, the firm, which initially reduced the price, will not be in any way better off. If a firm increases its price, other firms in the industry will not increase their price. Hence, the firm which initially increased the price will suffer a loss. Hence, firms are unwilling to change the price of their good.

The assumptions in the model are as follows:

(i) The firms recognize their interdependence but do not collude in any way.

(ii) The behavioural assumption is that firms in the industry match decreases in the price but not any increases. A price decrease by one firm in the industry leads to a decrease in the price by the others and hence the firm will not benefit in any way. A price increase by one firm is not matched by a price increase by the others and hence the firm would lose its customers. Thus, there is a non-price competition between the firms.

In Figure 12.3, the oligopoly firm faces the demand curve *dED*. The curve has a kink at P^*, the currently prevailing price. The demand curve can be divided into two parts:

(i) At prices below P^*, the *dE* part of the demand curve is inelastic because the firm is of the belief that if it reduces its price below P^*, the other firms in the industry will also reduce their price since they do not want to decrease their share of demand in the market. Thus, the increase in demand will be only to the extent that a fall in the price increases the total demand in the market.

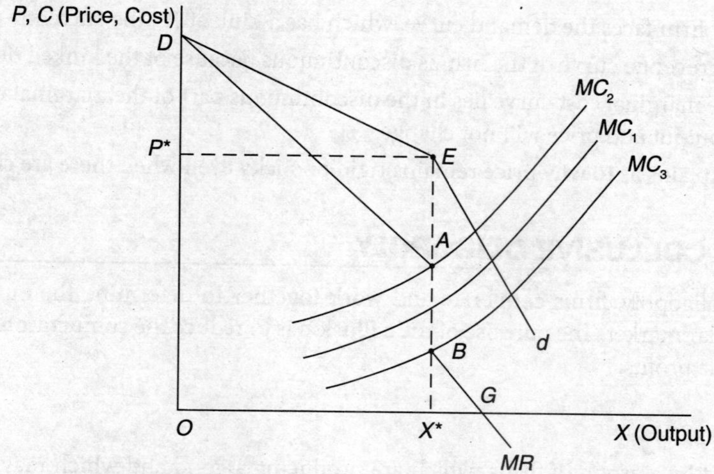

Figure 12.3 Sweezy's Kinked Demand Curve Model

(ii) At prices above P^*, the *ED* part of the demand curve is elastic because the firm is of the belief that if it raises its price above P^*, the other firms in the industry will not increase their price. Thus, the firm will experience a decrease in its sales and also in its share of the market demand.

The marginal revenue curve of the firm, *DABG*, is discontinuous because of the Kinked demand curve. The segment *BG* corresponds to the elastic part *dE*, while the segment *DA* corresponds to the inelastic part *ED* of the demand curve. Due to the kink, there exists a gap or discontinuity *AB* in the marginal revenue curve.

If the marginal cost is given by the curve MC_1, the firm will be in equilibrium producing an output OX^* and selling it at a price OP^*. Suppose that the marginal cost increases to MC_2 or decreases to MC_3, the firm's equilibrium output will continue to be OX^* and the equilibrium price will be OP^*. Thus, as long as the marginal cost curve lies in the discontinuous part of the marginal revenue curve, the equilibrium output and price will not change. Thus, the model explains as to why price remains rigid or sticky even when there are changes in costs.

Criticism

(i) The theory is not able to explain as to how the firms arrive at the particular price OP^*. The theory also does not explain as to how one can arrive at the price or the height at which the kink will occur.

(ii) Empirical evidence shows that often firms may match not only price decreases, but also price increases.

RECAP

- The kinked demand curve model was developed by Paul Sweezy in 1939.
- The model attempts at explaining as to why prices are rigid or sticky in spite of moderate changes in demand and cost under the conditions of oligopoly.

- The oligopoly firm faces the demand curve, which has a kink at P^*, the currently prevailing price.
- The marginal revenue curve of the firm is discontinuous because of the kinked demand curve.
- As long as the marginal cost curve lies in the discontinuous part of the marginal revenue curve, the equilibrium output and price will not change.
- The model explains as to why price remains rigid or sticky even when there are changes in costs.

MODELS OF COLLUSIVE OLIGOPOLY

Under collusive oligopoly, firms cooperate and work together to determine the output and the price levels in a particular market. The purpose of the collusion is to reduce the competition between the firms and to increase the profits.

Cartels

A cartel is formed by a group of firms, which are producing a good and which may explicitly agree to coordinate their policies to set a price and to increase the profits of the member firms. Often quotas may be fixed for each member. The Organization of Petroleum Exporting Countries (OPEC) is an international cartel of the oil-producing countries.

There are different types of cartels. Figure 12.4 depicts the centralized cartel. Suppose that there are four firms in the cartel producing a homogenous good. The prices of the input remain constant. *D* is the market demand curve while *MR* is the corresponding marginal revenue curve. By summing horizontally the short-run marginal cost curves of the four firms in the industry, one can obtain ΣMC. *MR* intersects ΣMC at point *E* to determine the equilibrium, which is a monopoly solution. The equilibrium output is OX^* while the equilibrium price is OP^*. Once the equilibrium output is determined, it is allocated among the member firms. The profits are also distributed among the members depending on the size of the firm.

The conditions necessary for a cartel to be successful are as follows:

(i) The member firms should agree on the output and the price to be charged by the cartel.
(ii) It is necessary that the demand for the good is not price elastic.
(iii) A major part of the world's production of the good must be controlled by the cartel.

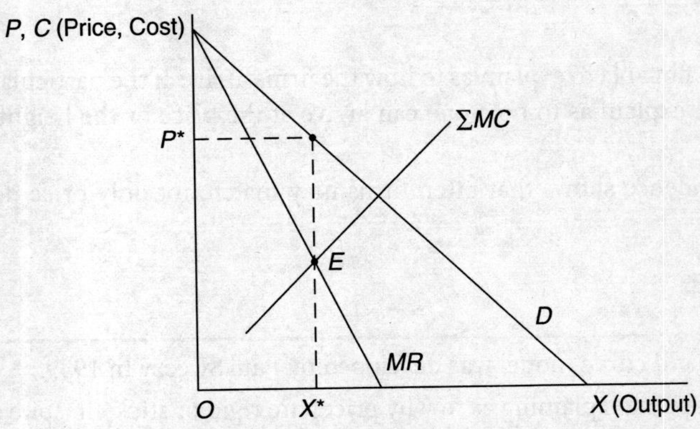

Figure 12.4 Centralized Cartel

Criticism

(i) There may be mistakes in estimating the market demand, which may affect the marginal revenue curve and thus the estimation of the equilibrium price.

(ii) Due to the problems in the availability of data, there may be mistakes in estimating the marginal cost.

(iii) The negotiations in the cartel may take too long, thus making the estimations obsolete.

(iv) The threat of entry may prevent the cartel from charging a high price for their product.

RECAP

- Under collusive oligopoly, firms cooperate and work together to determine the output and the price levels in a particular market.
- The purpose of the collusion is to reduce the competition between the firms and to increase the profits.
- A cartel is formed by a group of firms, which are producing a good and which may explicitly agree to coordinate their policies to set a price and to increase the profits of the member firms.
- In a centralized cartel, the equilibrium is a monopoly solution.
- Once the equilibrium output is determined, it is allocated among the member firms.

PRICE LEADERSHIP

Price leadership is another oligopoly model, where one firm sets the price while the other firms in the industry follow the firm. One firm may be recognized as the leader implicitly and the other firms in the industry become the price followers of this firm. There are different forms of price leadership. We here focus on price leadership by a dominant firm.

In Figure 12.5, there is a dominant firm, which supplies a large portion of the industry output while the remainder of the output is supplied by the group of the smaller firms or the fringe firms. The large firm may fix a price at which it maximizes its profits and then the smaller firms, acting as perfect competitors, accept the price and determine its output.

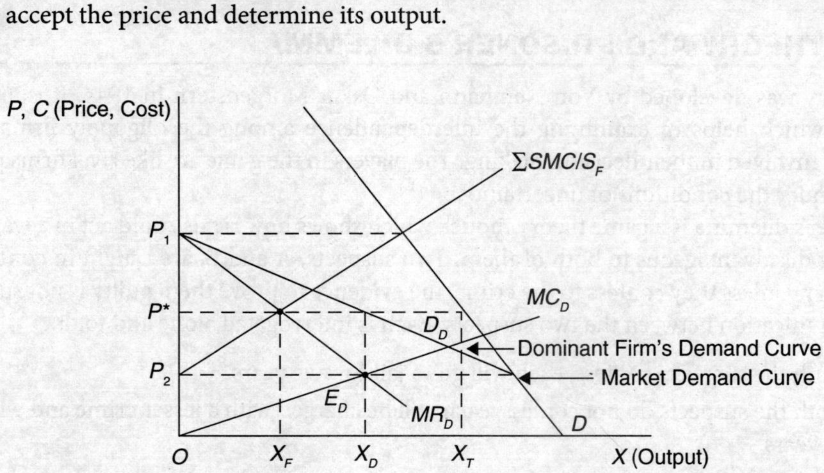

Figure 12.5 Price Leadership by a Dominant Firm

In the figure, the market demand curve is given by D while the supply curve is given by S_F. In fact, S_F is the aggregate of the marginal cost curve of the fringe (or the smaller) firms. D_D, the demand curve of the dominant firm, can be drawn as the difference between the market demand curve and the supply curve of the fringe firms.

At price P_1, since the entire market demand can be satisfied by the fringe firms, the demand from the dominant firm is zero. At price P_2, since the supply by the fringe firms is zero, the entire market demand is satisfied by the dominant firm. Between the prices P_1 and P_2, the dominant firm's demand curve is given by D_D. MR_D is the marginal revenue curve while MC_D is the marginal cost curve corresponding to the demand curve D_D.

MR_D and MC_D intersect at point E_D to determine the dominant firm's equilibrium output at OX_D and the equilibrium price at OP^*. The output of the fringe firms at this price is OX_F. Thus,

$$OX_T = OX_D + OX_F$$

Criticism

(i) It has often been noticed that the price leader is not only a large firm but it should also be a low-cost firm. Then, alone it can survive as the price leader.

(ii) Under barometric price leadership, the leader is one with a good knowledge about the conditions in the market. He may not be a large firm or a low-cost firm.

(iii) Often the leadership may undergo a change due to inventions and innovations.

RECAP

- Price leadership is an oligopoly model, where one firm sets the price while the other firms in the industry follow this firm.
- One firm may be recognized as the leader implicitly and the other firms in the industry become the price followers of the firm.

GAMES THEORY AND PRISONER'S DILEMMA

Game theory was developed by Von Neumann and Oskar Morgenstern in 1944. It is a mathematical technique, which helps in examining the interdependence among the oligopoly firms and also the uncertainty involved in their decision making. The players in the game are like rival firms planning their strategies under the conditions of uncertainty.

Prisoner's dilemma is a game theory model, which shows how rivals could act in a way which could be mutually disadvantageous to both of them. Two suspects, A and B, are caught in connection with a bank robbery. Unless they confess to the crime, the evidence to prove them guilty is not sufficient. There is no communication between the two suspects. Each is interrogated alone and told:

(i) If both the suspects confess, each will go to jail for five years.

(ii) If both the suspects do not confess, each will be charged with a lesser crime and will go to jail for two years.

(iii) If one of the suspects alone confesses, then his sentence will be reduced to just one year while the other who does not confess will get a 10 year sentence.

BOX 12.1

The Prisoner's Dilemma was first presented by Merrill Flood and Melvin Dresher in the year 1950. Later it was formalized by Albert W. Trucker. Many articles have been published about this game. It is a zero sum game. It is often applied in situations where there are two entities who could actually gain if they cooperate with each other but due to circumstances are not able to do so.

The outcomes given above can be illustrated in the form of a payoff matrix as in Table 12.1 below.

Table 12.1 Payoff Matrix for the Two Prisoners Under Prisoner's Dilemma

		Prisoner A	
		Confesses	**Does not confess**
Prisoner B	**Confesses**	Prisoner A gets 5 years Prisoner B gets 5 years	Prisoner A gets 10 years Prisoner B gets 1 year
	Does not confess	Prisoner A gets 1 year Prisoner B gets 10 years	Prisoner A gets 2 years Prisoner B gets 2 years

If both the prisoners confess, both get a sentence of five years. If both the prisoners do not confess, both get a sentence of two years. If one confesses and the other does not, the one who confesses gets a reduced sentence of one year while the other who does not confess gets 10 years.

Given the above situation, it is obvious that there are two options before a prisoner: to confess or not confess. Prisoner A might try to reason out that if he does not confess (and if prisoner B confesses), he will go to jail for 10 years and if he confesses he will go to jail for five years (if prisoner B confesses) and for one year (if prisoner B does not confesses). Thus, prisoner A might find it best to confess. Similarly, prisoner B might arrive at the same conclusion and confess to the crime. By confessing, each prisoner is trying to get the best out of the worst possible outcomes. Actually, the better strategy for the two would be to not confess as then both get a sentence of just two years.

The prisoner dilemma model of game theory can be applied to oligopoly theory as the interdependence of the rival firms in an oligopoly is similar to that of the players in the model.

In Table 12.2, we consider a duopoly situation, where there are two firms, Firm A and Firm B producing a homogenous product. The two firms form an agreement to fix the price of the good. The options before them are to cheat or not to cheat on the agreement represented by the payoff matrix.

If both the firms collude, both share the monopoly profits. If Firm A cheats on Firm B, Firm A will earn an even higher level of profits. If Firm B cheats on Firm A, Firm B will earn an even higher level of profits. However, if both Firm A and Firm B cheat, then the cartel will not be successful and profits will be low for each firm.

Given the above situation, it is obvious that there are two options before the firms: to cheat or not to cheat. Firm A might try to reason out that

(i) If Firm A cheats, then Firm B's profits will be at a low level if it also cheats and at a very low level if it does not cheat.

(ii) If Firm A does not cheat, then Firm B's profits will be at a very high level (if Firm B cheats) and at a high level if it does not cheat.

Table 12.2 Payoff Matrix for the Two Firms Under Prisoner's Dilemma

		Firm A	
		Cheats	**Does not cheat**
Firm B	**Cheats**	Firm A earns low level of profits. Firm B earns low level of profits.	Firm A earns a very low level of profits. Firm B earns a very high level of profits.
	Does not cheat	Firm A earns a very high level of profits. Firm B earns a very low level of profits.	Firm A earns a high level of profits. Firm B earns a high level of profits.

Thus, Firm A might find it best to cheat. Similarly, Firm B might arrive at the same conclusion and cheat. Thus, the outcome in this model is similar to the prisoner's dilemma in that the two firms follow the strategies, which may appear to be the best if followed independently but when the two firms are considered together it may be the worst outcome possible. It is important to note that in case the game is repeated, a number of times between the firms the outcome may undergo a change. Both the firms may learn from their past mistakes and may not indulge in cheating.

RECAP

- Game theory is a mathematical technique, which helps in examining the interdependence among oligopoly firms and also the uncertainty involved in their decision making.
- Prisoner's dilemma is a game theory model, which shows how rivals could act in a way, which is mutually disadvantageous to both of them.
- By confessing, each prisoner is trying to get the best out of the worst possible outcomes.
- Actually, the better strategy for the two would be to not confess as then both get a sentence of just two years.
- The prisoner dilemma model of game theory can be applied to oligopoly theory.
- Two firms form an agreement to fix the price of the good.
- If both the firms collude, both share the monopoly profits.
- The outcome in this model is similar to the prisoner's dilemma in that the two firms follow the strategies, which may appear to be the best if followed independently but when the two firms are considered together it may be the worst outcome possible.

SUMMARY

INTRODUCTION

1. Oligopoly is a market structure, where there are a few sellers of the product, which may be homogenous or differentiated.
2. Duopoly is a situation, where there are just two sellers of the product.
3. Oligopoly may be a pure oligopoly when the product is homogenous or it may be a differentiated oligopoly when the product is differentiated.

CAUSES OF OLIGOPOLY

1. **Product Differentiation:** The firm may be in a position to control a large part of the sales of the good, thus providing a barrier to entry.
2. **Large Capital Investment:** Some industries which are capital intensive involve huge investments, for example, iron and steel and shipbuilding.
3. **Absolute Cost Advantages:** In case the existing firms in the industry have cost advantages, a new firm will not find it easy to enter and operate in the industry.
4. **Mergers Between Firms:** Firms in an industry may often reduce the competition among themselves by merging with each other.
5. **Economies of Large Scale:** When a firm goes in for large-scale production and reaps the benefit of the economies of scale, the smaller firms in the industry, which cannot join the rat race, may opt out of the industry.

CHARACTERISTICS OF OLIGOPOLY

1. A few dominant firms, which produce a major part of the total industry output.
2. Since there are only a few firms in the industry, the actions of one firm influence the other firm in the industry. Thus, there exists mutual interdependence between the firms.
3. The barrier to entry reduces the threat of entry into the industry, thus enabling the firms to maximize their profits in the long run.
4. There is no set pattern in an oligopoly. There exist many models each based on a different set of behavioural assumptions.

MODELS OF NON-COLLUSIVE OLIGOPOLY

Non-collusive oligopoly is one where there are no implicit or explicit agreements relating to price or to the sharing of the market.

Cournot Duopoly Model

1. The model was developed by the French economist, Augustin Cournot, in 1838.
2. The assumptions in the model are: there are only two firms, Firm A and Firm B, in the industry selling spring water, which is assumed to be a homogenous good; there are constant costs of production; the firms sell their good in a market, where the demand curve is linear; each firm in its attempt at profit maximization assumes that the other firm will keep its output constant.
3. One can arrive at Firm A's reaction curve. A reaction curve shows the profit-maximizing output that a firm will produce expressed as a function of what it thinks will be produced by the other firm.
4. Firm A's reaction curve, $Q_A^*(Q_B)$ shows the profit-maximizing output that it will produce expressed as a function of what it thinks will be produced by Firm B.
5. Firm B's reaction curve, $Q_B^*(Q_A)$ shows the profit-maximizing output that it will produce expressed as a function of what it thinks will be produced by Firm A.
6. Cournot equilibrium exists at the point *C*, where the two reaction curves intersect.
7. At the Cournot equilibrium, each firm is correct in its assumption about the other firm's output and thus it maximizes its profits according to that output.
8. This equilibrium is a stable equilibrium.
9. **Criticism:** The firms in the model are naïve and do not learn from their mistakes about the past pattern of output of their rival firm; no mention is made about the time involved in making the adjustments.

Sweezy's Kinked Demand Curve Model

1. The kinked demand curve model was developed by Paul Sweezy in 1939.
2. The model attempts at explaining as to why prices are rigid or sticky in spite of moderate changes in demand and cost under the conditions of oligopoly.

3. The assumptions in the model are: the firms recognize their interdependence but do not collude in any way; firms in the industry match decreases in the price but not any increases.
4. The oligopoly firm faces the demand curve, which has a kink at P^*, the currently prevailing price.
5. The demand curve can be divided into two parts.
6. At prices below P^*, the dE part of the demand curve is inelastic.
7. At prices above P^*, the ED part of the demand curve is elastic.
8. The marginal revenue curve of the firm is discontinuous because of the kinked demand curve.
9. Due to the kink, there exists a gap or discontinuity AB in the marginal revenue curve.
10. As long as the marginal cost curve lies in the discontinuous part of the marginal revenue curve, the equilibrium output and price will not change.
11. Thus, the model explains as to why price remains rigid or sticky even when there are changes in costs.
12. Criticism: The theory is not able to explain as to how the firms arrive at the particular price OP^*; the theory also does not explain as to how one can arrive at the price or the height at which the kink will occur; empirical evidence shows that often firms may match not only price decreases, but also price increases.

MODELS OF COLLUSIVE OLIGOPOLY

Cartels

1. A cartel is formed by a group of firms, which are producing a good and which may explicitly agree to coordinate their policies to set a price and to increase the profits of the member firms.
2. In a centralized cartel, the equilibrium is a monopoly solution.
3. Once the equilibrium output is determined, it is allocated among the member firms.
4. The conditions necessary for a cartel to be successful are: the member firms should agree on the output and the price to be charged by the cartel; the demand for the good should not be price elastic; a major part of the world's production of the good must be controlled by the cartel.
5. **Criticism:** There may be mistakes in estimating the market demand; due to the problems in the availability of data there may be mistakes in estimating the marginal cost; threat of entry may prevent the cartel from charging a high price for their product.

Price Leadership

1. Price leadership is another oligopoly model, where one firm sets the price while the other firms in the industry follow this firm.
2. One firm may be recognized as the leader implicitly and the other firms in the industry become the price followers of this firm.
3. We here focus on price leadership by a dominant firm.
4. At the equilibrium price OP^*, the dominant firm's output and the fringe firm's output equal the total industry output or $OX_T = OX_D + OX_F$.
5. **Criticism:** It has often been noticed that the price leader is not only a large firm, but it should also be a low-cost firm. Then, alone it can survive as the price leader; under barometric price leadership, the leader is one with a good knowledge about the conditions in the market; often, the leadership may undergo a change due to inventions and innovations.

Games Theory and Prisoner's Dilemma

1. Game theory was developed by Von Neumann and Oskar Morgenstern in 1944.
2. It is a mathematical technique, which helps in examining the interdependence among the oligopoly firms and also the uncertainty involved in their decision making.
3. The players in the game are like rival firms planning their strategies under the conditions of uncertainty.

4. Prisoner's dilemma is a Game theory model, which shows how rivals could act in a way, which is mutually disadvantageous to both of them.
5. Two suspects, A and B, are caught in connection with a bank robbery. Unless they confess to the crime, the evidence to prove them guilty is not sufficient.
6. There is no communication between the two suspects.
7. It is obvious that there are two options before a prisoner: to confess or not to confess.
8. Prisoner A might find it best to confess. Similarly, prisoner B might arrive at the same conclusion and confess to the crime.
9. By confessing, each prisoner is trying to get the best out of the worst possible outcomes.
10. Actually, the better strategy for the two would be to not confess as then both get a sentence of just two years.
11. The prisoner dilemma model of game theory can be applied to oligopoly theory as the interdependence of the rival firms in an oligopoly is similar to that of the players in the model.
12. We consider a duopoly situation, where there are two firms, Firm A and Firm B, producing a homogenous product.
13. The two firms form an agreement to fix the price of the good.
14. The options before them are to cheat or not to cheat as represented by the payoff matrix.
15. If both the firms collude, both share the monopoly profits.
16. The outcome in this model is similar to the prisoner's dilemma in that the two firms follow the strategies, which may appear to be the best if followed independently but when the two firms are considered together it may be the worst outcome possible.
17. In case the game is repeated, a number of times between the firms the outcome may undergo a change.

REVIEW QUESTIONS

TRUE OR FALSE QUESTIONS

1. Oligopoly is a market structure, where there are a few sellers of the product, which may be homogenous or differentiated.
2. Under oligopoly since there are only a few firms in the industry, the actions of one firm do not influence the other firm in the industry.
3. Under collusive oligopoly, there are no implicit or explicit agreements relating to price or to the sharing of the market.
4. The Kinked demand curve model attempts at explaining as to why prices are rigid or sticky.
5. Under collusive oligopoly, firms cooperate and work together to determine the output and the price levels in a particular market.

SHORT ANSWER QUESTIONS

1. What are the causes of oligopoly? Discuss.
2. Discuss the characteristics of oligopoly?
3. 'Cournot equilibrium exists at the point, where the two reaction curves intersect'. Comment.
4. In the kinked demand curve model, why do firms match only price decreases and not price increases?
5. What is the prisoner's dilemma? Explain briefly.

LONG ANSWER QUESTIONS

1. Explain Cournot's Duopoly model. What are reaction curves?
2. Explain Sweezy's kinked demand curve model? Why does the demand curve have a kink?

3. What is a cartel? How is the equilibrium price and output determined in a cartel?
4. What is price leadership? Analyse the model of price leadership by a dominant firm.
5. 'Prisoner's dilemma is a game theory model, which shows how rivals could act in a way, which could be mutually disadvantageous to both of them'. Comment.

ANSWERS

TRUE OR FALSE QUESTIONS

1. **True.** Oligopoly may be a pure oligopoly when the product is homogenous or it may be a differentiated oligopoly when the product is differentiated.
2. **False.** Under oligopoly, since there are only a few firms in the industry, the actions of one firm influence the other firm in the industry. The output and price decisions made by one firm in the industry have a significant impact on the profits of the other firm in the industry.
3. **False.** Under Non-collusive oligopoly, there are no implicit or explicit agreements relating to price or to the sharing of the market.
4. **True.** The kinked demand curve model was developed by Paul Sweezy in 1939. The model attempts at explaining as to why prices are rigid or sticky in spite of moderate changes in demand and cost under the conditions of oligopoly.
5. **True.** Under collusive oligopoly, firms cooperate and work together to determine the output and the price levels in a particular market. The purpose of the collusion is to reduce the competition between the firms and increase the profits.

Capital Budgeting and the Decision to Invest

13

After studying this chapter, you should be able to understand:

- ✓ *Capital budgeting is the process, which involves the planning of the capital expenditures in the various investment projects.*
- ✓ *Capital budgeting or the planning of long-term expenditures is very crucial for a firm.*
- ✓ *Capital budgeting can increase the value of a firm.*
- ✓ *If the present value of the future cash flow from the project is smaller than the initial cost of the project, then the firm should not undertake the project.*
- ✓ *The firm will determine its optimum stock of capital by producing at the level, where the marginal revenue productivity of capital equals the marginal cost of capital.*
- ✓ *In deciding among two or more projects, the decision rule using the payback criterion is to opt for that project, which has the shortest payback period.*
- ✓ *In deciding among two or more projects, the decision rule for a firm using the net discounted present value criterion is to opt for that project whose net present value is positive and reject a project with a negative net present value.*
- ✓ *In deciding among two or more projects, the decision rule for a firm using the internal rate of return criterion is to opt for that project whose internal rate of return is greater than the market rate of interest.*

INTRODUCTION

Our focus till now has been on issues relating to demand, production, cost and the market structure, where all along we had assumed that the stock of capital is given. This chapter deals with the investment. Investment involves an increase in the capital stock. In other words, it is an addition to the capital stock.

It is important to note that as a factor of production capital has certain features, which make it possible to distinguish it from the other factors. Unlike the other factors, it yields returns over a number of years. These returns have to be discounted to find the present value and then compared with the cost of the capital asset before a final decision is made relating to the investment in the capital asset.

WHAT IS CAPITAL BUDGETING?

Capital budgeting is the process, which involves the planning of the capital expenditures in the various investment projects. Only those investment projects are included here, which are expected to yield returns beyond one year. It is also called long-term investment analysis as it involves only long-term capital expenditure.

Capital budgeting is the process, which involves the planning of the capital expenditures in the various investment projects.

Capital expenditure is expenditure on the projects, which yield a return beyond one year, for example, expenditure on building, machinery and research and development. Short-term capital expenditures, for example, expenditure on inventories, which can be adjusted in the short run are not included. Only capital expenditures, which are at least for a year, are considered under capital budgeting.

RECAP

- Capital budgeting is the process which involves the planning of the capital expenditures in the various investment projects.
- Capital expenditure is expenditure on the projects, which yield a return beyond one year, for example, expenditure on building, machinery and research and development.
- Only capital expenditures, which are at least for a year, are considered under capital budgeting.

SIGNIFICANCE OF CAPITAL BUDGETING

Capital budgeting or the planning of long-term expenditures is very crucial for a firm. This is due to many following reasons:

(i) Capital expenditure is very expensive and, in general, irreversible. This is because investments in machinery, capital equipments and others cannot be reverted back as their resale value is very low and involves heavy costs. Hence, a careful planning is essential before long-term capital expenditure is undertaken.

(ii) A firm cannot survive in the long run, unless a well-planned capital expenditure is undertaken. Given the objectives of the firm, the various investment projects must be evaluated and then only the projects which are profitable for the firm must be undertaken. These projects affect the profitability of the firm in the long run and thus increase the firm's value.

RECAP

- Capital budgeting or the planning of long-term expenditures is very crucial for a firm.
- Capital expenditure is very expensive and, in general, irreversible.
- A firm cannot survive in the long run, unless a well-planned capital expenditure is undertaken.

STEPS IN CAPITAL BUDGETING

As already discussed, capital budgeting can increase the value of a firm. The steps involved in capital budgeting are as follows:

(i) **Determination of the Cost of the Project:** In capital budgeting, it is most important at the outset to determine the cost of the project under consideration. The cost of the project will include the capital expenditure on the machinery and equipment to be bought, the foreign exchange required if equipment is to be imported and the necessary expenses involved in the installation of the machinery.

(ii) **Estimation of the Cash Flows from the Project:** The next step involves the estimation of the net cash flows from the project to be undertaken. The cash flows will include cash outflows, which are the incremental costs incurred over the years when the project is operational while cash inflows are the incremental revenues generated over the years when the project is operational. The incremental net cash flows, which a project generates, are determined by taking the difference between the incremental cash inflows and the incremental cash outflows.

(iii) **Measurement of the Risk Involved in the Cash Flows:** As the cash flows from the investments occur in the future, which is uncertain, there is an element of risk attached to the cash flows. This risk factor has to be accounted for in estimating the cash flows and in deciding whether the investment project should be undertaken.

(iv) **Determination of the Appropriate Discount Rate:** The next step is to decide on the rate at which the cash flows should be discounted to arrive at the present value of the cash flows. In general, the opportunity cost of funds, which is the market rate of interest, is used for the purposes of discounting.

(v) **Obtaining the Present Value of the Future Cash Flows:** Once the decision has been made on the discount rate, the cash inflows and the cash outflows are both discounted to arrive at the net cash flows.

(vi) **Comparing the Present Value of the Future Cash Flow with the Project's Cost:** Once the present value of the future cash flow is arrived at, it is compared with the initial cost of the project, which is to be undertaken. If the present value of the future cash flow from the project is greater than the initial cost of the project, then in that case the firm should undertake the project as it will increase the value of the firm. If the present value of the future cash flow from the project is smaller than the initial cost of the project, then the firm should not undertake the project.

RECAP

- Capital budgeting can increase the value of a firm.
- In capital budgeting, it is most important at the outset to determine the cost of the project under consideration.
- The next step involves the estimation of the net cash flows from the project to be undertaken.
- The risk factor has to be accounted for in estimating the cash flows and in deciding whether the investment project should be undertaken.
- The next step is to decide on the rate at which the cash flows should be discounted to arrive at the present value of the cash flows.
- If the present value of the future cash flow from the project is smaller than the initial cost of the project, then the firm should not undertake the project.

DETERMINATION OF THE OPTIMUM LEVEL OF CAPITAL

We have seen that a profit maximizing firm will determine its optimum output at the level, where the marginal revenue equals the marginal cost of production. Similarly, the firm will determine its optimum stock of capital by producing at the level, where the marginal revenue productivity of capital equals the marginal cost of capital. Thus,

$$MRP_K = MC_K$$

where MRP_K is marginal revenue productivity of capital and MC_K is marginal cost of capital.

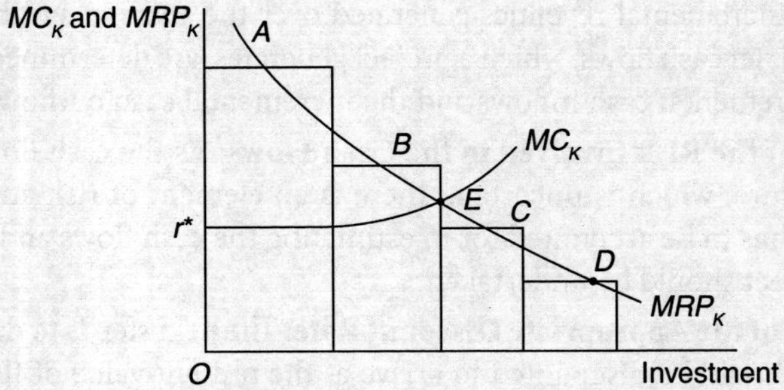

Figure 13.1 Optimum Level of Capital Stock

Figure 13.1 depicts the determination of the optimum stock of capital. The marginal cost of capital is given by the market rate of interest. Under a perfectly competitive market since the market rate of interest is given, marginal cost of capital will thus be constant at the rate of interest r^* as shown in the figure by the curve MC_K, which initially is parallel to the X axis. However, as the demand for capital increases, there is an increase in the market rate of interest as depicted by the rising part of the MC_K curve.

As far as marginal revenue productivity of capital is concerned, it can be written as

$$MRP_K = MPP \times P$$

where MPP is marginal physical productivity of capital and P is price of the good.

It is assumed that as the stock of capital increases, there occur diminishing returns or that the marginal physical productivity of capital diminishes. Thus, the marginal revenue productivity of capital curve slopes downwards. In fact, the marginal revenue productivity of capital curve represents the firm's demand curve for its capital stock.

Assume that a firm has four investment projects A, B, C and D from which it has to make a choice as to which project to undertake. Each project has a different marginal revenue productivity of capital. In Figure 13.1, the projects have been arranged in a descending order of marginal revenue productivity of capital to yield the demand curve for capital, which is step shaped. By joining the central points of the tops of the step-shaped curve, one can obtain a smooth marginal revenue productivity of capital curve as in the figure.

The figure shows that the marginal revenue productivity of capital curve intersects the marginal cost of capital curve at point E. Thus, the firm will invest only in projects A and B. As far as the other projects C and D are concerned, the marginal revenue productivity of capital from these projects is less than the marginal cost of capital. Hence, the firm will incur losses if it invests in these projects.

The optimum level of capital is determined theoretically at the intersection of the marginal revenue productivity of capital curve with the marginal cost of capital curve at point E. However, in practice, the projects under consideration have to be carefully evaluated before making the decision to invest.

RECAP

- The firm will determine its optimum stock of capital by producing at the level, where the marginal revenue productivity of capital equals the marginal cost of capital.
- It is assumed that as the stock of capital increases, there occur diminishing returns or that the marginal physical productivity of capital diminishes.

- The marginal revenue productivity of capital curve slopes downwards.
- The marginal revenue productivity of capital curve represents the firm's demand curve for its capital stock.

DECISION TO INVEST UNDER CERTAINTY

We are now in a position to discuss the decision to invest by the firm. We first discuss the case, where the decisions are taken under the conditions of certainty or in other words when there exists perfect knowledge. The investor possesses complete knowledge regarding the conditions prevailing in the market, about the availability of the different investment opportunities and also the costs and the returns on the various alternative projects. Three criteria are used to evaluate the profitability of projects under the conditions of certainty:

Payback Period Method

The payback period of a project is the number of years that it takes for the total net cash flows from the project to become equal to the total investment outlay involved in the project. In other words, it is the time taken by a project to recover the total investment outlay from its total net cash outflows.

$$\text{Payback period} = \frac{\text{Total investment outlay}}{\text{Total net cash outflows per period}}$$

Example 13.1: Suppose the total investment outlay on a project is ₹50,000 and the total net cash outflows per year are ₹10,000. The payback period can be calculated as follows:

$$\text{Payback period} = \frac{50{,}000}{10{,}000} = 5 \text{ years}$$

In deciding among two or more projects, the decision rule using the payback criterion is to opt for that project, which has the shortest payback period.

The limitations of the payback criterion are as follows:

(i) The method assumes that the cash flows are known by the firm with certainty. This may not always be true.

(ii) The total net cash flows from the projects after the payback period are not taken into account. It is necessary that the total net cash flows from the projects must be analysed.

(iii) The payback criterion does not discount the future net cash flows and thus does not consider the time value of money. The net cash flows earned by the firm in the earlier years have a greater value than those earned in the later years as they can be invested and a return can be earned on them.

Net Discounted Present Value Method

Here, the time value of money is involved since cash in hand has a greater value in that it provides liquidity and also can be invested to earn a return on it. In fact, a unit of money in the future is much less than a unit of money today.

To analyse the net discounted present value method, we examine the two aspects to an investment project, for example, the investment in a machine:

(i) The cost of the project which is to be incurred in the current year.

(ii) The returns from the project in the form of cash flows in the future, which cannot be simply added to arrive at the total net cash flows. This is because the returns accrue at different points in time. They have to be discounted at an interest rate.

To obtain the net present value of a project, a firm has to calculate the present value of the expected future net cash flows from the investment project under consideration and then to compare the value so obtained with the cost of the project. In deciding among two or more projects, the decision rule for a firm using the net discounted present value criterion is to opt for that project whose net present value is positive and reject a project with a negative net present value. The *NPV* can be calculated as follows:

$$NPV = -C + \frac{R_1}{1+i} + \frac{R_2}{(1+i)^2} + \frac{R_3}{(1+i)^3} + \cdots + \frac{R_N}{(1+i)^N}$$

where *NPV* is net present value, *C* is cost of the investment project, *i* is market rate of interest, and R_1, R_2, R_3, …, R_N is positive net cash flows from the project in 1, 2, 3 to *N* years.

The decision rules are as follows:

(i) The firm can accept the project if $NPV > 0$.

(ii) The firm can reject the project if $NPV < 0$.

(iii) The firm can accept or reject the project if $NPV = 0$.

An important consideration for the firm here is the choice of the discount rate, *i*. The firm can opt for the opportunity cost, which is the rate of return that the firm can earn by investing its funds in an alternative project with the same element of risk. Since here we are doing away with all uncertainties, the opportunity cost used for the purposes of discounting is the risk-free return, for example, the return that a firm can earn on investments made in government bonds.

Internal Rate of Return Method

The internal rate of return or the marginal efficiency of investment is another method of evaluating the profitability of a project. It is based on the concept of the net present value of the future cash flows from a project. The internal rate of return is the rate of discount, which equates the net present value of the future net cash flows to the investment cost of the project. In other words, it is the internal rate of return. Thus,

$$C = \frac{R_1}{1+r} + \frac{R_2}{(1+r)^2} + \frac{R_3}{(1+r)^3} + \cdots + \frac{R_N}{(1+r)^N}$$

where *C* is initial cost of the investment project, *r* is internal rate of return and R_1, R_2, R_3, …, R_N is positive net cash flows from the project in 1, 2, 3 to *N* years.

To obtain the internal rate of return on a project, the above equation will have to be solved. After finding the internal rate of return, the firm should compare the value so obtained with the market rate of interest (or the cost at which the firm obtains the capital). In deciding among two or more projects, the decision rule for a firm using the internal rate of return criterion is to opt for that project, whose internal rate of return is greater than the market rate of interest. Thus, it will be worthwhile for the firm to borrow from the market and invest in the project. Thus,

(i) The firm can invest in the project if $r > i$.

(ii) The firm can invest in the project if $r < i$.

(iii) The firm can invest in or reject the project if $r = i$.

BOX 13.1

For a financial manager, one of the most crucial decisions that he has to take is of capital budgeting. Past studies show that managers often prefer the internal rate of return method as compared with some of the other methods. However, recent data shows that the net present value method is the most popular method as a tool of capital budgeting.

Often a firm has only limited funds for purposes of investment. If a decision has to be made between several projects, then the firm can rank the projects in descending order of their internal rate of return. Then, the firm can opt for those projects, where the internal rate of return is highest.

RECAP

- In deciding among two or more projects, the decision rule using the payback criterion is to opt for that project, which has the shortest payback period.
- In deciding among two or more projects, the decision rule for a firm using the net discounted present value criterion is to opt for that project whose net present value is positive and reject a project with a negative net present value.
- In deciding among two or more projects, the decision rule for a firm using the internal rate of return criterion is to opt for that project, whose internal rate of return is greater than the market rate of interest.

SOURCES AND THE COST OF CAPITAL

In the earlier sections, we have focused on the demand for capital and the decision to invest under certainty. It is equally important for us to understand the two aspects to the supply of capital, the sources and the cost of capital.

Sources of Capital

The various sources of capital to a firm can be divided into internal and external sources.

(i) **Internal Sources:** These include

— Depreciation reserves, which a firm creates to replace the worn out capital.

— Retained earnings, which are the profits retained by a firm for purposes of investment.

Firms often rely on their internal sources of funds for reinvestments because there are large costs involved in raising funds from the market. Also, there are uncertainties involved when funds are raised from external sources. Use of internal funds for investments increases the market value of the stock of the firm.

(ii) **External Sources:** These are the funds raised by a firm from the market. They include:

— Issue of preferred and equity shares, which may involve heavy transaction costs and also have tax implications as dividend distributed thereon is not only tax deductible but is also subject to dividend distribution tax.

— Issue of bonds, where the total interest on the bonds is allowable as a business expenditure under income tax laws. However, too much borrowing through bonds may affect adversely the stocks of the firm. In case of liquidation of a company, the claims of the bondholders are settled before those of the shareholders.

— Borrowing from the financial institutions, for example, commercial banks and development banks.

Cost of Capital

The cost of capital is the price of capital. The cost may be implicit in terms of the opportunity cost, which is the return on the next best alternative use of the capital. Alternatively, the cost may be explicit in terms of the interest to be paid on the capital. It is because of this cost that the firm has to be careful in the selection of its investment projects.

RECAP

- Internal sources of capital to a firm include the depreciation reserves and the retained earnings.
- Use of internal funds for investments increases the market value of the stock of the firm.
- External sources of capital to a firm include the issue of preferred and equity shares, issue of bonds and borrowing from the financial institutions.
- The cost of capital is the price of capital.

DECISION TO INVEST UNDER RISK AND UNCERTAINTY

In the earlier section, we have discussed the decision to invest by a firm under the conditions of certainty. However, in reality, most of the decisions to invest are taken under situations of risk and certainty. The present section focuses on this aspect of the problem and on the different techniques, which a firm applies to find a solution to the problem.

Some Concepts

The following are some of the situations when a decision to invest under risk and uncertianity is made.

Certainty

Certainty is a situation, where there exists only one outcome to an investment decision and the investor is aware of that outcome.

It is a situation, where there exists perfect knowledge about the conditions prevailing in the market. Under the state of certainty, there exists only one outcome to an investment decision and the investor is aware of that outcome. For example, as far as investment in a fixed deposit is concerned, there is only one outcome of which the investor is aware. There are no possibilities of the investor not getting the interest on the fixed deposit or in facing problems in converting the deposit into cash.

Risk

Risk is a situation, where there exists more than one outcome to an investment decision and the investor is aware of (or can calculate) the probability of each outcome.

It is a situation, where there exists more than one outcome to an investment decision and the investor is aware of (or can calculate) the probability of each outcome. For example, as far as investment in a stock is concerned, there is more than one possible outcome of which the investor is aware of and can calculate the probability of each outcome on the basis of past experience.

Uncertainty

It is a situation, where there exists more than one outcome to an investment decision and the investor is not aware of (and cannot calculate) the probability of each outcome. For example, as far as the drilling of oil in a field is concerned, there are no past experiences in that field.

Uncertainty is a situation, where there exists more than one outcome to an investment decision and the investor is not aware of (and cannot calculate) the probability of each outcome.

Strategy

It is one of the various alternative actions that can be taken to achieve a desired goal.

States of Nature

It refers to the conditions, which exist in the long run and over which the investor does not have any control. These conditions influence the results of the strategy, for example recession, boom, etc.

Outcome

It is the result, which appears due to the implementation of the strategy.

Probability

It is the possibility of the occurrence of a given outcome. The sum of probabilities of all possible outcomes of each strategy will be equal to one.

Expected Value

It is the sum of the different outcomes of an investment multiplied by the probability of their occurrence.

Decision to Invest Under Risk

As already discussed, risk is a situation, where there exists more than one outcome to an investment decision and the investor is aware of (or can calculate) the probability of each outcome. Following are the methods used to make the decision to invest under risk.

Payoff Matrix Method

A payoff matrix lists the various outcomes, which are associated with the different strategies under various states of nature.

Each decision maker has to perform the following tasks:

(i) Give the objective of making a particular decision.
(ii) Make a decision on the strategies to be followed under the various states of nature, which can occur in an economy.
(iii) Each strategy under each of the states of nature should be assigned a pay-off.

Example 13.2: Table 13.1 depicts a payoff matrix, where an investor has to make a choice between two projects, A and B, under three different states of the economy, a boom, a normal situation and a recession.

It is obvious from Table 13.1 that since project A gives a higher expected value than project B, the investor will opt for project A. In case the expected values are the same for the different projects, then the standard deviation of the different projects can be used to arrive at a decision.

Table 13.1 A Payoff Matrix

Project A			
States of the Economy	**Probability**	**Outcome of the Investment**	**Expected Value**
Boom	0.25	₹300	₹ 75
Normal	0.50	₹250	₹125
Recession	0.25	₹200	₹ 50

Total expected value of Project A = 250

Project B			
Boom	0.25	₹300	₹ 75
Normal	0.50	₹250	₹125
Recession	0.25	₹100	₹ 25

Total expected value of Project B = 200

Risk-adjusted Discount Rate Method

In the calculation of the net present value, a risk-adjusted discount rate is used. Thus,

$$D = \frac{1}{i+\beta}$$

where D is risk-adjusted discount rate, i is market rate of interest (which is a risk-free discount rate) and β is risk probability.

$$\text{Risk-adjusted } NPV = -C + \frac{R_1}{1+i+\beta} + \frac{R_2}{(1+i+\beta)^2} + \frac{R_3}{(1+i+\beta)^3} + \cdots + \frac{R_N}{(1+i+\beta)^N}$$

where NPV is net present value, C is cost of the investment project, i is market rate of interest and R_1, R_2, R_3, … , R_N is positive net cash flows from the project in 1, 2, 3 to N years.

The decision rule is that the firm can accept the project if the risk-adjusted $NPV > 0$.

Probability Theory Approach

Under this method, the alternative outcomes of a project with the risks and the returns and the associated probabilities are considered. The returns are discounted to arrive at their present discounted values. The decision rule is the same that the firm can accept the project if the $NPV > 0$. The probability theory approach can be applied only if there are many investment projects, which involve a similar investment so that if one project is not successful the other projects can compensate for the loss.

Decision Tree Method

This is a graphical representation, where all the alternative investment decisions before a firm are arranged in a sequence with their expected outcomes under the various states of nature. Since the decisions and their outcomes are depicted in the form of the branches of a tree, this technique is called the decision tree approach.

In the construction of a decision tree, first the investor has to make a choice from the alternative investment strategies available to him. Then, the outcomes to the chosen strategies are arranged as branches of a tree. After determining the net-expected value of each project, the one with the greatest net-expected value is chosen. Thus, the decision tree depicts the whole range of decision options and their possible outcomes, thus guiding the investor in making a profitable and rational decision.

There are many other methods of making decisions to invest under the risk, which include the simulation and the sensitivity analysis.

Decision to Invest Under Uncertainty

We have observed that uncertainty is a situation, where there exists more than one outcome to an investment decision and the investor is not aware of the probability of each outcome. Thus, the decisions made here will be subjective. Following are the methods used to make the decision to invest under uncertainty.

Maximin Decision Criterion

Under this criterion, an investor first considers the various strategies and then finds the worst outcome possible under the different states of nature from those strategies. Then, from the worst possible outcomes, the outcome that gives the highest pay-off is chosen.

This criterion is criticized as a pessimistic way of making an investment decision. It assumes that the investor does not want to bear risks and thus aims at minimizing his risks. Thus, this decision criterion can be applied to the risk averters and not so much to those who are willing to take risks.

Minimax Regret Criterion

Under this criterion, an investor should choose a strategy, which minimizes the maximum regret from making a wrong decision. Regret is the difference between the pay-off from the best strategy and the given strategy under the state of nature, which is exactly the same in the two situations. In other words, regret can be said to be the opportunity cost of making an alternative investment decision.

This criterion is criticized as being subjective. However, it is considered to be better than the maximin criterion as it takes into consideration the opportunity cost of making an investment decision.

RECAP

- A payoff matrix lists the various outcomes, which are associated with different strategies under various states of nature.
- If project A gives a higher expected value than project B, the investor will opt for project A.
- Under the risk-adjusted discount rate method, the decision rule is that the firm can accept the project if the risk-adjusted $NPV > 0$.
- Under the Probability Theory Approach, the decision rule is the same that the firm can accept the project if the $NPV > 0$.
- Under the decision tree method, after determining the net-expected value of each project, the one with the greatest net-expected value is chosen.
- Under the maximin decision criterion from the worst possible outcomes, the outcome that gives the highest pay-off is chosen.
- Under the minimax regret criterion, an investor should choose a strategy, which minimizes the maximum regret from making a wrong decision.

SUMMARY

INTRODUCTION

1. The present chapter deals with investment.
2. Investment involves an increase in the capital stock.
3. It is important to note that as a factor of production capital has certain features, which make it possible to distinguish it from the other factors.
4. Unlike the other factors, capital yields returns over a number of years.
5. The returns have to be discounted to find the present value and then compared with the cost of the capital asset before a final decision is made relating to the investment in the capital asset.

WHAT IS CAPITAL BUDGETING?

1. Capital budgeting is the process, which involves the planning of the capital expenditures in the various investment projects.
2. It is also called long-term investment analysis as it involves only long-term capital expenditure.
3. Capital expenditure is expenditure on the projects, which yield a return beyond one year, for example, expenditure on building, machinery and research and development.
4. Only capital expenditures, which are at least for a year, are considered under capital budgeting.

SIGNIFICANCE OF CAPITAL BUDGETING

1. Capital expenditure is very expensive and, in general, irreversible.
2. A firm cannot survive in the long run, unless a well-planned capital expenditure is undertaken.

STEPS IN CAPITAL BUDGETING

1. **Determination of the Cost of the Project:** In capital budgeting, it is most important at the outset to determine the cost of the project under consideration.
2. **Estimation of the Cash Flows from the Project:** The incremental net cash flows, which a project generates, are determined by taking the difference between incremental cash inflows and incremental cash outflows.
3. **Measurement of the Risk Involved in the Cash Flows:** This risk factor has to be accounted for in estimating the cash flows and in deciding whether the investment project should be undertaken.
4. **Determination of the Appropriate Discount Rate:** In general, the opportunity cost of funds, which is the market rate of interest, is used for the purposes of discounting.
5. **Obtaining the Present Value of the Future Cash Flows:** Once the decision has been made on the discount rate, the cash inflows and the cash outflows are both discounted to arrive at the net cash flows.
6. **Comparing the Present Value of the Future Cash Flow with the Project's Cost:** If the present value of the future cash flow from the project is greater than the initial cost of the project, then, in that case, the firm should undertake the project as it will increase the value of the firm.

DETERMINATION OF THE OPTIMUM LEVEL OF CAPITAL

1. The firm will determine its optimum stock of capital by producing at the level, where the marginal revenue productivity of capital equals the marginal cost of capital. Thus $MRP_K = MC_K$.
2. In practice, the projects under consideration have to be carefully evaluated before making the decision to invest.

Decision to Invest Under Certainty

1. The investor possesses complete knowledge regarding the conditions prevailing in the market, about the availability of the different investment opportunities and also the costs and the returns on the various alternative projects.
2. Three criteria are used to evaluate the profitability of projects under the conditions of certainty.

3. **Payback Period Method:** The payback period is the time taken by a project to recover the total investment outlay from its total net cash outflows.
4. In deciding among two or more projects, the decision rule using the payback criterion is to opt for that project, which has the shortest payback period.
5. **Net Discounted Present Value Method:** Here, the time value of money is involved since cash in hand has a greater value in that it provides liquidity and also can be invested to earn a return on it.
6. In deciding among two or more projects, the decision rule for a firm using the net discounted present value criterion is to opt for that project whose net present value is positive and reject a project with a negative net present value.
7. The *NPV* can be calculated as follows:

$$NPV = -C + \frac{R_1}{1+i} + \frac{R_2}{(1+i)^2} + \frac{R_3}{(1+i)^3} + \cdots + \frac{R_N}{(1+i)^N}$$

8. **Internal Rate of Return Method:** The internal rate of return is the rate of discount, which equates the net present value of the future net cash flows to the investment cost of the project. In other words, it is the internal rate of return. Thus,

$$C = \frac{R_1}{1+r} + \frac{R_2}{(1+r)^2} + \frac{R_3}{(1+r)^3} + \cdots + \frac{R_N}{(1+r)^N}$$

9. In deciding among two or more projects, the decision rule for a firm using the internal rate of return criterion is to opt for that project, whose internal rate of return is greater than the market rate of interest.

Sources and the Cost of Capital

In the earlier sections, we have focused on the demand for capital and the decision to invest under certainty. It is equally important for us to understand the two aspects to the supply of capital, the sources and the cost of capital.

Sources of Capital

1. **Internal Sources:** These include depreciation reserves and retained earnings.
2. Firms often rely on their internal sources of funds for reinvestments because there are large costs involved in raising the funds from the market.
3. Also, there are uncertainties involved when funds are raised from external sources.
4. Use of internal funds for investments increases the market value of the stock of the firm.
5. **External Sources:** These are the funds raised by a firm from the market. They include issue of preferred and equity shares, sale of bonds and borrowing from the financial institutions.

Cost of Capital

1. The cost of capital is the price of capital.
2. The cost may be implicit in terms of the opportunity cost.
3. The cost may be explicit in terms of the interest to be paid on the capital.

Decision to Invest Under Risk and Uncertainty

1. In reality, most of the decisions to invest are taken under situations of risk and certainty.
2. The present section focuses on this aspect of the problem and on the different techniques, which a firm applies to find a solution to the problem.

Some Concepts

1. Certainty is a situation, where there exists perfect knowledge about the conditions prevailing in the market.
2. Risk is a situation, where there exists more than one outcome to an investment decision and the investor is aware of (or can calculate) the probability of each outcome.

3. Uncertainty is a situation, where there exists more than one outcome to an investment decision and the investor is not aware of (and cannot calculate) the probability of each outcome.
4. Strategy is one of the various alternative actions that can be taken to achieve a desired goal.
5. States of nature refers to the conditions, which exist in the long run and over which the investor does not have any control.
6. Outcome is the result, which appears due to the implementation of the strategy.
7. Probability is the possibility of the occurrence of a given outcome. The sum of probabilities of all possible outcomes of each strategy will be equal to one.
8. Expected value is the sum of the different outcomes of an investment multiplied by the probability of their occurrence.

Decision to Invest Under Risk

1. **Payoff Matrix Method:** A payoff matrix lists the various outcomes, which are associated with different strategies under various states of nature.
2. Each decision maker has to perform the following tasks:
   (a) Give the objective of making a particular decision.
   (b) Make a decision on the strategies to be followed under the various states of nature, which can occur in an economy.
   (c) Each strategy under each of the states of nature should be assigned a pay-off.
3. If project A gives a higher expected value than project B, the investor will opt for project A.
4. **Risk-adjusted Discount Rate Method:** In the calculation of the net present value, a risk-adjusted discount rate is used. Thus,

$$D = \frac{1}{i+\beta}$$

5. Risk-adjusted $NPV = -C + \frac{R_1}{1+i+\beta} + \frac{R_2}{(1+i+\beta)^2} + \frac{R_3}{(1+i+\beta)^3} + \cdots + \frac{R_N}{(1+i+\beta)^N}$
6. The decision rule is that the firm can accept the project if the risk-adjusted $NPV > 0$.
7. Under the probability theory approach, the alternative outcomes of a project with the risks and the returns and the associated probabilities are considered. The returns are discounted to arrive at their present discounted values. The decision rule is the same that the firm can accept the project if the $NPV > 0$.
8. The decision tree method is a graphical representation, where all the alternative investment decisions before a firm are arranged in a sequence with their expected outcomes under the various states of nature. Since the decisions and their outcomes are depicted in the form of the branches of a tree, this technique is called the decision tree approach.
9. After determining the net-expected value of each project, the one with the greatest net-expected value is chosen.

Decision to Invest Under Uncertainty

1. Uncertainty is a situation, where there exists more than one outcome to an investment decision and the investor is not aware of the probability of each outcome.
2. Under the maximin decision criterion, an investor first considers the various strategies and then finds the worst outcome possible under the different states of nature from those strategies. Then, from the worst possible outcomes, the outcome that gives the highest pay-off is chosen.
3. This criterion is criticized as a pessimistic way of making an investment decision.
4. Under the minimax regret criterion, an investor should choose a strategy, which minimizes the maximum regret from making a wrong decision.
5. Regret can be said to be the opportunity cost of making an alternative investment decision.
6. This criterion is considered to be better than the maximin criterion.

REVIEW QUESTIONS

TRUE OR FALSE QUESTIONS

1. Capital budgeting is the process, which involves the planning of the capital expenditures in the various investment projects.
2. Capital budgeting can decrease the value of a firm.
3. The firm will determine its optimum stock of capital by producing at the level, where the marginal revenue productivity of capital equals the marginal cost of capital.
4. Certainty is a situation, where there exists only one outcome to an investment decision and the investor is aware of that outcome.
5. Risk is a situation, where there exists more than one outcome to an investment decision and the investor is not aware of the probability of each outcome.

SHORT ANSWER QUESTIONS

1. What is capital budgeting?
2. What is the significance of capital budgeting? Discuss.
3. What is the internal rate of return method? Discuss.
4. Analyse the various sources of capital to a firm?
5. Discuss the following concepts:
   (a) Certainty
   (b) Risk
   (c) Uncertainty

LONG ANSWER QUESTIONS

1. What are the steps involved in capital budgeting? Discuss.
2. How does a firm determine its optimum level of capital? Discuss.
3. Discuss any two criteria used to evaluate the profitability of projects under the conditions of certainty.
4. How does a firm make its decision to invest under risk? Discuss with the help of the
   (a) Payoff matrix method
   (b) Risk-adjusted discount rate method
5. How does a firm make its decision to invest when there exists uncertainty? Explain using the maximin decision criterion and the minimax regret criterion.

ANSWERS

TRUE OR FALSE QUESTIONS

1. **True.** Capital budgeting is the process, which involves the planning of the capital expenditures in the various investment projects. Only those investment projects are included here, which are expected to yield returns beyond one year. It is also called long-term investment analysis as it involves only long-term capital expenditure.
2. **False.** Capital budgeting can increase the value of a firm. The investment projects affect the profitability of the firm in the long run and thus increase the firm's value.
3. **True.** The firm will determine its optimum stock of capital by producing at the level, where the marginal revenue productivity of capital equals the marginal cost of capital. Thus $MRP_K = MC_K$.
4. **True.** Certainty is a situation, where there exists perfect knowledge about the conditions prevailing in the market. Under the state of certainty, there exists only one outcome to an investment decision and the investor is aware of that outcome.
5. **False.** Risk is a situation, where there exists more than one outcome to an investment decision and the investor is aware of or can calculate the probability of each outcome.

Theories of Distribution

14

After studying this chapter, you should be able to understand:

- ✓ *The theory of distribution deals with the determination of the price of the different factors of production.*
- ✓ *The marginal productivity theory was formulated by J. B. Clark to explain the determination of the price of the factors of production.*
- ✓ *According to the marginal productivity theory, the price of a factor like labour is determined by the marginal productivity of labour.*
- ✓ *The $VMP_L = MRP_L$ is the firm's demand curve for labour when labour is the single variable factor.*
- ✓ *Under perfect competition, the wage rate equals the value of the marginal product.*
- ✓ *David Ricardo believed that rent was a payment by the tenant to the landlord for using the soil, which possessed some indestructible powers.*
- ✓ *Transfer earnings are the amount that the factor should earn if it has to remain in its present use.*
- ✓ *Economic rent is the excess of what a factor earns over its transfer earnings.*
- ✓ *Profit is a reward for entrepreneurship. It is a reward for the inventions and innovations that an entrepreneur undertakes in a dynamic world.*
- ✓ *Profit is the compensation given to the person, who is undergoing the disutility and the discomforts which accompany the risk.*
- ✓ *According to the innovation theory, profits occur when there are innovations.*
- ✓ *Interest is a payment made for the services of capital.*
- ✓ *According to the classical theory, since interest is determined by the real forces, it is a real theory of interest.*
- ✓ *The loanable funds theory incorporates both the monetary and the nonmonetary factors in the analysis.*
- ✓ *According to J. M. Keynes, money is demanded due to three motives.*
- ✓ *The existence of an uncertainty about the future gives rise to what is called the speculative demand for money.*
- ✓ *There exists an inverse relationship between the interest rate and the speculative demand for money.*
- ✓ *In Keynes theory, the rate of interest is a monetary phenomenon determined by the equality between the demand for and supply of money.*

INTRODUCTION

In this chapter, we are concerned with the theory of distribution. The theory of distribution deals with the determination of the price of the different factors of production. It shows as to how the national output is distributed between the different factors of production, labour, land, capital and entrepreneurship. The price of these factors is called wages, rent, interest and profits, respectively.

The price of a factor of production is determined by the demand and the supply of the factor. As far as the demand for the factor is concerned, it is a derived demand as it is derived from the demand for the good that the factor produces. Also, it is joint demand in that different factors are used in conjunction to produce a good. As far as the supply of a factor is concerned, unlike a good, the price of a factor does not depend on its cost of production.

WAGES

As a factor of production, labour is unique in that the owner of the factor is physically present. There are many theories, which explain as to how the wage rate is determined:

(i) **Subsistence Theory of Wages:** Subsistence level is the minimum level, which is required for survival. In his theory of population, Malthus had put forward the view that wages will be equal to the subsistence level. In case wages are higher than the subsistence level, the population will increase until the wages become equal to the subsistence level. Ricardo also believed in the subsistence theory of wages.

> Subsistence level is the minimum level, which is required for survival.

(ii) **Wages Fund Theory:** Wages fund is the stock out of which the wages are paid. According to the theory, wages are determined by the amount of the wages fund.

> Wages fund is the stock out of which the wages are paid.

(iii) **Marginal Productivity Theory:** The marginal productivity theory was formulated by J. B. Clark to explain the determination of the price of the factors of production. According to the theory, the price of a factor like labour is determined by the marginal productivity of labour. The marginal product of factor can be expressed in three ways:

> Marginal revenue product, MRP, is the change in the total revenue due to the employment of an additional unit of the variable factor, all other factors remaining the same. We can write $MRP = MPP \times MR$.

- **Marginal Physical Product:** MPP, which is the change in the total product due to the employment of an additional unit of the variable factor, all other factors remaining the same.
- **Marginal Revenue Product:** MRP, which is the change in the total revenue due to the employment of an additional unit of the variable factor, all other factors remaining the same. We can write $MRP = MPP \times MR$.
- **Value of Marginal Product:** VMP, is the value of the additional product due to the employment of an additional unit of the variable factor, all other factors remaining the same. We can write $VMP = MPP \times P_x$.

> Value of the marginal product, VMP, is the value of the additional product due to the employment of an additional unit of the variable factor, all other factors remaining the same. We can write $VMP = MPP \times P_x$.

We can examine wage determination under different kinds of situations in the market.

RECAP

- Malthus had put forward the view that wages will be equal to the subsistence level. Ricardo also believed in the subsistence theory of wages.
- Wages fund is the stock out of which the wages are paid. According to the wages fund theory, wages are determined by the amount of the wages fund.

- The marginal productivity theory was formulated by J. B. Clark to explain the determination of the price of the factors of production. According to the marginal productivity theory, the price of a factor like labour is determined by the marginal productivity of labour.

WAGE DETERMINATION UNDER PERFECT COMPETITION

Demand for Labour

Since a firm aims at maximizing the profits, it will employ the factors of production such that two conditions are satisfied:

(i) The least cost combination of factors condition which occurs at the producer's equilibrium, where the isoquant is tangential to the isocost line as discussed in Chapter 8. Thus,

$$MRTS_{LK} = \frac{P_L}{P_K}$$

But $$MRTS_{LK} = \frac{\Delta K}{\Delta L} = \frac{MP_L}{MP_K}$$

Thus, $$\frac{P_L}{P_K} = \frac{MP_L}{MP_K}$$

Or $$\frac{MP_K}{P_K} = \frac{MP_L}{P_L}$$

(ii) The profit maximizing condition can be shown by using the marginal approach as discussed in Chapter 10. Thus,

$$MR = MC$$

and $$\text{Slope of } MR < \text{Slope of } MC$$

Now, $$\frac{P_L}{MP_L} = MC_x$$

This is because given P_L, when the firm employs an additional unit of labour, the total cost increases by P_L while the total product increases by MP_L. Hence, P_L/MP_L is the change in the firm's total cost per unit change in its total product. But, in Chapter 9, we have observed that the marginal cost is the change in the total cost or total variable cost due to a unit change in the level of output (or total product).

Similarly, $$\frac{P_K}{MP_K} = MC_x$$

Combining the two conditions for profit maximization, we get

$$\frac{P_L}{MP_L} = \frac{P_K}{MP_K} = MC_x = MR_x$$

where P_L is price of labour, P_K is price of capital, MC_x is marginal cost of good x, MR_x is marginal revenue of good x, MP_L is marginal product of labour and MP_K is marginal product of capital.

Firm's Demand Curve When Labour Is the Single Variable Factor

We have
$$\frac{P_L}{MP_L} = \frac{P_K}{MP_K} = MC_x = MR_x$$

Thus,
$$\frac{P_L}{MP_L} = MC_x = MR_x$$

Or
$$P_L = MR_x \times MP_L = MRP_L$$

But under perfect competition,
$$MR_x = P_x$$

Hence,
$$P_L = P_x \times MP_L = VMP_L$$

Or
$$P_L = MRP_L = VMP_L$$

where MRP_L is marginal revenue product of labour and VMP_L is value of the marginal product of labour.

Figure 14.1(a) depicts only the falling part of the marginal product of labour curve as a rational producer operates in stage 2 of production. In Figure 14.1(b), we have $P_x = MR_x$ as a straight line parallel to the X axis as there exists perfect competition in the goods market. In Figure 14.1(c), the $MRP_L = VMP_L$ has been constructed from Figures 14.1(a) and (b) by multiplying the MP_L with P_x at each level of employment of labour.

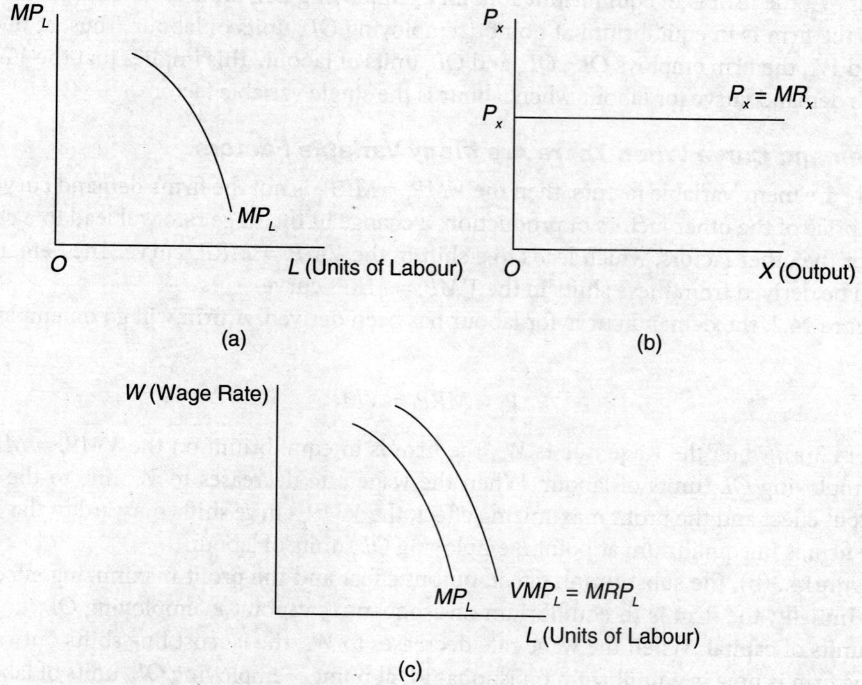

Figure 14.1 Construction of the MRP_L/VMP_L Curve

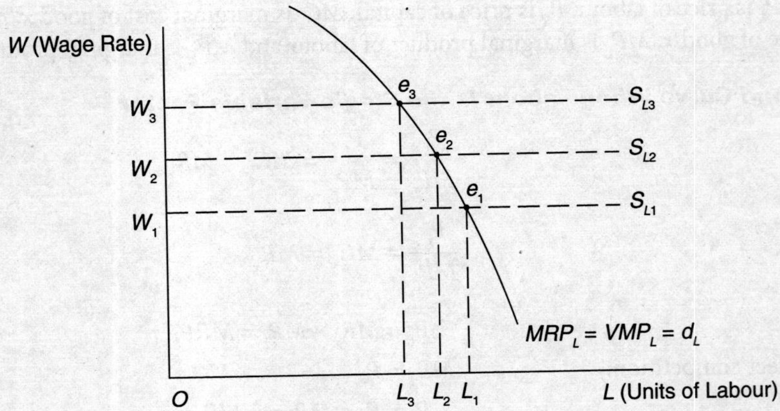

Figure 14.2 Firm's Demand Curve When Labour Is the Single Variable Factor—MRP_L or VMP_L Curve

In Figure 14.2, the demand curve for labour has been derived. A firm will go on employing labour until

$$P_L(\text{or } W) = MRP_L = VMP_L$$

When the wage rate is W_1, the firm is in equilibrium at point e_1 employing OL_1 units of labour. When the wage rate is W_2, the firm is in equilibrium at point e_2 employing OL_2 units of labour and when the wage rate is W_3, the firm is in equilibrium at point e_3 employing OL_3 units of labour. Thus, at the wage rates W_1, W_2 and W_3, the firm employs OL_1, OL_2 and OL_3 units of labour. This implies that the $VMP_L = MRP_L$ is the firm's demand curve for labour when labour is the single variable factor.

Firm's Demand Curve When There Are Many Variable Factors

When there are many variable factors, then the $VMP_L = MRP_L$ is not the firm's demand curve for labour. Given the price of the other factors of production, a change in the wage rate will lead to a change in the demand for the other factors, which leads to a shift in the $VMP_L = MRP_L$ curve. The demand curve for labour will be derived from these shifts in the $VMP_L = MRP_L$ curve.

In Figure 14.2, the demand curve for labour has been derived. A firm will go on employing labour until

$$P_L = MRP_L = VMP_L$$

In Figure 14.3(a), when the wage rate is W_1, the firm is in equilibrium on the $VMP_L = MRP_L$ curve at point A employing OL_1 units of labour. When the wage rate decreases to W_2 due to the substitution effect, output effect and the profit maximizing effect, the VMP_L curve shifts outward to the VMP'_L curve, where the firm is in equilibrium at point B employing OL_2 units of labour.

In Figure14.3(b), the substitution effect, output effect and the profit maximizing effect have been analysed. Initially, the firm is in equilibrium on isoquant I_1 at point e_1 employing OL_1 units of labour and OK_1 units of capital. When the wage rate decreases to W_2, the isocost line shifts outward from AB to AB'. The firm is now in equilibrium on isoquant I_2 at point e_2 employing OL_2 units of labour and OK_2 units of capital. This movement from point e_1 to point e_2 can be split up to depict the substitution effect and the output effects.

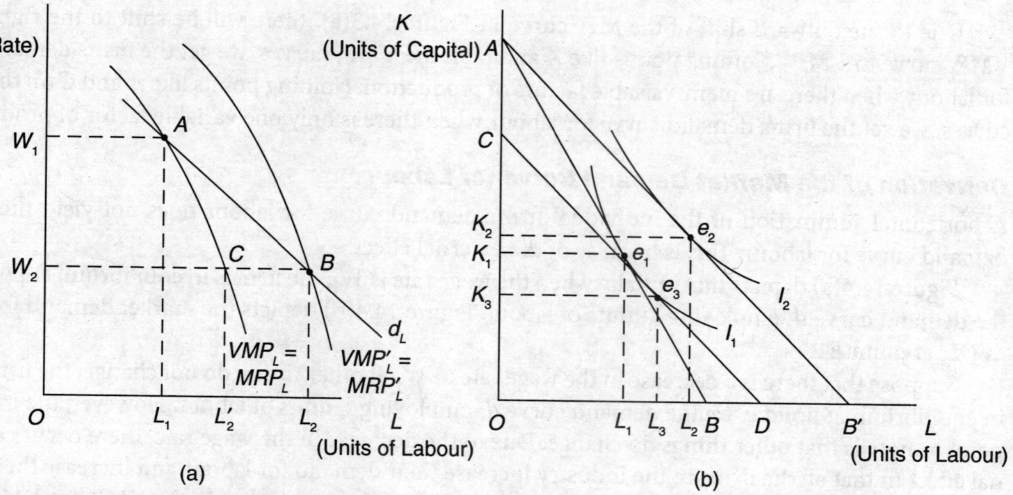

Figure 14.3 Firm's Demand Curve When There Are Many Variable Factors

Substitution Effect

To analyse the substitution effect, the isocost line *CD* is drawn such that it is parallel to the new isocost line represented by *AB′* and tangential to the original isoquant I_2.

The firm is now on the original isoquant I_1 but with the new price ratio. It is in equilibrium at point e_3 employing OL_3 units of labour and OK_3 units of capital. The movement from e_1 to e_3 is the substitution effect leading to an increase in the employment of labour by L_1L_3 caused by a decrease in the wage rate.

According to the substitution effect, a change in the price of one factor leads to a change in the relative prices of the factors leading to a change in the employment of the factors of production.

When there is a decrease in the wage rate, the relative factor price ratio undergoes a change in that labour is relatively cheaper when compared with capital. Thus, the firm will now substitute labour for capital. This will lead to an increase in the employment of labour by L_1L_3 and a decrease in the employment of capital by K_1K_3.

The movement from e_3 to e_2 is the output effect leading to an increase in employment of labour by L_3L_2 and of capital by K_3K_2 caused by a decrease in the wage rate. Thus, according to the output effect with a decrease in the wage rate with the same total outlay, the firm can employ more of labour or more of capital or more of both labour and capital.

Profit Maximizing Effect

It is important to note that the firm will not be maximizing profits at e_2. With the new wage rate, the firm will increase its total outlay and total profits. The isocost line will shift outwards and will be tangential to higher level of isoquant. Hence, due to the profit maximizing effect, more of both labour and capital will be employed to produce a larger output.

Combining the three effects, while, due to the substitution effect, the MP_L curve shifts inwards since there is less of the capital which labour needs to work with, due to the output and profit maximizing effect, the MP_L curve shifts outwards since there is more of both labour and capital. In total, the substitution effect is outweighed by the output and profit maximizing effect. This leads to a shift outwards of the MP_L curve when there is a decrease in the wage rate.

Due to the outward shift of the MP_L curve in Figure 14.3(a), there will be shift to the right of the VMP_L curve to VMP'_L. Joining points like *A* and *B* on the VMP_L curves, we get the firm's demand curve for labour when there are many variable factors of production. (Joining points like *A* and *C* on the VMP_L curves, we get the firm's demand curve for labour when there is only one variable factor of production.)

Derivation of the Market Demand Curve for Labour

A horizontal summation of the individual firm's demand curve for labour does not yield the market demand curve for labour. This is because of the external effect.

Figure 14.4(a) depicts that initially when the wage rate is W_1, the firm is in equilibrium at point e_1 on the demand curve d_L employing l_1 units of labour. Figure 14.4(b) depicts the market demand for labour as OL_1 at point E_1.

Suppose that there is a decrease in the wage rate to W_2. If other things do not change, the firm will be in equilibrium at point e_3 on the demand curve d_L employing l_3 units of labour. However, the important point to note is that other things do change. Due to the decrease in the wage rate, there occurs an external effect in that all the firms in the industry increase their demand for labour and increase their output of good *x*. This leads to a decrease in the price of good *x* and thus a decrease in the VMP_L (as $VMP = MPP \times P_x$). This leads to an inwards shift of the firm's demand curve from d_L to d'_L in Figure 14.4(a). Hence, when the wage rate is W_2, the firm is in equilibrium at point e_2 on the demand curve d'_L employing l_2 units of labour. In Figure 14.4(b), the market demand for labour at the wage rate W_2 is OL_2 at point E_2. Joining points like E_1 and E_2 in Figure 14.4(b), we get the market demand curve for labour, D_L.

RECAP

- Since a firm aims at maximizing the profits, it will employ the factors of production such that two conditions are satisfied.
- The least cost combination of factors condition occurs at the producer's equilibrium, where the isoquant is tangential to the isocost line.
- The profit maximizing condition can be shown by using the marginal approach.
- When there are many variable factors, then the $VMP_L = MRP_L$ is not the firm's demand curve for labour.
- The demand curve for labour will be derived from these shifts in the $VMP_L = MRP_L$ curve.

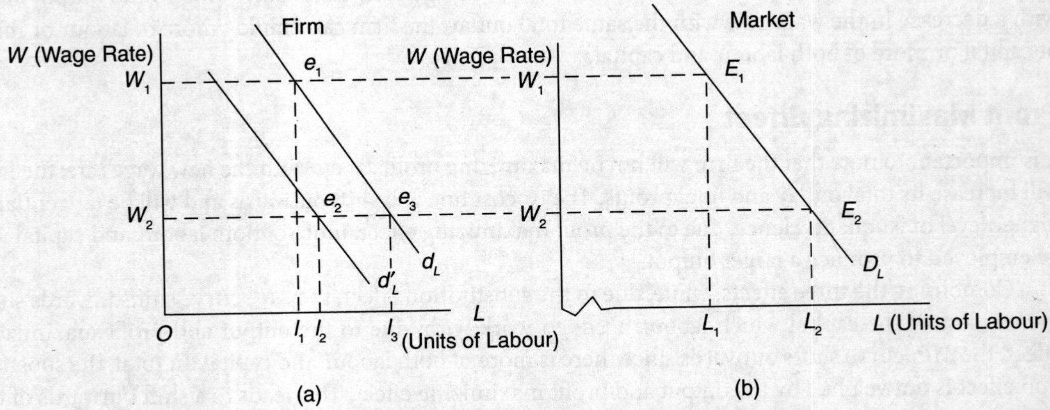

Figure 14.4 Substitution Effect and Output Effect

SUPPLY OF LABOUR

Individual Supply of Labour

Figure 14.5 depicts the backward-bending supply of labour to an individual firm. Till the wage rate *OW*, the supply curve is upward sloping showing that as the wage rate increases the supply of labour also increases and the individual cuts down on his hours of leisure. However, beyond the wage rate *OW* as the wage rate increases the supply of labour decreases while the hours of leisure increase. (Total number of hours which are available to an individual are limited to 24 h, which he can utilize either to work and earn an income or for leisure activities). It is not necessary that the supply curve of labour will always be backward bending.

Market Supply of Labour

Figure 14.6 depicts the market supply of labour as positively sloped showing that as the wage rate increases the supply of labour also increases.

Determination of the Wage Rate

Figure 14.7(a) depicts the determination of the equilibrium wage rate. The market supply of labour and the market demand for labour curves intersect at point *E* to determine the equilibrium wage rate at *W** and the equilibrium level of employment at *OL**.

Figure 14.7(b) shows that given the market equilibrium wage rate at *W**, the perfectly competitive firm's supply curve of labour is perfectly elastic. The supply curve intersects the $VMP_L = MRP_L = d_L$ at point *e* showing that the wage rate equals the value of the marginal product. Thus, under perfect competition, labour exploitation does not take place.

RECAP

- The market supply of labour and the market demand for labour curves intersect to determine the equilibrium wage rate and the equilibrium level of employment.
- The wage rate equals the value of the marginal product.
- Under perfect competition, labour exploitation does not take place.

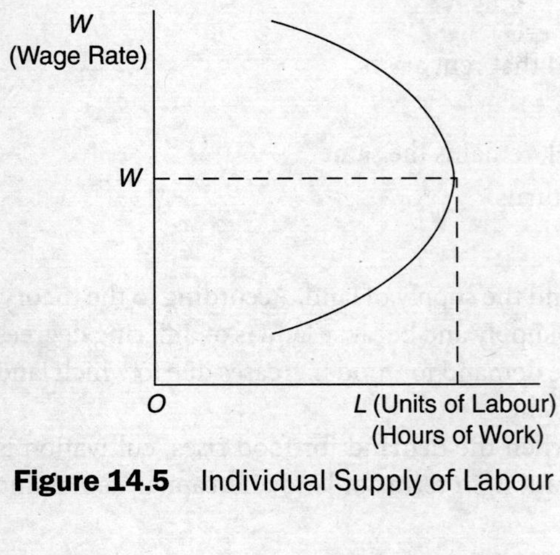

Figure 14.5 Individual Supply of Labour

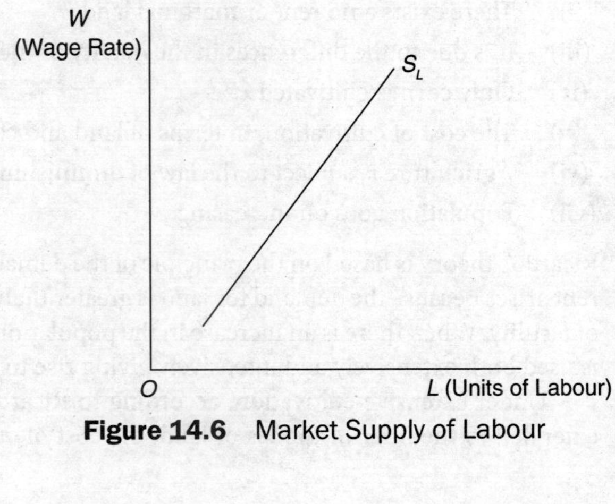

Figure 14.6 Market Supply of Labour

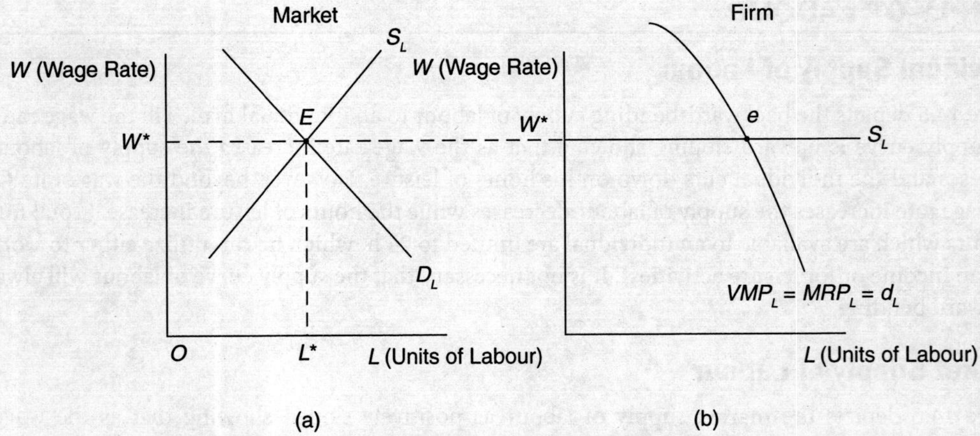

Figure 14.7 Determination of the Wage Rate

RENT

> Rent is the payment, which is made to a factor of production, whose supply is fixed.

In general, rent is the payment made for the hiring of a good. However, in economics, rent has a different connotation. Rent is the payment, which is made to a factor of production, whose supply is fixed. We will now focus on two theories of rent.

RECAP

- Rent is the payment which is made to a factor of production, whose supply is fixed.

RICARDIAN THEORY OF RENT

David Ricardo, a British economist, had formulated this theory in the nineteenth century. He believed that rent was a payment by the tenant to the landlord for using the soil, which possessed some indestructible powers. Rents are high because the supply of land is scarce or inelastic. The theory is based on some assumptions:

(i) In every country, initially the most fertile land is cultivated.
(ii) There exists a no rent or marginal land.
(iii) It is due to the differences in the quality of the land that rent arises.
(iv) Only corn is cultivated.
(v) The cost of cultivation, in terms of land and capital, remains the same.
(vi) Agriculture is subject to the law of diminishing returns.
(vii) Population goes on increasing.

Ricardo's theory is based on the principle of the demand and the supply of land. According to the theory, rent arises because the demand for land is greater than the supply and because land is of differing degrees of fertility. When there is an increase in the population, the demand for food increases due to which land is used both extensively and intensively giving rise to the rent.

Under extensive cultivation, according to Ricardo, when the demand for food rises, cultivation is extended to the inferior grades of land, the cost of cultivation, in terms of land and capital, remaining the same. Thus, rent arises on the superior land as the difference between the output of the superior and the inferior land.

Assume that only corn is cultivated on the three grades of land A, B and C, where A is the superior grade while C is the inferior grade. The cost of cultivation, in terms of land and capital, remains the same. The yields on land A, B and C are 90, 70 and 60 kg of corn. Initially, only grade A land is cultivated and thus there is no rent on grade A land. When the population increases, the demand for corn also increases. Thus, demand for land increases and grade B land is brought under cultivation. Due to the difference in the yields of the grades A and B land, rent arises on grade A land and is equal to 20 (90 – 70) kg of corn. When the population increases further, the demand for corn also increases. Thus, demand for land increases and grade C land is brought under cultivation. Due to the difference in the yields of the grades A, B and C, land rent arises on grades A and B land. The rents are equal to

Rent on grade A land = 90 – 70 = 20 kg of corn
Rent on grade B land = 70 – 60 = 10 kg of corn
Rent on grade C land = 60 – 60 = 0 kg of corn

Grade C is the no rent or marginal land. It will continue to remain so, until cultivation is extended further to the lower grades of land.

Under intensive cultivation, according to Ricardo, additional doses of capital and labour are employed on grade A land so that its productivity can be increased. However, due to the law of diminishing returns, output will increase at a diminishing rate. A stage will be reached, where the marginal revenue product of labour is equal to the marginal cost of labour. These are the marginal doses of labour and capital. Thus, the intensive margin of cultivation is reached with all the earlier doses of labour and capital yielding a rent on the grade A land.

There are many criticisms against Ricardo's theory:

(i) Ricardo believed that rent was a payment by the tenant to the landlord for using the soil, which possessed some indestructible powers. However, the powers of the soil are often destroyed due to soil erosion, floods and an intensive use of land.
(ii) The concept of rent can also be applied to the other factors of production like capital.
(iii) Ricardo had assumed that supply of land is scarce or inelastic. But that is no longer true as more land can be reclaimed.

RECAP

- David Ricardo believed that rent was a payment by the tenant to the landlord for using the soil, which possessed some indestructible powers.
- According to the Ricardian theory, rent arises because the demand for land is greater than the supply and because land is of differing degrees of fertility.

MODERN THEORY OF RENT

J. Robinson has differentiated between two concepts, transfer earnings and economic rent.

Transfer earnings can be defined as the amount that a factor of production expects to earn if transferred to its next best use. Thus, it is the amount that the factor should earn if it has to remain in its present use. It is also called the reservation price or the opportunity cost.

Transfer earnings are the amount that a factor of production expects to earn if transferred to its next best use. Thus, it is the amount that the factor should earn if it has to remain in its present use.

Economic rent is the payment to a factor of production, which is over and above the amount that the factor should earn if it has to remain in its present use.

Economic rent can be defined as the payment to a factor of production, which is over and above the amount that the factor should earn if it has to remain in its present use. In other words, it is the excess of what a factor earns over its transfer earnings. We can write

$$\text{Economic Rent} = \text{Actual Earnings} - \text{Transfer Earnings}$$

We can examine three situations in Figure 14.8:

(i) **Supply of a Factor Is Perfectly Elastic:** Figure 14.8(a) depicts a perfectly elastic supply of a factor. In such a situation, the entire payment made to the factor is transfer earnings. The payment is made to the factor to prevent it from moving to its next best use. Thus, the factor's total earnings, OP^*EQ^*, are transfer earnings. Economic rent is zero.

(ii) **Supply of a Factor Is Perfectly Inelastic:** Figure 14.8(b) depicts a perfectly inelastic supply of a factor. This may happen if a factor has only a specific use. In such a situation, the entire payment made to the factor is economic rent. Thus, the factor's total earnings, OP^*EQ^*, are economic rent. Transfer earnings are zero.

(iii) **Supply of a Factor Is Elastic:** Figure 14.8(c) depicts an elastic supply of a factor. Thus, the supply curve is upward sloping. The demand and the supply curves intersect at point E to determine

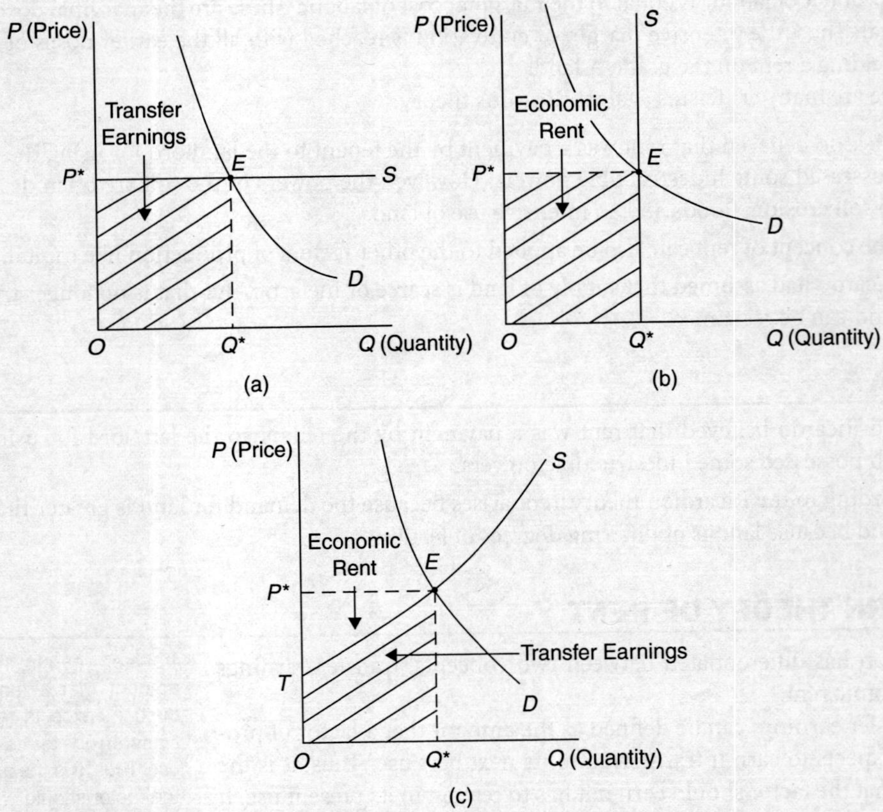

Figure 14.8 Transfer Earnings and Economic Rent

the equilibrium price as OP^* and the equilibrium quantity as OQ^*. The factor's total earnings, OP^*EQ^*, can be split into:

— Transfer earnings as equal to $OTEQ^*$. Since the supply curve depicts the minimum payment that must be paid to a factor to keep it in its present use, the area below the supply curve represents the transfer earnings of the factor.

— Economic rent as equal to TP^*E. It is the excess of what the factor earns over its transfer earnings.

$$\text{Actual Earnings} = \text{Transfer Earnings} + \text{Economic Rent}$$

Or

$$OP^*EQ^* = OTEQ^* + TP^*E$$

RECAP

- J. Robinson has differentiated between two concepts, transfer earnings and economic rent.
- Transfer earnings are the amount that the factor should earn if it has to remain in its present use. It is also called the reservation price or the opportunity cost.
- Economic rent is the excess of what a factor earns over its transfer earnings.

PROFIT

The marginal productivity theory applies to all the factors of production, including the profit, which is the reward for entrepreneurship. To a businessman, profit must be sufficiently large enough to cover the opportunity cost. To an economist, economic profit or pure profit is the return that is in addition to the opportunity cost. Thus, profit is the residual that is left after all the costs of production have been covered. Many profit theories have been put forward by the different economists.

> Profit is the residual that is left after all the costs of production have been covered.

Dynamic Theory

The dynamic theory of profits was given by J. B. Clark in 1900. According to the theory, it is only in a dynamic world that profits accrue.

In a static world, there is

(i) No change in the population.
(ii) No changes in the capital formation and no new techniques of production are invented.
(iii) There is no change in the process of production.
(iv) Though there is perfect mobility of factors of production, yet the factors do not move because their marginal product is the same in all industries.
(v) There is no uncertainty and thus no risk.

Thus, the remuneration of the entrepreneur is the wages he earns in managing the firm.

In contrast in a dynamic world, there are many changes.

(i) An increase in the population.
(ii) An increase in the capital formation and new techniques of production are invented leading to an improvement in the production process.
(iii) There are changes, which occur in the business organizations.

In such a dynamic world, the entrepreneur takes advantages of the different opportunities available to him to innovate, reduce the costs and expand the production, thus increasing the sales. It is because of these strategies adopted by the entrepreneur that profits emerge in a dynamic world.

The profits so earned by the entrepreneur are temporary. Due to the competition between the firms once the new techniques are adopted by the other firms, there is an increase in the demand for the factors of production leading to an increase in the price of these factors and thus in the cost of production. On the other hand, due to an increase in the production by all the firms in the industry, there is a decrease in the prices of the goods, which are being produced. Thus, the net result is that profits tend to disappear.

But in a dynamic world, change is an ongoing process. New techniques are invented at different points in time and thus profits appear at some stages and disappear at other times. Thus, it is a continuous process with profits appearing and disappearing.

Profit is a reward for entrepreneurship. It is a reward for the inventions and innovations that an entrepreneur undertakes in a dynamic world.

Criticism

(i) Clark's division of the earnings of a firm between profits and the wages of the management has been criticized by many economists.

(ii) In the modern world, profits are paid to the shareholders of the firm. These shareholders do not perform any functions relating to the coordination of the activities of a firm. It is often argued that what is paid out to the shareholders is actually a return earned on their investments.

(iii) Clark's view that profit is a reward for the inventions and innovations that an entrepreneur undertakes in a dynamic world has been criticized because often firms, which are past their dynamic stages, are continuing to make the profits.

RECAP

- Profit is the residual that is left after all the costs of production have been covered.
- According to the dynamic theory, it is only in a dynamic world that profits accrue.
- Profit is a reward for entrepreneurship. It is a reward for the inventions and innovations that an entrepreneur undertakes in a dynamic world.

RISK THEORY

The risk theory of profits was given by F. B. Hawley in 1893. According to the theory, profit is a reward for undertaking the risk in a dynamic world. Undertaking the risk gives rise to uncertainty and also a disutility. Profit is the compensation given to the person, who is undergoing the disutility and the discomforts which accompany the risk.

Hawley had realized that in certain situations in spite of undergoing the risk profit may not accrue, for example, under some situations in monopoly. He had analysed monopoly gains in a separate theory.

Criticism

(i) According to Clark, risk involves the loss of capital. Thus, the reward for undertaking the risk is actually the interest on capital.

(ii) Hawley's theory emphasizes only the risk-bearing function performed by the entrepreneur. It ignores the other functions, for example, administration and organization, which are performed by the entrepreneur, which also give rise to profits.

(iii) Hawley fails to distinguish between insurable risk and uninsurable risk. Profits arise due to the uninsurable risk.

Of the different theories of profits, Hawley's risk theory is one of the most widely accepted theories today.

RECAP

- According to the risk theory, profit is a reward for undertaking the risk in a dynamic world.
- Profit is the compensation given to the person, who is undergoing the disutility and the discomforts, which accompany the risk.
- Of the different theories of profits, Hawley's risk theory is one of the most widely accepted theories today.

UNCERTAINTY THEORY

The uncertainty theory of profits was developed by F. H. Knight. According to the theory, profit is a return on uncertainty bearing.

Knight had distinguished between the risk and the uncertainty. According to him, risks are of two kinds:

(i) **Calculable Risks:** These are risks for which their probability of occurring can be calculated and thus they can be insured against, for example, the risk of theft and fire.

(ii) **Incalculable Risks:** These are risks for which their probability of occurring cannot be calculated and thus they cannot be insured against, for example, the effects of a recession on the profits of a firm. Thus, here there is an element of uncertainty involved.

Since often the entrepreneur makes decisions under conditions of uncertainty, for example, decisions relating to the market, he may earn profits if the decisions turn out to be correct.

Criticism

(i) Often the dividing line between risk and uncertainty is very thin. Hence, it is difficult to make a distinction between the two.

(ii) Knight's theory does not often apply to the situations in the real world. In certain areas like agriculture, there is uncertainty but the returns are low. Thus, uncertainty does not necessarily lead to profits.

RECAP

- According to the uncertainty theory, profit is a return on uncertainty bearing.
- According to Knight, risks are of two kinds: calculable risks and incalculable risks.

INNOVATION THEORY

The innovation theory of profits was given by J. A. Schumpeter in 1934. It is a part of his theory of economic development. Schumpeter's starting point is an economy, which is in a stationary equilibrium, where the total receipts equal the total outlays. There are no profits.

Profits occur when there are innovations, for example, introduction of new methods in the production of goods and introduction of some new sources of obtaining the raw materials. Innovations create a surplus, provided there is no decrease in the price of the good and no increase in the cost of production.

The profits may be short lived. The innovations may be imitated by the other entrepreneurs, which may lead to an increase in the demand for the limited factors of production leading to an increase in the price of these factors of production. Thus, the cost of production will increase. On the other hand, since many firms opt for the new technology, the supply of the good may increase leading to a decrease in the price of the good. Thus, overtime, the difference between total receipts and total outlays may disappear and the economy may reach a new stationary equilibrium, which is at a higher level.

Criticism

- Schumpeter ignores the importance given to risk and uncertainty in the earlier theories of profit.
- Schumpeter's theory emphasizes only the importance of innovations as performed by the entrepreneur. It ignores the other functions, for example, administration and organization, which are performed by the entrepreneur, which also give rise to profits.

RECAP

- According to the innovation theory, profits occur when there are innovations.
- Innovations create a surplus, provided there is no decrease in the price of the good and no increase in the cost of production.
- The profits may be short lived.

INTEREST

Interest is a payment made for the services of capital. It is often defined as the price, which is paid for borrowed funds.

Like wages, rent and profit, interest is also a payment to a factor of production. It is a payment made for the services of capital. It is often defined as the price, which is paid for borrowed funds. Thus, it is the amount, which is paid by the borrowers to the lenders for using their funds. Many theories have been put forward to determine the rate of interest.

RECAP

- Like wages, rent and profit, interest is also a payment to a factor of production.
- Interest is a payment made for the services of capital.

CLASSICAL THEORY

The theories of Marshall, Cassel, Tausig and Walras are referred to as the classical theory. According to the theory, since interest is determined by the real forces including saving and investment, it is a real theory of interest.

According to the classical theory, the price of a good is determined by the demand and the supply of the good. Similarly, interest, which is the price of capital, is determined by the supply of saving (which is the supply of investible funds) and the demand for investible funds. Figure 14.9 depicts the determination of the rate of interest in the classical model. The savings curve, *S*, is downward sloping

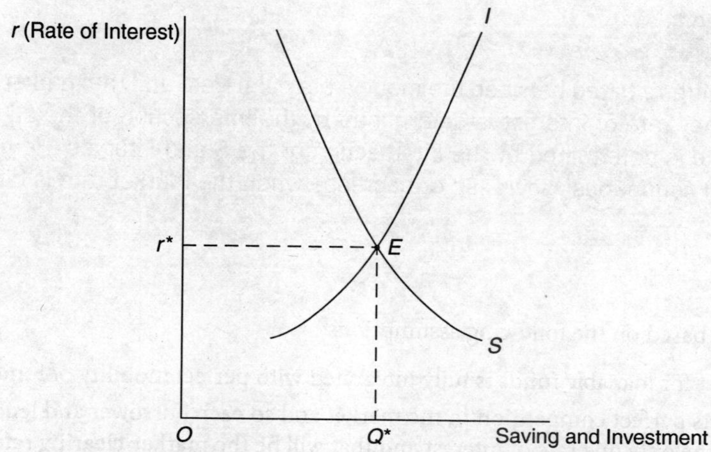

Figure 14.9 A Determination of the Interest Rate: Classical Theory

showing a positive relationship between savings and the rate of interest. The investment demand curve, *I*, is upward sloping showing a negative relationship between investment and the rate of interest. The investment demand curve and the savings curve intersect at point *E* to determine the equilibrium rate of interest at *Or**, where the supply of saving equals the demand for investible funds. If there is a change in the supply of saving or the demand for investible funds, the equilibrium rate of interest will change.

Criticism

(i) The classical theory assumes that the income level is given. Also, savings are assumed to be a function only of the interest rate, which is not true as savings depend on the income level also. The classical theory ignored the all important relationship between savings and income.

(ii) According to Keynes, the classical theory is indeterminate in that the savings and investment schedule cannot shift independently of each other. Since a shift in one curve leads to a shift in the other curve, it will be difficult to determine the equilibrium.

RECAP

- According to the classical theory, since interest is determined by the real forces, including saving and investment, it is a real theory of interest.
- Interest, which is the price of capital, is determined by the supply of saving and the demand for investible funds.

NEO-CLASSICAL THEORY

The neo-classical theory, also known as the loanable funds theory, is an extension of the classical saving and investment theory of interest. While the classical theory had incorporated only the nonmonetary (real) factors, the loanable funds theory incorporates both the monetary and the non-monetary factors in the analysis. It is associated with Wicksell, D. H. Robertson and others.

BOX 14.1

Wicksell had differentiated between the money rate of interest and the market rate of interest. While the money rate of interest is determined by the intersection of the *LD* and *LS* curves, the natural rate is determined by the intersection of the S and *I* curves. He had emphasized that prices will continuously increase or decrease when the market rate is different from the natural rate.

The theory is based on the following assumptions:

(i) The market for loanable funds is fully integrated with perfect mobility of funds.

(ii) There exists perfect competition in the market and so each borrower and lender is a price taker. There will be only one rate of interest and that will be the market-clearing rate of interest.

(iii) All factors, other than the rate of interest, are assumed to be constant. The rate of interest does not respond to or interfere with the other macroeconomic variables. In other words, the theory uses a partial equilibrium analysis.

(iv) The theory is in 'flow' terms, where the flow demand and supply of loanable funds are analysed to determine the rate of interest.

The rate of interest is determined by standard demand supply analysis. According to the loanable funds theory, the rate of interest, which is the price of loanable funds, is determined by the demand for and supply of loanable funds.

Demand for Loanable Funds, LD

The demand for loanable funds can be expressed as

$$LD = I + \Delta MD$$

where LD is demand for loanable funds, I is gross investment expenditure and ΔMD is incremental demand for money.

Since both I and ΔMD are a decreasing function of the rate of interest, LD is also a decreasing function of the rate of interest. While investment (which was present in the classical theory also) is a real factor, the incremental demand for money is a monetary factor. Hence, both real and monetary factors are included in the demand for money.

Supply of Loanable Funds, LS

The sources of supply of loanable funds are

$$LS = S + DH + \Delta M$$

where LS is supply of loanable funds, S is aggregate saving of all the households and firms in the economy net of their dissaving, DH is aggregate dishoarding of previously accumulated cash balances and ΔM is incremental supply of money.

Since both S and DH are an increasing function of the rate of interest, while ΔM is given autonomously, LS is also an increasing function of the rate of interest. While S, the aggregate saving of all the households and firms (which was present in the classical theory also), is a real factor, DH (the aggregate dishoarding of previously accumulated cash balances) and ΔM, the incremental supply of money, are both monetary factors. Hence, both real and monetary factors are included in the supply of money.

Interest Rate Determination

In Figure 14.10, S represents the saving curve while LS represents the supply of loanable funds. The horizontal distance between the S and LS curves is the sum of DH and ΔM. This distance increases as r increases because while, ΔM is given exogenously, DH is an increasing function of r. Similarly, I represents the investment curve while LD represents the demand for loanable funds. The horizontal distance between I and LD curves is ΔMD. This distance increases as r decreases because ΔMD is a decreasing function of r.

According to the standard demand supply theory, equilibrium is determined at the level where

$$\text{Demand for Loanable Funds} = \text{Supply of Loanable Funds}$$

or

$$LD = LS$$

or

$$I + \Delta MD = S + DH + \Delta M$$

On the other hand, in the classical theory, equilibrium is determined at the level where

$$I(r) = S(r)$$

In Figure 14.10, the LD and LS curves intersect each other at point E. The equilibrium rate of interest is r^{**}. The S–I equilibrium of the classical theory yields r^* as the equilibrium rate of interest.

A Critical Appraisal

The positive points of the loanable funds theory are:

(i) It is an improvement over the classical theory in that it recognizes the fact that loanable funds are demanded for purposes other than the investment expenditures and also that besides saving there exist other sources of loanable funds also.

(ii) While the classical theory considers only the real factors in the determination of the interest rate, the loanable funds theory takes into consideration both the real and the monetary factors.

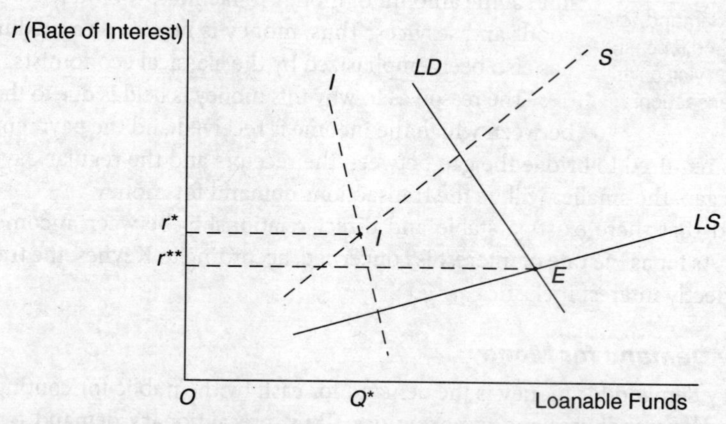

Figure14.10 Interest Rate Determination in the Loanable Funds Theory

(iii) The theory recognizes that like saving and investment, the aggregate dishoarding of previously accumulated cash balances and the incremental demand for money also exercise a strong influence on the rate of interest.

The negative points of the loanable funds theory are as follows:

(i) The theory is unable to specify in a clear manner the different sources of the supply and demand for loanable funds.

(ii) On the supply side,

(a) Some savings may not come through the loan market. Firms and households may invest their savings directly into physical assets.

(b) Not all dishoarding of cash balances are lent out. The dishoarders may spend them directly.

RECAP

- The neo-classical theory, also known as the loanable funds theory, is an extension of the classical saving and investment theory of interest.
- While the classical theory had incorporated only the non-monetary (real) factors, the loanable funds theory incorporates both the monetary and the nonmonetary factors in the analysis.
- The rate of interest, which is the price of loanable funds, is determined by the demand for and supply of loanable funds.

KEYNESIAN THEORY

According to the classical theory, money is demanded as a medium of exchange or in other words for conducting the transactions. But, according to J. M. Keynes who formulated his theory of demand for money in his well-known book *The General Theory of Employment, Interest and Money* in 1936, money is demanded due to three motives.

Transactions Demand for Money

The transactions demand for money is the demand for cash by the public for carrying on its various current transactions. The transactions motive creates transactions demand for money. Everyone needs to hold some amount of money to facilitate their day-to-day transactions in goods and services. Thus, money is needed as a medium of exchange, as has also been emphasized by the classical economists.

> The transactions demand for money is the demand for cash by the public for carrying on its various current transactions.

The reason as to why this money is held is due to the time gap involved between which the income is received and the payments are made out. In other words, it is required to bridge the gap between the receipts and the regular payments to be made. The closer is this gap, the smaller will be the transactions demand for money.

It is believed that there exists a stable and direct relationship between income and transactions money balances. As far as the rate of interest is concerned, according to Keynes, the transactions demand for money is perfectly interest inelastic.

Precautionary Demand for Money

The precautionary demand for money is the demand for cash by the public for contingencies, which may involve unexpected expenditures and opportunities. Thus, precautionary demand for money exists due to uncertainties. It is for those payments which are neither regular nor planned. Hence, it enables individuals to meet unexpected increases in expenditure or unexpected delays in receipts. The precautionary demand for money varies with the income level. For the sake of convenience and following the conventional procedure, transactions and precautionary balances are often put together as a function primarily of the income level and as being interest inelastic.

The precautionary demand for money is the demand for cash by the public for contingencies, which may involve unexpected expenditures and opportunities.

Speculative Demand for Money

While the transactions demand and precautionary demand for money do not in any way conflict with the views of the classical theory, the speculative demand for money (also called the asset demand for money) represents a complete break from the classical theory. It is one of the most important contributions made by Keynes to the theory of demand for money. It is the speculative motive, which gives rise to the speculative demand for money.

Often people hold money, which is in excess of their transactions and precautionary demand for money. This is money, which is held for purposes of speculation in the stock market. It is called the speculative demand for money and is inversely related to the rate of interest.

Often people hold money, which is in excess of their transactions and precautionary demand for money. This is money, which is held for purposes of speculation in the stock market. It is called the speculative demand for money and is inversely related to the rate of interest.

The classical economists had put forward the view that an individual would not hold money in excess of what he requires for transactions and precautionary purposes. For in doing so, he would be losing the interest, which he could have earned by putting that amount of money in a bond. Even if the interest rate is extremely low, it would still be advantageous for him to earn whatever interest he can earn from it.

Keynes, however, had different opinions. First of all to present his views, he assumed that individuals hold only two kinds of financial assets in their asset portfolio, namely, money and perpetual (or irredeemable) bonds. A bond is an asset that carries a promise to pay to its owner a fixed amount of income per annum. This income entitles the owner of the bond to a future income stream.

The market price of the bond will depend to a large extent on the rate of interest fixed in terms of money. Keynes had pointed out that an individual who is purchasing bonds does so because he expects that in the near future there will not occur an increase in the interest rates. In case he expects an increase in the interest rates, he should not be purchasing bonds and instead would be holding money. Thus, the existence of an uncertainty about the future gives rise to what is called the speculative demand for money. There exists an inverse relationship between the interest rate and the speculative demand for money.

BOX 14.2

J. M. Keynes is largely recognized for having created the shape and terminology of modern macroeconomics. His book, *General Theory of Employment, Interest and Money* brought about a revolution in the thinking of economists. The book is the foundation of Keynesian thought. It provided a great challenge for the classical school of thought by introducing some new and revolutionary concepts. Keynes is perhaps one of the greatest and most prominent economists of the twentieth century. He is often known as the father of modern economics.

Interest Rate Determination

In the classical theory, the rate of interest is a real phenomenon determined by the equality between savings and investment in the commodity market. In contrast, in Keynes theory, the rate of interest is a monetary phenomenon determined by the equality between the demand for and supply of money. It is in fact a compensation for parting with liquidity.

The total demand for money can be expressed as

$$m_d = m_t + m_{sp}$$

where m_d is total demand for money, m_t is transactions demand for money and m_{sp} is speculative demand for money.

But we can write $m_t = k(Y)$ and $m_{sp} = g(r)$.

Thus, combining we have

$$m_d = k(Y) + g(r)$$

Regarding the supply of money, Keynes assumed that the supply of money is exogenously determined by the monetary authorities. Hence, in Figure 14.11, it is shown by a line parallel to the vertical axis and is interest inelastic.

The money market will be in equilibrium when the demand for money is equal to the supply of money. Thus,

$$m_d = m_s$$

Or $k(Y) + g(r) = m_s$

According to Keynes, r^* represents a stable equilibrium value of r, which is determined by the monetary forces of demand and supply of money.

RECAP

- According to J. M. Keynes, money is demanded due to three motives.
- The transactions demand for money is the demand for cash by the public for carrying on its various current transactions.

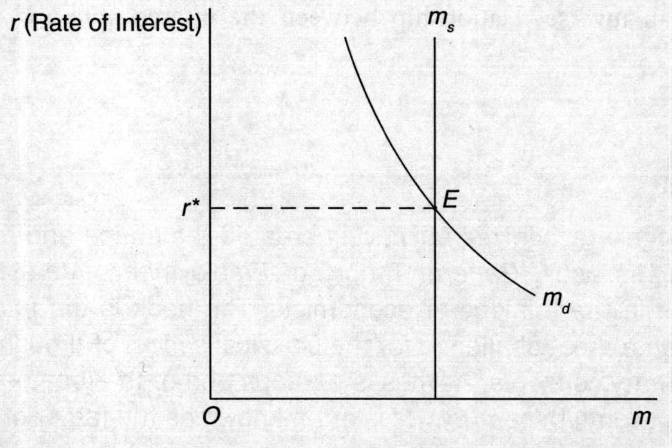

Figure 14.11 Determination of the Rate of Interest: The Keynesian Theory

- The precautionary demand for money is the demand for cash by the public for contingencies, which may involve unexpected expenditures and opportunities.
- The existence of an uncertainty about the future gives rise to what is called the speculative demand for money.
- There exists an inverse relationship between the interest rate and the speculative demand for money.
- In Keynes theory, the rate of interest is a monetary phenomenon determined by the equality between the demand for and supply of money.

SUMMARY

INTRODUCTION

1. The theory of distribution deals with the determination of the price of the different factors of production.
2. It shows as to how the national output is distributed between the different factors of production, labour, land, capital and entrepreneurship.
3. The price of these factors is called wages, rent, interest and profits, respectively.
4. The price of a factor of production is determined by the demand and the supply of the factor.
5. As far as the demand for the factor is concerned, it is a derived demand as it is derived from the demand for the good that the factor produces.
6. As far as the supply of a factor is concerned, unlike a good, the price of a factor does not depend on its cost of production.

WAGES

1. As a factor of production, labour is unique in that the owner of the factor is physically present.
2. **Subsistence Theory of Wages:** Malthus had put forward the view that wages will be equal to the subsistence level. Ricardo also believed in the subsistence theory of wages.
3. **Wages Fund Theory:** Wages fund is the stock out of which the wages are paid. According to the theory, wages are determined by the amount of the wages fund.
4. **Marginal Productivity Theory:** The marginal productivity theory was formulated by J. B. Clark to explain the determination of the price of the factors of production. According to the theory, the price of a factor like labour is determined by the marginal productivity of labour.
5. MRP is the change in the total revenue due to the employment of an additional unit of the variable factor, all other factors remaining the same. $MRP = MPP \times MR$.
6. VMP is the value of the additional product due to the employment of an additional unit of the variable factor, all other factors remaining the same. $VMP = MPP \times P_x$.

WAGE DETERMINATION UNDER PERFECT COMPETITION

Demand for Labour

1. Since a firm aims at maximizing the profits, it will employ the factors of production such that two conditions are satisfied.
2. The least cost combination of factors condition, which occurs at the producer's equilibrium, where the isoquant is tangential to the isocost line.
3. Thus, $\frac{MP_K}{P_K} = \frac{MP_L}{P_L}$.
4. The profit maximizing condition, which can be shown by using the marginal approach
5. Thus, $\frac{P_K}{MP_L} = \frac{P_K}{MP_K} = MC_x = MR_x$.

Firm's Demand Curve When Labour Is the Single Variable Factor

1. $P_L = MRP_L = VMP_L$.
2. The $VMP_L = MRP_L$ is the firm's demand curve for labour when labour is the single variable factor.

Firm's Demand Curve When There Are Many Variable Factors

1. When there are many variable factors, then the $VMP_L = MRP_L$ is not the firm's demand curve for labour.
2. Given the price of the other factors of production, a change in the wage rate will lead to a change in the demand for the other factors, which leads to a shift in the $VMP_L = MRP_L$ curve.
3. When the wage rate decreases due to the substitution effect, output effect and the profit maximizing effect, the VMP_L curve shifts outward to the VMP'_L curve.
4. The demand curve for labour will be derived from these shifts in the $VMP_L = MRP_L$ curve.
5. According to the substitution effect when there is a decrease in the wage rate, the relative factor price ratio undergoes a change in that labour is relatively cheaper when compared with capital. Thus, the firm will now substitute labour for capital. This will lead to an increase in the employment of labour.
6. According to the output effect with a decrease in the wage rate with the same total outlay, the firm can employ more of labour or more of capital or more of both labour and capital.
7. Due to the profit maximizing effect, more of both labour and capital will be employed to produce a larger output.
8. In total, the substitution effect is outweighed by the output and profit maximizing effect. This leads to a shift outwards of the MP_L curve when there is a decrease in the wage rate.
9. There will be shift to the right of the VMP_L curve.
10. Joining points on the VMP_L curves, we get the firm's demand curve for labour when there are many variable factors of production.

Derivation of the Market Demand Curve for Labour

A horizontal summation of the individual firm's demand curve for labour does not yield the market demand curve for labour. This is because of the external effect.

SUPPLY OF LABOUR

Individual Supply of Labour

1. The individual supply of labour curve is backward bending.
2. It is not necessary that the supply curve of labour will always be backward bending.

Market Supply of Labour

The market supply of labour is positively sloped showing that as the wage rate increases the supply of labour also increases.

Determination of the Wage Rate

1. The market supply of labour and the market demand for labour curves intersect to determine the equilibrium wage rate and the equilibrium level of employment.
2. The wage rate equals the value of the marginal product.
3. Under perfect competition, labour exploitation does not take place.

RENT

Rent is the payment, which is made to a factor of production, whose supply is fixed.

Ricardian Theory of Rent

1. David Ricardo believed that rent was a payment by the tenant to the landlord for using the soil, which possessed some indestructible powers.
2. Rents are high because the supply of land is scarce or inelastic.

3. Ricardo's theory is based on the principle of the demand and the supply of land.
4. According to the theory, rent arises because the demand for land is greater than the supply and because land is of differing degrees of fertility.
5. When there is an increase in the population, the demand for food increases due to which land is used both extensively and intensively giving rise to the rent.
6. There are many criticisms against Ricardo' theory: The powers of the soil are often destroyed due to soil erosion, floods and an intensive use of land; Ricardo had assumed that supply of land is scarce or inelastic but that is no longer true as more land can be reclaimed.

Modern Theory of Rent

1. J. Robinson has differentiated between two concepts, transfer earnings and economic rent.
2. Transfer earnings are the amount that the factor should earn if it has to remain in its present use. It is also called the reservation price or the opportunity cost.
3. Economic rent is the excess of what a factor earns over its transfer earnings.
4. Actual Earnings = Transfer Earnings + Economic Rent.

PROFIT

1. Profit is the reward for entrepreneurship.
2. Profit is the residual that is left after all the costs of production have been covered.

Dynamic Theory

1. The dynamic theory of profits was given by J. B. Clark in 1900.
2. According to the theory, it is only in a dynamic world that profits accrue.
3. Thus, it is a continuous process with profit appearing and disappearing.
4. Profit is a reward for entrepreneurship. It is a reward for the inventions and innovations that an entrepreneur undertakes in a dynamic world.
5. **Criticism:** It is often argued that what is paid out to the shareholders is actually an interest earned on their investments; often, firms, which are past their dynamic stages, are continuing to make the profits.

Risk Theory

1. The risk theory of profits was given by F. B. Hawley.
2. According to the theory, profit is a reward for undertaking the risk in a dynamic world.
3. Undertaking the risk gives rise to uncertainty and also a disutility. Profit is the compensation given to the person, who is undergoing the disutility and the discomforts, which accompany the risk.
4. **Criticism:** Hawley's theory emphasizes only the risk-bearing function performed by the entrepreneur. It ignores the other functions, for example, administration and organization, which are performed by the entrepreneur, which also give rise to profits; Hawley fails to distinguish between insurable risk and uninsurable risk. Profits arise due to the uninsurable risk.
5. Of the different theories of profits, Hawley's risk theory is one of the most widely accepted theories today.

Uncertainty Theory

1. The uncertainty theory of profits was developed by F. H. Knight.
2. According to the theory, profit is a return on uncertainty bearing.
3. According to Knight, risks are of two kinds: calculable risks and incalculable risks.
4. Since often the entrepreneur makes decisions under conditions of uncertainty, for example, decisions relating to the market, he may earn profits if the decisions turn out to be correct.
5. **Criticism:** Often the dividing line between risk and uncertainty is very thin. Often, it is difficult to make a distinction between the two; Knight's theory does not often apply to the situations in the real world.

Innovation Theory

1. The innovation theory of profits was given by J. A. Schumpeter in 1934.
2. Profits occur when there are innovations, for example, introduction of new methods in the production of goods and introduction of some new sources of obtaining the raw materials.
3. Innovations create a surplus, provided there is no decrease in the price of the good and no increase in the cost of production.
4. The profits may be short lived.
5. **Criticism:** Schumpeter ignores the importance given to risk and uncertainty in the earlier theories of profit; Schumpeter theory emphasizes only the importance of innovations as performed by the entrepreneur.

INTEREST

1. Like wages, rent and profit, interest is also a payment to a factor of production.
2. It is a payment made for the services of capital.

Classical Theory

1. The theories of Marshall, Cassel, Tausig and Walras are referred to as the classical theory.
2. According to the theory, since interest is determined by the real forces including saving and investment, it is a real theory of interest.
3. Interest, which is the price of capital, is determined by the supply of saving and the demand for investible funds.
4. **Criticism:** The classical theory ignored the all important relationship between savings and income; According to Keynes, the classical theory is indeterminate in that the savings and investment schedule cannot shift independently of each other.

Neo-Classical Theory

1. The neo-classical theory, also known as the loanable funds theory, is an extension of the classical saving and investment theory of interest.
2. While the classical theory had incorporated only the nonmonetary (real) factors, the loanable funds theory incorporates both the monetary and the nonmonetary factors in the analysis.
3. The rate of interest, which is the price of loanable funds, is determined by the demand for and supply of loanable funds.
4. The demand for loanable funds can be expressed as
$$LD = I + \Delta MD$$
5. Since both I and ΔMD are a decreasing function of the rate of interest, LD is also a decreasing function of the rate of interest.
6. The sources of supply of loanable funds are
$$LS = S + DH + \Delta M$$
7. Since both S and DH are an increasing function of the rate of interest, while ΔM is given autonomously, LS is also an increasing function of the rate of interest.
8. The horizontal distance between the S and LS curves is the sum of DH and ΔM. This distance increases as r increases.
9. The horizontal distance between I and LD curves is ΔMD. This distance increases as r decreases.
10. Equilibrium is determined at the level, where the demand for loanable funds is equal to the supply of loanable funds.
11. The negative points of the loanable funds theory are: The theory is unable to specify in a clear manner the different sources of the supply and demand for loanable funds; the flow equilibrium approach of the theory has also been subjected to a lot of criticism; for the determination of the interest rate, a general equilibrium approach, and not a partial equilibrium approach is required.

Keynesian Theory

1. According to J. M. Keynes, money is demanded due to three motives.
2. The transactions demand for money is the demand for cash by the public for carrying on its various current transactions. Everyone needs to hold some amount of money to facilitate their day-to-day transactions in goods and services.
3. It is believed that there exists a stable and direct relationship between income and transactions money balances. As far as the rate of interest is concerned, according to Keynes, the transactions demand for money is perfectly interest inelastic.
4. The precautionary demand for money is the demand for cash by the public for contingencies, which may involve unexpected expenditures and opportunities.
5. For the sake of convenience and following the conventional procedure, transactions and precautionary balances are often put together as a function primarily of the income level and as being interest inelastic.
6. The speculative demand for money represents a complete break from the classical theory. It is one of the most important contributions made by Keynes to the theory of demand for money. It is the speculative motive, which gives rise to the speculative demand for money.
7. The existence of an uncertainty about the future gives rise to what is called the speculative demand for money.
8. There exists an inverse relationship between the interest rate and the speculative demand for money.
9. In Keynes theory, the rate of interest is a monetary phenomenon determined by the equality between the demand for and supply of money.

REVIEW QUESTIONS

TRUE OR FALSE QUESTIONS

1. The marginal productivity theory was formulated by J. B. Clark to explain the determination of the price of the good.
2. The market supply of labour is backward bending.
3. Under perfect competition, the wage rate equals the value of the marginal product.
4. Transfer earnings are the amount that the factor should earn if it has to remain in its present use. It is also called the reservation price or the opportunity cost.
5. When the supply of a factor is perfectly elastic, the entire payment made to the factor is economic rent.

SHORT ANSWER QUESTIONS

1. Briefly discuss the theories of wage determination.
2. Is the individual firm's supply of labour curve backward bending? Explain.
3. Write short notes on
   (a) Transfer earnings
   (b) Economic rent
4. Discuss the classical theory of the determination of the rate of interest.
5. What are the three motives for holding money in Keynes's theory? Discuss.

LONG ANSWER QUESTIONS

1. 'According to the marginal productivity theory, the $VMP_L = MRP_L$ is the firm's demand curve for labour, when labour is the single variable factor'. Comment.
2. What are the two conditions that a profit maximizing firm will satisfy in deciding about its demand for labour?
3. Derive the firm's demand curve for labour, when there are many variable factors. Briefly discuss the substitution effect, output effect and the profit maximizing effect.

4. Explain the Ricardian theory of rent.
5. Analyse the dynamic theory of profits given by J. B. Clark.

ANSWERS

TRUE OR FALSE QUESTIONS

1. **False.** The marginal productivity theory was formulated by J. B. Clark to explain the determination of the price of the factors of production.
2. **False.** The market supply of labour is positively sloped showing that as the wage rate increases the supply of labour also increases.
3. **True.** Under perfect competition, the wage rate equals the value of the marginal product. Hence, there is no exploitation of labour.
4. **True.** Transfer earnings can be defined as the amount that a factor of production expects to earn if transferred to its next best use. Thus, it is the amount that the factor should earn if it has to remain in its present use. It is also called the reservation price or the opportunity cost.
5. **False.** When the supply of a factor is perfectly elastic, the entire payment made to the factor is transfer earnings.

General Equilibrium and Welfare Economics

15

After studying this chapter, you should be able to understand:

- ✓ *General equilibrium analysis involves a state, where all the markets and the decision-making units in the economy are in a simultaneous equilibrium.*
- ✓ *The general equilibrium of production in a two goods economy can be depicted with the help of the Edgeworth Box Diagram.*
- ✓ *Each point on the contract curve of production is an efficient allocation of the inputs and represents a general equilibrium of production.*
- ✓ *Each point on the production possibility frontier is an efficient allocation of the inputs.*
- ✓ *Each point on the contract curve of consumption is an efficient allocation of the goods and represents a general equilibrium of consumption.*
- ✓ *In welfare economics, we consider the welfare implications relating to the general equilibrium model.*
- ✓ *Each point on the utility possibility frontier is an efficient allocation of the goods between the two consumers.*
- ✓ *The society maximizes its welfare at the point, where the grand utility possibility curve is tangential to a social welfare curve.*

INTRODUCTION

A general equilibrium analysis deals with the study of an economic system and as to how a simultaneous equilibrium is reached in all the markets of an economy. We then consider the welfare implications relating to this general equilibrium model.

General equilibrium analysis involves a state, where all the markets and the decision-making units in the economy are in a simultaneous equilibrium. Hence, it studies the simultaneous equilibria in a group of interrelated markets emphasizing the interdependence between the different economic units in the economy.

RECAP

- General equilibrium is a state, where all the markets and the decision-making units in the economy are in a simultaneous equilibrium.

GENERAL EQUILIBRIUM OF PRODUCTION AND EXCHANGE

We consider a model, where there exists a perfectly competitive market with two factors, two goods and two consumers.

Assumptions

(i) There are two factors of production, labour, L and capital, K. The quantities of these two homogenous and perfectly divisible factors are given exogenously.

(ii) There are two goods, x and y, with the isoquants depicting the constant returns to scale and a diminishing marginal rate of technical substitution.

(iii) There are two consumers, A and B, with their indifference curves as convex to the origin and depicting a diminishing marginal rate of substitution.

(iv) Each firm aims at maximizing its profits, given the techniques of production.

(v) Each consumer aims at maximizing his utility, given his income.

(vi) The consumers own the factors, labour and capital and spend the entire income that they receive as owners of the factors. There exists full employment of the factors.

(vii) There exists perfect competition in both the factor and the goods market. Thus, the price of the goods P_x and P_y and the price of the factors, w (price of labour) and r (price of capital), remain the same for the firm and the consumer.

General Equilibrium of Production

The equilibrium of the firm exists at the point, where it is maximizing its profits. Thus, as already discussed in Chapter 8, in case of one good, the equilibrium of the firm exists at the point, where the slope of the isoquant is equal to the slope of the isocost line. In other words

$$MRTS_{LK} = \frac{P_L}{P_K}$$

In case of two goods, the general equilibrium of production exists at the point where

$$(MRTS_{LK})^x = (MRTS_{LK})^y$$

> The Edgeworth box diagram has been named after F. Y. Edgeworth. It is a graphical technique to show the optimum allocation of given amounts of two factors between two goods and also the allocation of the two goods between two consumers.

The general equilibrium of production in a two goods economy can be depicted in Figure 15.1 with the help of the Edgeworth box diagram. The Edgeworth box diagram has been named after F. Y. Edgeworth. It is a graphical technique to show the optimum allocation of given amounts of two factors between two goods and also the allocation of the (given amounts of) two goods between two consumers.

Figure 15.1 depicts the following:

(i) Point O_x marks the origin for good x while point O_y marks the origin for good y.

(ii) The horizontal axis measures the units of labour while the vertical axis measures the units of capital.

(iii) Each point in the box shows the specific combination of labour and capital that can be utilized to produce the two goods. For example, at point R.

- x_1 units of good x are produced by using L_x units of labour and K_x units of capital.
- y_1 units of good y are produced by using L_y units of labour and K_y units of capital.

(iv) The isoquants for good x are plotted with O_x as the origin while the isoquants for good y are plotted with O_y as the origin.

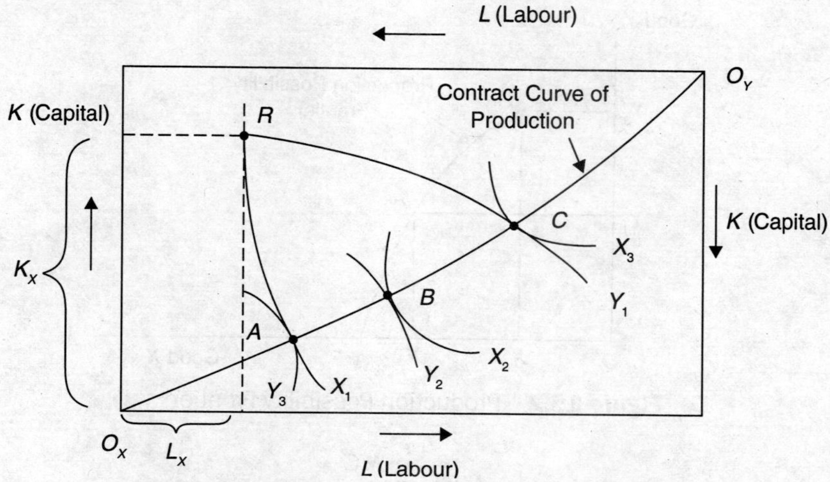

Figure 15.1 General Equilibrium of Production

(v) The locus of points of tangencies of the isoquants of goods *x* and *y* is called the contract curve of production. Once the economy is on this contract curve, it can increase the output of one good only by reducing the output of the other good. All the factor combinations on this curve O_xABCO_y are Pareto efficient in production.

(vi) All points, which are not on the contract curve, are inefficient combinations of inputs. Point *R* represents an inefficient allocation of inputs because with a reallocation of the factors production may be possible at points like *A* or *C*, which represent more of at least one of the goods *x* and *y*.

Each point on the contract curve of production is an efficient allocation of the inputs and represents a general equilibrium of production.

Production Possibility Frontier

By mapping the contract curve of production given in the input space in Figure 15.1 to the output space, one can derive the production possibility frontier as in Figure 15.2. The production possibility frontier depicts the different combinations of the two goods *x* and *y* that an economy can produce by utilizing all of its resources of capital and labour given the techniques of production. Each point on the production possibility frontier is an efficient allocation of the inputs.

> The production possibility frontier depicts the different combinations of the two goods *x* and *y* that an economy can produce by utilizing all of its resources of capital and labour given the techniques of production.

Point *A′* in Figure 15.2 corresponds to point *A* in Figure 15.1 representing x_1 units of good *x* and y_3 units of good *y*. Similarly, point *C′* corresponds to point *C* in Figure 15.1 representing x_3 units of good *x* and y_1 units of good *y*.

The production possibility frontier is concave to the origin implying an increase in its slope as one moves down the curve. The slope of the production possibility frontier is called the marginal rate of transformation. It measures the amount by which an economy must decrease its output of good *y* and release a sufficient amount of the factors, labour and capital, to increase the output of good *x* by one more unit. Thus,

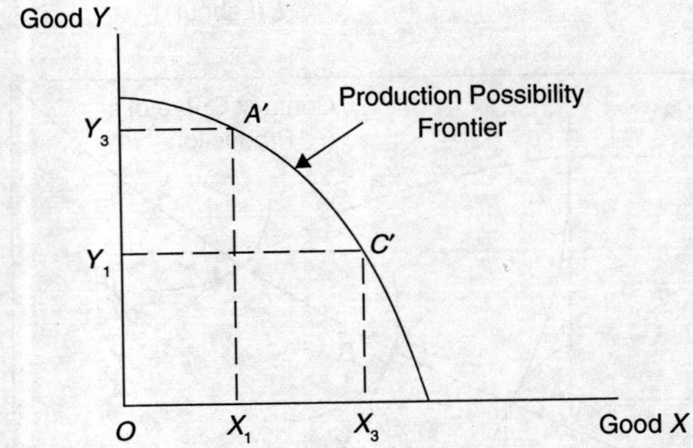

Figure 15.2 Production Possibility Frontier

$$MRT_{xy} = \frac{MC_x}{MC_y}$$

General Equilibrium of Exchange (Consumption)

A consumer achieves the equilibrium when he maximizes his utility, given his money income and the prices of the two goods. Thus, a consumer is in equilibrium when he is able to reach the highest indifference curve given the budget constraint or where the slope of the indifference curve is equal to the slope of the budget line. In other words,

$$MRS_{xy} = \frac{P_x}{P_y}$$

In case of two consumers, *A* and *B*, the general equilibrium of consumption exists at the point where

$$(MRS_{xy})^A = (MRS_{xy})^B$$

The general equilibrium of consumption can be depicted in Figure 15.3 with the help of the Edgeworth box diagram.

Figure 15.3 depicts the following:

(i) Point O_A marks the origin for consumer *A* while point O_B marks the origin for consumer *B*.

(ii) The horizontal axis measures units of good *x* while the vertical axis measures units of good *y*.

(iii) Each point in the box shows the specific combinations of goods *x* and *y* that are available to the consumers *A* and *B*.

(iv) The indifference curves for consumer *A* are plotted with O_A as the origin while the indifference curves for consumer *B* are plotted with O_B as the origin.

(v) The locus of points of tangencies of the indifference curves for consumers *A* and *B* is called the contract curve of consumption. Once the economy is on this contract curve, it cannot make one consumer better off without making the other consumer worse off. All the factor combinations on this curve $O_A L\ MNO_B$ are Pareto efficient in consumption.

(vi) All points, which are not on the contract curve, are inefficient allocation of the goods between the consumers. Point *D* represents an inefficient allocation of the goods because with a reallocation

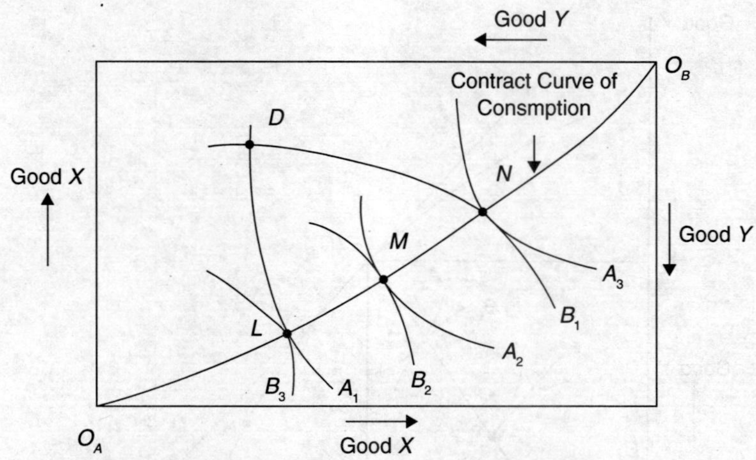

Figure 15.3 General Equilibrium of Consumption

of the goods it is possible for the consumers to achieve points like L and N, which represent a greater utility to at least one of the consumers.

(vii) The distribution of goods among the consumers is said to be Pareto efficient or optimal if it is not possible to reallocate the goods and make one consumer better off without making the other consumer worse off.

Each point on the contract curve of consumption is an efficient allocation of the goods and represents a general equilibrium of consumption.

General Equilibrium in Production and Exchange

For a general equilibrium of production and exchange to exist, it is necessary that the slope of the production possibility frontier is equal to the slope of the indifference curve. Thus,

$$MRT_{xy} = MRS_{xy}$$

In Figure 15.4, every point on the production possibility frontier represents a point of general equilibrium of production. Suppose that the economy is at point E producing x_E units of good x and y_E units of good y. In the Edgeworth box diagram, $O_A\ x_E\ Ey_E$, the consumption contract curve is given by $O_A L MNO_B$. Every point on the consumption contract curve represents a point of general equilibrium in exchange.

A simultaneous general equilibrium in production and exchange will exist at point M where

Slope of the indifference curves = Slope of the production possibility frontier

Or

Slope of the tangent to the indifference curves A_2 and B_2 = Slope of the tangent to the production possibility frontier

Or

Slope of the tangent ff' = Slope of the tangent pp'

$$(MRS_{xy})^A = (MRS_{xy})^B = MRT_{xy}$$

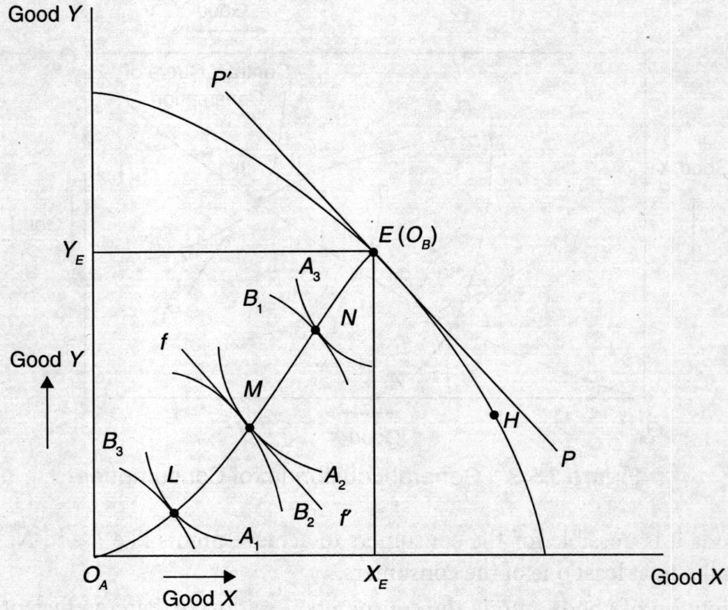

Figure 15.4 General Equilibrium of Production and Consumption

We have observed that three conditions should be satisfied if one has to achieve a Pareto optimum or Pareto efficient situation in both the production and the consumption. These conditions are as follows:

(i) $(MRTS_{LK})^x = (MRTS_{LK})^y$

(ii) $(MRS_{xy})^A = (MRS_{XY})^B$

(iii) $(MRS_{XY})^A = (MRS_{XY})^B = MRT_{xy}$

In a perfectly competitive market, all the three conditions are satisfied. If any of the conditions is not satisfied, it leads to a market failure.

RECAP

- In case of two goods, the general equilibrium of production exists at the point where $(MRTS_{LK})^x = (MRTS_{LK})^y$.
- Each point on the contract curve of production is an efficient allocation of the inputs and represents a general equilibrium of production.
- In case of two consumers, *A* and *B*, the general equilibrium of consumption exists at the point where $(MRS_{xy})^A = (MRS_{xy})^B$.
- Each point on the contract curve of consumption is an efficient allocation of the goods and represents a general equilibrium of consumption.
- For a general equilibrium of production and exchange to exist, it is necessary that the slope of the production possibility frontier is equal to the slope of the indifference curve.

BOX 15.1

An Indian economist, Professor Amartya Sen, made valuable contributions to the basic problems in welfare economics and the theory of social choice. For these contributions, he received the Nobel Memorial Prize in Economic Sciences 1998. Professor Sen has also worked on the causes of famines and thus in finding ways to prevent food shortages. He has given some new indexes of poverty. He helped in forming the United Nations Human Development Index. At present, he is at the Harvard University.

WELFARE ECONOMICS

As already mentioned in welfare economics, we consider the welfare implications relating to the general equilibrium model. We analyse the conditions under which the general equilibrium model results in an optimal solution. This is possible only if there exists

(i) An optimal allocation of the factors of production among the goods. The allocation of factors in a two good economy is said to be Pareto optimal or efficient if it is not possible to reorganize the production to increase the output of one good without decreasing the output of the other good. All the factor combinations on the contract curve of production curve O_xABCO_y in Figure 15.1 are Pareto efficient in production.

(ii) An optimal allocation of the goods among the consumers. The allocation of goods is said to be Pareto optimal or efficient if it is not possible to reorganize the distribution to increase the utility of one consumer without decreasing the utility of the other consumer. All the factor combinations on the contract curve of consumption O_ALMNO_B in Figure 15.3 are Pareto efficient in consumption.

RECAP

- The allocation of factors in a two good economy is said to be Pareto optimal or efficient if it is not possible to reorganize the production to increase the output of one good without decreasing the output of the other good.
- The allocation of goods is said to be Pareto optimal or efficient if it is not possible to reorganize the distribution to increase the utility of one consumer without decreasing the utility of the other consumer.

UTILITY POSSIBILITY FRONTIER

By mapping the contract curve of consumption given in the output space in Figure 15.3 to the utility space, one can derive the utility possibility frontier as in Figure 15.5. The utility possibility frontier depicts the different combinations of utility of the two goods x and y that are received by the consumers when the economy is in a general equilibrium of exchange. It is also called the welfare frontier. Each point on the utility possibility frontier is an efficient allocation of the goods between the two consumers. Each point on the frontier is equally efficient. Points lying inside the frontier represent an inefficient allocation of the goods between the two consumers since both the consumers can be made better off.

The utility possibility frontier depicts the different combinations of utility of the two goods x and y that are received by the consumers when the economy is in a general equilibrium of exchange.

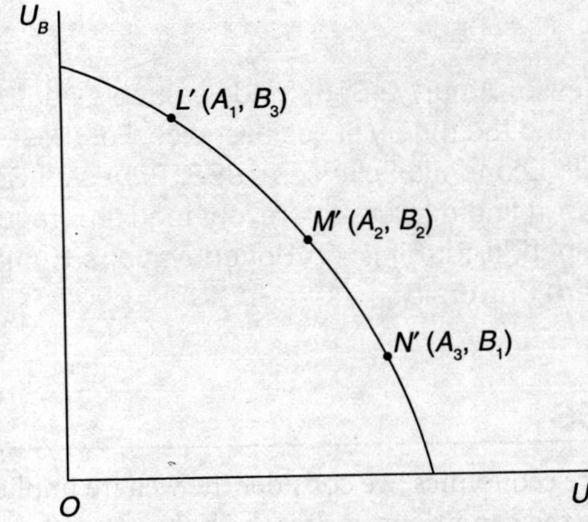

Figure 15.5 Utility Possibility Curve

Point L' in Figure 15.5 corresponds to point L in Figure 15.3. Similarly, point M' corresponds to point M in Figure 15.3.

Grand Utility Possibility Curve

In Figure 15.4 by selecting a point on the production possibility frontier like point E, we have constructed a box diagram with a consumption contract curve drawn from point O_A to point E. From the consumption contract curve, one can derive the utility possibility curve, F'_E in Figure 15.6 and arrive at a Pareto optimum point like W.

By selecting another point on the production possibility frontier like point H, one can construct another box diagram with a consumption contract curve drawn from point O_A to point H. From the consumption contract curve, one can derive the utility possibility curve, F'_H in Figure 15.6 and arrive at a Pareto optimum point like V.

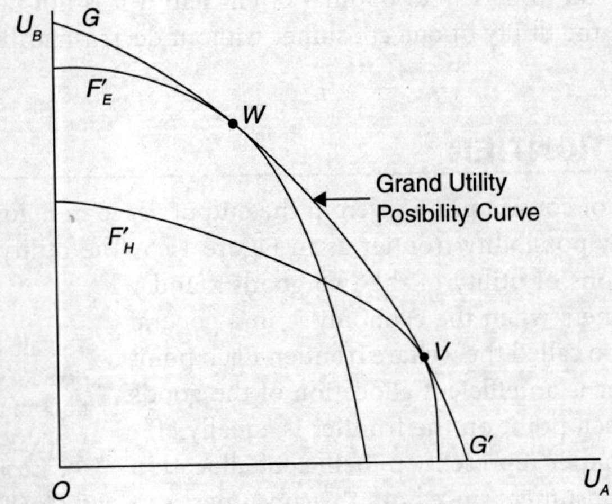

Figure 15.6 Grand Utility Possibility Curve

Joining points like W and V, one can derive the grand utility possibility curve GG' in the figure, which is a locus of points, which are Pareto optimum in production and consumption. This curve is an envelope of the utility possibility curves.

RECAP

- The utility possibility frontier depicts the different combinations of utility of the two goods x and y that are received by the consumers when the economy is in a general equilibrium of exchange.
- Each point on the utility possibility frontier is an efficient allocation of the goods between the two consumers.
- The grand utility possibility curve is a locus of points, which are Pareto optimum in production and consumption.

SOCIAL WELFARE FUNCTION

A social welfare function or a social welfare curve depicts the various combinations of the utilities of the two consumers, U_A and U_B, which give the same level of satisfaction or welfare to the society.

Figure 15.7 depicts three social welfare curves W_1, W_2 and W_3. All the combinations on a social indifference curve represent the same level of satisfaction or welfare to the society. A higher social welfare curve depicts a higher level of welfare. It is important to note that to draw social welfare functions, it is necessary to make interpersonal comparisons of utility.

Point of Maximum Social Welfare

The society maximizes its welfare at the point, where the grand utility possibility curve is tangential to a social welfare curve as depicted in Figure 15.8 at point S. Given the resources and the technology in the society, this is the highest level of social welfare that the society can achieve. It is also called the Point of Bliss. Thus, we have determined the general equilibrium solution that maximizes the welfare of the society.

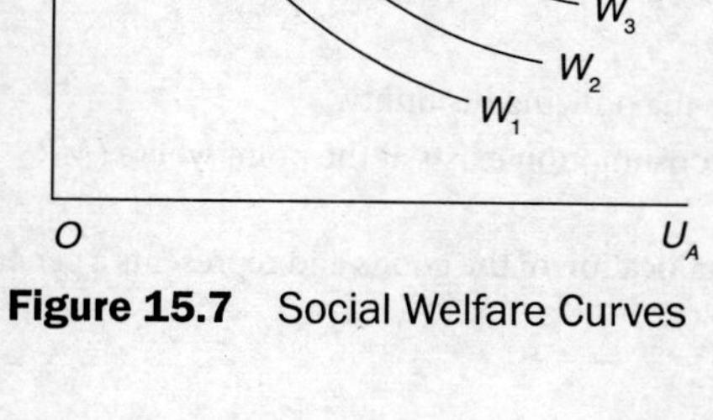

Figure 15.7 Social Welfare Curves

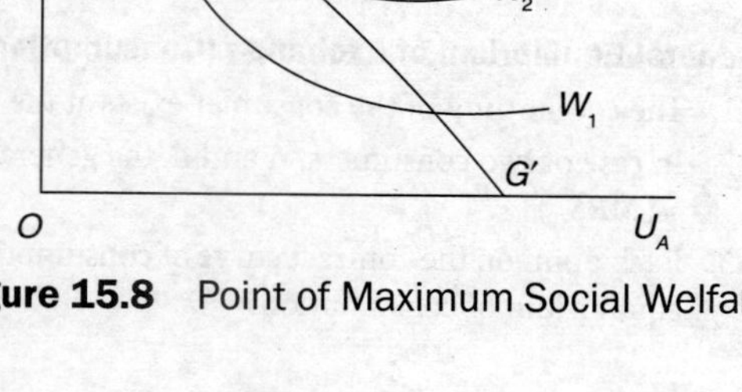

Figure 15.8 Point of Maximum Social Welfare

RECAP

- A social welfare function or a social welfare curve depicts the various combinations of the utilities of the two consumers, which give the same level of satisfaction or welfare to the society.
- A higher social welfare curve depicts a higher level of welfare.
- The society maximizes its welfare at the point, where the grand utility possibility curve is tangential to a social welfare curve.

SUMMARY

INTRODUCTION

1. A general equilibrium analysis deals with the study of an economic system and as to how a simultaneous equilibrium is reached in all the markets of an economy.
2. We then consider the welfare implications relating to this general equilibrium model.
3. General equilibrium analysis involves a state, where all the markets and the decision-making units in the economy are in a simultaneous equilibrium.

GENERAL EQUILIBRIUM OF PRODUCTION AND EXCHANGE

1. We consider a model, where there exists a perfectly competitive market with two factors, two goods and two consumers.
2. Each firm aims at maximizing its profits given the techniques of production.
3. Each consumer aims at maximizing his utility given his income.
4. There exists perfect competition in both the factor and the goods market.

General Equilibrium of Production

1. The equilibrium of the firm exists at the point, where it is maximizing its profits.
2. In case of two goods, the general equilibrium of production exists at the point, where $(MRTS_{LK})^x = (MRTS_{LK})^y$.
3. The general equilibrium of production in a two goods economy can be depicted with the help of the Edgeworth Box Diagram.
4. Each point on the contract curve of production is an efficient allocation of the inputs and represents a general equilibrium of production.

Production Possibility Frontier

1. By mapping the contract curve of production given in the input space to the output space, one can derive the production possibility frontier.
2. The production possibility frontier depicts the different combinations of the two goods x and y that an economy can produce by utilizing all of its resources of capital and labour given the techniques of production.
3. Each point on the production possibility frontier is an efficient allocation of the inputs.
4. The slope of the production possibility frontier is called the marginal rate of transformation. $MRT_{xy} = \frac{MC_x}{MC_y}$.

General Equilibrium of Exchange (Consumption)

1. The equilibrium of the consumer exists at the point, where he is maximizing his utility.
2. In case of two consumers, A and B, the general equilibrium of consumption exists at the point where $(MRS_{xy})^A = (MRS_{xy})^B$.
3. Each point on the contract curve of consumption is an efficient allocation of the goods and represents a general equilibrium of consumption.

General Equilibrium in Production and Exchange

1. For a general equilibrium of production and exchange to exist, it is necessary that the slope of the production possibility frontier is equal to the slope of the indifference curve.
2. Three conditions should be satisfied if one has to achieve a Pareto optimum or Pareto efficient situation in both the production and the consumption.
3. In a perfectly competitive market, all the three conditions are satisfied. If any of the conditions is not satisfied, it leads to a market failure.

WELFARE ECONOMICS

1. In welfare economics, we consider the welfare implications relating to the general equilibrium model.
2. We analyse the conditions under which the general equilibrium model results in an optimal solution.
3. The allocation of factors in a two good economy is said to be Pareto optimal or efficient if it is not possible to reorganize the production to increase the output of one good without decreasing the output of the other good.
4. The allocation of goods is said to be Pareto optimal or efficient if it is not possible to reorganize the distribution to increase the utility of one consumer without decreasing the utility of the other consumer.

Utility Possibility Curve

1. By mapping the contract curve of consumption given in the output space to the utility space, one can derive the utility possibility frontier.
2. The utility possibility frontier depicts the different combinations of utility of the two goods x and y that are received by the consumers when the economy is in a general equilibrium of exchange.
3. Each point on the utility possibility frontier is an efficient allocation of the goods between the two consumers.

Grand Utility Possibility Curve

1. From the consumption contract curve, one can derive the utility possibility curve.
2. Joining the Pareto optimum points on the utility possibility curve, one can derive the grand utility possibility curve, which is a locus of points, which are Pareto optimum in production and consumption.

SOCIAL WELFARE FUNCTION

1. A social welfare function or a social welfare curve depicts the various combinations of the utilities of the two consumers, U_A and U_B, which give the same level of satisfaction or welfare to the society.
2. All the combinations on a social indifference curve represent the same level of satisfaction or welfare to the society.
3. A higher social welfare curve depicts a higher level of welfare.

Point of Maximum Social Welfare

1. The society maximizes its welfare at the point, where the grand utility possibility curve is tangential to a social welfare curve.
2. Given the resources and the technology in the society, this is the highest level of social welfare that the society can achieve. It is also called the Point of Bliss.

REVIEW QUESTIONS

TRUE OR FALSE QUESTIONS

1. Under a general analysis, all the markets and the decision-making units in the economy are in a simultaneous equilibrium.
2. The general equilibrium of production in a two goods economy can be depicted with the help of the Edgeworth box diagram.

3. The locus of points of tangencies of the isoquants is called the contract curve of consumption.
4. By mapping the contract curve of production given in the input space to the output space, one can derive the production possibility frontier.
5. Each point on the contract curve of production is an inefficient allocation of the inputs.

SHORT ANSWER QUESTIONS

1. What is a general equilibrium analysis?
2. How can one derive the production possibility frontier from the contract curve of production?
3. Show how a firm reaches a general equilibrium of consumption in case of two consumers, with the help of the Edgeworth box diagram.
4. Analyse the conditions under which the general equilibrium model results in an optimal solution.
5. 'The utility possibility frontier depicts the different combinations of utility of the two goods x and y that are received by the consumers when the economy is in a general equilibrium of exchange'. Comment.

LONG ANSWER QUESTIONS

1. Show how a firm reaches a general equilibrium of production in a two goods economy with the help of the Edgeworth box diagram.
2. How does a firm reach the general equilibrium of production?
3. How does a firm reach the general equilibrium of consumption?
4. 'For a general equilibrium of production and exchange to exist, it is necessary that the slope of the production possibility frontier is equal to the slope of the indifference curve'. Comment.
5. 'The grand utility possibility curve is an envelope of the utility possibility curves'. Comment.

ANSWERS

TRUE OR FALSE QUESTIONS

1. **True.** General equilibrium analysis involves a state, where all the markets and the decision-making units in the economy are in a simultaneous equilibrium.
2. **True.** The Edgeworth box diagram is a graphical technique to show the optimum allocation of given amounts of two factors between two goods and also the allocation of the two goods between two consumers.
3. **False.** The locus of points of tangencies of the isoquants of goods x and y is called the contract curve of production.
4. **True.** The production possibility frontier depicts the different combinations of the two goods x and y that an economy can produce by utilizing all of its resources of capital and labour given the techniques of production. Each point on the production possibility frontier is an efficient allocation of the inputs.
5. **False.** Each point on the contract curve of production is an efficient allocation of the inputs.

National Income

16

After studying this chapter, you should be able to understand:

- ✓ *GNP is a measure of the value of goods and services, which the nationals or residents of the country produce regardless of where they are located.*
- ✓ *GDP is the total value of all the final goods and services produced by all the enterprises within the domestic territory of a country in a particular year.*
- ✓ *Personal income is the income received by households and the non-corporate businesses.*
- ✓ *Disposable personal income is the amount, which is actually available to the households and to the non-corporate business after they have fulfilled their tax obligations to the government.*
- ✓ *GDP is one of the most important macroeconomic variables and one of the best measures to judge an economy's performance.*
- ✓ *Three approaches to calculating the GDP are the output approach, the income approach and the expenditure approach.*

INTRODUCTION

In macroeconomics, we deal with economic aggregates such as saving, consumption, investment, employment, national income and the national product. This chapter focuses on an analysis of the national income, national product and related aggregates such as personal income and disposable personal income. It is not only important to have an understanding of the different concepts, but also equally important is to understand as to how these aggregates are measured.

NATIONAL INCOME AGGREGATES

If we look at the different countries in the world, we find that some are rich; some are not so rich while the others are in between. The performance and the standard of living of a country can be evaluated by looking at the amount of goods that the country produces. It is again necessary to measure the national income to plan for the economy's future. Here, we focus on the different concepts of the national income and the related aggregates.

Gross National Product (GNP)

Gross national product is a measure of the value of goods and services, which the nationals or residents of the country produce regardless of where they are located.

GNP is defined as the total value of all the final goods and services produced in a country in a particular year, and the income which is earned by its citizens, who are located abroad minus the income of non-residents located within that country. GNP is a measure of the value of goods and services, which the nationals or residents of the country produce

BOX 16.1

The need for accurate measures of aggregate economic activity was felt somewhere around the Great Depression. Thus, the initial efforts to develop such measures date back to the late 1920s and 1930s. Colin Clark and Simon Kuznets initiated the process followed later by Richard Stone. In the USA, the first formal national accounts were available by 1947. The United Nations System of National Accounts defines the international rules relating to national accounting.

regardless of where they are located. It is thus the total income of a nation as earned by the citizen's of a nation.

Gross Domestic Product (GDP)

Gross domestic product is the total value of all final goods and services produced by all the enterprises within the domestic territory of a country in a particular year.

GDP is defined as the total value of all the final goods and services produced by all the enterprises (both the resident and the non-resident) within the domestic territory of a country in a particular year.

One of the most essential macroeconomic variables, the GDP, can be said to measure both a nation's total income and its total output of goods and services. *It is taken to be one of the best indicators of judging an economy's performance.*

In calculating the GDP:

(i) Only market prices are used as they reveal the willingness of the public to pay for a good or a service.

(ii) Only the value of currently produced goods and services are included.

Treatment of Inventories in GDP

In general, when a firm adds to its inventories of goods, it involves expenditure by the firms. Hence, like production for the final sale of the product, the production of inventories also increases the GDP.

Treatment of Intermediate Goods in the GDP

Production involves many stages starting with the raw materials, intermediate goods and then the finished goods. It is important to note that in the GDP, only the values of the final goods are included. The values of the intermediate goods are already a part of the market price of the final goods in the production of which they are used. This avoids duplication.

Imputations in the GDP

For goods, which are not sold in the market, imputed values have to be used in the GDP calculations. For example, imputations are used for people living in their own houses, for durable goods which are owned by households and meals which are cooked at home.

Nominal GDP is the total of the value of the goods and services calculated at current prices.

Real GDP is the total of the value of goods and services calculated at constant prices.

Nominal GDP and Real GDP

Nominal GDP is the total of the value of the goods and services calculated at current prices. Real GDP is the total of the value of goods and services calculated at constant prices.

In Table 16.1, the overall growth of GDP in India (at factor cost at 2004–05 prices), in 2011–12, as per advanced estimates released by the

BOX 16.2

The GDP deflator or the implicit deflator is the ratio of the nominal GDP to the real GDP. GDP Deflator = Nominal GDP/Real GDP. This deflator deflates (or in other words takes out inflation from) the nominal GDP to give the real GDP. Hence, it reflects as to what is really happening to the general price level in an economy.

Table 16.1 Overall GDP Growth in India

Year	Rate of Growth of Total GDP at Factor Cost at 2004–05 Prices in India
2005–06	9.5
2006–07	9.6
2007–08	9.3
2008–09	6.7
2009–10	8.4
2010–11	8.4
2011–12	6.9

Source: *Economic Survey, 2011–12.*

Central Statistical Organization (CSO) was 6.9 per cent. The growth of GDP represents a deceleration from high growth years of 9.3 per cent and 9.6 per cent in 2007–08 and 2006–07, respectively.

GDP and Economic Activity

It is important to note that often the value of many goods and services do not get included in the GDP. Also, the imputations involved in the calculations of the GDP may not be accurate. Hence the *GDP is an imperfect measure of economic activity.*

To some extent, it can be pointed out that real GDP, when compared with nominal GDP, is a better measure of economic well-being because it is not affected by a change in the prices.

Measurement of Real GDP

Real GDP can be calculated in two ways:

(i) By using base year prices.
(ii) By using chain-weighted measures.

In general and most often, the two methods are interlinked and used to measure variations in the production of goods and services in the economy.

GDP and the Other Measures of Income

From the GDP, we can arrive at the other measures of income in the national income accounts.

Gross National Product (GNP)

GNP = GDP + Factor payments from abroad – Factor payments to abroad.

Net National Product (NNP)

$$NNP = GNP - Depreciation$$

National Income (NI)

$$NI = NNP - Indirect\ business\ taxes$$

where depreciation is quantity of the economy's stock of plants and equipment that wears out during the period of a year, indirect business taxes like sales tax and value-added taxes account for the difference between the price received by the firms and the price paid by the consumers for a good.

Personal Income

Personal income is the income received by households and the non-corporate businesses.

Personal income is the income received by households and the non-corporate businesses. It includes income from all sources.

Personal income = National income − (Corporate profits + Social security contributions + Net interest) + (Dividends + Transfers from government to individuals + Personal interest income)

We can arrive at the personal income from the national income by making some adjustments in the following sectors.

Corporate Sector

(i) Deduction to be made from the national income of undistributed corporate profits (or retained earnings) and the corporate taxes paid to the state.

(ii) Addition to be made to the national income of dividends.

Government Sector

(i) Deduction of the contributions to social insurance.

(ii) Addition to be made of the net amount the government pays as transfer payments to the individuals.

Household Sector

(i) Deduction of the net interest.

(ii) Addition to be made of the personal interest income.

Disposable Personal Income

Disposable personal income is the amount, which is actually available to the households and to the non-corporate business after they have fulfilled their tax obligations to the government.

Disposable personal income or personal disposable income is the amount, which is actually available to the households and to the non-corporate business after they have fulfilled their tax obligations to the government. It is the income available to the households for saving and consumption.

Disposable personal income = Personal income − Personal tax and non-tax payments

RECAP

- Real GDP, when compared with nominal GDP, is a better measure of economic well-being because it is not affected by a change in the prices.
- Real GDP can be calculated in two ways: by using base year prices and by using chain-weighted measures.

MEASUREMENT OF NATIONAL INCOME

To estimate the aggregate economic activity in a country, many measures are used mainly GDP, GNP and NNP. Among these, GDP is perhaps one of the most important macroeconomic variables and one of the best measures to judge an economy's performance. Three approaches to calculating the GDP are the output approach, the income approach and the expenditure approach. Theoretically, the three approaches must yield the same result because the total expenditures on goods and services (GNE) must be equal to the total income paid out to the producers (GNI), and that in turn must also be equal to the total value of the output of goods and services (GNP).

We now attempt an analysis of the three approaches.

Output Approach

It is also called the product method or the value-added method. To estimate the GDP by this approach, the total value of all the final goods and services produced in an economy during a given time are estimated.

The stages involved are:

(i) **Estimation of Gross Value of the Domestic Product:** This involves, firstly, a classification of the enterprises involved in the production according to their activities. The three sectors here are the primary sector, which relates to agriculture and allied activities, secondary sector (manufacturing sector), which includes all units engaged in producing material goods, and tertiary sector (services sector) which includes all units engaged in producing services such as banking and transport.

Secondly, the gross value or the value of the output is estimated from all the sectors in two ways.

— Multiplying the output of each sector with the respective price and then summing them up.

— Adding up the sales and change in stocks.

(ii) **Estimation of the Intermediate Cost of Production and Depreciation:** While intermediate costs are estimated by including expenditure on non-factor inputs such as raw materials, electricity and fuel used in the production process, depreciation may be estimated as a percentage of output or as a percentage of capital.

(iii) **Deduction of the Intermediate Cost of Production** and depreciation from the gross value to arrive at the net value of the domestic product.

BOX 16.3

In the US economy, the output flow method is accepted. It is also called the total product method or the goods flow method.

Income Approach

It is also called the factor income method or factor share method. To estimate the GDP by this approach, *the total sum of factor payments received during a given time is estimated.* Depending on the way the income is earned, it can be classified into five components:

(i) **Employee's Compensation** includes the wages, salaries, and the fringe benefits received by the workers.

(ii) **Proprietor's Income** includes the incomes of non-corporate businesses including the small firms.

(iii) **Rental Income** includes all the rental income earned by the owners of properties including the imputed rent on the houses, which are self-owned.

(iv) **Corporate Profits** include the incomes of corporations after having made payments to the workers, creditors and others.

(v) **Net Interest** includes the interest, which is paid by the domestic business after deducting the interest received and also the interest earned from abroad.

All the different categories of income are added together to obtain the GDP from the income method.

Expenditure Approach

The GDP can be classified into four components of expenditure:

(i) **Private Consumption Expenditure** includes goods and services, which are purchased by households. These can be further grouped into three categories:
- Non-durable goods are goods, which last only for a short period such as food and clothing.
- Durable goods are goods, which last for a long period such as cars and electronic goods.
- Services include the work performed or services provided by firms, individuals and others for the benefit of the consumer such as banking, accounting and auditing services.

(ii) **Investment Expenditure** consists of goods and services bought for use in the future. It can be further grouped into three categories:
- Business-fixed investment is the purchase of new plant and equipment by firms.
- Residential investment is the purchase of new housing by households and others.
- Inventory investment is the change in the inventory of goods of the firm. This change can be positive or negative depending on whether inventories increase or decrease.

(iii) **Government Purchases** include the goods and services bought by the different governments such as defense equipments. It is to be noted that transfer payments to the individuals such as social security payments are not included in the GDP as they are not a payment for any goods and services.

(iv) **Net Exports** are the values of goods and services exported to other countries minus the value of goods and services imported into the country.

A sum of all these different expenditures will give the GDP by the expenditure method.

Net Income from Abroad

It is important to understand that all the three methods discussed above yield the GDP at market price or in other words the GDP for a closed economy. To arrive at the GDP for an open economy, we need to

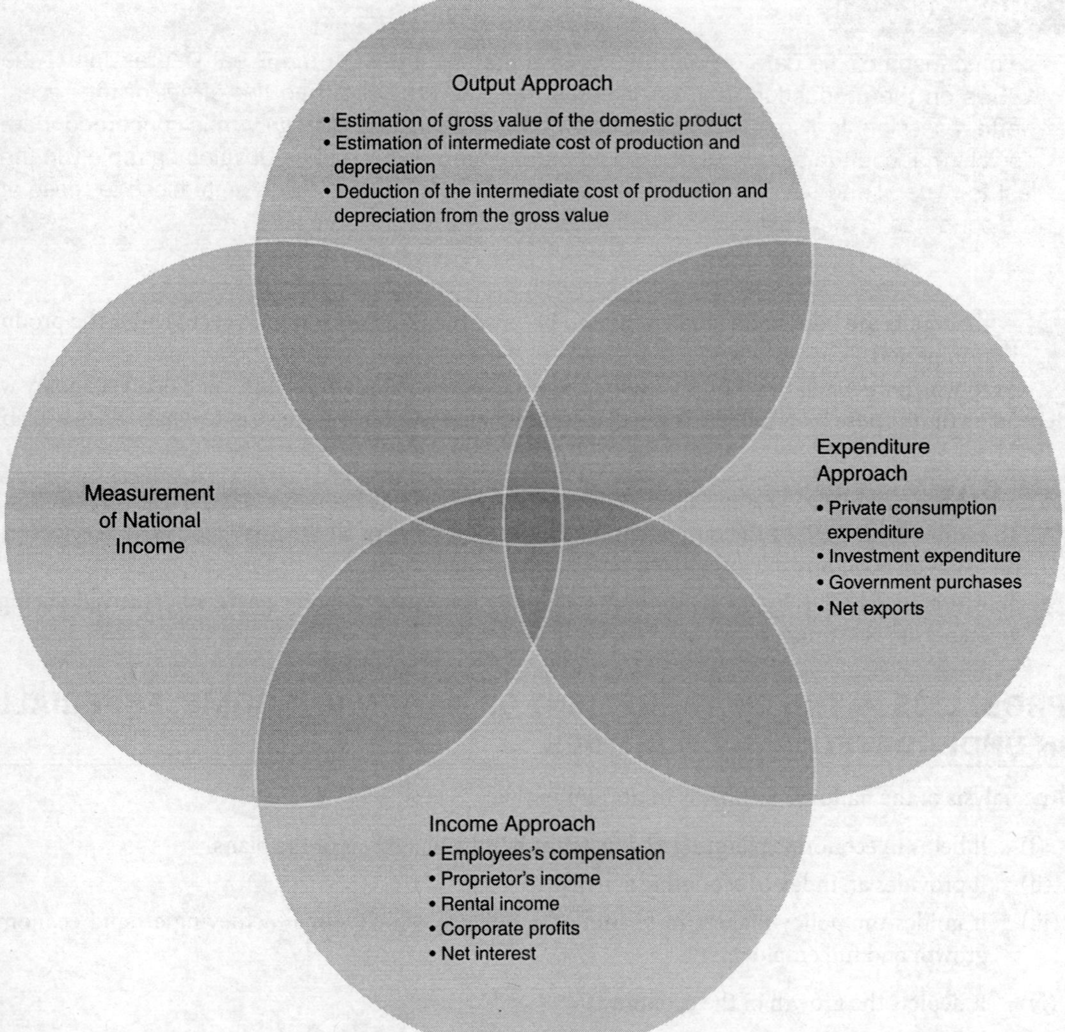

Figure 16. 1 Measurement of National Income

add to it the net factor incomes earned from abroad. Hence, we will now obtain what is called the Gross National Income (GNI).

The three approaches have been depicted in Figure 16.1. As already mentioned, theoretically, the three approaches must yield the same result. However, in practice, there exist minor differences from the various methods for several reasons:

(i) Changes in inventory levels and errors in the statistics. This occurs because the goods, which are in inventory, have been produced (and are therefore included in GNP) but they are not yet sold (and are therefore not yet included in GNE).

(ii) Issues relating to timing can cause a slight difference between the value of goods produced (GNP) and the payments to the factors involved in the production of the goods. This is, particularly so if

BOX 16.4

A comparison of the data on real GDP shows that the effect of the Great Depression of the 1930s on the production and the incomes was more severe than the effect of the recent world recession. It also appears that as far as the per capita GDP growth is concerned, data depicts that countries such as China and other countries have been developing rapidly in the last few years, and have succeeded in raising their standards of living quite close to those of the countries in the West.

the inputs are bought on credit, and also because the wages are often collected after the production period.

As to which particular method should be chosen to estimate the national income of an economy will depend on the purpose for which the national income is being estimated and also as to what data is available.

RECAP

- To estimate the GDP by the output approach, the total value of all the final goods and services produced in an economy during a given time are estimated.
- To estimate the GDP by the income approach, the total sum of factor payments received during a given period is estimated.

PROBLEMS IN THE MEASUREMENT OF NATIONAL INCOME, ESPECIALLY IN UNDERDEVELOPED COUNTRIES

An analysis of the national income is important in that:

(i) It helps in economic planning and in achieving the objectives of the plans.
(ii) It provides an index of economic activity.
(iii) It guides the policy makers in forming the policies, which aim at achieving a rapid economic growth and full employment.
(iv) It depicts the growth of the economy.

To calculate the national income of a country is not an easy task. The first person who made an attempt to calculate the national income of India was Dadabhai Naroji in 1867–68. Professor V. K. R. V. Rao made another attempt in 1931–32. Professor P. C. Mahalnobis conducted another attempt in 1948–49 as chairman of the National Income Committee. This committee made some very important recommendations on the basis of which the National Sample Survey and later the CSO was set up in 1967 for the estimation of the national income. Table 16.2 depicts some selected indicators for the Indian economy.

BOX 16.5

The United Nations has developed the Human Development Index. This index ranks the different countries according to their level of human development. It gives the same weightage to the GDP, the level of education and life expectancy. Some economists are of the opinion that the national income accounts are of more use than the Human Development Index.

Table 16.2 Selected Indicators of the Indian Economy

Key Indicators							
Data Categories and Components	**Units**	**2006–07**	**2007–08**	**2008–09**	**2009–10**	**2010–11**	**2011–12**
GDP and Related Indicators							
GDP (current market prices)	₹ crore	4294706	4987090	5630063	6457352[PE]	7674148[QE]	8912178[AE]
Growth rate	%	16.3	16.1	12.9	14.7	18.8	16.1
GDP (factor cost 2004–05 prices)	₹ crore	3564364	3896636	4158676	4507637[PE]	4885954[QE]	5222027[AE]
Growth rate	%	9.6	9.3	6.7	8.4	8.4	6.9
Savings rate	% of GDP	34.6	36.8	32.0	33.8	32.3	na
Capital formation (rate)	% of GDP	35.7	38.1	34.3	36.6	35.1	na
Per capita net national income (factor cost at current prices)	₹	31206	35825	40775	46117	53331	60972
Production							
Foodgrains	Mn tonnes	217.3	230.8	234.5	218.1	244.8	250.4[a]
Index of industrial production[b] (growth)	Per cent	12.9	15.5	2.5	5.3	8.2	3.6[c]
Electricity generation (growth)	Per cent	7.3	6.3	2.7	6.1	5.5	9.4[c]
Prices							
Inflation (WPI) (52-week average)	% change	6.6	4.7	8.1	3.8	9.6	9.1[d]
Inflation CPI (IW) (average)	% change	6.7	6.2	9.1	12.4	10.4	8.4[d]
External Sector							
Export growth (US$)	% change	22.6	29.0	13.6	–3.5	40.5	23.5[d]
Import growth (US$)	% change	24.5	35.5	20.7	–5.0	28.2	29.4[d]
Current account balance (CAB)/GDP	Per cent	–1.0	–1.3	–2.3	–2.8	–2.7	–3.6[e]

(Continued)

Table 16.2 **(Continued)**

Key Indicators							
Data Categories and Components	**Units**	**2006–07**	**2007–08**	**2008–09**	**2009–10**	**2010–11**	**2011–12**
Foreign exchange reserves	US$ Bn.	199.2	309.7	252.0	279.1	304.8	292.8[f]
Average exchange rate	₹/US$	45.25	40.26	45.99	47.44	45.56	47.70[g]
Money and Credit							
Broad money (M3) (annual)	% change	21.3	21.4	19.3	16.8	16.0	14.4[h]
Scheduled commercial bank credit (growth)	% change	28.1	22.3	17.5	16.9	21.5	16.4[h]
Fiscal Indicators (Centre)							
Gross fiscal deficit	% of GDP	3.3	2.5	6.0	6.5	4.8[i]	4.6[j]
Revenue deficit	% of GDP	1.9	1.1	4.5	5.2	3.2[i]	3.4[j]
Primary deficit	% of GDP	–0.2	–0.9	2.6	3.2	1.8[i]	1.6[j]
Population	Million	1122	1138	1154	1170	1210[k]	na

[AE] GDP figures for 2011–12 are advance estimates; [QE] Quick estimates; [PE] Provisional estimates.

na not available

[a] Second advance estimates.

[b] The Index of Industrial Production has been revised since 2005–06 on base (2004–05 = 100).

[c] April–December 2011.

[d] April 2011 to January 2012.

[e] CAB to GDP ratio for 2011–12 is for the period April–September 2011.

[f] At end January, 2012.

[g] Average exchange rate for 2011–12 (April 2011–February 2012).

[h] Provisional (upto January 27, 2012).

[i] Fiscal indicators for 2010–11 are based on the provisional actuals.

[j] Budget estimates.

[k] Census 2011.

Source: *Economic Survey, 2011–12.*

The CSO estimates the national income by using a combination of the income and the output approach. As far as the agriculture and industry sectors are concerned, the output approach is used. As far as the service sector including banking, transport and commerce are concerned, the income approach is used.

The estimation of the national income is not an easy task, especially in the underdeveloped countries. The problems involved include:

(i) One of the major difficulties relates to the availability of reliable statistical data. Often, it is formed on the basis of assumptions.

(ii) Often, the data is underreported because of the vast area, huge population, the existence of an unorganized sector and the black market.

(iii) When calculating the national income of a country, it is necessary to include the income of all the residents of the country whether they are living within the country or outside the country.

(iv) A major problem is the presence of a non-monetized sector. A major part of the agricultural output does not enter the market and is used for self-consumption.

(v) Most producers are illiterate and thus do not maintain proper accounts. Hence, it is difficult to obtain the information data from them.

(vi) Another problem relates to illegal activities, income from which should not be included in the national income.

In spite of all the limitations, which exist in the estimation of the national income, it is still the most useful and best method for measuring the output in an economy, comparing it overtime and with the other countries in the world.

RECAP

- An analysis of the national income is important in that it provides an index of economic activity, depicts the growth of the economy and guides the policy makers in forming the policies.
- The CSO estimates the national income by using a combination of the income and the output approach.
- The problems involved in the estimation of the national income include the lack of availability of reliable statistical data, the presence of a non-monetized sector, and existence of illegal activities.
- The national income estimates are still the most useful and best method for measuring the output in an economy.

SUMMARY

INTRODUCTION

This chapter focuses on an analysis of the national income, national product and related aggregates such as personal income and disposable personal income.

NATIONAL INCOME AGGREGATES

1. GNP is the total value of all the final goods and services produced in a country in a particular year, and the income which is earned by its citizens who are located abroad minus the income of non-residents located within that country.
2. GDP is the total value of all the final goods and services produced by all the enterprises (both the resident and the non-resident) within the domestic territory of a country in a particular year. It is taken to be one of the best indicators of judging an economy's performance.

3. In calculating the GDP, only market prices are used and only the value of currently produced goods and services is included.
4. As far as inventories are concerned, production of inventories also increases the GDP.
5. As far as intermediate goods are concerned, in the GDP, only the value of the final goods (and not the intermediate goods) is included. This avoids duplication.
6. For goods, which are not sold in the market, imputed values have to be used in the GDP calculations.
7. Nominal GDP is the total of the value of the goods and services calculated at current prices while real GDP is the total of the value of goods and services calculated at constant prices.
8. GDP is an imperfect measure of economic activity because often the value of many goods and services do not get included in the GDP and the imputations involved in the calculations of the GDP may not be accurate. Real GDP is a better measure of economic well-being because it is not affected by a change in the prices.
9. Real GDP can be calculated either by using base year prices or by using chain-weighted measures.
10. GNP = GDP + Factor payments from abroad – Factor payments to abroad.
11. NNP = GNP – Depreciation.
12. NI = NNP – Indirect business taxes.

Personal Income

1. Personal income is the income received by households and the non-corporate businesses from all sources.
2. Personal income = National income – (Corporate profits + Social security contributions + Net interest) + (Dividends + Transfers from government to individuals + Personal interest income).

Disposable Personal Income

1. Disposable personal income or personal disposable income is the amount, which is actually available to the households and to the non-corporate business after they have fulfilled their tax obligations to the government.
2. Disposable personal income = Personal income – Personal tax and non-tax payments.

MEASUREMENT OF NATIONAL INCOME

1. GDP is one of the most important macroeconomic variables and one of the best measures to judge an economy's performance.
2. Three ways of calculating the GDP are the output approach, the income approach and the expenditure approach.
3. The output approach is also called the product method or the value-added method. Here, the total value of all the final goods and services produced in an economy during a given time are estimated in three stages.
4. The income approach is also called the factor income method or factor share method. To estimate the GDP by this approach, the total sum of factor payments received during a given period is estimated.
5. In the expenditure approach, there are four components: private consumption expenditure, investment expenditure, government purchases and net exports.
6. Net income from abroad is to be added to the GDP to arrive at the GNI.
7. Theoretically, the three approaches must yield the same result. However, in practice, there exist minor differences in the various methods due to changes in inventory levels and errors in the statistics and due to issues relating to timing.

PROBLEMS IN THE MEASUREMENT OF NATIONAL INCOME, ESPECIALLY IN UNDERDEVELOPED COUNTRIES

1. An analysis of the national income is important in that it provides an index of economic activity, depicts the growth of the economy and guides the policy makers in forming the policies.
2. The first person who made an attempt to calculate the national income of India was Dadabhai Naroji in 1867–68.

3. Professor V. K. R. V. Rao made another attempt in 1931–32.
4. Professor P. C. Mahalnobis conducted another attempt in 1948–49 as chairman of the National Income Committee.
5. The CSO was set up in 1967 for the estimation of the national income.
6. The CSO estimates the national income by using a combination of the income and the output approach.
7. The problems involved in the estimation of the national income include the lack of availability of reliable statistical data, the presence of a non-monetized sector, and existence of illegal activities.
8. The national income estimates are still the most useful and best method for measuring the output in an economy.

REVIEW QUESTIONS

TRUE OR FALSE QUESTIONS

1. GDP is a measure of the value of goods and services, which the nationals or residents of the country produce regardless of where they are located.
2. Personal income is the income received by households and the non-corporate businesses.
3. Disposable personal income is the amount, which is actually available to the households and to the non-corporate business after they have fulfilled their tax obligations to the government.
4. Personal income is perhaps one of the most important macroeconomic variables and one of the best measures to judge an economy's performance.
5. Three approaches to calculating the GDP are the output approach, the income approach and the expenditure approach.

SHORT ANSWER QUESTIONS

1. What is personal income? How can one arrive at the personal income from the national income?
2. How is the GDP calculated by the output approach? What are the different stages?
3. How is the GDP calculated by the income approach? What are the different components of income?
4. How is the GDP calculated by the expenditure approach? What are the different components of expenditure?
5. Differentiate between the GNP and the GDP? In the computation of the GDP, what is the treatment given to:
   (a) Inventories
   (b) Intermediate goods and
   (c) Goods not sold in the market

LONG ANSWER QUESTIONS

1. Write a short note on the GNP and the GDP bringing out the difference between the two national income aggregates. Is the GDP a perfect measure of economic activity? Discuss.
2. Which are the three approaches to calculating the GDP? Discuss.
3. Write short notes on the following:
   (a) GNP
   (b) GDP
   (c) Nominal GDP and real GDP
   (d) Personal income
   (e) Disposable personal income
4. (a) How is the real GDP measured?
   (b) How can we arrive at the other measures of income in the national income accounts from the Gross Domestic Product, namely, Gross National Product, Net National Product (NNP) and National Income (NI)?
5. 'A sum of all the different expenditures will give the GDP by the expenditure method'. Which are these expenditures? Discuss.

ANSWERS

TRUE OR FALSE QUESTIONS

1. **False.** GNP is a measure of the value of goods and services, which the nationals or residents of the country produce regardless of where they are located.
2. **True.** Personal income is the income received by households and the non-corporate businesses. It includes income from all sources.
3. **True.** Disposable personal income is the amount, which is actually available to the households and to the non-corporate business after they have fulfilled their tax obligations to the government. It is, in fact, the income available to the households for saving and consumption.
4. **False.** GDP is one of the most important macroeconomic variables and one of the best measures to judge an economy's performance.
5. **True.** Three approaches to calculating the GDP are the output approach, the income approach and the expenditure approach. Theoretically, the three approaches must yield the same result.

Classical Model of Income Determination

17

After studying this chapter, you should be able to understand:

- ✓ *With advent of Keynes' book, The General Theory of Employment, Interest and Money, in the year 1936, began the Keynesian era.*
- ✓ *It was followed by the development of the supply side economics.*
- ✓ *Whether it is the individual, the consumer, the firm or the government, macroeconomics is important for all.*
- ✓ *The variables in any economic model can be a stock or a flow.*
- ✓ *A static relationship exists when all variables relate to the same time and a dynamic relationship exists when all the variables relate to different times.*
- ✓ *A given set of relationships between the variables may lead to equilibrium or a disequilibrium solution.*
- ✓ *Say's law states that 'supply creates its own demand'.*
- ✓ *The aggregate of the demand in all the markets will be always equal to the aggregate of the supply.*
- ✓ *The production function describes the relationship between the inputs and the output.*
- ✓ *The marginal product schedule is the firm's demand curve for labour.*
- ✓ *The classical economists had propagated a free market economy, which they believed that it would automatically lead to full employment.*

INTRODUCTION

Macroeconomic is the study of how the national economy as a whole grows and the changes which occur over time. Thus, it analyses the big or the macropicture. Hence, the basic concerns of macroeconomics are to measure as to how well an economy is performing, as to how the economy works and then to try to improve the performance of the economy.

> Macroeconomics is the study of how the national economy as a whole grows and the changes which occur over time.

BACKGROUND OF MACROECONOMICS

The founder of the field of microeconomics is thought to be Adam Smith. It is that branch of economics, which is concerned with the behaviour of individual entities such as firms, households and markets. These are the very issues, which Adam Smith has addressed in his book *The Wealth of Nations*.

Macroeconomics, the other major branch of economics, is of relatively recent origin when compared with microeconomics. However, it did exist earlier also but not with the same popularity that it gained with Keynes. One can trace the origin of macroeconomics by dividing it into three stages.

Classical School of Thought

Karl Marx was responsible for the origin of the term 'classical'. He used the term to include the theories of David Ricardo, James Mill and the other economists who preceded him. Later on, Keynes extended the term classical to include the followers of Ricardo including Marshall, J. S. Mill, Pigou and Edgeworth.

Keynesian Economics

In the 1930s, the most dramatic developments took place. The US economy, even with a quarter of its resources lying idle (a less than full employment situation), plunged into a depression. The classical school failed to provide any explanation to this turn of events.

The answer to the problems, which the US economy faced, came in the form of Keynes book, *The General Theory of Employment, Interest and Money*, in the year 1936. This book provided a theory to explain the events, which plagued the US economy at that particular time. The book with its embedded theories was so well received that with it began the Keynesian era.

The response of the classical school to the situation was the argument that full employment was the normal situation in any economy. However, departures in the form of less than full employment could temporarily occur. But, the automatic forces present in a competitive market would push the economy back to the full employment equilibrium. The experiences of the US economy with the relatively few but temporary depressions in the early twentieth century lend credence to these views. Their basic tenet was that it was not possible for aggregate demand for goods and services to fall short of aggregate supply except for a temporary period.

Keynes' General Theory was an alternative theory, which explained the determination of employment and output and also gave an explanation as to why the market forces in an economy would not automatically generate a level of aggregate demand, which was required for full employment. Keynes' theory addressed the issues pertaining to the economic disaster in the form of the Great Depression and provided an explanation for this disaster. In his new theory, Keynes had developed an analysis as to what causes unemployment and the downturns, how the consumption and investment levels are determined, as to how a Central Bank manages the money and the interest rates in an economy, and most important of all as to why some nations prosper while others stagnate.

Keynes' theory was followed by refinements, termed as Keynesian economics, which were later applied to tackle the analysis of inflation during and after the Second World War. With its growing success in providing a solution to the major macroeconomic issues, the Keynesian theory held sway into the 1960s.

The success faced by the US economy was, however, short lived. The various restrictive policy measures, recommended by the Keynesian theory, were not successful in checking the inflation and were, in fact, responsible for pushing the US economy towards a recession in 1970, which was later followed by double digit rate of inflation that gripped the US economy. In such a situation, Keynesian economics, where the tools were designed for the specific purpose of controlling aggregate demand, could not provide a solution to the problem of controlling inflation and a recession simultaneously. What were required were tools to manage the long-neglected supply side. This was followed by the development of what is called the supply side economics.

Post-Keynesian Economics

Notwithstanding the tremendous success, which Keynes and his book received, it could not in any way prevent the further developments, which occurred on the classical front to appear under the heading of neo-classical, especially during the 1950s.

BOX 17.1

It was the Keynesian macroeconomics and the implementation of the proper plans and in the right directions which were responsible, to some extent, in building up the US economy in the aftermath of the Great Depression. Today, most of the economies in Africa and even in parts of South America are facing a struggle, which is worse than what the US did at the time of the Great Depression. Faced with the problems of poverty, the issues of health and education, these economies are in a dire need of economic policies, which can help them in coming out of such doldrums. However, these policies can be determined only after a thorough study of the macroeconomic issues, which affect these economies.

Starting in the 1950s and continuing till today is the development of another extension of the classical theory, which assigns a very critical role to money as a major factor in determining whatever happens in an economy. The theory is known as the *monetarism*. In fact, in the 1960s and the 1970s, the theory gained so much importance that it was thought to be a counter-revolution. Monetarists such as Milton Friedman were responsible for making the theory popular worldwide.

In the 1970s, the classical theory took a new turn with the introduction of the concept of *rational expectations*. This was the latest theoretical development on the classical front, whose roots were firmly embedded in the classical theory. The emphasis here was on the role played by the individual's rational expectations regarding the future economic events. Later on, there appeared the supply side economists with their emphasis on the factors operating on the supply side.

RECAP

- The answer to the problems in the US economy came in the form of Keynes book.
- In the 1960s and the 1970s, the theory which gained popularity is known as monetarism.

NEED TO STUDY MACROECONOMICS

From the Viewpoint of an Individual

Macroeconomics may exercise a strong influence on the individual investor. For understanding and analysing the long-term trends and also the aggregate market behaviour, the principles of macroeconomics play a very important role. Thus, for an individual, who is managing his own asset portfolio, it may be of considerable importance to be aware of the current fiscal policy and also as to what will be its repercussions on the value of the government bond holdings. Depending on the objectives of the fiscal policy, the government may buy back the bonds or it may issue more bonds.

From the Viewpoint of the Consumers, Firms and Governments

The macroeconomists try to anticipate the economic conditions to be able help the consumers, the firms and the governments in making their decisions.

(i) The consumers' interest lies in wanting to know how easy or difficult it will be for them to be able to find work. They are also concerned about the price of the goods and service and also as to how much may be the cost of borrowing.

(ii) The interest of the business lies in knowing whether or not to expand the production. They are also concerned about whether the consumer will have sufficient purchasing power to buy the product.

(iii) The government is concerned with the macroeconomy when planning its budget and taxes, deciding on the interest rates and making its other policy decisions in the national interest.

From the Viewpoint of an Economy's Performance

An economy's performance is of considerable importance to all of us. We evaluate the performance of the macroeconomy by essentially looking at the national output, the rate of unemployment, the inflation rate and the trade performance. Even though it is the consumers who play the most important role in determining the direction that an economy traverses, the government also plays its role through the fiscal and the monetary policy. A study of macroeconomics helps us evaluate the success or failure of the economic policies of the government and the Central Bank of the country.

From the Viewpoint of an Economy's Stability and Growth

Although macroeconomics involves a wide field of study, there are two areas, which are typical of the discipline.

Business Cycle

Macroeconomists are involved in trying to analyse the short-run fluctuations in the national income, which lead to the business cycles.

Increases in the National Income

Of great interest to the macroeconomists are the determinants of long-run economic growth, which are responsible for the increases in the national income.

Both the government and the corporations utilize the macroeconomic models and their forecasts to further the process of development and also in the evaluation of economic policies and the business strategies. This would help in maintaining the stability and also in attaining the growth.

In the present scenario with the world in the grips of a recession, macroeconomists are busy in trying to diagnose the cause of the recession and to find the policies or the mix of policies, which will help the different economies of the world to pull out of the recession.

RECAP

- Macroeconomics helps evaluate the performance of the economy, in terms of the national output, the rate of unemployment, the inflation rate and the trade performance.

CONCEPTS IN MACROECONOMICS

The variables in any economic model can be a stock and/or a flow. A relationship is postulated among these variables in the model. If all the variables in the model relate to the same time, then it is a static relationship while, if the variables relate to different times, it is a dynamic relationship. A given set of relationships between the variables may lead to equilibrium or a disequilibrium solution. An equilibrium solution can be analysed through a static methodology, while a disequilibrium solution can be analysed through a dynamic methodology. If the model pertains to a situation, where one equilibrium position is succeeded by another equilibrium position, then it can be analysed through the comparative statics.

Stocks and Flows

Both the stocks and the flows are variables. Both are quantities, which may increase or decrease over time. However, there is a difference between them. While stock is a quantity, which is measured at a point in time, flow is a quantity measured overtime.

Stock is a quantity, which is measured at a point in time.

Flow is a quantity measured over time.

Some macrostock variables are the money supply, total number of people employed in an economy, total stock of capital, the total labour force, etc. Some macroflow variables are the savings, investment, change in inventories, change in the money supply, etc.

It is important to note that often stock and flow are related. This is because flow is actually the change in the stock. For example, while the total number of people employed in an economy is a stock variable, the numbers of people who take up new jobs or leave jobs are flow variables. While money is a stock variable, the expenditures in money or the spending of money is a flow variable. While inventories are stock variables, the change in inventories is a flow variable.

It is not necessary for there to be a flow counterpart to every stock variable. Imports and exports, taxes, wages and salaries and dividends are flows. There is no direct stock counterpart to them. However, though they do not have a stock counterpart, it is important to note that they do influence the other stock variables. For example, imports may affect the size of the stock of capital and also the stock of inventories.

While a change in stock occurs due to a change in the flow, a change in flow may also be influenced by a change in stock. For example, a change in inventories is brought about by many factors including a change in the stock of capital. An excessive stock of capital may necessitate a decrease in the flow of investment and may thus be responsible for a business going downhill. However, it is important to note that stock can influence flows only in the long run.

Equilibrium and Disequilibrium

In the simplest terms, equilibrium is a state of balance or a state, where there is no change. The forces acting in the system may bring about a change in the economy. However, the net effect of the change is that the equilibrium position does not in any way gets disturbed. On the other hand, disequilibrium is a state of imbalance.

Equilibrium is a state of balance or a state, where there is no change.

The macroeconomic model, which can be considered here, relates to aggregate demand and aggregate supply as in Figure 17.1, where X axis

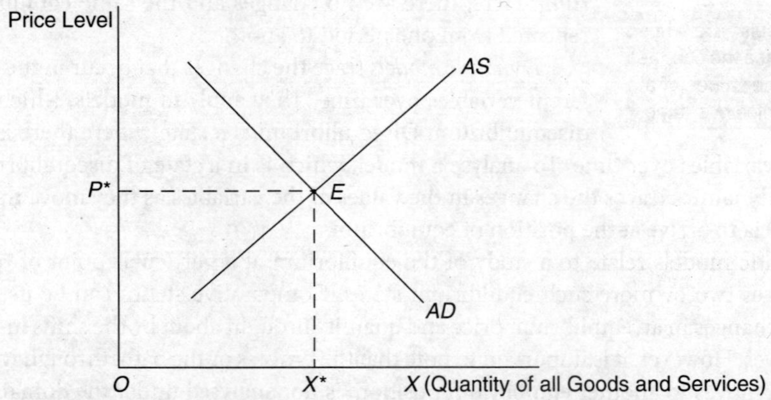

Figure 17.1 Aggregate Demand and Aggregate Supply

is aggregate quantities of all the commodities in the economy, *Y* axis is the price level, *AD* is aggregate demand, *AS* is aggregate supply and *E* is equilibrium.

The *AD*, aggregate demand curve relates to the aggregate quantity of all the goods and services demanded or in other words it is the summation of the spending by the individuals, businesses, government and the net exports at each price level. The *AS*, aggregate supply, is the amount produced and supplied by the business at each price level. Equilibrium is determined at the intersection of the aggregate demand and aggregate supply curves at point *E* with the equilibrium output at X* and the equilibrium price at P^*. Thus, at P^*, the aggregate quantity of the goods and services demanded and supplied are equal.

Disequilibrium will exist at any price higher or lower than P^*. At a price higher than P^*, the aggregate quantity of the goods and services demanded will be less than the aggregate quantity supplied and therefore the price level will fall until equilibrium is achieved. At a price lower than P^*, the aggregate quantity of the goods and services demanded will be more than the aggregate quantity supplied and therefore the price level will rise until equilibrium is achieved.

Flow equilibrium can be taken as short-run equilibrium, while a stock equilibrium can be taken as long-run equilibrium. It is necessary to remember that a stock equilibrium cannot exist without flow equilibrium because long-run equilibrium cannot exist without short-run equilibrium.

The concept of equilibrium is of immense importance in that it identifies that position, where the variables are in a state of balance. Disequilibrium is again of importance in that it is closer to economic reality than equilibrium. The Keynesian model is, in fact, built upon the disequilibrium analysis.

Statics, Dynamics and Comparative Statics

We have already focused on the stock and flow variables found in the economic models. Equilibrium and disequilibrium are the two positions, which these models are in at any point in time. Two methods employed in the construction of these economic models are statics and dynamics.

In *static models*, the relations between the different variables relate to the same period in time. There is no need to be concerned about the problem of dating. Thus, static models are not able to trace the changes in the values of the different variables over time. Hence, these models are unable to explain the process of change. They apply to models, which are in a state of equilibrium.

> Static models are those models, where the relationship between the different variables relates to the same period in time.

> Dynamic models are those models that trace the changes that occur in the values of the different variables over time.

A special case of a static model is what is called a *stationary equilibrium*. Here, there are no changes and the same equilibrium position is repeated from one period to another.

Dynamic models trace the changes that occur in the values of the different variables over time. They apply to models, which are in a state of disequilibrium. Disequilibrium is a state, where there is a change in the values of the variables over time. To analyse a model, which is in a state of disequilibrium, dynamics is used. Hence, dynamics traces the changes in the values of the variables as they move through the different disequilibria to arrive at the position of equilibrium.

While static models relate to a study of the equilibrium at a particular point of time, *comparative statics* compares two or more such equilibrium states. Comparative statics can be used to analyse, for example, the changes in an equilibrium price and quantity brought about by the shifts in the demand and/or supply curves. However, it is important to note that the process or the path. through which one equilibrium position moves to another equilibrium position, is not analysed under the domain of comparative statics, which is discussed under dynamics. Comparative statics performs the task of bridging the gap between the two equilibrium positions, but is unable to explain the path, which has been traversed.

Comparative statics is of relevance only when an old equilibrium is succeeded by a new equilibrium position. When the old equilibrium is succeeded by a new disequilibrium position, comparative statics is not relevant.

Partial Equilibrium and General Equilibrium

Economists often distinguish between partial and general equilibrium analysis.

In a partial equilibrium analysis, which is the basis of study in microeconomics, more factors are assumed to be held constant when compared with a general equilibrium analysis.

A partial equilibrium analysis is based on the assumption of *ceteris paribus*, that is we assume everything, other than the market we are analysing, to be constant. For example, in an analysis of the maximization of the utility of the consumer, we assume that his income is constant. In analysing the demand, for say commodity *X*, we assume all factors, other than the price of commodity *X*, including income, tastes and price of other commodities to be constant. In the product market, the interaction of the buyers and sellers determines the equilibrium price and output, *ceteris paribus*, or in other words ignoring the relationship with the other markets. Thus, a partial equilibrium approach involves the determination of the equilibrium price and output in each market, *ceteris paribus*.

> Partial equilibrium approach involves the determination of the equilibrium price and output in each market, *ceteris paribus*.

The main problem with a partial equilibrium approach is that it ignores the interdependence and the linkages between the different markets. For example, in analysing the demand, for say commodity *X*, we assume all factors other than the price of commodity *X*, including income, tastes and price of other commodities to be constant. However, in reality, the demand for commodity *X* depends not only on the price of commodity *X*, but also on the individual's income, his tastes and the price of the other commodities, which may be substitutes or complements to the commodity.

As already discussed in Chapter 15, general equilibrium analysis involves a state, where all the markets and the decision-making units in the economy are in a simultaneous equilibrium. Hence, it studies the simultaneous equilibria in a group of interrelated markets emphasizing the interdependence between the different economic units in the economy.

> General equilibrium approach involves a state, where all the markets and the decision-making units in the economy are in a simultaneous equilibrium.

A general equilibrium approach analyses an economy in its totality taking into consideration the linkages between the different sectors in the economy. It does not consider the restrictive assumptions used in the partial equilibrium analysis. When compared with a partial equilibrium analysis, it allows many more variables to change.

While Marshall's name is associated with partial equilibrium analysis, general equilibrium analysis is associated with the French economist, Leon Walrus. He analysed an economic system, where the firms were perfectly competitive and the consumers were utility maximizers. The model showed that under such conditions a unique stable equilibrium can exist. However, economists have raised doubts about the stability and the uniqueness of such equilibrium.

In the modern world economics, while Marshall's partial equilibrium analysis is said to be relevant for the learners as well as the noninterventionist arts academicians, real economists are more interested in Walrus's general equilibrium analysis.

RECAP

- While a stock is measured at a point in time, flow is measured over time.
- Equilibrium is a state of balance, where there is no change.

- In static models, the relations between the different variables relate to the same period in time.
- General equilibrium is a state, where all the markets and the decision-making units in the economy are in a simultaneous equilibrium.

SAY'S LAW

Say's law is named after the famous economist J. B. Say, who refused to believe that general overproduction and unemployment are common occurrences. Many economists of the early nineteenth century accepted this law as a true explanation of the working of any economic system.

Some assumptions, which are implicit in the Say's law, are as follows:

(i) The income, which the households receive, is spent on goods and services. Hence, the average propensity to consume is one. This obviously implies that savings will be zero.

(ii) The government does not perform any economic functions. This implies that there are no government expenditures, no taxation or subsidies or government borrowing.

(iii) The economy is a closed economy. This implies that there is no trade or any other links with the rest of the world.

(iv) The prices are flexible in that they can rapidly adjust upwards or downwards.

In the economy, which is under consideration, basically there are only two sectors. These two sectors, the firms and households, are engaged in production and consumption, respectively. There is a circular flow of money from firms to households and from households to firms.

The most famous tenet of Say's law is 'supply creates its own demand'.

The most famous tenet of Say's law is 'supply creates its own demand'. By the very act of production, each producer aims at either the direct satisfaction of his wants or to exchange the goods that he produces for the other goods that he requires. Thus, the production of the goods itself involves a creation of demand for them.

In a *barter economy*, there is no doubt that this law will function. When a producer produces a good, he does so with the specific purpose of exchanging it for another good. Thus, the production or supply of the good creates a direct demand for the good in a barter economy.

In a *money economy*, goods are sold in the market for a price, which is expressed in terms of money. According to the classical economists, the producers of the goods, once they receive the money for the goods sold, use this money to buy more factors of production. The only function of money, according to the classical school, is to facilitate the process of exchange or to solely act as a medium of exchange.

BOX 17.2

J. B. Say was born in Lyon to a Protestant family. Say was expected to take up a commercial career. He went to England to a merchant for whom he acted as a clerk. Later, he moved to London under another employer. Then, he returned to France to work in a life assurance company. Say first wrote a pamphlet on the liberty of the press in 1789. In the year 1793, Say got married to the daughter of a former lawyer. Later, he edited a periodical, in which he developed the doctrines of Adam Smith. In 1831, Say became a professor of political economy at the college in France. His wife passed away in 1830 and since then his health started declining. He passed away in Paris on 15 November 1832.

BOX 17.3

An important point to note is that Say had himself not used any of the short definitions of Say's law. Some of his contemporaries and those who came after him developed this law. The 'law of markets' evolved from the work of James Mill, David Ricardo, John Stuart Mill and many others. It formed the basic framework of macroeconomics.

Its purpose is to avoid the problems faced in a barter economy. Thus, it is obvious that in any economy, the supply of any commodity implies a demand for the other commodities in the economy. Hence, *the aggregate of the demand in all the markets will be always equal to the aggregate of the supply.* It is possible that, for an individual market, the equality between supply and demand may not hold. But, an excess supply or overproduction in one market will necessarily be accompanied by an excess demand or under-production in the other market for Say's law to hold.

RECAP

- In a barter economy, there is no doubt that Say's law will function.
- In a money economy, for Say's law to hold, an excess supply in one market should necessarily be accompanied by an excess demand in the other market.

OUTPUT AND EMPLOYMENT IN CLASSICAL MODEL

The classical model, which is being discussed here, is highly simplified. It is limited to the determination of employment, output and price level.

Production Function

The production function describes the input–output relationship. Here, it is being defined for the short run. Short run is the length of time, which is too short for the firms to be able to vary the plants and equipment, which they use in production. In addition, the technology or the production method is also assumed to be constant in the short run. Thus, we can represent our short-run aggregate production function as

> The production function describes the input–output relationship.

$$Y = f(L, K)$$

where Y is real output, L is labour input and K is capital input.

As already discussed, it is being assumed that

(i) the stock of capital, or in other words, the plant and equipment are constant.
(ii) the technology is constant.

In Figure 17.2, the production function has been shown. It can be divided into three parts:

(i) Up to labour input, L_1 is the linear portion of the production function. It indicates *proportional returns* or in other words the output varies proportionately with labour.
(ii) Between L_1 and L_2 units of labour, the output increases less than proportionately for every unit of increase in labour. This is because increasing units of labour are applied to fixed amounts of plant

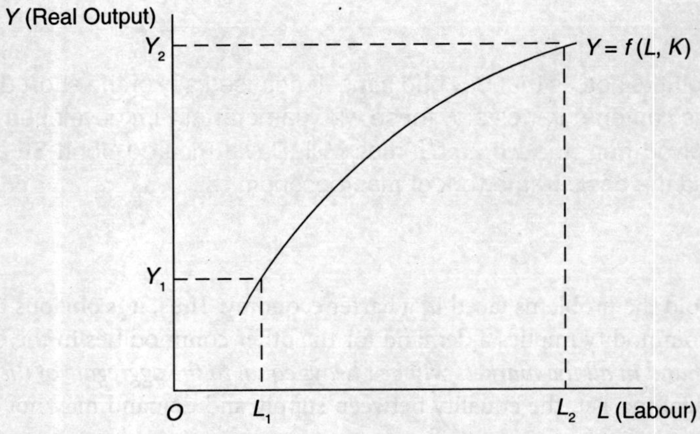

Figure 17.2 The Short-run Aggregate Production Function

and capital equipment. Hence, this is the stage of *diminishing returns* as the marginal product of labour (the increase in the total product due to a unit increase in labour) decreases as the quantity of labour input increases. Thus, the diminishing returns begin at L_1 units of labour and keep diminishing to become zero at L_2 units of labour.

(iii) Beyond L_2 units of labour, further additions to the labour input will not lead to an increase in the output. In fact, at some higher levels of the labour input, the output may start decreasing if more labour is hired.

Given the production function, it is obvious that a firm will not hire labour beyond L_2 units.

Labour Market in Classical Theory

It is assumed that

(i) The workers and the firms have complete knowledge about the prices, which are prevailing in the market.

(ii) The money wages adjust and thus the market clears. There is flexibility in the wages and prices.

Demand for Labour

A perfectly competitive profit-maximizing firm will go on increasing the output level till the marginal cost of producing an additional unit of the output is equal to the marginal revenue from the sale of the unit. Thus,

$$W/P = MPL$$

> The marginal product schedule is the firm's demand curve for labour.

where W/P is real wage and MPL is marginal product of labour.

Thus, a profit-maximizing firm will go on hiring labour till the MPL is equal to the real wage. In other words, the marginal product schedule is the firm's demand curve for labour.

The individual firms demand curve for labour can be summed up horizontally to arrive at the aggregate demand curve for labour. Thus, the aggregate demand schedule for labour can be expressed as

$$L^d = L^d(W/P)$$

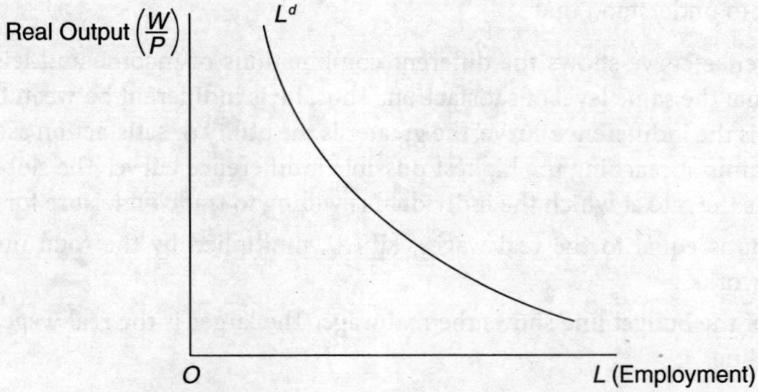

Figure 17.3 Aggregate Demand Curve for Labour

In Figure 17.3, the short-run aggregate demand for labour curve has been shown. L^d is downward sloping showing that decrease in the real wage rate will lead to an increase in the aggregate demand for labour.

Supply of Labour

The labour in an economy is supplied by the individual workers, who aim at maximizing their utility. Utility depends on both the leisure and the real income. While income can be increased by putting in more work, work leads to a reduction in the leisure time. Hence, *there appears to be a trade-off between leisure and income* (or work).

The derivation of the individual's supply curve of labour has been depicted in Figure 17.4, where *X* axis is total number of hours available for leisure or work to an individual over a given time, *Y* axis is real income, I_1, I_2, I_3 are indifference curves and $Z\text{-}W_1/P_1$, $Z\text{-}W_2/P_2$, $Z\text{-}W_3/P_3$ are individual's budget lines.

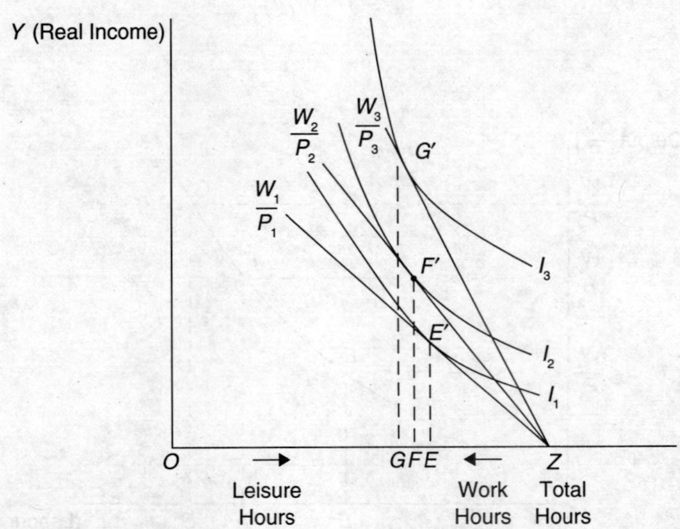

Figure 17.4 Derivation of the Individual's Supply Curve of Labour

It is important to understand that

(i) An indifference curve shows the different combinations of income and leisure, which give to the individual the same level of satisfaction. Thus, he is indifferent between these combinations. The higher is the indifference curve, the greater is the utility or satisfaction associated with it. The individual aims at reaching the highest possible indifference curve. The slope of an indifference curve shows the rate at which the individual is willing to trade off leisure for income.

(ii) Real income is equal to the real wages, (W/P), multiplied by the total number of hours the individual works.

(iii) The slope of the budget line shows the real wage. The larger is the real wage, the steeper will be the budget line.

The individual aims at maximizing his utility for any given real wage. He will do so by choosing that particular point on the indifference curve, where the budget line (which corresponds to that particular wage rate) is tangential to the indifference curve. At this particular point, the slope of the indifference curve is equal to the slope of the budget line. This implies that the rate at which he is willing to trade off the leisure for income is equal to the rate at which he is actually able to trade off.

In Figure 17.4,

(i) When the real wage rate is W_1/P_1, the individual is in equilibrium at point E' working for EZ hours, earning an income of EE' and spending OE hours on leisure.

(ii) When the real wage increases to W_2/P_2, the individual is in equilibrium at point F' working for FZ hours, earning an income of FF' and spending OF hours on leisure.

Similarly, the other points like G' can be derived. Joining these points such as E', F' and G', we can derive the supply curve for labour in Figure 17.5.

The aggregate supply curve for labour can be arrived at by summing up horizontally the individual supply curves of labour. The aggregate supply curve of labor can be expressed as

$$L^s = L^s\,(W/P)$$

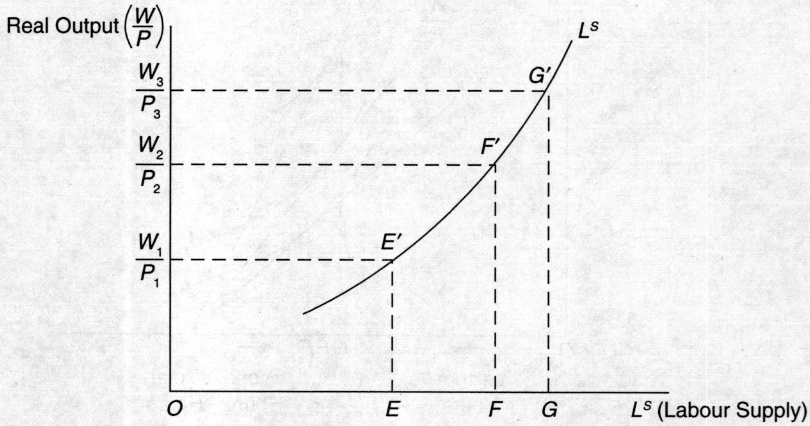

Figure 17.5 The Individual's Supply Curve of Labour

The aggregate supply curve of labour portrays the following two characteristics:

(i) The wage is the real wage rate.
(ii) The curve is positively sloped showing that the supply of labour increases as the real wage rate increases. (This relationship may not exist at some very high wage rate and in that case the supply curve of labour may bend backwards.)

Determination of Employment, Real Wage Rate and Output

The aggregate demand and aggregate supply curves of labour can now be utilized to determine the equilibrium level of output, employment and the real wage rate.

Figure 17.6(a) depicts the intersection of the aggregate demand curve for labour and aggregate supply curve for labour. The two curves intersect at point E^*. Thus, the equilibrium level of employment will

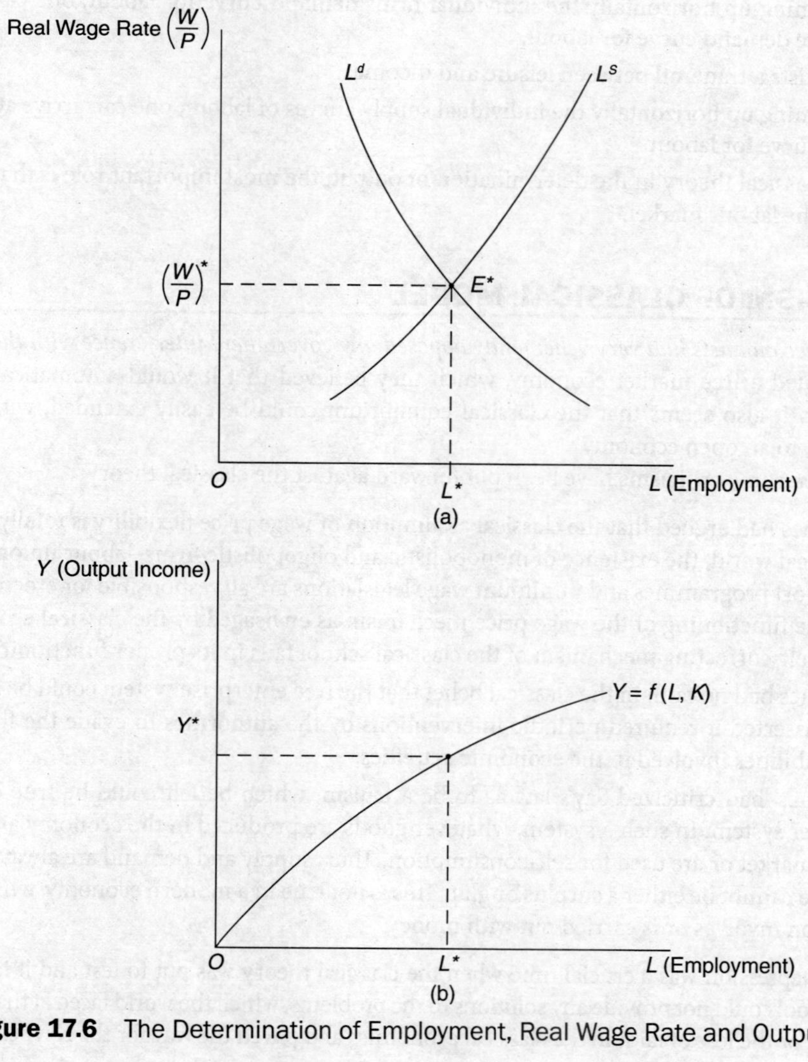

Figure 17.6 The Determination of Employment, Real Wage Rate and Output

be L^* and the real wage rate will be $(W/P)^*$. The classical economists had proposed that this will be the full employment level, which will prevail in the long run.

Figure 17.6(b) depicts the short-run production function. Given the equilibrium level of employment at L^*, as determined in Figure 17.6(a), the corresponding equilibrium level of output can be determined from the production function at Y^*. Hence, this implies that, according to the classical theory, L^* amount of labour will produce an output of Y^*, given the fixed capital and the technology.

It is obvious from the above that *in the classical theory, the main role in the determination of output, employment and the real wage rate is played by the supply side in the labour market.* The demand for labour is directly derived from the production function. Thus, the factors operating on the supply side in the labour market determine the level of employment, output and the wage rate.

RECAP

- By summing up horizontally the individual firms demand curve for labour, one can arrive at the aggregate demand curve for labour.
- There exists a trade-off between leisure and income.
- By summing up horizontally the individual supply curves of labour, one can arrive at the aggregate supply curve for labour.
- In the classical theory in the determination of output, the most important role is that of the supply side in the labour market.

A CRITICISM OF CLASSICAL MODEL

The classical economists had very vehemently opposed any government interference with the market. They had propagated a free market economy, which they believed that it would automatically lead to full employment. It also seems that the classical equilibrium could be easily extended, with some minor adjustments, to an open economy.

However, some criticisms have been put forward against the classical theory:

(i) Keynes had argued that the classical assumption of wage price flexibility is totally unrealistic. In the real world, the existence of monopolistic and oligopolistic firms, labour unions, government support programmes and minimum wage legislations are all responsible for erecting the barriers in the functioning of the wage price mechanism as envisaged by the classical economists. Thus, the self-correcting mechanism of the classical school fails in its proper functioning.

(ii) Keynes had no faith in the classical belief that the free enterprise system could be self-regulating. He asserted it required periodic interventions by the authorities to evade the fluctuations and instabilities involved in the economic activities.

(iii) Keynes' had criticized Say's law as to be a truism, which he felt could be true only under the barter system. In such a system, whatever goods are produced in the economy are either sold in the market or are used for self-consumption. Thus, supply and demand are always equal. Hence, there cannot be either a surplus or glut. This is not true in a modern economy, where every transaction involves or is carried out with money.

The Great Depression was a crucial time when the classical theory was put to test and it failed in that the classical school could not provide any solutions to the problems, which the world faced at that time. This was responsible for the loss of faith in the classical economics and paved the way for the Keynesian economics.

RECAP

- The classical economists believed that voluntary and frictional unemployment were consistent with a full employment level.
- Keynes had criticized the classical assumption of wage price flexibility as totally unrealistic.
- Keynes' had criticized Say's law as to be a truism.

SUMMARY

BACKGROUND OF MACROECONOMICS

1. The founder of the field of microeconomics is thought to be Adam Smith.
2. Macroeconomics, the other major branch of economics, is of relatively recent origin when compared with microeconomics. One can trace the origin of macroeconomics by dividing it into three stages.
3. The classical school of thought includes the theories of David Ricardo, James Mill, Marshall, J. S. Mill, Pigou and Edgeworth.
4. The Keynesian Economics provided an alternative theory to explain the determination of employment and output.
5. The post-Keynesian economics, the monetarism, assigns a critical role to money.
6. In the 1970s, the classical theory took a new turn with the introduction of the concept of rational expectations.

NEED TO STUDY MACROECONOMICS

1. From the viewpoint of an individual, macroeconomics may exercise a strong influence on the individual investor. For an individual, who is managing his own asset portfolio, it may be of considerable importance to be aware of the current fiscal policy.
2. From the viewpoint of the consumers, firms and governments, macroeconomics is again important. The consumer's interest lies in wanting to know how easy or difficult it will be for them to be able to find work, about the price of the goods and service and also as to how much may be the cost of borrowing. The interest of the business lies in wanting to whether or not to expand the production. The government turns to macroeconomy when planning its budget and taxes, deciding on the interest rates and making its other policy decisions.
3. From the viewpoint of an economy, its performance is evaluated by the national output, the rate of unemployment, the inflation rate and the trade performance.
4. From the viewpoint of an economy's stability and growth, macroeconomists are involved in trying to analyse the short-run fluctuations in the national income, which lead to the business cycles.

CONCEPTS IN MACROECONOMICS

1. While stock is a quantity, which is measured at a point in time, flow is a quantity measured over time.
2. While a change in stock occurs due to a change in the flow, a change in flow may also be influenced by a change in stock.
3. Equilibrium is a state of balance or a state, where there is no change. On the other hand, disequilibrium is a state of imbalance.
4. Flow equilibrium can be taken as short-run equilibrium while a stock equilibrium can be taken as long-run equilibrium.
5. Two methods employed in the construction of these economic models are statics and dynamics.
6. In static models, the relations between the different variables relate to the same period in time. Hence, these models are unable to explain the process of change.
7. A special case of a static model is what is called a stationary equilibrium, where there are no changes and the same equilibrium position is repeated from one period to another.
8. Dynamic models trace the changes that occur in the values of the different variables over time.

Partial Equilibrium and General Equilibrium

1. Economists often distinguish between partial and general equilibrium analysis.
2. A partial equilibrium analysis is based on the assumption of *ceteris paribus*, that is we assume everything, other than the market we are analysing, to be constant.
3. General equilibrium analysis involves a state, where all the markets and the decision-making units in the economy are in a simultaneous equilibrium.
4. While Marshall's name is associated with partial equilibrium analysis, general equilibrium analysis is associated with the French economist, Leon Walrus.
5. In the modern world of the twentieth century economics, while Marshall's partial equilibrium analysis is said to be relevant for the learners as well as the noninterventionist arts professors, real economists are more interested in Walrus's general equilibrium analysis.

SAY'S LAW

1. Say's law is one of the most important conclusions, which have been provided by the classical economists. It is named after the famous economist J. B. Say, who refused to believe that general overproduction and unemployment are common occurrences.
2. Some assumptions which are implicit in Say's law are: the average propensity to consume is one and thus savings will be zero; government does not perform any economic functions; the economy is a closed economy; the prices are flexible.
3. There are only two sectors in the economy, the firms and households, who are engaged in production and consumption, respectively.
4. The most famous tenet of the classical theory is Say's law 'supply creates its own demand'. Thus the production of the goods itself creates a demand for them.
5. In a barter economy, there is no doubt that this law will function, where the production or supply of the good creates a direct demand for the good.
6. In a money economy, goods are sold in the market for a price, which is expressed in terms of money. The only function of money is to act as a medium of exchange. The aggregate of the demand in all the markets will be always equal to the aggregate of the supply.

OUTPUT AND EMPLOYMENT IN CLASSICAL MODEL

1. The production function describes the input–output relationship.
2. We can represent our short-run aggregate production function as $Y = f(L, K)$. A profit-maximizing firm will operate in the stage of diminishing returns.
3. As far as the labour market is concerned, it is assumed that the workers and the firms have complete knowledge about the prices, which are prevailing in the market and also there exists wage price flexibility.
4. As far as the demand for labour is concerned, a perfectly competitive profit-maximizing firm will go on hiring labour till the *MPL* is equal to the real wage. Thus, the marginal product schedule is the firm's demand curve for labour.
5. The individual firms demand curve for labour can be summed up horizontally to arrive at the downward sloping aggregate demand curve for labour, $L^d = L^d(W/P)$.
6. As far as the supply of labour is concerned, there appears to be a trade-off between leisure and income.
7. The individual's supply curve of labour can be derived diagrammatically through indifference curves and budget lines, where the indifference curve shows the different combinations of income and leisure, which give to the individual the same level of satisfaction while the slope of the budget line shows the real wage.
8. The individual aims at maximizing his utility for any given real wage. He will do so by choosing that particular point on the indifference curve, where the budget line (which corresponds to that particular wage rate) is tangential to the indifference curve.

9. We can derive the individual's supply curve for labour.
10. The aggregate supply curve for labour can be arrived at by summing up horizontally the individual supply curves of labour, $L^s = L^s(W/P)$.

Determination of Employment, Real Wage Rate and Output

1. The intersection of the aggregate demand and aggregate supply curves of labour determines the equilibrium level of output, employment and the real wage rate.
2. Given the conditions in the short run, the classical economists had proposed that this will be the full employment level.
3. Given the equilibrium level of employment, the corresponding equilibrium level of output can be determined from the production function.
4. In the classical theory, the main role in the determination of output, employment and the real wage rate is played by the supply side in the labour market.

A CRITICISM OF CLASSICAL MODEL

1. The classical theory had opposed any government interference with the market and had propagated a free market economy, which they believed that it would automatically lead to full employment.
2. However, many criticisms have been put forward against the classical theory: Keynes had argued that the classical assumption of wage price flexibility is totally unrealistic. He had criticized Say's law as to be a truism only under the barter system.
3. The Great Depression was a crucial time when the classical theory was put to test and it failed. And this was responsible for the loss of faith in the classical economics and paved the way for the Keynesian economics.

REVIEW QUESTIONS

TRUE OR FALSE QUESTIONS

1. While flow is a quantity, which is measured at a point in time, stock is a quantity measured over time.
2. Static Models are those models that trace the changes that occur in the values of the different variables over time.
3. The general opinion among the classical economists was that it was impossible to have a situation of full employment.
4. The most famous tenet of Say's law is 'demand creates its own supply'.
5. While Marshall's name is associated with general equilibrium analysis, partial equilibrium analysis is associated with the French economist, Leon Walrus.

SHORT ANSWER QUESTIONS

1. Briefly trace the origin of macroeconomics through its three stages.
2. Distinguish between static and dynamic models.
3. Differentiate between a partial equilibrium approach and a general equilibrium approach.
4. What is Say's law? Discuss in brief.
5. Write a short note on the production function in the classical theory.

LONG ANSWER QUESTIONS

1. What is the relationship between a stock and a flow? Explain with examples.
2. In the classical theory, 'the individual firms demand curve for labour can be summed up horizontally to arrive at aggregate demand curve for labour'. Elaborate.
3. How can the aggregate supply curve for labour be arrived at from the individual supply curve of labour? Discuss by throwing light on the trade-off between leisure and income.

4. How are the equilibrium levels of employment, real wage rate and output determined in the classical theory? Explain.
5. What are the criticisms leveled against the classical theory of employment, real wage rate and output? Discuss.

ANSWERS

TRUE OR FALSE QUESTIONS

1. **False.** Stock is a quantity, which is measured at a point in time while flow is a quantity measured over time.
2. **False.** Dynamic models are those models that trace the changes that occur in the values of the different variables over time.
3. **False.** The classical economists believed that it was impossible to have a situation of unemployment.
4. **False.** The most famous tenet of Say's law is 'supply creates its own demand'.
5. **False.** While Marshall's name is associated with partial equilibrium analysis, general equilibrium analysis is associated with the French economist, Leon Walrus.

Keynesian Model of Income Determination in a Two-sector Economy, Shifts in Aggregate Demand and Multiplier

18

After studying this chapter, you should be able to understand:

- ✓ *Aggregate demand is the total amount of goods demanded in an economy.*
- ✓ *The consumption function is a relationship between income and consumption.*
- ✓ *Saving is income that is not spent on consumption.*
- ✓ *The aggregate demand function is obtained by a vertical summation of the investment function and consumption function.*
- ✓ *In the Keynesian theory, there are two approaches to the determination of income and output: aggregate demand–aggregate supply approach and saving–investment approach.*
- ✓ *A shift in the aggregate demand function results in a change in the equilibrium income or output.*
- ✓ *The multiplier is of great importance in planning the economic growth of a nation.*
- ✓ *The existence of certain limitations prevents the multiplier from working.*
- ✓ *The multiplier may not always work, especially in the less-developed countries (LDCs).*
- ✓ *Keynes argued that if the whole economy becomes thrifty or in other words starts saving more, there will be a decrease in the total consumption in the economy.*

INTRODUCTION

In this chapter, we focus on the determination of the equilibrium level of income in the simple Keynesian model. This chapter is limited to only a two-sector model which includes only the households and the firms.

This model assumes that the aggregate supply curve is perfectly elastic (or parallel to the horizontal axis) up to the full employment level of output after which it becomes perfectly inelastic (or parallel to the vertical axis). Hence, the price level, until the full employment level, will be determined solely by the height of the supply curve. Thus, the price variable gets less attention while the entire focus is on the determination of the equilibrium level of income, which is determined solely by the aggregate demand (or aggregate spending). Thus, the basic question relates to the determination of the aggregate demand.

BOX 18.1

In 1913, Keynes published his first book, *Indian Currency and Finance*. In 1919, Keynes wrote *The Economic Consequences of the Peace*, which was a controversial book but made Keynes a famous economist. In 1926, he published the book *The End of Laissez-Faire*. He later wrote a series of articles, *The Means to Prosperity*, in *The Times of London*. In 1930, Keynes published *A Treatise on Money*, which was his first major work in economics. In 1936, Keynes published *The General Theory of Employment, Interest and Money* and in 1940, he wrote on *How to Pay for the War*.

AGGREGATE DEMAND IN A TWO-SECTOR ECONOMY

The basic assumptions in this analysis are:

(i) The prices are constant or do not change.
(ii) Given the price level, the firms are willing to sell any amount of the output at that price level.
(iii) The short-run aggregate supply curve is perfectly elastic or flat.
(iv) Investment is assumed to be autonomous and thus independent of the income level.
(v) There exist only two sectors in the economy, the households and firms.

Aggregate demand is the total amount of goods demanded in an economy. The aggregate demand function can be expressed as

$$AD = C + I \tag{18.1}$$

where C is aggregate demand for consumers' goods and I is aggregate demand for investment goods.

Aggregate demand is the total amount of goods demanded in an economy.

Since we have already assumed that investment is autonomous and independent of the income level, the aggregate demand function will thus depend mainly on the consumption function. Our focus will be mainly on the consumption function, which is one of the biggest sectors in any economy.

RECAP

- As investment is autonomous, aggregate demand function will depend mainly on the consumption function.

CONSUMPTION

Consumption Spending

The consumption spending or the aggregate amount of goods bought in any time will depend upon the real income of the households. Other factors are also important but here we assume that the aggregate amount of goods bought is determined only by the real income of the households.

BOX 18.2

According to the under consumption theory of the classical economists such as Thomas Malthus, aggregate demand was unable to achieve the potential output or the output level corresponding to the full employment level. Hence, their focus was on the demand side. In this connection, many concepts were developed. The multiplier concept is associated with Julius Wulff, Nicholas Johannsen and Alfred De Lissa. The paradox of thrift is associated with J. M. Robertson. However, nowadays, these concepts are referred to under Keynesian economics as Keynes had made them popular.

Consumption Function

The consumption function is a relationship between income and consumption expenditure.

The two important aspects are as follows:

(i) Consumption expenditure varies directly with disposable income or it is a positive function of income.

(ii) Keynes had stated in his 'fundamental psychological law' that, in general, an individual increases his consumption expenditure when his income increases. However, the increase in consumption is less than the increase in income.

> The consumption function is a relationship between income and consumption expenditure.

Non-linear Consumption Function

The most general *non-linear form* of the consumption function can be expressed as

$$C = C(Y) \tag{18.2}$$

where C is consumption expenditure and Y is disposable income.

The consumption function equation (18.2), which is a *non-linear consumption function*, has been depicted in Figure 18.1.

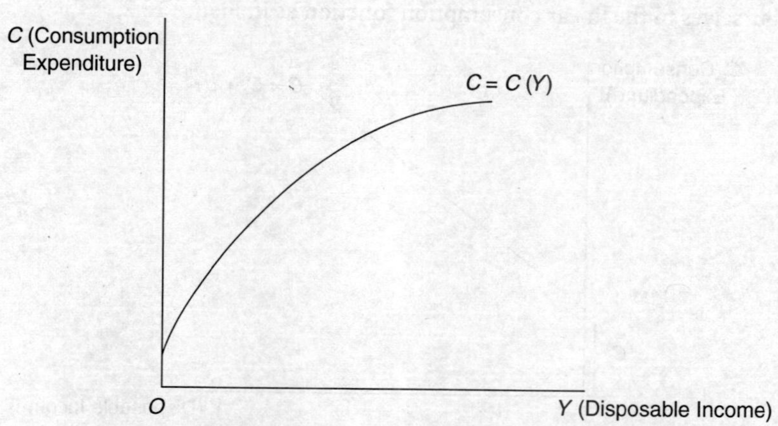

Figure 18.1 The Non-linear Consumption Function

Linear Consumption Function

The consumption function equation in a linear form can be expressed as

$$C = C_a + bY \tag{18.3}$$

where C is consumption expenditure, Y is disposal income, $C_a > 0$ and $0 < b < 1$.

In this equation,

(i) C_a is the intercept of the consumption function on the Y axis. It shows the level of consumption at zero level of income. It is known as *autonomous consumption*.

(ii) The constant 'b' denotes the slope of the consumption function. It is known as the *marginal propensity to consume* (MPC). It indicates the increase in the consumption per unit of increase in the income.

> The Average Propensity to Consume (APC) is defined as the ratio of consumption to income for different levels of income.

Average Propensity to Consume (APC)

The APC is defined as the ratio of consumption to income for different levels of income. Thus,

$$APC = \frac{C}{Y}$$

> The Marginal Propensity to Consume (MPC) is defined as the increase in the consumption per unit of increase in the income.

Marginal Propensity to Consume (MPC)

The MPC is defined as the increase in the consumption per unit of increase in the income. Thus,

$$MPC = \frac{\Delta C}{\Delta Y}$$

Since b is <1, it implies that if income increases by a rupee, only a fraction, b will be spent on consumption.

Illustration 1: If the value of the marginal propensity to consume 'b' is 0.60, then for every rupee of increase in income, what will be the increase in consumption?

Solution:

For every rupee of increase in income, there will be an increase in consumption of 60 paisa. Here, we will be restricting ourselves to the linear consumption function as in Figure 18.2.

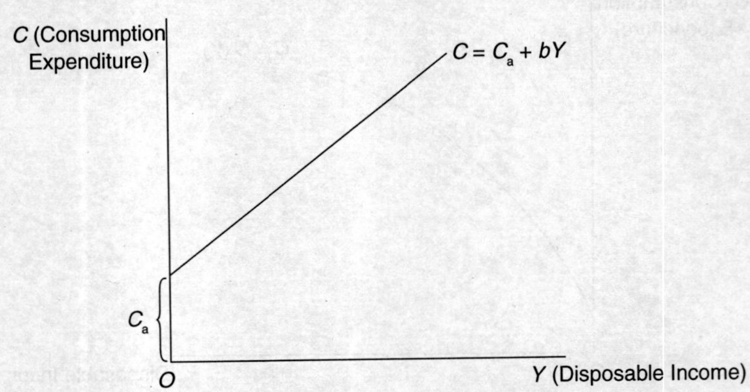

Figure 18.2 The Linear Consumption Function

RECAP

- Consumption expenditure varies directly with disposable income.

SAVING AS A COUNTERPART OF THE CONSUMPTION FUNCTION

As there are only two uses of income–consumption and saving, income that is not spent on consumption is saved.

Saving Function

The saving function is the counterpart of the consumption function. In its most general form, the saving function can be written as

$$S = S(Y) \tag{18.4}$$

We know that

$$Y = C + S \tag{18.5}$$

Or

$$S = Y - C \tag{18.6}$$

Equation (18.6) is actually the budget constraint showing that, by definition, savings will equal income net of consumption.

By substituting equation (18.3), the consumption function, in equation (18.6), which is the budget constraint, we can arrive at the savings function

$$S = Y - C$$
$$S = Y - C_a - bY$$
$$S = -C_a + (1 - b)Y$$
$$S = -C_a + sY \tag{18.7}$$

where s is $1 - b$ and $s > 0$.

In this equation, the constant s denotes the slope of the saving function. It is the marginal propensity to save. It indicates the increase in the savings per unit of increase in the income.

Average Propensity to Save (APS)

The APS is the saving counterpart to the APC. APS is defined as the ratio of saving to income for different levels of income. Thus,

$$APS = \frac{S}{Y}$$

Marginal Propensity to Save (MPS)

The MPS is defined as the increase in the saving per unit of increase in the income. Thus,

$$MPS = \frac{\Delta S}{\Delta Y}$$

Since the MPS or s is always positive, savings will be an increasing function of income.

Illustration 2: If the value of the marginal propensity to consume b is 0.60, then what is the marginal propensity to save?

Solution:

The marginal propensity to save = 1 – 0.60 = 0.40. This implies that of every rupee of income 40 paisa is saved.

The saving function equation (18.7) has been shown in Figure 18.3.

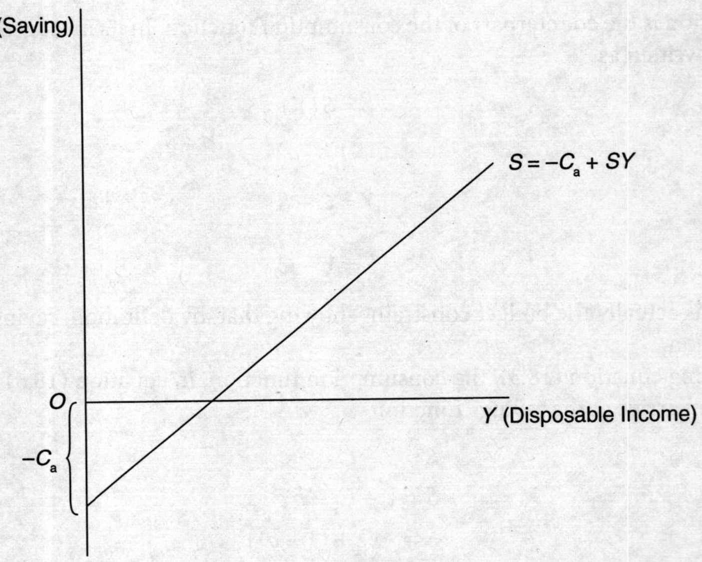

Figure 18.3 Saving Function

Relationship Between APC and APS

From equation (18.5),

$$Y = C + S$$

Dividing both sides of the equation by Y, we get

$$1 = \frac{C}{Y} + \frac{S}{Y}$$

Or

$$1 = APC + APS$$

Hence, the sum of APC and APS is always equal to 1.

Relationship Between MPC and MPS

From equation (18.5),

$$Y = C + S$$

Since a change in income can be split up into a change in consumption and a change in saving, we have

$$\Delta Y = \Delta C + \Delta S$$

Dividing both sides of the equation by ΔY, we get

$$1 = \frac{\Delta C}{\Delta Y} + \frac{\Delta S}{\Delta Y}$$

Or

$$1 = MPC + MPS$$

Hence, the sum of MPC and MPS is always equal to 1.

Illustration 3: If the consumption function is $C = 40 + 0.75Y$, then what is the saving function?

Solution:

Since $S = Y - C$, we can write

$$S = Y - (40 + 0.75Y)$$
$$S = Y - (40 - 0.75Y)$$

Thus, the saving function $S = -40 + 0.25Y$.

Aggregate Demand Function

After having determined the consumption and the saving function, we can now determine the aggregate demand function in a two-sector economy. We are assuming that investment is constant, or $I = \overline{I}$. From the aggregate demand equation (18.1) and consumption function equation (18.3), we have

$$AD = C + I \tag{18.1}$$
$$C = C_a + bY \tag{18.3}$$

Substituting for C from equation (18.3) and $I = \overline{I}$ in equation (18.1), we get

$$AD = C_a + bY + \overline{I} \tag{18.8}$$

Figure 18.4 depicts the derivation of the aggregate demand curve. While investment has been shown as a straight line parallel to the horizontal axis, $I = \overline{I}$, consumption has been shown as an upward sloping straight line, $C = C_a + bY$. The aggregate demand function has been obtained by a vertical summation of the investment function and consumption function as $AD = C_a + bY + \overline{I}$.

RECAP

- The saving function is the counterpart of the consumption function.
- The APS is the saving counterpart to the APC. APS is defined as the ratio of saving to income for different levels of income.
- The MPS is defined as the increase in the saving per unit of increase in the income.
- The sum of APC and APS is always equal to 1.
- The sum of MPC and MPS is always equal to 1.

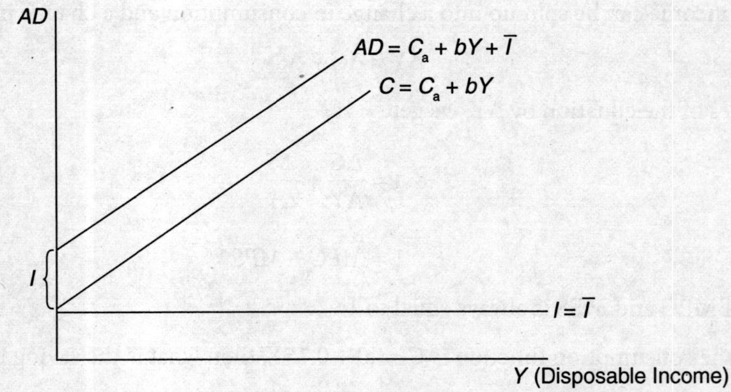

Figure 18.4 Aggregate Demand Function

DETERMINATION OF EQUILIBRIUM INCOME OR OUTPUT IN A TWO-SECTOR ECONOMY

In the most basic terms, an economy can be said to be in equilibrium when the production plans of the firms and the expenditure plans of the households are realized.

Some assumptions (already mentioned) necessary are as follows:

(i) There exist only two sectors in the economy, the households and the firms. There is no government sector and no foreign sector.
(ii) All the factors of production are owned by the households, who sell the factor services to earn an income. With a part of this income, they purchase goods and services and save the rest.
(iii) Since there is no government in the economy, there are no taxes and subsidies and no government expenditures.
(iv) Since there is no foreign sector in the economy, there are no exports and imports and no external inflows and outflows.
(v) As far as firms are concerned, there are no undistributed profits.
(vi) All the prices are constant and do not change.
(vii) Investment is assumed to be autonomous and thus independent of the income level.
(viii) The technology and the supply of capital are given.

According to the Keynesian theory, there are two approaches to the determination of income and output:

(i) Aggregate demand–aggregate supply approach
(ii) Saving–investment approach

Equilibrium Income and Output: A Theoretical Explanation

Aggregate Demand–Aggregate Supply Approach

Equilibrium: The equilibrium national income is determined at that level, where the aggregate demand is equal to the aggregate supply. Thus,

$$\text{Aggregate demand} = \text{Aggregate supply}$$

However, Keynes had argued that it is not necessary that aggregate demand will be always equal to aggregate supply. As far as aggregate supply is concerned, it can be assumed to be relatively stable as production depends on factors, which do not change much in the short run. However, aggregate demand depends on the planned consumption expenditure of households and planned investment expenditure of firms. Aggregate demand is relatively unstable. This instability of aggregate demand can, to some extent, explain the changes in the real income.

Disequilibrium: In an economy, since the production and expenditure decisions are taken by different groups of people, it is possible that aggregate demand may not be equal to aggregate supply.

Consider a situation, where the firms underestimate the demand. Thus, a situation arises where the production is insufficient to meet the demand or, in other words, aggregate demand is greater than the aggregate supply. There is a run down on inventories to meet the excess demand. The firms revise their production plans upwards till aggregate demand becomes equal to aggregate supply.

Now, we consider another situation, where the firms overestimate the demand. Thus, a situation arises, where the production is in excess of demand or, in other words, aggregate demand is less than the aggregate supply. There is an involuntary accumulation of inventories. The firms revise their production plans downwards till aggregate demand becomes equal to aggregate supply.

It is, thus, obvious that if any disequilibrium occurs, then the forces inbuilt in the system would operate in such a manner that equilibrium is restored.

Saving–Investment Approach

Equilibrium: Before going into the depth of the saving investment approach, it is necessary to understand the difference between *ex ante* and *ex post* saving and investment.

In the national income accounting, saving is said to be identically equal to investment. Thus,

(i) National income is equal to the sum of income generated in the production of consumer goods and investment goods, or that $Y = C + I$.

(ii) National expenditure is equal to the sum of income spent on consumption and income that is saved or that $Y = C + S$.

But we know that national income = national expenditure.

Or
$$C + I = C + S$$

Therefore,
$$I = S$$

Hence, as an identity, saving is always equal to investment.

However, if we bring in the concepts of *ex ante* and *ex post*, it is not so simple. *Ex ante* (planned or desired) saving is not always equal to *ex ante* (planned or desired) investment. This is because while the households save, it is the firms that invest. There is no reason as to why the two will be the same. However, *ex post* (actual or realized) saving is always equal to *ex post* (actual or realized) investment. Thus, while *ex ante* saving and investment may differ, *ex post* saving and investment are always equal.

The equilibrium national income is determined where not only the aggregate demand and the aggregate supply are equal but at that level where planned saving is also equal to planned investment. Thus,

$$\text{Planned saving} = \text{Planned investment}$$

This is possible because in a two-sector economy while saving is the only leakage investment is the only injection into the system.

Disequilibrium: Consider a situation, where the firms underestimate the demand. Thus, planned saving will be less than the planned investment. This implies that the consumption of goods is more than the current production. There will be a run down on inventories. Firms will expand production till the output increases to the level, where planned investment is equal to planned saving.

Consider another situation, where the firms overestimate the demand. Thus planned saving will be more than the planned investment. The consumption of goods is less than the current production. There will be an involuntary accumulation of inventories. Firms will cut back on production till the output decreases to the level, where planned investment is equal to planned saving.

Equilibrium Income and Output: An Algebraic Explanation

Aggregate Demand–Aggregate Supply Approach

$$\text{Aggregate demand} = \text{Total value of output (or income)}$$

Or

$$Y = C + I$$

But the consumption function is $C = C_a + bY$ while investment has been assumed to be autonomous or $I = \bar{I}$. Thus,

$$Y = C_a + bY + \bar{I}$$

Hence, equilibrium income is

$$Y - bY = C_a + \bar{I}$$

Or

$$Y = \frac{1}{1-b}\left(C_a + \bar{I}\right) \qquad (18.9)$$

Saving–Investment Approach

In equilibrium,

$$AD = AS$$

Or

$$C + I = C + S$$

Since C is common in both the sides, the equilibrium condition can be written as

$$I = S$$

But the saving function is $S = -C_a + (1 - b)Y$ while investment has been assumed to be autonomous or $I = \bar{I}$. Thus,

$$\bar{I} = -C_a + (1 - b)Y$$

Or

$$Y = \frac{1}{1-b}\left(C_a + I\right)$$

This is the same equation as (18.9) above.

Hence, both the approaches yield the same equilibrium level of income.

Illustration 4: In a two-sector economy, when the level of the national income is ₹500 crore, savings are ₹50 crore and when the national income is ₹550 crore savings are ₹70 crore. If planned investment is ₹70 crore, what is the equilibrium level of the national income?

Solution:

In an economy, equilibrium exists when planned saving equals planned investment. Since planned investment is ₹70 crore, equilibrium will occur at an income level of ₹550 crore because at that income level alone planned investment equals planned saving of ₹70 crore. Thus, the equilibrium level of the national income is ₹550 crore.

Equilibrium Income and Output: A Graphical Explanation

Aggregate Demand–Aggregate Supply Approach

Equilibrium: The determination of the equilibrium income by the aggregate demand–aggregate supply approach in a two-sector economy has been depicted in Figure 18.5(a). C is aggregate consumption function, $C = C_a + bY$, C_a is the intercept of the consumption function on the Y axis showing the consumption spending at zero income level, b is the MPC or the slope of the consumption function (it will remain constant since, in our analysis, the consumption function is a linear function), AD is aggregate demand function (obtained by adding the consumption function and the investment function), and AS is aggregate supply function (also called the guideline or the 45° line). Aggregate demand and aggregate supply curves intersect at point E to determine the equilibrium income at Y^*. It is also called the Keynesian cross.

Disequilibrium: Consider a situation, where the firms produce an output equal to OY_1. At this level of output, the aggregate demand Y_1A, consisting of consumption demand of Y_1C and investment demand of CA, is in excess of the aggregate supply of Y_1B. There is a run down on inventories to meet the excess demand. This excess demand will induce the firms to expand their output till equilibrium is reached at an income level of OY^*, where the aggregate demand is equal to aggregate supply.

Suppose the firms produce an output equal to OY_2. At this level of output, the aggregate demand Y_2E, consisting of consumption demand of Y_2F and investment demand of FE, is insufficient to exhaust the aggregate supply of Y_2D. There is an involuntary accumulation of inventories. Thus, the firms will cut down on production till equilibrium is reached at an income level of OY^*, where aggregate demand is equal to aggregate supply.

Saving–Investment Approach

Equilibrium: The determination of the equilibrium income by the saving–investment approach in a two-sector economy has been depicted in Figure 18.5(b).

In Figure 18.5(b), S is aggregate saving function (it can be easily obtained from the consumption function), $-C_a$ is the intercept of the saving function on the Y axis, s is the MPS or the slope of the saving function (it will remain constant since the saving function, in our analysis, is a linear function), I is aggregate investment function (it is parallel to the X axis because investment is independent of the income level). Planned saving and planned investment functions intersect at point E' to determine the equilibrium income at Y^*.

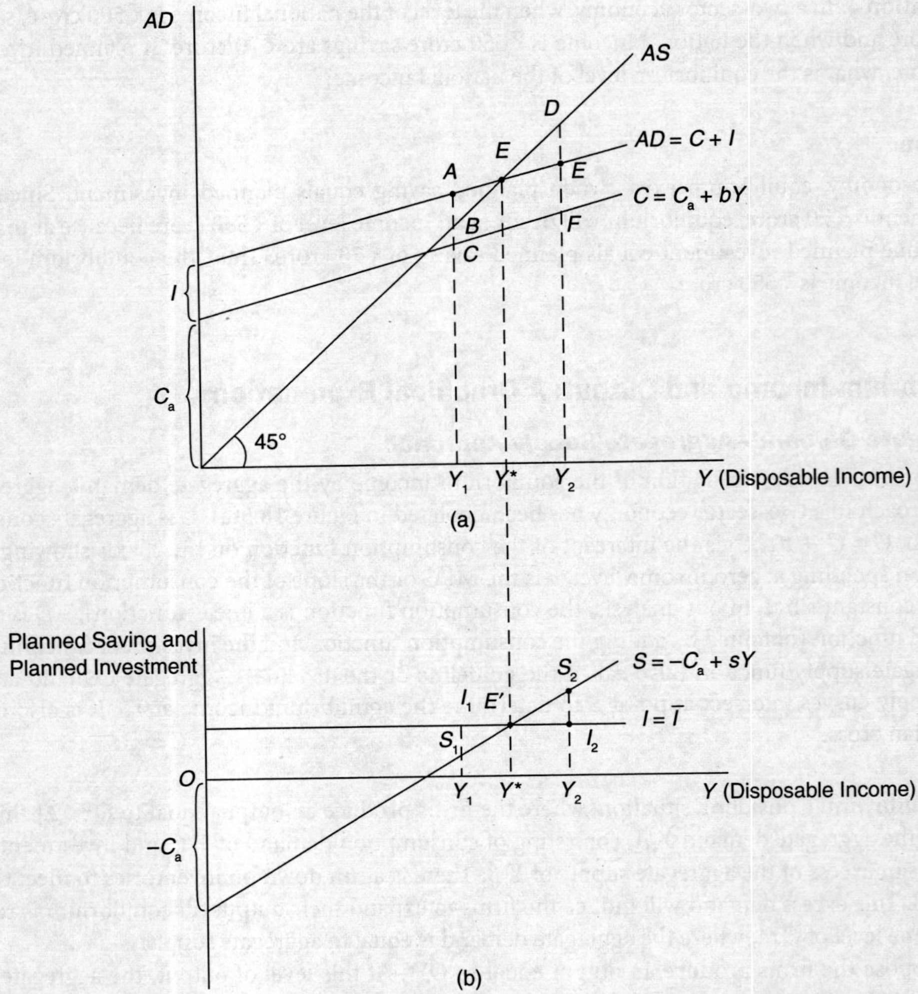

Figure 18.5 Determination of Equilibrium Income or Output in a Two-sector Economy

Disequilibrium: Consider a situation, where the firms produce an output equal to OY_1. At this level of output, the planned saving S_1Y_1 is less than the planned investment I_1Y_1. Thus, the consumption of goods is larger than the current production. Thus, inventories will fall. Firms will be tempted to hire more workers and expand production till the output increases to Y^*, where planned investment is equal to planned saving.

Suppose the firms produce an output equal to OY_2. At this level of output, the planned saving S_2Y_2 is greater than the planned investment I_2Y_2. There will be an involuntary accumulation of inventories. Firms will lay off workers and cut back on production till it decreases to Y^*, where planned investment is equal to planned saving.

The equilibrium level of income will be determined at the point, where planned saving is equal to planned investment. At any other income level, there will be disequilibrium which will make the firms change their production and employment in such a manner that the system returns to the initial point of equilibrium. Thus, it is clear that while actual saving is always equal to actual investment, planned saving is only equal to planned investment at the equilibrium point.

We find that the two approaches to the determination of the equilibrium income, the aggregate demand–aggregate supply approach and the saving–investment approach, both yield the same result.

RECAP

- While actual saving always equals actual investment, planned saving equals planned investment only at the equilibrium point.
- In an economy, disequilibrium exists when aggregate demand is not equal to aggregate supply or planned saving is not equal to planned investment.
- The two approaches to the determination of the equilibrium income, the aggregate demand–aggregate supply approach and the saving–investment approach, both yield the same equilibrium level of income.

SHIFTS IN AGGREGATE DEMAND AND MULTIPLIER

Till now, we had focused on the determination of equilibrium income and output. Here, we analyse the changes in the equilibrium income and output in a two-sector model.

In a two-sector economy, the aggregate demand is a sum of consumption and investment expenditures. It is generally agreed that though both the consumption and the investment functions undergo a change from one period to another, the consumption function is relatively more stable than the investment function. Thus, the initial changes in income occur more due to the shifts in the investment function. This implies that, in Figure 18.6, it is not the consumption function or the saving function, which shifts up and down. It is the investment function, which shifts up and down and is responsible for the shift in the $C + I$ curve. Hence, our analysis will be in terms of the shift in the investment function (though the same analysis will apply for a shift in the consumption function).

In Figure 18.6, C is consumption function, I is investment function, ΔI is change in investment, S is saving function and $Y = C + S$ is the guideline or the 45° line.

In Figure 18.6(a), suppose that initially the $C + I$ function intersects the guideline to determine the equilibrium at point E_1 with the equilibrium level of income at Y_1. The same can be illustrated in Figure 18.6(b), where the saving function intersects the I function to determine the equilibrium at point E_1 with the equilibrium level of income at Y_1.

Assume that, due to an improvement in the business expectations, there is a permanent increase in investment expenditures per time by an amount equal to ΔI at all the levels of output. In Figure 18.6(a), this shift has been illustrated by a shift in the $C + I$ curve to $C + I + \Delta I$ while in Figure 18.6(b) the same shift has been illustrated by a shift in the I curve to the $I + \Delta I$ curve. In both the figures, the new equilibrium will be at point E_2 with the equilibrium level of income at Y_2.

It is of extreme importance to note that an increase in the income from Y_1 to Y_2 (national income) can occur if and only if the economy is operating at less than full employment. Otherwise, there cannot be an increase in the income.

One would expect that the increase in income from Y_1 to Y_2, say ΔY would be by the same amount as the increase in the investment expenditure, that is ΔI or that $\Delta Y = \Delta I$. However, *one finds that the*

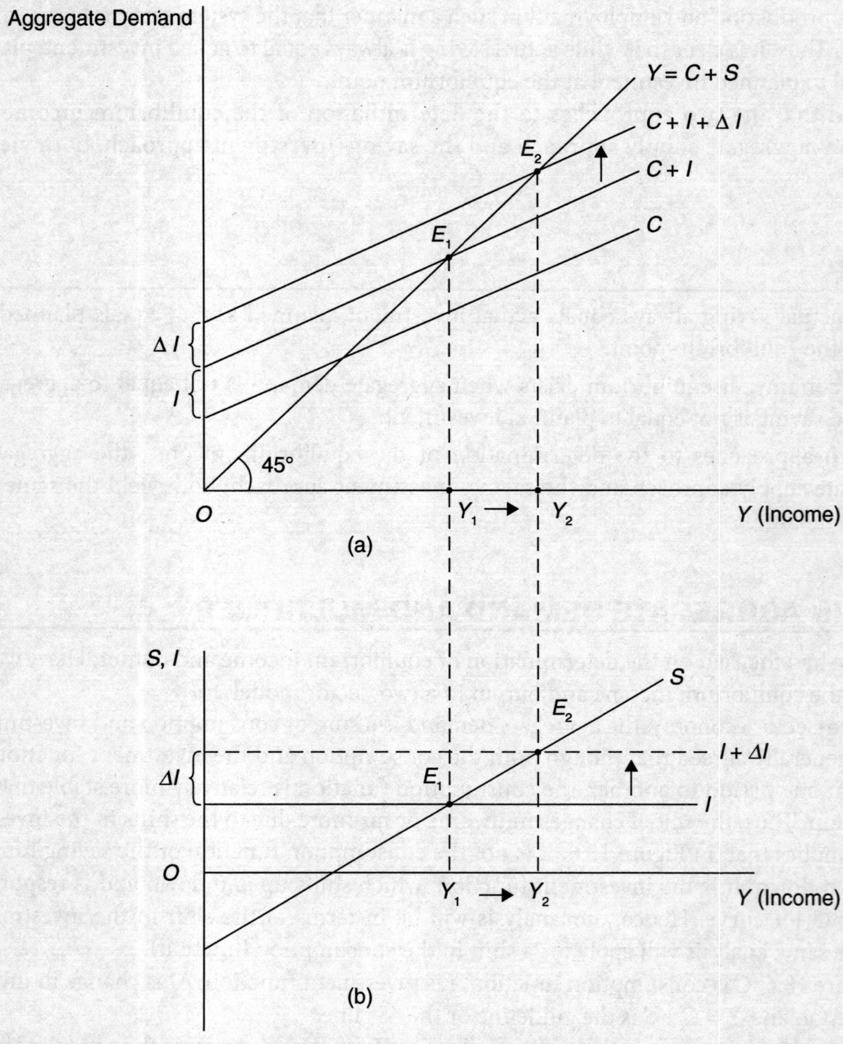

Figure 18.6 Effect of Change in Investment on the Equilibrium Income or Output

increase in income is much more than the increase in investment expenditure, which was responsible for bringing about that increase in the income, or in other words $\Delta Y > \Delta I$. In fact $\Delta Y = m\Delta I$, where m is what is known as the investment multiplier and has a value >1. Thus,

$$\Delta Y = m\Delta I \quad (18.10)$$

The multiplier can be defined as the amount by which there occurs a change in the equilibrium level of income due to a change in autonomous aggregate expenditure by one unit.

or

$$m = \Delta Y/\Delta I \quad (18.11)$$

The multiplier can be defined as the amount by which there occurs a change in the equilibrium level of income due to a change in autonomous aggregate expenditure by one unit.

Working of Multiplier

Suppose the economy is initially in equilibrium. Let there be an increase in autonomous investment by ₹1 million (ΔI). If the economy is operating at less than full employment, this will be matched by an increase in production and output equal to ₹1 million to meet the increased demand. The increase in the production will lead to an equal increase in income of ₹1 million (ΔY) in the form of wages, interest and profits. This is the first round of income generation due to the additional investment of ₹1 million.

Those who receive the additional income will consume only a part of it, depending on their marginal propensity to consume, and will save the rest of this income. Suppose the marginal propensity to consume, or b is 0.8. Hence, they will spend ₹1 million × 0.8 = 0.80 million (or $b \times \Delta I = b\Delta I$) on the consumer goods and services and save ₹0.20 million. Thus, in the second round, there is an increase in consumption and expenditure by ₹0.80 million (or $b\Delta I$). Again production and income will increase to match the increase in the expenditure.

This will lead to a third round of induced expenditures by the recipients of the income in the second round. There will be an increase in consumption and expenditure by ₹0.80 million × 0.8 = ₹0.64 million (or $b\Delta I \times b = b^2\Delta I$). Hence, an additional income of ₹0.64 million is generated in the third round.

It is important to note that the additional income generated in the second round, ₹0.80 million ($b\Delta I$) is certainly less than the additional income generated in the first round, ₹1 million (ΔI). Similarly, the additional income generated in the third round, ₹0.64 million ($b^2\Delta I$) is less than the additional income generated in the second round, 0.80 million ($b\Delta I$). Thus, the induced expenditures in the second round are smaller than those in the first round while those in the third round are smaller than those in the second round. Hence, the induced expenditures and thus the additional income generated in each round go on becoming smaller and smaller. The rounds of income generation will continue till the additional income generated falls to zero.

The total increase in the income in all the rounds can be summed as

$$\Delta Y = \Delta I + b\Delta I + b^2\Delta I + b^3\Delta I + \cdots + b^{n-1}\Delta I$$

$$\Delta Y = \Delta I(1 + b + b^2 + b^3 + \cdots + b^{n-1}) \qquad (18.12)$$

This is a geometric series and can be put in a simpler form as follows.

Multiplying both sides of equation (18.12) by b, we get

$$b\Delta Y = \Delta I(b + b^2 + b^3 + b^4 + \cdots + b^n) \qquad (18.13)$$

Subtracting equation (18.13) from (18.12), we get

$$\Delta Y - b\Delta Y = \Delta I(1 + b + b^2 + b^3 + \cdots + b^{n-1}) - \Delta I(b + b^2 + b^3 + b^4 + \cdots + b^n)$$

$$\Delta Y(1 - b) = \Delta I(1 - b^n)$$

Thus,

$$\frac{\Delta Y}{\Delta I} = \frac{(1-b^n)}{1-b} \qquad (18.14)$$

If the multiplier process continues for a very long period, the value of n will become very large and b^n (b is a fraction with its value between zero and one) will approach zero. Hence,

$$\frac{\Delta Y}{\Delta I} = m = \frac{1}{1-b} \qquad (18.15)$$

where m is the investment multiplier.

Table 18.1 Working of Multiplier

Round	Increase in Aggregate Demand (or Aggregate Expenditure)	Total Increase in Income
1	ΔI	ΔI
2	$b\Delta I$	$\Delta I + b\Delta I = \Delta I\ (1 + b)$
3	$b^2\Delta I$	$\Delta I + b\Delta I + b^2\Delta I = \Delta I\ (1 + b + b^2)$
4	—	—
—	—	$1/(1 - b) \times \Delta I$

Thus, we have

$$m = \frac{1}{1 - mpc} \tag{18.16}$$

Or

$$m = \frac{1}{mps}$$

Table 18.1 depicts the working of the multiplier.

An Alternative Derivation of Multiplier

The equilibrium level of income is

$$Y = C + I \tag{18.17}$$

Let there be an increase in autonomous investment by ΔI. This will result in an induced increase in income, which will lead to an increase in consumption, or ΔC. Thus, now the equilibrium level of income will be

$$Y + \Delta Y = C + \Delta C + I + \Delta I \tag{18.18}$$

Subtracting equation (18.17) from equation (18.18), we get

$$\Delta Y = \Delta C + \Delta I \tag{18.19}$$

But the consumption function is $C = C_a + bY$. Thus,

$$\Delta C = b\Delta Y \tag{18.20}$$

Substituting for ΔC from equation (18.20) in equation (18.19), we get

$$\Delta Y = b\Delta Y + \Delta I$$

Or

$$\Delta Y(1 - b) = \Delta I$$

Or

$$\Delta Y = \frac{\Delta I}{1 - b}$$

Or

$$\frac{\Delta Y}{\Delta I} = m = \frac{1}{1 - b}$$

where m is the investment multiplier.

It is obvious that the value of the multiplier depends on *b*, the marginal propensity to consume. *The larger is the marginal propensity to consume, the larger will be the multiplier*. When the marginal propensity to consume is 0.5, the multiplier is 2 and when the marginal propensity to consume increases to 0.9 the multiplier increases to 10.

RECAP

- A shift in the investment function results in a change in the equilibrium income or output.
- The ratio of the change in income is a multiple of the change in the investment.
- $\Delta Y = m\Delta I$ where m is the investment multiplier and has a value >1.
- The larger is the marginal propensity to consume, the larger will be the multiplier.

USES AND LIMITATIONS OF MULTIPLIER

The importance of the multiplier is more obvious in a three-sector and a four-sector economy. However, it plays an important role even in a two-sector economy in that it helps in evaluating the effects of an increase in the investment on the national income. Thus, it is able to determine the investment, which would be required for a certain planned growth in the national income. Hence, the multiplier is of great importance in planning the economic growth of a nation.

In spite of its utility in economic planning, the multiplier has certain limitations, which may prevent it from working:

(i) **Existence of Leakages from the Income Stream:** Keynes was of the view that the marginal propensity to consume remains constant overtime. However, empirical evidence does not lend credence to this view. It has been observed that, as income increases often, consumption may not increase proportionately and hence the value of the multiplier may be reduced. Other than consumption, individuals may utilize their increased income for different purposes as the following:
- They may increase their holdings of money.
- They may use a part of the increased income to pay off their old debts.
- They may purchase old securities and property with the additional income.
- They may purchase imported goods and services, the income spent on which will certainly be a leakage out of the economy.

(ii) **Availability of the Consumer Goods:** For the multiplier principle to work, it is necessary that the consumer goods are available in the right quantities and at the right time. Often, this may not be the case and this may hinder the multiplier from working properly.

(iii) **There May Exist Time Lags:** The supply of goods may increase in response to demand but only with a time gap. Also consumption may not increase immediately in response to an increase in income.

(iv) **Full Employment Ceiling:** When an economy is at the full employment level, any further increases in the income and output are not possible. Whatever is the marginal propensity to consume, the multiplier principle will not be able to work. In fact, any increases in investment will trigger off inflationary expectations in the economy.

These limitations do not in any way undermine the importance of the multiplier. In fact, due to these limitations, economists have time and again modified the multiplier, which has further enhanced its utility in analysing the changes in income in response to an increase in the aggregate demand.

RECAP

- The multiplier plays a very important role in planning the economic growth of a nation.
- The multiplier suffers from many limitations, which may prevent it from working.
- These limitations have been responsible for the modifications in the multiplier.

APPLICABILITY OF MULTIPLIER TO LDCs

In the article *Investment, Income and the Multiplier in an Underdeveloped Economy* in the *Indian Economic Review*, February 1953, Dr V. K. R. V. Rao raised doubts regarding the applicability of the multiplier principle to the LDCs.

The LDCs have a lower per capita income when compared with the other countries. It is also an established fact that, at low levels of income, the marginal propensity to consume is always high. According to the Keynesian theory, the higher the b or the marginal propensity to consume, the higher is the value of the multiplier $m = 1/(1-b)$. Thus, it is to be expected that the multiplier should apply with a stronger effect in LDCs when compared with the developed countries of the world. This would imply that even a small increase in the investment in the LDCs would result in an increase in the income and output, which would be much larger than the increase in the income and output experienced in the developed countries. However, this does not seem to be the case. The reason for this, according to Dr V. K. R .V. Rao, is that the conditions necessary for the multiplier principle to work do not exist in the LDCs. They are satisfied only in the developed countries.

The conditions necessary for the multiplier principle to work are:

(i) *There should exist only involuntary unemployment and no other form of unemployment.* Such unemployment is characteristic of the developed countries, where there exists wage employment in almost all the sectors of the economy. When compared with the developed countries, in the LDCs, wage employment is a feature found only in the secondary sector, which again is a very small sector when compared with the other sectors in the economy. Hence, involuntary unemployment, which is associated with wage employment, is not so predominant in these countries.

The type of unemployment most predominant in the LDCs is what is known as disguised unemployment. This is a type of unemployment, which is most prevalent in agriculture in a country like India, where there exist plots of land on which the whole family may be employed. The additions to the total output and the income by the last few units of labour employed may actually be zero. Yet, they continue to till the land simply because they are not aware that they are actually not contributing to the total output. Hence, their unemployment is a kind of concealed one of which even they themselves are not aware. The existence of this disguised unemployment prevents the working of the multiplier principle in the LDCs.

(ii) *It must be mainly an industrial economy with an upward sloping supply curve for the consumer goods.* In the developed economies, the supply curve is reasonably elastic in that an increase in demand results in an increase in the supply with not much of an inflationary increase in the prices. However, the situation is different in the LDCs, where an increase in the demand is not followed by an increase in the supply. This is because due to the low incomes and poverty in the LDCs, any increases in income generates a demand largely for the agricultural goods. But agriculture is subject to the vagaries of nature. Hence, the multiplier may work in the first stage in that an increase in investment may result in a primary increase in the incomes. But, the increase in demand in response to an increase in these incomes may not result in an increase in the production, especially in the agricultural goods sector. The story is not any different for the non-agricultural goods sector, which is characterized by an outdated technology, lack of skilled workers and other problems. Thus, in the LDCs, while there occurs an increase in the money incomes due to an increase in the investment, there is no perceptible increase in the output level. Thus, it is often argued that in the LDCs, the multiplier principle functions only with respect to the money incomes and not with respect to the real incomes.

(iii) *There should exist excess capacity in the consumer goods industries.* In the Keynesian theory, which came at the time of the Great Depression, it was not unusual to assume the existence of idle capacity in the consumer goods industry. Thus, an increase in demand could be immediately satisfied by an increase in the production. However, this is not the situation in the LDCs, especially in the agriculture sector. Hence, in these countries, the multiplier does not work except in that it is responsible for contributing to the inflationary fires in the economy whenever there occurs an increase in demand in response to an increase in investment.

(iv) *There should exist an elastic supply of capital.* This is a necessary accompaniment to the labour if there has to occur an increase in the production in response to an increase in the demand. Since the developed countries face no problem on this front, the multiplier functions quite efficiently in these countries. In the LDCs, while there is not only a sufficient, but, in fact, a surplus supply of labour, as far as capital is concerned, there is a shortage of capital in these countries. Hence, again the multiplier principle does not work in the LDCs due to the acute shortage of capital that these countries face.

RECAP

- Dr V. K. R. V. Rao had raised doubts regarding the applicability of the multiplier principle to the LDCs.
- It seems that the conditions, which are necessary for the multiplier principle to work, are not satisfied in the LDCs.

MULTIPLIER AND PARADOX OF THRIFT

It was widely believed, especially by the classical economists, that saving or thrift was a 'virtue' for not only an individual, but also for an economy. An individual has to refrain from consumption if he wishes to save. By saving, he is able to amass huge amounts of wealth. Similarly, it was believed that an economy could become rich if every individual in the economy became thrifty.

Keynes, in his *General Theory*, criticized these beliefs. He argued that what applies to an individual was not necessarily true for the economy. Contrary to the popular beliefs at that time, *Keynes argued that if the whole economy becomes thrifty or in other words starts saving more, there will be a decrease in the total consumption in the economy.* Hence, there will be a decrease in the aggregate demand, and thus the income and output will decrease. Since saving is a function of income, a decrease in income

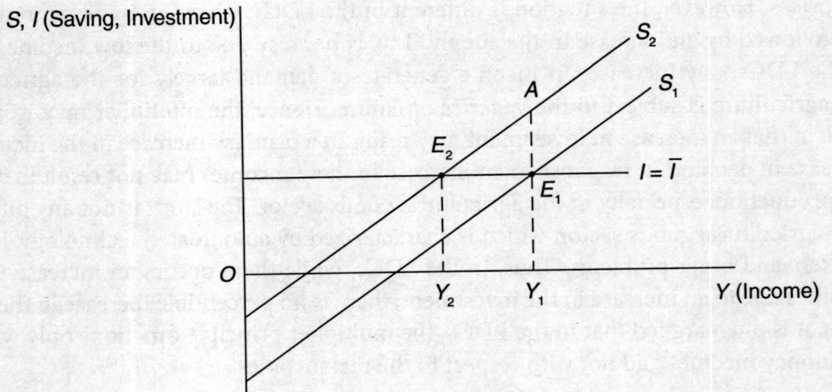

Figure 18.7 Paradox of Thrift

will ultimately lead to a decrease in the savings. This is what Keynes called the paradox of thrift. It is a contradiction in that what is good for an individual is not good for an economy.

In Figure 18.7, I is investment demand schedule, where I is assumed to be constant at $\bar{I}$ and S_1 is saving schedule, where saving is positively related to income. E_1 is the equilibrium point at which the saving schedule, S_1, and investment schedule, I, intersect to determine the equilibrium income at OY_1. S_2 is saving schedule when the economy becomes thriftier. E_2 is the equilibrium point at which the saving schedule, S_2, and investment schedule, I, intersect to determine the equilibrium income at OY_2.

Figure 18.7 depicts the paradox of thrift. If everyone in the economy becomes thriftier, the saving schedule will shift upwards from S_1 to S_2. The equilibrium point will move from E_1 to E_2 while the equilibrium income decreases from Y_1 to Y_2. This lends credence to the paradox of thrift that an increase in the thrift by one individual may be good in that it may help in increasing his fortunes in the long run, but if the whole economy becomes thrifty, the economy's equilibrium income and output may, in fact, actually decrease, rather than increase!

Some economists describe this process, where through the paradox of thrift, there is ultimately a decrease in the economy's savings as a reverse multiplier. The increase in savings, by a reduction in consumption expenditures, will lead to a decrease in the aggregate demand. Thus, there will be a decrease in production leading to a decrease in the income, which will further lead to a decrease in savings (which are a function of the income level). The economy will finally reach a new equilibrium at which saving is equal to investment. It is imperative to remember that the paradox of thrift will operate only if the increase in the economy's saving is not accompanied by an increase in the investment. If there is an increase in investment, then, in that case, there will occur an increase in the income through the multiplier, which will lead to additional savings and investment in the economy, rather than a decrease.

RECAP

- The classical economists believed that saving or thrift was a 'virtue' for both an individual and also for an economy.
- Keynes was of the view that an increase in the thrift by one individual may be good but if the whole economy becomes thrifty, then the economy's equilibrium income may decrease.

INCOME DETERMINATION IN A TWO-SECTOR ECONOMY

SOLVED NUMERICAL

1. In an economy, the basic equations are as follows: the consumption function is $C = 120 + 0.80Y$ and investment is $\overline{I} = 250$. Find
   (a) The equilibrium level of income.
   (b) The equilibrium level of consumption.
   (c) The equilibrium level of saving.
   (d) Show that at the equilibrium level aggregate demand equals aggregate supply and saving leakages equals investment injections.

Solution:

(a) The equilibrium condition is given as $Y = C + I$.

Thus,
$$Y = 120 + 0.80Y + 250$$
$$Y - 0.80Y = 120 + 250$$
$$0.20Y = 370$$
$$Y = 370/0.20$$
$$Y = 1850$$

The equilibrium level of income is 1850.

(b) The consumption function is $C = 120 + 0.80Y$.
When $Y = 1850$, $C = 120 + 0.80\ (1850)$
$$C = 120 + 1480$$
$$C = 1600$$

The equilibrium level of consumption is 1600.

(c) The saving equation is $S = Y - C$.
When $Y = 1850$ and $C = 1600$, we have
$$S = 1850 - 1600$$
$$S = 250$$

The equilibrium level of saving is 250.

(d) Aggregate demand equals aggregate supply.
$$C + I = C + S$$
$$1600 + 250 = 1600 + 250$$
$$\text{Or } 1850 = 1850$$

Saving equals investment.
$$S = I$$
$$250 = 250$$

2. The fundamental equations in an economy are given as: consumption as $C = 150 + 0.80Y$, investment as $\overline{I} = 200$.
   (a) Derive the saving function.
   (b) Find the equilibrium level of output by equating the saving leakages to the investment injections.

Solution:

(a) The saving function is given by $S = Y - C$.

$$S = Y - (150 + 0.80Y)$$

$$S = -150 + 0.20Y$$

The saving function is given by $S = -150 + 0.20Y$.

(b) The equilibrium level of output can be determined by equating the saving leakages to the investment injections.

Thus, $$-150 + 0.20Y = 200$$

Or $$-150 + 0.20Y = 200$$

$$0.20Y = 350$$

$$Y = 350/0.20$$

$$Y = 1750$$

The equilibrium level of output is 1750.

3. If in an economy $C = 450 + 0.80Y$, investment is $I = 540$.
   (a) Determine the equilibrium level of income and consumption.
   (b) Derive the saving function and determine the savings at the equilibrium level.
   (c) Determine the equilibrium level of income by equating planned saving and planned investment.

Solution:

(a) The equilibrium condition is given as $Y = C + I$.

Thus, $$Y = 450 + 0.80Y + 540$$

$$Y - 0.80Y = 450 + 540$$

$$0.20Y = 990$$

$$Y = 990/0.20$$

$$Y = 4950$$

The equilibrium level of income is 4950.
The consumption function is $C = 450 + 0.80Y$.
When $Y = 4950$, $C = 450 + 0.80\ (4950)$

$$C = 450 + 3960$$

$$C = 4410$$

The equilibrium level of consumption is 4410.

(b) The saving function is given by $S = Y - C$.

$$S = Y - (450 + 0.80Y)$$

$$S = 0.20Y - 450$$

$$S = -450 + 0.20Y$$

The saving function is given by $S = -450 + 0.20Y$.
At the equilibrium level, $$S = -450 + 0.20\ (4950)$$

$$S = -450 + 990$$

$$S = 540$$

(c) The planned saving is given by $S = -450 + 0.20Y$.
In equilibrium, planned saving equals planned investment.

Thus,

$$-450 + 0.20Y = 540$$
$$0.20Y = 540 + 450$$
$$Y = 990/0.20$$
$$Y = 4950$$

The equilibrium level of income is 4950.

4. In an economy, the basic equations are as follows: the consumption function is $C = 150 + 0.80Y$ and investment is $\overline{I} =$ ₹180 crore. Find
(a) The equilibrium level of income.
(b) The equilibrium level of income when planned investment increases from ₹180 to ₹200 crore, a total increase of ₹20 crore.
(c) The multiplier effect of the ₹20 crore increase in planned investment.

Solution:

(a) The equilibrium condition is given as $Y = C + I$.

Thus,

$$Y = 150 + 0.80Y + 180$$
$$Y - 0.80Y = 150 + 180$$
$$0.20Y = 330$$
$$Y = 330/\ 0.20$$
$$Y = 1650$$

The equilibrium level of income is ₹1650 crore.

(b) The equilibrium condition is given as $Y = C + I$.

Thus now

$$Y = 150 + 0.80Y + 200$$
$$Y - 0.80Y = 150 + 200$$
$$0.20Y = 350$$
$$Y = 350/0.20$$
$$Y = 1750$$

The equilibrium level of income is ₹1750 crore.

(c) The equilibrium level of income increases from ₹1650 to ₹1750 crore when planned investment increases from ₹180 to ₹200 crore. There is an increase in income by ₹100 crore. Hence, the multiplier effect is 5 ($m = 1/1 - b = 1/1 - 0.80 = 5$).

5. Assume that in a two-sector economy the income is ₹500 billion while the marginal propensity to consume is 40 per cent. Suppose the government wants to increase the income to ₹800 billion, by an amount of ₹300 billion. By how much should the autonomous investment be increased?

Solution:

The income level = ₹500 billion

The planned income level = ₹800 billion

Change in income = $\Delta Y = 800 - 500 =$ ₹300 billion

But,
$$\frac{\Delta Y}{\Delta I} = m = m\Delta I = \Delta I \frac{1}{1-b}$$

$$\Delta Y = \Delta I \frac{1}{1-b}$$

Thus,
$$300 = \Delta I \frac{1}{1-0.4}$$

$$\Delta I = ₹\,180 \text{ billion}$$

Autonomous investment should be increased by ₹180 billion for the income to increase to ₹800 billion, an increase in income by ₹300 billion.

SHIFTS IN AGGREGATE DEMAND AND MULTIPLIER

SOLVED NUMERICAL

1. In an economy, the basic equations are as follows: the consumption function is C = 80 + 0.75Y and investment is $\overline{I} = ₹\,100$ crore. Find
   (a) The equilibrium level of income.
   (b) The equilibrium level of income when planned investment increases from ₹100 to ₹120 crore, a total increase of ₹20 crore.
   (c) The multiplier effect of the ₹20 crore increase in planned investment.

   Solution:

   (a) The equilibrium condition is given as $Y = C + I$.
   Thus,
   $$Y = 80 + 0.75Y + 100$$
   $$Y - 0.75Y = 80 + 100$$
   $$0.25Y = 180$$
   $$Y = 180/0.25$$
   $$Y = 720$$
   The equilibrium level of income is ₹720 crore.

   (b) The equilibrium condition is given as $Y = C + I$.
   Thus,
   $$Y = 80 + 0.75Y + 120$$
   $$Y - 0.75Y = 80 + 120$$
   $$0.25Y = 200$$
   $$Y = 200/0.25$$
   $$Y = 800$$
   The equilibrium level of income, when planned investment increases from ₹100 to ₹120 crore, is ₹800 crore.

   (c) The equilibrium level of income increases from ₹720 to ₹800 crore when planned investment increases from ₹100 to ₹120 crore. There is an increase in income by ₹80 crore. Hence, *the multiplier effect is* 4.
   $$m = 1/1 - b = 1/1 - 0.75 = 4$$

2. Suppose in an economy the marginal propensity to consume is 0.80. The autonomous investment rises by ₹40 crore. Find
   (a) The change in the equilibrium level of income.
   (b) The change in consumption expenditures.

Solution:

(a) We know that

$$\frac{\Delta Y}{\Delta I} = m = \frac{1}{1-b}$$

Where m is the investment multiplier

$$m = \frac{1}{1-mpc}$$

Thus, $$\Delta Y = \Delta Im = \Delta I\frac{1}{1-b} = (40)\times\frac{1}{1-0.80} = 200$$

Hence, the increase in autonomous investment causes an increase in the equilibrium level of income by ₹200 crore. This effect occurs due to the multiplier.

(b) $Y = C + I$

Thus,

$$\Delta Y = \Delta C + \Delta S$$

$$200 = \Delta C + 40$$

(Since autonomous investment decreases by ₹20 crore, the saving will also decrease by ₹20 crore.)

$$\Delta C = 200 - 40 = ₹160 \text{ crore}$$

$$\Delta C = ₹160 \text{ crore}$$

The consumption expenditure increases by ₹160 crore.

3. In a two-sector economy, the income is ₹200 billion while the marginal propensity to consume is 60 per cent. Suppose the government wants to increase the income by a 100 per cent. By how much should the autonomous investment be increased?

Solution:

The income level = ₹200 billion

The planned income level = ₹400 billion

Change in income = ΔY = 400 – 200 = ₹200 billion

But $$\frac{\Delta Y}{\Delta I} = m = m\Delta I = \Delta I\frac{1}{1-b}$$

$$\Delta Y = \Delta I\frac{1}{1-b}$$

Thus, $$200 = \Delta I\frac{1}{1-0.6}$$

$$\Delta I = ₹80 \text{ billion}$$

Autonomous investment should be increased by ₹80 billion for a 100 per cent increase in the income level.

4. In an economy, the marginal propensity to consume is 0.75. The level of autonomous investment decreases by ₹40 crore. Find
   (a) The change in the equilibrium level of income.
   (b) The change in autonomous demand.
   (c) The induced change in the consumption expenditures.

Solution:

(a) We know that

$$\frac{\Delta Y}{\Delta I} = m$$

But, m is the investment multiplier.

Also, $$m=\frac{1}{1-mpc}$$

Thus, $$\Delta Y=\Delta Im=\Delta I\frac{1}{1-b}=(-40)\times\frac{1}{1-0.75}=-160$$

Hence, the decrease in autonomous investment causes a decrease in the equilibrium level of income by ₹160 crore. This effect occurs due to the reverse multiplier.

(b) The decrease in investment by ₹40 crore is the change in the level of autonomous demand.

(c) $Y=C+I$

Therefore,

$$\Delta Y=\Delta C+\Delta S$$

$$-160=\Delta C-40$$

(Since autonomous investment decreases by ₹40 crore, the saving will also decrease by ₹40 crore.)

$$\Delta C=-160+40=-₹120 \text{ crore}$$

$$\Delta C=-₹120 \text{ crore}$$

The consumption expenditure falls by ₹120 crore.

5. Suppose the marginal propensity to consume is (i) 0.40, (ii) 0.50, (iii) 0.80, (iv) 1.0 and (v) 0
   (a) Calculate the marginal propensity to save.
   (b) Calculate the value of the multiplier.
   (c) Using the values of the marginal propensity to consume, find the effect of an increase in the equilibrium income when autonomous investment increases by ₹40 crore.

Solution:

(a) We know that, $mpc+mps=1$

Thus, $$mps=1-mpc$$

Hence,

(i) $mps=1-mpc=1-0.40=0.60$

(ii) $mps=1-mpc=1-0.50=0.50$

(iii) $mps=1-mpc=1-0.80=0.20$

(iv) $mps=1-mpc=1-1.0=0$

(v) $mps=1-mpc=1-0=1$

(b) The value of the investment multiplier is

$$m=\frac{1}{1-mpc}=\frac{1}{1-mps}$$

Thus, $$m=\frac{1}{1-mps}$$

(i) $m=1.67$

(ii) $m=2$

(iii) $m=5$

(iv) $m=\infty$ (infinity)

(v) $m=1$

(c) We know that

$$\frac{\Delta Y}{\Delta I} = m$$

Thus, $$\Delta Y = \Delta Im$$

The effect of an increase in the equilibrium income when autonomous investment decreases by ₹30 crore is

(i) $\Delta Y = \Delta Im = 40 \times 1.67 = 67$

(ii) $\Delta Y = \Delta Im = 40 \times 2 = 80$

(iii) $\Delta Y = \Delta Im = 40 \times 5 = 200$

(iv) $\Delta Y = \Delta Im = 40 \times \infty$ (infinity) $= \infty$ (infinity)

(v) $\Delta Y = \Delta Im = 40 \times 1 = 40$

SUMMARY

INTRODUCTION

Here, we focus on the determination of the equilibrium level of income in the simple Keynesian model in a two-sector economy.

AGGREGATE DEMAND IN A TWO-SECTOR ECONOMY

1. Aggregate demand is the total amount of goods demanded in an economy. The aggregate demand function can be expressed as:
$$AD = C + I$$
2. The consumption spending or the aggregate amount of goods bought in any time will depend upon the real income of the households.
3. The consumption function is a relationship between income and consumption expenditure.
4. The most general non-linear form of the consumption function can be expressed as $C = C(Y)$.
5. The consumption function equation in a linear form can be expressed as $C = C_a + bY$.
6. C_a, also known as autonomous consumption, is the intercept of the consumption function on the Y axis while the constant b known as the MPC denotes the slope of the consumption function.
7. The APC is defined as the ratio of consumption to income.
8. The MPC is defined as the increase in the consumption per unit of increase in the income.

SAVING AS A COUNTERPART OF THE CONSUMPTION FUNCTION

1. Income that is not spent on consumption is saved.
2. The saving function is the counterpart of the consumption function and can be written as $S = -C_a + sY$, where the constant s is the MPS and denotes the slope of the saving function.
3. The APS is the saving counterpart to the APC and is defined as the ratio of saving to income.
4. The MPS is defined as the increase in the saving per unit of increase in the income. Since the MPS or s is always positive, savings will be an increasing function of income.
5. The sum of APC and APS is always equal to 1.
6. The sum of MPC and MPS is always equal to 1.

Aggregate Demand Function

1. To determine the aggregate demand function in a two-sector economy, we assume investment is constant and $C = C_a + bY$.
2. Thus, the aggregate demand function can be written as:
$$AD = C_a + bY + \overline{I}$$

DETERMINATION OF EQUILIBRIUM INCOME OR OUTPUT IN A TWO-SECTOR ECONOMY

1. In the most basic terms, an economy can be said to be in equilibrium when the production plans of the firms and the expenditure plans of the households are realized.
2. According to the Keynesian theory, there are two approaches to the determination of income and output: aggregate demand–aggregate supply approach and saving–investment approach.

Equilibrium Income and Output

Aggregate Demand–Aggregate Supply Approach

1. The equilibrium national income is determined at that level, where the aggregate demand = aggregate supply.
2. Keynes had argued that it is not necessary that aggregate demand will be always equal to aggregate supply.
3. Disequilibrium occurs if aggregate demand is not equal to aggregate supply. However, if any disequilibrium occurs, then the forces inbuilt in the system would operate in such a manner that equilibrium is restored.

Saving–Investment Approach

1. While *ex ante* saving and investment may differ, *ex post* saving and investment are always equal.
2. The equilibrium national income is determined, where not only the aggregate demand and the aggregate supply are equal, but at that level where planned saving is also equal to planned investment.
3. Disequilibrium occurs when planned saving is not equal to planned investment. However, firms expand production or cut back on production till planned investment is equal to planned saving.
4. The two approaches to the determination of the equilibrium income, the aggregate demand–aggregate supply approach and the saving–investment approach, both yield the same result.

SHIFTS IN AGGREGATE DEMAND AND MULTIPLIER

1. In a two-sector economy, the initial changes in income occur more due to the shifts in the investment function.
2. It is to be noted that the increase in income is much more than the increase in investment expenditure, or in other words $\Delta Y > \Delta I$.
3. In fact $\Delta Y = m\Delta I$, where m is what is known as the investment multiplier and has a value >1.

Working of Multiplier

1. Suppose the economy is initially in equilibrium.
2. Let there be an increase in autonomous investment by ₹1 million (ΔI).
3. If the economy is operating at less than full employment, this will be matched by an increase in production and output equal to ₹1 million, which will lead to an equal increase in income of ₹1 million (ΔI) in the form of wages, interest and profits. This is the first round of income generation due to the additional investment of ₹1 million. Similarly, there will occur other rounds of income generation.
4. The induced expenditures and thus the additional income generated in each round go on becoming smaller and smaller.
5. We have $\frac{\Delta Y}{\Delta I} = m = \frac{1}{1-b}$, where m is investment multiplier and b is marginal propensity to consume.
6. The value of the multiplier depends on b, the marginal propensity to consume. The larger is the marginal propensity to consume, the larger will be the multiplier.

USES AND LIMITATIONS OF MULTIPLIER

1. The multiplier plays an important role even in a two-sector economy in that it is able to determine the investment, which would be required for a certain planned growth in the national income.
2. The multiplier suffers from many limitations, which may prevent it from working.

APPLICABILITY OF MULTIPLIER TO LDC

1. Dr V. K. R.V. Rao has raised doubts regarding the applicability of the multiplier principle to the underdeveloped countries.
2. The conditions necessary for the multiplier principle to work do not exist in the LDCs.

MULTIPLIER AND PARADOX OF THRIFT

1. It was widely believed, especially by the classical economists, that saving or thrift was a 'virtue' for not only an individual, but also for an economy.
2. Keynes argued that what applies to an individual was not necessarily true for the economy. This is what Keynes called the paradox of thrift.
3. An increase in the thrift by one individual may be good in that it may help in increasing his fortunes in the long run, but if the whole economy becomes thrifty, the economy's equilibrium income may, in fact, actually decrease.

REVIEW QUESTIONS

TRUE OR FALSE QUESTIONS

1. The MPC is defined as the ratio of consumption to income for different levels of income.
2. The APS is defined as the increase in the saving per unit of increase in the income.
3. In an economy, disequilibrium exists when aggregate demand is not equal to aggregate supply.
4. The multiplier is the amount by which there is a change in autonomous investment when income or output increases by one unit.
5. The larger is the marginal propensity to consume, the larger will be the multiplier.

SHORT ANSWER QUESTIONS

1. Write a short note on the consumption function?
2. Write a short note on the saving function?
3. 'As an identity saving is always equal to investment'. Comment.
4. What is the Paradox of Thrift? Discuss.
5. 'The multiplier has certain limitations, which may prevent it from working'. Comment.

LONG ANSWER QUESTIONS

1. Discuss the aggregate demand–aggregate supply approach to the determination of the equilibrium income and output in the Keynesian theory.
2. Discuss the saving–investment approach to the determination of the equilibrium income and output in the Keynesian theory.
3. Give the algebraic explanation to the determination of equilibrium income and output in the Keynesian theory.
4. Explain the working of the multiplier.
5. Analyse the effects of a change in investment on the equilibrium income or output?

NUMERICAL QUESTIONS

1. If the consumption function is $C = 70 + 0.8Y$ and investment is $\overline{I} = 70$. Find
   (a) The equilibrium level of income.
   (b) The equilibrium level of consumption.
   (c) The equilibrium level of saving.

2. In an economy, planned consumption is $C = 50 + 0.60Y$ and planned investment is $\overline{I} = 70$. Find
   (a) The equilibrium level of income.
   (b) The equilibrium level of consumption.
   (c) The equilibrium level of saving.
   (d) Show that at the equilibrium level aggregate demand equals aggregate supply and saving leakages equals investment injections.

3. In an economy, the basic equations are as follows: the consumption function is $C = 80 + 0.75Y$ and investment is $\overline{I} =$ ₹100 crore. Find
   (a) The equilibrium level of income.
   (b) The equilibrium level of income when planned investment increases from ₹100 to ₹120 crore, a total increase of ₹20 crore.
   (c) The multiplier effect of the ₹20 crore increase in planned investment.

4. In an economy, the marginal propensity to consume is 0.75. The level of autonomous investment decreases by ₹40 crore. Find
   (a) The change in the equilibrium level of income.
   (b) The change in autonomous demand.
   (c) The induced change in the consumption expenditures.

5. Suppose the marginal propensity to consume is (i) 0.40, (ii) 0.50, (iii) 0.80, (iv) 1.0 and (v) 0.
   (a) Calculate the marginal propensity to save.
   (b) Calculate the value of the multiplier.
   (c) Using the values of the marginal propensity to consume, find the effect of an increase in the equilibrium income when autonomous investment increases by ₹40 crore.

ANSWERS

NUMERICAL QUESTIONS

1. (a) $Y = 700$
   The equilibrium level of income is 700.
   (b) $C = 630$
   The equilibrium level of consumption is 630.
   (c) $S = 70$
   The equilibrium level of saving is 70.
2. (a) $Y = 300$
   The equilibrium level of income is 600.
   (b) $C = 230$
   The equilibrium level of consumption is 230.
   (c) $S = 70$
   The equilibrium level of saving is 70.
   (d) $C + I = C + S$
   $300 = 300$
   Saving equals investment
   $S = I$
   $300 = 300$
3. (a) $Y = 720$
   The equilibrium level of income is ₹720 crore.
   (b) $Y = 800$

The equilibrium level of income, when planned investment increases from ₹100 to ₹120 crore, is ₹800 crore.

(c) The multiplier effect is 4.
$m = 4$

4. (a) $\Delta Y = -160$.
The decrease in autonomous investment causes a decrease in the equilibrium level of income by ₹160 crore. This effect occurs due to the reverse multiplier.

(b The decrease in investment by ₹40 crore is the change in the level of autonomous demand.

(c) $\Delta C = -$₹120 crore.
The consumption expenditure falls by ₹120 crore.

5. (a) (i) $mps = 1 - mpc = 1 - 0.40 = 0.60$
(ii) $mps = 1 - mpc = 1 - 0.50 = 0.50$
(iii) $mps = 1 - mpc = 1 - 0.80 = 0.20$
(iv) $mps = 1 - mpc = 1 - 1.0 = 0$
(v) $mps = 1 - mpc = 1 - 0 = 1$

(b) (i) $m = 1.67$
(ii) $m = 2$
(iii) $m = 5$
(iv) $m = \infty$ (infinity)
(v) $m = 1$

(c) (i) $\Delta Y = \Delta Im = 40 \times 1.67 = 67$
(ii) $\Delta Y = \Delta Im = 40 \times 2 = 80$
(iii) $\Delta Y = \Delta Im = 40 \times 5 = 200$
(iv) $\Delta Y = \Delta Im = 40 \times \infty$ (infinity) $= \infty$ (infinity)
(v) $\Delta Y = \Delta Im = 40 \times 1 = 40$

TRUE OR FALSE QUESTIONS

1. **False.** The APC is defined as the ratio of consumption to income for different levels of income.
2. **False.** The MPS is defined as the increase in the saving per unit of increase in the income.
3. **True.** In an economy, disequilibrium exists when aggregate demand is not equal to aggregate supply or planned saving is not equal to planned investment.
4. **False.** The multiplier is the amount by which there is a change in equilibrium income or output when autonomous investment increases by one unit.
5. **True.** Since the value of the multiplier depends on b, the marginal propensity to consume or $m = 1/1 - b$; the larger is the marginal propensity to consume, the larger will be the multiplier.

Keynesian Model of Income Determination in Three-sector and Four-sector Economies

19

After studying this chapter, you should be able to understand:

- ✓ *Three main activities of the government are government expenditure, transfers and taxes.*
- ✓ *Income leakages are in the form of saving and taxes, and injections in the form of investment and government expenditure.*
- ✓ *There are two approaches to income determination in a three-sector model, aggregate demand–aggregate supply approach and leakages equals injections approach.*
- ✓ *An economy can achieve a full employment output by an expansion in its budget, financing every rupee of additional expenditure with a rupee of additional taxes.*
- ✓ *Introduction of government transfer payments has an expansionary effect on the income level.*
- ✓ *The expansionary effect on the income level will be smaller with a proportional income tax than with a lump sum income tax.*
- ✓ *The government expenditure multiplier, tax multiplier and the balanced budget multiplier have an impact on the equilibrium level of income.*
- ✓ *In a four-sector economy, the export and import of goods and services affect the level of aggregate demand.*
- ✓ *There are two approaches to the determination of the equilibrium income and output in a four-sector model, the aggregate demand–aggregate supply approach and leakages equals injections approach.*
- ✓ *The four-sector equilibrium exists where the C + I + G + X – M curve and aggregate supply curve intersect.*
- ✓ *A zero marginal propensity to import implies a multiplier, which has the same value as the ordinary multiplier.*
- ✓ *In an open economy, the value of the multiplier is less than that in a closed economy.*

INTRODUCTION

The earlier chapters have focused on income determination and the multiplier in a two-sector economy, where there exist the households and the firms. This chapter focuses on extending the theory of income determination and the multiplier to three- and four-sector models.

In a three-sector model, the third sector is the government sector. Thus, the economy, which is being analysed, is a closed economy and is in isolation from the rest of the world. The action of the government relating to its expenditures, transfers and taxes is called the fiscal policy. Here, we focus on three fiscal policy models, which are in increasing order of complexity, with the emphasis being on the government expenditure, taxation and the income level. We also discuss some of the fiscal policy multipliers including the balanced budget multiplier.

The four-sector model or in other words an open economy is engaged in trade with the rest of the world. Thus, the aggregate demand will be now determined by the spending of four sectors, namely, households, firms, government and the foreign sector. The foreign sector will include the foreign consumers, the foreign business and the foreign governments. The chapter also discusses the foreign trade multiplier.

DETERMINATION OF EQUILIBRIUM INCOME OR OUTPUT IN A THREE-SECTOR ECONOMY

Though the government is involved in a variety of activities, three of them are of greater relevance to us in the present context. Hence, we will focus on these activities of the government, which are discussed below:

(i) **Government Expenditure** (or spending), which includes goods purchased by the central, state and the local governments and also the payments made to the government employees.

(ii) **Transfers** are those government payments, which do not involve any direct services by the recipient, for example, welfare payments, unemployment insurance and others.

(iii) **Taxes**, which include taxes on property, income and goods. Taxes can be classified into two categories, direct taxes and indirect taxes. Direct taxes are levied directly and include personal income and corporate income taxes. Indirect taxes are levied indirectly and include sales tax and excise tax. They are paid as a part of the price of the goods.

Transfer payments are those government payments, which do not involve any direct services by the recipient, for example, welfare payments, unemployment insurance and others.

Indirect taxes are levied indirectly and include sales tax and excise tax. They are paid as a part of the price of the goods.

Direct taxes are levied directly and include personal income and corporate income taxes.

We simplify our analysis by making a few assumptions, which are as follows:

(i) The government purchases factor services from the household sector and goods and services from the firms.

(ii) Transfer payments include subsidies to the firms and pensions to the household sector.

(iii) The government levies only direct taxes on the household sector.

We here introduce the notion of an income leakage and an injection. In a two-sector model, a part of the current income stream (which is not spent on consumption) 'leaked' out as saving while injections in the form of 'investment' were injected into the system. In a three-sector model, taxes, like saving, are income leakages while government expenditures, like investment, are injections.

RECAP

- We will focus on three activities of the government including government expenditure, transfers and taxes.
- In a three-sector model, taxes, like saving, are income leakages while government expenditures, like investment, are injections.

FIRST MODEL OF INCOME DETERMINATION (INTRODUCING GOVERNMENT EXPENDITURE AND TAX)

This model is an extension of the two-sector model with the following modifications:

(i) Government expenditure is determined autonomously.

(ii) There is only one kind of tax, lump sum income tax (which is independent of the income level).

(iii) The government expenditure equals the tax revenue. This implies that the government follows a balanced budget.

Given the above modifications, we can now analyse the equilibrium in a three-sector model.

Equilibrium Income and Output

Aggregate Demand–Aggregate Supply Approach

Aggregate demand = total value of output (or income)

Or $$Y = C + I + G \tag{19.1}$$

where $C = C_a + bY_d$ is the consumption function, $Y_d = Y - T$ is disposable income, $T = \overline{T}$ is tax (lump sum income tax), $I = \overline{I}$ is investment (assumed to be autonomous) and $G = \overline{G}$ is government expenditure (assumed to be autonomous).

Substituting for these values in the basic equation (19.1), we get $Y = C_a + bY_d + \overline{I} + \overline{G}$

$$Y = C_a + b(Y - T) + \overline{I} + \overline{G}$$

Or $$Y - bY = C_a + \overline{I} + \overline{G} - b\overline{T}$$

Or $$Y(1 - b) = C_a + \overline{I} + \overline{G} - b\overline{T}$$

Thus, $$Y = \frac{1}{1-b}(C_a + \overline{I} + \overline{G} - b\overline{T}) \tag{19.2}$$

Equation (19.2) gives the equilibrium income in a three-sector economy.

Leakages Equal Injections Approach

In equilibrium, in a three-sector model,

$$AD = AS$$

Or $$C + I + G = C + S + T$$

Since C is common in both the sides, the equilibrium condition can be written as

$$I + G = S + T \tag{19.3}$$

where $I = \overline{I}$ is investment (assumed to be autonomous), $G = \overline{G}$ is government expenditure (assumed to be autonomous), $S = Y_d - C$ is saving function, $C = C_a + bY_d$ is consumption function and $T = \overline{T}$ is tax (lump sum income tax).

Substituting for these values in the equation (19.3), we get

$$\overline{I} + \overline{G} = S + \overline{T}$$

$$\overline{I}+\overline{G}=(Y_d-C)+\overline{T}$$

$$\overline{I}+\overline{G}=\{Y-\overline{T}-[C_a+bY_d]\}+\overline{T}$$

$$\overline{I}+\overline{G}=\{Y-\overline{T}-C_a-b(Y-\overline{T})\}+\overline{T}$$

$$Y-bY=C_a+\overline{I}+\overline{G}-b\overline{T}$$

$$Y(1-b)=C_a+\overline{I}+\overline{G}-b\overline{T}$$

Or
$$Y(1-b)=C_a+\overline{I}+\overline{G}-b\overline{T}$$

Thus,
$$Y=\frac{1}{1-b}(C_a+\overline{I}+\overline{G}-b\overline{T})$$

The above equation is the same as equation (19.2) above. Hence, both the approaches yield the same equilibrium level of income.

Equilibrium Income and Output: A Graphical Explanation

Aggregate Demand–Aggregate Supply Approach

Equilibrium: The determination of the equilibrium income by the aggregate demand–aggregate supply approach in a three-sector economy has been depicted in Figure 19.1(a), where

C = aggregate consumption function $C=C_a+bY_d=C_a+b(Y-\overline{T})$.

C_a = the intercept of the consumption function on the Y axis showing consumption spending at zero income level.

b = the MPC or the slope of the consumption function. (It will remain constant since, in our analysis, the consumption function is a linear function.)

$I=\overline{I}$ = investment (assumed to be autonomous).

$G=\overline{G}$ = government expenditure (assumed to be autonomous).

AD_1 = aggregate demand function before a tax. (This is obtained by adding the consumption function, the investment function and the government expenditures.)

AS = aggregate supply function. (Also called the guideline or the 45° line.)

Point E depicts the two-sector equilibrium or the initial equilibrium, where the aggregate demand curve AD (= C + I) and aggregate supply curves intersect to determine the equilibrium income at Y^*.

Point E_1 shows the three-sector equilibrium, where the aggregate demand curve $AD_1(=C+I+G)$ and aggregate supply curves intersect to determine the equilibrium income at Y_1. It is important to note that at this stage the entire government expenditure is deficit financed and that the taxes are zero. Thus, increase in government spending will lead to an increase in income, where $\Delta Y>\Delta G$ or that $\Delta Y=m\Delta G$. Hence, the multiplier, $m>1$.

C' = the consumption function after the tax. Since a tax is a withdrawal, it reduces the disposable income, Y_d, thus leading to a shift of the consumption function from C to C' and a shift of the aggregate demand curve from AD_1 to AD_2.

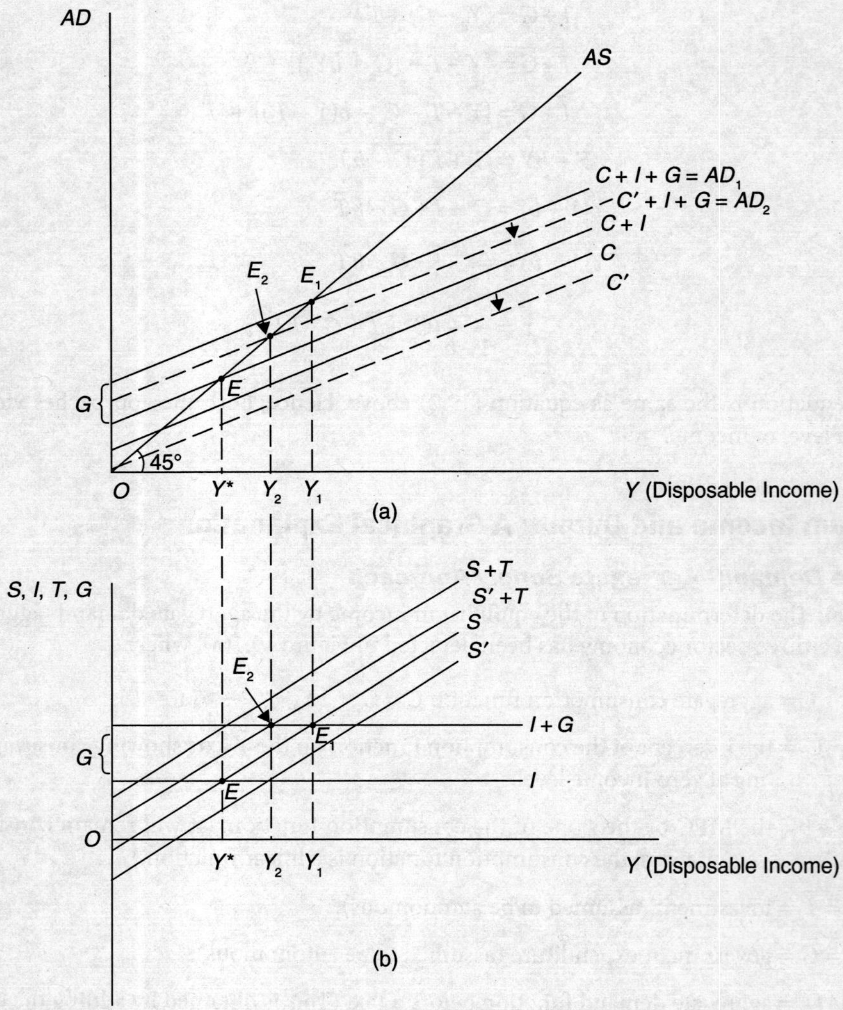

Figure 19.1 Determination of Equilibrium Income or Output in a Three-sector Economy

AD_2 = aggregate demand function after a tax and

> A balanced budget exists when the entire government expenditure is financed by taxes or that $G = T$.

Point E_2 shows the three-sector equilibrium, where the aggregate demand curve $AD_2(C' + I + G)$ and aggregate supply curves intersect to determine the equilibrium income at Y_2. The entire government expenditure is financed by taxes or that $G = T$. In other words, it is a balanced budget.

Leakages Equal Injections Approach

Equilibrium: The determination of the equilibrium income by the leakages and injections approach in a three-sector economy has been depicted in Figure 19.1(b).

In Figure 19.1(b),

X axis = disposable income.
Y axis = planned saving, planned investment, taxes and government expenditure.
S = planned saving.
$I = \overline{I}$ = investment function.
$S + \overline{T}$ = planned saving plus taxes.
$\overline{I} + \overline{G}$ = planned investment plus government expenditure.
E = the two-sector equilibrium or the initial equilibrium, where the saving curve, S, and the investment curve, $\overline{I}$, intersect to determine the equilibrium income at Y^*.

Point E_1 shows the three-sector equilibrium, where the saving curve, S, and the investment plus government expenditure curve, $\overline{I} + \overline{G}$, intersect to determine the equilibrium income at Y_1. Here, taxes are zero.

S' = saving after the imposition of the tax and

Point E_2 depicts the three-sector equilibrium, where the planned saving and taxes curve, $S' + \overline{T}$, and the investment plus government expenditure curve, $\overline{I} + \overline{G}$, intersect to determine the equilibrium income at Y_2. The entire government expenditure is financed by taxes or that $\overline{G} = \overline{T}$. In other words, it is a balanced budget.

We find that the two approaches to the determination of the equilibrium income, the aggregate demand–aggregate supply approach and the leakages equals injections approach, both yield the same result.

It is important to observe that while government expenditure has an expansionary effect taxes have a contractionary effect on the income level. However, the contractionary effect of taxes is less than the expansionary effect of government expenditure, even though $\Delta G = \Delta T$. This is because while an increase in government spending is entirely an addition to the aggregate demand, an increase in T is not entirely a decrease in the aggregate demand. Some part of the increase in T involves a reduction in the savings while the rest is absorbed by a reduction in consumption and hence in aggregate demand.

While, before the imposition of the tax, the equilibrium level of income was Y_1 after the tax, it reduces to Y_2 and not to Y^* (even though $G = T$). Hence, the imposition of a tax, given the level of government expenditure, causes a reduction in the equilibrium level of income, from Y_1 to Y_2, though it is still larger than the initial income level Y^*.

An important implication for fiscal policy is that an economy can achieve full employment output by an expansion in its budget, financing every rupee of additional expenditure with a rupee of additional taxes.

RECAP

- In a three-sector model, taxes and saving are the income leakages while government expenditures and investment are the injections.
- The First Model of Income Determination introduces the government expenditure and tax.
- The two approaches to the determination of the equilibrium income, the aggregate demand–aggregate supply approach and the leakages equals injections approach, both yield the same result.
- The imposition of a tax, given the government expenditure, reduces the equilibrium level of income.
- The contractionary effect of taxes on the income level is less than the expansionary effect of government expenditure.

BOX 19.1

During the period 1500 to 1776, the nation states in Europe were involved in strengthening themselves. The philosophy that gained importance was mercantilism. The need to accumulate gold was emphasized to achieve the nation's military and political dreams. It was realized that the sectors, which led to a favourable balance of trade, should be encouraged. The needs of the people were neglected and the production was only for purposes of exports. A famous writer Thomas Mun wrote in his book, *England's Treasure by Foreign Trade*, that a nation's treasure could be increased through encouraging exports. He advocated that those goods should be exported, which had an inelastic demand so that a higher price could be charged.

Illustration 1: The fundamental equations in an economy are given as

$$C = 150 + 0.75(Y - T)$$

$$\overline{I} = 300$$

$$T = 40 + 0.2Y$$

$$\overline{G} = 150$$

Find the equilibrium level of income.

Solution:

The equilibrium condition in a three-sector economy is given as

$$Y = C + I + G$$

Thus,

$$Y = 150 + 0.75[Y - (40 + 0.2Y)] + 300 + 150$$

$$Y = 150 + 0.75[Y - 40 - 0.2Y] + 300 + 150$$

$$Y = 600 + 0.75[-40 - 0.8Y]$$

$$Y = 600 - 30 - 0.6Y$$

$$Y - 0.6Y = 570$$

$$0.4Y = 570$$

$$Y = 570/0.4$$

$$Y = 1425$$

The equilibrium level of income is 1425.

SECOND MODEL OF INCOME DETERMINATION (INTRODUCING GOVERNMENT TRANSFER PAYMENTS)

In the first model, we had included only two activities of the government, namely, government expenditure and taxes. Here, in this second model, we bring transfer payments also into the picture.

As already mentioned, transfer payments are those government payments, which do not involve any *quid pro quo* or in other words do not involve any direct services by the recipient, for example, welfare payments. Transfer payments are, in fact, just the reverse of taxes or in other words they are negative taxes. While taxes reduce the spending capacity, transfer payments increase the spending capacity of the households leading to ultimately an increase in the equilibrium level of income.

We have our basic equation (19.1)

$$Y = C + I + G$$

where $C = C_a + bY_d$ is consumption function, $Y_d = Y - T + R$ is disposable income, $T = \overline{T}$ is tax (lump sum income tax), $I = \overline{I}$ is investment (assumed to be autonomous), $G = \overline{G}$ is government expenditure (assumed to be autonomous) and $R = \overline{R}$ is transfer payments (assumed to be autonomous).

Substituting for these values in the basic equation, we get

$$Y = C_a + b(Y - \overline{T} + \overline{R}) + \overline{I} + \overline{G}$$

Or $$Y - bY = C_a + \overline{I} + \overline{G} - b\overline{T} + b\overline{R}$$

Or $$Y(1 - b) = C_a + \overline{I} + \overline{G} - b\overline{T} + b\overline{R}$$

Thus, $$Y = \frac{1}{1-b}(C_a + \overline{I} + \overline{G} - b\overline{T} + b\overline{R})$$

Similar to the first model, here also, a change in any of the values within brackets will lead to a change in income, which will be equal to the change in that particular value times the multiplier.

It is important to observe that both the transfer payments and the government expenditure have an expansionary effect on the income level. However, the expansionary effect of an increase in transfer payments will be less than the effect of an increase in government expenditure even though $\Delta G = \Delta R$ (as long as the marginal propensity to consume is <1). Thus,

$$\frac{1}{1-b}\Delta G > \frac{1}{1-b} b\Delta R$$

This is because while the entire increase in government spending is an addition to the aggregate demand, only a part of the increase in R will be an addition to the aggregate demand (through an increase in the consumption spending). Some part of the increase in R is directed towards savings. Hence, the increase in income:

(i) In case of an increase in government expenditure is equal to the increase in the government expenditure times the multiplier.

(ii) In case of an increase in transfers is equal to only b (b is the marginal propensity to consume.) part of the increase in the transfers times the multiplier.

It is important to note that while a change in government expenditure affects aggregate demand directly, a change in transfer payments affects aggregate demand indirectly through a change in disposable income.

RECAP

- As long as the marginal propensity to consume is <1, the expansionary effect of an increase in transfer payments will be less than the effect of an increase in government expenditure even when ΔG = ΔR.
- A change in government expenditure affects aggregate demand directly.
- A change in transfer payments affects aggregate demand indirectly through a change in disposable income.

THIRD MODEL OF INCOME DETERMINATION (INCLUDING GOVERNMENT EXPENDITURES, TRANSFER PAYMENTS AND INTRODUCING TAX AS A FUNCTION OF THE INCOME LEVEL)

In recent years, a large part of the tax receipts of the government consists of personal and corporate income taxes. Other taxes such as sales tax, excise duty and service taxes also vary indirectly with the income level though less when compared with personal and corporate income taxes. Thus, we introduce tax as a linear function of income in this model.

$$T = \overline{T} + tY + \overline{R}$$

where T is the total tax, $T = \overline{T}$ is autonomous tax receipts (tax receipts at, theoretically zero income level), t is proportional income tax rate (the fraction of any income that will be taxed) and $\overline{R}$ is transfers.

$$Y = C + I + G$$

where $C = C_a + bY_d$ is consumption function, $Y_d = Y - T + \overline{R}$ is disposable income, $T = \overline{T} + tY + \overline{R}$ is net tax (where the tax is a function of the income level), $\overline{R}$ is transfer payments, $I = \overline{I}$ is investment (assumed to be autonomous) and $G = \overline{G}$ is government expenditure (assumed to be autonomous).

Substituting for these values in the equation (19.1), we get

$$Y = C_a + b\,[Y - (\overline{T} + tY + \overline{R})] + \overline{I} + \overline{G}$$

Or

$$Y - bY = C_a + \overline{I} + \overline{G} - b\overline{T} - btY + b\overline{R}$$

Or

$$Y - bY + btY = C_a + \overline{I} + \overline{G} - b\overline{T} + b\overline{R}$$

$$Y(1 - b + bt) = C_a + \overline{I} + \overline{G} - b\overline{T} + b\overline{R}$$

Thus,

$$Y = \frac{1}{1 - b(1 - t)}(C_a + \overline{I} + \overline{G} - b\overline{T} + b\overline{R}) \tag{19.4}$$

In the second model, where the tax receipts are independent of the income level, the multiplier is larger than the multiplier in the third model, where the tax receipts are dependent on the income level.

Given an increase in government expenditure, the expansion in income will be smaller with a proportional income tax than for a lump sum income tax.

RECAP

- The multiplier in the second model, where the tax receipts are independent of the income level, is larger than the multiplier in the third model, where the tax receipts are dependent on the income level.
- The increase in income will be smaller in the case of a proportional income tax than for a lump sum income tax.

Illustration 2: In illustration 1, suppose the government transfer payments are at ₹60 crore. Find the equilibrium level of income.

Solution:

The equilibrium condition in the three-sector economy is given as

$$Y = C_a + b(Y - \overline{T} + \overline{R}) + \overline{I} + \overline{G}$$

Thus,
$$Y = 150 + 0.75[Y - (40 + 0.2Y) + 60] + 300 + 150$$
$$Y = 150 + 0.75[Y - 40 - 0.2Y + 60] + 300 + 150$$
$$Y = 600 + 0.75[20 - 0.8Y]$$
$$Y = 600 + 15 - 0.6Y$$
$$Y - 0.6Y = 615$$
$$0.4Y = 615$$
$$Y = 615/0.4$$
$$Y = 1537.50$$

The equilibrium level of income is 1537.50.

MULTIPLIERS IN A THREE-SECTOR ECONOMY–FISCAL MULTIPLIERS

Through its fiscal policy, the government is in a position to influence the economic activities in an economy. To what extent its fiscal operations have an impact on the equilibrium level of income depends on the fiscal multipliers. Here, we analyse three multipliers.

Government Sector Multipliers with Lump Sum Tax

Government Expenditure Multiplier

In the first model, we had arrived at

$$Y = C + I + G \tag{19.1}$$

where $C = C_a + bY_d$ is consumption function, $Y_d = Y - T$ is disposable income, $T = \overline{T}$ is tax (lump sum income tax), $I = \overline{I}$ is investment (assumed to be autonomous) and $G = \overline{G}$ is assumed to be autonomous.

Substituting for these values in the basic equation (19.1), we get the equilibrium level of income as:

$$Y = \frac{1}{1-b}(C_a + \overline{I} + \overline{G} - b\overline{T}) \tag{19.2}$$

Assume that there is an increase in government expenditure by ΔG. Hence,

$$Y + \Delta Y = \frac{1}{1-b}(C_a + \overline{I} - b\overline{T} + \overline{G} + \Delta G) \tag{19.5}$$

Subtracting equation (19.2) from equation (19.5), we get

$$\Delta Y = \frac{1}{1-b}(\Delta G)$$

Or
$$G_M = \frac{\Delta Y}{\Delta G} = \frac{1}{1-b}$$

where ΔG is change in government expenditure, b is marginal propensity to consume, ΔY is change in income and G_M is government expenditure multiplier.

An increase in government expenditure by ΔG leads to an increase in aggregate demand and hence in the equilibrium level of income by ΔY. The government expenditure multiplier has the same value as the investment multiplier in the two-sector model of $\frac{1}{1-b}$ or $\frac{1}{1-mpc}$. Since the value of b is always between 0 and 1, the multiplier will always have a value >1. Hence, a change in government expenditure by ΔG will lead to a change in the equilibrium level of income by ΔY, where $\Delta Y > \Delta G$.

Tax Multiplier (Lump Sum Tax)

We have equation (19.2) as

$$Y = \frac{1}{1-b}(C_a + \bar{I} + \bar{G} - b\bar{T})$$

Assume that there is a change in tax by $\Delta \bar{T}$. Hence, we get

$$Y + \Delta Y = \frac{1}{1-b}(C_a + \bar{I} - b(\bar{T} + \Delta\bar{T}) + \bar{G}) \tag{19.6}$$

Subtracting equation (19.2) from equation (19.6), we get

$$\Delta Y = \frac{1}{1-b}(-b\Delta\bar{T})$$

Or

$$G_T = \frac{\Delta Y}{\Delta \bar{T}} = \frac{-b}{1-b}$$

where $\Delta\bar{T}$ is change in tax, b is marginal propensity to consume, ΔY is change in income and G_T is government tax multiplier. Since the tax multiplier is negative, an increase in tax leads a decrease in the equilibrium level of income.

Similarly, the transfer multiplier can be written as

$$\frac{\Delta Y}{\Delta R} = \frac{b}{1-b}$$

Balanced Budget Multiplier

The budget is in balance when the government expenditures plus transfer payments equal the gross tax receipts or, in other words, G = T.

The budget is in balance when the government expenditures plus transfer payments equal the gross tax receipts or, in other words, $G = T$. It follows that when there is an increase in government expenditure, it will be financed by an increase in taxation. Thus, $\Delta G = \Delta T$.

It is important to note that an increase in the government expenditures, which is balanced by an increase in taxes of an equal amount, will not leave the income level unchanged. In fact, there will be an increase in income by the same amount as the increase in the government expenditures and the tax. This implies that it is incorrect to assert that government expenditures and taxes of an equivalent amount offset one another and that there is no increase in the income level if the budget is balanced. In fact, the increase in the income is exactly equal to the amount by which there is an increase in the government expenditures and tax. Hence, the value of the 'balanced budget' multiplier, which is the increase in the output as a consequence of equal increases in the government expenditure and taxes, is equal to 1. This is what is known as the 'balanced budget' or 'unit multiplier' theorem.

Balanced budget multiplier is the increase in the output as a consequence of equal increases in the government expenditure and taxes.

We have equation (19.2) as

$$Y = \frac{1}{1-b}(C_a + \bar{I} + \bar{G} - b\bar{T})$$

Assume that there is a change in government expenditure by ΔG and in tax by ΔT and where $\Delta G = \Delta T$. Hence, we get

$$Y + \Delta Y = \frac{1}{1-b}(C_a + \bar{I} - b(\bar{T} + \Delta\bar{T}) + (\bar{G} + \Delta\bar{G})) \tag{19.7}$$

Subtracting equation (19.2) from equation (19.7), we get

$$\Delta Y = \frac{1}{1-b}(-b\Delta T + \Delta\bar{G}) \tag{19.8}$$

But

$$\Delta G = \Delta T$$

Thus, we can write

$$\Delta Y = \frac{1}{1-b}(-b\Delta\bar{G} + \Delta\bar{G})$$

Or

$$\Delta Y(1-b) = \Delta\bar{G}(-b+1)$$

Or

$$\Delta Y(1-b) = \Delta\bar{G}(1-b)$$

Or

$$\frac{\Delta Y}{\Delta G} = \frac{1-b}{1-b} = 1$$

where ΔG is change in government expenditure, ΔT is change in tax, b is marginal propensity to consume and ΔY is change in income.

Alternatively, the balanced budget multiplier can also be obtained by summing up the government expenditure multiplier and the tax multiplier to get

$$\frac{\Delta Y}{\Delta G} + \frac{\Delta Y}{\Delta T} = \frac{1}{1-b} + \frac{-b}{1-b} = \frac{1-b}{1-b} = 1$$

Whatever the value of b, the sum of the government expenditure multiplier and the tax multiplier will always be equal to unity.

Government Sector Multipliers with Income Tax

Government Expenditure Multiplier

$$G_M = \frac{\Delta Y}{\Delta G} = \frac{1}{1-b(1-t)}$$

Tax Multiplier

$$G_T = \frac{\Delta Y}{\Delta T} = \frac{-b}{1-b(1-t)}$$

RECAP

- The government expenditure multiplier has the same value as the investment multiplier of $\frac{1}{1-b}$ or $\frac{1}{1-mpc}$.

- Since the tax multiplier is negative, an increase in tax will lead to a decrease in the equilibrium level of income.
- An increase in the government expenditures, which is balanced by an increase in taxes of an equal amount, will lead to an increase in income by the same amount as the increase in the government expenditures and the tax.

DETERMINATION OF EQUILIBRIUM INCOME OR OUTPUT IN A FOUR-SECTOR ECONOMY

The inclusion of the foreign sector in our analysis influences the level of aggregate demand through the export and import of goods and services. Hence, it is necessary to understand the factors that influence the exports and imports.

The volume of exports in any economy depends on the following factors:

(i) The prices of the exports in the domestic economy relative to the price in the other economies.
(ii) The income level in the other economies.
(iii) Tastes, preferences, customs and traditions in the other economies.
(iv) The tariff and trade policies between the domestic economy and the other economies.
(v) The domestic economy's level of imports.

Open economy is an economy, which is engaged in trade with the rest of the world.

To simplify our analysis, we assume that the exports in any economy are determined by external factors or, in other words, forces which are external to the domestic economy. Thus, the level of *exports is assumed to be an autonomous variable.*

As far as imports are concerned, the volume of imports in any economy depends on the following factors:

(i) The prices of the imports relative to the domestic prices.
(ii) The income level in the domestic economy.
(iii) The tastes and preferences for imports when compared with the domestic goods.
(iv) The tariff and trade policies of the domestic economy *vis-a-vis* the other economies.
(v) The domestic economy's exchange rate policies.

To simplify our analysis, we assume that the *imports in any economy are determined by the income level* in the domestic economy. This brings us to the import function, which, in its simplest form, can be expressed as a linear function.

$$M = M_a + mY$$

Figure 19.2 depicts the import function as an upward sloping line and the exports function as a line parallel to the X axis (as they are assumed to be determined autonomously).

The marginal propensity to import is the fraction of any change in income that will be devoted to imports.

In Figure 19.2, M is imports, M_a is autonomous imports (imports at a theoretically zero level of income), $m = \Delta M/\Delta Y$ is marginal propensity to import (fraction of any change in income that will be devoted to imports) and Y is income level.

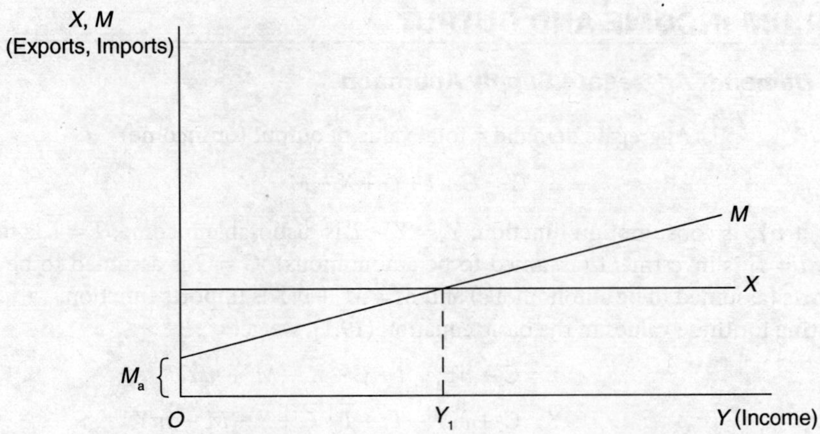

Figure 19.2 The Import Function and the Export Function

In Figure 19.2,

(i) At all the income levels below Y_1, since exports are greater than imports, there exists a net export balance or a favourable balance of trade.

(ii) At all the income levels above Y_1, since exports are less than imports, there exists a net import balance or an unfavourable balance of trade.

It is important to note that

(i) A change in the factors that influence the exports such that there is an upward shift in the exports function will lead to an increase in the net export balance or a decrease in the net import balance at each income level.

(ii) A change in the factors that influence the imports such that there is a downward shift in the imports function (a decrease in M_a) or a decrease in the slope of the import function (decrease in M) will lead to an increase in the net export balance or a decrease in the net import balance at each income level.

Export, Import and Aggregate Demand

While exports must be added to the total final expenditures to arrive at the aggregate demand, all spending on imports do not contribute to the domestic demand, and thus must be deducted from the total final expenditures to arrive at the aggregate demand.

RECAP

- The level of exports is assumed to be an autonomous variable.
- The imports in any economy are determined by the income level in the domestic economy.
- When exports are greater than imports, there exists a net export balance or a favourable balance of trade.
- While exports need to be added to the total final expenditures, imports need to be deducted from the total final expenditures to arrive at the aggregate demand.

EQUILIBRIUM INCOME AND OUTPUT

Aggregate Demand–Aggregate Supply Approach

Aggregate demand = total value of output (or income)

Or $$Y = C + I + G + X - M \quad (19.9)$$

where $C = C_a + bY_d$ is consumption function, $Y_d = Y - T$ is disposable income, $T = \overline{T}$ is tax (lump sum income tax), $I = \overline{I}$ is investment (assumed to be autonomous), $G = \overline{G}$ is assumed to be autonomous, $X = \overline{X}$ is exports (assumed to be autonomous) and $M = M_a + mY$ is imports function.

Substituting for these values in the basic equation (19.1), we get

$$Y = C_a + bY_d + \overline{I} + \overline{G} + \overline{X} - (M_a + mY)$$

$$Y = C_a + b(Y - T) + \overline{I} + \overline{G} + \overline{X} - M_a - mY$$

Or $$Y - bY + mY = C_a + \overline{I} + \overline{G} + \overline{X} - b\overline{T} - M_a$$

Or $$Y(1 - b + m) = C_a + \overline{I} + \overline{G} + \overline{X} - b\overline{T} - M_a$$

Thus $$Y = \frac{1}{1-b+m} C_a + \overline{I} + \overline{G} + \overline{X} - b\overline{T} - M_a \quad (19.10)$$

Leakages Equal Injections Approach

In equilibrium in a four-sector model,

$$AD = AS$$

Or $$C + I + G + X = C + S + T + M$$

(In a four-sector model, the injections include investment, government expenditures and exports while the leakages include saving, taxes and imports.)

Since C is common in both the sides the equilibrium, condition can be written as

$$I + G + X = S + T + M \quad (19.11)$$

where $I = \overline{I}$ is investment (assumed to be autonomous), $G = \overline{G}$ is government expenditure (assumed to be autonomous), $X = \overline{X}$ is exports (assumed to be autonomous), $S = Y_d - C$ is saving function, $C = C_a + bY_d$ is consumption function, $T = \overline{T}$ = tax (lump sum income tax) and $M = M_a + mY$ is imports function.

Substituting for these values in the equation (19.11), we get

$$\overline{I} + \overline{G} + \overline{X} = S + \overline{T} + M_a + mY$$

$$\overline{I} + \overline{G} + \overline{X} = (Y_d - C) + \overline{T} + M_a + mY$$

$$\overline{I} + \overline{G} + \overline{X} = \{Y - \overline{T} - [C_a + bY_d]\} + \overline{T} + M_a + mY$$

$$\overline{I} + \overline{G} + \overline{X} = \{Y - \overline{T} - C_a - b(Y - \overline{T})\} + \overline{T} + M_a + mY$$

$$Y - bY + mY = C_a + \overline{I} + \overline{G} + \overline{X} - b\overline{T} - M_a$$

$$Y(1 - b + m) = C_a + \overline{I} + \overline{G} + \overline{X} - b\overline{T} - M_a$$

Thus $$Y = \frac{1}{1-b+m} (C_a + \overline{I} + \overline{G} + \overline{X} - b\overline{T} - M_a) \quad (19.10)$$

The above equation is the same as equation (19.10) above. Hence, *both the approaches yield the same equilibrium level of income.*

RECAP

- Both the approaches to income determination yield the same equilibrium level of income.

INTRODUCTION OF GOVERNMENT TRANSFER PAYMENTS IN A FOUR-SECTOR MODEL

Till now, we have not included transfer payments in our analysis. As already mentioned, transfer payments increase the spending capacity of the households leading to an increase in the equilibrium level of income.

We have our basic equation (19.9)

$$Y = C + I + G + X - M$$

where $C = C_a + bY_d$ is consumption function, $Y_d = Y - T$ is disposable income, $T = \overline{T}$ is tax (lump sum income tax), $I = \overline{I}$ is investment (assumed to be autonomous), $G = \overline{G}$ is government expenditure (assumed to be autonomous), $X = \overline{X}$ is exports, $M = M_a + mY$ is imports function and $R = \overline{R}$ is transfer payments (assumed to be autonomous).

Substituting for these values in the basic equation, we get

$$Y = C_a + b(Y - \overline{T} + \overline{R}) + \overline{I} + \overline{G} + \overline{X} - M_a - mY$$

Or
$$Y - bY + mY = C_a + \overline{I} + \overline{G} + \overline{X} - b\overline{T} + b\overline{R} - M_a$$

Or
$$Y(1 - b + m) = C_a + \overline{I} + \overline{G} + \overline{X} - b\overline{T} + b\overline{R} - M_a$$

Thus
$$Y = \frac{1}{1 - b + m}(C_a + \overline{I} + \overline{G} + \overline{X} - b\overline{T} + b\overline{R} - M_a)$$

Determination of Equilibrium Income and Output: A Graphical Explanation

Aggregate Demand–Aggregate Supply Approach

Equilibrium: The determination of the equilibrium income by the aggregate demand–aggregate supply approach in a four-sector economy has been depicted in Figure 19.3(a), where

C = aggregate consumption function, $C = C_a + bY_d = C_a + b(Y - \overline{T})$.

C_a = the intercept of the consumption function on the y axis showing consumption spending at zero income level.

b = the MPC or the slope of the consumption function (it will remain constant since, in our analysis, the consumption function is a linear function).

$I = \overline{I}$ is investment (assumed to be autonomous).

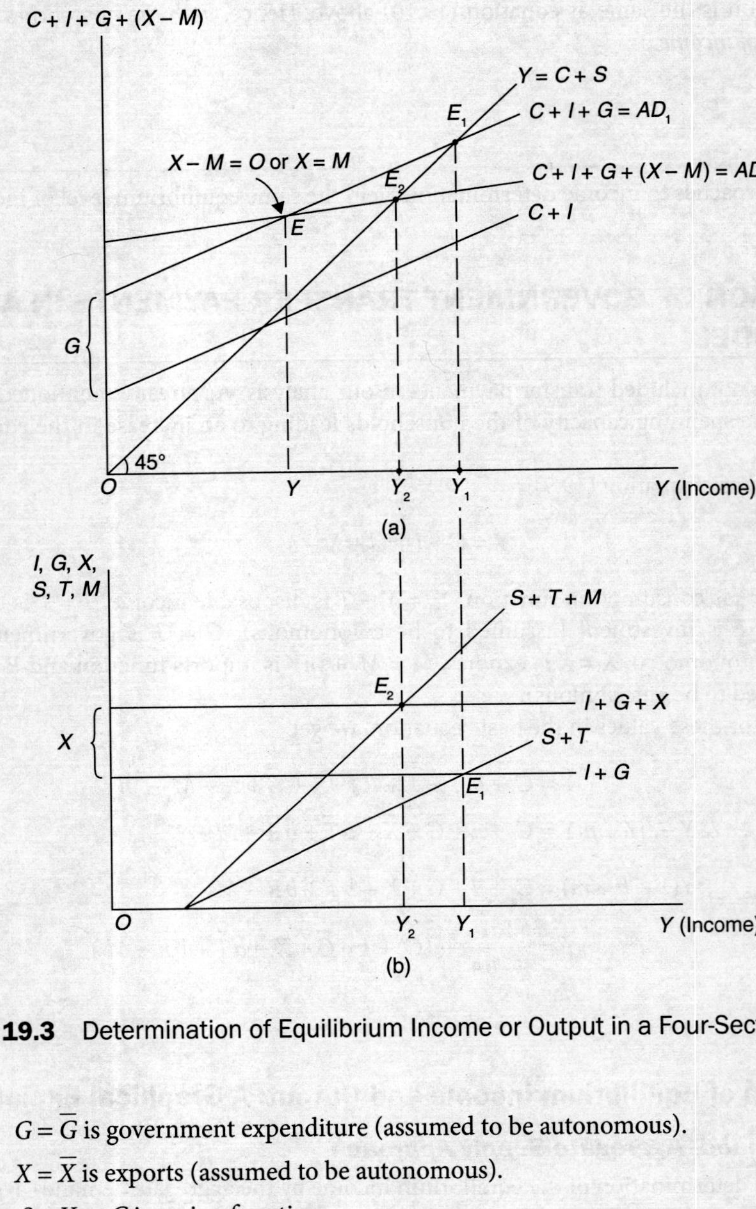

Figure 19.3 Determination of Equilibrium Income or Output in a Four-Sector Economy

$G = \overline{G}$ is government expenditure (assumed to be autonomous).

$X = \overline{X}$ is exports (assumed to be autonomous).

$S = Y_d - C$ is saving function.

$C = C_a + bY_d$ is consumption function.

$T = \overline{T}$ is tax (lump sum income tax).

$M = M_a + mY$ is imports function, $C + I$ line is consumption plus saving line.

AD_1 = aggregate demand function (this is obtained by adding the consumption function, the investment function and the government expenditures).

AS = aggregate supply function (also called the guideline or the 45° line).

Point E_1 shows the three-sector equilibrium or the initial equilibrium, where the aggregate demand curve AD_1 $(= C + I + G)$ and aggregate supply curves intersect to determine the equilibrium income at Y_1.

Point E_2 depicts the four-sector equilibrium, where the aggregate demand curve AD_2 $(= C + I + G + X - M)$ and aggregate supply curves intersect to determine the equilibrium income at Y_2.

At point E, curves AD_1 and AD_2 intersect to determine the equilibrium income at Y. At this level of income, exports equal imports or $X = M$.

To the left of point E, curve AD_2 is above AD_1 indicating that exports exceed imports or $X > M$.

To the right of point E, curve AD_2 is below AD_1 indicating that imports exceed exports or $X < M$.

Leakages Equal Injections Approach

Equilibrium: The determination of the equilibrium income by the leakages and injections approach in a four-sector economy has been depicted in Figure 19.3(b).

The leakages now include saving, taxation and imports while the injections are investment, government expenditure and imports.

In Figure 19.3(b),

S = planned saving.

$I = \overline{I}$ = investment function.

$X = \overline{X}$ = exports.

M = imports function.

$S + \overline{T} + M$ = planned saving plus taxes plus imports.

$\overline{I} + \overline{G} + \overline{X}$ = planned investment plus government expenditure plus exports.

Point E_1 shows the three-sector equilibrium, where the planned saving and taxes curve, $S + \overline{T}$, and investment plus government expenditure curve, $\overline{I} + \overline{G}$, intersect to determine the equilibrium income at Y_1.

Point E_2 depicts the four-sector equilibrium, where the planned saving, taxes and imports curve, $S + \overline{T} + M$, and investment plus government expenditure plus exports curve, $\overline{I} + \overline{G} + \overline{X}$, intersect to determine the equilibrium income at Y_2.

We find that, in a four-sector economy, the two approaches to the determination of the equilibrium income, the aggregate demand–aggregate supply approach and the leakages equals injections approach, both yield the same result.

The introduction of foreign trade has the affect of reducing the equilibrium level of income from Y_1 to Y_2.

RECAP

- In an economy, while the exports are assumed to be exogenous, imports are assumed to be a linear function of the income level.
- At the level of income, where the $C + I + G$ and $C + I + G + X - M$ curves intersect exports equal imports or $X = M$.
- The introduction of foreign trade has the affect of reducing the equilibrium level of income.

MULTIPLIER IN A FOUR-SECTOR ECONOMY–FOREIGN TRADE MULTIPLIER

The size of the multiplier will be lower when the marginal propensity to import is positive.

To have an understanding of the multiplier in the foreign sector, we assume that due to an increase in the income level in the other countries there occurs an increase in the exports of the domestic country. To meet this increased demand for exports, there is an increase in the domestic production, which leads to an increase in the income and hence in the consumption expenditure (depending on the marginal propensity to consume). A part of this increase in the consumption expenditure will be directed towards imports, depending on the marginal propensity to import. This will further lead to a second stage of expansion though due to the leakage from the economy in the form of imports, there will occur only a restricted increase in the income. Further increases in the income will become smaller and smaller. The size of the multiplier will be lower when the marginal propensity to import is positive.

In a four-sector economy, the equilibrium level of income is

$$Y = \frac{1}{1-b+m}(C_a + \overline{I} + \overline{G} + \overline{X} - b\overline{T} - M_a) \tag{19.10}$$

Assume that there is an increase in exports by ΔX. Hence,

$$Y + \Delta Y = \frac{1}{1-b+m}(C_a + \overline{I} - b\overline{T} + \overline{G} + \Delta\overline{G} + \overline{X} + \Delta X) \tag{19.12}$$

Subtracting equation (19.10) from equation (19.12), we get

$$\Delta Y = \frac{1}{1-b+m}(\Delta X)$$

$$\frac{\Delta Y}{\Delta \text{X}} = \frac{1}{1-b+m}$$

where ΔX is change in exports, b is marginal propensity to consume, ΔY is change in income and $\frac{\Delta Y}{\Delta \text{X}} = \frac{1}{1-b+m}$ is foreign trade multiplier.

The value of the multiplier in an open economy is less than that in a closed economy. This is because in the open economy there is an additional leakage in the form of imports. Thus, as long as the marginal propensity to import is positive, the size of the multiplier gets reduced. A zero marginal propensity to import implies a multiplier, which is the same as the ordinary multiplier, $1/1 - b$.

Another way of analysing the effect of the marginal propensity to import on the multiplier is by expressing the multiplier as $1/1 - (b - m)$.

Here, we can write

b = marginal propensity to purchase both domestically and foreign-produced goods.
m = marginal propensity to purchase foreign-produced goods.
$b - m$ = marginal propensity to purchase domestically produced goods.

It is to be observed that

(i) If $b = m$, the value of the multiplier is equal to 1. The increase in income would be equal to the increase in the autonomous expenditure since all the increases in income would be towards the purchase of only imports.

(ii) If $b < m$, the value of the multiplier would be greater than 1. The increase in income would be equal to the increase in the autonomous expenditure since all the increases in income would be towards the purchase of only imports.

(iii) If the value of m were zero, then the multiplier would become equal to the ordinary multiplier.

RECAP

- When the marginal propensity to import is positive, the size of the multiplier will be lower.
- When the marginal propensity to import is zero, then the multiplier would become equal to the ordinary multiplier.

SOLVED NUMERICAL

1. In a two-sector economy, the basic equations are as follows: the consumption function is $C = 100 + 0.80Y_d$ and investment is $\bar{I} =$ ₹150 crore. The equilibrium level of income is ₹1250 crore. Suppose the government sector is added to this two-sector model, which then becomes a three-sector economy. The government expenditure is at ₹50 crore.
   (a) Find the equilibrium level of income in the three-sector economy.
   (b) What is the multiplier affect of the government expenditure? Is it of the same magnitude as the multiplier effect of a change in the autonomous investment?
   (c) Suppose that there is a balanced budget in that the entire government expenditure is financed from a lump sum tax. Find the new equilibrium level of income in the three-sector economy.

Solution:

(a) The equilibrium condition in the three-sector economy is given as $Y = C + I + G$

Thus,

$$Y = 100 + 0.80Y + 150 + 50$$
$$Y - 0.80Y = 100 + 150 + 50$$
$$0.20Y = 300$$
$$Y = 300/0.20$$
$$Y = 1500$$

The equilibrium level of income in the three-sector economy is ₹1500 crore, which is an increase by ₹250 crore over the two-sector economy.

(b) Government expenditure multiplier

$$G_M = \frac{\Delta Y}{\Delta G} = \frac{1}{1-b} = \frac{1}{1-0.80} = 5$$

Investment multiplier

$$m = \frac{\Delta Y}{\Delta I} = \frac{1}{1-b}$$

(Where b is the marginal propensity to consume.)

Thus, the magnitude of the multiplier effect (of a change in the autonomous investment) is the same as that of a change in government expenditure.

(c) $G = T =$ ₹50 crore

Thus,

$$C = 100 + 0.80(Y - 50)$$
$$C = 100 - 40 + 0.80Y$$
$$C = 60 + 0.80Y$$

But

$$Y = C + I + G$$
$$Y = 60 + 0.80Y + 150 + 50$$
$$Y - 0.80Y = 60 + 150 + 50$$
$$0.20Y = 260$$
$$Y = 26/0.20$$
$$Y = 1300$$

The new equilibrium level of income in the three-sector economy when there exists a balanced budget is ₹1300 crore.

2. In an economy, the full employment output occurs at ₹1000 crore. The marginal propensity to consume is 0.80 and the equilibrium level of output is currently at ₹800 crore. Suppose the government aspires to achieve the full employment output. Find the change in
   (a) The level of government expenditures.
   (b) Net lump sum tax.
   (c) The level of government expenditures and the net lump sum tax when the government aims at bringing the output to the full employment while keeping the budget balanced.

Solution:

(a) We have $G_M = \dfrac{\Delta Y}{\Delta G} = \dfrac{1}{1-b}$

where ΔG is change in government expenditure, b is marginal propensity to consume, ΔY is change in income and G_M is government expenditure multiplier.
In the present example,

$$b = 0.80$$
$$\Delta Y = 1000 - 800 = 200$$

Thus,

$$\frac{200}{\Delta G} = \frac{1}{1-0.80}$$
$$\Delta G = 200(0.20) = 40$$

The level of government expenditures required to achieve the full employment output is ₹40 crore.

(b) We have $G_T = \dfrac{\Delta Y}{\Delta T} = \dfrac{-b}{1-b}$

where ΔT is change in tax, b is marginal propensity to consume, ΔY is change in income and G_T is government tax multiplier.
Since the tax multiplier is negative, an increase in tax leads a decrease in the equilibrium level of income.

In the present example,

$$b = 0.80$$

$$\Delta Y = 1000 - 800 = 200$$

Thus,
$$\frac{200}{\Delta T} = \frac{-0.80}{1-0.80}$$

$$-0.80\Delta T = 200(0.20) = -50$$

The net lump sum tax is –₹50 crore. There should be a decrease in lump sum tax by ₹50 crore.

(c) We have $\Delta Y = \frac{1}{1-b}(-b\Delta T + \Delta\overline{G})$

But, $\Delta G = \Delta T$.

Thus, we can write
$$\Delta Y = \frac{1}{1-b}(-b\Delta\overline{G} + \Delta\overline{G})$$

Or
$$\Delta Y(1-b) = \Delta\overline{G}(-b+1)$$

Or
$$\Delta Y(1-b) = \Delta\overline{G}(1-b)$$

Or
$$\frac{\Delta Y}{\Delta G} = \frac{1-b}{1-b} = 1$$

Thus, $\Delta Y = \Delta G =$ ₹200 crore.

The required increase in the level of government expenditures and the net lump sum tax is ₹200 crore.

3. In an economy, $C = 50 + 0.80Y_d$, $\overline{I} =$ ₹100 crore, government expenditure is at ₹50 crore while $T =$ ₹20 crore.
   (a) Find the equilibrium level of income in the three-sector economy.
   (b) Find the equilibrium level of consumption and saving at the equilibrium level of income.
   (c) Depict the injections leakages equality at the equilibrium level.

Solution:

(a) The equilibrium condition in the three-sector economy is given as

$$Y = C + I + G$$

Here,
$$C = 50 + 0.80Y_d$$
$$C = 50 + 0.80\,(Y - T)$$
$$C = 50 + 0.80\,(Y - 20)$$
$$C = 50 + 0.80\,(Y - 16)$$
$$C = 50 + 0.80\,(Y - 16)$$

Thus,
$$Y = 50 + 0.80Y - 16 + 100 + 50$$

$$Y - 0.8Y = 50 - 16 + 100 + 50$$

$$0.2Y = 184$$

$$Y = 184/0.2$$
$$Y = 920$$

The equilibrium level of income is ₹920 crore.

(b) When the equilibrium level of income is ₹920 crore,
Equilibrium level of consumption:

$$C = 50 + 0.80Y_d$$
$$C = 50 + 0.80\ (Y - T)$$
$$C = 50 + 0.80\ (Y - 20)$$
$$C = 50 + 0.80\ (Y - 16)$$
$$C = 50 + 0.80\ (Y - 16)$$
$$C = 50 + 0.80\ (920) - 16$$
$$C = 770$$

The equilibrium level of consumption is ₹770 crore.
Equilibrium level of saving: $S = Y - C - T$

$$S = 920 - 770 - 20 = 130$$

The equilibrium level of saving is ₹130 crore.

(c) Injections $= I + G = 100 + 50 = 150$
Leakages $= S + T = 130 + 20 = 150$
This depicts the injections leakages equality at the equilibrium level.

4. The fundamental equations in an economy are given as
Consumption function $C = 100 + 0.80Y_d$
Investment function $\bar{I} = 150$
Tax $T = 60$
Government expenditure $G = 100$
Exports $X = 50$
Imports $M = 0.05Y$
(a) Find the equilibrium level of income.
(b) Find the net exports.

Solution:

(a) The consumption function is

$$C = 100 + 0.8Y_d$$
$$C = 100 + 0.8(Y - T)$$
$$C = 100 + 0.8\ (Y - 60)$$

The equilibrium condition is given as $Y = C + I + G + X - M$. Thus,

$$Y = 100 + 0.8(Y - 60) + 150 + 100 + (50 - 0.05Y)$$
$$Y = 100 + 0.8\ Y - 48 + 300 - 0.05Y$$
$$Y - 0.8Y + 0.05Y = 352$$
$$0.25Y = 352$$

$$Y = 352/0.25$$

$$Y = 1408$$

The equilibrium level of income is 1408.

Checking the answer: In equilibrium in a four-sector model,
Leakages Equals Injections

Or $$C + I + G + X = C + S + T + M$$

The consumption function is $C = 100 + 0.8\ Y_d$

$$C = 100 + 0.8\ (1408 - 60)$$

$$C = 100 + 0.8(1348)$$

$$C = 1178.4$$

The saving function is $S = Y_d - C$

$$S = (Y - 60) - 1178.4$$

$$S = (1408 - 60) - 1178.4 = 169.6$$

$$S = 169.6$$

Thus, $$I + G + X = S + T + M$$

$$150 + 100 + 50 = 169.6 + 60 + 0.05Y$$

$$300 = 229.6 + 0.05\ (1408)$$

$$300 = 300$$

(b) Imports: $M = 0.05Y = 0.05\ (1408) = 70.4$
Net Exports: $X - M = 50 - 70.4 = -20.4$

$$X - M = -20.4$$

There is a deficit in the balance of trade.

5. Suppose the basic functions in an economy are as follows:

$C = 130 + 0.80Y_d$

$\overline{I} = 160$

$T = 150$

$G = 150$

$X = 150 - 0.05Y$

(a) Find the equilibrium level of income.

(b) Find the net exports at equilibrium level of income.

(c) Find the equilibrium level of income and the net exports when there is an increase in investment from 160 to 170.

(d) Find the equilibrium level of income and the net exports when the net export function becomes $140 - 0.05Y$.

Solution:

(a) The consumption function is

$$C = 130 + 0.8Y_d$$

$$C = 130 + 0.8\ (Y - T)$$

$$C = 130 + 0.8\,(Y - 150)$$

The equilibrium condition is given as $Y = C + I + G + X - M$. Thus,

$$Y = 130 + 0.8(Y - 150) + 160 + 150 + (150 - 0.05Y)$$
$$Y = 130 + 0.8Y - 120 + 460 - 0.05Y$$
$$Y - 0.8Y + 0.05Y = 470$$
$$0.25Y = 470$$
$$Y = 470/0.25$$
$$Y = 1880$$

The equilibrium level of income is 1880.

(b) Imports: $M = 0$

Net Exports: $X - M = 150 - 0.05(1880) - 0$

$X - M = 56$

There is a surplus in the balance of trade.

(c)
$$Y = 130 + 0.8(Y - 150) + 170 + 150 + (150 - 0.05Y)$$
$$Y = 130 + 0.8Y - 120 + 470 - 0.05Y$$
$$Y - 0.8Y + 0.05Y = 480$$
$$0.25Y = 480$$
$$Y = 480/0.25$$
$$Y = 1920$$

The equilibrium level of income is 1920, which is an increase by 40.

Imports: $M = 0$

Net Exports: $X - M = 150 - 0.05(1920) - 0$

$X - M = 54$

There is a surplus in the balance of trade.

(d)
$$Y = 130 + 0.8(Y - 150) + 160 + 150 + (140 - 0.05Y)$$
$$Y = 130 + 0.8Y - 120 + 450 - 0.05Y$$
$$Y - 0.8Y + 0.05Y = 460$$
$$0.25Y = 460$$
$$Y = 460/0.25 = 1840$$
$$Y = 1840$$

The equilibrium level of income is 1840, which is a decrease by 40.

Imports: $M = 0$

Net Exports: $X - M = 140 - 0.05(1840) - 0$

$X - M = 48$

There is a surplus in the balance of trade.

SUMMARY

INTRODUCTION

1. This chapter focuses on extending the theory of income determination and the multiplier to three- and four-sector models.
2. The action of the government relating to its expenditures, transfers and taxes is called the fiscal policy.

3. Here, we focus on three fiscal policy models.
4. We also discuss some of the fiscal policy multipliers including the balanced budget multiplier.
5. The four-sector model or, in other words, an open economy is engaged in trade with the rest of the world.
6. Thus, the aggregate demand will be now determined by the spending of four sectors, namely, households, firms, government and the foreign sector.
7. The chapter also discusses the foreign trade multiplier.

DETERMINATION OF EQUILIBRIUM INCOME OR OUTPUT IN A THREE-SECTOR ECONOMY

1. Three activities of the government are important: government expenditure, transfers and taxes.
2. We simplify our analysis by making a few assumptions like the government levies only direct taxes on the household sector.
3. In a three-sector model, taxes are income leakages while government expenditures are injections.

FIRST MODEL OF INCOME DETERMINATION (INTRODUCING GOVERNMENT EXPENDITURE AND TAX)

1. This model is an extension of the two-sector model in that it includes autonomous government expenditure and a lump sum income tax. Also, the government follows a balanced budget, or $\overline{G}=\overline{T}$.
2. There are two approaches to the determination of equilibrium income and output: aggregate demand–aggregate supply approach and leakages equals injections approach. Both the approaches yield the same equilibrium level of income.
3. The contractionary effect of taxes is less than the expansionary effect of government expenditure even when $G=T$.

SECOND MODEL OF INCOME DETERMINATION (INTRODUCING GOVERNMENT TRANSFER PAYMENTS)

1. In this model, in addition to government expenditure and taxes, we bring transfer payments also into the picture.
2. Transfer payments are just the reverse of taxes or, in other words, they are negative taxes.
3. While taxes reduce the spending capacity, transfer payments increase the spending capacity of the households leading to ultimately an increase in the equilibrium level of income.
4. The expansionary effect of an increase in transfer payments will be less than the effect of an increase in government expenditure even when $\Delta G=\Delta R$.
5. It is important to note that while a change in government expenditure affects aggregate demand directly a change in transfer payments affects aggregate demand indirectly through a change in disposable income.

THIRD MODEL OF INCOME DETERMINATION (INCLUDING GOVERNMENT EXPENDITURES, TRANSFER PAYMENTS AND INTRODUCING TAX AS A FUNCTION OF INCOME LEVEL)

1. In this model, tax is a linear function of income.
2. In the model where the tax receipts are independent of the income level, the multiplier is larger than the multiplier in the model, where the tax receipts are dependent on the income level.
3. Given an increase in government expenditure, the expansion in income will be smaller with a proportional income tax than for a lump sum income tax.

MULTIPLIERS IN A THREE-SECTOR ECONOMY–FISCAL MULTIPLIERS

1. To what extent fiscal operations of the government have an impact on the equilibrium level of income depends on the fiscal multipliers.
2. Government expenditure multiplier:

$$G_M=\frac{\Delta Y}{\Delta G}=\frac{1}{1-b}$$

3. The government expenditure multiplier has the same value as the investment multiplier of $1/1 - b$ or $1/1 - mpc$.
4. Tax multiplier:

$$G_T = \frac{\Delta Y}{\Delta T} = \frac{-b}{1-b}$$

   Since the tax multiplier is negative, an increase in tax leads to a decrease in the equilibrium level of income.
5. Whatever the value of b, the sum of the government expenditure multiplier and the tax multiplier will always be equal to unity.
6. The budget is in balance when $\Delta G = \Delta T$.
7. An increase in the government expenditures, which is balanced by an increase in taxes of an equal amount, will lead to an increase in income by the same amount as the increase in the government expenditures and the tax.
8. The value of the 'balanced budget' multiplier, which is the increase in the output as a consequence of equal increases in the government expenditure and taxes, is equal to 1.
9. The sum of the government expenditure multiplier and the tax multiplier will always be equal to unity.

DETERMINATION OF EQUILIBRIUM INCOME OR OUTPUT IN A FOUR-SECTOR ECONOMY

1. The inclusion of the foreign sector influences the level of aggregate demand through the export and import of goods and services.
2. The volume of exports in any economy depends on many factors including prices of the exports and income level in the other economies.
3. The level of exports is assumed to be an autonomous variable.
4. The volume of imports in any economy depends on many factors including the prices of the imports, and the income level in the domestic economy.
5. We assume that the imports in any economy are determined by the income level in the domestic economy with the import function as $M = M_a + mY$.
6. When exports are greater than imports, there exists a net export balance or a favourable balance of trade. When exports are less than imports, there exists a net import balance or an unfavourable balance of trade.
7. Although exports must be added to the total final expenditures to arrive at the aggregate demand, all spending on imports do not contribute to the domestic demand, and thus must be deducted from the total final expenditures to arrive at the aggregate demand.

EQUILIBRIUM INCOME AND OUTPUT

1. There are two approaches to the determination of the equilibrium income and output, the aggregate demand–aggregate supply approach, where $Y = C + I + G + X - M$ and leakages equals injections approach, where $I + G + X = S + T + M$.
2. Both the approaches yield the same equilibrium level of income

$$Y = \frac{1}{1-b+m}(C_a + \overline{I} + \overline{G} + \overline{X} - b\overline{T} - M_a)$$

INTRODUCTION OF GOVERNMENT TRANSFER PAYMENTS IN A FOUR-SECTOR MODEL

1. Transfer payments increase the spending capacity of the households leading to an increase in the equilibrium level of income.
2. The equilibrium level of income is thus

$$Y = \frac{1}{1-b+m}(C_a + \overline{I} + \overline{G} + \overline{X} - b\overline{T} + b\overline{R} - M_a)$$

Equilibrium Income and Output: A Graphical Explanation

1. According to the aggregate demand–aggregate supply approach, in figure 19.3(a), the four-sector equilibrium exists at point E_2, where the aggregate demand curve AD_2 $(= C + I + G + X - M)$ and aggregate supply curves intersect to determine the equilibrium income at Y_2.
2. At point E, the curves AD_1 and AD_2 intersect to determine the equilibrium income at Y. At this level of income, exports equal imports or $X = M$.
3. According the leakages equals injections approach, in figure 19.3(b), the four-sector equilibrium exists at point E_2, where the $S + \overline{T} + M$ curve and $\overline{I} + \overline{G} + \overline{X}$ curve intersect to determine the equilibrium income at Y_2.
4. The introduction of foreign trade has the affect of reducing the equilibrium level of income.

MULTIPLIER IN A FOUR-SECTOR ECONOMY–FOREIGN TRADE MULTIPLIER

1. The size of the multiplier will be lower when the marginal propensity to import is positive.
2. The foreign trade multiplier can be expressed as:

$$\frac{\Delta Y}{\Delta X} = \frac{1}{1 - b + m}$$

3. The value of the multiplier in an open economy is less than that in a closed economy.
4. A zero marginal propensity to import implies a multiplier, which is the same as the ordinary multiplier, $1/1 - b$.
5. It is to be observed that if $b = m$ the value of the multiplier is equal to 1, if $b < m$ the value of the multiplier would be greater than 1, if the value of m were zero, then the value of the multiplier would become equal to the ordinary multiplier.

REVIEW QUESTIONS

TRUE OR FALSE QUESTIONS

1. The action of the government relating to its expenditures, transfers and taxes is called the monetary policy.
2. Transfer payments are just the reverse of taxes or in other words they are negative taxes.
3. The sum of the government expenditure multiplier and the tax multiplier will always be equal to unity.
4. When exports are greater than imports, there exists a net import balance or an unfavourable balance of trade.
5. While exports must be added to the total final expenditures, imports must be deducted from the total final expenditures to arrive at the aggregate demand.

SHORT ANSWER QUESTIONS

1. Show as to how the imposition of a tax, given the level of government expenditure, causes a reduction in the equilibrium level of income in a three-sector economy?
2. Differentiate between the expansionary effect of an increase in transfer payments and that of an increase in government expenditure.
3. How is income determined in a model, where there exists government expenditure, transfer payments and proportional income tax? Explain.
4. Describe the import function and the exports function.
5. How does the introduction of government transfer payments affect a four-sector model?

LONG ANSWER QUESTIONS

1. How is income determined in a model, where there exists government expenditure, lump sum income taxes and transfer payments? Explain.
2. Write short notes on the following:
   (a) Government expenditure multiplier
   (b) Tax multiplier

3. What is the balanced budget multiplier? Discuss.
4. How is the equilibrium level of income and output determined in a four-sector model? Explain using both the aggregate demand–aggregate supply and the leakages equals injections approach.
5. Show a graphical explanation to the determination of the equilibrium income and output in a four-sector model.

NUMERICAL QUESTIONS

1. Given the proportional tax function as $t = 10$ per cent $= 0.1$ and the marginal propensity to consume as 0.75, find the change which will occur in the equilibrium level of income when there is
   (a) An increase in government expenditure by 100.
   (b) An increase in autonomous tax by 150.
   (c) An increase in transfers by 150.
2. Given the marginal propensity to consume as 0.75 and the proportional tax function as $t = 20$ per cent $= 0.2$. Find the change which will occur in the equilibrium level of income, when there is
   (a) An increase in government expenditure by 50.
   (b) An increase in autonomous tax by 30.
   (c) An increase in transfers by 20.
3. In an economy, the consumption function is $C = 40 + 0.80Y_d$ and investment is $\overline{I} =$ ₹80 crore. The government expenditure is at ₹40 crore while the tax is a lump sum tax, where $T = 0.10$.
   (a) Find the equilibrium level of income in the three-sector economy.
   (b) Find the equilibrium level of consumption and saving at the equilibrium level of income.
   (c) Depict the injections leakages equality at the equilibrium level.
4. The fundamental equations in an economy are given as:
   Consumption function $C = 50 + 0.50Y_d$
   Investment function $\overline{I} = 350$
   Tax $T = 60$
   Government expenditure $G = 200$
   Exports $X = 90$
   Imports $M = 0.05Y$
   (a) Find the equilibrium level of income.
   (b) Find the net exports.
5. The equations in an economy are given as:
   Consumption function $C = 50 + bY_d$
   Investment function $\overline{I} = 40$
   Tax $T = 20$
   Government expenditure $G = 40$
   Exports $X = 20$
   Imports $M = 20 + 0.1Y$
   Marginal propensity to consume $b = 0.75$
   (a) Find the equilibrium level of income.
   (b) Find the value of the foreign trade multiplier.
   (c) Find the equilibrium level of imports.

ANSWERS

NUMERICAL QUESTIONS

1. (a) The equilibrium level of income increases by 307.70 ,when there is an increase in government expenditure by 100.
   (b) The equilibrium level of income decreases by 346.15, when there is an increase in autonomous tax by 150.
   (c) The equilibrium level of income decreases by 230.77, when there is an increase in transfers by 150.
2. (a) The equilibrium level of income increases by 125, when there is an increase in government expenditure by 50.
   (b) The equilibrium level of income decreases by 56.25, when there is an increase in autonomous tax by 150.
   (c) The equilibrium level of income decreases by 37.5, when there is an increase in transfers by 150.
3. (a) The equilibrium level of income is ₹760 crore.
   (b) The equilibrium level of consumption is ₹640 crore.
   The equilibrium level of saving is ₹130 crore.
   (c) Injections $= I + G = 80 + 40 = 120$
   Leakages $= S + T = 110 + 10 = 120$
   This depicts the injections leakages equality at the equilibrium level.
4. (a) $Y = 1200$
   The equilibrium level of income is 1200.
   (b) $X - M = 30$
   There is a surplus in the balance of trade.
5. (a) $Y = 328.57$
   The equilibrium level of income is 328.57.
   (b) Foreign trade multiplier = 2.86
   (c) $M = 52.86$
   The equilibrium level of imports is 52.86.

TRUE OR FALSE QUESTIONS

1. **False.** The action of the government relating to its expenditures, transfers and taxes is called the fiscal policy.
2. **True.** While taxes reduce the spending capacity, transfer payments increase the spending capacity of the households leading to ultimately an increase in the equilibrium level of income.
3. **True.** Whatever is the value of b, the sum of the government expenditure multiplier and the tax multiplier will always be equal to unity.
4. **False.** When exports are greater than imports, there exists a net export balance or a favourable balance of trade. When exports are less than imports, there exists a net import balance or an unfavourable balance of trade.
5. **True.** While exports must be added to the total final expenditures to arrive at the aggregate demand, all spending on imports do not contribute to the domestic demand, and thus must be deducted from the total final expenditures to arrive at the aggregate demand.

IS–LM Model for a Two-sector Economy

20

After studying this chapter, you should be able to understand:

- ✓ *The IS curve represents the goods market equilibrium.*
- ✓ *The LM curve represents the money market equilibrium.*
- ✓ *The simultaneous equilibrium in the goods and money markets exists where the IS curve intersects the LM curve.*
- ✓ *At all points, other than the point where the IS and LM curves intersect, there will exist disequilibrium.*
- ✓ *The equilibrium is disturbed due to a shift in the IS or LM curves.*

INTRODUCTION

This chapter is a synthesis of the theory of income and output and the theory of money and interest. It analyses the linkages and the interactions between the goods and money markets to determine that level of income and the interest rate, which bring about a simultaneous equilibrium in both the markets. The focus of this chapter is limited to a two-sector economy.

The *IS–LM* model, which is the foundation of the short-run macroeconomics, was first introduced by J. R. Hicks in his famous article *Mr Keynes and the Classics* in 1937. While the *IS* curve represents the goods market equilibrium, investment (*I*) equals saving (*S*), the *LM* curve represents the money market equilibrium, and demand for money (*L*) equals the supply of money (*M*).

Even today, after a period of more than 70 years since its inception, the *IS–LM* model continues to be popular because it is a useful tool for analysing the effects of monetary and fiscal policy on the level of output and the rate of interest.

We can analyse the *IS–LM* model in two ways. The earlier books on macroeconomics follow a four figure quadrants approach to derive the *IS* and *LM* curves while the recent books on the subject follow a different approach. It is difficult to say as to which of the two approaches is more correct.

IS–LM MODEL IN A TWO-SECTOR ECONOMY

Many authors prefer the approach discussed in the chapter when compared with the recent approach to determine the simultaneous equilibrium in the goods and money markets.

The analysis is based on certain following assumptions:

(i) The price level is not a variable or it is constant.
(ii) At that price level, the firms are willing to supply whatever output is demanded.
(iii) The short-run aggregate supply curve is perfectly elastic till the full employment level of output.

Thus, changes in aggregate demand alone can influence the output.

RECAP

- Changes in aggregate demand alone can influence the output.

GOODS MARKET EQUILIBRIUM IN A TWO-SECTOR ECONOMY: *IS* CURVE

We have observed that there are two approaches to determine the equilibrium level of income or, in other words, the goods market equilibrium:

(i) **Aggregate Demand–Aggregate Supply Approach**, where aggregate demand is total value of output (or income).

Or
$$Y = C + I$$

(ii) **Saving–Investment Approach**, where
$$I = S$$

From the aggregate demand–aggregate supply approach, we have
Consumption function as $C = C(Y)$
Investment function as $I = I(r)$
Equilibrium condition as $Y = C(Y) + I(r)$

From the saving–investment approach, we have
Saving function as $S = S(Y)$
Investment function as $I = I(r)$
Equilibrium condition as $S(Y) = I(r)$

The two equilibrium conditions can be used to develop a graphical approach to the derivation of the *IS* curve as in Figure 20.1.

In Figure 20.1, there are four quadrants.

(i) Quadrant *A* depicts the investment function showing an inverse relationship between investment and the rate of interest.
(ii) Quadrant *B* gives the saving investment equality in the form of a 45° line drawn through the origin. At all points along this 45° line, saving equals the investment.
(iii) Quadrant *C* depicts the saving function showing a direct relationship between saving and the income level.
(iv) Quadrant *D* shows the goods market equilibrium, where the *IS* curve depicts the different combinations of the output levels and the interest rates at which planned investment equals saving (or planned spending is equal to income).

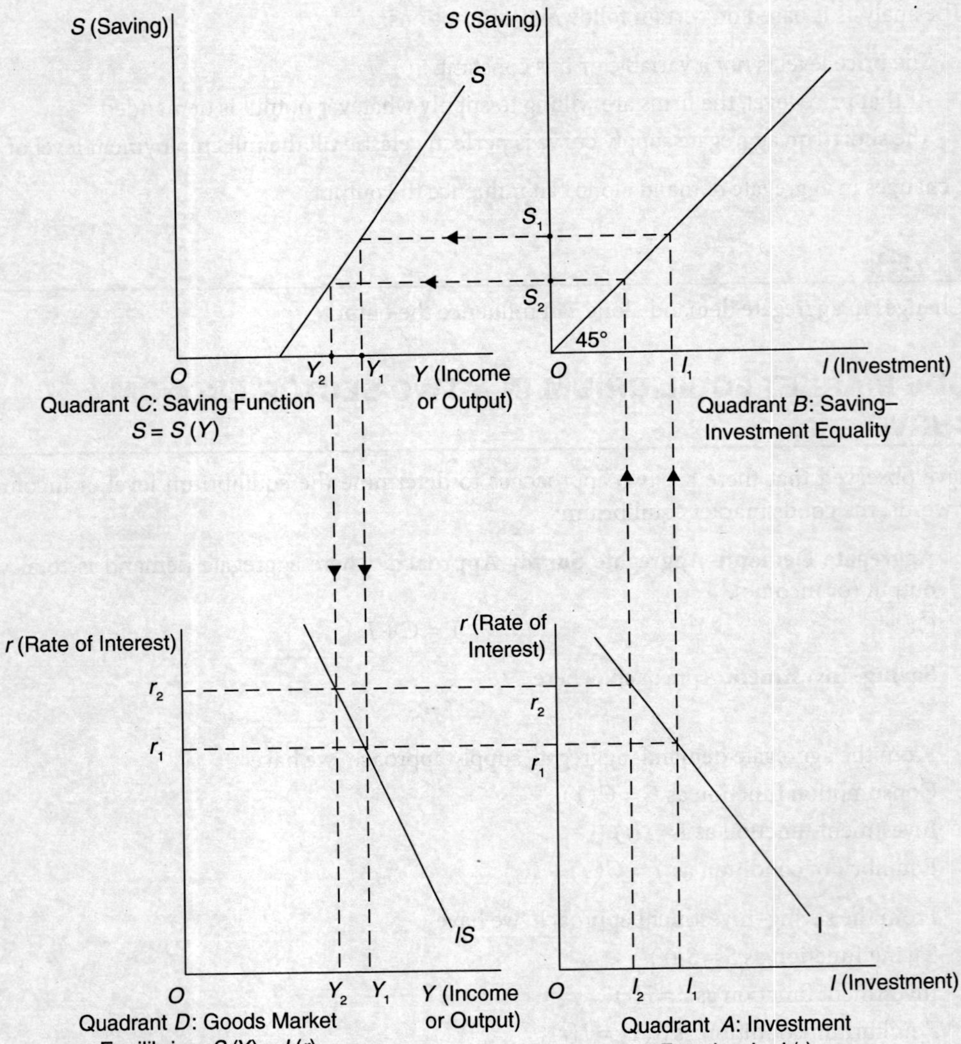

Figure 20.1 Goods Market Equilibrium in a Two-sector Economy: *IS* Curve

To understand the derivation of the *IS* curve in Quadrant *D*, we start in Quadrant *A*. Assume that the interest rate is r_1 indicating an investment at the level of I_1. Quadrant *B* shows that for saving investment equality to be maintained, saving must be equal to S_1 (where because of the 45° line $I_1 = S_1$). Quadrant *C* shows that saving will be S_1 only when the income level is Y_1. Bringing together r_1 of Quadrant *A* and Y_1 of Quadrant *C* gives one combination of income and the rate of interest at which the goods market is in equilibrium in Quadrant *D*.

Now assume that the interest rate increases is r_2 indicating an investment at I_2. Quadrant *B* shows that saving must be equal to S_2. Quadrant *C* depicts that saving will be S_2 when income is Y_2. Once again bringing together r_2 of Quadrant *A* and Y_2 of Quadrant *C* yields another combination of income and the rate of interest at which the goods market is in equilibrium.

BOX 20.1

Economists have attempted to analyse the world around them by using different frameworks. The quantity-theory framework followed by the Keynesian framework of the income-expenditure model, the *IS–LM* framework, which brings together the Keynesian framework and the quantity-theory framework, the business-cycle framework, which accepts the existence of a disequilibrium, and the aggregate-supply aggregate-demand framework. Though each framework carries an element of truth, none of them can be said to be perfect and satisfactory on its own.

Similarly, the other combinations of income and the rate of interest at which the saving investment equality exists, indicating equilibrium in the goods market, can be arrived at in Quadrant *D*. By joining such points, we can trace out the *IS* curve. The *IS* curve is a graphic representation of the goods market equilibrium showing the different combinations of the output levels and the interest rates at which saving equals investment (or planned spending is equal to income). At each point on the *IS* curve, the goods market is in equilibrium while at all other points there is disequilibrium in the goods market. The *IS* curve is downward sloping showing that there is an inverse relationship between income and the rate of interest.

> The *IS* curve is a graphic representation of the goods market equilibrium showing the different combinations of the output levels and the interest rates at which saving equals investment (or planned spending is equal to income).

RECAP

- There are two approaches to determine the equilibrium level of income or, in other words, the goods market equilibrium.
- The *IS* curve is downward sloping showing that there is an inverse relationship between income and the rate of interest.

MONEY MARKET EQUILIBRIUM IN A TWO-SECTOR ECONOMY: *LM* CURVE

The money market is in equilibrium when the demand for money is equal to the supply of money. Thus, we have

$$m_s = m_d$$

As far as the supply of money is concerned, it is determined by the monetary authorities and hence assumed to be exogenous. Thus, we can express the supply of money as

$$m_s = \overline{m}_s$$

Regarding the demand for money according to the Keynesian theory, the demand for money consists of the transactions demand (including the precautionary demand for money), which is a direct function of the income level and the speculative demand, which is an indirect function of the interest rate. Thus, the total demand for money can be expressed as

$$m_d = m_t + m_{sp}$$

where m_d is total demand for money, $m_t = k(Y)$ is transactions demand for money and $m_{sp} = g(r)$ is speculative demand for money. Thus, we can write

$$m_d = k(Y) + g(r)$$

From the above, we have

Supply of money: $m_s = \overline{m}_s$
Demand for money: $m_d = k(Y) + g(r)$
Money market equilibrium condition: $\overline{m}_s = k(Y) + g(r)$

The money market equilibrium condition can be used to develop a graphical approach to the derivation of the *LM* curve as in Figure 20.2.

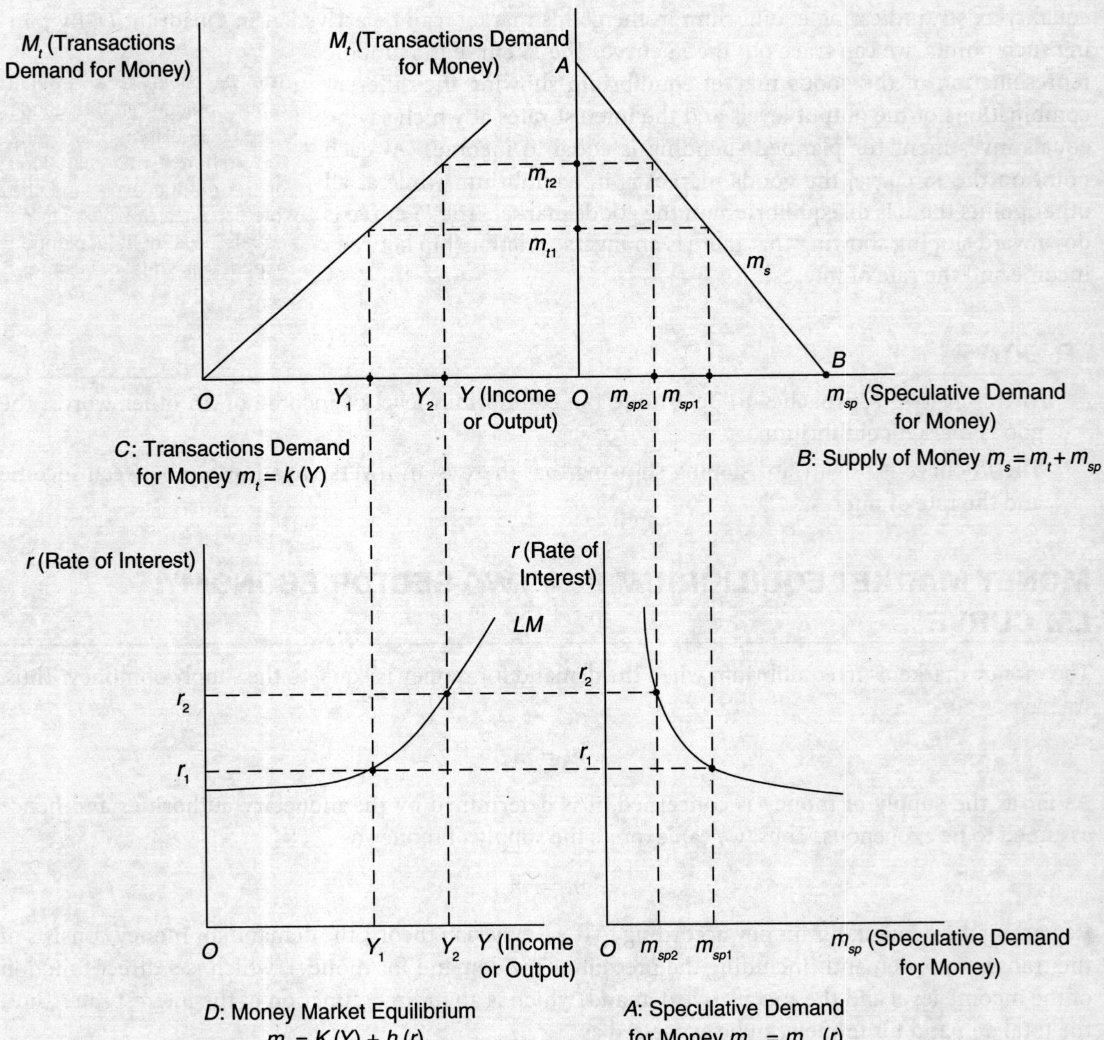

Figure 20.2 Money Market Equilibrium in a Two-sector Economy: *LM* Curve

In Figure 20.2, there are four quadrants.

(i) Quadrant *A* depicts the speculative demand for money showing an inverse relationship between speculative demand for money and the rate of interest.

(ii) Quadrant *B* shows the supply of money as a straight line meeting the two axis. At point *A* where it is meeting the *Y* axis indicates that the entire supply of money is used for transactions demand while at point *B* where it is meeting the *X* axis indicates that the entire supply of money is used for purposes of speculative demand. All points along the line *AB* show the different ways in which the supply of money can be divided between the transactions demand and the speculative demand.

(iii) Quadrant *C* depicts the income level that will support the transactions demand determined in Quadrant *B* (given the transactions demand function as $m_t = k(Y)$).

(iv) Quadrant *D* shows the money market equilibrium, where the *LM* curve shows the different combinations of the output levels and the interest rates at which the demand for money is equal to the supply of money.

To understand as to how the *LM* curve has been derived in Quadrant *D*, we start in Quadrant *A*. Assume that the interest rate is r_1 indicating that the public wants to hold a speculative demand for money equal to m_{sp1}.

Quadrant *B* shows that when the speculative demand is m_{sp1}, the amount of money left as transactions balances will be m_{t1}. Quadrant *C* shows that transactions balances of m_{t1} will be consistent with an income level of Y_1. Hence, combining together r_1 of Quadrant *A* and Y_1 of Quadrant *C* gives one combination of income and the rate of interest at which the money market is in equilibrium in Quadrant *D*.

Next assume that the interest rate increases is r_2 indicating that the speculative demand must be m_{sp2}. Quadrant *B* shows that the money available for transactions will be equal to m_{t2}. Quadrant *C* depicts that transactions balances of m_{t2} will be consistent with an income level of Y_2. Once again bringing together r_2 of Quadrant *A* and Y_2 of Quadrant *C* yields another combination of income and the rate of interest at which the money market is in equilibrium.

In a similar manner, the other combinations of income and the rate of interest at which the demand for money equals the supply of money, indicating equilibrium in the money market, can be arrived at. By joining all such points, we can trace out the *LM* curve in Quadrant *D*. The *LM* curve is a graphic representation of the money market equilibrium showing the different combinations of the output levels and the interest rates at which the demand for money is equal to the supply of money. It is important to note that at each point on the *LM* curve, the money market is in equilibrium and at all other points there exists disequilibrium in the money market. The *LM* curve is upward sloping showing that there is a direct relationship between income and the rate of interest. This is because when the rate of interest increases, individuals demand less for speculative purposes and more for transactions, which is consistent only with a higher level of income.

> The *LM* curve is a graphic representation of the money market equilibrium showing the different combinations of the output levels and the interest rates at which the demand for money is equal to the supply of money.

RECAP

- The money market is in equilibrium when the demand for money is equal to the supply of money.
- The *LM* curve is upward sloping showing that there is a direct relationship between income and the rate of interest.

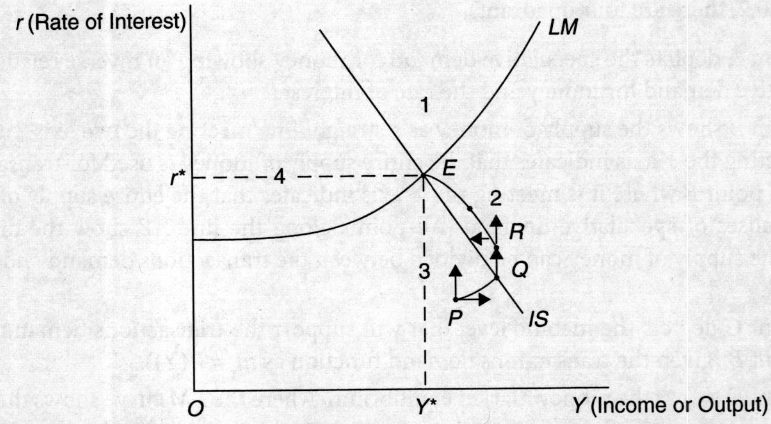

Figure 20.3 Equilibrium in Two Markets: Goods Market and Money Market

EQUILIBRIUM IN TWO MARKETS: GOODS MARKET AND MONEY MARKET

The *IS* curve represents all combinations of income and the rate of interest at which saving equals the investment (or planned spending is equal to income) or, in other words, where the goods market is in equilibrium. The *LM* curve represents all combinations of income and the rate of interest at which the demand for money equals the supply of money or, in other words, where the money market is in equilibrium. But, there is only one combination of income and the rate of interest at which both the goods and the money market are in equilibrium, as depicted in Figure 20.3. This combination is given by point *E* at which the *IS* and *LM* curves intersect to determine the equilibrium rate of interest at r^* and the equilibrium level of income at Y^*. At all other points, there exists disequilibrium in either the goods market or the money market or both the markets.

IS Curve: An Algebraic Explanation

Aggregate Demand–Aggregate Supply Approach

The goods market is in equilibrium when

Aggregate demand = Total value of output (or income)

Or

$$Y = C + I$$

But the linear forms of the consumption function is $C = C_a + bY$ while investment function can be expressed as $I = \overline{I} - hr$. Thus,

$$Y = C_a + bY + \overline{I} - hr$$

Hence,

$$Y - bY = C_a + \overline{I} - hr$$

Or

$$Y = \frac{1}{1-b}(C_a + \overline{I}) - \frac{hr}{1-b}$$

$$Y = \frac{1}{1-b}(C_a + \overline{I} - hr) \tag{20.1}$$

Equation (20.1) represents the *IS* curve.

Saving–Investment Approach

In equilibrium, $I = S$

But the saving function is $S = -C_a + (1 - b)Y$ while investment function is taken as $I = \overline{I} - hr$. Thus,

$$\overline{I} - hr = -C_a + (1 - b)Y$$

Or
$$Y = \frac{1}{1-b}(C_a + \overline{I} - hr)$$

This is the same equation as equation (20.1) above.

Hence, both the approaches yield the same equation for the *IS* curve.

Illustration 1: Suppose the consumption and investment functions are as follows:

$C = 100 + 0.75Y$

$I = 250 - 5i$

Find the equation of the *IS* curve.

Solution:

The equation of the *IS* curve is

$$Y = C + I$$
$$Y = 100 + 0.75Y + 250 - 5i$$
$$Y - 0.75Y = 350 - 5i$$
$$0.25Y = 350 - 5i$$
$$Y = 1400 - 20i$$

Figure 20.4 shows the *IS* curve $Y = 1400 - 20i$.

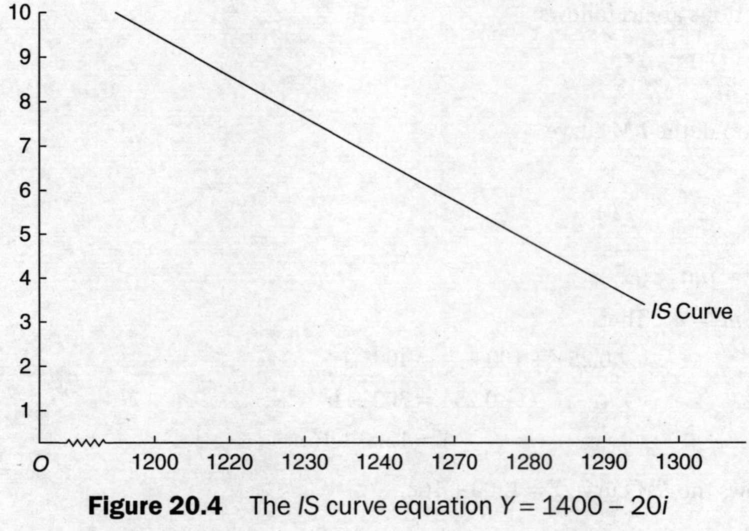

Figure 20.4 The *IS* curve equation $Y = 1400 - 20i$

LM Curve: An Algebraic Explanation

The money market is in equilibrium when

$$m_d = m_s$$

But

$$m_d = m_t + m_{sp}$$

where m_d is total demand for money, m_t *IS kY* is transactions demand for money and $m_{sp} = g(r)$ is speculative demand for money.

However, for the sake of convenience, we assume that the speculative demand for money is a linear function (rather than a curve). Hence, we have

$$m_{sp} = \overline{m}_{sp} - g(r)$$

From the above, we have

Supply of money as $m_s = \overline{m}_a$

Demand for money as $m_d = k(Y) + \overline{m}_{sp} - g(r)$

The money market equilibrium condition can be written as

$$\overline{m}_s = kY + \overline{m}_{sp} - g(r)$$

Thus,

$$Y = \frac{1}{k}[\overline{m}_s - \overline{m}_{sp} + g(r)] \tag{20.2}$$

Equation (20.2) represents the *LM* curve.

Illustration 2: Suppose that the supply of money is ₹400. The transactions and speculative demand for money functions are as follows:

$m_t = 0.25Y$

$m_{sp} = 100 - 4r$

Find the equation of the *LM* curve.

Solution:

$m_d = m_t + m_{sp}$

$m_d = 0.25Y + 100 - 4r$

In equilibrium, $m_d = m_s$. Thus,

$$0.25Y + 100 - 4r = 400$$

$$0.25Y = 300 + 4r$$

$$Y = 1200 + 16r$$

Figure 20.5 shows the *LM* curve $Y = 1200 + 16r$.

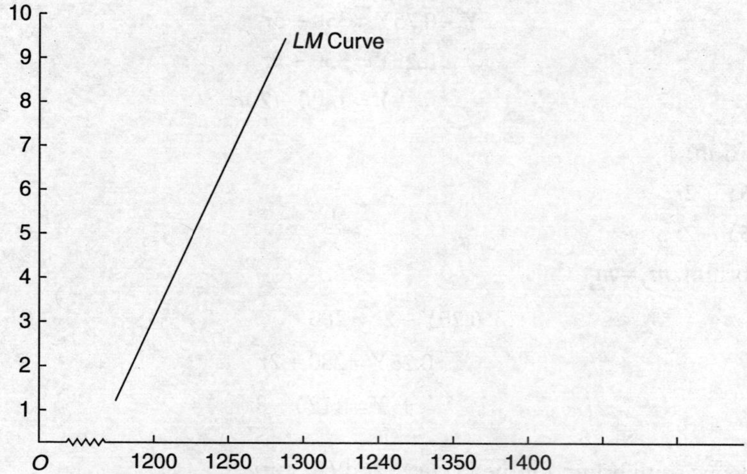

Figure 20.5 *LM* Curve Equation $Y = 1200 + 16r$

EQUILIBRIUM IN THE TWO MARKETS (GOODS MARKET AND MONEY MARKET): AN ALGEBRAIC EXPLANATION

A simultaneous equilibrium in both the goods and money markets can be determined by solving the equations for the *IS* and *LM* curves.

Equation of the *IS* curve:

$$Y = \frac{1}{1-b}(C_a + \overline{I} - hr)$$

Equation of the *LM* curve:

$$Y = \frac{1}{k}[\overline{m}_s - \overline{m}_{sp} + g(r)]$$

These are a set of simultaneous equations, which can be solved to determine the equilibrium values of *Y* and *r*.

Illustration 3: Suppose the consumption and investment functions are as follows:

$C = 100 + 0.75Y$

$I = 250 - 5r$

Also, assume that the supply of money is ₹280. The demand for money function is as follows:

$m_d = 0.25Y - 2r$

(i) Find the equation of the *IS* curve.

(ii) Find the equation of the *LM* curve.

(iii) Find the simultaneous equilibrium for the *IS* curve and *LM* curves.

Solution:

(i) ***IS* Equation:**

$$Y = C + I$$

$$Y = 100 + 0.75Y + 250 - 5r$$

$$Y - 0.75Y = 350 - 5r$$
$$0.25Y = 350 - 5r$$
$$Y = 1400 - 20r$$

(ii) ***LM* Equation:**

$m_d = 0.25Y - 2r$

$m_d = 0.25Y - 2r$

In equilibrium, $m_d = m_s$. Thus,

$$0.25Y - 2r = 280$$
$$0.25Y = 280 + 2r$$
$$Y = 1120 + 8r$$

(iii) Simultaneous equilibrium for the *IS* curve and *LM* curves.

$$IS = LM$$
$$1400 - 20r = 1120 + 8r$$
$$28r = 280$$
$$r = 10 \text{ per cent}$$
$$Y = 1400 - 20 \times 10$$
$$Y = 1200$$

Simultaneous equilibrium for the *IS* curve and *LM* curves exists when $Y = 1200$ and $r = 10$ per cent. Figure 20.6 shows the simultaneous equilibrium for the *IS* curve and *LM* curves when $Y = 1200$ and $r = 10$ per cent.

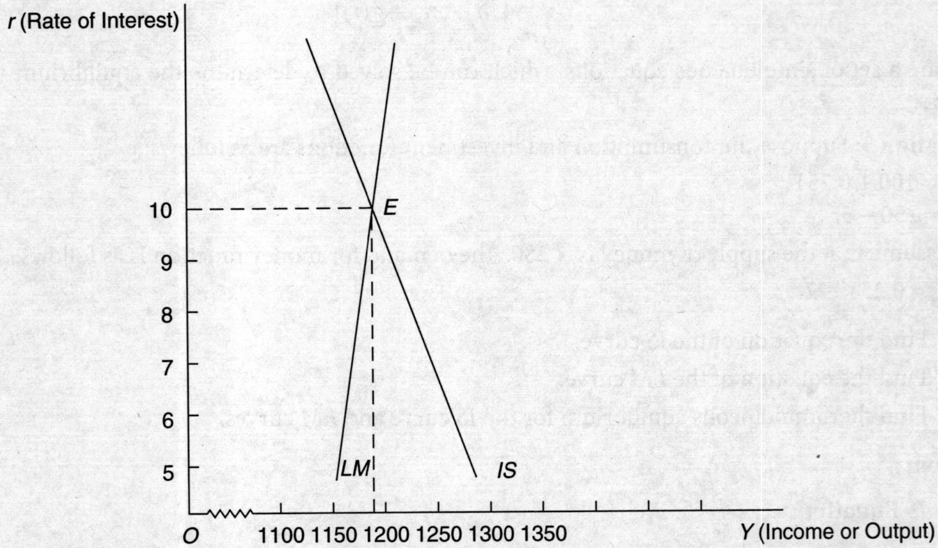

Figure 20.6 Simultaneous Equilibrium for the *IS* Curve and *LM* Curves When $Y = 1200$ and $r = 10\%$

RECAP

- The *IS* curve is downward sloping because there exists an inverse relationship between income and the rate of interest.
- The *LM* curve is upward sloping because there is a direct relationship between income and the rate of interest.
- It is only at the intersection of the *IS* and *LM* curves that both the goods and the money market are in equilibrium.

DISEQUILIBRIUM TO EQUILIBRIUM: THE PROCESS OF ADJUSTMENT

In Figure 20.3, we have already observed that at points, other than point E^*, there will exist disequilibrium in either the goods market, or the money market or in both the markets.

As far as the *IS* curve is concerned, any combination of income and interest that lies on the *IS* curve represents a goods market equilibrium. However, at all other points, there exists goods market disequilibrium.

(i) All combinations of income and interest that lie above and towards the right of the *IS* curve indicate a situation, where $Y > C + I$ or saving is greater than planned investment. Hence, the level of income will fall.

(ii) All combinations of income and interest that lie below and towards the left of the *IS* curve indicate a situation, where $Y < C + I$ or saving is less than planned investment. Hence, the level of income will rise.

Regarding the *LM* curve, any combination of income and interest that lies on the *LM* curve represents money market equilibrium. However, at all other points, there exists money market disequilibrium.

(i) All combinations of income and interest that lie below and towards the right of the *LM* curve indicate a situation, where the demand for money is greater than the supply of money or there is an excess demand for money. Hence, the rate of interest will rise.

(ii) All combinations of income and interest that lie above and towards the left of the *LM* curve indicate a situation, where the demand for money is less than the supply of money or there is an excess supply of money. Hence, the rate of interest will fall.

Figure 20.3 has been divided into four spaces:

Space	Goods Market	Money Market
Space 1	$S > I, Y > C + I$	$m_d < m_s$
Space 2	$S > I, Y > C + I$	$m_d > m_s$
Space 3	$S < I, Y < C + I$	$m_d > m_s$
Space 4	$S < I, Y < C + I$	$m_d < m_s$

As far as the goods market is concerned,

(i) When $S > I$, or $Y > C + I$, there will occur a decrease in income.

(ii) When $S < I$, or $Y < C + I$, there will occur an increase in income.

As far as the money market is concerned,

(i) When $m_d < m_s$, there will occur a decrease in the rate of interest.

(ii) When $m_d > m_s$, there will occur an increase in the rate of interest.

In Figure 20.3, suppose that the economy is at point *P*, a position of a disequilibrium located in the space 3. Here, there exists

(i) An excess demand for goods or $S < I$, or $Y < C + I$. Thus, there will occur an increase in the income.

(ii) An excess demand for money or $m_d > m_s$. Thus, there will occur an increase in the rate of interest.

The economy will gradually move to a point like *Q*. But, since point *Q* is on the *IS* curve, the goods market will be in equilibrium. However, the demand for money is greater than the supply of money since point *Q* is located to the right of the *LM* curve. Thus, there will occur an increase in the interest rate and a movement to a point like *R*. Thus, adjustments will occur and ultimately the forces that are pushing the income level and the interest rate will move the economy to point *E*, which is the only point at which the goods and the money markets are both in equilibrium.

The economy could be anywhere in the system in any of the different spaces. However, it is important to remember that the forces which are at work will go on till the final equilibrium is attained at point *E*. Once point *E* is reached, the income level and the rate of interest will remain unchanged until there occurs a shift in the *IS* or *LM* curve or in both of them which can disturb the equilibrium and start of a new rounds of adjustments.

RECAP

- If there exists disequilibrium in the economy, then the forces will be at work till the final equilibrium is attained at the intersection of the *IS–LM* curves.

A SHIFT IN *IS–LM* CURVES

A shift in the *IS* or *LM* curve or in both of them will disturb the equilibrium. Hence, it is imperative to examine these shifts.

A Shift in *IS* Curve

The shifts in the *IS* curve can occur due to a shift in the investment function or the saving function or due to a change in any of the factors, which are responsible for a shift in these functions.

In Figure 20.7, the IS_1 curve has been derived diagrammatically from the investment curve I_1 in Quadrant *A*, the saving–investment equality in Quadrant *B* and the saving function in Quadrant *C*. The intersection of IS_1 and the *LM* curves at point E_1 determines the equilibrium income as Y_1 and the equilibrium interest rate at r_1.

Assume that there is rightward shift in the investment function from I_1 to I_2 in Quadrant *A* of Figure 20.7. This implies an increase in investment at all interest rates. Given the interest rate at r_2, to match the increase in the investment, the equilibrium level of saving in Quadrant *B* will also increase from S_1 to S_2 leading to an increase in the income level from Y_1 to Y_2 in the Quadrant *C*. Thus, combining the income

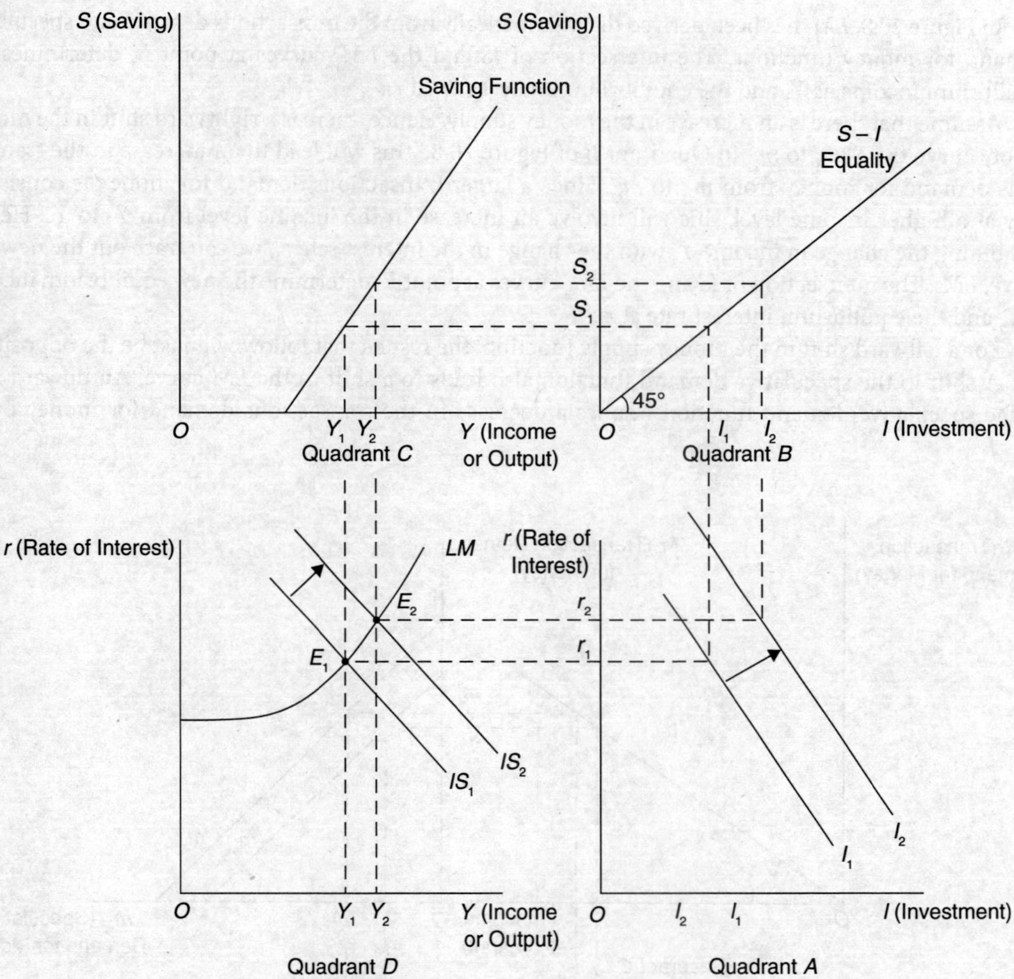

Figure 20.7 A Shift in the *IS* Curve

Y_2 with the interest rate r_2, we can trace out the new is curve IS_2. The intersection of IS_2 and the *LM* curves at point E_2 determines the new equilibrium income as Y_2 and the equilibrium interest rate at r_2.

For a leftward shift in the investment function, the results that follow will just be the opposite.

A shift in the consumption function also leads to a shift in the *IS* curve. An upward shift in the consumption function (or, in other words, a downward shift in the saving function) implies a decrease in the saving at any income level. To maintain the saving investment equality, the income level would have to increase leading to eventually a rightward shift in the *IS* curve. For a downward shift in the investment function, the results that follow will just be the opposite.

A Shift in *LM* Curve

The shift in the *LM* curve can occur due to a shift in the transactions demand, speculative demand or the money supply function.

In Figure 20.8, LM_1 has been derived diagrammatically from the transactions demand and speculative demand for money functions. The intersection of *IS* and the LM_1 curves at point E_1 determines the equilibrium income as Y_1 and the equilibrium interest rate at r_1.

Assume that there is an increase in the money supply. Hence, there is a rightward shift in the money supply curve from m_{s1} to m_{s2} in Quadrant *B* of Figure 20.8. This will lead to an increase in the transactions demand for money from m_{t1} to m_{t2}. Since a larger transactions demand for money is consistent only at a higher income level, this will involve an increase in the income level from Y_1 to Y_2. Hence, combining the change in income Y_2 with the change in the interest rate r_2, we can trace out the new *LM* curve, LM_2. The intersection of *IS* and the LM_2 curves at point E_2 determine the new equilibrium income as Y_2 and the equilibrium interest rate at r_2.

For a leftward shift in the money supply function, the results that follow will just be the opposite.

A shift in the speculative demand function also leads to a shift in the *LM* curve. An upward shift in the speculative demand function implies a decrease in the transactions demand for money by an

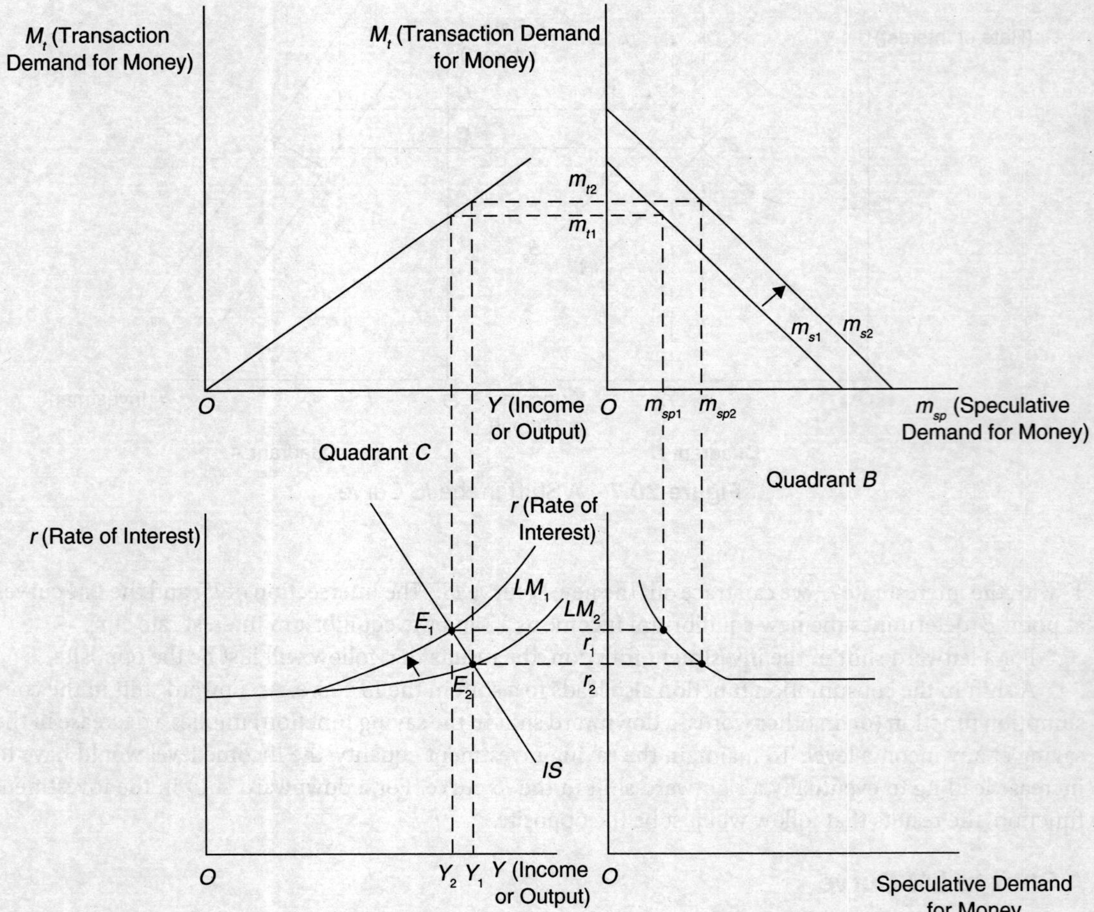

Figure 20.8 A Shift in *LM* Curve

equal amount. This would necessitate a decrease in the income level. Hence, for an upward shift in the speculative demand function, the *LM* curve will shift to the left. Similarly, a shift in the transactions demand for money function will lead to a shift in the *LM* curve.

A Simultaneous Shift in Both *IS* and *LM* Curves

Till now, we have analysed the shifts in the *IS* and *LM* curves separately. Now, we analyse the two shifts simultaneously.

In Figure 20.9, suppose the initial *IS* and *LM* curves are given as IS_1 and LM_1. They intersect at point E_1 to determine the equilibrium income at Y_1 and the rate of interest at r_1.

Next, suppose there is

(i) An increase in investment (or a rightward shift in the investment function), which shifts the *IS* curve from IS_1 to IS_2.

(ii) An increase in the money supply (or a rightward shift in the money supply function), which shifts the *LM* curve from LM_1 to LM_2.

The curves IS_2 and LM_2 intersect at point E_2 to determine the equilibrium income at Y_2 while the rate of interest remains unchanged at r_1. The reason as to why there is no change in the interest rate is that the extent of the shifts in the *IS* and *LM* curves is equal. However, in reality, the extent of the shifts may not be equal in which case there will not only be a change in the income level, but also a change in the interest rate.

RECAP

- The shifts in the *IS* curve occur due to a shift in the investment function or the saving function.
- The shift in the *LM* curve can occur due to a shift in the transactions demand, speculative demand or the money supply function.

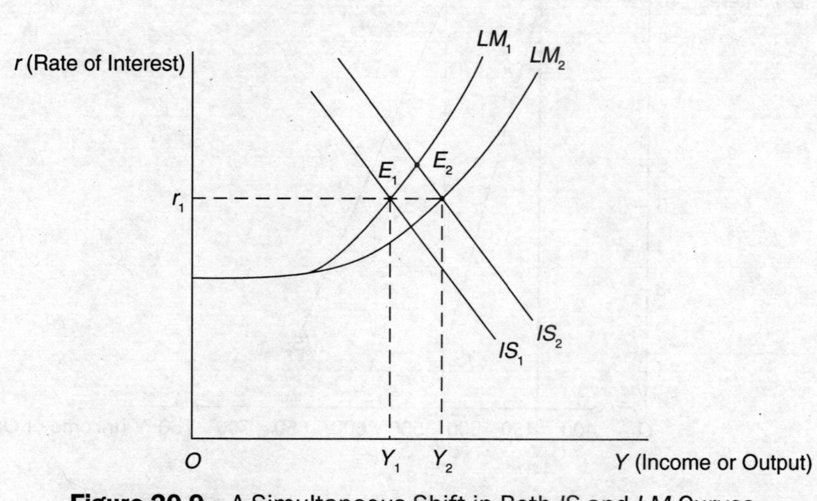

Figure 20.9 A Simultaneous Shift in Both *IS* and *LM* Curves

SOLVED NUMERICAL

1. Suppose the consumption and investment functions are as follows:

   $C = 50 + 0.75Y$

   $I = ₹80 \text{ crore} - 2r$

   Find

   (a) The equation of the *IS* curve and plot it.

   (b) The equation of the *IS* curve when investment increases by ₹20 crore.

   (c) By how much does the *IS* curve shift?

Solution:

(a) Equation of the *IS* curve:

$$Y = C + I$$
$$Y = 50 + 0.75Y + 80 - 2r$$
$$Y - 0.75Y = 130 - 2r$$
$$0.25Y = 130 - 2r$$
$$Y = 520 - 8r$$

(b) Equation of the *IS* curve when investment increases by ₹20 crore:

$$Y = C + I$$
$$Y = 50 + 0.75Y + 100 - 2r$$
$$Y - 0.75Y = 150 - 2r$$
$$0.25Y = 150 - 2r$$
$$Y = 600 - 8r$$

(c) When investment increases by ₹20 crore, the *IS* curve shifts horizontally by ₹80 crore, which is equal to the increase in investment times the multiplier, ₹20 crore × 4:
Figure 20.10 gives the diagrammatic picture of the *IS* curves, where equation $Y = 520 - 8r$ is represented by IS_1 and equation $Y = 600 - 8r$ is represented by IS_2.

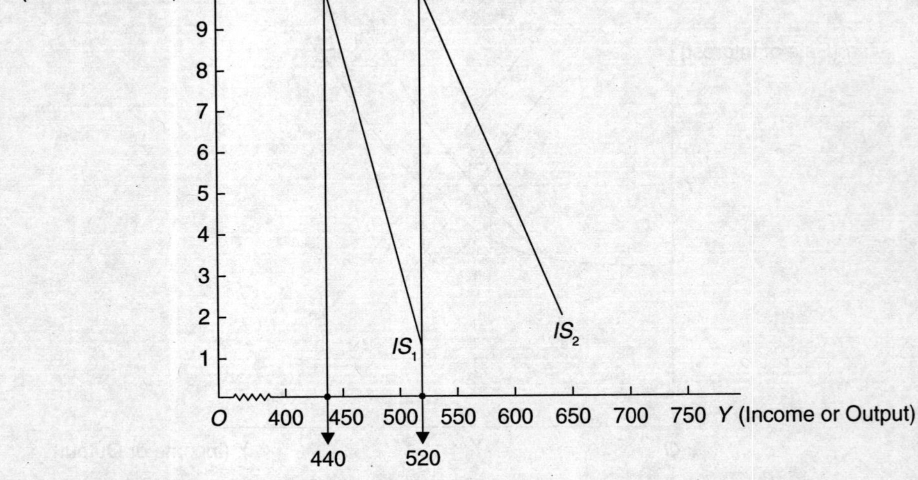

Figure 20.10 The *IS* Curves Equations $Y = 520 - 8r$ and $Y = 600 - 8r$

2. Suppose that the supply of money is ₹240 crore. The demand for money is $m_d = 0.20Y - 5r$. Find
   (a) The equation of the *LM* curve and plot it.
   (b) The equation of the *LM* curve when the supply of money increases by ₹60 crore to ₹300 crore.
   (c) By how much does the *LM* curve shift?

Solution:

(a) Equation of the *LM* curve:
In equilibrium, $m_d = m_s$. Thus,

$$0.20Y - 5r = 240$$
$$0.20Y = 240 + 5r$$
$$Y = 1200 + 25r$$

(b) Equation of the *LM* curve when the supply of money increases by ₹60 crore to ₹300 crore:
In equilibrium, $m_d = m_s$. Thus,

$$0.20Y - 5r = 300$$
$$0.20Y = 300 + 5r$$
$$Y = 1500 + 25r$$

(c) When the supply of money increases by ₹60 crore, the *LM* curve shifts horizontally by ₹300 crore, which is equal to $1/k$ times delta m_s, ₹60/0.20 crore:
Figure 20.11 gives the diagrammatic picture of the *LM* curves, where equation $Y = 1200 + 25r$ is represented by LM_1 and equation $Y = 1500 + 25r$ is represented by LM_2.

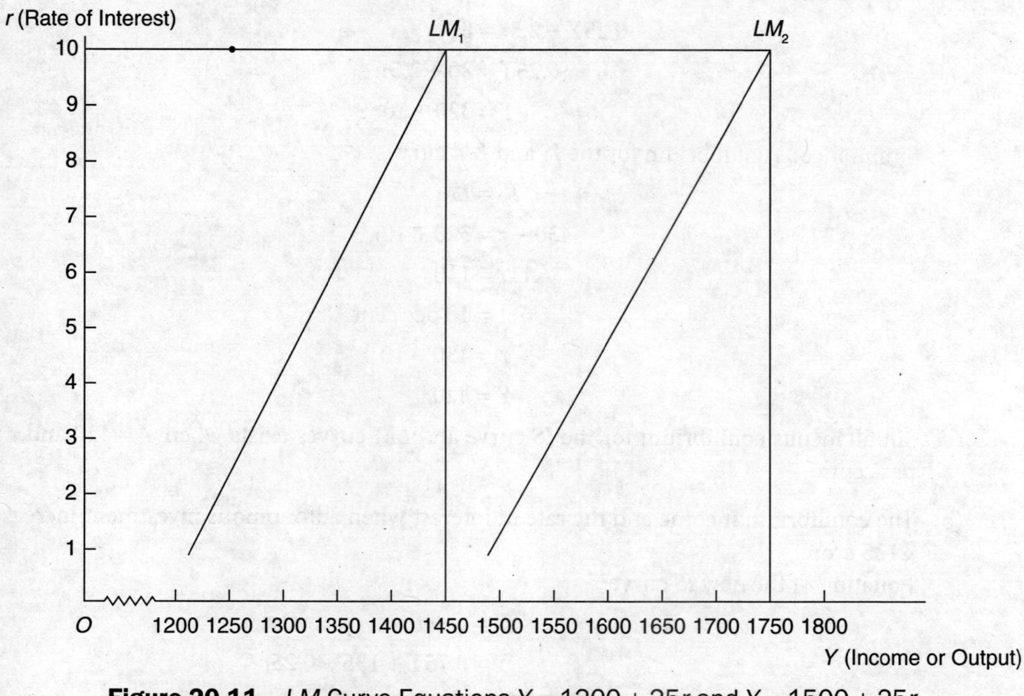

Figure 20.11 *LM* Curve Equations $Y = 1200 + 25r$ and $Y = 1500 + 25r$

3. Suppose the consumption, investment, demand for money and supply of money functions are as follows:

$C = 0.75Y$

$I = ₹107.5 \text{ crore} - 0.25r$

$m_d = 0.25Y - 2.5i$

$m_s = ₹80 \text{ crore}$

Find

(a) The equilibrium income and the rate of interest.

(b) The equilibrium income and the rate of interest when autonomous investment increases to ₹135 crore.

Solution:

(a) Equilibrium income and the rate of interest:
Equation of the *IS* curve:

$$Y = C + I$$
$$Y = 0.75Y + 107.5 - 0.25r$$
$$Y - 0.75Y = 107.5 - 0.25r$$
$$0.25Y = 107.5 - 0.25r$$
$$Y = 430 - r$$

Equation of the *LM* curve:
In equilibrium, $m_d = m_s$. Thus,

$$0.25Y - 2.5r = 80$$
$$0.25Y = 80 + 2.5r$$
$$Y = 320 + 10r$$

Simultaneous equilibrium for the *IS* and *LM* curves:

$$IS = LM$$
$$430 - r = 320 + 10r$$
$$11r = 110$$
$$r = 10 \text{ per cent}$$
$$Y = 430 - 10$$
$$Y = 420$$

Simultaneous equilibrium for the *IS* curve and *LM* curves exists when $Y = 420$ and $r = 10$ per cent.

(b) The equilibrium income and the rate of interest when autonomous investment increases to ₹135 crore.
Equation of the new *IS* curve:

$$Y = C + I$$
$$Y = 0.75Y + 135 - 0.25r$$
$$Y - 0.75Y = 135 - 0.25r$$

$$0.25Y = 135 - 0.25r$$
$$Y = 540 - r$$

Equation of the *LM* curve: $Y = 320 + 10r$
Simultaneous equilibrium for the *IS* curve and *LM* curves.

$$IS = LM$$
$$540 - r = 320 + 10r$$
$$11r = 220$$
$$r = 20 \text{ per cent}$$
$$Y = 540 - 20$$
$$Y = 520$$

Simultaneous equilibrium for the *IS* curve and *LM* curves exists when $Y = 520$ and $r = 20$ per cent.

4. Suppose autonomous consumption is ₹60 crore, investment is ₹120 crore, marginal propensity to consume is 0.75 and the value of *h*, the behavioural coefficient which measures the sensitivity of investment to the rate of interest, is 4. Find
   (a) The equation of the *IS* curve and plot it.
   (b) The equation of the *IS* curve when *h* increases to 8.
   (c) What is the effect on the slope of the *IS* curve when the value of *h* increases?

Solution:

(a) Equation of the *IS* curve:
The consumption and investment functions are as follows:

$$C = 60 + 0.75Y$$
$$I = 120 - 4r$$

We have

$$Y = C + I$$
$$Y = 60 + 0.75Y + 120 - 4r$$
$$Y - 0.75Y = 180 - 4r$$
$$0.25Y = 180 - 4r$$
$$Y = 720 - 16r$$

This is represented by the IS_1 curve in Figure 16.12.

(b) Equation of the *IS* curve when *h* increases to 8.
The consumption and the new investment functions are as follows:

$$C = 60 + 0.75Y$$
$$I = 120 - 8r$$

We have

$$Y = C + I$$
$$Y = 60 + 0.75Y + 120 - 8r$$
$$Y - 0.75Y = 180 - 8r$$
$$0.25Y = 180 - 8r$$
$$Y = 720 - 32r$$

This is represented by IS_2 in Figure 20.12.

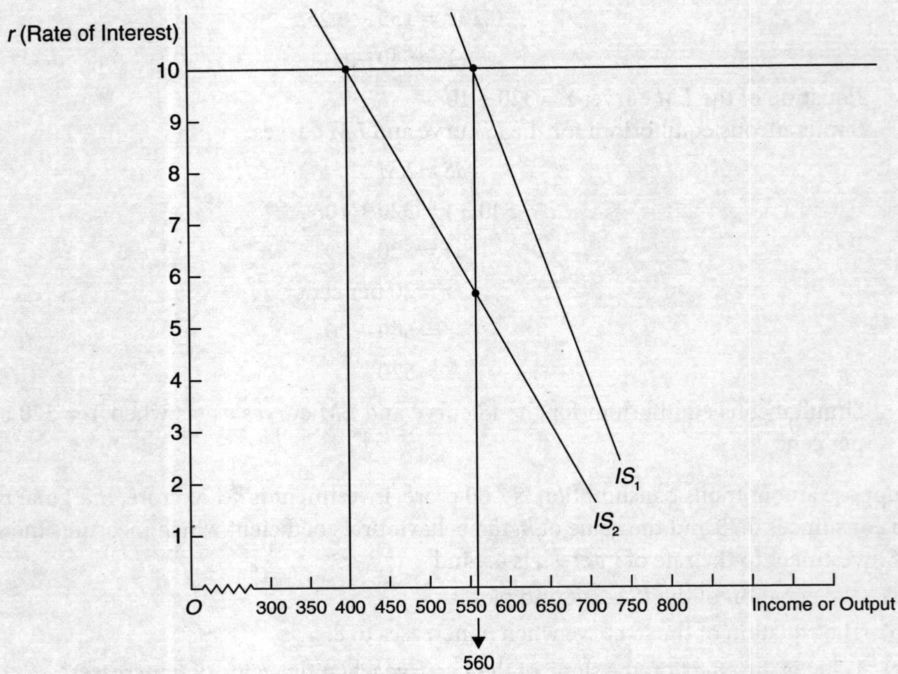

Figure 20.12 *IS* Curve Equations $Y = 720 - 16r$ and $Y = 720 - 32r$

(c) The effect on the slope of the *IS* curve when the value of h increases: The slope of the IS_2 curve is less than that of IS_1.

5. Suppose that the value of k is 0.25. Find the direction and the amount of shift in the *LM* curve when
   (a) The increase in the money supply is ₹10 crore.
   (b) The decrease in the money supply is ₹25 crore.

Solution:

(a) The direction and the amount of shift in the *LM* curve when the increase in the money supply is ₹10 crore:
Amount of shift in the *LM* curve:

$$\frac{1}{0.25} \times 20 = 80$$

Since there is an increase in the money supply, the *LM* curve will shift to the right.

(b) The direction and the amount of shift in the *LM* curve when the increase in the money supply is ₹25 crore:
Amount of shift in the *LM* curve:

$$\frac{1}{0.25} \times 25 = 100$$

Since there is a decrease in the money supply, the *LM* curve will shift to the left.

SUMMARY

INTRODUCTION

1. This chapter analyses the linkages and the interactions between the goods and money markets to determine that level of income and the interest rate, which bring about a simultaneous equilibrium in both the markets.
2. The *IS–LM* model, which is the foundation of the short-run macroeconomics, was first introduced by J.R. Hicks.
3. The *IS* curve represents the goods market equilibrium.
4. The *LM* curve represents the money market equilibrium.
5. We can analyse the *IS–LM* model in two ways.

IS–LM MODEL FOR A TWO-SECTOR ECONOMY

The analysis is based on certain assumptions: price level is constant; at that price level, the firms are willing to supply whatever output is demanded; short-run aggregate supply curve is perfectly elastic till the full employment level of output.

GOODS MARKET EQUILIBRIUM: *IS* CURVE

1. There are two approaches to determine the goods market equilibrium.
2. According to the *AD–AS* approach, the goods market equilibrium exists where $Y = C(Y) + I(r)$.
3. According to the *S–I* approach, the goods market equilibrium exists where $S(Y) = I(r)$.
4. The two equilibrium conditions can be used to develop a graphical approach to the derivation of the *IS* curve.
5. The *IS* curve is a graphic representation of the goods market equilibrium showing the different combinations of the output levels and the interest rates at which saving equals the investment. (Or planned spending is equal to income.)
6. The *IS* curve is downward sloping showing that there is an inverse relationship between income and the rate of interest.

MONEY MARKET EQUILIBRIUM: *LM* CURVE

1. The money market is in equilibrium when the demand for money is equal to the supply of money or $m_s = m_d$.
2. The supply of money is assumed to be exogenous or as $m_s = \overline{m}_s$.
3. The total demand for money can be expressed as $m_d = m_t + m_{sp}$.
4. The money market equilibrium condition can be used to develop a graphical approach to the derivation of the *LM* curve.
5. The *LM* curve is a graphic representation of the money market equilibrium showing the different combinations of the output levels and the interest rates at which the demand for money is equal to the supply of money.
6. The *LM* curve is upward sloping showing that there is a direct relationship between income and the rate of interest. This is because when the rate of interest increases, individuals demand less for speculative purposes and more for transactions, which is consistent only with a higher level of income.

EQUILIBRIUM IN THE TWO MARKETS: GOODS MARKET AND MONEY MARKET

1. The *IS* curve represents all combinations of income and the rate of interest at which the goods market is in equilibrium.
2. The *LM* curve represents all combinations of income and the rate of interest at which the money market is in equilibrium.
3. There is only one combination of income and the rate of interest at which both the goods and the money market are in equilibrium, point *E* at which the *IS* and *LM* curves intersect.

IS Curve: An Algebraic Explanation

Both the aggregate demand–aggregate supply approach and the saving–investment approach yield

$$Y = \frac{1}{1-b}(C_a + \bar{I} - hr)$$

as the equation of the *IS* curve.

LM Curve: An Algebraic Explanation

$$Y = \frac{1}{k}[\bar{m}_s - \bar{m}_{sp} + g(r)]$$

is the equation of the *LM* curve.

EQUILIBRIUM IN THE TWO MARKETS (GOODS MARKET AND MONEY MARKET): AN ALGEBRAIC EXPLANATION

A simultaneous equilibrium in both the goods and money markets can be determined by solving the equations for the *IS* and *LM* curves and thus the equilibrium values of *Y* and *r* can be determined.

A SHIFT IN *IS–LM* CURVES

1. A shift in the *IS* or *LM* curve or in both of them will disturb the equilibrium. Hence, it is imperative to examine these shifts.
2. The shifts in the *IS* curve can occur due to a shift in the investment function or the saving (or consumption) function.
3. A rightward shift in the investment function leads to a rightward shift in the *IS* curve. For a leftward shift in the investment function, the results that follow will just be the opposite.
4. The shift in the *LM* curve can occur due to a shift in the transactions demand, speculative demand or the money supply function.
5. A rightward shift in the money supply curve leads to a leftward shift in the *LM* curve. For a leftward shift in the money supply function, the results that follow will just be the opposite.
6. A simultaneous shift in both *IS* and *LM* curves brings about a change in the income level and also a change in the interest rate.

REVIEW QUESTIONS

TRUE OR FALSE QUESTIONS

1. The *IS–LM* model is the foundation of long-run macroeconomics.
2. The *IS* curve is upward sloping showing that there is a direct relationship between income and the rate of interest.
3. The *LM* curve is upward sloping showing that there is a direct relationship between income and the rate of interest.
4. There is only one combination of income and the rate of interest at which both the goods and the money market are in equilibrium.
5. The shift in the *LM* curve can occur due to a shift in the in the investment function or the saving function.

SHORT ANSWER QUESTIONS

1. Write a short note on the *IS* curve.
2. Write a short note on the *LM* curve.
3. 'There is only one combination of income and the rate of interest at which both the goods and the money market are in equilibrium'. Explain.

4. Show the algebraic derivation of
   (a) *IS* curve
   (b) *LM* curve
5. Examine the effects of a simultaneous shift in both the *IS* and *LM* curves.

LONG ANSWER QUESTIONS

1. 'The two equilibrium conditions *AD–AS* approach and *S–I* approach can be used to develop a graphical approach to the derivation of the *IS* curve'. Explain.
2. 'The money market equilibrium condition can be used to develop a graphical approach to the derivation of the *LM* curve'. Explain.
3. How is simultaneous equilibrium in the goods and money market achieved? Explain with the help of diagram/diagrams.
4. Examine the effects of a shift in the *IS* curve.
5 Examine the effects of a shift in the *LM* curve.

NUMERICAL QUESTIONS

1. Suppose the saving and investment functions are as follows:
   $S = -50 + 0.5Y$
   $I = 120$ crore $- 5r$
   Find the equation of the *IS* curve and plot it.
2. Suppose the consumption and investment functions are as follows:
   $C = 20 + 0.5Y$
   $I = 120$ crore $- 5r$
   Find
   (a) The equation of the *IS* curve and plot it.
   (b) The equation of the *IS* curve when the investment function changes to $I = 120$ crore $- 10r$.
3. Suppose the consumption and investment functions are as follows:
   $C = 20 + 0.75Y.$
   $I = 400 - 2500r$
   Find
   (a) The equation of the *IS* curve by the aggregate demand–aggregate supply approach.
   (b) The equation of the *IS* curve by the saving–investment approach.
4. In a two-sector model, assume that the consumption and investment functions are as follows:
   $C = 100 + 0.75Y$
   $I = 1500 - 10r$
   Find
   (a) The equation of the *IS* curve.
   (b) The equation of the *IS* curve when the investment function changes to $I = 1500 - 5r$ while the consumption function remains the same.
5. Suppose in a two-sector model, consumption and investment functions are as follows:
   $C = 600 + 0.80Y$
   $I = 1160 - 20r$

The demand for money and the supply of money are

$L = 0.20Y - 50r$

$M = 1200$

(a) Find the equation of the *IS* curve.
(b) Find the equation of the *LM* curve.
(c) Find the simultaneous equilibrium for the *IS* and *LM* curves.

ANSWERS

NUMERICAL QUESTIONS

1. Equation of the *IS* curve: $Y = 340 - 10r$
   Different values of r can be taken with the corresponding values of Y and then the *IS* curve can be plotted. When $r = 5$, $Y = 290$; $r = 7$, $Y = 270$; and $r = 10$, $Y = 240$.
2. (a) Equation of the *IS* curve: $Y = 280 - 10r$.
   (b) Equation of the *IS* curve when investment changes: $Y = 280 - 20r$.
3. (a) Equation of the *IS* curve by the aggregate demand–aggregate supply approach: $Y = 1680 - 10{,}000r$.
   (b) Equation of the *IS* curve by the saving–investment approach: $Y = 1680 - 10{,}000r$.
4. (a) Equation of the *IS* curve: $Y = 6400 - 40r$.
   (b) Equation of the *IS* curve when the investment function changes to $I = 1500 - 5r$ while the consumption function remains the same: $Y = 6400 - 20r$.
5. (a) *IS* equation: $Y = 8800 - 100r$.
   (b) *LM* equation: $Y = 6000 + 250r$.
   (c) Simultaneous equilibrium for the *IS* and *LM* curves: $r = 8$ per cent, $Y = 8000$.

TRUE OR FALSE QUESTIONS

1. **False.** The *IS–LM* model is the foundation of the short-run macroeconomics and was first introduced by J.R. Hicks.
2. **False.** The *IS* curve is downward sloping showing that there is an inverse relationship between income and the rate of interest.
3. **True.** The *LM* curve is upward sloping showing that there is a direct relationship between income and the rate of interest. This is because when the rate of interest increases, individuals demand less for speculative purposes and more for transactions, which is consistent only with a higher level of income.
4. **True.** There is only one combination of income and the rate of interest at which both the goods and the money market are in equilibrium and that is the point at which the *IS* and *LM* curves intersect. At all other points, there exists disequilibrium.
5. **False.** The shift in the *LM* curve can occur due to a shift in the transactions demand, speculative demand or the money supply function.

Theories of Investment Spending

21

After studying this chapter, you should be able to understand:

- ✓ *Investment can be defined as the value of that portion of an economy's output for any time that takes the form of new producer's durable equipment, new structures and the change in inventories.*
- ✓ *To arrive at net investment, a deduction is made from gross investment for producer's durable equipments and the existing structures that are used in the production process.*
- ✓ *The decision to invest is different when compared with the decision to buy consumer goods.*
- ✓ *Once the marginal efficiency of capital (MEC) is determined, a comparison of the market rate of interest with the MEC will enable one to make a decision as to whether the investment in the capital asset is profitable or not.*
- ✓ *The marginal efficiency of investment (MEI) schedule depicts the relationship between the economy's investment and rate of interest when the change in the price of capital goods is taken into consideration.*
- ✓ *MEI schedule represents the true investment demand schedule for the economy as a whole.*
- ✓ *The concavity of the MEI schedule is due to the increasing cost of the capital goods.*
- ✓ *Given the MEC schedule, net investment is determined by the rate of interest and the size of the capital stock.*
- ✓ *An upward shift in the MEC schedule leads to an increase in the profit-maximizing capital and thus to capital accumulation.*
- ✓ *According to the accelerator theory, the desired stock of capital depends on the economy's output level.*
- ✓ *The main idea in the flexible accelerator model is that whenever there exists a large gap between the firms existing capital stock and the desired capital stock, the firm's investment is swifter.*

INTRODUCTION

One of the most important components of the gross national product (GNP) is investment. In the earlier chapters of the simple model of income determination, investment was assumed to be given at some particular level. This chapter analyses the relationship between investment and the rate of interest and also the responsiveness of investment to the rate of interest.

Investment expenditure constitutes an extremely volatile component of the aggregate demand. The fluctuations in investment cause fluctuations in the production and income levels. They are responsible for much of the business cycles. In this chapter, we attempt at determining the factors that influence the investment decisions. We also examine some of the theories of investment spending.

BASIC CONCEPTS

Before we embark on our analysis of investment, we will discuss some of the concepts relating to investment.

Investment

> Capital is the accumulated stock of plant and equipment, which is held by the business firms.

> Investment can be defined as the value of that portion of an economy's output for any time that takes the form of new producer's durable equipment, new structures and the change in inventories.

Capital is the accumulated stock of plant and equipment, which is held by the business firms. It is the stock of the productive facilities, which are available to produce the output. Hence, capital is a stock concept. On the other hand, investment is a flow concept. In the simplest terms, investment can be defined as the value of that portion of an economy's output for any time that takes the form of new producer's durable equipment, new structures and the change in inventories. It is the flow of spending, which makes an addition to the physical stock of capital. In the long run, it is investment, which determines the stock of capital and hence the long-run growth in the economy. It is to be noted that compared with the stock of capital, the flow of investment is quite small.

Investment expenditure is expenditure on goods and services bought for use in the future. It can be grouped into three categories:

(i) Business fixed investment is the purchase of new plant and equipment by firms.
(ii) Residential investment is the purchase of new housing by households and others.
(iii) Inventory investment is the change in the inventory of goods by the firm. This chapter focuses on specifically, the business fixed investment.

It is obvious that different factors influence the different types of investment. Thus, there can be no single investment theory, which is applicable to all the different types of investment.

Gross and Net Investments

Investment can be in net terms or in gross terms. Gross investment consists of two parts:

(i) The replacement investment, which is required to keep the capital stock intact.
(ii) The net investment, which is required to expand the existing capital stock.

BOX 21.1

All human beings attempt to increase their wealth. But they try to do so in a way that their savings, wealth and investments are not put at an undue risk. Though all investments involve some element of risk, however, through cautious investments one can attempt to reduce such risk. This has over time given rise to many theories of investment. These investment theories attempt at explaining and supporting the different types of investment strategies. Some of these popular investment theories include: diversification theory, Bernstein's psychology of successful investing, efficient market theory and life cycle investment theory.

To arrive at net investment, a deduction is made from gross investment for producer's durable equipments and the existing structures that are used in the production process. Net investment is equal to gross investment less depreciation. In fact, net investment is an accretion to the stock of capital.

Net investment is an accretion to the stock of capital.

If, in a particular period of time,

(i) The gross investment is equal to the amount of capital that is used up in that particular period (in other words, the cumulative depreciation thereon), then there will not be net investment.

(ii) The gross investment is greater than the amount of capital that is used up in that particular period, then there will be positive net investment, which involves an increase in the stock of capital.

(iii) The gross investment is smaller than the amount of capital that is used up in that particular period, then there will be negative net investment or, in other words, there will be a disinvestment. This involves a reduction in the stock of capital.

Other things remaining unchanged, for example, given the labour force, technology and natural resources, an accretion to the stock of capital increases the economy's productive capacity. However, in practice as the stock of capital increases, the other things do not remain unchanged. But, it is necessary to separate the growth in the other factors if one wishes to isolate the effect of the growth of capital stock on the potential output. Thus, for the sake of convenience, we assume that all the variables such as labour force, technology and natural resources are assumed to be constant. Hence, we can associate all increases in the capital stock with increases in the productive capacity of an economy.

Public and Private Investments

It is important to differentiate between public investment and private investment. Public investment refers to the investment in the public sector and private investment refers to the investment in the private sector. While the motivating factor behind public investment is social welfare, private investment is guided by the profit motive. Our analysis primarily relates to the private investment.

Public investment refers to the investment in the public sector while private investment refers to the investment in the private sector.

Induced and Autonomous Investments

Investment can be divided into two categories: induced and autonomous.

Induced Investment

In general, the investment function can be expressed as

$$I = I(Y, r)$$

where I is investment, Y is income level and r is rate of interest (rate of return).

While investment is positively related to the income level, there is a negative relationship between investment and the rate of interest. Investment which changes due to a change in income and the interest rate is called the induced investment.

In the short run as income remains more or less constant, the investment function can be expressed as

Investment which changes due to a change in income and the interest rate is called induced investment.

$$I = I(r)$$

Autonomous Investment

> Investment which does not change due to the change in income and the interest rate is called autonomous investment.

Investment which does not change due to a change in income and the interest rate is called the autonomous investment. This is the investment, which depends on the other factors such as inventions, population and future expectations. While most investment in the public sector is autonomous as they are made for considerations other than the profit, some of the investments in the private sector may also be autonomous.

RECAP

- In the long run, it is investment, which determines the stock of capital and hence the long-run growth in the economy.
- We can associate all increases in the capital stock with increases in the productive capacity of an economy.
- While most investment in the public sector is autonomous as they are made for considerations other than the profit, some of the investments in the private sector may also be autonomous.

DECISION TO INVEST

The decision to invest is different when compared with the decision to buy the consumer goods. This is due to the following reasons:

(i) A firm must make a decision whether to go for capital expansion or buy an existing asset like equity in another company.

(ii) Most capital goods have a long life and one can learn only several years later as to whether the investment in these capital goods has been profitable or not.

(iii) When a firm has decided to expand, it will have to decide as to whether the cost of borrowing is greater than the return expected on the new investment undertaken by the firm.

A firm's investment decision is based on the relationship between the following three elements:

(i) Expected income flow from capital good under consideration. Since the future is uncertain, a crucial decision for the firm in making its investment decision is regarding two aspects:
   - An estimate of the future flow of income that the capital asset under consideration is expected to yield over its entire life.
   - The expected life of the capital good, which may last more than expected or may become obsolete before its lifetime due to technological advancements.

(ii) The purchase price of the good in question. Often, there exists uncertainty regarding the price at which the good is to be purchased. This is more for projects, where new machines and equipment are involved and where the cost may undergo change over time.

(iii) The rate of interest prevailing in the market, which again is subject to fluctuations.

It is important to note that any calculations, which relate to the future, must take into consideration the fact that the returns over the future have a much lower worth when compared with the same returns today. While making an investment decision relating to the future, a calculation may be made regarding the present value of the capital asset and the discounted rate of return on the asset.

BOX 21.2

It is only recently that there has arisen some interest in the theory of finance. This is because the theory of finance was a neglected part of the theories of investment. According to the traditional theory, investment depends on the marginal efficiency of capital and also the purchase price of the capital good. As far as finance is concerned, these theories assumed that there is a perfect capital market from which funds will be forthcoming. Thus, finance has been given a back seat as it was assumed that finance presented no problem. It was only later on that work was done by the different economists to remedy the neglect which the theory of finance had suffered.

Present Value of a Capital Asset and Discounting

To make its investment decision, a firm compares the present value of the capital asset with its purchase price or the supply price.

The supply price of a capital asset is the cost of replacing the capital asset, which is under consideration, with a new one.

The supply price of a capital asset is the cost of replacing the capital asset, which is under consideration, with a new one.

The present value of a capital asset is the sum obtained after discounting the expected future yields over its entire life at the market rate of interest. The higher is the market rate of interest, the lower is the present value. In the extreme case if the market rate of interest is zero, then the present value is equal to the expected future yield.

The present value of a capital asset is the sum obtained after discounting the expected future yields over its entire life at the market rate of interest.

The discounting process is the process by which a future sum is converted into its present value. It is just the reverse of the process by which a sum of money grows as it is invested in the future.

Suppose that an amount R_0 is invested for 1 year at a market rate of interest, r. The amount the individual will receive at the end of year 1:

$$R_1 = R_0(1 + r) \tag{21.1}$$

Suppose that the amount R_1 is invested for another year.

The amount the individual will receive at the end of year 2:

$$R_2 = R_1(1 + r)$$

But

$$R_1 = R_0(1 + r)$$

Thus,

$$R_2 = R_0(1 + r)(1 + r) = R_0(1 + r)^2$$

If R_2 is invested for another year, then at the end of year 3, the individual will receive

$$R_3 = R_0(1 + r)^3$$

In general, if an amount R_0 is invested for n years at a market rate of interest, r, the amount the individual will receive at the end of the n years:

$$R_n = R_0(1 + r)^n \tag{21.2}$$

Equation (21.1) can be written as

$$R_0 = \frac{R_1}{(1+r)}$$

where $(1 + r)$ is discount rate, and $\frac{R_1}{(1+r)}$ = the discounted present value of R_1.

Illustration 1: Suppose that ₹ 100 is to be received by an individual after 1 year. The market rate of interest is 10 per cent. How much must he invest today?

Solution:

The discounted present value of ₹ 100 is

$$R_0 = \frac{100}{(1+0.10)} = 90.91$$

This implies that to get a sum of ₹ 100 at the end of year, ₹ 90.91 must be invested today at an interest rate of 10 per cent.

Equation (21.2) can be written as

$$R_0 = \frac{R_n}{(1+r)^n}$$

where $(1+ r)$ is discount rate and $\frac{R_n}{(1+r)^n}$ = the discounted present value of R_n.

We consider the determination of the present value of a bond. A bond yields a yearly income, say R, until it reaches the maturity at the end of n years when it returns the principal amount, P. The present value of the bond is

$$V = \frac{R}{(1+r)} + \frac{R}{(1+r)^2} + \frac{R}{(1+r)^3} + \cdots + \frac{R}{(1+r)^n} + \frac{P}{(1+r)^n}$$

Alternatively, a machine is expected to yield an income stream of $R_1, R_2, R_3, \ldots, R_n$ over its entire life. At the end, it has a scrap value of J. The market rate of interest is r. The present value of the returns from the machine is

$$V = \frac{R_1}{(1+r)} + \frac{R_2}{(1+r)^2} + \frac{R_3}{(1+r)^3} + \cdots + \frac{R_n}{(1+r)^n} + \frac{J}{(1+r)^n}$$

Illustration 2: Suppose the annual expected returns from a machine are ₹ 35,000 over 5 years, which is the expected economic life of the machine. The scrap value of the machine is ₹ 20,000. The market rate of interest is 10 per cent. The cost of the machine is ₹ 100,000. Find the present value of the expected returns from the machine? Is it profitable to invest in the machine?

Solution:

The present value of the expected returns from the machine is

$$V = \frac{R_1}{(1+r)} + \frac{R_2}{(1+r)^2} + \frac{R_3}{(1+r)^3} + \cdots + \frac{R_n}{(1+r)^n} + \frac{J}{(1+r)^n}$$

$$V = \frac{35{,}000}{1.10} + \frac{35{,}000}{(1.10)^2} + \frac{35{,}000}{(1.10)^3} + \frac{35{,}000}{(1.10)^4} + \frac{35{,}000}{(1.10)^5} + \frac{20{,}000}{(1.10)^5}$$

$$V = 31{,}818 + 28{,}925 + 26{,}296 + 23{,}905 + 21{,}732 + 12{,}418$$

$$= 1{,}45{,}904$$

As the discounted present value of the returns from the machine is ₹1,45,904, which is greater than the cost of the machine, ₹1,00,000, the investment in the machine is profitable.

RECAP

- The decision to invest is different when compared with the decision to buy consumer goods.
- To make its investment decision, a firm compares the present value of the capital asset with its purchase price or the supply price.

MARGINAL EFFICIENCY OF CAPITAL

Till now, we have focused on the determination of the present value of a given income stream and the market rate of interest. We now assume that we are given the following:

(i) The income stream from the capital asset, $R_1, R_2, R_3, \ldots, R_n$.

(ii) The cost or purchase price of the capital asset, *C*.

We wish to find the rate of interest that will make the cost or purchase price of the capital asset equal to the present value of a given income stream. Thus, given *C* and $R_1, R_2, R_3, \ldots, R_n$, we wish to find *i*, which is the rate of return expected from a particular capital asset. It is also called the MEC. Thus,

$$C = \frac{R_1}{(1+i)} + \frac{R_2}{(1+i)^2} + \frac{R_3}{(1+i)^3} + \cdots + \frac{R_n}{(1+i)^n} + \frac{J}{(1+i)^n}$$

Illustration 3: Suppose the income stream from an investment project is R_1 = ₹500 million, R_2 = ₹600 million, R_3 = ₹600 million, R_4 = ₹400 million and R_5 = ₹400 million. The cost of the machine is ₹2000 million. Find the internal rate of return (IRR).

Solution:

The MEC is

$$C = \frac{R_1}{(1+i)} + \frac{R_2}{(1+i)^2} + \frac{R_3}{(1+i)^3} + \cdots + \frac{R_n}{(1+i)^n} + \frac{J}{(1+i)^n}$$

We get the IRR, $i = 8.397$ per cent or, in other words, the MEC as 8.397 per cent. Hence, if market rate of interest is >8.397 per cent, the project is not profitable and hence not acceptable. If the cost of borrowing funds is lower than the IRR threshold of 8.397 per cent, the project can be taken up.

It is important to note that

(i) For a given level of the income stream the higher the cost or purchase price of the capital asset, *C* the lower is the value of *i*, the MEC.

(ii) For a given level of the income stream the lower the cost or purchase price of the capital asset, *C* the higher is the value of *i*, the MEC.

Once the MEC is determined, a comparison of the market rate of interest with the MEC will enable one to make a decision as to whether the investment in the capital asset is profitable or not. The level of *r* determines as to whether the capital asset will be purchased or not, given the MEC. However, *r* does not, in any way, determine the MEC of the capital asset.

The difference between the MEC and the market rate of interest is the net rate of return expected after allowance is made for all costs. Though both the MEC and *r* are percentages, they are totally different.

The MEC will increase when

(i) Given an unchanged price of the capital good, business expectations improve leading to an upward revision of the expected income flow from the capital asset.

(ii) There is a decrease in the purchase price of the capital asset, and no change in the expected income flow from the capital asset.

The MEC will decrease when

(i) Given an unchanged price of the capital good, business expectations worsen leading to a downward revision of the expected income flow from the capital asset.

(ii) There is an increase in the purchase price of the capital asset, and no change in the expected income flow from the capital asset.

Hence, we find that the basic rule for making a decision is that

(i) If the MEC is greater than the market rate of interest, then the purchase of the capital asset is worthwhile.

(ii) If the MEC is smaller than the market rate of interest, then the purchase of the capital asset is not worthwhile.

Marginal Efficiency of Capital Schedule and the Rate of Investment

A firm has, often, variety of investment projects among which it has to make a choice. These may involve new projects or even the expansion of existing buildings and purchase of more equipment of a similar type. In making its decision, a firm will compare the MEC of the capital asset with the current market rate of interest. Once it has estimated the MEC from all the projects, the firm's MEC would be as in Figure 21.1.

In Figure 21.1, a firm can invest in four different projects: Project 1 requires an investment of ₹20 crore with an MEC of 10 per cent. Project 2 involves an investment of ₹15 crore and the MEC is 8 per cent. Project 3 requires an investment of ₹10 crore with an MEC of 6 per cent. Project 4 involves an investment of ₹5 crore with an MEC of 4 per cent. If the market rate of interest is 6 per cent, the firm will invest in projects 1, 2 and 3 with a total investment of ₹45 crore. Once the investment has increased to the point, where the last project yields an MEC, which equals the market rate of interest, the firm will stop with its expansion drive unless there is a further change in the market rate of interest. The firm has achieved its desired capital stock. For an individual firm, the lower is the rate of interest, the higher is its investment expenditures.

For every firm, the MEC schedule will resemble the stair-like curve in Figure 21.1 with an obvious difference in the heights and the lengths of the steps depending on the investment opportunities available to the firm. However, once the MECs for all the firms are added together horizontally, the steps would all even out and we can arrive at the aggregate MEC schedule as in Figure 21.2. The aggregate MEC schedule slopes downwards from left to right. *The economy is in equilibrium at the point, where the*

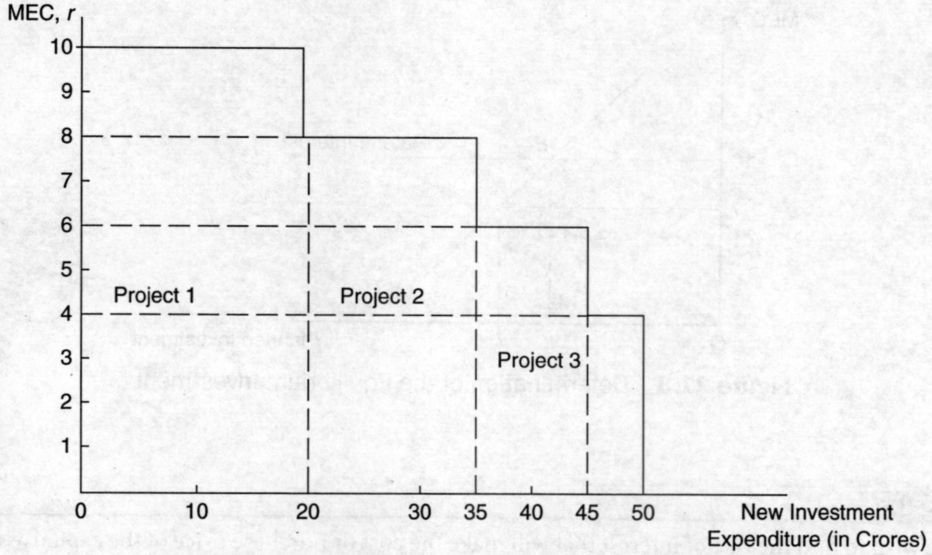

Figure 21.1 Marginal Efficiency of Capital Schedule

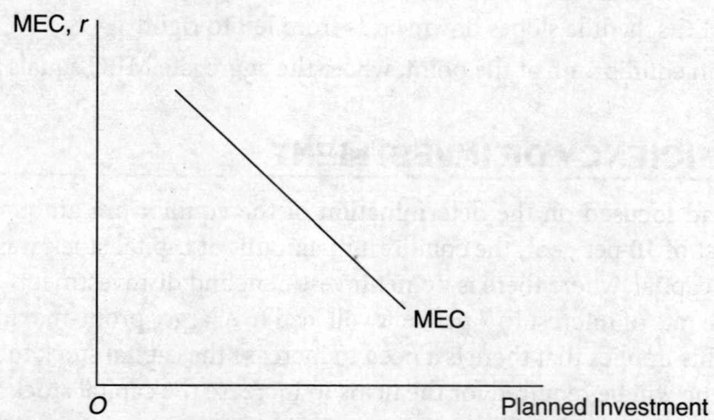

Figure 21.2 Aggregate Marginal Efficiency of Capital Schedule

aggregate MEC equals the rate of interest. Thus, the equilibrium aggregate stock of capital is determined and there is no net investment and disinvestment. This equilibrium stock of capital is the desired stock of capital.

The determination of the equilibrium amount of investment has been depicted in Figure 21.3. Given a market rate of interest equal to 10 per cent, the equilibrium point will be at point *E* with the capital stock at I^*. It is determined at the intersection of the aggregate MEC schedule and the curve representing the rate of interest.

A decrease in the rate of interest will lead to a larger investment while an increase in the rate of interest will lead to a smaller investment.

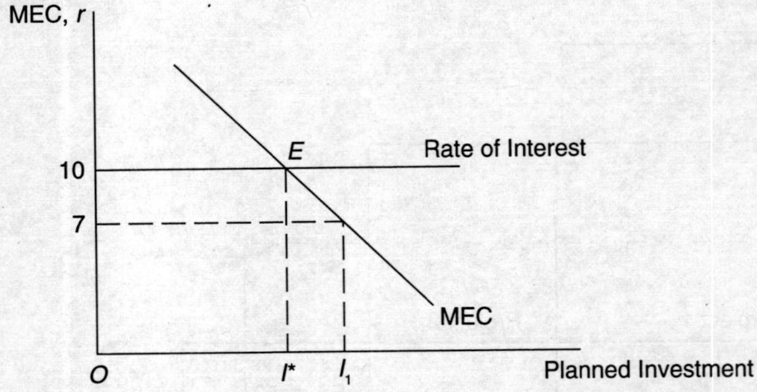

Figure 21.3 Determination of the Equilibrium Investment

RECAP

- We wish to find the rate of interest that will make the cost or purchase price of the capital asset equal to the present value of a given income stream.
- Once the MEC is determined, a comparison of the market rate of interest with the MEC will enable one to make a decision as to whether the investment in the capital asset is profitable or not.
- The aggregate MEC schedule slopes downwards from left to right.
- The economy is in equilibrium at the point, where the aggregate MEC equals the rate of interest.

MARGINAL EFFICIENCY OF INVESTMENT

In Figure 21.3, we had focused on the determination of the equilibrium amount of investment. At a market rate of interest of 10 per cent, the equilibrium amount of capital stock was I^*. This is the profit-maximizing stock of capital, where there is no net investment and disinvestment.

A decrease in the rate of interest to 7 per cent will lead to a larger profit-maximizing stock of capital at I_1 in Figure 21.3. This implies that there is a need to increase the capital stock to I_1, a net investment of $I_1 - I^*$. How much time will be required for the firms to increase the capital stock from I^* to I_1? This is a crucial question and needs considerable attention.

There can be two totally diverse situations:

(i) The capital goods industry has unlimited capacity with a supply curve, which is perfectly elastic. In such a case, the net investment will increase at a faster rate and the optimum capital stock will be achieved quickly.

(ii) The capital goods industry has limited capacity with a supply curve, which is upward sloping. The marginal costs increase as the level of output increases, which leads to increasing prices of the capital goods. In such a case, due to the increasing prices of the capital goods, the rate of investment will slow down and thus more time will be taken to achieve the optimum capital stock.

When we were analysing the investment expenditures by a single firm, we could increase the capital stock overnight because the capitals goods industry may be able to cater to the increased demands of a single firm at short notice and without much increase in the price of the capital goods. However, when all the firms in the industry increase their stock of capital, the capitals goods industry will not only take a long time to produce the additional output, but also it may have to install extra capacity, which may lead to increased costs and thus increasing the price of the capital goods.

> The marginal efficiency of investment schedule depicts the relationship between the economy's investment and rate of interest when the change in the price of capital goods is taken into consideration.

It is necessary at this stage of our analysis to distinguish between the MEC and MEI. The MEI schedule depicts the relationship between the economy's investment and rate of interest when the change in the price of capital goods is taken into consideration.

Figure 21.4 distinguishes between the MEC and MEI schedules.

(i) When the rate of interest is 10 per cent, all the firms taken as a group decide only to replace worn out capital and not to go in for any new investments. Thus, net investment is zero. The capital goods price remains unchanged. Thus, MEC equals MEI at a rate of interest of 10 per cent.

(ii) When the rate of interest decreases to 7 per cent, given the price of capital goods, all the firms taken as a group decide not only to replace worn out capital, but also to increase the new investment to I_1'. Thus, net investment is now >0. Since all the firms decide to increase their investment simultaneously, there is an increase in the demand for the capital goods, which leads to an increase in their price. This leads to a decrease in the MEC or the IRR for all the new investments. Hence, the firms reduce their investment to I_1 instead of I_1'. This is clearly the result of an increase in the price of capital goods. Thus, given a market rate of interest equal to 7 per cent, the equilibrium point will be at point *A* (and not point *C*) with the capital stock at I_1. This gives one point on the MEI schedule.

(iii) Similarly, if the rate of interest falls to 5 per cent, the equilibrium point will be at point *B* with the capital stock at I_2. This gives another point on the MEI schedule.

By joining such points, we can arrive at the MEI schedule, which represents the true investment demand schedule for the economy as a whole. The MEI schedule is downward sloping showing a negative relationship between the level of investment and the rate of interest.

RECAP

- A firm's investment decision is based on the relationship between three elements, which are the expected income flow from capital good under consideration, purchase price of the good in question and the rate of interest prevailing in the market.

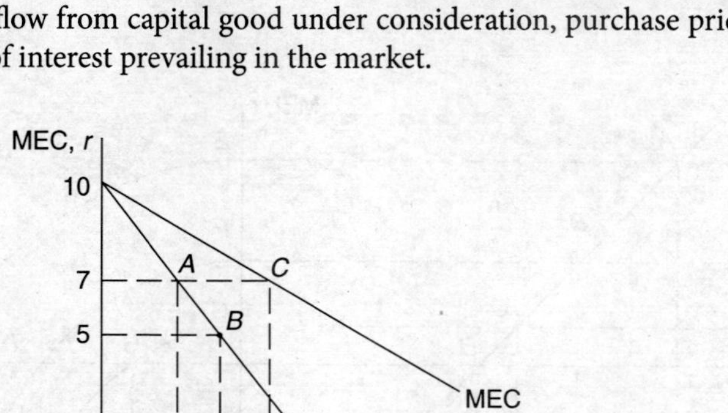

Figure 21.4 Marginal Efficiency of Capital Schedule and Marginal Efficiency of Investment Schedule

- For every firm, the MEC schedule is a stair-like curve while the aggregate MEC schedule is downward sloping and a smooth curve.
- When all the firms in the industry increase their stock of capital, there will be increases in the price of the capital.
- The MEI schedule is downward sloping showing a negative relationship between the level of investment and the rate of interest.

CHANGES IN THE RATE OF INTEREST, MEC AND CAPITAL ACCUMULATION

This section is concerned with answering two questions:

(i) When do the firms attain the desired stock of capital?

(ii) What is capital accumulation?

Fall in the Rate of Interest and Capital Accumulation

Here, we attempt at explaining the process by which capital accumulation occurs in response to a decrease in the market rate of interest.

We assume that increased supplies of capital goods are possible only at higher prices. In such a scenario, the supply curve of capital goods is upward sloping or, in other words, it is upward bending.

In Figure 21.5(a), the MEC is downward sloping. In Figure 21.5(b), the MEI also slopes downwards from left to right because the supply curve of capital is upward sloping. In fact, the concavity of the MEI schedule is due to the increasing cost of the capital goods. It is important to note that with a given stock of capital there is only one MEI.

In Figure 21.5(a), assume that

(i) At point *A* on the MEC, the economy's actual stock of capital is of ₹400 crore. This is also the desired stock of capital as the MEC equals the market rate of interest, r_1. Thus, the net investment is zero.

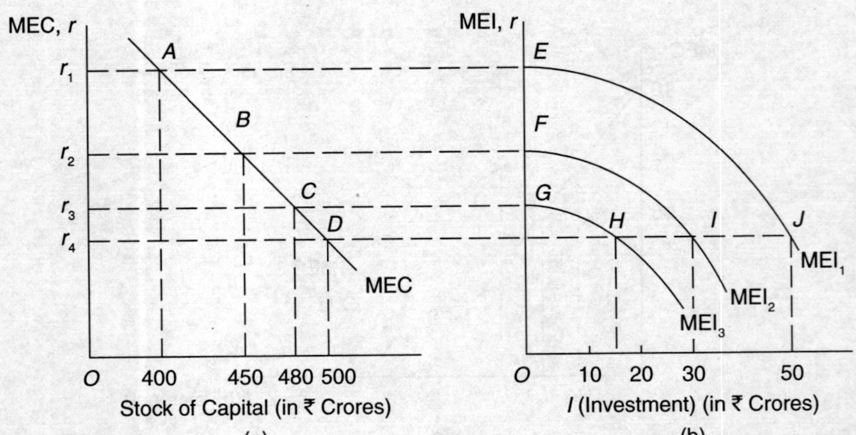

Figure 21.5 Fall in the Rate of Interest and Capital Accumulation

(ii) There is a decrease in the market rate of interest to r_4. At this rate of interest, the equilibrium occurs at point *D* (since the MEC equals the market rate of interest). The desired stock of capital increases to ₹500 crore. This is a difference of ₹100 crore from the existing actual stock. Thus, ₹100 crore of net investment is required to increase the capital stock to the desired level.

The important question here is how long will it take the firms to increase the capital stock by ₹100 crore? If the production capacity of the capital goods industry were unlimited, the firm could increase its capital goods to ₹500 crore in just one time. However, the production capacity of the capital goods industry is limited and increasing the capital goods to the desired level will take more than one time.

Figure 21.5(b) shows that

(i) In period 1, given MEI_1, due to the decrease in the rate of interest to r_4, net investment will increase but only by ₹50 crore. This is because the horizontal line, which corresponds to the rate of interest r_4, meets MEI_1 at point *J*. Hence, the stock of capital increases to ₹450 crore at the end of period 1.

(ii) In period 2, the actual stock of capital in the beginning of the period is ₹450 crore. In Figure 10.5(a), corresponding to this stock of capital of ₹450 crore, the equilibrium occurs at point *B*, where the MEC equals the market rate of interest, which is r_2. The corresponding MEI curve is MEI_2. The net investment will increase by ₹30 crore. Again, this is because the horizontal line, which corresponds to the rate of interest r_4, meets MEI_2 at point *I*. The stock of capital increases to ₹480 crore at the end of period 2.

Similarly, in the next period, there will be a further increase in the capital stock and the process will continue till the actual stock of capital gradually increases over time to ₹500 crore, which is the desired capital stock. It is obvious from the above analysis that in each period the net investment is smaller when compared with the previous period. Thus,

(i) Given the MEC schedule (which does not shift), net investment is determined by the rate of interest and the size of the capital stock.

(ii) Given the stock of capital, MEC can be determined. If the MEC is greater than the market rate of interest, then there will be positive net investment and hence an increase in the capital stock.

(iii) The rate at which net investment will increase in every time will depend on the steepness of the slope of the MEI schedule.

(iv) The steepness of the slope of the MEI schedule, in turn, depends on the slope of the supply curve of the capital goods.

Shift in the MEC Schedule and Capital Accumulation

In this section, we attempt at explaining the process by which capital accumulation occurs in response to a shift in the MEC schedule, given the market rate of interest. We will analyse an upward shift in the MEC schedule, which leads to an increase in the profit-maximizing capital and thus to capital accumulation.

Figure 21.6(a) depicts the effect of a shift in the MEC schedule on capital accumulation. The figure depicts:

(i) The original MEC schedule is MEC_1. At a rate of interest of r_1, the profit-maximizing or the desired capital stock is at ₹400 crore. Since the actual capital stock is also ₹400 crore, net investment is zero.

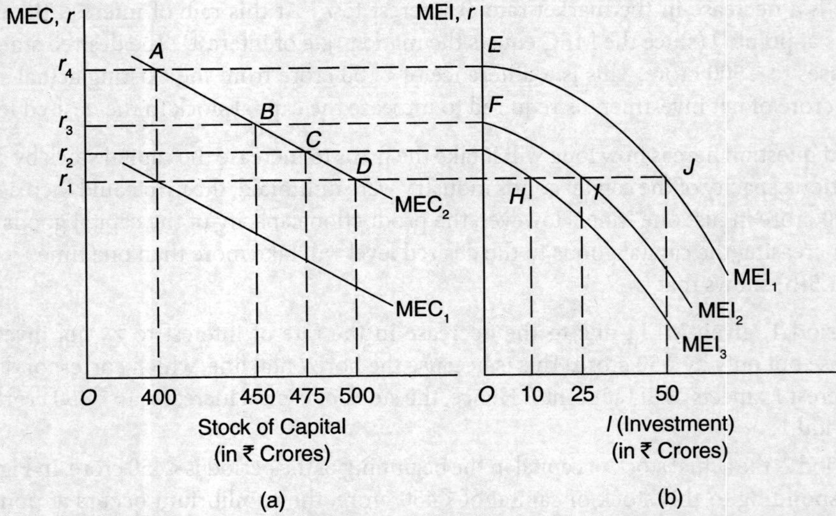

Figure 21.6 Shift in the MEC Schedule and Capital Accumulation

(ii) Suppose the MEC schedule shifts upwards to MEC$_2$. At a rate of interest of r_1, the profit-maximizing or the desired capital stock is now at ₹500 crore. Since the actual capital stock is at ₹400 crore, there is a difference of ₹100 crore from the optimum or desired capital stock. Thus, ₹100 crore of net investment is required implying that net investment is positive or >0.

The important question here again is how long will it take the firms to increase the capital stock by ₹100 crore? Since the production capacity of the capital goods industry is limited, increasing the capital goods to the desired level will take more than one time.

Figure 21.6(b) shows that

(i) In period 1, given MEI$_1$, net investment will increase but only by ₹50 crore. This is because the horizontal line, which corresponds to the rate of interest r_1, meets MEI$_1$ at point *J*. Thus, the stock of capital increases to ₹450 crore at the end of period 1.

(ii) In period 2, the actual stock of capital in the beginning of the period is ₹450 crore. In Figure 10.6(a), corresponding to this stock of capital of ₹450 crore is point *B* on MEC$_2$. The corresponding MEI curve is MEI$_2$. The net investment will increase by ₹25 crore. Again this is because the horizontal line, which corresponds to the rate of interest r_1, meets MEI$_2$ at point *I*. The stock of capital increases to ₹475 crore at the end of period 2. However, the actual stock of capital is still less than the desired stock of capital.

Thus, in the next period, there will be a further increase in the capital stock and the process of capital accumulation will continue till the actual stock of capital gradually increases over time to ₹500 crore, which is the desired capital stock. Thus,

(i) Given the rate of interest, an upward shift in the MEC schedule generates conditions, which are apt for investment.

(ii) Due to the upward shift in the MEC schedule, the MEC becomes greater than the current market rate of interest (given the actual capital stock). This leads to a situation, which initiates the investment activity or the net investment is >0. The process of investment, or, in other words, the process of capital accumulation will continue till the actual capital stock is equal to the desired capital stock. At this level, investment activity will cease as the MEC is equal to the market rate of interest.

RECAP

- In each period, the net investment is smaller when compared with the previous period.
- The rate at which net investment will increase in every time will depend on the steepness of the slope of the MEI schedule.
- Given the rate of interest, an upward shift in the MEC schedule generates conditions, which are apt for investment.

THEORIES OF INVESTMENT

Many theories have been put forward to explain the investment demand. It is difficult and complex subject and one of the most controversial subjects. We throw light on some of these theories.

Accelerator Theory of Investment

The simple accelerator model states that investment is proportional to the change in the level of output and is not influenced by the cost of capital.

According to the accelerator theory, the desired stock of capital depends on the economy's output level. An increase in the output leads to an outward shift in the MEC schedule implying that at each interest rate a larger capital stock is desired. Thus, changes in investment can be explained in terms of shifts in the MEC schedule. The increases in the output put pressures on the existing stock of capital or, in other words, on the existing productive capacity. An increase in the productive capacity is possible only by an expansion of the existing capital stock, thus providing the incentive to the firm to obtain more capital goods and a higher rate of investment.

According to this approach, the rate of investment spending depends on the output level. To produce more output, more capital is required. Within limits, it is possible to increase the output by using the existing capacity more intensively. But, there exists a particular capital output ratio, which the firms consider to be the ideal ratio. This ratio differs from industry to industry being higher in some industries and lower in the others. However, at a particular point in time, there exists a particular capital output ratio, which is considered to be the desired ratio for the economy as a whole. As there occurs technological and other changes in the economy, this ratio will undergo a change. However, for simplifying our analysis, we assume that the ratio remains unchanged over time.

We have

$$K = kY$$

where K is capital stock, k is capital output ratio and Y is output level.

Given an unchanged capital output ratio, as the output changes, the desired stock of capital will also change. Suppose

$$K_{t-1} = kY_{t-1}$$

where t is some particular time, $t-1$, $t-2$ are preceding times and $t+1$, $t+2$ are subsequent times.

Suppose there is an increase in the output level in period *t*. Hence,

$$K_t = kY_t$$

The increase in the desired stock of capital = $K_t - K_{t-1}$.

The capital will increase only when net investment equals the increase in the capital stock or

$$I_t = K_t - K_{t-1}$$

where I_t is net investment in period *t*.

We can also write

$$I_t = K_t - K_{t-1} = kY_t \;\; kY_{t-1} = k(Y_t - Y_{t-1})$$

The above equation indicates that the net investment in time *t* depends on the change in the output level between time *t* and *t* – 1 multiplied by the capital output ratio. It is clear that

(i) If $Y_t > Y_{t-1}$, there is a positive net investment in period *t*.
(ii) If $Y_t < Y_{t-1}$, there is a negative net investment or disinvestment in period *t*.
(iii) If $Y_t = Y_{t-1}$, there is a zero net investment in period *t*.

To net investment if replacement investment (which we assume to be equal to depreciation) is added, we get gross investment.

Thus, we have

$$I_t + D_t = k(Y_t - Y_{t-1}) + D_t$$

where D_t is depreciation in period *t*. Thus,

$$I_{gt} = k(Y_t - Y_{t-1}) + D_t$$

where I_{gt} is gross investment.

Investment will change if there is a change in the output level. However, it is assumed that there is no excess capacity. We allow for excess capacity by including X_t, which is the excess capacity in period *t* in our analysis. Thus,

$$I_{gt} = k(Y_t - Y_{t-1}) + D_t - X_t$$

The basic relationship, which exists between the investment and the change in the output level, is known as the accelerator principle.

The capital output ratio, *k*, is known as the accelerator.

where X_t is excess capacity in period *t*.

If $k(Y_t - Y_{t-1}) + D_t$ is equal to or less than X_t, then I_{gt} will be zero.

The basic relationship, which exists between the investment and the change in the output level, is known as the accelerator principle. The capital output ratio, *k*, is known as the accelerator. The investment theory, which is based on the above relationship, is known as the accelerator theory.

The following points are important in the context of the theory:

(i) If the economy is in a position, where the existing capital stock is fully utilized and there is no excess capacity, and the capital output ratio is constant, then in that case an expansion of output is possible only with an expansion in the existing stock of capital.
(ii) If the accelerator is >1, then the increase in the capital stock will be greater than the increase in the output. Thus, the increase in the investment is greater than the increase in the output.

For the accelerator principle to work, certain conditions must be satisfied:

(i) The firms must operate without any excess capacity. During periods of excess capacity, the accelerator principle is temporarily inactive.
(ii) The firms increase their capacity so as to able to meet every increase in the level of real spending. This implies that whenever there is an increase in the quantity of goods sold, there is an increase in investment by the firms and whenever there is a decrease in the quantity of goods sold, there is a decrease in investment by the firms.
(iii) The capital output ratio, *k*, or, in other words, the accelerator must be constant.
(iv) The gap between the desired output and the actual output of the firms is closed within a single time. In practice, this will depend on the production capacity of the capital goods industries.

Criticism

Due to its rigid assumptions, the accelerator theory has been subject to severe criticisms. Also, it appears that the accelerator principle does not work during periods of recession when there exists excess capacity. The accelerator principle is based on calculations about the future, which are not necessarily accurate. Thus, doubts have been raised about the validity of the accelerator principle. However, its basic idea remains that investment depends upon changes in the level of output. It does not depend upon changes in the cost of capital.

Flexible Accelerator Model

Many theories have been put forward regarding the speed at which firms fine-tune their stock of capital over time. The main idea in the flexible accelerator model is that whenever there exists a large gap between the firms existing capital stock and the desired capital stock, the firm's investment is swifter.

According to the model, the firm, in each period, plans on bridging only a fraction of the gap, which exists between the desired and the actual capital stocks.

At the end of current period, the actual stock of capital is

$$K_0 = K_{-1} + \beta(K^* - K_{-1})$$

where K_{-1} is capital stock at the end of preceding period, K^* is desired capital stock and $(K^* - K_{-1})$ is gap between the desired and the actual capital stock.

Net investment to be achieved by the firm is

$$I = K_0 - K_{-1}$$

$$I = \beta(K^* - K_{-1})$$

The larger is the value of β, the quicker is the reduction in the gap between the desired and the actual capital stock. The investment function shows that the desired stock of capital, K^*, and the actual stock of capital, K_{-1}, together determine the level of current spending. Any factor that is responsible for an increase in the desired capital stock also leads to an increase in the rate of investment.

The factors that are responsible for the increase the rate of investment are

(i) An increase in the investment tax credit.
(ii) An increase in the expected level of output.
(iii) A decrease in the real rate of interest.

The flexible accelerator theory emphasizes that

(i) Net investment adjusts gradually over time.

(ii) Investment shows the various aspects of a firm's dynamic behaviour.

q Theory of Investment

This theory is based on the relationship between investment and the stock market. The relationship between the stock market and investment was first put forward by James Tobin.

According to the theory, q is the ratio of a firm's market value (capitalization) to the replacement cost of capital. Hence, it is an assessment of the value placed on the firm's assets by the stock market in comparison with the cost of producing those assets.

A high q ratio implies that a firm will like to increase the production. Thus, there will be an increase in investment. Hence, a high q indicates a high investment. For example, if the value of q is larger than 1, it implies that a firm should increase the investment level. For every rupee worth of new machinery, a firm will be able to sell rupee q worth of stocks and hence make a profit equal to $q - 1$. Hence, when the value of a q is >1, it implies a flurry of investment.

RECAP

- According to the accelerator theory, given an unchanged capital output ratio, as the output changes, the desired stock of capital will also change.
- If the accelerator is >1, then the increase in the capital stock will be greater than the increase in the output.
- The flexible accelerator theory emphasizes that net investment adjusts gradually over time.
- The q Theory of Investment is based on the relationship between investment and the stock market.

SUMMARY

INTRODUCTION

1. This chapter analyses the relationship between investment and the rate of interest and also the responsiveness of investment to the rate of interest.
2. We attempt at determining the factors that influence the investment decisions. We also examine some of the theories of investment spending.

BASIC CONCEPTS

1. Capital is the accumulated stock of plant and equipment, which is held by the business firms.
2. Investment can be defined as the value of that portion of an economy's output for any time that takes the form of new producer's durable equipment, new structures and the change in inventories. In the long run, it is investment, which determines the stock of capital and hence the long-run growth in the economy.
3. As different factors influence the different types of investment, there can be no single investment theory, which is applicable to all the different types of investment.

Gross and Net Investments

1. Gross investment consists of two parts: the replacement investment, which is required to keep the capital stock intact and the net investment, which is required to expand the existing capital stock.

2. Net investment is equal to gross investment less depreciation. In fact, net investment is an accretion to the stock of capital.
3. Other things remaining unchanged, for example, given the labour force, technology and natural resources, an accretion to the stock of capital increases the economy's productive capacity.

Public and Private Investments

1. Public investment refers to the investment in the public sector and private investment refers to the investment in the private sector.
2. While the motivating factor behind public investment is social welfare, private investment is guided by the profit motive.

Induced and Autonomous Investments

1. Investment which changes due to a change in income and the interest rate is called the induced investment.
2. In general, the investment function can be expressed as $I = I(Y, r)$. While investment is positively related to the income level, there is a negative relationship between investment and the rate of interest.
3. Investment which does not change due to a change in income and the interest rate is called the autonomous investment.
4. While most investment in the public sector is autonomous as they are made for considerations other than the profit, some of the investments in the private sector may also be autonomous.

DECISION TO INVEST

1. The decision to invest is different when compared with the decision to buy the consumer goods.
2. Most capital goods have a long life and one can learn only several years later as to whether the investment in these capital goods has been profitable or not.
3. A firm's investment decision is based on the relationship between three elements: expected income flow from capital good under consideration, the purchase price of the good in question and the rate of interest prevailing in the market.

Present Value of a Capital Asset and Discounting

1. To make its investment decision, a firm compares the present value of the capital asset with its purchase price or the supply price.
2. The supply price of a capital asset is the cost of replacing the capital asset, which is under consideration, with a new one.
3. The present value of a capital asset is the sum obtained after discounting the expected future yields over its entire life at the market rate of interest. The higher is the market rate of interest, the lower is the present value.
4. The discounting process is the process by which a future sum is converted into its present value.
5. In general, if an amount R_0 is invested for n years at a market rate of interest, r, the amount the individual will receive at the end of the n years: $R_n = R_0 (1+r)^n$.
6. $\dfrac{R_n}{(1+r)^n}$ = the discounted present value of R_n.
7. The present value of the bond is

$$V = \frac{R}{(1+r)} + \frac{R}{(1+r)^2} + \frac{R}{(1+r)^3} + \cdots + \frac{R}{(1+r)^n} + \frac{P}{(1+r)^n}$$

8. The present value of a machine is

$$V = \frac{R_1}{(1+r)} + \frac{R_2}{(1+r)^2} + \frac{R_3}{(1+r)^3} + \cdots + \frac{R_n}{(1+r)^n} + \frac{J}{(1+r)^n}$$

MARGINAL EFFICIENCY OF CAPITAL

1. We assume that we are given the following: The income stream from the capital asset, $R_1, R_2, R_3, \ldots, R_n$; cost or purchase price of the capital asset, C.
2. Given C and $R_1, R_2, R_3, \ldots, R_n$, we wish to find i, which is the rate of return expected from a particular capital asset. It is also called the MEC.
3. Once the MEC is determined, a comparison of the market rate of interest with the MEC will enable one to make a decision as to whether the investment in the capital asset is profitable or not.
4. The difference between the MEC and the market rate of interest is the net rate of return expected after allowance is made for all costs.
5. The basic rule for making a decision is that if the MEC is greater than the market rate of interest, then the purchase of the capital asset is worthwhile and if the MEC is smaller than the market rate of interest, then the purchase of the capital asset is not worthwhile.

Marginal Efficiency of Capital Schedule and the Rate of Investment

1. A firm has often variety of investment projects among which it has to make a choice.
2. In making its decision, a firm will compare the MEC of the capital asset with the current market rate of interest.
3. For every firm, the MEC schedule will resemble the stair-like curve.
4. Once the MECs for all the firms are added together horizontally, the steps would all even out and we can arrive at the downward sloping and a smooth aggregate MEC schedule.
5. The equilibrium amount of investment is determined at the intersection of the aggregate MEC schedule and the curve representing the rate of interest.

MARGINAL EFFICIENCY OF INVESTMENT

1. When all the firms in the industry increase their stock of capital, the capitals goods industry will not only take a long time to produce the additional output, but also it may have to install extra capacity, which may lead to increased costs and thus increasing the price of the capital goods.
2. The MEI schedule depicts the relationship between the economy's investment and rate of interest when the change in the price of capital goods is taken into consideration.
3. The MEI schedule represents the true investment demand schedule for the economy as a whole. The MEI schedule is downward sloping showing a negative relationship between the level of investment and the rate of interest.

CHANGES IN THE RATE OF INTEREST, MEC AND CAPITAL ACCUMULATION

Fall in the Rate of Interest and Capital Accumulation

1. Here, we attempt at explaining the process by which capital accumulation occurs in response to a decrease in the market rate of interest.
2. We assume that the supply curve of capital goods is upward sloping.
3. The concavity of the MEI schedule is due to the increasing cost of the capital goods.
4. There is a decrease in the market rate of interest. The desired stock of capital increases.
5. The important question here is how long will it take the firms to increase the capital stock to the desired level?
6. In each period, there is an increase in the capital stock and the process will continue till the actual stock of capital gradually increases over time to the optimum level.
7. In each period, the net investment is smaller when compared with the previous period.
8. Given the MEC schedule (which does not shift), net investment is determined by the rate of interest and the size of the capital stock.

A Shift in the MEC Schedule and Capital Accumulation

1. We attempt at explaining the process by which capital accumulation occurs in response to an upward shift in the MEC schedule, given the market rate of interest.
2. Suppose the MEC schedule shifts upwards. Given the market rate of interest, there is an increase in the profit-maximizing or the desired capital stock.
3. The important question here again is how long it will take the firms to increase the capital stock.
4. In each period, there is an increase in the capital stock and the process will continue till the actual stock of capital gradually increases over time to the optimum level.
5. Thus given the rate of interest, an upward shift in the MEC schedule generates conditions, which are apt for investment.
6. The process of investment or, in other words, the process of capital accumulation will continue till the actual capital stock is equal to the desired capital stock. At this level, investment activity will cease as the MEC is equal to the market rate of interest.

THEORIES OF INVESTMENT

Accelerator Theory of Investment

1. The simple accelerator model states that investment is proportional to the change in the level of output and is not influenced by the cost of capital.
2. According to this approach, the rate of investment spending depends on the output level. At a particular point in time, there exists a particular capital output ratio, which is considered to be the desired ratio for the economy as a whole.
3. The net investment in time t depends on the change in the output level between time t and $t - 1$ multiplied by the capital output ratio.
4. Investment will change if there is a change in the output level. However, it is assumed that there is no excess capacity.
5. The basic relationship, which exists between the investment and the change in the output level, is known as the accelerator principle. The capital output ratio, k, is known as the accelerator. The investment theory, which is based on the above relationship, is known as the accelerator theory.
6. If the accelerator is >1, then the increase in the capital stock will be greater than the increase in the output. Thus, the increase in the investment is greater than the increase in the output that is responsible for the increase in it.
7. Due to its rigid assumptions, the accelerator theory has been subject to severe criticisms. Also, it appears that the accelerator principle does not work during periods of recession when there exists excess capacity. The accelerator principle is based on calculations about the future, which are not necessarily accurate.

Flexible Accelerator Model

1. The main idea in the flexible accelerator model is that whenever there exists a large gap between the firms existing capital stock and the desired capital stock, the firm's investment is swifter.
2. According to the model, the firm, in each period, plans on bridging only a fraction of the gap, which exists between the desired and the actual capital stocks.
3. The investment function shows that the desired stock of capital and the actual stock of capital together determine the level of current spending.
4. The flexible accelerator theory emphasizes that net investment adjusts gradually over time.

q Theory of Investment

1. This theory is based on the relationship between investment and the stock market. The relationship between the stock market and investment was first put forward by James Tobin.
2. According to the theory, q is the ratio of a firm's market value (capitalization) to the replacement cost of capital.
3. A high q indicates a high investment

REVIEW QUESTIONS

TRUE OR FALSE QUESTIONS

1. Investment which changes due to a change in income and the interest rate is called the autonomous investment.
2. The present value of a capital asset is the sum obtained after discounting the expected future yields over its entire life at the market rate of interest.
3. The supply price of a capital asset is the cost of replacing the capital asset, which is under consideration, with an old one.
4. For every firm, the MEC schedule is a stair-like curve while the aggregate MEC schedule is a downward sloping curve.
5. The MEC schedule represents the true investment demand schedule for the economy as a whole.

SHORT ANSWER QUESTIONS

1. What is capital? How is it different from investment?
2. Distinguish between gross investment and net investment.
3. 'The decision to invest is different when compared with the decision to buy consumer goods'. Comment.
4. On which three factors does a firm's investment decision depend? Discuss.
5. 'MEI schedule represents the true investment demand schedule for the economy as a whole'. Comment.

LONG ANSWER QUESTIONS

1. Write short notes on the following:
   (a) Capital and investment
   (b) Gross and net investment
   (c) Public and private investment
   (d) Induced and autonomous investment
2. What is the present value of a capital asset? How is it related to discounting? Explain.
3. What is the MEC? How can we arrive at the aggregate MEC schedule?
4. (a) Analyse the effect of a decrease in the rate of interest on capital accumulation.
   (b) Analyse the effect of an upward shift in the MEC schedule on capital accumulation.
5. Write short notes on the following theories of investment:
   (a) Accelerator theory of investment
   (b) The flexible accelerator model
   (c) The *q* theory of investment

ANSWERS

TRUE OR FALSE QUESTIONS

1. **False.** Investment which changes due to a change in income and the interest rate is called the induced investment.
2. **True.** The higher is the market rate of interest, the lower is the present value. In the extreme case, if the market rate of interest is zero, then the present value is equal to the expected future yield.
3. **False.** The supply price of a capital asset is the cost of replacing the capital asset, which is under consideration, with a new one.
4. **True.** For every firm, the MEC schedule will resemble the stair-like curve. However, once the MECs for all the firms are added together horizontally, the steps would all even out and we can arrive at the aggregate MEC schedule, which is a downward sloping and smooth curve.
5. **False.** The MEI schedule represents the true investment demand schedule for the economy as a whole.

Economic Growth, Business Cycles and Stabilization Policy

22

After studying this chapter, you should be able to understand:

- ✓ *Economic growth refers to an increase in the amount of goods and services which are produced in an economy over time.*
- ✓ *The Harrod–Domar model is a long-run model, which is an extension of the Keynesian model of income and employment.*
- ✓ *The views of Robert Solow, Trevor Swan, James Tobin and many others have been put together as the neo-classical growth theory, which was developed in the 1950s.*
- ✓ *Business cycles relate to economic changes in the short run in production.*
- ✓ *A business cycle generally moves between periods of expansions and contractions with the peaks and the troughs forming the extremes.*
- ✓ *According to the pure monetary theory, the basic cause of business cycles is the fluctuations in the bank credit and the supply of money in the economy.*
- ✓ *According to the monetary overinvestment theory, presented by Professor Hayek, the industries fall under two categories, consumer goods industries and capital goods industries.*
- ✓ *According to the multiplier–accelerator interaction theory, the different phases of a business cycle can be explained in terms of the interaction between the accelerator and the multiplier.*
- ✓ *According to Schumpeter's innovation theory, business cycles can be explained in terms of industrial innovations.*
- ✓ *Stabilization means controlling the ups and downs of a business cycle without interfering in any way with the economic growth of the country.*
- ✓ *The two most common economic policies, which are used to achieve stabilization, are monetary policy and fiscal policy.*
- ✓ *An automatic stabilizer is a built-in mechanism in any economy, which automatically reduces the change in the output in response to a change in the level of the autonomous demand.*

INTRODUCTION

It was in the early 1930s and the 1940s that attempts were made to develop a theory of economic growth. The foundations for a theory of economic growth were laid by Evsey D. Domar in the USA and Sir Roy Harrod in the UK.

The study of economic growth is very complicated. But, nevertheless it is very important for the not only the policy makers but also for the business to be aware of the logistics involved including the determinants of economic growth.

Every economy is subject to ups and downs in the form of business cycles. It is also of great importance for both the policy makers and business to analyse the environment in the economy before making their decisions.

ECONOMIC GROWTH

Concept of Economic Growth

Economic growth refers to an increase in the amount of goods and services, which are produced in an economy over time. Thus, it is an increase in the economy's capacity to produce goods and services in the long run. It can be shown by a shift to the right of the production possibility curve.

> Economic growth refers to an increase in the amount of goods and services, which are produced in an economy over time.

> Economic growth could be defined in terms of a sustained increase in the per capita national product over time.

To measure economic growth, the percentage increase in the Gross Domestic Product is calculated. If economic growth is to be adjusted for inflation, it can be measured in real terms; otherwise, it can be measured in nominal terms.

It is important to understand that if the purpose of focusing on economic growth rests on the desire to bring about improvements in the standard of living in an economy, then in that case economic growth could be defined in terms of a sustained increase in the per capita national product over time.

For making comparisons between countries in relation to economic growth, the per capita GDP or the per capita GNP should be compared as these take into consideration the differences, which exist in the population between the countries. It is essential that economic growth is not linked to just an enhancement of the capacity to produce but that there should be an improvement in the standard of living of the people in the country.

RECAP

- Economic growth refers to an increase in the amount of goods and services which are produced in an economy over time.
- It is essential that economic growth is not linked to just an enhancement of the capacity to produce but that there should be an improvement in the standard of living of the people in the country.

FACTORS DETERMINING ECONOMIC GROWTH

To examine the factors that determine economic growth, it is necessary to understand as to how output is produced. Firms employ a combination of capital and labour to produce the output. While the physical capital consists of the machinery and equipment, labour relates to the workers and employees, and human capital refers to the intellectual property, which is required in the production process.

Development of Technology

Technology is the skill and expertise involved in the production of a good. Thus, one can say that technology refers to the machinery and equipment used in production. The growth in technology plays a key role in the improvements in productivity and also in economic growth. The choice of the technique of production is very crucial. The capital–labour ratio is important in this context. A country, which is abundant in labour, should use a labour-intensive technique while a country, which is abundant in capital, should use a capital-intensive technique.

Technological development involves research, inventions and innovations. A major factor influencing growth is innovations. Innovations not only lower the production costs, but also create new markets for the product, both within the country and outside the country. It leads to an increase in the output.

Formation of Capital and Development of the Infrastructure

Capital formation refers to that fraction of the present income, which is set aside as savings and invested so that there is an increase in the future level of output and income in the economy. It involves not only an investment in machinery, plant and equipment but also an improvement in the infrastructure including roads, transport and communication. Capital formation increases the productivity of the worker. Unless a country possesses the necessary infrastructure, it cannot increase its production levels and experience growth. Often, the lack of infrastructural development may be an important factor in holding back an economy.

> Capital formation refers to that fraction of the present income, which is set aside as savings and invested so that there is an increase in the future level of output and income in the economy.

Human Capital Formation

Human capital is the level of knowledge and the skill of the labour. The better is the quality of the human capital, the more is the adaptability of the labour to the latest techniques and thus the more will be the productivity of the labour. The labour productivity depends on the education levels and the training provided to the labour. An increase in the productivity of labour can be a crucial factor in economic growth.

Natural Resources

Natural resources are those objects that are present naturally and are of tremendous use to mankind. At its basic level, every man-made product consists of natural resources. Natural resources may exist in the form of land water and air, or as a living organism like a fish or it may be in the form of minerals, oil and energy, which may need to be processed further. They are very essential for economic growth. But it is important to note that for the exploitation of natural resources, it is necessary for the country to possess the necessary technology, capital, infrastructure and manpower or human capital.

Other Factors

Social factors, which include the customs and the traditions prevailing in the society, affect the economic growth. A society, which is progressive and ready to accept new inventions and ideas, is bound to experience a higher economic growth than one, which is shrouded with superstitions and traditional ways of life.

The political situation, which prevails in the country, is again important as far as economic growth is concerned. While a stable government can encourage growth, the existence of political instability can act as a shock, thus acting as an impediment in the path of growth.

RECAP

- Economic growth refers to an increase in the amount of goods and services, which are produced in an economy over time.
- The factors that affect the economic growth are the development of technology, formation of capital and development of the infrastructure and human capital formation.

THEORIES OF ECONOMIC GROWTH

The earlier schools of thought like mercantalism laid emphasis on the wealth of the ruler and the accumulation of gold. The Physiocrats developed the economic theory called physiocracy, which emphasized that the source of wealth of a nation was its productive capacity.

According to the classical economics, which started with Adam Smith's *An Enquiry into the Nature and Causes of Wealth of Nations*, 1776, the wealth of a nation depended on the division of labour. Later, the views given by Malthus, Ricardo and others gained popularity.

This chapter focuses on two theories. The Harrod–Domar theory of growth was presented by two famous economists, Sir Roy Harrod of the UK and Evesey Domar of the USA in the late 1930s. The neo-classical theory of economic growth came in the 1950s.

Harrod–Domar Theory of Growth

Two important historical developments occurred, which played a very significant role in influencing the views of the development economists. The Great Depression, which occurred in the 1930s, led to a sharp increase in the unemployment and thus affected the economic growth. The Second World War again was responsible for destroying the economies of the countries, which were involved in the war.

It was under these circumstances that doubts were raised regarding the instability associated with the Keynesian model, which is a short-run model. Two models were presented independently on the requirements and conditions relating to the achievement of a steady economic growth: by Sir Roy F. Harrod in the year 1939 and Evsey Domar in the year 1946. Though these models follow different approaches, yet they more or less reach the same conclusion. Hence, their models are collectively known as the Harrod–Domar model.

The Harrod–Domar model is a long-run model, which is an extension of the Keynesian model of income and employment. It has gained popularity as a planning model for the developing economies. One of the main approaches to development is to mobilize the savings, both domestic and foreign. Savings are imperative not only for the replacement of the worn-out existing capital goods, but also to make new additions to the stock of capital. The accumulation of capital is the key to the achievement of the economic growth.

Capital accumulation plays a dual role in economic growth:

(i) It leads to an increase in the productive capacity by increasing the economy's total capital stock.

(ii) It leads to the generation of income in that those who are engaged in the production of the capital goods experience an increase in their income levels. Once this income is spent, it creates an additional increase in the goods and services.

It is important to note that the additional demand for the goods and services should be sufficient to absorb the increase in output from the additional productive capacity installed in the economy. It is necessary that this condition is satisfied year after year if the economy has to achieve a steady economic growth and full employment in the long run. If the condition is not satisfied, then problems may crop up in the form of idle capacity in production. This is the crux of the Harrod–Domar model.

Assumptions

The Harrod–Domar model is based on certain assumptions:

(i) The capital output ratio is assumed to be constant. In every economy, there exists a direct relation between the total stock of capital, K and the GNP or the total national output or income, Y. Hence, to produce a total output of, for example, of ₹300, a stock of ₹100 of capital is required. For any additions in the national output to occur, it is necessary that there occur additions to the capital stock taking the form of new investments. Thus, the output/capital ratio,

k (It is a reciprocal of the capital/output ratio)(3:1 in the above example), plays a very crucial role in the Harrod–Domar model. It can be expressed as:

$$Y = kK \tag{22.1}$$

where Y is national output, GNP, k is output capital ratio and K is capital stock.

Since k, the output capital ratio, is assumed as constant in the model, it follows that any increases in the GNP must be equal to k times the increase in the capital stock. The increase in the capital stock is actually the net investment in the economy. Thus,

$$\Delta Y = k\Delta K = kI \tag{22.2}$$

where ΔY is change in the national output, GNP, k is output capital ratio, ΔK is change in the capital stock and I = net investment in the economy.

(ii) The national savings S, is assumed to be a fixed proportion of the GNP or the national output. Thus,

$$S = sY \tag{22.3}$$

where S is national savings, s is propensity to save and Y is national output, GNP.

It is important to note that, according to the model, in equilibrium, the desired savings are equal to the desired investment.

$$S = sY = I \tag{22.4}$$

Harrod–Domar Model: From equation (22.2), we get

$$\Delta Y_n = kI_n \tag{22.5}$$

But

$$\Delta Y_n = Y_n - Y_{n-1}$$

where ΔY_n is change in the national output in period n, k is capital output ratio, Y_n is national output in period n and Y_{n-1} is national output in period $n - 1$.

Hence, equation (22.5) can be written as

$$Y_n - Y_{n-1} = kI_n \tag{22.6}$$

From equation (22.4),

$$sY_n = I_n$$

Thus, equation (22.6) can be written as

$$Y_n - Y_{n-1} = ksY_n \tag{22.7}$$

Dividing both sides of equation (22.7) by Y_n, we get

$$\frac{Y_n - Y_{n-1}}{Y_n} = \frac{ksY_n}{Y_n}$$

$$\frac{\Delta Y}{Y_n} = ks$$

$$\frac{\Delta Y}{Y_n} = W_G = ks$$

Or $$W_G = ks \qquad (22.8)$$

In this model, W_G is the warranted rate of growth, which is the rate of growth of the output, where the firms are of the opinion that given the expectations regarding the future demand, they have achieved the accurate amount of the capital and hence are not interested in increasing or decreasing the capital stock or, in other words, the net investment in the economy.

The model also discusses the actual growth rate, which is the actual change in the aggregate output. According to the model, the natural rate of growth relates to the rate at which the labour force grows implying that when the labour force is large, the output is also large. This determines the natural rate of growth, the factor of production, labour is introduced in the model, where

(i) The capital–labour ratio is assumed to be a constant.
(ii) Capital and labour are assumed to be perfect complements.

It is obvious from the above assumptions that for growth to occur beyond the full employment level there should be an increase in the supply of labour. Thus,

$$N_G = m + \frac{\Delta L}{L}$$

where N_G is natural rate of growth, m is rate at which capital substitutes for labour and $\frac{\Delta L}{L}$ is rate of growth of the labour force.

Hence, the natural rate of growth of the economy will depend on the rate at which the labour force grows in the long run and also on the rate at which the economy is able to substitute the capital for labour or, in other words, the development of labour-saving techniques of production in the economy.

Limitations

(i) According to the model, in equilibrium, the desired savings are equal to the desired investment. The basis of this assumption is that the warranted rate of growth will equal the actual growth rate or, in other words, that the expected rate of growth will be always realized. This is possible only under very stringent and unrealistic conditions such as a constant marginal propensity to consume, a constant output capital ratio, and no changes in the techniques of production.
(ii) Some of the parameters used in the model like the marginal propensity to save and development of labour-saving techniques of production are determined outside the model. Hence, in the long run, the model may not be able to achieve the equilibrium level of the growth rate.
(iii) The model was formulated for the problems relating to the developed countries and was not meant to address the problems of the developing countries, which are of a different nature.

The model cannot be given up due to the above problems. With some modifications, it can be applied even to solve the problems of the developing countries.

Neo-Classical Growth Theory

The views of Robert Solow, Trevor Swan, James Tobin and many others have been put together as the neo-classical growth theory, which was developed in the 1950s.

BOX 22.1

The neo-classical growth theory is an extension of the Harrod–Domar Model, which came up in 1946. Robert Solow and T. W. Swan made some significant contributions to the model. Solow had developed some growth models independently, which were applicable to the USA and for which he received the Nobel Prize in Economics in 1987. According to Solow, new capital is of more value and is more productive than vintage (old) capital. This is because over time there is an improvement in technology and the production of capital is based on this technology.

The assumptions on which the theory has been based are as follows:

(i) The capital output ratio and the capital labour ratios are assumed to be variable.
(ii) There exists perfect competition in both the commodity and the factor markets.
(iii) The remuneration to the factors is equal to their marginal revenue product.
(iv) There exists full employment.

The model emphasizes that in an economy the rate of economic growth is determined by the supply of labour, the stock of capital and the growth of technology over time. The optimum amounts of labour, capital and technology will accomplish for an economy a steady economic growth. If this economic growth has to continue, then in that case there is a need for progress in technology. The theory is based on the concept of diminishing returns.

Hence, the production function can be expressed as:

$$Y = f(L, K, T) \tag{22.9}$$

where Y is national output, GNP, L is supply of labour, K is stock of capital and T is growth of technology over time.

If the growth of technology over time is taken as a constant, then the production function can be written as:

$$Y = f(L, K) \tag{22.10}$$

Assuming constant returns to scale,

$$\Delta Y = MP_L \Delta L + MP_K \Delta K \tag{22.11}$$

where MP_L is marginal physical product of labour and MP_K is marginal physical product of capital.

Divide both sides of equation (22.11) by Y. Thus,

$$\frac{\Delta Y}{Y} = \frac{MP_L}{Y}\Delta L + \frac{MP_K}{Y}\Delta K \tag{22.12}$$

Multiply the first term on the right hand side by $\frac{L}{L}$ and the second term by $\frac{K}{K}$. Thus,

$$\frac{\Delta Y}{Y} = \frac{MP_L L}{Y}\frac{\Delta L}{L} + \frac{MP_K K}{Y}\frac{\Delta K}{K} \tag{22.13}$$

As already discussed, the model assumes that there exists perfect competition in both the commodity and the factor markets and also that the remuneration to the factors is equal to their marginal revenue product (MP_X price of the product). Now $MP_L L$ and $MP_K K$ indicate the total share of labour and capital in the national output.

Thus,
$$MP_L L + MP_K K = Y$$

$$\frac{MP_L L}{Y} + \frac{MP_K K}{Y} = 1 \qquad (22.14)$$

Assume $\frac{MP_K K}{Y} = y$

Thus, $\frac{MP_L L}{Y} = 1 - y$

Substituting for y in equation (22.13), we get

$$\frac{\Delta Y}{Y} = 1 - y\frac{(\Delta L)}{L} + y\frac{(\Delta K)}{K}$$

$$\frac{\Delta Y}{Y} = y\frac{\Delta K}{K} + (1-y)\frac{\Delta L}{L} \qquad (22.15)$$

It is important to note that:

(i) $(MP_K K)/Y$ or y depict the elasticity of output with respect to the changes in the stock of capital assuming that the supply of labour is constant. Thus, it shows the responsiveness of output to the changes in the stock of capital

(ii) $(MP_L L)/Y$ or $y - 1$ depict the elasticity of output with respect to the changes in the supply of labour assuming that the stock of capital is constant. Thus, it shows the responsiveness of output to the changes in the supply of labour.

According to the neo-classical growth theory, given the technology, the rate of economic growth is equal to the elasticity of output with respect to the changes in the stock of capital plus the elasticity of output with respect to the changes in the supply of labour.

The modern economic research does not support the baseline version of the neo-classical growth theory. In addition, there are certain limitations of the model. Entrepreneurship, which is often a catalyst to economic growth, is not taken into account by the model. The model is unable to explain as to how and why there is a growth in technology.

RECAP

- The Harrod–Domar model is a long-run model and has gained popularity as a planning model for the developing economies.
- The natural rate of growth relates to the rate at which the labour force grows implying that when the labour force is large the output is also large.
- The views of Robert Solow, Trevor Swan, James Tobin and many others have been put together as the neo-classical growth theory.
- According to the neo-classical growth theory, given the technology, the rate of economic growth is equal to the elasticity of output with respect to the changes in the stock of capital plus the elasticity of output with respect to the changes in the supply of labour.

BUSINESS CYCLES AND STABILIZATION

What Are Business Cycles?

Often, economists make a distinction between economic changes in the short run in production and economic growth in the long run. Business cycles relate to economic changes in the short run in production. In production, there occur booms and busts over time. The booms and busts may occur due to many reasons including an overproduction of goods, which may lead to an accumulation of inventories, political upheavals, wars and others. These ups and downs in the business cycles lead to fluctuations in the economic growth in the long run.

Figure 22.1 depicts the phases in a business cycle. It starts from a trough going through a phase of recovery and expansion. It is then followed by a phase of prosperity. Once the peak is reached, there follows the recession phase and then the depression. Hence, the cycle starts again with its ups and downs.

The phases in a business cycle are:

(i) **Phase of Prosperity:** In this stage, the economy is in a phase of expansion with an increase in the economic activity. The demand for goods increases and exceeds the supply leading to an increase in the prices. Thus, prices and profits increase with the economy experiencing an inflation. There is an increase in the output and employment. Credit expansion occurs. There is a rise in the standard of living. Thus, there is optimism in the economy with an increase in the GNP. The expansion in the economy goes on till the production levels reach a maximum and the peak is reached, which is the highest level of a business cycle. This is also the boom period.

(ii) **Phase of Recession:** Once the peak is reached, the recession starts. In this stage, there occurs a slowdown in the economic activity. The prices are too high and there is a fall in demand. The profits start decreasing. There is a contraction in credit. The expansion in business and production stops. Businessmen start losing confidence and thus there is a decrease in investments and workers are laid off. The expansion in the economy comes to a standstill. In general, a recession continues for short time.

(iii) **Phase of Depression:** In this stage, there is a decrease in the economic activity and thus a decrease in the output and employment. The prices and profits decrease. There is a fall in the standard of living. A pessimistic atmosphere prevails in the economy with a decrease in the GNP.

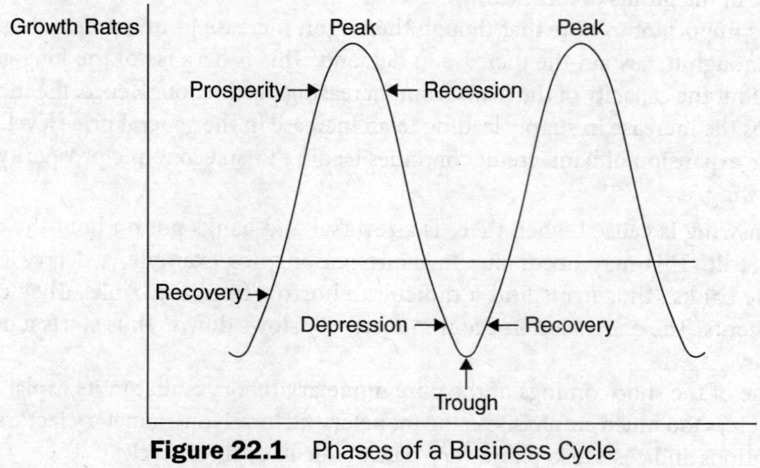

Figure 22.1 Phases of a Business Cycle

The resources in the economy are underutilized and the decline in economic activity continues till the economy reaches the trough. This is the period of shutdowns and unemployment. In the USA, there occurred a Depression in 1929, which affected every sector of the economy.

(iv) **Phase of Recovery:** When the economy starts moving from a depression to an expansion, the recovery phase starts. Economic activity starts rising. The low prices lead to an increase in demand. Businessmen become optimistic leading to an increase in investments. Production levels expand leading to an increase in output and employment. The economy starts recovering and moves towards the phase of prosperity. Hence, the business cycle is repeated.

A business cycle generally moves between periods of expansions and contractions with the peaks and the troughs forming the extremes.

The different phases of a business cycle depict the changes in the level of economic activity, production level, employment levels and others. It has a profound effect on the lives of the investor, employer and the employee.

Theories of Business Cycle

There are many schools of economic thought – classical, monetarists, Keynesian and others – who accept that in a market economy business cycle is a reality. However, the explanation given to these cycles differ depending on their perception of the working of the market. Hence, the solution to these business cycles and the stabilization policies will vary.

Some of the business cycle theories are:

Pure Monetary Theory

According to this theory, the basic cause of business cycles is the fluctuations in the bank credit and the supply of money in the economy.

In a modern economy, the supply of money in the economy is influenced by the creation of credit by the banking system.

(i) An upswing is caused when there is an expansion in the bank credit. The conditions in the economy are conducive for credit creation. The rates at which the loans are offered are low. Thus, firms borrow from the banks and increase their investments leading to capital formation. There is an increase in the profits of business.

It is important to note that though there is an increase in investment, however, the supply is not enough to sustain the increase in demand. This is because of the long gestation periods, which limit the capacity of the firms from increasing production. Hence, the increase in demand outstrips the increase in supply leading to an increase in the general price level.

The expansion of bank credit continues leading to an economic prosperity, thus sustaining the upswing.

(ii) A downswing is caused when there is a reversal and banks put on hold the expansion in the bank credit. This may occur due to many reasons, for example, a decrease in the deposits with the banks. Thus firms find it difficult to borrow from the banks. They cut back on their investments. The expansion in economic activity slows down. Thus starts a downswing in the economy.

One of the shortcomings of the pure monetary theory is that in its explanation of business cycles it lays too much emphasis on the monetary factors. Non-monetary factors such as business expectations and costs also play a very crucial role in business cycles.

Monetary Overinvestment Theory

The theory has been presented by Professor Hayek. The industries fall under two categories, consumer goods industries and capital goods industries, which produce machinery and equipment. According to this theory, there occurs an expansion in the economy when the expansion in the capital goods industry is greater than the expansion in the consumer goods industry. In a similar manner, there occurs a contraction in the economy when the contraction in the capital goods industry is greater than the contraction in the consumer goods industry.

The growth of the consumer goods industries are dependent on the consumer's demand. The demand for capital goods depends on the demand for consumer goods and is thus a derived demand. The capital goods industries reflect the demand for consumer goods.

Suppose the market rate of interest is lower than the natural rate of interest. This will lead to an increase in the demand for bank credit and hence there will be an increase in investment in the economy. The level of employment will also increase and ultimately a full employment situation will be achieved. Due to the full employment scenario, the expansion in the capital goods industry will involve a shift of factors from the consumer goods industry to the capital goods industry. Hence, the expansion in the capital goods industry will be greater than the expansion in the consumer goods industry leading to an expansion in the economy.

With an expansion in the economy, the demand for consumer goods will increase leading to an increase in the price of these goods, which now overtakes the increase in the price of the capital goods. Thus, the profitability in the capital goods industry decreases when compared with that in the consumer goods industry. Hence, there is a shift in investment from the capital goods industry to the consumer goods industry. In addition, the contraction in the capital goods industry is greater than the contraction in the consumer goods industry. This results in a contraction in the economy, which will continue until steps are taken to revive the economy. According to the theory, fluctuations in economic activities are caused by overinvestment.

The theory has been criticized on many grounds. It lays undue emphasis on the rate of interest as the most important factor determining investment. Other factors which influence the investment are not considered.

Multiplier–Accelerator Interaction Theory

The Keynesians have attempted to explain the business cycles in terms of the multiplier. According to the multiplier theory, changes in investment cause multiple changes in the level of income and employment thus deepening a depression or heightening a boom. However, the theory is unable to explain the cyclical nature of a business cycle.

According to the accelerator theory, the current level of investment is positively related to the expected rate of growth of the GDP.

According to J. R. Hicks and Professor Samuelson, the different phases of a business cycle can be explained in terms of the interaction between the accelerator and the multiplier. While the multiplier shows how changes in investment cause multiple changes in the level of income and employment, the accelerator shows how the current level of investment is positively related to the expected rate of growth of the GDP.

To understand the theory, it is assumed that there is an injection of a certain quantity of autonomous investment in the economy. Due to the multiple effect, this leads to an increase in income, which is equal to the multiplier times the increase in investment.

Due to the increase in income, there occurs an increase in the demand for consumer goods. This increase in the demand induces the firms to increase their investment in capital goods. This is called derived investment, which is investment undertaken to cater to the increase in the demand for consumer goods. Due to the accelerator, the increase in investment by the firms would be greater than the increase in the demand for consumer goods. This leads to a further increase in the income level. Thus, an upswing of the business cycle is set in due to the interaction of the accelerator and the multiplier.

A downswing of the business cycle is set in due to the reverse working of both the multiplier and the accelerator.

The model has been criticized in that it is based on some very simple assumptions and also in that it ignores the importance of consumer's preferences and producer's expectations in a business cycle.

Schumpeter's Innovation Theory

Joseph Schumpeter, an Austrian economic theoretician, published a paper *The Explanation of the Business Cycles* in 1927. Schumpeter explained business cycles in terms of industrial innovations.

Innovations may involve a change in the method of production, transportation or in the industrial organization, new markets, etc. Whatever the reason for the innovation, the result is economic prosperity. Thus, non-monetary factors are the cause of the booms as industrial history also depicts.

Starting with an initial equilibrium in the economy, suppose a new technique of production is discovered, which leads to an increase in productivity. To finance this new technique, firms need funds and hence they go to the banks for credit. With these funds, the firms increase their demand for the factors of production.

It is important to note that since there are no unemployed resources in the economy, the increase in the demand for the factors of production will lead to an increase in their price. Other firms in the economy also adopt the innovation. Thus due to the new technique, there will be an increase in the output initiating the phase of economic expansion and economic growth. However, beyond a certain stage, the effects of the innovation will wear off and firms will start paying back to the banks the money that they had borrowed. The supply of money in the economy will contract. A recession commences. This continues until the economy reaches equilibrium.

Schumpeter's innovation theory suffers from the fact that its explanation of business cycles is in terms of innovation. It neglects the role played by the other factors in a business cycle.

Many other theories have been presented to explain the business cycles, for example, Hicks' theory of trade cycle and under consumption theories.

Stabilization Policies

The world over, business cycles have played havoc with the lives of people. The ups and downs, which accompany a business cycle, lead to fluctuations in the level of income, output employment and price levels. Hence, the governments and central banks of the different countries are evolving ways to tackle the problems associated with these cycles.

Stabilization means controlling the ups and downs of a business cycle without interfering in any way with the economic growth of the country. Thus, it involves the application of economic policies, which do not in any way obstruct the functioning of the economy and, in fact, encourages an optimum utilization of the resources of an economy.

Stabilization policies are also called counter-cyclical policies as they are used to counteract the ups and downs of the business cycles. The two most common economic policies, which are used to achieve stabilization, are:

(i) Monetary policy
(ii) Fiscal policy

The policies have been discussed in detail in Chapter 25.

During the expansionary phases of a business cycle to counteract the effects of a rising inflation, contractionary policies are used. While contractionary fiscal policy involves an increase in taxes or a decrease in government expenditure, contractionary monetary policy involves an increase in the rate of interest or a decrease in money supply.

During the contractionary phases of a business cycle accompanied by rising unemployment, to stimulate the economy, expansionary policies are used. While expansionary fiscal policy involves an increase in government expenditure or a decrease in taxes, expansionary monetary policy involves an increase in the money supply or a decrease in the rate of interest.

Monetary Policy

Monetary policy is an operation by the monetary authorities of the country to achieve certain well-defined macroeconomic objectives/goals. It is generally the central bank of the country, which undertakes the implementation of the monetary policy. It operates through changes in the quantity of money, interest rates and credit rationing.

The main objectives, which the monetary policy aims at achieving, include economic growth, a higher rate of employment, stable prices, equality in the distribution of income and wealth, a stable balance of payments and many others depending on the need of the time.

To achieve these objectives, monetary policy has at its disposal instruments, which give the central bank the power to control the money supply and hence achieve these objectives.

Quantitative Measures of Monetary Policy

The quantitative measures control the total volume of credit and the cost of credit in the economy and hence the expansion or contraction in the total amount of credit and thus the supply of money.

Open Market Operations

It is the sale and purchase of government securities and treasury bills by the central bank. It is an instrument of monetary control, which is the most powerful and which is most widely used by the central bank. The central bank carries out the open market operations through the commercial banks. Hence, these operations affect the bank deposits and reserves and thus influence their capacity to create money.

Variations in Reserve Requirements

Commercial banks maintain a certain proportion of their time and demand liabilities in the form of cash reserves. These can be divided under two heads:

(i) **Required Reserves:** These are cash balances, which banks hold to meet their statutory reserve requirements. This is a legal requirement imposed on the banks by the central bank.

(ii) **Excess Reserves:** These are reserves in excess of the required reserves.

Statutory Liquidity Requirement

Besides the cash reserve ratio (CRR), banks are subject to control through yet another requirement, the statutory liquidity ratio (SLR) as it is often known. Under the SLR, banks are statutorily required to maintain a certain fixed proportion of their demand and time liabilities in the form of designated liquid assets.

Bank Rate Policy

The bank rate or the discount rate is the rate of interest at which the central bank rediscounts eligible bills of exchange or other commercial papers. When the banks are short of reserves, they borrow from the central bank by getting their bills of exchange rediscounted.

Repo Rate and Reverse Repo Rate

The repo rate is the rate at which the central bank infuses short-term liquidity into the system. The reverse repo rate is the rate at which banks park their short-term excess liquidity with the central bank in exchange for government securities.

Qualitative or Selective Measures of Monetary Policy

The qualitative measures control the direction and distribution of credit in the economy. Some qualitative credit control measures are:

Rationing of Credit

Credit rationing is resorted to when there occurs a shortage of institutional credit. The sectors, which may in fact be in dire need of funds, may not be able to procure them. To prevent such a situation from occurring, the central bank may resort to credit rationing.

Change in Margin Requirements

The margin requirement specifies the minimum maintainable ratio of the value of the securities charged to the amount borrowed. Changes in margin requirements are used to control speculative activities.

Moral Suasion

This is a combination of persuasion and pressures, which a central bank asserts to bring the erring banks in line so that they function in accordance with the central bank's directives.

Direct Action

This refers to the coercive actions resorted to by the central bank against those banks which do not function according to its directives.

Fiscal Policy

Fiscal policy refers to the government's policy regarding government expenditure, taxation and public borrowing with the view to achieving certain well-defined macroeconomic objectives. To implement fiscal policy, the government has at its behest several instruments.

Taxation

One of the most important sources of revenue for the government in most countries is taxation. Taxes can be analysed under two headings:

Direct taxes include *corporate income taxes*, personal *income tax and taxes on wealth and property; Indirect taxes* include *sales tax*, *excise duty* and *customs duty.*

Government Expenditure

It was realized that government expenditure is imperative for an economy in the form of investments in capital goods industries, building the infrastructure and payments of wages and salaries.

Public Borrowing

Public borrowing is the second most important source of revenue.

Stabilization in the Economy

In any economy, due to the business cycles, there are many ups and downs causing the instability in the economy.

Automatic Stabilizer

An automatic stabilizer is a built-in mechanism in any economy, which automatically reduces the change in the output in response to a change in the level of the autonomous demand. The changes in the taxes and in the government expenditures vary automatically and in the desired direction to bring about stability in the economy.

> An automatic stabilizer is a built-in mechanism in any economy, which automatically reduces the change in the output in response to a change in the level of the autonomous demand.

The business cycles are often caused due to the changes in the level of the autonomous demand, particularly, investment. At some times, the investors are optimistic and go in for high levels of investment while at other times the investors are pessimistic and go in for low levels of investment. The automatic stabilizer diminishes the effects on the output level due to the swings in the investment. There is no deliberate action or interference by the government to bring about stability.

Two automatic stabilizers are:

(i) **Proportional Income Tax:** When the gross national product of an economy increases, the tax revenue increases automatically because some tax payers progress into the higher income and tax brackets. When the gross national product of an economy decreases, the tax revenue decreases automatically because some tax payers retreat into the lower brackets. Hence, the tax revenues automatically move in the requisite direction, thus bringing about stabilization in the economy.

(ii) **Unemployment Benefits:** In many economies, unemployment benefits are paid to the workers, who are without a job. These make it possible for the unemployed to consume even during a recession. Hence, there is no decrease in the level of consumption and in aggregate demand. As a result, output remains stable even during recessions due to the unemployment benefits. On the other hand, during a boom, the number of unemployed falls and hence there is a decrease in the unemployment benefits. Hence, the increases in the level of consumption and in aggregate demand are controlled to some extent. Thus, output remains stable even during periods of boom.

Existence of automatic stabilizers reduces the fluctuations, which occur in the output due to the business cycles. However, a major limitation of automatic stabilizers is that though they can prevent a downturn in the output level from becoming worse, but they cannot prevent a downturn from taking place. This is because they come into effect only when a downturn has occurred. Hence, they cannot, on their own, prevent a downturn and initiate an upturn.

Discretionary Fiscal Policy

It refers to the deliberate changes in the government expenditure and the tax rates by the government in an economy in order to bring about stability in the economy.

It is important to note that the above explanation of discretionary fiscal policy is more applicable for a developed country, where the main concern is with stabilization. However, as far as a developing country is concerned, the discretionary fiscal policy would be designed more towards achieving economic development.

A major limitation in the implementation of fiscal policy is the time lag involved in its implementation. Not only is there a delay in making decisions relating to the fiscal policy actions to achieve a particular goal, even once the decision has been made there are innumerable delays in the implementation and the execution of the policies. The time lag involved at the different stages of the fiscal policy actions leads to a decrease in the effectiveness of the policy.

RECAP

- Business cycles relate to economic changes in the short run in production.
- The phases in a business cycle are: phase of prosperity, phase of recession, phase of depression and phase of recovery.
- Some of the business cycle theories are: the pure monetary theory, monetary overinvestment theory, multiplier–accelerator interaction theory and Schumpeter's innovation theory.
- Stabilization policies are also called counter-cyclical policies as they are used to counteract the ups and downs of the business cycles.
- The two most common economic policies, which are used to achieve stabilization, are: monetary policy and fiscal policy.

SUMMARY

INTRODUCTION

1. It was in the early 1930s and the 1940s that attempts were made to develop a theory of economic growth.
2. The foundations for a theory of economic growth were laid by Evsey D. Domar in the USA and Sir Roy Harrod in the UK.

ECONOMIC GROWTH

Concept of Economic Growth

1. Economic growth refers to an increase in the amount of goods and services, which are produced in an economy over time.
2. To measure the economic growth, the percentage increase in the Gross Domestic Product (GDP) is calculated.
3. If economic growth is to be adjusted for inflation, it can be measured in real terms; otherwise, it can be measured in nominal terms.
4. If the purpose of focusing on economic growth rests on the desire to bring about improvements in the standard of living in an economy, then in that case economic growth could be defined in terms of a sustained increase in the per capita national product over time.
5. For making comparisons between countries in relation to economic growth, the per capita GDP or the per capita GNP should be compared.

FACTORS DETERMINING ECONOMIC GROWTH

The factors that affect the economic growth are as follows:

1. **Development of Technology:** Technology is the skill and expertise involved in the production of a good.
2. **Formation of Capital and Development of the Infrastructure:** Capital formation refers to that fraction of the present income, which is set aside as savings and invested so that there is an increase in the future level of output and income in the economy.

3. **Human Capital:** Human capital is the level of knowledge and the skill of the labour.
4. **Natural Resources:** Natural resources are those objects that are present naturally and are of tremendous use to mankind.
5. **Other Factors:** Social factors, which include the customs and the traditions prevailing in the society, affect economic growth.

THEORIES OF ECONOMIC GROWTH

1. The earlier schools of thought like mercantalism laid emphasis on the wealth of the ruler and the accumulation of gold.
2. The Physiocrats developed the economic theory called physiocracy, which emphasized that the source of wealth of a nation was its productive capacity.
3. This chapter focuses on two theories. The Harrod–Domar theory of growth was presented by two famous economists, Sir Roy Harrod of the UK and Evesey Domar of the USA in the late 1930s. The neo-classical theory of economic growth came in the 1950s.

Harrod–Domar Theory of Growth

1. The Harrod–Domar model is a long-run model, which is an extension of the Keynesian model of income and employment.
2. It has gained popularity as a planning model for the developing economies.
3. One of the main approaches to development is to mobilize the savings, both domestic and foreign.
4. Savings are imperative not only for the replacement of the worn-out existing capital goods, but also to make new additions to the stock of capital.
5. The accumulation of capital is the key to the achievement of the economic growth.
6. Capital accumulation plays a dual role in economic growth:
   (a) It leads to an increase in the productive capacity by increasing the economy's total capital stock.
   (b) It leads to the generation of income in that those who are engaged in the production of the capital goods experience an increase in their income levels.
7. It is important to note that the additional demand for the goods and services should be sufficient to absorb the increase in output from the additional productive capacity installed in the economy.
8. It is necessary that this condition is satisfied year after year if the economy has to achieve a steady economic growth and full employment in the long run.
9. If the condition is not satisfied, then problems may crop up in the form of idle capacity in production. This is the crux of the Harrod–Domar model.
10. The Harrod–Domar model is based on certain assumptions:
    (a) The output/capital ratio, k, is assumed to be constant. It can be expressed as $Y = kK$. Thus, $Y = k\Delta K = kI$.
    (b) The national savings S, is assumed to be a fixed proportion of the GNP or the national output. Thus, $S = sY$.

    In equilibrium, the desired savings are equal to the desired investment, $S = sY = I$.
11. Also $W_G = ks$, where W_G is the warranted rate of growth.
12. The natural rate of growth relates to the rate at which the labour force grows implying that when the labour force is large the output is also large. Thus,

$$N_G = m + \frac{\Delta L}{L}$$

13. The limitations of the model are as follows:
    (a) In equilibrium, the desired savings are equal to the desired investment. This is possible only under very stringent and unrealistic conditions.

(b) Some of the parameters used in the model like the marginal propensity to save and development of labour-saving techniques of production are determined outside the model. Hence, in the long run, the model may not be able to achieve the equilibrium level of the growth rate.
(c) The model was formulated for the problems relating to the developed countries and was not meant to address the problems of the developing countries, which are of a different nature.

14. The model cannot be given up due to the above problems. With some modifications, it can be applied even to solve the problems of the developing countries.

Neo-Classical Growth Theory

1. The views of Robert Solow, Trevor Swan, James Tobin and many others have been put together as the neo-classical growth theory, which was developed in the 1950s.
2. The assumptions on which the theory has been based are:
   (a) The capital output ratio and the capital labour ratios are assumed to be variable.
   (b) There exists perfect competition in both the commodity and the factor markets.
   (c) The remuneration to the factors is equal to their marginal revenue product.
   (d) There exists full employment.
3. The model emphasizes that in an economy the rate of economic growth is determined by the supply of labour, the stock of capital and the growth of technology over time.
4. $\frac{\Delta Y}{Y} = y\frac{\Delta K}{K} + (1-y)\frac{\Delta L}{L}$

   According to the neo-classical growth theory, the rate of economic growth is equal to the elasticity of output with respect to the changes in the stock of capital plus the elasticity of output with respect to the changes in the supply of labour, given the technology.
5. The modern economic research does not support the baseline version of the neo-classical growth theory.
6. In addition, there are certain limitations of the model. Entrepreneurship, which is often a catalyst to economic growth, is not taken into account by the model. The model is unable to explain as to how and why there is a growth in technology.

BUSINESS CYCLES AND STABILIZATION

What Are Business Cycles?

1. Business cycles relate to economic changes in the short run in production.
2. In production, there occur booms and busts over time.
3. The booms and busts may occur due to many reasons including an overproduction of goods, which may lead to an accumulation of inventories, political upheavals, wars and others.
4. These ups and downs in the business cycles lead to fluctuations in economic growth in the long run.
5. The phases in a business cycle are:
   (a) **Phase of Prosperity:** In this stage, the economy is in a phase of expansion with an increase in the economic activity. The expansion in the economy goes on till the production levels reach a maximum and the peak is reached, which is the highest level of a business cycle.
   (b) **Phase of Recession:** Once the peak is reached, there starts the recession. In this stage, there starts a slowdown in the economic activity. The expansion in the economy comes to a standstill. In general, a recession continues for short time.
   (c) **Phase of Depression:** In this stage, there is a decrease in the economic activity. The resources in the economy are underutilized and the decline in economic activity continues till the economy reaches the trough. This is the period of shutdowns and unemployment.
   (d) **Phase of Recovery:** When the economy starts moving from a depression to an expansion, the recovery phase starts. Economic activity starts rising. The economy starts recovering and moves towards the phase of prosperity. Hence, the business cycle is repeated.

6. A business cycle generally moves between periods of expansions and contractions with the peaks and the troughs forming the extremes.
7. The different phases of a business cycle depict the changes in the level of economic activity, production level, employment levels and others. It has a profound effect on the lives of the investor, employer and the employee.

Theories of Business Cycle

1. There are many schools of economic thought – classical, monetarists, Keynesian and others – who accept that in market economy business cycles is a reality. However, the explanation given to these cycles differ depending on their perception of the working of the market. Hence, the solution to these business cycles and the stabilization policies will vary.
2. **Pure Monetary Theory:** According to this theory, the basic cause of business cycles is the fluctuations in the bank credit and the supply of money in the economy.
3. An upswing is caused when there is an expansion in the bank credit. The conditions in the economy are conducive for credit creation. The rates at which the loans are offered are low. Thus, firms borrow from the banks and increase their investments leading to capital formation. There is an increase in the profits of business. The expansion of bank credit continues leading to an economic prosperity, thus sustaining the upswing.
4. A downswing is caused when there is a reversal and banks put on hold the expansion in the bank credit. Thus, firms find it difficult to borrow from the banks. They cut back on their investments. The expansion in economic activity slows down.
5. One of the shortcomings of the pure monetary theory is that in its explanation of business cycles it lays too much emphasis on the monetary factors. Non-monetary factors such as business expectations and costs also play a very crucial role in business cycles.
6. **Monetary Overinvestment Theory:** The theory has been presented by Professor Hayek. The industries fall under two categories, consumer goods industries and capital goods industries.
7. According to this theory, there occurs an expansion in the economy when the expansion in the capital goods industry is greater than the expansion in the consumer goods industry.
8. In a similar manner, there occurs a contraction in the economy when the contraction in the capital goods industry is greater than the contraction in the consumer goods industry.
9. The theory has been criticized because of its assumption of unemployment, which is not realistic. Also, the theory lays undue emphasis on the rate of interest as the most important factor determining the investment. Other factors, which influence the investment, are not considered.
10. **Multiplier–Accelerator Interaction Theory:** The Keynesians have attempted to explain the business cycles in terms of the multiplier.
11. According to the multiplier theory, changes in investment cause multiple changes in the level of income and employment, thus deepening a depression or heightening a boom. However, the theory is unable to explain the cyclical nature of a business cycle.
12. According to the accelerator theory, the current level of investment is positively related to the expected rate of growth of the GDP.
13. According to J. R. Hicks and Professor Samuelson, the different phases of a business cycle can be explained in terms of the interaction between the accelerator and the multiplier.
14. While the multiplier shows how changes in investment cause multiple changes in the level of income and employment, the accelerator shows how the current level of investment is positively related to the expected rate of growth of the GDP.
15. The model has been criticized in that it is based on some very simple assumptions and also in that ignores the importance of consumer's preferences and producer's expectations in a business cycle.
16. **Schumpeter's Innovation Theory:** Schumpeter explained business cycles in terms of industrial innovations. Innovations may involve a change in the method of production, transportation or in the industrial organiza-

tion, new markets, etc. Whatever the reason for the innovation, the result is economic prosperity. Thus, non-monetary factors are the cause of the booms.

17. Schumpeter's innovation theory suffers from the fact that its explanation of business cycles is in terms of innovation. It neglects the role played by the other factors in a business cycle. Many other theories have been presented to explain the business cycles, for example, Hicks' theory of trade cycle and under consumption theories.

Stabilization Policies

1. The world over, business cycles have played havoc with the lives of people.
2. The ups and downs, which accompany a business cycle, lead to fluctuations in the level of income, output employment and price levels.
3. Hence, the governments and central banks of the different countries are evolving ways to tackle the problems associated with these cycles.
4. Stabilization means controlling the ups and downs of a business cycle without interfering in any way with the economic growth of the country.
5. Thus, it involves the application of economic policies, which do not in any way obstruct the functioning of the economy and, in fact, encourages an optimum utilization of the resources of an economy.
6. Stabilization policies are also called counter-cyclical policies as they are used to counteract the ups and downs of the business cycles.
7. The two most common economic policies, which are used to achieve stabilization, are:
   (a) Monetary policy
   (b) Fiscal policy
8. During the expansionary phases of a business cycle to counteract the effects of a rising inflation, contractionary policies are used to dampen the economy.
9. While contractionary fiscal policy involves an increase in taxes or a decrease in government expenditure, contractionary monetary policy involves an increase in the rate of interest or a decrease in money supply.
10. During the contractionary phases of a business cycle accompanied by rising unemployment, to stimulate the economy, expansionary policies are used.
11. While expansionary fiscal policy involves an increase in government expenditure or a decrease in taxes, expansionary monetary policy involves an increase in the money supply or a decrease in the rate of interest.

Monetary Policy

1. Monetary policy is an operation by the monetary authorities of the country to achieve certain well-defined macroeconomic objectives/goals.
2. It is generally the central bank of the country, which undertakes the implementation of the monetary policy.
3. It operates through changes in the quantity of money, interest rates and credit rationing.
4. To achieve these objectives, monetary policy has at its disposal instruments, which give the central bank the Power to control the money supply and hence achieve these objectives.

Quantitative Measures of Monetary Policy

Open Market Operations

It is the sale and purchase of government securities and treasury bills by the central bank.

Variations in Reserve Requirements

Commercial banks maintain a certain proportion of their time and demand liabilities in the form of cash reserves. These can be divided under two heads: *Required Reserves:* These are cash balances, which banks hold to meet their statutory reserve requirements. This is a legal requirement imposed on the banks by the central bank; *Excess Reserves:* These are reserves in excess of the required reserves.

Statutory Liquidity Requirement

Under the SLR, banks are statutorily required to maintain a certain fixed proportion of their demand and time liabilities in the form of designated liquid assets.

Bank Rate Policy

The bank rate or the discount rate is the rate of interest at which the central bank rediscounts eligible bills of exchange or other commercial papers.

Repo Rate and Reverse Repo Rate

The repo rate is the rate at which the central bank infuses short-term liquidity into the system. The reverse repo rate is the rate at which banks park their short-term excess liquidity with the central bank in exchange for government securities.

Qualitative or Selective Measures of Monetary Policy

The quantitative measures control the total volume of credit and the cost of credit in the economy. Some qualitative credit control measures are:

Rationing of Credit

Credit rationing is resorted to when there occurs a shortage of institutional credit.

Change in Margin Requirements

The margin requirement specifies the minimum maintainable ratio of the value of the securities charged to the amount borrowed.

Moral Suasion

This is a combination of persuasion and pressures, which a central bank asserts to bring the erring banks in line so that they function in accordance with the central bank's directives.

Direct Action

This refers to the coercive actions resorted to by the central bank against those banks which do not function according to its directives.

Fiscal Policy

1. Fiscal policy refers to the government's policy regarding government expenditure, taxation and public borrowing with the view to achieving certain well-defined macroeconomic objectives.
2. To implement the fiscal policy, the government has at its behest several instruments.

Taxation

One of the most important sources of revenue for the government in most countries is taxation.

Government Expenditure

It was realized that government expenditure is imperative for an economy in the form of investments in capital goods industries, building the infrastructure and payments of wages and salaries.

Public Borrowing

Public borrowing is the second most important source of revenue.

Stabilization in the Economy

In any economy, due to the business cycles, there are many ups and downs causing instability in the economy.

Automatic Stabilizer

1. An automatic stabilizer is a built-in mechanism in any economy, which automatically reduces the change in the output in response to a change in the level of the autonomous demand.

2. The changes in the taxes and in the government expenditures vary automatically and in the desired direction to bring about stability in the economy.
3. Two automatic stabilizers are:
   (i) **Proportional Income Tax:** When the Gross National Product of an economy increases, the tax revenue increases automatically because some tax payers progress into the higher income and tax brackets. When the Gross National Product of an economy decreases, the tax revenue decreases automatically because some tax payers retreat into the lower brackets. Hence, the tax revenues automatically move in the requisite direction, thus bringing about stabilization in the economy.
   (ii) **Unemployment Benefits:** In many economies, unemployment benefits are paid to the workers who are without a job. These make it possible for the unemployed to consume even during a recession. Hence, there is no decrease in the level of consumption and in aggregate demand. As a result, output remains stable even during recessions due to the unemployment benefits.
4. Existence of automatic stabilizers reduces the fluctuations, which occur in the output due to the business cycles.
5. However, a major limitation of automatic stabilizers is that though they can prevent a downturn in the output level from becoming worse, but they cannot prevent a downturn from taking place.
6. Discretionary fiscal policy refers to the deliberate changes in the government expenditure and the tax rates by the government in an economy in order to bring about stability in the economy.
7. A major limitation in the implementation of fiscal policy is the time lag involved in its implementation.

REVIEW QUESTIONS

TRUE OR FALSE QUESTIONS

1. The neo-classical growth theory was presented by two famous economists, Sir Roy Harrod of the UK and Evesey Domar of the USA in the late 1930s.
2. Business cycles relate to economic changes in the long run in production.
3. During the phase of prosperity, the economy is in a phase of expansion with an increase in the economic activity.
4. According to the pure monetary theory, the different phases of a business cycle can be explained in terms of the interaction between the accelerator and the multiplier.
5. Stabilization policies are also called counter-cyclical policies.

SHORT ANSWER QUESTIONS

1. What are business cycles?
2. Depict the different phases of a business cycle in a diagram.
3. What are stabilization policies? Discuss.
4. What is an automatic stabilizer? How does it bring about stability in the economy?
5. To implement the fiscal policy, the government has at its behest several instruments. Discuss.

LONG ANSWER QUESTIONS

1. What is economic growth? What are the factors that determine economic growth?
2. 'The Harrod–Domar model is a long-run model'. Comment.
3. Discuss the neo-classical growth theory.
4. What are business cycles? What are the different phases in a business cycle?
5. How is monetary policy used to achieve the stabilization in an economy? Discuss.

ANSWERS

TRUE OR FALSE QUESTIONS

1. **False.** The Harrod–Domar theory of growth was presented by two famous economists, Sir Roy Harrod of the UK and Evesey Domar of the USA in the late 1930s.
2. **False.** Business cycles relate to economic changes in the short run in production.
3. **True.** During the phase of prosperity, the demand for goods increases and exceeds the supply leading to an increase in the prices. Thus, prices and profits increase with inflation in the economy. There is an increase in the output and employment.
4. **False.** According to the pure monetary theory, the basic cause of business cycles is the fluctuations in the bank credit and the supply of money in the economy.
5. **True.** Stabilization policies are also called counter-cyclical policies as they are used to counteract the ups and downs of the business cycles.

Theory of International Trade, Trade Policy and Foreign Exchange

23

After studying this chapter, you should be able to understand:

- ✓ *The classical approach considered the differences in productive efficiencies between nations as the reason for the motivation to trade between countries.*
- ✓ *When two countries are involved in trade with each other producing only those goods in which they have an absolute advantage, it results in an increased production for the two combined.*
- ✓ *According to the Heckscher–Ohlin theory of trade, international trade takes place due to the comparative advantage in the cost of production, which can be explained in terms of differences in factor endowments between countries.*
- ✓ *The 'terms of trade' is the rate at which the goods of one country are exchanged for the goods of another country.*
- ✓ *The measures of the terms of trade are net barter terms of trade, gross barter terms of trade and income terms of trade.*
- ✓ *Under free trade, there is no interference by the government in matters relating to trade. There is a free and an unhindered movement of goods and services between countries.*
- ✓ *The most commonly used form of protection for trade is in the form of tariffs.*
- ✓ *Tariffs are levied by a country on its exports and imports to influence not only the direction but also the pattern and volume of trade.*
- ✓ *In a foreign exchange market, foreign currency (or foreign exchange) is purchased and sold by individuals, firms, commercial banks and the central banks of the different countries.*
- ✓ *Two types of foreign exchange transactions are spot transaction and forward transaction.*
- ✓ *The exchange rate reflects the purchasing power of one country's currency in terms of the purchasing power of another country's currency.*
- ✓ *Two nominal exchange rate systems are flexible or floating exchange rate system and fixed exchange rate system.*
- ✓ *As to how the exchange rate is determined will depend on whether the exchange rates system is a flexible or a fixed exchange rate system.*
- ✓ *In a flexible exchange rate system, the equilibrium rate of exchange is determined at the point at which the demand for foreign exchange equals the supply of foreign exchange.*
- ✓ *Under a fixed exchange rate, the exchange rate is set by the government in consultation with the other concerned countries.*
- ✓ *There are gains and losses connected with both the major exchange rate systems, fixed and flexible exchange rate.*

INTRODUCTION

One of the most important questions that the theory of international trade has to deal with is as to what determines the trade that takes place between the different countries. What do the countries gain by trading?

One of the earliest explanations of international trade to emerge was the mercantilist doctrine in the UK from 1500 to 1800. According to this doctrine, the government of a country could increase its wealth by the acquisition of precious metals, especially gold. In addition, to extract the gains from trade, the government should control trade such that exports were a maximum and imports were a minimum.

Today, all economies are open and dealing in transactions with the rest of the world. They all are involved in the export and import of goods and services. They are also engaged in borrowing and lending in the financial markets of the different countries.

These different countries have their own currencies, which are generally (the exception being the Euro) legal tender only within the territories of the country. While the rupee is acceptable within India, the dollar is acceptable within the US economy. The problem occurs when one country trades with another. This problem can be solved by fixing the rate of exchange between the different currencies. Here, we discuss the determination of the foreign exchange rate and also the fixed and the flexible exchange rates.

CLASSICAL APPROACH

The classical approach did not accept the mercantilist doctrine. It was argued that the main source of wealth for a nation was its domestic production. Thus, the differences in productive efficiencies between nations were considered as the reason for the motivation to trade between countries. The two classical theories, which gained popularity were, Adam Smith's theory of absolute advantage and Ricardo's theory of comparative advantage.

Adam Smith's Theory of Absolute Advantage

Adam Smith published his famous book *An Inquiry into the Nature and Causes of the Wealth of Nations* in 1776, in which he promoted the doctrine of *laissez faire*, which encouraged a market which could function without any interference.

The mercantilist doctrine had advocated trade as a zero sum game, where the gain of one country is the loss of another country. According to Adam Smith gain in trade is a positive sum game, where each of the participating countries gains from trade. He used the concept of absolute advantage, where each country specializes in the production of a commodity in which it is more efficient than the other countries. It may have a natural advantage in the production of the good in terms of climatic conditions and the availability of natural resources or labour. For example, the land and climate in India are very suitable for the production of cotton while in Brazil it is suitable for the production of coffee. It may also have an acquired advantage in the technological process involved in the production of the good. For example, the handicrafts of India are famous all over the world.

> Adam Smith published his famous book *An Inquiry into the Nature and Causes of the Wealth of Nations* in 1776, in which he promoted the doctrine of *laissez faire*, which encouraged a market which could function without any interference.

> Adam Smith used the concept of absolute advantage, where each country specializes in the production of a commodity in which it is more efficient than the other countries.

The theory of absolute advantage is of the view that the intervention by the government should be at a minimum whether it is trade or the economic activity in a country. The invisible hand, according to Adam Smith, would act as a guide in maximizing the welfare of the individual and thus of the society.

A simple example of two countries and two commodities can be used to show as to how the countries can gain from trade. Assume that two countries, India and China, possess the same quantity of resources, say 1000 units, which are utilized to produce either iron ore or electronic goods. Further assume, in India, to produce one tonne of iron ore, 40 units of the resources are required and that to produce one unit of the electronic goods 50 units of the resources are required. Also assume that in China, to produce one tonne of iron ore, 50 units of the resources are required and that to produce one unit of the electronic goods 40 units of the resources are required.

India can produce

(i) Twenty-five tonnes of iron ore and 0 units of electronic goods.
(ii) Twenty units of electronic goods and 0 tonne of iron ore.
(iii) A combination of iron ore and electronic goods.

China can produce

(i) Twenty tonnes of iron ore and 0 units of electronic goods.
(ii) Twenty-five units of electronic goods and 0 tonne of iron ore.
(iii) A combination of iron ore and electronic goods.

It is obvious from the above that while India has an absolute advantage in the production of iron ore China has an absolute advantage in the production of electronic goods. Hence, India should specialize in the production of iron ore while China should specialize in the production of electronic goods. In such a situation, both the countries will reap the gains from producing and trading in those goods in which they have an absolute advantage.

Suppose the two countries remain in isolation and do not indulge in trade with each other. We can simplify our example by assuming that each country devotes half of its resources to the production of iron ore and the rest half of its resources to the production of electronic goods.

In the absence of trade,

(i) India can produce 12.5 tonnes of iron ore and 10 units of electronic goods.
(ii) China can produce 10 tonnes of iron ore and 12.5 units of electronic goods.
(iii) India and China can jointly produce 22.5 tonnes of iron ore and 22.5 units of electronic goods.

When the two countries are involved in trade with each other, India will specialize in the production of iron ore while China will specialize in the production of electronic goods:

(i) India will produce 25 tonnes of iron ore and import electronic goods from China.
(ii) China will produce 25 units of electronic goods and import iron ore from India.
(iii) India and China will jointly produce 25 tonnes of iron ore and 25 units of electronic goods.

When two countries are involved in trade with each other, producing only those goods in which they have an absolute advantage, it results in an increased production for the two combined. The increase in production would be:

(i) 2.5 (25–22.5) tonnes of iron ore.
(ii) 2.5 (25–22.5) units of electronic goods.

Ricardian Theory of Comparative Advantage

Ricardo did not disagree with Adam Smith's analysis. If one country has an absolute advantage, over another country, in the production of a good while the other country has an absolute advantage, over the first country, in the production of another good, the two countries can gain from trade.

The problem to be faced is when one country is more efficient than the other country in all lines of production. David Ricardo tackled this problem in his book *On the Principles of Political Economy and Taxation* in 1817. Ricardo believed that even if one country is more efficient in the production of both the goods, both the countries would gain from trading with each other. Hence, trade flows are determined by the comparative advantage, which a country has in the production of a good relative to the other country.

> Ricardo believed that even if one country is more efficient in the production of both the goods, both the countries would gain from trading with each other.

Our example of two countries and two commodities can be used to show as to how the countries can gain from trade. Assume that our two countries, India and China, possess the same quantity of resources, say 1000 units, which are utilized to produce either iron ore or electronic goods. Further assume, that in India, to produce one tonne of iron ore, 80 units of the resources are required and that to produce one unit of the electronic goods, 90 units of the resources are required. Also, assume that, in China, to produce one tonne of iron ore, 120 units of the resources are required and that to produce one unit of the electronic goods, 100 units of the resources are required.

According to Ricardo's theory, when compared with China, India has an absolute advantage in the production of iron ore because it takes 80 units of the resources to produce one tonne of iron ore. However, in China, it takes 120 units of the resources to produce one tonne of iron ore.

Similarly, when compared with China, India also has an absolute advantage in the production of electronic goods because it takes 90 units of the resources to produce one unit of the electronic good. However, in China, it takes 100 units of the resources to produce one unit of the electronic good.

India has a comparative advantage in the production of iron ore since she can produce one tonne of iron ore with only $80/120 \times 100 = 67$ per cent of the effort required in China. However, to produce one unit of the electronic good in India, it takes $90/100 \times 100 = 90$ per cent of the effort required in China.

China has an absolute disadvantage in the production of both iron ore and electronic goods. However, it has a comparative advantage in the production of electronic goods. China can produce one unit of the iron ore with $120/80 \times 100 = 150$ per cent of the effort required in India. However, to produce one unit of the electronic goods in China, it takes $100/ 90 \times 100 = 111$ per cent of the effort required in India. Thus, China is comparatively more efficient in producing electronic goods than in iron ore. It has a greater absolute disadvantage in the production of iron ore and a comparative advantage in the production of electronic goods.

We can compare the ratios of the cost of production of the two goods in both the countries. If the two ratios differ, then there is a basis for trade between the two countries. For example, the ratio of the cost of production of iron ore, in both the countries, in our example, is $80/120 = 0.67$ while the ratio of the cost of production of electronic goods is $90/100 = 0.9$. Since the two ratios are different, one country will have a comparative advantage in the production of one good while the other country will have a comparative advantage in the production of the other good.

To analyse the gains from trade, we initially assume that the two countries are in isolation. Both the countries produce and consume their own production of the two goods, iron ore and electronic goods.

In India, it takes 80 units of the resources to make one ton of iron ore. However, it takes 90 units of the resources to make one unit of electronic goods. This implies that in India per unit electronic goods must be more expensive than iron ore. One tonne of iron ore will cost $80/90 = 0.89$ units of electronic goods.

In China, it takes 120 units of the resources to make one tonne of iron ore. However, it takes 100 units of the resources to make one unit of electronic goods. This implies that in China per unit iron ore must be more expensive than electronic goods. One tonne of iron ore will cost 120/100 = 1.2 units of electronic goods.

Suppose we now examine the possibility of trade between the two countries. If China could import, from India, one unit of iron ore at a price, which is <1.2 units of the electronic goods, she could gain from trade. If India could import, from China, more than 0.89 units of electronic goods in exchange for one tonne of iron ore, she could also gain from trade.

Suppose that in the international market the exchange rate is one tonne iron ore for one unit of electronic goods. In this case, China would export electronic goods and import iron ore. If China does not go in for trade, then in that case it would have to use 120 units of the resources to produce one tonne of iron ore. The alternative for China is to produce one unit of the electronic good by using 100 units of the resources and then to exchange it for one tonne of iron ore, through trade. In the process, it would save 20 units of the resources, which can be used to produce more electronic goods and hence China would be better off.

Similarly, India could export iron ore and import electronic goods. If India does not go in for trade, then in that case it would have to use 90 units of the resources to produce one unit of the electronic goods. The alternative for India is to produce one unit of iron ore by using 80 units of the resources and then exchanging it for one unit of the electronic goods, through trade. In the process, she would save 20 units of the resources, which can be used to produce more electronic goods and hence India would be better off.

Through trade, each country is able to specialize in the production of the good in which it has a comparative advantage. It can then exchange these goods for those in which it has a comparative disadvantage. Thus, in this manner each country, given its resources, can consume more with trade than without trade.

The Ricardian theory of comparative advantage has often been criticized:

(i) It assumes that labour is the only factor of production. However, to produce goods, other factors like capital are also required.

(ii) Resources are assumed to be mobile only within the country and immobile internationally. However, this is not true in a world where factors of production often move between countries.

(iii) Differences in transport costs are not taken into consideration in the theory.

(iv) The theory does not take into consideration the demand side of trade. According to this theory as long as there exists a comparative advantage, trade will take place. It concentrates only on the supply side of trade. Later, other economists introduced the relevance of the demand side in trade.

RECAP

- Adam Smith used the concept of absolute advantage, where each country specializes in the production of a commodity in which it is more efficient than the other countries.
- When two countries are involved in trade with each other producing only those goods in which they have an absolute advantage, it results in an increased production for the two combined.
- Ricardo believed that even if one country is more efficient in the production of both the goods, both the countries would gain from trading with each other.
- Trade flows are determined by the comparative advantage, which a country has in the production of a good relative to the other country.
- If the two ratios of the cost of production of the two goods in both the countries differ, then there is a basis for trade between the two countries.

HECKSCHER–OHLIN THEORY OF TRADE

According to the Ricardian theory of comparative advantage, international trade takes place due to the comparative advantage in the cost of production.

The Heckscher–Ohlin theory of trade was developed by the Swedish economist Eli Heckscher in 1919 and later developed further by another Swedish economist Bertil Ohlin in 1933. According to this theory, international trade takes place due to the comparative advantage in the cost of production, which can be explained in terms of differences in factor endowments between countries. Thus, the basis of trade is the differences in factor endowments between countries.

> According to the Heckscher–Ohlin theory of trade, international trade takes place due to the comparative advantage in the cost of production, which can be explained in terms of differences in factor endowments between countries.

As far as factor endowments are concerned, according to the theory, only labour and capital are considered. While some countries are abundant in labour, others are abundant in capital. Countries that are abundant in labour will have a comparative cost advantage in the production of those goods, where the technology is labour intensive. Hence, these countries, such as India and China, will export labour-intensive goods. Similarly, countries that are abundant in capital will have a comparative cost advantage in the production of those goods, where the technology is capital intensive. Hence, countries, such as the USA, will export capital-intensive goods.

For the Heckscher–Ohlin theory to hold there should be two countries, *I* and *II*, two goods, *x* and *y*, and two factors of production, labour (*L*) and capital (*K*). The model is based on certain assumptions:

(i) There exist no transport costs or any other barriers to trade. Hence, the prices of the goods will be the same in both the countries.

(ii) In both the countries, there exists perfect competition, in the factor markets and the goods market. Hence, the factors of production will be allocated optimally.

(iii) The factors of production, labour and capital, are homogenous. Also, the countries differ as far as the availability of the factors of production is concerned.

(iv) The production functions are homogenous of degree one.

(v) While the technology for production for good *x* is labour intensive, the technology for production for good *y* is capital intensive.

The Heckscher–Ohlin theory implies that there will occur an equalization of the factor prices under free trade. This is called the Heckscher–Ohlin factor price equalization theorem. Due to free trade, the differences in factor prices between countries are eliminated.

As far as the meaning of factor abundance is concerned, there can be two alternative definitions:

(i) Factor abundance in terms of factor prices. According to this definition, Country *I* is abundant in capital when compared with Country *II* if capital is comparatively cheaper in country *I* than in Country *II*. Thus, country *I* is capital abundant if

$$\frac{P_L^I}{P_K^I} < \frac{P_L^{II}}{P_K^{II}}$$

where P_L^I is the price of labour in country *I*, P_K^I is the price of capital in country *I*, P_L^{II} is the price of labour in country *II* and P_K^{II} is the price of capital in country *II*.

(ii) Factor abundance in physical terms. According to this definition, Country *I* is abundant in capital when compared with Country *II* if the ratio of capital to labour is comparatively greater in country *I* than in Country *II*. Thus, country *I* is capital abundant if

$$\frac{K^I}{L^I} > \frac{K^{II}}{L^{II}}$$

where K^I is the total amount of capital in Country *I*, L^I is the total amount of labour in Country *I*, K^{II} is the total amount of capital in Country *II* and L^{II} is the total amount of labour in Country *II*.

Autarky Equilibrium

To analyse the effect of factor abundance, we have the production possibility curve in Figure 23.1. It is assumed that

(i) While the production for good *x* is labour intensive, the production for good *y* is capital intensive.

(ii) Country *I* is abundant in labour and Country *II* is abundant in capital.

Figure 23.1 depicts the autarky equilibrium (no trade situation) through the production possibility curves, the indifference curves and the factor price line.

The production possibility curve of Country *I*, which is the labour abundant country, is shown by *I–I′*. It shows that with the given resources Country *I* is in a position to produce a larger quantity of good *x*, which is labour intensive when compared with good *y*, which is capital intensive.

The production possibility curve of Country *II*, which is the capital abundant country, is shown by *II–II′*. It shows that with the given resources Country *II* is in a position to produce a larger quantity of good *y*, which is capital intensive when compared with good *x*, which is labour intensive.

The indifference map for the two countries is represented by the curves I_1, I_2 and I_3. The lines *jj′* and *mm′* are the factor price lines for Country *I* and Country *II*, respectively, assuming that factor prices remain constant.

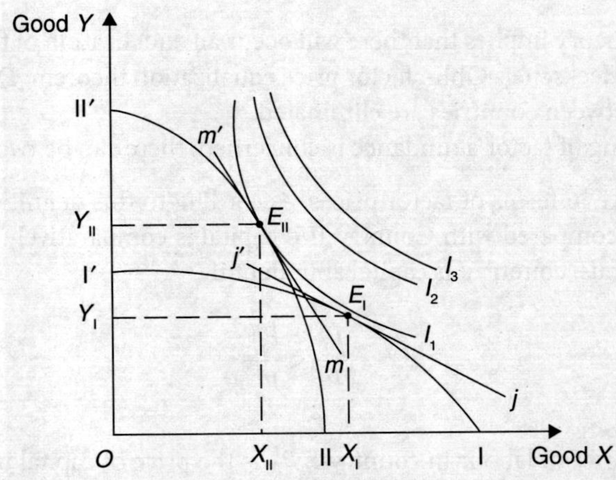

Figure 23.1 Autarky Equilibrium

The figure shows that

(i) Under autarky, Country *I* is in equilibrium at point E_I, where the indifference curve I_1 and the factor price line *jj′* are tangential to the production possibility curve of Country *I*, *I–I′*. At this point,

$$MRT^{I}_{xy} = MRS^{I}_{xy} = \frac{P^{I}_{K}}{P^{I}_{L}}$$

where MRT^{I}_{xy} is the marginal rate of transformation between goods *x* and *y* given by the slope of the production possibility curve of Country *I*, *I–I′*, MRS^{I}_{xy} is the marginal rate of substitution between goods *x* and *y* given by the slope of the indifference curve I_1, $\frac{P^{I}_{K}}{P^{I}_{L}}$ is the slope of the factor price line *jj′*.

At point E_I, Country *I* produces and consumes Ox_I units of good *x* and Oy_I units of good *y*.

(ii) Under autarky, Country *II* is in equilibrium at point E_{II}, where the indifference curve I_1 and the factor price line *mm′* are tangential to the production possibility curve of Country *II*, *II–II′*. At this point,

$$MRT^{II}_{xy} = MRS^{II}_{xy} = \frac{P^{II}_{K}}{P^{II}_{L}}$$

where MRT^{II}_{xy} is the marginal rate of transformation between goods *x* and *y* given by the slope of the production possibility curve of Country *II*, *II–II′*, MRS^{II}_{xy} is the marginal rate of substitution between goods *x* and *y* given by the slope of the indifference curve I_1, $\frac{P^{II}_{K}}{P^{II}_{L}}$ is the slope of the factor price line *mm′*.

At point E_{II}, Country *II* produces and consumes Ox_{II} units of goods *x* and Oy_{II} units of good *y*.

It is obvious from the above analysis that, in autarky,

(i) A country which is abundant in labour, Country *I*, produces and consumes more of the labour-intensive good *x* ($x_I > x_{II}$).

(ii) A country which is abundant in capital, Country *II*, produces and consumes more of the capital-intensive good *x* ($y_{II} > y_I$).

Equilibrium with Trade

Suppose our two countries are now in a position to trade with each other. Figure 23.2 illustrates the Heckscher–Ohlin theorem.

According to the theorem, countries that are abundant in labour will have a comparative cost advantage in the production of those goods, where the technology is labour intensive and thus will export labour-intensive goods, which are comparatively cheaper to produce. Hence, on the one hand, the demand for labour will increase leading to an increase in the price of labour and on the other hand, the demand for capital will decrease leading to a decrease in the price of capital. There will be a change in the factor price ratio, with the factor price line now approaching *kk′*. Thus, in Figure 23.2, Country *I*, which is a labour-intensive country, experiences a rightward shift in its equilibrium, along the production possibility curve, from point E_I to point T_I.

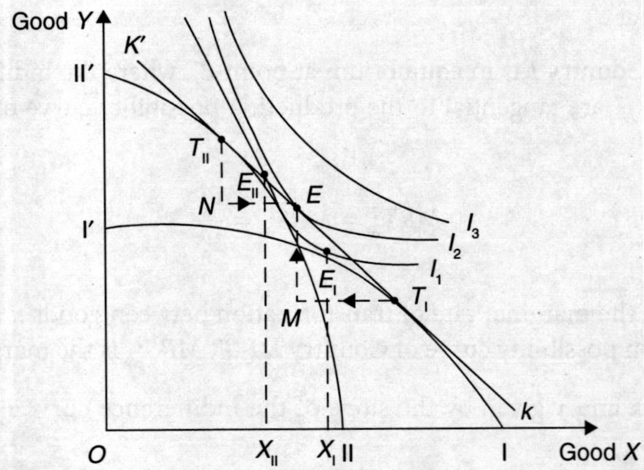

Figure 23.2 Heckscher–Ohlin Trade Theorem

On the other hand, countries that are abundant in capital will have a comparative cost advantage in the production of those goods, where the technology is capital intensive and thus will export capital-intensive goods. Hence, on the one hand, the demand for capital will increase leading to an increase in the price of capital and on the other hand, the demand for labour will decrease leading to a decrease in the price of labour. There will be a change in the factor price ratio, with the factor price line now approaching *kk′*. Thus, in Figure 23.2, Country *II*, which is a capital-intensive country, experiences an upwards shift in its equilibrium, along the production possibility curve, from point E_{II} to point T_{II}.

The above analysis depicts that

(i) A labour-intensive country, like Country *I*, will specialize in the production of the labour-intensive good *x*. A capital-intensive country, like Country *II*, will specialize in the production of the capital-intensive good *y*.

(ii) The larger is the degree of specialization the greater will be the amount of trade between the two countries. The degree of specialization will continue to increase until the marginal rates of transformation between goods *x* and *y*, given by the slope of the production possibility curves, are the same in both the countries.

In Figure 23.2, at point T_I, the production possibility curve of Country *I*, *I–I′* is tangential to the factor price line *kk′*. Similarly, at point T_{II}, the production possibility curve of Country *II*, *II–II′* is tangential to the factor price line *kk′*. Since both are tangential to the same line *kk′*, it implies that the slopes of the two production possibility curves are equal at the points T_I and T_{II}.

As far as the gains from trade are concerned, both the countries will gain from trade as shown by the trade patterns of triangles EMT_I and ENT_{II}:

(i) Country *I*, which is in equilibrium at point T_I will move along triangle EMT_I exporting T_IM units of good *x* and importing *ME* units of good *y*. Hence, after trade, Country *I* will be in equilibrium at point *E* on a higher indifference curve I_2.

(ii) Country *II*, which is in equilibrium at point T_{II} will move along triangle ENT_{II} exporting $T_{II}N$ units of good *y* and importing *NE* units of good *x*. Hence, after trade, Country *II* will be in equilibrium at point *E* on a higher indifference curve I_2.

The Heckscher–Ohlin theorem has often been criticized:

(i) The assumption that there exist no transport costs is not realistic. In fact, it has been shown that the inclusion of transport costs in the analysis does affect the volume of trade.

(ii) The assumption regarding the existence of perfect competition is again doubtful in that there exists imperfect competition in most of the world markets.

(iii) The factors of production, labour and capital are assumed to be homogenous. However, the factors of production are different in quality and thus difficult to compare and measure.

RECAP

- According to the Heckscher–Ohlin theory of trade, international trade takes place due to the comparative advantage in the cost of production which can be explained in terms of differences in factor endowments between countries.
- Countries that are abundant in labour will have a comparative cost advantage in the production of those goods, where the technology is labour intensive. Hence, these countries will export labour-intensive goods.
- Countries that are abundant in capital will have a comparative cost advantage in the production of those goods, where the technology is capital intensive. Hence, these countries will export capital-intensive goods.
- According to the Heckscher–Ohlin factor price equalization theorem, there will occur an equalization of the factor prices under free trade.

TERMS OF TRADE

In the literal sense, the 'terms of trade' refers to the relative price between two goods or a group of goods. We can be more specific and define the 'terms of trade' as the rate at which the goods of one country are exchanged for the goods of another country. The measures of the terms of trade are:

The 'terms of trade' can be defined as the rate at which the goods of one country are exchanged for the goods of another country.

Net Barter Terms of Trade

Given by Taussig and Viner, it is one of the most commonly used measures of the terms of trade. It can be written as

$$T_N = \frac{P_X}{P_M}$$

where T_N is net barter terms of trade, P_X is price of exports and P_M is price of imports.

A comparison of the net barter terms of trade at two points in time yields the trends in the terms of trade.

Gross Barter Terms of trade

This measure was again given by Taussig and Viner and is one of the key measures of the terms of trade. It was developed to overcome the deficiency in the net barter terms of trade. Instead of relating the prices of exports and imports, it relates the quantities of exports and imports. It can be written as

$$T_G = \frac{M}{X}$$

where T_G is Gross Barter Terms of Trade, X is quantity of exports and M is quantity of imports.

If $M < X$, the terms of trade will be favourable. If $M > X$, the terms of trade will be unfavourable.

When there is a balance in the trade between two countries, then the net barter terms of trade is equal gross barter terms of trade

$$T_N = T_G$$

Or
$$\frac{P_X}{P_M} = \frac{M}{X}$$

Thus,
$$P_X \times X = P_M \times M$$

The implications of the above are as follows:

(i) If the price and quantity of imports are constant, that is P_M and M are constant, and there is an increase in the price of exports, P_X, in that case the terms of trade will be favourable and to balance the trade a smaller quantity of exports, X, will be required.

(ii) If the price and quantity of imports are constant, that is P_M and M are constant, and there is a decrease in the price of exports, P_X, in that case the terms of trade will be unfavourable and to balance the trade a larger quantity of exports, X, will be required.

(iii) If the price and quantity of exports are constant, that is P_X and X are constant, and there is an increase in the price of imports, P_M, in that case the terms of trade will be unfavourable and to balance the trade a larger quantity of imports, M, will be required.

(iv) If the price and quantity of exports are constant, that is P_X and X are constant, and there is a decrease in the price of imports, P_M, in that case the terms of trade will be favourable.

Income Terms of Trade

The income terms of trade can be written as

$$T_I = \frac{P_X \times X}{P_M}$$

where T_I = Income terms of trade.

The income terms of trade is considered to be a step more advanced than the net barter terms of trade as far as the underdeveloped countries are concerned.

RECAP

- The 'terms of trade' is the rate at which the goods of one country are exchanged for the goods of another country.
- The measures of the terms of trade are net barter terms of trade, gross barter terms of trade and income terms of trade.

TRADE POLICY

The trade policy relates to the rules, regulations and measures, which are adopted by a country in relation to its exports and imports. Often, there is a controversy surrounding the trade policy in that whether a country should pursue a policy of free trade or that there should be a policy of trade protection.

Policy of Free Trade

Adam Smith was one of the first economists to advocate the policy of free trade. Under free trade, there is no interference by the government in matters relating to trade. There is a free and an unhindered movement of goods and services between countries. The arguments in favour of free trade are as follows:

(i) As already explained in the theory of comparative advantage through trade, each country is in a position to specialize in the production of the good in which it has a comparative advantage. It can then exchange these goods for those in which it has a comparative disadvantage. It can consume more with trade than without trade, especially where there exists a free trade. Thus, in this manner each country, given its resources, is able to enjoy a larger national product, a better availability of goods and services and an improved standard of living across the globe.

(ii) Free trade prevents an increase in the price of the goods and services, which are imported into the country. In this manner, it prevents monopolies from growing within the country. The domestic industry has to compete with the imports and thus have to increase their competitive efficiency through improved technology and an efficient allocation of resources.

(iii) Free trade leads to a maximization of the production of the goods and services across the globe, a maximization of the economic efficiency across the globe leading to a maximization of the world economic welfare.

Policy of Trade Protection

In spite of the many arguments in favour of free trade, free trade remains to be an idealist situation only theoretically, with most countries indulging in protectionist policies.

The most commonly used form of protection for trade is in the form of tariffs. Tariffs are levied by a country on its exports and imports to influence not only the direction but also the pattern and volume of trade. The arguments in favour of tariffs are as follows:

(i) **Need for a Balanced Growth:** According to the theory of comparative advantage, each country should specialize in the production of the good in which it has a comparative advantage. If one goes by this argument, the countries would specialize only in the production of a very limited range of goods, which it can then exchange for those goods, which it needs from the other countries of the world. Thus, the country, in question, is dependent on the other countries of the world for many of its requirements.

Such a trade policy may lead to a very comfortable situation in the country as long as there are no major upheavals on the global front. In times of World Wars, depressions and recessions and also political upheavals between countries, such countries will be left stranded and unable to meet its requirements.

In such countries, tariffs are advocated on the grounds that they not only make a country self-reliant but also encourage a balanced growth by providing protection to the industry and its different sectors.

(ii) **Infant Industry Argument:** Often when the industry of an economy is in its early stages, most industries are infants and need support to grow and mature. They need to be nurtured in this infant stage. They should be protected from the competition from the goods of the developed countries, which use the latest technologies to produce the goods not only of the best quality, but also at prices which are lower. This can be done by imposing tariffs on the imports, which are competing with these industries, hence leading to an increase in the price of these imports. Here, it is important to note that the protection should be just a temporary phenomenon, which should be provided only in the infant stage; otherwise, the industry would not be able to come up and survive the international completion.

(iii) **Increase in Employment:** A tariff on the imports of goods, which are in competition with the domestic industries, helps in the growth of these industries including a growth in the employment provided by these industries. This growth spreads further to the industries, which have a link with these industries, thus increasing the employment in these industries also.

RECAP

- The trade policy relates to the rules, regulations and measures, which are adopted by a country in relation to its exports and imports.
- Under free trade, there is no interference by the government in matters relating to trade. There is a free and an unhindered movement of goods and services between countries.
- The most commonly used form of protection for trade is in the form of tariffs.
- Tariffs are levied by a country on its exports and imports to influence, not only the direction, but also the pattern and volume of trade.

FOREIGN EXCHANGE MARKET

The foreign exchange market is a market, where foreign currencies (or foreign exchange) are purchased and sold by individuals, firms, commercial banks and the central banks of the different countries.

The *foreign exchange market* is a market, where foreign currencies (or foreign exchange) are purchased and sold by individuals, firms, commercial banks and the central banks of the different countries.

Types of Foreign Exchange Transactions

Foreign exchange transactions are of two kinds:

Spot Transaction

A spot transaction is one where the seller of the foreign exchange has to deliver the exchange to the buyer on the spot, that is, within two days of the deal.

A *spot transaction* is one where the seller of the foreign exchange has to deliver the exchange to the buyer on the spot, that is, within two days of the deal.

The *spot market* is one, where there are spot sales and purchases of the foreign exchange.

The *spot exchange* rate is the rate at which the foreign exchange is bought and sold in the spot market.

Forward Transaction

A forward transaction is one which involves an agreement between the buyer and the seller to purchase or sell a fixed amount of currency for a predetermined rate at a specified date in the future.

A *forward transaction* is one which involves an agreement between the buyer and the seller to purchase or sell a fixed amount of currency for a predetermined rate at a specified date in the future. Usually, a forward contract is for three months.

The *forward exchange market* is one, where there is a forward sale and purchase of foreign exchange.

The *forward exchange rate* is the rate at which the foreign exchange is bought and sold in the forward exchange market.

Functions of the Foreign Exchange Market

The foreign exchange market performs many functions:

International Transfer of Purchasing Power Between Different Countries

In foreign trade, there are two types of transfers of purchasing power:

(i) From one country to another country.
(ii) From one currency to another currency.

These transfers take place through a clearing mechanism. When a firm in a country exports some goods to a firm in another country, the exporting firm acquires a claim on the foreign firm while the foreign firm is under a debt obligation to the exporting firm. Hence, there arise counter claims, which are settled in the foreign exchange market through bills of exchange.

Provision of Credit for Foreign Trade

Similar to the domestic trade, for the smooth functioning of the foreign trade, credit is essential. There is a considerable time gap involved in the movement of the goods between the exporter and the importer. Hence, there is need for some form of institutional credit to finance the transactions of the goods between the time periods.

Hedging Risks of Foreign Exchange

In a situation when the exchange rate fluctuates freely, any forward foreign exchange transaction will be subject to great risks. To avoid such risks, the buyers and sellers of foreign exchange resort to hedging facilities.

Hedging is an attempt at covering the risk involved in a foreign exchange transaction through a forward transaction. The exporters and importers are subject to risks relating to the exchange rate in conducting their business. This risk can be avoided through a forward transaction where they can enter into an agreement regarding the buying and selling of goods at a future date at a contracted rate of exchange. However, where the rates of exchange are stable over long time, hedging is not required.

> Hedging is an attempt at covering the risk involved in a foreign exchange transaction through a forward transaction.

Some Related Concepts

Arbitrage

It is the simultaneous buying and selling of different foreign currencies in the different foreign exchange markets to take advantage of the difference in the prices. An arbitrageur is the person, who is engaged in these buying and selling of the foreign currencies.

> Arbitrage is the simultaneous buying and selling of different foreign currencies in the different foreign exchange markets to take advantage of the difference in the prices.

Speculation

It is an activity relating to the sale and purchase of foreign exchange in which risk is undertaken to take advantage of the fluctuations in the

> Speculation is an activity relating to the sale and purchase of foreign exchange in which risk is undertaken to take advantage of the fluctuations in the exchange rate.

exchange rate. The speculative buying and selling of the foreign currency depends the speculator's expectations regarding the future exchange rates.

Speculative Attacks

It is a situation, which causes a change in the investors' perception.

Currency board is an arrangement under which the central bank of a country holds enough amount of a foreign currency to back, in a fixed ratio, each and every unit of the domestic currency.

Currency Board

It is an arrangement under which the central bank of a country holds enough amount of a foreign currency to back, in a fixed ratio, each and every unit of the domestic currency. Thus, under a currency board, a country is in a position to commit itself to some strong currency like the dollar. Also, whenever the need arises, it should be ready to convert its own currency to the foreign currency.

Dollarization is a situation, where a country abandons its domestic currency and adopts a strong foreign currency like the dollar.

Dollarization

It is a step further than the currency board, where a country abandons its domestic currency and adopts a strong foreign currency like the dollar. Thus, the domestic currency is converted into the US dollar.

RECAP

- The foreign exchange market performs many functions, which include international transfer of purchasing power between different countries, provision of credit for foreign trade and hedging risks of foreign exchange.

EXCHANGE RATE SYSTEMS

The exchange rate is the rate at which one country's currency exchanges for another country's currency. Hence, it reflects the purchasing power of one country's currency in terms of the purchasing power of another country's currency. It is actually the price at which the residents of one country conduct trade with the residents of another country.

The exchange rate is the rate at which one country's currency exchanges for another country's currency.

One can distinguish between the nominal exchange rate and the real exchange rate. *The nominal exchange rate is the rate at which the currency of one country is traded for the currency of another country.* Thus, it signifies the relative price of one currency *vis-a-vis* the currency of another country. *The real exchange rate is the rate at which the goods of one country are traded for the goods of another country.* Hence, the real exchange rate takes into consideration the relative purchasing power of the currency as well. The real exchange rate is also called the terms of trade.

Two nominal *exchange rate systems are as follows:*

(i) **Flexible or Floating Exchange Rate:** Flexible or floating exchange rate is a system, where the exchange rate fluctuates freely in response to the changes in the economic conditions and without any government intervention. Hence, the exchange rate is determined by the market forces.

(ii) **Fixed Exchange Rate:** Fixed exchange rate is a system, where the exchange rate does not fluctuate in response to the changes in the economic conditions. The exchange rate is maintained through government intervention in the foreign exchange market and also by the central bank through its buying and selling of currencies.

BOX 23.1

Till recently, the countries of East Asia experienced the most impressive growth rates ever possible. However, in the year 1997, there occurred the Asian Crisis, when speculative attacks affected the currencies of these countries. Thailand was the first country, which was forced to devalue its currency followed by South Korea, Indonesia and Malaysia. There was a financial and banking crisis. This attack on the currencies affected these economies adversely in many aspects. By 1999, the financial assistance from the International Monetary Fund and the other world agencies embarked these countries on the path to recovery.

At this stage, a brief history of the exchange rate systems adopted by the different countries is required. When the Second World War ended, there was a need for a new international monetary and exchange rate system, which would promote growth of world trade. Thus, at Bretton Woods, New Hampshire, in the year 1944, delegates from 44 nations converged. They adopted the fixed exchange rate system in which each country pegged its currency to the dollar and since all currencies were pegged to the dollar, they were pegged to each other also. The International Monetary Fund (IMF) and the World Bank were two new organizations, which emerged from the Bretton Woods conference.

There occurred, in succession, many crises in the exchange rate. At a meeting held in 1971 at the Smithsonian Institution in Washington, DC between the finance ministers of the leading countries of the world, the Bretton Woods system was officially dissolved. The dollar was devalued. The major industrial countries of the world adopted the flexible exchange rate in 1973. Thus, as of today, there are many exchange rate arrangements, while some countries operate under the flexible exchange rates, others operate under the floating exchange rates and there are some for whom the exchange rate systems lie somewhere in between.

RECAP

- While the nominal exchange signifies the relative price of one currency vis-á-vis the currency of another country, the real exchange rate takes into consideration the relative purchasing power of the currency as well.
- As of today, there are many exchange rate arrangements, while some countries operate under the flexible exchange rates, others operate under the floating exchange rates and there are some for whom the exchange rate systems lie somewhere in between.

EXCHANGE RATE DETERMINATION

How the exchange rate is determined will depend on whether the exchange rate system is a flexible or a fixed exchange rate system.

Determination of Exchange Rate in a Flexible or Floating Exchange Rate

As already mentioned, the exchange rate is the price of one currency in terms of another currency. *In a flexible exchange rate system, the exchange rate is determined by the market forces of the demand and supply of foreign exchange.* Here, we will consider two countries, say India, as the home country and the USA, as the foreign country and two currencies, rupee and the dollar.

Demand for Foreign Exchange

Foreign exchange is demanded by the citizens of a country to make payments outside the country. From the view point of a country, say India, the demand for foreign exchange (say, dollar) arises to make payments for the following items:

(i) Imports of commodities.
(ii) Imports of services, including banking, insurance, shipping and tourism.
(iii) Interest, royalties, payment for technical services and dividend payments on securities in India owned by the foreigners.
(iv) Expenditures by the government abroad.
(v) Remittances by NRI's of capital out of India from realized capital gains.
(vi) Exports of short-term capital.
(vii) Exports of long-term capital.
(viii) Unrequited payments including gifts to foreigners.
(ix) Gold imports.
(x) Payment to foreign universities for education.

In all these items, perhaps the most important item is the imports of commodities since India, like any other developing country, imports commodities such as petroleum and machinery, which require huge amounts of foreign exchange. In the context of this analysis, as far as India is concerned, the demand for foreign exchange is the demand for dollars.

Figure 23.3 depicts the derivation of the demand curve for foreign exchange. Suppose

(i) Initially, the foreign exchange rate as determined at 1\$ = ₹50 (by autonomous factors). Suppose the price of a basket of goods imported from the USA is \$5 (or ₹250) per unit. Thus, to import 100 units of the good, India's demand for dollars will be \$500 or in other words ₹25,000.
(ii) Suppose that the value of the rupee depreciates in terms of dollars to 1\$ = ₹60. Since the price of the basket of goods imported from the USA is in terms of dollars (which is not affected), it will

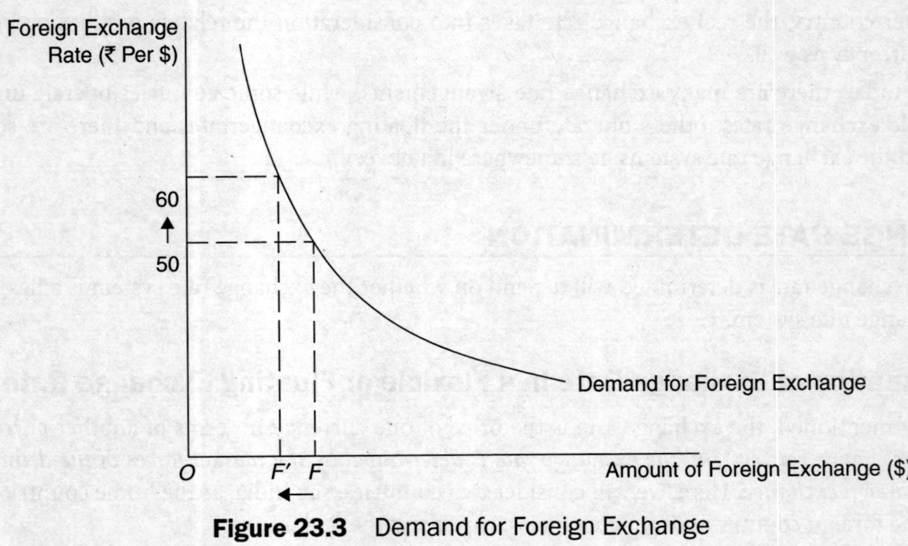

Figure 23.3 Demand for Foreign Exchange

remain at \$5 (or ₹300) per unit. Thus, to import 100 units of the good, India's demand for dollars will also remain unchanged at \$500. But in terms of rupees, India will now have to spend ₹30,000 on its imports from the USA.

The net effect of the depreciation of the rupee will be an increase in the price of imports and hence a decrease in the demand for imports from the USA by India. Hence, there will be a decrease in demand for dollars by India.

In Figure 23.3, an increase in the price of the dollar (or depreciation of the rupee) from 1\$ = ₹50 to 1\$ = ₹60 leads to a decrease in the demand for foreign exchange from *OF* to *OF′*. Hence, an increase in the exchange rate leads to a decrease in demand for the imports from the USA leading to a decrease in demand for the foreign exchange (or dollars), It is obvious from this analysis that the demand curve for foreign exchange (or dollars) will be a downward sloping curve as in Figure 23.3.

The shape and slope of the demand curve for foreign exchange depend on certain factors:

(i) The extent of the decrease in the demand for foreign exchange, in response to an increase in the foreign exchange rate, will depend on *elasticity of demand for the imported goods.* This is because *the demand for foreign currency is a derived demand* in that it is derived from the demand for the foreign goods and services. For a given depreciation of the rupee
 - If the elasticity of demand for the US goods is large, then the decrease in demand for the US imports and thus for the dollar will be high. This is the case especially for luxuries and goods for which there exist substitutes.
 - If the elasticity of demand for the US goods is small, then the decrease in demand for the US imports and thus for the dollar will be small. This is the case especially for necessities and raw materials.

(ii) *The existence of import-competing industries in the country.* If the import-competing industries in the country are well developed, then the elasticity of demand for imports will be high. This is because any increase in the price of imports (due to the depreciation of the domestic currency) will be accompanied by an increase in the share of the import-competing industries and decrease in the share of the imports.

(iii) *Time is also an important factor* here because
 - In the short run, a reallocation of factors of production in response to a price change may be a difficult task. Hence, the elasticity of demand for imports may be low.
 - In the long run, it is possible to reallocate factors of production in response to a price change, and thus to change the production pattern accordingly. Hence, the elasticity of demand for imports may be high.

Supply of Foreign Exchange

The supply of foreign exchange to a country arises from the payments made by the foreigners to the residents of the country within a specified time. From the view point of a country, say India, the supply of foreign exchange (the dollar) arises from payments made for the following items:

(i) Exports of commodities.
(ii) Exports of services, including banking, insurance, shipping and tourism.
(iii) Interest and dividend payments on securities in the USA owned by the Indians.
(iv) Imports of short-term capital.

(v) Imports of long-term capital, including foreign loans to India.
(vi) Unrequited receipts including gifts from foreigners.
(vii) Gold exports.

As far as India is concerned, the supply of foreign exchange is the supply of dollars.

Figure 23.4 depicts the derivation of the supply curve of foreign exchange. Suppose

(i) Initially, the foreign exchange rate as determined at 1\$ = ₹50 (by autonomous factors). Suppose the price of a composite of goods exported by India to the USA is at ₹250 (or \$5) per unit. Thus, if India exports 100 units of the composite good, the supply of foreign exchange to India will be \$500 (25,000/50).

(ii) Suppose that the value of the rupee depreciates in terms of dollars to 1\$ = ₹60. Since the price of the composite of goods exported by India to the USA is in terms of rupees, it will remain at ₹250 (or \$4.17) per unit. Thus, if India exports 100 units of the composite good, the supply of foreign exchange to India will now be \$416.7 (25,000/60).

The net effect of the depreciation of the rupee will be a decrease in the price of the exports and hence an increase in the demand for exports to the USA from India. Hence, there will be an increase in supply of dollars to India.

In Figure 23.4, an increase in the price of the dollar (or depreciation of the rupee) from 1\$ = ₹50 to 1\$ = ₹60 leads to an increase in the supply of foreign exchange from OF to OF_1. Hence, an increase in the exchange rate leads to an increase in demand for the exports from India to the USA leading to an increase in supply of foreign exchange (or dollars). It is obvious from this analysis, the supply curve of foreign exchange (or dollars) will be an upward sloping curve as in Figure 23.4.

The shape and slope of the supply curve of foreign exchange will depend on the elasticity of demand for India's exports to the USA. *The supply of foreign currency is a derived demand in that it is derived from the demand for the exported goods and services.*

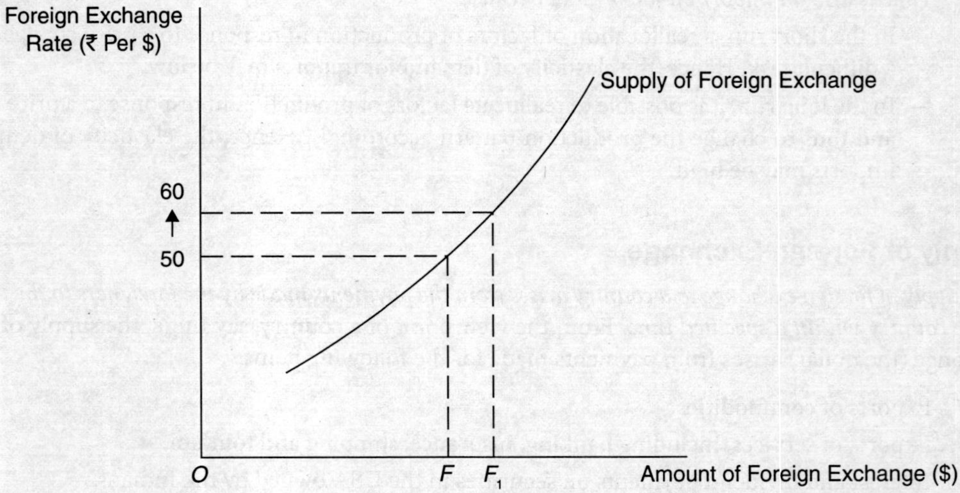

Figure 23.4 Supply of Foreign Exchange

(India's exports to the USA). For a given depreciation of the rupee

(i) If the elasticity of demand for India's exports to the USA is greater than unity, then the supply of foreign exchange to India (or dollar) will increase. Hence, the supply curve for foreign exchange is upward sloping as in Figure 23.4.

(ii) If the elasticity of demand for India's exports to the USA is smaller than unity, then the supply of foreign exchange to India (or dollar) will decrease. Hence, the supply curve for foreign exchange will be downward sloping.

Exchange Rate: Equilibrium

The equilibrium rate of exchange is determined at the point at which the demand for foreign exchange equals the supply of foreign exchange. Thus, it is determined by the unregulated forces of the market demand and market supply. Graphically, it is determined at the point of intersection of the demand and the supply curves of foreign exchange.

In Figure 23.5, the demand curve for foreign exchange (demand for dollars) and the supply curve of foreign exchange (supply of dollars) intersect at point *E*. The equilibrium exchange rate is thus at 1$ = ₹$50 with the equilibrium amount of foreign exchange at *OF*.

In such an exchange rate system, the government intervenes as and when it is required to make sure that the movements in the exchange rate are in order.

Exchange Rate: Disequilibrium

Figure 23.6 depicts the effect of a change in demand on the equilibrium rate of exchange. In the figure,

(i) Initially the demand curve for foreign exchange (demand for dollars) is given by the curve *DD*, while the supply curve of foreign exchange (supply of dollars) is given by the curve *SS*.

The curves *DD* and *SS* intersect to determine equilibrium at point *E*. The equilibrium exchange rate is 1$ = ₹$50 and the equilibrium amount of foreign exchange at *OF*.

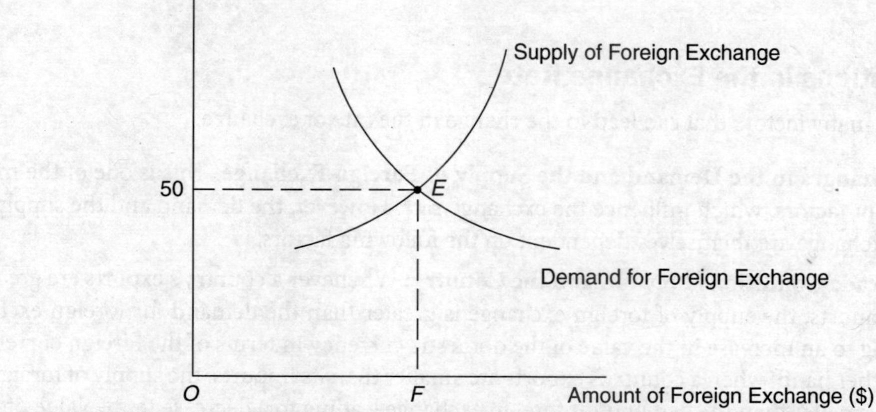

Figure 23.5 Determination of the Equilibrium Exchange Rate Under a Flexible Exchange Rate System

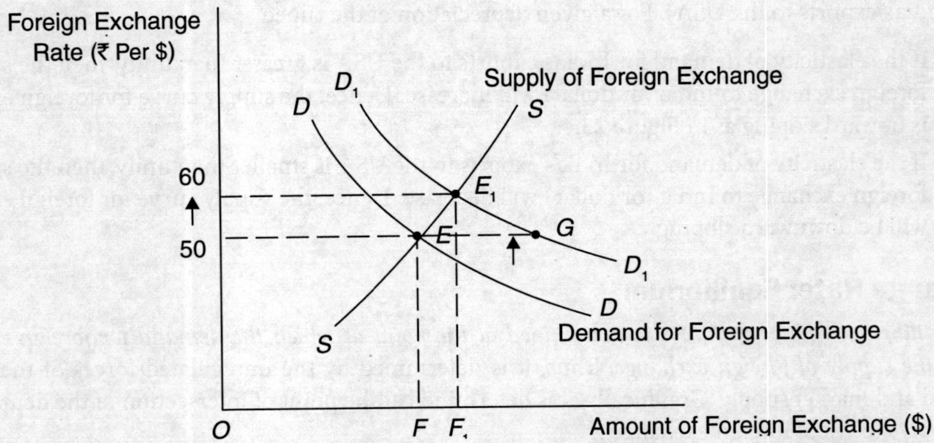

Figure 23.6 An Effect of a Change in Demand on the Equilibrium Exchange Rate

(ii) Suppose the demand curve for foreign exchange shifts outwards to D_1D_1 due perhaps to a change in tastes in India in favour of US goods. The supply curve of foreign exchange (supply of dollars) remains at *SS*.

At the given exchange rate, there occurs an excess demand for foreign exchange (or dollars) equal to *EG*. The foreign exchange market will clear only if there is an increase in the exchange rate to 1$ = ₹$60. Hence, the new equilibrium occurs at point E_1, where the curves D_1D_1 and *SS* intersect. The increase in the exchange rate (depreciation of the rupee), on the one hand, causes a decrease in the demand for India's imports and thus in the demand for dollars and on the other hand, an increase in the demand for India's exports and thus in the supply of dollars. At the new equilibrium exchange rate of 1$ = ₹$60, the equilibrium amount of foreign exchange at OF_1.

In a flexible exchange rate system, the exchange rate varies with changes in the demand and supply of foreign exchange. But, there is always an equilibrium exchange rate at which the demand for foreign exchange equals the supply of foreign exchange creating an external equilibrium.

Fluctuations in the Exchange Rate

There are many factors that can lead to the change in the rate of exchange:

(i) **Changes in the Demand and the Supply of Foreign Exchange:** This is one of the most important factors, which influence the exchange rate. However, the demand and the supply of foreign exchange are themselves dependent on the following factors.

(ii) **Trade Conditions Prevailing in the Country:** Whenever a country's exports are greater than its imports, the supply of foreign exchange is greater than the demand for foreign exchange leading to an increase in the value of the domestic currency in terms of the foreign currency. On the other hand, when a country's exports are smaller than its imports, the supply of foreign exchange is smaller than the demand for foreign exchange leading to a decrease in the value of the domestic currency in terms of the foreign currency.

(iii) **Changes in the Interest Rate in the Domestic Country:** An increase in the interest rates attracts capital leading to an increase in the supply of foreign exchange. Given the demand for foreign exchange, this will lead to an increase in the value of the domestic currency in terms of the foreign currency. On the contrary, a decrease in the interest rates encourages the export of capital leading to a decrease in the supply of foreign exchange. Given the demand for foreign exchange, this will lead to a decrease in the value of the domestic currency in terms of the foreign currency.

(iv) **Arbitrage Operations:** As discussed earlier, an arbitrage involves the simultaneous buying and selling of different foreign currencies in the different foreign exchange markets. The purpose of this exercise is to take advantage of the difference in the prices in the two markets. These operations have a singular impact on the foreign exchange market and in fact help in ensuring that there exists no major variation in the exchange rates in different currency markets.

(v) **Stock Exchange Influences:** If the individuals of a country purchase stocks in another country, there is an increase in demand for foreign currency. Given the supply of foreign currency, this will lead to a decrease in the value of the domestic currency in terms of the foreign currency. If, on the other hand, foreigners purchase stocks in the country, there is an increase in supply of foreign currency. Given the demand for foreign currency, this will lead to an increase in the value of the domestic currency in terms of the foreign currency. The fall in the value of rupee in the fiscal 2008–09 could partly be explained by the flight of foreign capital away from the Indian Stock markets, which, in turn, also sent the market indices spiraling down.

Determination of Exchange Rate in a Fixed Exchange Rate System

Many countries have a fixed exchange rate. In contrast to the flexible exchange rate system, where the demand and supply of foreign exchange determine the exchange rate, *under a fixed exchange rate, the exchange rate is set by the government in consultation with the other concerned countries.*

It is not necessary that the exchange rate set by the government is one, where the demand for foreign exchange is equal to the supply of foreign exchange. Figure 23.7 depicts the determination of the exchange rate under a fixed exchange rate system. The official exchange rate at e_1 is higher than the basic exchange rate determined by the demand and supply of foreign exchange at e. Thus, the exchange rate is overvalued.

The question arises as to *what a country should do when its official exchange rate is higher than the basic exchange rate*? It has several alternatives to choose from:

(i) *Change the value of the official exchange rate* so that it is equal to or nearer to the basic exchange rate. Thus, in Figure 23.7, the country can lower the exchange rate from e_1 to e.

(ii) There can be a *direct intervention on the part of the government* to reduce imports through, say, taxation. Such a policy will decrease the demand for imports shifting the demand curve for foreign exchange raising the basic value of the exchange rate towards the fixed rate.

(iii) *The government of the country could supply or demand its currency in the foreign exchange market.* For example, in Figure 23.7, at the official exchange rate, the supply of foreign exchange is greater than the demand for foreign exchange by the amount *AB*. The government could, in such a situation, buy currency, using official reserve assets like gold.

It is important to note that when the exchange rate of a country is overvalued, then appropriate policy actions will have to be taken because an overvalued exchange rate cannot be sustained for long.

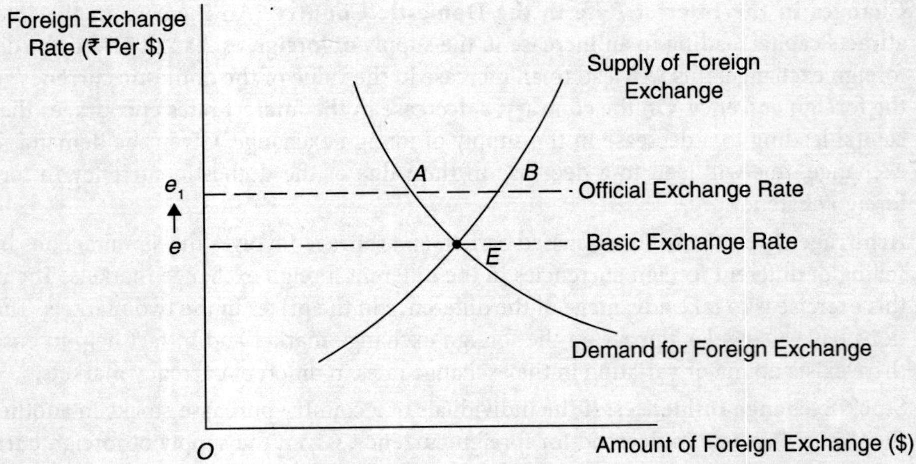

Figure 23.7 Determination of the Exchange Rate Under a Fixed Exchange Rate System

RECAP

- Foreign exchange is demanded by the citizens of a country to make payments outside the country.
- The net effect of the depreciation of the rupee will be on the one hand an increase in the price of imports and hence a decrease in the demand for imports from the USA by India and, on the other hand, a decrease in the price of the exports and hence an increase in the demand for exports to the USA from India.
- The supply of foreign exchange to a country arises from the payments made by the foreigners to the residents of the country within a specified time.

FIXED VERSUS FLEXIBLE EXCHANGE RATE

Most major economies now follow the flexible exchange rate system. Even China, where the Yuan was historically pegged to the dollar, lifted the peg finally in the year 2005. The value of the Yuan is now a managed floating exchange rate based on market demand and supply with reference to a basket of international currencies

It is now the appropriate time for us to evaluate the gains and losses connected with the two major exchange rate systems we have discussed.

BOX 23.2

Often, a group of countries come together to form a currency union, instead of fixing exchange rates. Under the currency union, the countries share a common currency and also agree to cooperate amongst themselves both economically and politically. They thus have a common currency, which not only reduces the costs of trading, but also prevents speculative attacks on the national currencies (which are eliminated in favor of a common currency). The major disadvantage of such a system is that the member countries have to share a common monetary policy and cannot use the monetary policy to pursue individual domestic goals. The euro was the common currency adopted by 11 countries in 1999.

Advantages and Disadvantages of the Fixed Exchange Rate System

Advantages of the fixed exchange rate system are as follows:

(i) It eliminates the uncertainties that are associated with international business transactions and hence creates a confidence in the foreign currency. A fixed exchange rate removes the uncertainties regarding the exchange rate.

(ii) In comparison with the floating exchange rate system, the fixed exchange rate system is simpler to implement because the money supply adjusts itself automatically to the required level.

(iii) It is often able to constrain the inflationary government policies and also acts as a safety device in controlling the import of inflation, which often accompanies a flexible exchange rate system. Since a fixed exchange rate shields an economy from the occurrences in the other countries, it is able to prevent any import of inflation.

(iv) It disciplines a country's monetary authority and thus improves the monetary policy preventing excessive growth in the money supply. Again, this may lead to a lower inflation rate in the long run.

(v) *It facilitates the movements of capital between countries* by providing a stability in the exchange rates and creating a confidence in the foreign currencies.

(vi) *It discourages speculative activity*, which is an important feature associated with the flexible exchange rate.

It is important to observe that a fixed exchange rate can be maintained only between countries, which have similar basic economic conditions and similar types of macroeconomic policies.

Disadvantages of the fixed exchange rate system are as follows:

(i) It reduces a country's ability to apply its monetary policy to deal with recessions. This problem is more acute when the different countries under the fixed exchange rate system aim at different policy goals. In fact, there may occur disagreements regarding the goals of monetary policy among the countries under the fixed exchange rate and may ultimately lead to a break down of the entire system.

(ii) As is obvious from the experience of the gold standard and the Bretton Woods systems, a fixed exchange system is rigid and this has unfavourable effects on economies of the countries.

Advantages and Disadvantages of the Flexible Exchange Rate System

Advantages of the flexible or market-determined exchange rate system are as follows:

(i) It enables countries to formulate their macroeconomic policies independently of the other countries. Hence, a country is not required to sacrifice full employment and other goals to achieve an external equilibrium.

(ii) It allows monetary and the fiscal policies to attain goals such as employment, stabilizing prices, etc.

(iii) It provides an automatic and smooth adjustment mechanism for correcting any disequilibrium in the balance of payments of a country concerned through the free market forces of demand and supply.

It seems that empirically the total amount of world trade has increased under the flexible exchange rate system.

Disadvantages of the flexible exchange rate system are as follows:

(i) It increases the uncertainty regarding the future exchange rates, thus affecting adversely the volume of world trade.

(ii) It may lead to speculation and may thus disturb the stability in the system.

(iii) It not only imparts an inflationary bias to the system, but is also not able to *prevent any import of inflation*, which often accompanies a flexible exchange rate system.

As to which exchange rate system is ideal differs according to the circumstances. When a group of countries are able to avail huge benefits from an increased trade and are able to coordinate their monetary policies, a fixed exchange rate system is more suitable. However, countries, which have their own policy goals relating to, for example, unemployment and inflation, should adopt a flexible exchange rate system.

RECAP

- A fixed exchange rate can be maintained only between countries, which have similar basic economic conditions and similar types of macroeconomic policies.
- It seems that empirically the total amount of world trade has increased under the flexible exchange rate system.
- As to which exchange rate system is ideal differs according to the circumstances.

SUMMARY

INTRODUCTION

1. One of the earliest explanations of international trade to emerge was the mercantilist doctrine in the UK from 1500 to 1800.
2. Today, all economies are open and dealing in transactions with the rest of the world.
3. The different countries have their own currencies, which are generally (the exception being the Euro) legal tender only within the territories of the country. While the rupee is acceptable within India, the dollar is acceptable within the US economy.
4. The problem occurs when one country trades with another. This problem can be solved by fixing the rate of exchange between the different currencies. Here, we discuss the determination of the foreign exchange rate and also the fixed and the flexible exchange rates.

CLASSICAL APPROACH

1. The classical approach argued that the main source of wealth for a nation was its domestic production.
2. The differences in productive efficiencies between nations were considered as the reason for the motivation to trade between countries.
3. The two classical theories, which gained popularity, were Adam Smith's theory of absolute advantage and Ricardo's theory of comparative advantage.

Adam Smith's Theory of Absolute Advantage

1. Adam Smith promoted the doctrine of *laissez faire*, which encouraged a market, which could function without any interference.
2. According to Adam Smith, gain in trade is a positive sum game, where each of the participating countries gains from trade.

3. He used the concept of absolute advantage, where each country specializes in the production of a commodity in which it is more efficient than the other countries.
4. The theory of absolute advantage is of the view that the intervention by the government should be at a minimum whether it is trade or the economic activity in a country.
5. When two countries are involved in trade with each other, producing only those goods in which they have an absolute advantage, it results in an increased production for the two combined.

Ricardian Theory of Comparative Advantage

1. Ricardo did not disagree with Adam Smith's analysis.
2. Ricardo believed that even if one country is more efficient in the production of both the goods, both the countries would gain from trading with each other.
3. Trade flows are determined by the comparative advantage, which a country has in the production of a good relative to the other country.
4. We can compare the ratios of the cost of production of the two goods in both the countries.
5. If the two ratios differ, then there is a basis for trade between the two countries.
6. Through trade, each country is able to specialize in the production of the good in which it has a comparative advantage.
7. It can then exchange these goods for those in which it has a comparative disadvantage.
8. Thus, each country, given its resources, can consume more with trade than without trade.
9. The Ricardian theory of comparative advantage has often been criticized.
10. It assumes that labour is the only factor of production. However, to produce goods other factors like capital are also required.
11. Resources are assumed to be mobile only within the country and immobile internationally. However, this is not true in a world, where factors of production often move between countries.
12. Differences in transport costs are not taken into consideration in the theory.
13. The theory does not take into consideration the demand side of trade.

HECKSCHER–OHLIN THEORY OF TRADE

1. The Heckscher–Ohlin theory of trade was developed by the Swedish economist Eli Heckscher in 1919 and later developed further by another Swedish economist Bertil Ohlin in 1933.
2. According to this theory, international trade takes place due to the comparative advantage in the cost of production, which can be explained in terms of differences in factor endowments between countries.
3. The basis of trade is the differences in factor endowments between countries.
4. As far as factor endowments are concerned, according to the theory, only labour and capital are considered.
5. Countries that are abundant in labour will have a comparative cost advantage in the production of those goods, where the technology is labour intensive. Hence, these countries will export labour-intensive goods.
6. Countries that are abundant in capital will have a comparative cost advantage in the production of those goods, where the technology is capital intensive. Hence, these countries will export capital-intensive goods.
7. The Heckscher–Ohlin theory implies that there will occur an equalization of the factor prices under free trade. This is called the Heckscher–Ohlin factor price equalization theorem. Due to free trade, the differences in factor prices between countries are eliminated.
8. According to the theory, a labour-intensive country will specialize in the production of the labour-intensive good x. A capital-intensive country will specialize in the production of the capital-intensive good y.
9. The larger is the degree of specialization, the greater will be the amount of trade between the two countries.
10. The Heckscher–Ohlin theorem has often been criticized.

11. The assumption that there exist no transport costs is not realistic.
12. The assumption regarding the existence of perfect competition is again doubtful in that there exists imperfect competition in most of the world markets.
13. The factors of production, labour and capital are assumed to be homogenous. However, the factors of production are different in quality and thus difficult to compare and measure.

TERMS OF TRADE

1. We can define the 'terms of trade' as the rate at which the goods of one country are exchanged for the goods of another country.
2. The measures of the terms of trade are: net barter terms of trade, gross barter terms of trade and income terms of trade.
3. Net barter terms of trade has been given by Taussig and Viner and is one of the most commonly used measures of the terms of trade. It can be written as:

$$T_N = \frac{P_X}{P_M}$$

4. Gross barter terms of trade was again given by Taussig and Viner and is one of the key measures of the terms of trade.
5. It was developed to overcome the deficiency in the net barter terms of trade. It relates the quantities of exports and imports. It can be written as:

$$T_G = \frac{M}{X}$$

6. The income terms of trade can be written as:

$$T_I = \frac{P_X \times X}{P_M}$$

TRADE POLICY

1. The trade policy relates to the rules, regulations and measures, which are adopted by a country in relation to its exports and imports.
2. Should a country pursue a policy of free trade or a policy of trade protection?

Policy of Free Trade

1. Adam Smith was one of the first economists to advocate the policy of free trade.
2. Under free trade, there is no interference by the government in matters relating to trade.
3. There is a free and an unhindered movement of goods and services between countries.
4. Through trade, each country is in a position to specialize in the production of the good in which it has a comparative advantage. It can then exchange these goods for those in which it has a comparative disadvantage. It can consume more with trade than without trade, especially where there exists a free trade.
5. Free trade prevents an increase in the price of the goods and services, which are imported into the country. In this manner, it prevents monopolies from growing within the country.
6. Free trade leads to a maximization of the production of the goods and services across the globe, a maximization of the economic efficiency across the globe leading to a maximization of the world economic welfare.

Policy of Trade Protection

1. The most commonly used form of protection for trade is in the form of tariffs.
2. Tariffs are levied by a country on its exports and imports to influence, not only the direction, but also the pattern and volume of trade.

3. According to the theory of comparative advantage, each country should specialize in the production of the good in which it has a comparative advantage. However in times of World Wars, depressions and recessions and also political upheavals between countries, such countries will be left stranded and unable to meet its requirements.

   In such countries, tariffs are advocated on the grounds that they not only make a country self-reliant, but also encourage a balanced growth by providing protection to the industry and its different sectors.
4 According to the infant industry argument when the industry of an economy is in its early stages, most industries are infants and need support to grow and mature. They should be protected from the competition from the goods of the developed countries, which use the latest technologies to produce the goods not only of the best quality, but also at prices which are lower. This can be done by imposing tariffs on the imports, which are competing with these industries, hence, leading to an increase in the price of these imports.
5. A tariff on the imports of goods, which are in competition with the domestic industries, helps in the growth of these industries including a growth in the employment provided by these industries.

FOREIGN EXCHANGE MARKET

1. In a foreign exchange market, foreign currencies (or foreign exchange) are purchased and sold by individuals, firms, commercial banks and the central banks of the different countries.
2. Two types of foreign exchange transactions are spot transaction and forward transaction.
3. The foreign exchange market performs many functions, which include international transfer of purchasing power between different countries, provision of credit for foreign trade and hedging risks of foreign exchange.
4. Hedging is an attempt at covering the risk involved in a foreign exchange transaction through a forward transaction.
5. Arbitrage is the simultaneous buying and selling of different foreign currencies in the different foreign exchange markets to take advantage of the difference in the prices.
6. Speculation is an activity relating to the sale and purchase of foreign exchange in which risk is undertaken to take advantage of the fluctuations in the exchange rate.

EXCHANGE RATE SYSTEMS

1. The exchange rate reflects the purchasing power of one country's currency in terms of the purchasing power of another country's currency.
2. The nominal exchange rate is the rate at which the currency of one country is traded for the currency of another country.
3. The real exchange rate is the rate at which the goods of one country are traded for the goods of another country.
4. Two nominal exchange rate systems are flexible or floating exchange rate and fixed exchange rate.
5. Flexible or floating exchange rate is a system, where the exchange rate fluctuates freely in response to the changes in the economic conditions and without any government intervention. Hence, the exchange rate is determined by the market forces.
6. Fixed exchange rate is a system, where the exchange rate does not fluctuate in response to the changes in the economic conditions.

EXCHANGE RATE DETERMINATION

1. As to how the exchange rate is determined will depend on whether the exchange rates system is a flexible or a fixed exchange rate system.
2. In a flexible exchange rate system, the equilibrium rate of exchange is determined at the point at which the demand for foreign exchange equals the supply of foreign exchange.
3. Foreign exchange is demanded by the citizens of a country to make payments outside the country.
4. The net effect of the depreciation of the rupee will be an increase in the price of imports and hence a decrease in the demand for imports from the USA by India.

5. The supply of foreign exchange is a derived demand in that it is derived from the demand for the exported goods and services.
6. The net effect of the depreciation of the rupee will be a decrease in the price of the exports and hence an increase in the demand for exports to the USA from India.
7. Under a fixed exchange rate, the exchange rate is set by the government in consultation with the other concerned countries.

FIXED VERSUS FLEXIBLE EXCHANGE RATE

1. There are gains and losses associated with both the major exchange rate systems, fixed and flexible exchange rate.
2. Advantages of the fixed exchange rate system are it eliminates the uncertainties that are associated with international business transactions, is simpler to implement, and is often able to constrain the inflationary government policies.
3. Disadvantages of the fixed exchange rate system are it reduces a country's ability to apply its monetary policy to deal with recessions and it is rigid.
4. Advantages of the flexible or market-determined exchange rate system are it enables countries to formulate their macroeconomic policies independently of the other countries, it allows monetary and the fiscal policies to attain goals such as employment and stabilizing prices and it provides an automatic and smooth adjustment mechanism for correcting any disequilibrium in the balance of payments.
5. Disadvantages of the flexible exchange rate system are it increases the uncertainty regarding the future exchange rates. It may lead to speculation and also prevent any import of inflation.
6. When a group of countries are able to avail huge benefits from an increased trade and are able to coordinate their monetary policies, a fixed exchange rate system is more suitable. However, countries, which have their own policy goals relating to, for example, unemployment and inflation, should adopt a flexible exchange rate system.

REVIEW QUESTIONS

TRUE OR FALSE QUESTIONS

1. The two classical theories, which gained popularity, were Adam Smith's theory of comparative advantage and Ricardo's theory of absolute advantage.
2. The gross barter terms of trade can be written as

$$T_N = \frac{P_X}{P_M}$$

3. The foreign exchange market is a market, where foreign currencies are purchased and sold.
4. Currency board is an arrangement, where a country abandons its domestic currency and adopts a strong foreign currency like the dollar.
5. The real exchange rate is the rate at which the currency of one country is traded for the currency of another country.

SHORT ANSWER QUESTIONS

1. Write a short note on the terms of trade.
2. What is hedging? Explain.
3. (a) What is the exchange rate? Differentiate between the nominal and real exchange rates.
   (b) Which are the two nominal exchange rate systems? Explain.

4. What are the factors that determine the shape and slope of the demand curve for foreign exchange in a flexible exchange rate system?
5. What are the factors that lead to fluctuations in the exchange rate under a flexible exchange rate system? Explain.

LONG ANSWER QUESTIONS

1. What is Adam Smith's theory of absolute advantage? Explain.
2. What are the functions performed by the foreign exchange market? Discuss.
3. Which are the two nominal exchange rate systems? Analyse with the help of a brief history of the exchange rate systems adopted by the different countries.
4. Explain the determination of the demand for foreign exchange in a flexible or floating exchange rate system.
5. Analyse the determination of the supply of foreign exchange in a flexible or floating exchange rate system.

ANSWERS

TRUE OR FALSE QUESTIONS

1. **False.** The two classical theories, which gained popularity, were Adam Smith's theory of absolute advantage and Ricardo's theory of comparative advantage.
2. **False.** Gross barter terms of trade was given by Taussig and Viner. It relates the quantities of exports and imports. It can be written as $T_G = \dfrac{M}{X}$.
3. **True.** The foreign exchange market is a market, where foreign currencies (or foreign exchange) are purchased and sold by individuals, firms, commercial banks and the central banks of the different countries.
4. **False.** Dollarization is a step further than the currency board, where a country abandons its domestic currency and adopts a strong foreign currency like the dollar. Thus, the domestic currency is converted into the US dollar.
5. **False.** The nominal exchange rate is the rate at which the currency of one country is traded for the currency of another country.

Balance of Payments and the International Monetary System

24

After studying this chapter, you should be able to understand:

- ✓ *The balance of payment is a statement, which summarizes the exports and imports and the other international transactions between the countries.*
- ✓ *The transactions entering into the balance of payments can be grouped under three broad accounts: Current Account, Capital Account and Official International Reserve Account.*
- ✓ *The current account of the balance of payments measures the flow of goods, services and income, which occur across the national borders. The capital account of the balance of payments measures the outflow and inflow of capital into the economy.*
- ✓ *The balance of payments of a country will always balance because of the double entry system of bookkeeping.*
- ✓ *Autonomous transactions are transactions that take place for the satisfaction that they give or for the profit that they yield.*
- ✓ *Accommodating transactions take place for balancing a deficit or surplus in the foreign account.*
- ✓ *The macroeconomic policies that are utilized for correcting disequilibrium in the balance of payments include the expenditure-reducing and expenditure-switching policies.*
- ✓ *Expenditure-reducing policies can be divided under two broad groups: monetary policy and fiscal policy.*
- ✓ *Expenditure-switching policies work mainly through changing the relative price of exports and imports.*
- ✓ *Once the global crisis deepened, it spread to most of the countries including India through the capital and current account of the balance of payments.*

INTRODUCTION

In the earlier chapters, we had developed the model for a closed economy and then moved on to the model of an open economy. However, the discussion was limited to only the economy's exports and imports of goods and services and the affect of a change in the net exports on the aggregate demand and the equilibrium level of income and output. However, there is much more to the international economic relationships than just simple exports and imports of goods and services. Transfer payments between the individuals of the different countries and also the governments are of extreme importance. Capital flows between countries is again important.

The balance of payment is a statement, which summarizes the exports and imports and the other international transactions between the countries. This chapter analyses the different aspects of the balance of payments.

MEANING AND STRUCTURE OF BALANCE OF PAYMENTS

The balance of payments is a summary statement of all the economic transactions between the residents of one country with the rest of the world during a particular time, which is usually a year.

In the balance of payments accounting any transaction that involves a payment by the residents of a country will be shown as a debit item while any transaction that involves a receipt by the residents of a country will be shown as a credit item in the balance of payments of that country.

The balance of payments is a summary statement of all the economic transactions between the residents of one country with the rest of the world during a particular time, which is usually a year.

The transactions entering into the balance of payments can be grouped under three broad accounts:

(i) Current account
(ii) Capital account
(iii) Official international reserve account

Current Account

The current account of the balance of payments measures the flow of goods, services and income, which occur across the national borders. The current account of the balance of payments includes the following items.

The current account of the balance of payments measures the flow of goods, services and income, which occur across the national borders.

Balance of Trade

It includes the export and import of goods (or merchandise). It is also called the balance of visible trade. The balance of trade is the difference between the exports and imports of goods. While exports of goods are entered as a positive entry or credit claims in the balance of payments, imports of goods are entered as a negative entry or debits in the balance of payments.

The balance of trade is the difference between the exports and imports of goods.

The balance of trade is one of the most important components of the balance of payments. It is not necessary for the balance of trade to be always in balance. If in a country:

(i) Exports are greater than the imports, there is a trade surplus. Hence, the country has a favourable balance of trade.
(ii) Exports are smaller than the imports, there is a trade deficit. Hence, the country has an unfavourable balance of trade.

Balance of Invisible Trade

It includes the export and import of services. The balance of invisible trade is the difference between the exports and imports of services. The services include the following:

The balance of invisible trade is the difference between the exports and imports of services.

(i) Travel, for example, expenditure by foreign tourists in India on hotels, will be a credit entry in India's balance of payments.
(ii) Insurance, banking, shipping, freight services and others, provided, for example, by Indian firms to foreigners, will again be a credit entry in India's balance of payments.
(iii) Expenditure abroad by the government agencies (in India) will be a debit entry in India's balance of payments.
(iv) Interest and dividend on foreign investment earned by domestic entities will be a credit entry in India's balance of payments.

While the exports of services are entered as a positive entry or credit claims in the balance of payments, imports of services are entered as a negative entry or debits in the balance of payments.

Unilateral Transfers

These are also called unrequited transfers since they are one way transactions as there is no claim involved as far as repayment is concerned, either at present or in the future. Unilateral transfers include gifts, personal remittances, indemnities and others. Unilateral transfers appearing on the

Unilateral transfers (also called unrequited transfers) are one way transactions since there is no claim involved as far as repayment is concerned, either at present or in the future.

(i) Credit side of the balance of payments include personal remittances of the emigrants to relatives in the country, gifts, and grants, which are received by the country from the individuals, institutions and governments of the foreign countries.

(ii) Debit side of the balance of payments include payments made by the country to the other countries in the form of personal remittances, gifts and grants.

The balance of current account or the current account balance includes the balance of trade, the balance of invisible trade and the balance of unrequited transfers or unilateral transfers. It represents the country's current receipts from abroad and unilateral receipts on the credit side and country's current international expenditures abroad and unilateral payments on the debit side. It has a flow dimension.

It is important to understand that

(i) If the sum of receipts (or credits) is greater than the sum of payments (or debits), then there will be a current account surplus. It implies that there is a net inflow of income into the country.

(ii) If the sum of receipts (or credits) is smaller than the sum of payments (or debits), then there will be a current account deficit. It implies that there is a net outflow of income from the country. It not only leads to a loss of income from the country, but also involves a problem in making the payments.

The transactions in the current account have an effect on the national income and thus the income and output levels in the economy.

Capital Account

The capital account of the balance of payments measures the outflow and inflow of capital into the economy. The outflow of capital occurs due to the purchase of foreign assets by the households and firms in the domestic country. The inflow of capital occurs due to the purchase of assets in the domestic country by the households and firms of the foreign countries. The capital account has a stock dimension.

The capital account of the balance of payments measures the outflow and inflow of capital into the economy.

The capital account of the balance of payments includes the following capital transactions:

Long-term Movements of Capital

(i) Portfolio investment, which refers to the purchase of long-term securities by foreigners from the residents of the domestic country. The holding/maturity period is normally greater than a year. This involves the acquiring of an asset, which does not give any control to the investor, for example, purchase of the shares of a company in the country by a foreigner.

(ii) Direct investment, which refers to the private direct foreign investment in shares, bonds, plant and machinery in the country. In direct investment, the investor has a controlling power.

Short-term Movements of Capital

(i) Purchase of short-term government and corporate securities (with a maturity period of one year or less than one year), for example, commercial bills and treasury bills.
(ii) Holdings of cash balances by foreigners due to, for example, political uncertainty.
(iii) Purchase of foreign currency for speculation.

Loan Repayments

(i) Loans by the international financial institutions to the government of a country.
(ii) Loans received by the government of the country from the government of another country.
(iii) Receipts of funds in the repayments of loans, for example, to loans extended to business firms and governments in the foreign countries.

All these involve an inflow of capital and are thus entered as a positive entry or credit claims in the balance of payments. Similarly, an outflow of capital is entered as a negative entry or debits in the balance of payments.

The transactions in the capital account influence the position of the economy as an international creditor or debtor.

Official International Reserve Account

The official reserves of a country include the following:

Foreign Currencies

Most countries prefer to hold their foreign exchange reserves in dollar, which is the most widely accepted and important currency in the world today.

Gold

As far as gold is concerned, it can be divided into two following categories:

(i) Monetary gold, where the movements occur when gold is used as a means of payment. Hence, all monetary gold movements are included under the official reserves.
(ii) Non-monetary gold according to which gold is a commodity. Hence all exports and imports of gold are treated like any other commodity in the balance of payments.

Special Depository Receipts (SDRs)

When a country becomes a member of the International Monetary Fund (IMF), it has to deposit a subscription of which twenty-five per cent is in the form of gold or even SDRs while the rest is in the form of the country's own currency. Depending on its subscription, a country can draw other convertible currencies from the IMF, and this enters as a positive entry or credit claims in the balance of payments.

The foreign exchange reserves are maintained not only to make payments in case of deficits in the balance of payments, but also to stabilize the foreign exchange rate.

The transactions in the international reserve account determine the foreign exchange reserves, which are available for settling a deficit in the current or capital account of the country.

The different components of the balance of payments can be shown as in Table 24.1.

Table 24.1 Balance of Payments

Current Account
(i) Balance of trade
(a) Export and import of goods
(b) Non-monetary gold (According to which, gold is a commodity and all exports and imports of gold are treated like any other commodity.)
(ii) Balance of invisible trade (It includes exports and imports of services.)
(a) Travel
(b) Insurance, banking, shipping, freight services and others
(c) Expenditure abroad by government agencies
(d) Interest and dividend income
(e) Miscellaneous
(iii) Unilateral transfers
(a) Personal remittances
(b) Transfers from the government
Capital Account
(i) Long-term movements of capital
(a) Portfolio investment
(b) Direct investment
(ii) Short-term movements of capital
(a) Purchase of short-term government and corporate securities
(b) Holdings of cash balances by foreigners
(c) Purchase of foreign currency for speculation
(iii) Repayment of loans
(a) Loans by the international financial institutions
(b) Loans received by the government
(c) Receipts of funds in the repayments of loans
Official International Reserve Accounts
(i) Foreign currencies
(ii) Monetary gold
(iii) SDRs
Errors and Omissions: In the balance of payments accounts of any country usually an item called errors and omissions are included to balance the balance of payments.

RECAP

- The current account of the balance of payments includes the following items: balance of trade, balance of invisible trade and unilateral transfers.
- The balance of trade is one of the most important components of the balance of payments.
- The transactions in the current account have an effect on the national income and thus the income and output levels in the economy.
- The transactions in the capital account influence the position of the economy as an international creditor or debtor.
- The transactions in the international reserve account determine the foreign exchange reserves, which are available for settling a deficit in the current or capital account of the country.

DOUBLE ENTRY BOOKKEEPING

It is important to note that the balance of payments of a country will always balance and thus will always be in equilibrium. This is based on the double entry system of bookkeeping, where each transaction is recorded twice, as a debit entry and as a credit entry.

Table 24.2 depicts a hypothetical example of the balance of payments of a country. The left side of the table shows the ways in which a country can acquire foreign currency while the right side of the table shows the ways in which the country spends the foreign currency.

Balance of Trade

In Table 24.2, row 1 indicates that the country earns ₹500 crore as foreign exchange by exporting goods. Similarly, row 6 indicates that the country spends ₹600 crore of the foreign exchange by importing goods. These two rows depict the balance of trade equal to –₹100 crore as row (a) in Table 24.3. This implies that there is an adverse balance of trade.

Balance of Services

In Table 24.2, row 2 indicates that the country earns ₹250 crore as foreign exchange by exporting services. Similarly, row 7 indicates that the country spends ₹50 crore of the foreign exchange by importing services. These two rows depict the balance of invisible trade equal to ₹200 crore as row (b) in Table 24.3. This implies that there is a favourable balance of services or invisible trade.

Table 24.2 Balance of Payments of a Country

S. No.	Receipts (Credit)	Amount (₹ in Crore)	S. No.	Payments (Debit)	Amount (₹ in Crore)
1.	Exports of goods	500	6.	Imports of goods	600
2.	Exports of services	250	7.	Imports of services	50
3.	Unilateral receipts	50	8.	Unilateral payments	80
4.	Capital receipts	100	9.	Capital payments	120
5.	Sale of gold	100	10.	Purchase of gold	150
	Total receipts	**1000**		**Total payments**	**1000**

Table 24.3 External Balances in the Balance of Payments

(a)	Balance of Trade (Rows (1) and (6) of Table 24.2)	500 – 600 = –100
(b)	Balance of Services (Rows (2) and (7) of Table 24.2)	250 – 50 = 200
(c)	Balance of Unilateral Transfers (Rows (3) and (8) of Table 24.2)	50 – 80 = –30
(d)	Balance of Current Account (Rows (a), (b) and (c) of Table 24.3)	–100 + 200 –30 = 70
(e)	Balance of Capital Account (Rows (4) and (9) of Table 24.2)	100 – 120 = –20
(f)	Balance of Official Reserve Account (Rows (5) and (10) of Table 24.2)	100– 150 = –50
(g)	Balance of Payments (Rows (d), (e) and (f) of Table 24.3)	1000 – 1000 = 0

Balance of Unilateral Transfers

In Table 24.2, row 3 indicates that the country earns ₹50 crore as foreign exchange from unilateral receipts. Similarly, row 8 indicates that the country spends ₹80 crore of the foreign exchange on unilateral payments. These two rows depict the balance of unilateral transfers or unrequited receipts equal to –₹30 crore as row (c) in Table 24.3. This implies that there is an unfavourable balance of unilateral transfers.

Balance of Current Account

In Table 24.2, the balance of current account includes rows 1, 2, 3 and 6, 7 and 8. In Table 24.3, the balance of current account includes rows (a), (b) and (c) to depict a surplus on the current account equal to ₹70 crore as in row (d).

Balance of Capital Account

In Table 24.2, row 4 indicates that the country earns ₹100 crore as foreign exchange from capital receipts. Similarly, row 9 indicates that the country spends ₹120 crore of the foreign exchange on capital payments. These two rows depict a deficit in capital account. Table 24.3 shows a balance of capital account equal to –₹20 crore as row (e).

Balance of Official Reserve Account

In Table 24.2, row 5 indicates that the country earns ₹100 crore as foreign exchange from the sale of gold. Similarly, row 10 indicates that the country spends ₹150 crore of the foreign exchange on purchase of gold. These two rows depict the balance of official reserve account equal to –₹50 crore as row (f) in Table 24.3.

Balance of Payments

In Table 24.3, the balance of payments includes rows (d), (e) and (f) to depict a balance in the balance of payments in an accounting sense. The balance of current account equals ₹70 crore while the balance of capital account depicts a deficit equal to –₹20 crore. The official reserve account provides the balancing factor through a net purchase of gold equal to ₹50 crore.

RECAP

- The official reserve account provides the balancing factor in the balance of payments.

DISEQUILIBRIUM IN THE BALANCE OF PAYMENTS

As we have already observed, the balance of payment always balances as it is prepared on the basis of the double entry system of bookkeeping. This leads us to the very important issue of as to how a surplus or a deficit occurs in the balance of payments or, in other words, as to how disequilibrium occurs in the balance of payments. To understand this very crucial aspect of the balance of payments, we first examine autonomous and accommodating transactions.

Autonomous and Accommodating Transactions

One can distinguish between two types of transactions, autonomous and accommodating transactions.

> Autonomous transactions are those transactions that take place independently of other items in the balance of payments.

Autonomous transactions are those transactions that take place independently of other items in the balance of payments. Thus, these are transactions that take place for the satisfaction that they give or for the profit that they yield. They take place in both the current and the capital accounts:

(i) **Current Account:** Here, autonomous transactions include the exports and imports of goods and services. Unilateral transfers are also included under the autonomous transactions though they are not commercial transactions (since they do not in any way bring about a balance in the balance of payments).

(ii) **Capital Account:** Here, autonomous transactions include the long-term movements of capital because they are commercial transactions for the explicit purpose of making the profits.

> Accommodating transactions are those transactions that take place for the specific purpose of equalizing the balance of payments from an accountant's point of view.

Accommodating transactions are those transactions that take place for the specific purpose of equalizing the balance of payments from an accountant's view. They take place for balancing a deficit or surplus in the foreign account. They are not motivated by profit. They include short-term movements of capital, monetary gold movements and variations in the foreign exchange reserves.

To determine whether the balance of payments is in equilibrium or disequilibrium, only the autonomous transactions are considered.

(i) If the total receipts from autonomous transactions are equal to the total payments from autonomous transactions, then there is equilibrium in the balance of payments.

(ii) If the total receipts from autonomous transactions are not equal to the total payments from autonomous transactions, then there is disequilibrium in the balance of payments. The disequilibrium is in the form of a

- Surplus if the total receipts from autonomous transactions are larger than the total payments from autonomous transactions.

— Deficit if the total receipts from autonomous transactions are smaller than the total payments from autonomous transactions.

Any disequilibrium in the balance of payments is offset by the accommodating transactions, which make up for any deficit or surplus. Hence, the sum of accommodating transactions and autonomous transactions will always be zero. Thus, theoretically speaking, from an accountant's view, the balance of payment always balances, yet there will exist disequilibrium in the balance of payments from an economist's view.

RECAP

- To determine whether the balance of payments is in equilibrium or disequilibrium, only the autonomous transactions are considered.

KINDS OF DISEQUILIBRIA IN THE BALANCE OF PAYMENTS

One can differentiate between different kinds of disequilibrium on the basis of the source of the disequilibrium.

Structural Disequilibrium

This occurs due to structural imbalances caused by the shifts in the international demand and/or the supply of the factors of production, goods or services. They persist for a long time and are difficult to eliminate. Some causes of structural disequilibrium are due to the

Change in Production Pattern

Some countries may experience a change in its factor endowments over long time. This happened in the case of Britain, which had to face competition in its exports, especially of manufactured goods, from countries of West Europe and the USA. Hence, there occurred a structural imbalance in its balance of payments, which Britain could not tackle even by changing its production pattern and shifting to new industries.

Loss of Capital

A country may experience a loss of capital. For example, during times of war, there is widespread destruction including that of industries. Hence, on the one hand, a country has to rely on imports, not only for goods, but also for capital, at least over a short time. On the other hand, its exports will experience a slow down. All this will lead to a structural disequilibrium in the country's balance of payments.

Resource Deficiencies

Many countries have to go through a shortage of resources, which prevents them from achieving the level of growth, which they desire to achieve. Hence, they have to face an increased dependence on imports, which creates a problem in their balance of payments. For example, India has to rely heavily on imports of petroleum for its development, thus putting a strain on India's balance of payments.

Change in the Supply of Long-term Flows of Capital

Often, a country, which depends heavily on foreign capital, may find a change in that it may stop coming perhaps because the investor may find other avenues of investment more attractive. This may have a serious affect on the production structure and thus on the balance of payments of the country.

Change in the Demand Pattern

Countries, which experience growth and change in the income distribution, experience a shift in the demand from agricultural goods to manufactured goods. Hence, countries, whose exports are primarily based on agricultural goods, suffer a setback as the demand for their exports fails to keep up with the growing world demand for exports. They face difficulties in their balance of payments. They can tackle this problem through a change in their production pattern and also through a diversification of their exports.

Changes in the Political, Economic and Social Environment

This again plays a crucial role in influencing the relations between countries and hence their exports and imports.

Cyclical Disequilibrium

Business cycles are another major cause of disequilibrium in the balance of payments. Business cycles, which are global, affect almost all the countries though to differing degrees. A recession or inflation is accompanied by a trade surplus in some countries and a deficit in the others depending on the nature of their exports and imports and also on the elasticity of demand for their exports and imports. Countries with a high marginal propensity to import experience huge trade deficits during inflation and smaller deficits during recession times.

Exchange Rate Disequilibrium

There often occurs an overvaluation or an undervaluation of a currency on the foreign scenario.

Overvaluation of a currency is said to occur when the official value of a currency is fixed at a higher rate than would have been determined by the free market forces of demand and supply. The effects of overvaluation are similar to that of inflation. It has an adverse affect on exports and a favourable effect on imports, thus producing a deficit in the balance of payments.

> Overvaluation of a currency is said to occur when the official value of a currency is fixed at a higher rate than would have been determined by the free market forces of demand and supply.

Undervaluation of a currency is said to occur when the official value of a currency is fixed at a lower rate than would have been determined by the free market forces of demand and supply. The effects of undervaluation are opposite to that of overvaluation. It has an adverse affect on imports and a favourable effect on exports, thus producing a surplus in the balance of payments.

> Undervaluation of a currency is said to occur when the official value of a currency is fixed at a lower rate than would have been determined by the free market forces of demand and supply.

Capital flows are also influenced by disequilibrium in the exchange rate. An undervaluation of the currency attracts foreign capital, thus adding to the surplus in the balance of payments.

Monetary Disequilibrium

Inflation and deflation are the accompaniments of a monetary disequilibrium. Inflation has a two- fold effect on trade. On the one hand, inflation makes imports relatively cheaper leading to an increase in the demand for imports.

On the other hand, inflation makes exports relatively costlier leading to a decrease in the demand for exports. Thus, inflation leads to a deficit in the balance of payments, which will persist if the inflation continues to persist.

PROCESS OF ADJUSTMENT IN THE BALANCE OF PAYMENTS

Disequilibrium in the balance of payments is a cause for concern for every economy, more so if the disequilibrium is in the form of a deficit. We here analyse the macroeconomic policies that are utilized for adjustment in the balance of payments. Since deficit is more of a basis for concern, our analysis will focus on a deficit. They can be grouped under two heads:

(i) **Expenditure-reducing or Expenditure-changing Policies:**
   — Monetary policy
   — Fiscal policy

(ii) **Expenditure-switching Policies:**
   — Devaluation: the elasticity approach
   — Devaluation: the absorption approach

Expenditure-reducing or Expenditure-changing Policies

Expenditure-reducing policies are aimed at bringing about a change in the aggregate expenditure in the country.

Expenditure-reducing policies are aimed at bringing about a change in the aggregate expenditure in the country. To simplify our analysis, we exclude autonomous capital movements. Thus, the balance of payments can be written as:

$$B = Y - E$$

where B is balance of payments (net), Y is domestic output and E is domestic expenditure.

If in a country:

(i) $Y > E$: The domestic output is greater than the domestic expenditure and there will be a surplus in the country's balance of payments.

(ii) $Y = E$: The domestic output is equal to the domestic expenditure and there will be balance of payments equilibrium.

(iii) $Y < E$: The domestic output is smaller than the domestic expenditure and there will be a deficit in the country's balance of payments.

It is a deficit in the balance of payments that is of concern for the policy makers. The deficit can be eliminated in two ways: either by increasing the domestic output, Y, or by reducing the domestic expenditure, E. However, in the short run, it may be difficult to increase the output if there are structural constraints. Hence, most economies prefer to resort to expenditure-reducing policies to reduce a balance of payments deficit.

Expenditure-reducing policies can be divided under two broad groups: monetary policy and fiscal policy.

Monetary Policy

During the gold standard, monetary policies were quite popular in correcting disequilibrium in the balance of payments. However, in the 1930s, they were not successful in bringing about stabilization during the Depression and they lost popularity. It was only in the 1950s that interest and belief in the effectiveness of monetary policy was once again revived.

The instruments of monetary policy are discussed in depth in Chapter 25. Here, we will throw light only on some of these instruments.

To tackle a deficit in the balance of payments, a contractionary or tight monetary policy is followed. The instruments of monetary policy, which are most effective and used, often include:

Changes in Interest Rates: The effect of an increase in the interest rates on the level of investment will depend on the general economic situation. Suppose there is a boom in the economy and

(i) If the producers expect prices and thus the interest rate to fall in the future, they will postpone all investments. Through the multiplier effect, this will lead to a decrease in the national income and thus a reduction in the imports, which will, to some extent, reduce the deficit in the balance of payments.

(ii) If the producers expect prices and thus the interest rate to rise in the future, they will go ahead with all investments. Through the multiplier effect, this will lead to an increase in the national income and thus an increase in the imports which will increase, rather than decrease, the deficit in the balance of payments.

Open Market Operations: Suppose the Central Bank sells bonds and securities in the open market. Commercial banks, insurance companies and others purchase it with liquid money. This will not only reduce the liquidity in the banking system, but will also decrease the availability of credit. The interest rates will also increase. This will have an adverse effect on investment and the national income, leading to a fall in the imports.

Other instruments of monetary policy like changes in reserve requirements are also often applied to correct a deficit in the balance of payments.

Fiscal Policy

Fiscal policies can also be used to reduce the expenditure. They can be divided into two groups:

Those That Work on the Income Side of the Government Budget: Here, the most important instrument is taxation. As far as taxes are concerned,

(i) an increase in direct taxes, for example, income tax, reduces the incomes of households leading to a decrease in consumption (and also in savings) and thus a decrease in imports.

(ii) an increase in indirect taxes, for example, sales tax, leads to a decrease in consumption and thus a decrease in imports.

Those That Work on the Expenditure Side of the Government Budget: As far as government expenditure is concerned,

(i) a reduction in transfer payments will immediately decrease consumption since it is the low-income group, with a high marginal propensity to consume, which are the main beneficiaries of transfer payments.

(ii) a decrease in public consumption expenditure will lead to a fall in income and thus in imports.

(iii) a decrease in public investment expenditure will, similar to private investment, leads to a decrease in national income and imports.

Monetary and fiscal policies are the two most important ways of implementing an expenditure-reducing policy. To eliminate a deficit in the balance of payments, a country can pursue a contractionary monetary policy or a restrictive fiscal policy. Both policies lead to the following:

(i) On the one hand, a deflationary impact on the national income leading to a decrease in imports.

(ii) On the other hand, a positive effect on the export- and the import-competing industries.

BOX 24.1

In the 1980s, the US dollar appreciated quite strongly, reached a peak in 1985 and then decreased for the next three years and then became stable at nearly the same rate as in the 1980s. The Keynesians explain these fluctuations in terms of the macroeconomic policies, which were a blend of expansionary fiscal policy and a tight monetary policy. The classical economists argue that the US dollar appreciated because of the increase in the desirability of the US assets when compared with the other foreign assets. However, later, when the foreign savers were satiated with the US assets, there occurred a decrease in the value of the dollar.

Thus, an expenditure-reducing policy affects exports favourably and imports adversely leading to a positive effect on the balance of payments.

Expenditure-switching Policies: Devaluation (Elasticity Approach)

The expenditure-switching policies work mainly through changing the relative price of exports and imports. This is achieved through a change in the exchange rates that is a revaluation or devaluation of the domestic currency. One can include direct controls, which include commercial controls (like limiting the volume of imports), financial controls and exchange restrictions, also as a switching device.

> The expenditure-switching policies work mainly through changing the relative price of exports and imports.

In a flexible exchange rate system, a country with a deficit in the balance of payments experiences depreciation or, in other words, a lowering in the value of its currency with respect to other currencies. Similarly, a country with a surplus in the balance of payments experiences appreciation or, in other words, a rise in the value of its currency with respect to other currencies.

Under a stable exchange rate system in case of a deficit or a surplus in the balance of payments, the authorities have to take a conscious decision to bring about changes in the value of the currency with respect to the price of gold or to some primary asset. Devaluation refers to a conscious action by the monetary authorities to lower the value of a currency with respect to the price of gold.

> Devaluation refers to a conscious action by the monetary authorities to lower the value of a currency with respect to the price of gold.

Devaluation leads to a change in the relative prices. A devaluation of 10 per cent leads to

(i) An increase in the price of imports by 10 per cent in the home currency, which will, on the one hand, discourage imports and on the other hand encourage the import-competing industries, which will be in a better position to compete.

(ii) A decrease in the price of exports by 10 per cent in the foreign currency, which will encourage the exports.

Devaluation of a currency improves the balance of payments by encouraging the exports and discouraging the imports. The extent to which devaluation encourages the exports and discourages the imports depends on the elasticity of demand for its exports and imports.

The traditional approach to the effects of devaluation has been analysed in the Marshall–Lerner condition in terms of elasticity. According to the Marshall–Lerner condition, for a devaluation to have a positive effect on a country's balance of payments, the sum of the absolute values of the elasticity of demand for its exports and imports should be greater than one. If the sum of the absolute values of the elasticity of demand for its exports and imports is less than one, then a country can improve its balance of payments through a revaluation.

The Marshall–Lerner condition can be expressed as follows:

$$\Delta B = kX_f(e_{1m} + e_{2m} - 1) \tag{24.1}$$

where ΔB is change in the trade balance, k is devaluation in percentage terms, X_f is value of exports in terms of foreign currency, e_{1m} is the elasticity of demand for imports of the devaluing country and e_{2m} is the elasticity of demand for exports (imports of the foreign country) of the devaluing country in the foreign country.

A devaluation leads to

(i) An increase in the price of imports. The larger is the elasticity of demand for imports, the greater will be the decrease in the volume of imports. The value of the elasticity of demand for imports will depend on the type of good that the country imports. In case a country imports goods such as necessities and raw materials, the elasticity of demand for imports will be low and devaluation may not be effective in correcting a balance-of-payment deficit.

(ii) A decrease in the price of exports. The larger is the elasticity of demand for exports of a country, the greater will be the increase in the volume of exports. The value of the elasticity of demand for exports will depend on the type of good that the country exports and also the conditions in the market. In case a country exports goods such as necessities and raw materials, the elasticity of demand for exports will be low and devaluation may not be effective in correcting a balance-of-payment deficit. On the other hand if a country exports industrial goods, the elasticity of demand for exports will be high and devaluation will be very effective in correcting a balance-of-payment deficit.

The Marshall–Lerner condition is based on some conditions, which should be satisfied:

(i) The supply elasticities should be large. This may be true in times of a recession when there are unemployed resources. However, when there exists full employment, an increase in the price of exports will fail to increase the supply of exports.

(ii) When devaluation takes place, the trade balance is in equilibrium, which again is not always possible.

Devaluation has some adverse effects on the economy. It has an inflationary impact which is, to some extent, limited if devaluation is pursued with a contractionary monetary and fiscal policy. It is also felt that devaluation leads to a redistribution of income from the labour class to the others.

In spite of all the restrictions and adverse effects, the Marshall–Lerner condition holds in that the larger are the elasticities of demand for a country's exports and imports, the greater is the favourable effect of devaluation on the balance of payments.

Expenditure-switching Policies: Devaluation (Absorption Approach)

Sidney Alexander in 1952 presented an alternative approach, the absorption approach, to the effects of devaluation. The approach is in macroterms.

$$B = Y - A \tag{24.2}$$

where B is balance of trade, Y is national income and A is total absorption or total expenditure or total demand.

Since total demand includes consumption and investment, for a two sector economy

$$A = C + I$$

Devaluation affects the balance of trade, *B*, either by influencing the national income, *Y*, or by influencing the total absorption, *A*. We have

$$\Delta B = \Delta Y - \Delta A \tag{24.3}$$

The effect of devaluation on absorption can be split into two parts;

(i) Direct effect on absorption, which depends mainly on the real income at which the devaluation occurs, ΔD.

(ii) Indirect effect on absorption, which depends on the propensity to absorb, *c* out of real income, $c\Delta Y$.

$$\Delta A = \Delta D + c\Delta Y \tag{24.4}$$

where ΔA is change in absorption, ΔD is direct effect on absorption and $c\Delta Y$ is indirect effect on absorption.

Combining equations (24.3) and (24.4), we get

$$\Delta B = \Delta Y - (\Delta D + c\Delta Y)$$

$$\Delta B = \Delta Y(1 - c) - \Delta D \tag{24.5}$$

It is obvious from the above equation that the effects of devaluation on the balance of trade depend on three factors. These three factors depend on as to how devaluation effects the

(i) National income, *Y*.

(ii) Propensity to absorb, *c*.

(iii) Direct absorption, *D*.

The effects of devaluation will be different according to whether there is full employment in the economy or whether there exist unemployed resources.

When there is full employment in the economy, devaluation will not have any influence on the national income. However, it will affect the economy to some extent through its affect on absorption.

When there are unemployed resources in the economy, devaluation leads to an expansionary effect on exports and hence on income and absorption. If the increase in income is greater than the increase in absorption, then there will be an improvement in the trade balance.

Policy Mix and Simultaneous External and Internal Balances

Trevor Swan had developed a diagrammatic analysis to explain the impact of expenditure changing and expenditure policies on the external and internal balance of a country, in what is called the Swan diagram.

Figure 24.1 depicts the impact of expenditure changing and expenditure switching policies on the external and internal balance of a country.

In Figure 24.1, *X* axis shows domestic absorption and *Y* axis shows real exchange rate (amount of the domestic currency that is required to purchase one unit of the domestic currency) Curve *IB* is combinations of the real exchange rate and domestic absorption at which there exists an internal balance

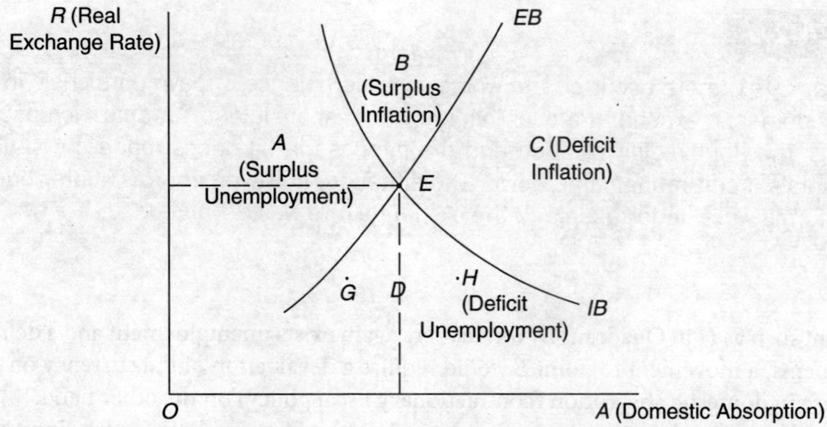

Figure 24.1 Policy Mix and a Simultaneous External and Internal Balance

and Curve *EB* is combinations of the real exchange rate and domestic absorption at which there exists an external balance.

An increase in *R*, the real exchange rate (amount of the domestic currency that is required to purchase one unit of the domestic currency), implies a devaluation of the domestic currency. A decrease in *R*, the real exchange rate, implies a revaluation of the domestic currency.

Curve *IB* is downward sloping because a lower rate of exchange worsens the balance of trade and thus a higher domestic absorption is required for the economy to maintain an internal balance. Curve *EB* is upward sloping because a higher rate of exchange improves the balance of trade and thus a higher domestic absorption is required for the economy to maintain an external balance.

In the figure,

(i) At all points to the right (and above) of the *IB* curve, there exists an inflationary situation while at all points to the left (and below) of the *IB* curve, there exists unemployment.

(ii) At all points to the left (and above) of the *EB* curve, there exists a surplus in the balance of payments while at all points to the right (and below) of the *EB* curve, there exists a deficit in the balance of payments.

In Figure 24.1, there are four quadrants:

(i) **Quadrant *A*:** Unemployment and Balance-of-Payments Surplus.

(ii) **Quadrant *B*:** Inflation and Balance-of-Payments Surplus.

(iii) **Quadrant *C*:** Inflation and Balance-of-Payments Deficit.

(iv) **Quadrant *D*:** Unemployment and Balance-of-Payments Deficit.

At a point such as *G* in Quadrant *D*, where there exists unemployment and a deficit in the balance of payments, a movement to point *E* (where there exists a simultaneous external and internal balance) would require a devaluation of the currency on the one hand and an increase in domestic absorption (expansionary fiscal policy) on the other hand. Thus, a combination of two policies is usually required to achieve two goals.

BOX 24.2

In the year 1991, there occurred the worst possible balance of payments crisis in India. The excess of domestic expenditure over income was responsible for a rapid increase in foreign borrowing. The double-digit inflation and the increase in oil prices made the situation even worse. India's credit rating came down. The situation, however, improved later on when economic reforms were undertaken and the exchange rate was devalued.

At a point such as *H* in Quadrant *D*, where there again exists unemployment and a deficit in the balance of payments, a movement to point *E* would require a devaluation of the currency on the one hand and a decrease in domestic absorption (contractionary fiscal policy) on the other hand.

Thus, we have observed that in most cases, a combination of both expenditure-reducing and -switching policies are required to achieve both the external and the internal balance in a country.

RECAP

- Most economies prefer to resort to expenditure-reducing policies to reduce a balance-of-payments deficit.
- The expenditure-switching policies work through a change in the exchange rates, that is a revaluation or devaluation of the domestic currency.
- The extent to which devaluation encourages the exports and discourages the imports depends on the elasticity of demand for its exports and imports.
- A combination of both expenditure-reducing and expenditure-switching policies are required to achieve both the external and the internal balance in a country.

PERFORMANCE OF INDIAN ECONOMY IN THE EXTERNAL SECTOR

In today's globalized world, no country is fully insulated from what is happening in the global economy and India can be no exception to the rule as it increasingly integrates into the world. The emerging euro zone crisis and the insecurity surrounding the global economy have adversely impacted the Indian economy triggering sharp drop in growth, higher current account deficit and diminishing capital inflows. As in 2008, the transmission of the crisis crept through the balance-of-payments channel. Fiscal 2011–12 witnessed deceleration in export while imports continued to remain high because of oil imports as shown in Table 24.4. At the same time, foreign institutional investment flows declined, straining the capital account and the dollar/rupee exchange rate continued to slide and touched an all-time low of ₹56.23 per US dollar on 30 May 2012.

RECAP

- The emerging euro zone crisis and the insecurity surrounding the global economy have adversely impacted the Indian economy triggering sharp drop in growth, higher current account deficit and diminishing capital inflows.

Table 24.4 India's Balance of Payments

Item	2006–07	2007–08	2008–09	2009–10	2010–11[PR]	2010–11 H1 (April–Sept. 2010)[PR]	2011–12 H1 (April–Sept. 2011)[P]
1	2	3	4	5	6	7	8
				(US$ million)			
Curent Account							
Exports	128888	166162	189001	182442	250468	107331	150909
Imports	190670	257629	308520	300644	381061	176213	236674
Trade balance	–61782	–91467	–119519	–118203	–130593	–68883	–85765
Invisibles (net)	52217	75731	91604	80022	84647	39283	52923
• Non-factor services	29469	38853	53916	36016	48816	21517	31060
• Income	–7331	–5068	–7110	–8038	–17309	–8238	–9025
• Transfers	30079	41945	44798	52045	53140	26004	30887
Goods & services balance	–32313	–52614	–65603	–82187	–81777	–47366	–54705
Current account balance	–9565	–15737	–27914	–38181	–45945	–29599	–32842
Capital Account							
Capital account balance	45203	106585	7395	51634	61989	38950	41061
• External assistance (net)	1775	2114	2439	2890	4941	3036	705
• External commercial borrowings (net)	16103	22609	7861	2000	12506	5674	10592
• Short-term debt	6612	15930	–1985	7558	10990	6937	5940
• Banking capital (net) of which	1913	11759	–3245	2083	4962	839	19344
– Non-resident deposits (net)	4321	179	4290	2922	3238	2163	3937
• Foreign inverstment (net) of which	14753	43326	8342	50362	39652	30836	13657
– FDI (net)	7693	15893	22372	17966	9360	7040	12311
– Portfolio (net)	7060	27433	–14030	32396	30293	23796	1346
• Rupee debt service	–162	–122	–100	–97	–68	–16	–32
• Other flows (net)	4209	10969	–5916	–13162	–10994	–8356	–9145
Errors and Omissions	968	1316	440	–12	–2993	–2320	–2500
Overall Balance	**36606**	**92164**	**–20080**	**13441**	**13050**	**7030**	**5719**

Source: RBI; *Indian Economic Survey, 2011–12.*
Notes: PR, partially revised; P, preliminary.

BOX 24.3

Foreign Exchange Reserves

India's foreign exchange reserves comprise foreign currency assets (FCA), gold, special drawing rights (SDRs) and reserve tranche position (RTP) in the International Monetary Fund (IMF). The level of foreign exchange reserves is largely the outcome of the RBI's intervention in the foreign exchange market to smoothen the exchange rate volatility and valuation changes due to movement of the US dollar against other major currencies of the world. Foreign exchange reserves are accumulated when there is absorption of the excess foreign exchange flows by the RBI through intervention in the foreign exchange market, aid receipts and interest receipts and funding from the International Bank for Reconstruction and Development (IBRD), Asian Development Bank (ADB), International Development Association (IDA), etc.

FCAs are maintained in major currencies such as the US dollar, euro, pound sterling, Australian dollar and Japanese yen. Both the US dollar and the euro are intervention currencies; however, reserves are denominated and expressed in the US dollar only, which is the international numeraire for the purpose. The movement of the US dollar against other currencies in which FCAs are held therefore impacts the level of reserves in US dollar terms. The level of reserves declines when the US dollar appreciates against major international currencies and vice versa. The twin objectives of safety and liquidity have been the guiding principles of foreign exchange reserves management in India with return optimization being embedded strategy within this framework.

India's Foreign Exchange Reserves: Beginning from a low level of US$ 5.8 billion at the end of March 1991, India's foreign exchange reserves gradually increased to US$ 25.2 billion by the end of March 1995, US$ 38.0 billion by the end of March 2000, US$ 113.0 billion by the end of March 2004, and US$ 199.2 billion by the end of March 2007. The reserves stood at US$ 314.6 billion at the end of May 2008, before declining to US$ 252.0 billion at the end of March 2009. The decline in reserves in 2008–09 was inter alia a fallout of the global crisis and strengthening of the US dollar vis-à-vis other international currencies. During 2009–10, the level of foreign exchange reserves increased to US$ 279.1 billion at the end of March 2010, mainly on account of valuation gain as the US dollar depreciated against most of the major international currencies. In fiscal 2010–11, foreign exchange reserves have shown an increasing trend and reached US$ 304.8 billion at the end of March 2011, up by US$ 25.7 billion from the US$ 279.1 billion level at the end of March 2010. In 2011–12, the reserves increased by US$ 6.7 billion from US$ 304.8 billion at the end of March. 2011 to US$ 311.5 billion at end September 2011.

Source: *Economic Survey*, http://indiabudget.nic.in

INTERNATIONAL MONETARY SYSTEM

A market is a place, where goods are bought and sold. In a foreign exchange market, one form of currency is converted into another form of currency. This is necessary because all international business activities require money to be transferred from one country to another and thus from one form of currency to another form.

The international monetary system refers to the institutions, rules, regulations and the policies, which are involved in determining the foreign exchange rates. It involves the currencies of the different countries and also the composite currency units such as the European Monetary Unit (EMU) and the Special Drawing Rights (SDR).

An Evolution of the International Monetary System

Gold Standard (1876–1914)

In 1821, Great Britain adopted the gold standard officially. Later, in 1879, the United States, Germany and France adopted the gold as the monetary standard.

It was in the 1870s that the gold standard was accepted as the international monetary system. Under the gold standard:

(i) Each country pegged its currency to gold.
(ii) The buying and selling of gold in each country by the government was at its own fixed parity rate.
(iii) Every country had to maintain gold reserves to back up the value of its currency.
(iv) There were no restrictions on the export and import of gold.

At the time of the First World War, the trade flows and the free movement of gold was disrupted. Also, there was an uneven distribution of the limited supplies of gold. Hence, some of the major trading countries suspended the gold standard. In 1914, the gold standard was abandoned.

After the First World War, attempts were made to re-establish the gold standard once again. As in the classical theory, the gold standard was based on the assumption of full employment and wage price flexibility. These assumptions of the classical theory were put to test at the time of the Great Depression. However, they did not hold ground and the need for government interference was felt. With the onset of the Great Depression, the gold standard was given up, by Great Britain in 1913, United States in 1933 and by the other nations in 1937. Thus, the gold standard was finally given up.

Period Between the Two World Wars (1914–1944)

At the time of the First World War, the currencies of the different countries were fluctuating widely not only in terms of each other, but also in terms of gold. This gave ample arbitrage opportunities to the international speculators. However, it had widespread ramifications in that it hindered trade between the different countries. All this ultimately contributed to the occurrence of the Great Depression.

In 1934, the United States opted for a modified gold standard. Under this system, the treasury traded gold with only the central banks and not the individual citizens. From 1934, till the end of the Second World War, the exchange rates were such that the value of each currency was determined in terms of gold. The important trading currencies were not convertible to other currencies, the dollar being the most important trading currency that was convertible.

Bretton Woods System (1944–1973)

At the end of the Second World War, there was a widespread belief that a fixed exchange rate would encourage the world trade. Hence, in 1944, the delegates from 44 nations across the world met at Bretton Woods, New Hampshire, and discussed as to how to create a fixed exchange rate system. From this conference, at the Bretton Woods, there emerged the gold exchange standard. Under this system:

(i) Each nation pegged (fixed) its currency in terms of gold or the dollar.
(ii) Each nation agreed to buy and sell the US dollar to maintain the value of its currency.

(iii) The reserve currency was the US dollar.
(iv) Devaluation of up to 10 per cent was allowed only if a currency became very weak.

From the conference at the Bretton Woods, two organizations emerged, the International Monetary Fund (IMF) and the World Bank. The fixed exchange rates were maintained through the government interference in the foreign exchange market and through the buying and selling of currency by the central bank.

Unfortunately, the US dollar ran into problems. In December 1971, at the meeting of the finance ministers of some of the leading nations at the Smithsonian Institution in Washington DC, the USA agreed to a devaluation of the dollar. By February 1973, it was realized that a fixed exchange rate system was no longer possible. Hence, in March 1973, some of the major industrial nations adopted a floating exchange rate system.

As of today, there are many exchange rate regimes. They include pegged exchange rates within horizontal bands, crawling pegs and currency board arrangement.

Special Drawing Rights (SDRs) VX–A Note

The Special Drawing Rights (SDRs) were created in 1969 by the IMF to meet the increasing need for international liquidity. Under the fixed exchange rate system of the Bretton Woods, to be able to maintain a fixed exchange rate, a country required official reserves so that it could buy domestic currency in the world foreign exchange markets. However, due to the expanding world trade, there seemed to be a shortage of the two most important official reserve assets, US dollar and gold. Thus, under the IMF, a new reserve asset, the SDR was formed.

The characteristics of an SDR are:

(i) It is a reserve asset.
(ii) Its allocation is done as per the IMF quota of the member countries.
(iii) The value of the SDR is determined on the basis of a basket of some important international currencies.
(iv) The SDR is a unit of account of the IMF and other international organizations.
(v) The SDR performs the function of a store of value, and as a means of payment.
(vi) It is in the form of an entry in the SDR Account of the countries involved in the SDR Scheme. They are then available for use as per the rules.

The importance of the SDR came down when the Bretton Woods system collapsed. Also, due to the growth of the international capital markets, borrowing by the governments became easy. Thus, the SDR's utility as a reserve asset declined.

RECAP

- The international monetary system refers to the institutions, rules, regulations and the policies, which are involved in determining the foreign exchange rates.
- It was in the 1870s that the gold standard was accepted as the international monetary system.
- In 1914, the gold standard was abandoned.
- From the conference at the Bretton Woods in 1944, there emerged the gold exchange standard.
- By February 1973, it was realized that a fixed exchange rate system was no longer possible.
- Hence, in March 1973, some of the major industrial nations adopted a floating exchange rate system.

- The Special Drawing Rights (SDRs) were created in 1969 by the IMF to meet the increasing need for international liquidity.
- The importance of the SDR came down when the Bretton Woods system collapsed.

SUMMARY

INTRODUCTION

The balance of payment is a statement, which summarizes the exports and imports and the other international transactions between the countries. This chapter analyses the different aspects of the balance of payments.

MEANING AND STRUCTURE OF BALANCE OF PAYMENTS

1. The balance of payment is a statement, which summarizes the exports and imports and the other international transactions between the countries.
2. The transactions entering into the balance of payments can be grouped under three broad accounts: Current Account, Capital Account and Official International Reserve Account.
3. The current account of the balance of payments measures the flow of goods, services and income, which occur across the national borders.
4. The capital account of the balance of payments measures the outflow and inflow of capital into the economy.

Current Account

1. The current account of the balance of payments includes the following items: Balance of Trade, which includes the export and import of goods (or merchandise); Balance of Invisible Trade, which includes the export and import of services; Unilateral Transfers, which are one way transactions as there is no claim involved as far as repayment is concerned, either at present or in the future.
2. The transactions in the current account have an effect on the national income and thus the income and output levels in the economy.

Capital Account

1. The capital account of the balance of payments measures the outflow and inflow of capital into the economy.
2. The capital account of the balance of payments includes the following capital transactions: Long-term movements of capital, which further includes portfolio investment and direct investment; Short-term movements of capital, which includes items such as purchase of short-term government and corporate securities; Loan Repayments, which includes the loans by the international financial institutions, etc.
3. The transactions in the capital account influence the position of the economy as an international creditor or debtor.

Official International Reserve Account

1. The official reserves of a country include: foreign currencies, monetary gold and SDRs.
2. The transactions in the international reserve account determine the foreign exchange reserves, which are available for settling a deficit in the current or capital account of the country.

DOUBLE ENTRY BOOKKEEPING

1. The balance of payments of a country will always balance because of the double entry system of bookkeeping and thus will always be in equilibrium.
2. The official reserve account provides the balancing factor in the balance of payments.

DISEQUILIBRIUM IN THE BALANCE OF PAYMENTS

1. Autonomous transactions are those transactions that take place independently of other items in the balance of payments. Thus, these are transactions that take place for the satisfaction that they give or for the profit that they yield.

2. Autonomous transactions include exports and imports of goods and services, unilateral transfers and long-term movements of capital.
3. Accommodating transactions are those transactions that take place for the specific purpose of equalizing the balance of payments from an accountant's view. They take place for balancing a deficit or surplus in the foreign account.
4. Accommodating transactions include short-term movements of capital, monetary gold movements and variations in the foreign exchange reserves.
5. To determine whether the balance of payments is in equilibrium or disequilibrium, only the autonomous transactions are considered.
6. Any disequilibrium in the balance of payments is offset by the accommodating transactions, which make up for any deficit or surplus. Hence, the sum of accommodating transactions and autonomous transactions will always be zero.

KINDS OF DISEQUILIBRIA IN THE BALANCE OF PAYMENTS

1. **Structural Disequilibrium:** It occurs due to structural imbalances caused by the shifts in the international demand and/or the supply of the factors of production, goods or services.
2. **Cyclical Disequilibrium:** It is caused by business cycles.
3. **Exchange Rate Disequilibrium:** Overvaluation of a currency has an adverse affect on exports and a favourable effect on imports, thus producing a deficit in the balance of payments. Undervaluation of a currency has an adverse affect on imports and a favourable effect on exports, thus producing a surplus in the balance of payments.
4. **Monetary Disequilibrium:** Inflation makes exports relatively costlier leading to a decrease in the demand for exports. Thus, inflation leads to a deficit in the balance of payments.

PROCESS OF ADJUSTMENT IN THE BALANCE OF PAYMENTS

The macroeconomic policies that are utilized for correcting disequilibrium in the balance of payments include expenditure-reducing and -switching policies.

Expenditure-reducing or Expenditure-changing Policies

1. Expenditure-reducing policies are aimed at bringing about a change in the aggregate expenditure in the country.
2. Expenditure-reducing policies can be divided under two broad groups: monetary policy and fiscal policy.
3. To tackle a deficit in the balance of payments, a contractionary or tight monetary policy is followed.
4. Fiscal policies can be divided into two groups: those that work on the income side of the government budget and those that work on the expenditure side of the government budget.

Expenditure-switching Policies: Devaluation (Elasticity Approach)

1. The expenditure-switching policies work mainly through changing the relative price of exports and imports.
2. Under a stable exchange rate system in case of a deficit or a surplus in the balance of payments, the authorities have to take a conscious decision to bring about changes in the value of the currency with respect to the price of gold or to some primary asset.
3. Devaluation refers to a conscious action by the monetary authorities to lower the value of a currency with respect to the price of gold.
4. Devaluation of a currency improves the balance of payments by encouraging the exports and discouraging the imports.
5. The extent to which devaluation encourages the exports and discourages the imports depends on the elasticity of demand for its exports and imports.
6. According to the Marshall–Lerner condition, for a devaluation to have a positive effect on a country's balance of payments, the sum of the absolute values of the elasticity of demand for its exports and imports should be greater than one.

Expenditure-switching Policies: Devaluation (Absorption Approach)

1. Sidney Alexander, in 1952, presented an alternative approach, the absorption approach, to the effects of devaluation.
2. Devaluation affects the balance of trade, *B*, either by influencing the national income, *Y*, or by influencing the total absorption, *A*.
3. The effects of devaluation will be different according to whether there is full employment in the economy or whether there exist unemployed resources.

Policy Mix and Simultaneous External and Internal Balances

1. Trevor Swan had developed a diagrammatic analysis to explain the impact of expenditure changing and expenditure switching policies on the external and internal balance of a country, in what is called the Swan diagram.
2. In most cases, a combination of both expenditure-reducing and -switching policies is required to achieve both the external and the internal balance in a country.

ANALYSIS OF PERFORMANCE OF INDIAN ECONOMY IN THE EXTERNAL SECTOR

1. Once the global crisis deepened, it spread to most of the countries including India through the capital and current account of the balance of payments.
2. Despite these adverse developments in the balance of payments of India, including a sharp deceleration in the net capital flows and a slowdown in the demand for exports, the foreign sector of the Indian economy showed resilience.
3. India continued to remain an attractive destination for Foreign Direct Investment while its foreign exchange reserves continued to be in comfortable position.

INTERNATIONAL MONETARY SYSTEM

1. In a foreign exchange market, one form of currency is converted into another form of currency.
2. The international monetary system refers to the institutions, rules, regulations and the policies, which are involved in determining the foreign exchange rates.
3. In 1821, Great Britain adopted the gold standard officially. It was in the 1870s that the gold standard was accepted as the international monetary system.
4. In 1914, the gold standard was abandoned.
5. At the time of the First World War, the currencies of the different countries were fluctuating widely not only in terms of each other, but also in terms of gold.
6. In 1934, the United States opted for a modified gold standard. The important trading currencies were not convertible to other currencies, the dollar being the most important trading currency that was convertible.
7. In 1944, the delegates from 44 nations across the world met at Bretton Woods, New Hampshire. From this conference at the Bretton Woods, there emerged the gold exchange standard.
8. From the conference at the Bretton Woods, two organizations emerged, the International Monetary Fund (IMF) and the World Bank. Unfortunately, the US dollar ran into problems.
9. In December 1971, at the meeting of the finance ministers of some of the leading nations at the Smithsonian Institution in Washington DC, the USA agreed to a devaluation of the dollar. By February 1973, it was realized that a fixed exchange rate system was no longer possible.
10. In March 1973, some of the major industrial nations adopted a floating exchange rate system. As of today, there are many exchange rate regimes. They include pegged exchange rates within horizontal bands, crawling pegs and currency board arrangement.

Special Drawing Rights (SDRs)–A Note

1. The Special Drawing Rights (SDRs) were created in 1969 by the IMF to meet the increasing need for international liquidity.

2. Under the fixed exchange rate system of the Bretton Woods, to be able to maintain a fixed exchange rate, a country required official reserves so that it could buy domestic currency in the world foreign exchange markets.
3. Under the IMF, a new reserve asset, the SDR was formed.
4. The characteristics of an SDR are: it is a reserve asset, its allocation is done as per the IMF quota of the member countries, it is a unit of account of the IMF and performs the function of a store of value, and as a means of payment.
5. The importance of the SDR came down when the Bretton Woods system collapsed.

REVIEW QUESTIONS

TRUE OR FALSE QUESTIONS

1. The capital account of the balance of payments measures the flow of goods, services and income, which occur across the national borders.
2. Autonomous transactions are those transactions that take place independently of other items in the balance of payments.
3. To determine whether the balance of payments is in equilibrium or disequilibrium, only the accommodating transactions are considered.
4. Structural disequilibrium occurs due to business cycles.
5. According to the Marshall–Lerner condition, for a devaluation to have a positive effect on a country's balance of payments, the sum of the absolute values of the elasticity of demand for its exports and imports should be greater than one.

SHORT ANSWER QUESTIONS

1. Write short notes on the
   (a) Balance of trade
   (b) Balance of invisible trade.
2. Write a short note on the Official International Reserve Account.
3. Differentiate between autonomous and accommodating transactions.
4. Briefly discuss the different kinds of disequilibria in the balance of payments.
5. Discuss the effectiveness of monetary and fiscal policies as expenditure-reducing policies in tackling a balance-of-payments deficit.

LONG ANSWER QUESTIONS

1. What does the current account of the balance of payments measure? Discuss the constituent of the current account of the balance of payments.
2. What does the capital account of the balance of payments measure? Discuss the constituent of the capital account of the balance of payments.
3. 'The balance of payments of a country will always balance because of the double entry system of bookkeeping'. Explain.
4. 'To determine whether the balance of payments is in equilibrium or disequilibrium, only the autonomous transactions are considered'. Explain.
5. What is devaluation? Discuss the conditions under which it is expected to improve a deficit in the balance of payments of a country?

ANSWERS

TRUE OR FALSE QUESTIONS

1. **False.** The current account of the balance of payments measures the flow of goods, services and income, which occur across the national borders. The capital account of the balance of payments measures the outflow and inflow of capital into the economy.
2. **True.** Autonomous transactions are those transactions that take place independently of other items in the balance of payments. Thus, these are transactions that take place for the satisfaction that they give or for the profit that they yield.
3. **False.** To determine whether the balance of payments is in equilibrium or disequilibrium, only the autonomous transactions are considered.
4. **False.** Structural disequilibrium. This occurs due to structural imbalances caused by the shifts in the international demand and/or the supply of the factors of production, goods or services.
5. **True.** If the sum of the absolute values of the elasticity of demand for its exports and imports is less than one, then a country can improve its balance of payments through a revaluation.

Monetary Policy and Fiscal Policy

25

After studying this chapter, you should be able to understand:

- ✓ *Macroeconomic policy is the action taken by the government through its different policies to achieve the macroeconomic objectives of the economy.*
- ✓ *Monetary policy is an operation by the monetary authorities of the country, whereas fiscal policy is an operation by the government.*
- ✓ *Monetary policy aims at achieving certain well-defined macroeconomic objectives.*
- ✓ *To achieve the objectives of monetary policy, the central bank has at its disposal the quantitative and the qualitative measures of the monetary policy.*
- ✓ *The effective working of monetary policy is hindered due to the existence of different obstacles.*
- ✓ *Fiscal policy refers to the government's policy regarding government expenditure, taxation and public borrowing with the view to achieving certain well-defined macroeconomic objectives.*
- ✓ *To implement fiscal policy, the government has at its behest several instruments which include taxation, government expenditure and public borrowing.*
- ✓ *Fiscal policy actions which can tackle the problem of instability include automatic stabilizers and discretionary fiscal policy.*
- ✓ *The full employment budget surplus differs from the actual budget surplus only in respect of tax collections.*

INTRODUCTION

Before the Second World War there was a strong conviction that a laissez-faire economy was the best. The government's role should be at a minimum, and the economy should function on the basis of the principle of the invisible hand as mentioned by Adam Smith in 1776 in his famous book, *An Inquiry into the Nature and Causes of the Wealth of Nations,* where each individual aimed at the maximization of his own welfare, and in the process the society's welfare was maximized. Smith was deeply religious, and saw the invisible hand as a device by which a generous and kind God administered the universe where happiness was at a maximum.

With the advent of Keynes, the role of the government in achieving the macroeconomic objectives was realized. The authorities in the United States and the other countries realized as to how important a role the government played in achieving the objectives of growth, employment and price stability, besides the other goals. Thus, laws were passed in many countries emphasizing the importance of the government in the different aspects of economic development. Although there were still doubts and differences relating to the extent of responsibility that the government should be assigned in achieving the different goals, it certainly was the beginning of an era where the role of the government in economic intervention gained importance. Slowly as time passed, the role of the government encompassed the different aspects of life.

Macroeconomic policy refers to the action taken by the government through different policies to achieve the macroeconomic objectives of the economy. These macro goals include economic growth, economic development, full employment, equality in the distribution of income, controlling inflation in the economy by maintaining price stability and others. The most popular macroeconomic policies are the fiscal policy and the monetary policy.

Monetary policy is an operation by the monetary authorities of the country and it operates through changes in the quantity of money. Thus, its immediate impact is felt in the money market. Fiscal policy is an operation by the government and it operates through changes in the government expenditure and tax collections. Thus, its immediate impact is felt in the goods market.

This chapter examines the monetary policy and the fiscal policy, and their functioning. An attempt has also been made at understanding the goals which these policies aim at achieving. Are they successful in achieving these goals or do they face some limitations which prevent them from achieving them? All these issues will be discussed at length in the chapter.

MONETARY POLICY

Meaning of Monetary Policy

Monetary policy is an operation by the monetary authorities of the country to achieve certain well-defined macroeconomic objectives/goals. It is generally the central bank of the country which undertakes the implementation of the monetary policy. It operates through changes in the quantity of money. Hence, monetary policy has its immediate impact in the money market.

> Monetary policy is an operation by the monetary authorities of the country to achieve certain well-defined macroeconomic objectives.

Monetary policy, it is to be noted, has much wider connotations than credit policy. While both are administered by the central bank of the country, the credit policy is concerned with changes in the supply of credit and the monetary policy with changes in the supply of money. To avoid confusion, often the two are clubbed together under the head of monetary policy.

RECAP

- The central bank of the country undertakes the implementation of the monetary policy through changes in the quantity of money.

INSTRUMENTS OF MONETARY POLICY

The main objectives which the monetary policy aims at achieving include economic growth, a higher rate of employment, stable prices, equality in the distribution of income and wealth, a stable balance of payments and many others depending on the need of the hour.

To achieve these objectives, monetary policy has at its disposal instruments which give the central bank the power to control the money supply, and hence achieve these objectives.

These instruments can be divided into two categories:

(i) Quantitative or general measures
(ii) Qualitative or selective measures

Quantitative or General Measures of Monetary Policy

Open Market Operations

It is the sale and purchase of government securities and treasury bills by the central bank. It is an instrument of monetary control which is most powerful and which is most widely used by the central bank.

> Open market operations are the sale and purchase of government securities and treasury bills by the central bank.

The central bank carries out the open market operations through the commercial banks. Hence, these operations affect the bank deposits and reserves, and thus influence their capacity to create money.

Suppose the central bank follows:

(i) **A Contractionary Monetary Policy:** It aims at reducing the supply of money in the hands of the public and also at decreasing the creation of credit. To achieve this, it offers government securities and treasury bills for sale through the commercial banks. When the public and other institutions purchase these securities through cheques drawn on the commercial banks, there is a withdrawal of money from their accounts with the banks. Hence, there occurs a decrease in the cash reserves of banks, thereby reducing their capacity to create credit. There is thus a decrease in the money supply.

(ii) **An Expansionary Monetary Policy:** It aims at raising the supply of money in the hands of the public and also at increasing the creation of credit. To achieve this, it purchases government securities and treasury bills through the commercial banks. When the public and other institutions sell these securities there is an increase in the flow of money to their accounts with the banks. Hence, there occurs an increase in the bank's deposits and also in their cash reserves. This improves their capacity to create credit. There is thus an increase in the money supply.

Effectiveness of Open Market Operations: Open market operations are one of the most popular instruments of monetary policy. In the United Kingdom, the United States and other countries they are regarded as one of the most efficient instruments of monetary control.

Advantages of Open Market Operations

(i) They are highly flexible and can be used in widely varying amounts.

(ii) They are easily reversible in time.

(iii) They can be often be used in widely differing amounts.

(iv) Unlike the other instruments of monetary policy, they do not involve any public announcements. Hence, they do not have any announcement effects, that is, there are no reactions in the market consequent to open market operations.

For open market operations to be successful, at least three conditions need to be satisfied:

(i) It is necessary that the market for government securities, the gilt edged market is well developed and well organized.

(ii) It is necessary that the central bank has enough capacity to buy and sell government securities.

(iii) It is necessary that in the pursuit of these operations, the chief consideration for the central bank is only of monetary control.

In India, it seems that out of all these conditions, only condition (ii) seems to be satisfied. The central bank of the country, the Reserve Bank of India, has sufficient capacity to buy and sell securities. As for condition (i), the market for government securities is not well organized. Regarding condition (iii), the

RBI has often been weighed down by considerations other than monetary control and more towards, say, public debt management.

Variations in Reserve Requirements

Commercial banks maintain a certain proportion of their time and demand liabilities in the form of cash reserves. These can be divided under two heads:

Required Reserves: These are cash balances which banks hold to meet their statutory reserve requirements. This is a legal requirement imposed on the banks by the central bank. The purpose of these reserves is to safeguard the interest of the depositors and to prevent the banking system from a total collapse. It also enables the central bank to be able to control the liquidity. As per these requirements, the banks have to maintain a certain minimum reserve deposit ratio. Hence, a fraction of each bank's total deposits have to be maintained as cash balance with the central bank.

> Required reserves are cash balances which banks hold to meet their statutory reserve requirements.

When the central bank pursues

(i) A contractionary monetary policy, it raises the cash reserve ratio(CRR). With an upward revision in the CRR, banks are required to hold larger proportion of their cash balances with the central bank for the same amount of their liabilities. This reduces the bank's ability to extend loans leading to a decrease in the money supply. In essence, the CRR impounds funds available with the banks.

(ii) An expansionary monetary policy, it will reduce the CRR. With a reduction in the reserve requirement ratio, banks are required to hold a smaller proportion of their cash balances with the central bank for the same amount of their liabilities. This improves the bank's ability to extend loans leading to an increase in the money supply.

Excess Reserves: These are reserves in excess of the required reserves. A part of these may be held as cash on hand or in the form of vault cash with the banks themselves. The rest may be kept as excess balances with the central bank. They are held by the banks for meeting basically two purposes:

> Excess reserves are reserves in excess of the required reserves.

(i) Currency drains which is the net withdrawal of the currency by the depositors.
(ii) Clearing drains which is the net loss of cash due to the interbank clearing of checks.

BOX 25.1

As per the existing law, the central bank of India, the RBI, has the power to impose statutorily a CRR on banks which can be anywhere between 3 per cent and 15 per cent of their net demand and time deposits. The RBI has been using this instrument often for monetary control. When the Reserve Bank of India (RBI) hiked the CRR by 25 basis points to 8.25 per cent with effect from 24 May 2008, the small – almost token – CRR hike led to a withdrawal of around US$ 2.22 billion from the banking system. During the fiscal year 2008–09, frequent changes in the CRR were resorted to in tandem with current and evolving macroeconomic situation and liquidity conditions in the global and domestic financial markets. In November 2008, CRR was down to 5.5 per cent. January 2009 saw another reduction of 50 basis points in CRR in order to gear up the economy to cope up with the global recession. From April 2010, CRR stood at 6 per cent till January 2012 when it was reduced to 5.5 per cent.

Effectiveness of Variations in Reserve Requirements: As compared to open market operations it is often alleged that variations in reserve requirements are an inferior tool of monetary policy because:

(i) They lead to lumpy and discontinuous changes in the deposits and the reserves.
(ii) Since changes in reserve requirements are newsworthy, they produce announcement effects.

However, the counter argument given in support of variations in reserve requirements is that:

(i) Banks can be given sufficient notice of the changes so that they can be introduced gradually with banks having sufficient time to adjust their portfolios accordingly.
(ii) During times of inflation, the reserves of banks would be increasing rapidly. Hence, banks would not find it difficult to meet a higher CRR and thus they would not face any problems in giving their complete cooperation to the monetary authorities in controlling the money supply.
(iii) Often the central bank is unable to use open market operations for purposes of monetary control. Hence, it has to resort to variations in reserve requirements if it wishes to ensure monetary stability in the economy.

It is increasingly felt that the variable reserve ratio, on its own, is not a sufficient instrument for controlling money supply. Thus to make it an effective instrument, it needs to be supplemented by the other instruments of monetary policy.

Statutory Liquidity Requirements

The statutory liquidity requirement is a statutory requirement where the banks are required to maintain a certain fixed proportion of their demand and time liabilities in the form of designated liquid assets.

Besides the CRR, banks are subject to control through yet another requirement, the statutory liquidity ratio, or SLR as it is often known.

Under the SLR, banks are statutorily required to maintain a certain fixed proportion of their demand and time liabilities in the form of designated liquid assets. This ratio of liquid assets to demand and time liabilities is known as SLR. The SLR can be defined as:

$$SLR = \frac{ER + I^* + CB}{L}$$

where ER is excess reserves which are total reserves minus the required reserves with the central bank; I^* is investment in unencumbered securities, which are securities against which no loans have been taken by the bank from the central bank; CB is current account balances with other banks and L is total demand and time liabilities of the bank.

The purpose behind the SLR is to prevent the commercial banks from negating the impact of an increase in CRR by converting their liquid assets into cash so that their loanable funds remain intact. An increase in SLR thus impedes the bank's leveraged capacity to pump more money into the economy.

By increasing the SLR, the central bank attempts to allocate an increasingly larger share of banks resources to the government and the specified public sector agencies. However, the central bank has

BOX 25.2

In India, the SLR was first imposed on the banks in the year 1949. It was fixed at 20 per cent. It remained at this level for about a period of 15 years until it was increased to 25 per cent in the year 1964. After that, it was often changed and stood at 24 per cent at end of fiscal 2008–09. RBI is empowered to increase this ratio up to 40 per cent. The rate stood at 24 per cent in January 2012.

not been very successful in its effort because in meeting the SLR, the banks have preferred to acquire other approved securities rather than the government securities, since these other securities give higher yields.

Effectiveness of SLR: In India, like the CRR, the SLR has not been very successful as an instrument of monetary policy. Also it has not been a very flexible instrument of monetary policy and has often been revised in the upward direction for considerations other than monetary control.

Bank Rate Policy

The bank rate or the discount rate is the rate of interest at which the central bank rediscounts eligible bills of exchange or other commercial papers. When the banks are short of reserves they borrow from the central bank by getting their bills of exchange rediscounted. In simpler terms, the bank rate is the rate of interest charged by the central bank on the loans and advances made by it to the commercial banks. The central bank is thus a 'lender of the last resort' for the commercial banks.

> Bank rate or the discount rate is the rate of interest at which the central bank rediscounts eligible bills of exchange or other commercial papers.

It is at the discretion of the central bank to change the bank rate.

(i) When the central bank pursues an expansionary monetary policy, it lowers the bank rate. Hence it becomes cheaper for the commercial banks to borrow from the central bank's discount window. Thus, a decrease in the bank rate increases the money supply. A decrease in the bank rate is followed by a fall in the market rates of interest all along the line, since the banks revise their lending rates downwards. This is followed by an expansion in bank credit and is a sign for the onset of a cheap money policy in the economy.

(ii) When the central bank pursues a contractionary monetary policy, it raises the bank rate. Hence it becomes costlier for the commercial banks to borrow from the central bank's discount window, discouraging them to borrow from the central bank. Thus, an increase in the bank rate decreases the money supply. An increase in the bank rate is followed by a rise in the market rates of interest all along the line, since the banks revise their lending rates upwards to absorb the higher cost of borrowed reserves. This is followed by a tighter bank credit, and is a sign for the onset of a tighter money policy in the economy.

Effectiveness of Bank Rate Policy: In reality, it is difficult to predict the effect of the changes in the bank rate on the amount of the banks borrowings. This effect will depend on a number of factors:

(i) The extent to which the bank is dependent on borrowed reserves.

(ii) The extent to which the differential between the banks' lending rates and borrowed rates is sensitive to the banks demand for borrowed reserves.

(iii) The extent to which the other rates of interest change, in response to the changes in the borrowed reserves.

(iv) The demand for loans and the extent to which loans are available from other sources.

Limitations of the Bank Rate Policy

(i) The bank rate is often more sticky in comparison to the other rates. Also the changes in it are discontinuous.

(ii) Changes in the bank rate have announcement effects, that is, there are reactions in the market due to a mere announcement of a change being brought about in the bank rate. Hence, the central bank may avoid bringing about changes in the bank rate.

BOX 25.3

Changes in the bank rate in India in the initial years were not very frequent. Since 1962 it has been varied more often. From 10 per cent in 1990–91 it came down to 6 per cent in 2006–07 and remained at that level till March 2009. The repo rate (in April 2009) stood at 4.75 per cent, while the reverse repo rate stood at 3.25 per cent. Between October 2008 and March 2009, the central bank cut the repo rate at which it lends to banks by 425 basis points in desperate attempts to help boost the economy. Post-2010, with very evident inflationary pressures, RBI has raised the repo rate 13 times by 375 bps between March 2010 and January 2012.

(iii) Over the years, the flexibility in the money market has gone down. Hence, the response of the money and credit markets to changes in the bank rate is not very adequate for monetary policy to be effective.

(iv) Most commercial banks nowadays are often financially self reliant and thus not fully dependent on the central bank for finance.

(v) In certain countries, there has developed a private market for loans and those banks which are in need of loans borrow from those who have excess reserves.

Repo Rate and Reverse Repo Rate

The repo rate is the rate at which the central bank infuses short-term liquidity into the system. In simpler terms, it is the rate at which the central bank lends to the banks.

Repo rate is the rate at which the Central Bank infuses short-term liquidity into the system.

Reverse repo rate is the rate at which banks park their short-term excess liquidity with the Central bank in exchange for government securities.

The reverse repo rate is the rate at which banks park their short-term excess liquidity with the central bank in exchange for government securities. It is the rate at which the central bank borrows from the banks. Hence, the reverse repo rate is the return earned by the banks on their excess funds with the central bank. An increase in this rate tempts banks to park their short-term excess liquidity with the central bank thus squeezing out loose cash from the system which in turn helps in reducing inflationary pressures. When yields on government securities go up, the financial markets feel the liquidity crunch, and the lending rates to the retail and corporate sector harden.

BOX 25.4

Difference Between Bank Rate and Repo Rate

Bank rate is the rate at which RBI provides finance to commercial banks in India. Banks can avail different types of refinance from RBI at rates that are linked to bank rate. Thus, banks can borrow at this rate depending on their eligibility for refinance.

Repo, on the other hand, is a money market instrument, which enables collateralized short-term borrowing and lending through sale/purchase operations in debt instruments. Under a repo transaction, a holder of securities (a bank) sells them to an investor (RBI, in this case) with an understanding to repurchase the same at a predetermined date and rate. Thus, in repo, the forward clean price of the bonds is determined in advance at a level which varies from the spot clean price by accounting for the disparity between repo interest and coupon earned on the security. Thus, a bank can borrow under repo provided it has the extra securities which it can lend temporarily to RBI for borrowing short-term funds.

Table 25.1 Changes in the Policy Rate and Inflation

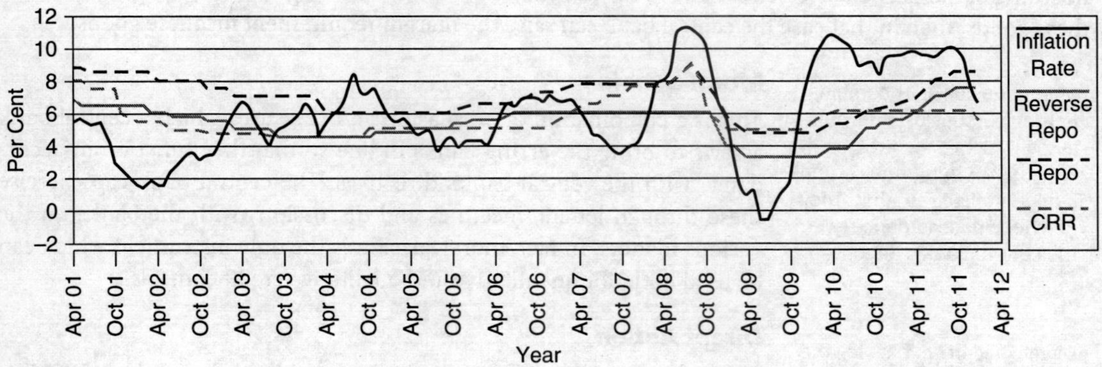

Source: *Economic Survey 2011–12*, Chapter 2.

The reverse repo rate is linked to the repo rate. The spread between the reverse repo rate and the repo rate is maintained generally at 100 basis points with the repo rate being the higher of the two.

Qualitative or Selective Measures of Monetary Policy

The quantitative measures control the total volume of credit and the cost of credit in the economy and hence the expansion or contraction in the total amount of credit and thus the supply of money.

On the other hand, the qualitative measures control the direction and distribution of credit in the economy. This can have two aspects:

(i) Positive aspect, in that these measures can be used to encourage the flow of credit in particular directions.

(ii) Negative aspect, in that these measures can be used to restrict the flow of credit to particular sectors.

The following are some of the qualitative credit control measures.

Rationing of Credit

This has been often used in many countries. Credit rationing is resorted to when there occurs a shortage of institutional credit. The more powerful and the financially strong sectors, which in fact may not really need the credit, may be able to capture the major share of the credit. The sectors, which may in fact be in dire need of funds, may not be able to procure them. To prevent such a situation from occurring, the central bank may resort to credit rationing. They may do so by

(i) Charging higher rates of interest on the bank loans which go beyond certain limits.

(ii) Setting limits on the quantum of loans to larger firms and industries.

Change in Margin Requirements

This is a tool of monetary policy that works indirectly to influence lending and thus regulate the capital markets. The margin requirement specifies the minimum maintainable ratio of the value of the securities charged to the amount borrowed.

Changes in margin requirements are used to control speculative activities. If the wholesalers start hoarding some particular essential goods so that they can create a shortage and push up the price of these goods, then in that case the central bank can raise the margin requirement for these goods.

Moral suasion is a combination of persuasion and pressures which a central bank asserts to bring the erring banks in line so that they function in accordance with the central bank's directives.

Moral Suasion

This is a combination of persuasion and pressures which a central bank asserts to bring the erring banks in line so that they function in accordance with the central bank's directives. The central bank can exercise these through letters, meetings and discussions with the banks on the various matters. In fact, moral suasion is the only instrument which can be used both, for quantitative and qualitative credit controls.

Direct action refers to the coercive actions resorted to by the central bank against those banks who do not function according to its directives.

Direct Action

This refers to the coercive actions resorted to by the central bank against those banks who do not function according to its directives. These may be by way of denial of discretionary rediscounting facilities, charging of penal interest rates, etc.

Effectiveness of Qualitative Credit Control Measures: This will depend on a number of factors:

(i) **The Extent of Restrictions on the Credit:** These may not be sufficient. The selective credit controls are generally security oriented and not purpose oriented. Hence, the influential borrowers may succeed in using the borrowed funds for purposes like speculation in the stock markets rather than for the priority sectors.

(ii) **The Availability of Finance from Other Sources:** Besides the availability of finance from banks, another major source of funds for the traders is the unregulated credit market. Further the existence of black money constraints the ability of the central bank to curtail speculative hoarding and other such activities.

(iii) **The Extent to which Supply Is Not Able to Fulfill the Demand:** The greater the shortage of funds, the more will be the speculation in the market. Hence, it is necessary that the credit controls are imposed well in advance so that timely action can be taken.

It is increasingly felt that the selective credit controls cannot be successful on their own. They need to be supplemented with the general credit controls. Also they are more in the form of short-term rather than long-term solutions.

Deficit Financing: Government's Instrument of Monetary Control

It refers to ways in which the deficit in the government's budget is financed. In less developed countries, it is financed by credit from the central bank. The central bank merely prints more currency and then puts them into circulation on behalf of the government.

Deficit financing leads to an increase in the money supply leading to an increase in the expenditure in the economy. Thus, whenever there arises a slack in demand, deficit financing is resorted to so as to increase the aggregate demand in the economy. Hence, deficit financing fills up the gap in the government expenditure and the revenue that it gets from taxation, public borrowing and external finance.

However, one major problem that is associated with deficit financing is that it always results in inflation. The increase in the money supply leads to an increase in the money in the hands of the public. This creates a demand for goods and services. However, the supply of goods is not able to keep up with the demand. Hence, there occurs an inflationary pressure in the economy.

Table 25.2 Monetary Policy Developments in India

Call Money Market
The call money market is an important segment of the money market where uncollateralized borrowing and lending of funds take place on overnight basis. Participants in the call money market in India currently include scheduled commercial banks (SCBs) (excluding regional rural banks), cooperative banks (other than land development banks), and primary dealers, both as borrowers and lenders (RBT's Master Circular dated 1 July 2011). Prudential limits in respect of both outstanding borrowing and lending transactions in the call money market for each of these entities are specified by the RBI.
Open Market Operations
OMOs are conducted by the RBI via the sale/purchase of government securities to/from the market with the primary aim of modulating rupees liquidity conditions in the market. OMOs are an effective quantitative policy tool in the armoury of the RBI, but are constrained by the stock of government securities available with at a point in time.
Liquidity Adjustment Facility
The LAF is the key element in the monetary policy operating framework of the RBI. On daily basis, the RBI stands ready to lend to or borrow money from the banking system, as per the latter's requirement, at fixed interest rates. The primary aim of such an operation is to assist banks to adjust to their day-to-day mismatches in liquidity, via repo and reverse repo operations. Under the repo or repurchase option, banks borrow money from the RBI via the sale of securities with an agreement to purchase the securities back at a fixed rate at a future date. The rate charged by the RBI to aid this process of liquidity injection is termed as the repo rate. Under the reverse repo operation, the RBI borrows money from the banks, draining liquidity out from the system. The rate at which the RBI borrows money is the reverse repo rate. The interest rate on the LAF is fixed by the RBI from time to time (with crucial changes introduced recently in the operating procedure of Monetary Policy detailed in the next paragraph). LAF operations help the RBI effectively transmit interest rate signals to the market.
Changes in the Operating Procedure of Monetary Policy
Effective 3 May 2011, based on the recommendations of the *Working Group on Operating Procedure of Monetary Policy*, the operating framework of monetary policy has been refined. The repo rate has been made the only independently varying policy rate. A new marginal standing facility (MSF) has been instituted, under which SCBs have been allowed to borrow overnight at their discretion, up to 1 per cent of their respective NDTL, at 100 bps above the repo rate. The revised MSF reverse repo corridor has been defined with a fixed width of 200 bps with the repo rate placed in the middle of the corridor. The reverse repo rate has been placed 100 bps below and the MSF rare 100 bps above the repo rate. It is expected that the fixed interest rate corridor, set by the MSF rate and reverse repo rate, by reducing uncertainty and avoiding difficulties in communication associated with a variable corridor, will help in keeping the overnight average call money rate close to the repo rate.

Source: *Economic Survey 2011–12.*

Table 25.3 Revision in Policy Rates

Effective Date	Repo Rate	Reverse Repo Rate	CRR	SLR	MSF Rate*
1	2	3	4	5	6
			(Per cent)		
2009–10					
21 April 2009	4.75	3.25	5.00	24.0	
7 November 2009	4.75	3.25	5.00	25.0	
13 February 2010	4.75	3.25	5.50	25.0	
27 February 2010	4.75	3.25	5.75	25.0	
19 March 2010	5.00	3.50	5.75	25.0	
2010–11					
20 April 2010	5.25	3.75	5.75	25.0	
24 April 2010	5.25	3.75	6.00	25.0	
2 July 2010	5.50	4.00	6.00	25.0	
27 July 2010	5.75	4.50	6.00	25.0	
16 September 2010	6.00	5.00	6.00	25.0	
2 November 2010	6.25	5.25	6.00	25.0	
18 December 2010	6.25	5.25	6.00	24.0	
25 January 2011	6.50	5.50	6.00	24.0	
17 March 2011	6.75	5.75	6.00	24.0	
2011–12					
3 May 2011	7.25	6.25	6.00	24.0	
9 May 2011	7.25	6.25	6.00	24.0	8.25
16 June 2011	7.50	6.50	6.00	24.0	8.50
26 July 2011	8.00	7.00	6.00	24.0	9.00
16 September 2011	8.25	7.25	6.00	24.0	9.25
25 October 2011	8.50	7.50	6.00	24.0	9.50
24 January 2012	8.50	7.50	5.50	24.0	9.50

* *The MSF commenced from 9 May 2011.*

Source: *Economic Survey 2011–12.*

RECAP

- Quantitative measures of monetary policy include open market operations, variations in reserve requirements, bank rate policy and repo rate.
- Qualitative measures of monetary policy include rationing of credit, change in margin requirements, moral suasion and direct action.

LIMITATIONS OF MONETARY POLICY

Existence of a Time Lag

This is perhaps one of the major problems in the path of the working of monetary policy. There exists a substantial time lag between the time that there is a realization for the need for a monetary policy and the time by which the response of the policy in bringing about changes in aggregate demand is felt.

The time lags can be divided under two heads:

(i) **Inside Lags**: These include the recognition lag and the action lag. The recognition lag relates to the considerable time taken by the central bank in realizing that there are problems and hence there is a need to tackle them through the monetary policy. The action lag may occur due to the considerable time gap involved during the recognition phase and the actual implementation of the policy.

(ii) **Outside Lags:** Once the policy has been implemented, the problem occurs in that it may take a considerable time for the households and firms to respond to those policies. Hence, there may occur a considerable time lapse for the impact of these changes to be felt on aggregate demand and the output.

The issue of time lags is very important for the success of the monetary policy in achieving its various goals. If the time lag is short then the chances of monetary policy being successful are strong. However, with long time gaps it is quite possible that the situation may have undergone a complete change and implementation of the policy, may worsen, rather than improve the situation.

Presence of Non-bank Financial Intermediaries

Besides commercial banks, the other entities which play a major role in the money and capital markets are the financial intermediaries. These include the development banks, mutual saving funds, insurance companies, etc.

Like banks these intermediaries cannot directly create money. However, they can influence money indirectly through their actions. Suppose the central bank is pursuing a tight monetary policy. These non-bank financial intermediaries can, to some extent, negate the impact of such a policy through an increase in the velocity of money by attracting idle funds and converting them into active balances.

Underdeveloped Nature of the Money and Capital Markets

One of the major problems in the implementation of monetary policy in less developed countries is that their money and the capital markets are highly fragmented, disconnected and disorganized. In such economies, sectors like the agriculture sector is unorganized and its main source of funds are the moneylenders who do not fall under the supervision of the central bank and are outside its control.

The presence of these factors not only increases the time lag involved but also to some extent limits the effectiveness of monetary policy in achieving its goals.

RECAP

- The existence of a time lag, presence of non bank financial intermediaries and the underdeveloped nature of the money and capital markets limit the effectiveness of monetary policy in achieving its goals.

FISCAL POLICY

Meaning of Fiscal Policy

The government of a country can influence the economy not only through the monetary policies but also through its fiscal policies. Fiscal policy refers to the government's policy regarding government expenditure, taxation and public borrowing with the view to achieving certain well-defined macroeconomic objectives.

> Fiscal policy refers to the government's policy regarding government expenditure, taxation and public borrowing with the view to achieving certain well-defined macroeconomic objectives.

It was only with the coming of Keynes that fiscal policy gained importance. Prior to Keynes, monetary policy was more popular. Also economists like Adam Smith strongly propagated the belief that in an economy the role of the government should be kept at a minimum. An economy which functioned on its own without any interference of any kind would be an ideal economy. It was believed that an economy would always function at the full employment level and hence the government's role should be limited to maintaining law and order and in providing essential services.

The coming of the Great Depression and the failure of monetary policy to tackle the severe unemployment problems arising from it made one realize the need for a fiscal policy. Further, the 'new economics' by Keynes' with the emphasis on aggregate demand strengthened the belief that the time was right to renew the dwindling faith of the public in the effectiveness of fiscal policy. Also, government expenditure and taxation were gaining importance. It was obvious that the government could increase or decrease aggregate demand through its expenditures, taxations and transfers. However, the monetarists attacked this argument because they believed that, with the exception of some circumstances, in general, increases in government expenditures do not add to aggregate demand but in fact are responsible for crowding out private investment of an equal amount.

Most economists do not agree with the crowding out arguments and promote the view that fiscal policy is certainly an effective instrument in achieving the macroeconomic policy objectives. In the developed countries, fiscal policy is effective in maintaining economic stability while in the developing countries its role is all the more important in achieving economic growth, development, and also in tackling employment and the problems emanating from it.

RECAP

- In the developed countries, fiscal policy is effective in maintaining economic stability while in the developing countries it is important in achieving economic growth, development and also in tackling employment.

INSTRUMENTS OF FISCAL POLICY

To implement fiscal policy, the government has at its behest several instruments.

Taxation

One of the most important sources of revenue for the government in most countries is taxation. In developing countries, the government is making an attempt at increasing the proportion of the national income which is collected as taxes. Taxes can be analysed under two headings.

Direct Taxes

(i) **Corporate Income Taxes** which are collected from firm's economic profits. These form a very small proportion of the total revenue of the government for many reasons:

— Since the corporate sector forms a very small part of the economy, its contribution to the total revenue will also be small.

— Often to encourage industrial development, the government offers incentives in the form of tax rebates and investment subsidies.

However, it is important to note that in spite of all problems corporate income taxes are easier to collect as compared to personal income tax.

(ii) **Personal Income Tax** again accounts for a very small proportion of the total revenue of the government for many reasons:

— Large proportions of the people have low incomes and are not in a position to pay taxes.

— There are administrative weaknesses which are responsible for tax evasions.

(iii) **Taxes on Wealth and Property** can account for a large proportion of the total revenue of the government for many reasons:

— Since they are collected from the rich class which has property, they are not likely to have an adverse influence on the incentive to work.

— Such taxes can reduce the income and wealth inequalities to some extent.

Indirect Taxes: They are also known as commodity taxes.

(i) **Sales Tax and Excise Duty** which are paid by all, the rich and the poor. However, luxury goods are taxed at a higher rate than the necessities.

(ii) **Customs Duty** includes exports duty and imports duty. They are easy to implement as the number of commodities involved in trade are limited and easy to monitor.

In developed countries, the direct taxes are a more important source of revenue for the government as compared to the developing countries where indirect taxes are more important.

Government Expenditure: Since the Great Depression, the government's role in economic intervention is continuously on the increase for several reasons:

(i) It was realized that the private sector was not in a position to pull the economy out of the depression on its own.

(ii) The private sector did not possess either the ability or the willingness to embark on ambitious projects which were necessary to put the economy on the path of growth and development.

Hence, it was realized that government expenditure is imperative for an economy in the form of investments in capital goods industries, building of the infrastructure, and payments of wages and salaries. Besides the government has to fulfill various social obligations which include expenditure on education, public health services, unemployment compensations, pensions and other welfare considerations.

Public Borrowing: Though public borrowing is the second most important source of revenue (after taxation) it is unlike taxes. All the borrowings from the public must be repaid back in the future.

Public borrowing can take two forms:

(i) Compulsory loans where bonds are issued by the government for a period varying from five to 10 years. Employees' contribution to provident fund falls under this category.

(ii) Voluntary loans where bills and securities are issued by the government.

Since taxation is insufficient to finance the growing public expenditures, the government in most countries has to resort to borrowing from the public. The developmental expenditures are increasing at such a great speed that in most countries the government has to finance these expenditures by raising loans from the public.

(Deficit financing has also often been included as an instrument of fiscal policy. Since it has already been discussed earlier in this chapter, it is not repeated again.)

RECAP

- One of the most important sources of revenue for the government in most countries is taxation.
- Since the Great Depression, the government's role in economic intervention is continuously on the increase.
- Public borrowing is the second most important source of revenue.

FULL EMPLOYMENT BUDGET SURPLUS

In any economy, the effect of any fiscal plan on the economic activity is associated with the size of the fiscal budget:

(i) When the government expenditure is greater than government revenue there exists a deficit in the budget and thus the government policy is stimulative or expansionary.

(ii) When government expenditure is lesser than the government revenue there exists a surplus in the budget and thus the government policy is restrictive or contractionary.

The budget surplus is the excess of government revenue over its total expenditures.

However, it is incorrect to measure the direction of the fiscal policy as expansionary or contractionary by analysing a budget deficit or a budget surplus. A budget may be in deficit during a recession when there is a decrease in the tax revenue. On the other hand, a budget may be in surplus during a boom when there is an increase in the tax revenue.

To measure the effect of fiscal policy on the level of output, a policy measure is necessary which is independent and not related to the business cycles. The full employment budget surplus is often quoted to be such a policy measure.

A related concept is the budget surplus (*BS*). The budget surplus is the excess of government revenue over its total expenditures. While the government revenue is in the form of taxes, its total expenditures are in the form of purchases of goods and services and transfer payments. Thus,

$$BS = TA - G - TR$$

where *BS* is budget surplus, $TA = tY$ is proportional tax, *G* is government expenditure on goods and services and *TR* is transfer payments. Thus,

$$BS = tY - G - TR$$

A negative budget surplus is an excess of government expenditure over government revenue. In simpler terms, it is a budget deficit.

The full employment budget surplus measures the budget surplus at the full employment level of income. It is also known as the high employment surplus, the standardized budget surplus or the cyclically adjusted surplus (or deficit).

The full employment budget surplus measures the budget surplus at the full employment level of income.

If Y^* is the full employment income level, then

$$BS^* = tY^* - G - TR$$

Thus,

$$BS^* - BS = t(Y^* - Y)$$

It is important to note that

(i) If the actual output level is higher than the full employment level, then the full employment budget surplus is lesser than the actual surplus.

(ii) If the actual output level is lesser than the full employment level, then the full employment budget surplus is larger than the actual budget surplus.

While the full employment budget and actual budget differs due to the cyclical factor in the budget, the full employment budget surplus differs from the actual budget surplus only in respect of tax collections.

The full employment budget surplus is a convenient way of analysing the impact of the budget and the effect of any fiscal plan on the economic activity.

The full employment budget surplus has been depicted in Figure 25.1 where BS is the line depicting the budget surplus. It has been plotted as a function of income, given the fiscal policy choices in terms

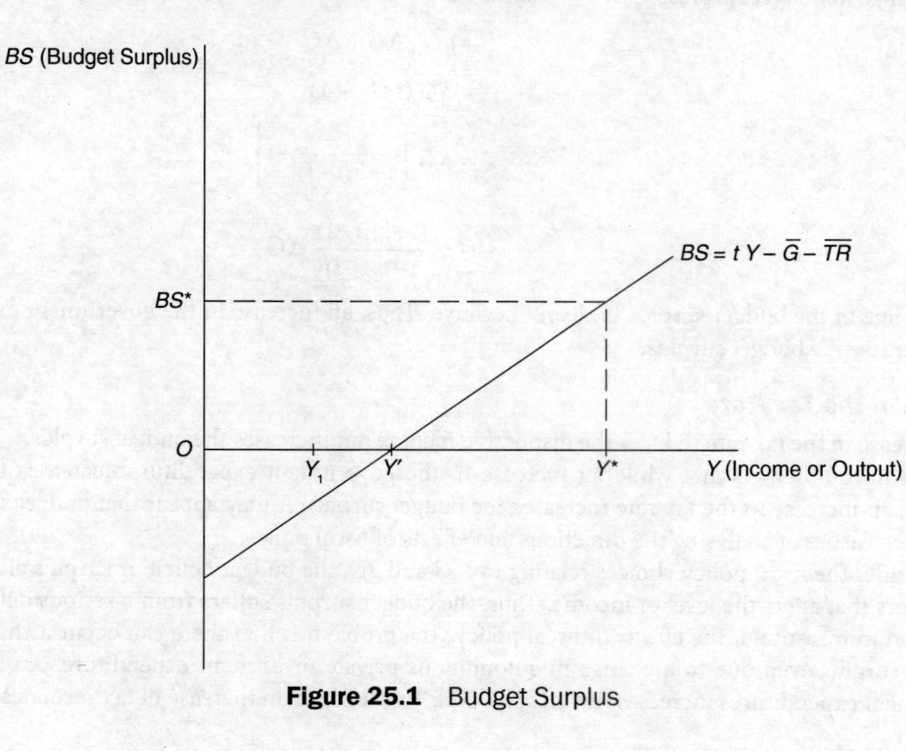

Figure 25.1 Budget Surplus

of t, G and TR. When the income level is high, the budget is in surplus or the budget surplus is high as the government revenue from tax is greater. When the income level is low, the budget is in deficit or there is a budget deficit as the government revenue from tax is less.

In the figure, suppose that the full employment level of output or income is at Y^*. The full employment budget surplus is BS^*. Also

(i) At an income level of Y', the government will have a balanced budget where the government expenditure matches the government revenue.

(ii) At lower levels of income, for example, if the income level is below Y', the budget will be in a deficit or there is a negative budget surplus. This may happen, for example, during recessions, when $G + TR$ are larger than the collections from taxes.

(iii) At higher levels of income, above Y' $G + TR$ is lesser than the collections from taxes.

The changes in the budget often occur due to changes in fiscal policy:

An Increase in the Government Expenditure

An increase in government expenditures will decrease the budget surplus.

Change in income due to the increase in government expenditures can be expressed as

$$\Delta Y = G_M \Delta \bar{G}.$$

(G_M is the multiplier when there exist income taxes.)

But a fraction of this increased income is collected as taxes. Thus, there is an increase in tax revenue equal to $\Delta T = t\, G_M \Delta \bar{G}$

Change in budget surplus:

$$\begin{aligned}\Delta \overline{BS} &= \Delta \bar{T} - \Delta \bar{G} \\ &= t\, G_M \Delta \bar{G} - \Delta \bar{G} \\ &= \Delta \bar{G}\,(t\, G_M - 1) \\ &= \Delta \bar{G}\left[\frac{t}{1-b(1-t)} - 1\right] \\ &= -\frac{(1-b)(1-t)}{1-b(1-t)}\,\Delta \bar{G}\end{aligned}$$

The change in the budget surplus is clearly negative. Thus, an increase in the government expenditure will decrease the budget surplus.

A Rise in the Tax Rate

An increase in the tax rate reduces the disposable income but increases the budget surplus.

We have observed that while an increase in the government expenditure decreases the budget surplus, an increase in the tax rate increases the budget surplus. It may appear that budget surplus is a suitable measure of analysing the directions and effects of fiscal policy.

Besides the fiscal policy choices relating to t, G and TR, the budget deficit or surplus also depends on factors that affect the level of income. Thus, the budget surplus suffers from a serious defect in case it is used to measure of the effects of fiscal policy. The problem is that there can occur a change in the budget surplus even due to a change in autonomous private investment expenditure. An increase in investment expenditures increases the income level. This leads to an increase in tax revenues and hence there is an increase in budget surplus or a decrease in the budget deficit. In this, it is quite obvious that the government has played no part in bringing about a change in the deficit.

RECAP

- An increase in the government expenditure or a decrease in the tax rate will decrease the budget surplus.
- Besides the fiscal policy choices relating to *t*, *G* and *TR*, the budget deficit or surplus also depends on factors that affect the level of income.

LIMITATIONS OF FISCAL POLICY

Existence of a Time Lag

Similar to monetary policy, this is perhaps one of the major problems in the path of the working of fiscal policy. There exists a considerable time lag between the time that there is a realization for the need for a fiscal policy and the time by which the response of the policy in bringing about changes in aggregate demand is felt.

The time lags can be divided under two heads:

(i) **Inside Lags**: These include the considerable time taken by the parliament or the state legislatures in giving their consent to the changes in the fiscal policy. There are long bureaucratic procedures which govern the changes required in taxation and government expenditures.

(ii) **Outside Lags:** Once the approvals have been given, the changes in the fiscal policy act directly on aggregate demand and the output which again may take some time.

It is imperative to observe that in case of fiscal policy inside lags are longer than the outside lags. However, the existence of the lags is certainly responsible for reducing the effectiveness of the fiscal policy. The policy makers, keeping in mind the existence of the lags, may often try to take the future into consideration in their attempts to bring about stability in the economy. But since the future is uncertain and difficult to predict, they may actually land up doing just the opposite, that is, destabilize the economy. Hence, the policy makers should refrain from intervening in the functioning of the economy unless it is absolutely necessary to do so since they may do more harm than good.

Underdeveloped Nature of the Less Developed Countries Limits the Effectiveness of the Fiscal Policy

The major problems in the implementation of fiscal policy in the less developed countries are:

(i) In such economies, sectors like the agriculture are often non-monetized. It is difficult for the administrators to assess the taxes to be paid by this sector which is formed mainly by the farmers and the self-employed. Often the agricultural sector is either exempt from taxation or subject to a minimal tax. Hence the entire burden of the tax has to be borne by the monetized sector, which is unjust and inequitable because the rich and the powerful landowners are able to get away without paying little or no tax.

(ii) In most such countries, the tax laws are highly complicated with various types of exemptions and deductions. As a result, many interpretations and loopholes co-exist which in turn make the tax laws a fertile ground for long drawn litigations. The tax rates which ideally should be progressive end up being regressive favouring the smart, who incidentally are also rich, and who are able to take advantage of the loopholes, while the general public and fixed income group bears the brunt of the tax. There are problems even at the level of the tax enforcement. The tax machinery is generally highly inefficient and prone to corruption which results in revenue leakages from the government coffers.

Excessive Burden of Public Debt

Often the resources which are generated through tax and other sources may prove to be insufficient for the ever increasing expenditures necessary for development of the economy. Hence, the authorities have to raise public debt, or in other words, borrowings both internal and external.

The problems associated with public debt are innumerable. Not only have the loans to be paid back the interest payments have also to be made at regular intervals. The problem is more acute in the case of external borrowings where all repayments are in terms of foreign currency. This will necessitate that the country earns sufficient foreign exchange to be in a position to pay back the debt. Often a country may be caught in an external debt trap where it is forced to take on a fresh loan to repay back just the interest on the earlier loan. Even with internal borrowings the government may have to take recourse to deficit financing which leads to inflation and related problems.

RECAP

- The existence of a time lag, underdeveloped nature of the less-developed countries and the excessive burden of public debt limit the effectiveness of the fiscal policy.

CROWDING OUT AND ITS IMPORTANCE

Crowding out is a situation which takes place when an expansionary fiscal policy causes an increase in the rate of interest leading to a decrease in private spending, especially the investment level.

Crowding out is a situation which takes place when an expansionary fiscal policy causes an increase in the rate of interest leading to a decrease in private spending, especially the investment level.

In Figure 25.2, the effects of an expansionary fiscal policy have been analysed in terms of the *IS–LM* framework. The initial equilibrium is determined by the intersection of the curves IS_1 and *LM* at point E_1. Due to an expansionary fiscal policy, the equilibrium shifts to E_2 and not E'. The income level increases to Y_2 and not Y'. The reason for this can be explained in terms of the rise in the rate of interest from r_1 to r_2. This increase in the rate of interest has a contractionary effect on investment. Thus, the increase in government spending crowds out private investment spending. The adjustments which occur in the interest rate have a dampening effect on the increase in output which is caused by the increase in government spending. It is to be noted that the higher the increase in the rate of interest rate due to increase in government spending, the greater will be the crowding out effect.

The crowding out depends on certain factors:

(i) The flatter is the *LM* curve, the lower is the increase in interest rates and thus the higher is the increase in income.

(ii) The flatter is the *IS* curve, the lower is the increase in the interest rate and thus the lower is the increase in income.

(iii) The larger the value of the multiplier, the higher the increase in the interest rate and the income.

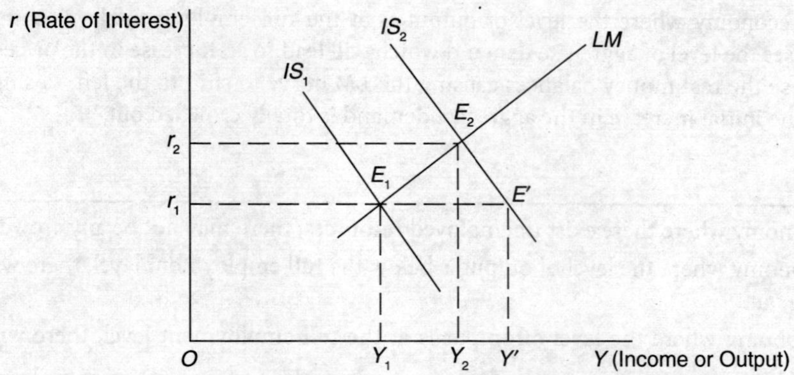

Figure 25.2 Effects of Expansionary Fiscal Policy

The importance of crowding out can be analysed by considering the following three cases:

(i) In an economy where there exist unemployed resources, a fiscal expansion may increase the level of output but it may not increase the interest rate as in Figure 25. 3. The reason may be the increase in the supply of money by the monetary authorities in order to accommodate the fiscal expansion. This would prevent the rise in the interest rate.

Monetary accommodation is also described as monetizing the budget deficit. It involves the printing of more money by the monetary authorities. Such a situation has been depicted in Figure 25.3 where both the *IS* and *LM* curves shift to the right and equilibrium shifts from E_1 to E'. The income level increases from Y_1 to Y' while the rate of interest remains unchanged at r_1.There need not occur a decrease in investment and hence there may not be any crowding out.

(ii) In an economy where the level of output is below the full employment level, a fiscal expansion increases the level of aggregate demand but now the firms can hire additional workers to increase the output level. There will be an increase in both the rate of interest and income level. However, there occurs an increase in savings in the economy which will make possible the financing of a larger budget deficit without there being a total displacement of private investment. Hence, there will not be a full crowding out.

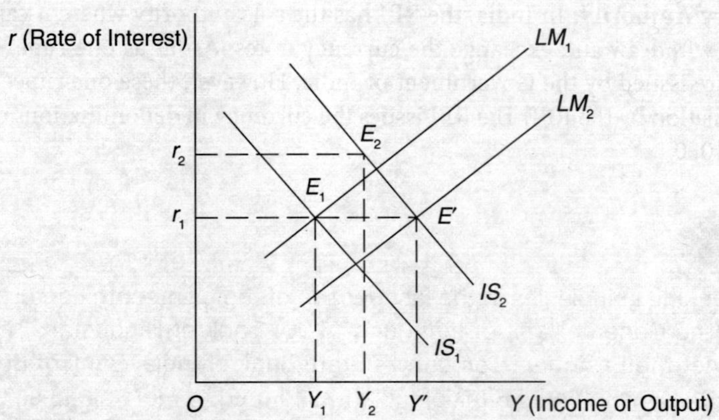

Figure 25.3 A Fiscal Expansion and Monetary Accommodation

(iii) In an economy where the level of output is at the full employment level, a fiscal expansion increases the level of aggregate demand which will lead to an increase in the price level. This will decrease the real money balances causing the *LM* curve to shift to the left, raising interest rates until the initial increase in the aggregate demand is totally crowded out.

RECAP

- In an economy where there exist unemployed resources, there may not be any crowding out.
- In an economy where the level of output is below the full employment level, there will not be a full crowding out.
- In an economy where the level of output is at the full employment level, there will be complete crowding out.

BANKING SECTOR

The banking sector plays a very important role in a country. Its structure differs from country to country, depending on the regulatory regime under which it functions.

In India, the banking system includes the central bank, commercial banks, and cooperative banks and developments banks.

Central Bank

The central bank of a country is the apex institution of the financial system. It plays an important role not only in the development of the financial system but also in the development of the economy.

The central bank of India, Reserve Bank of India (RBI), was established in 1935 under the Reserve Bank of India Act, 1934. It was formed as a private shareholder's bank and nationalized in 1949. As far as the administration of the RBI is concerned, the governor is the executive head and is assisted by the deputy governors and other officers. Its head office is in Bombay. There are many departments including the banking and issue departments.

The RBI performs all traditional functions that are performed by a central bank. In addition, it performs some promotional functions also.

Traditional Functions of the RBI

RBI as a Currency Authority: In India, the RBI has the sole authority where it can not only issue and circulate but also withdraw and exchange the currency notes. As far as one rupee notes and coins are concerned, they are issued by the Government of India. However, these one rupee notes and coins are added to the circulation by the RBI. The RBI issues the currency in denominations of rupees 2, 5, 10, 20, 50, 100, 500 and 1000.

BOX 25.5

The origin of banking in India lies in the last decade of the eighteenth century. The first banks include 1786, The General Bank of India and 1790, Bank of Hindustan. Three banks were established under the East India Company – State Bank of India, Bank of Bombay and Bank of Madras. In 1921, the Imperial Bank of India was formed by merging these three presidency banks. In 1955, this bank became the State Bank of India.

The RBI has two departments – the issue department and the banking department. The issue department looks after the issue of the currency. The currency which is issued by the RBI is a monetary liability of the RBI and must be backed by assets with an equal value. The assets may be in the form of gold coin, foreign securities, Government of India rupee securities and other assets. The composition of these assets determines the currency standard in the country.

RBI as a Banker's Bank: The RBI, as a banker's bank, performs many functions:

(i) All commercial and state cooperative banks, which are the scheduled banks, are required statutorily to deposit a stipulated ratio of their demand and time deposits as cash reserves with the RBI. This is as per the cash reserve ratio. Through this, the RBI is able to control the money supply and creation of credit in the economy.

(ii) It acts as a 'lender' of the last resort for the banks who can borrow funds from it in times of a temporary need.

(iii) The RBI supervises, regulates and controls the commercial and cooperative banks. As far as supervision is concerned, the RBI issues licenses for the opening up of new branches, regularly inspects the functioning of the scheduled banks, carries out ad hoc investigations into irregularities and complaints and exercises controls over appointments This ensures that a sound banking system develops in the country. Through the bank rate, the RBI is able to exercise control over the cost and hence the volume of bank credit.

RBI as a Banker to the Government: The RBI is a banker to the government, both central and state. It provides them with different banking services which include:

(i) Payments and receipt of money on behalf of the government.

(ii) Withdrawals and transfers of funds.

(iii) Managing public debt (for which it can charge a commission). It also manages the new issues of government loans.

The government, in return for all these services, maintains its cash balances on current account with the RBI.

As a banker to the government, the RBI provides the government with short-term credit whenever the government is in dire need of funds.

The state government is entitled to ways and means advances, which are temporary advances, from the RBI. Often some state governments even resort to overdrafts from the RBI.

As the central bank of India, the RBI imparts valuable guidance to the government on matters relating to banking and finance, including the financing of the five year plans, legislation relating to banking and other important matters.

RBI's Function of Exchange Management and Control: Under this head, the RBI's tasks include acting as a custodian of the foreign exchange reserves of the country, managing the exchange control, maintaining the external value of the rupee and acting as the government's agent as far as India's membership of the IMF is concerned.

At the time of the Second World War, exchange control was imposed in India for the first time. The control was exercised not only on the payments but also on the receipts of foreign exchange. All receipts of foreign exchange, whether from exports, investments and others were to be sold to the RBI. This facilitated a centralization of the foreign change reserves thus making possible a planned utilization of these reserves.

The RBI regulated the foreign exchange market through the Foreign Exchange Regulation (FERA) Act, 1947. However, later the FERA, was replaced by the Foreign Exchange Management Act (FEMA), 1999.

The tasks performed by the RBI in this regard include:

(i) Administering of the foreign exchange control through its exchange control department. For this purpose, it has authorized dealers who are involved in the foreign exchange transactions as per the guidelines issued to them.
(ii) Managing the exchange rate between the rupee and the foreign currencies. This is done through the purchase and sale of foreign exchange from the authorized dealers and others.
(iii) Managing the foreign exchange reserves and also maintaining the reserves in the form of gold and foreign securities.

RBI as a Controller of Credit and the Supply of Money: As the central bank of the country, the RBI performs the important task of controlling money supply, and also the volume and the cost of credit in the economy. This control has to be done keeping in mind the economy's objectives like a high rate of economic growth with distributional justice, a maximum output and employment with price stability and a balance in the country's balance of payments.

To exercise this control, the RBI has many instruments at its disposal which include open market operations, statutory liquidity ratio of banks and changes in the CRR.

RBI as a Source of Monetary Data: RBI acts as a source of banking and monetary data. For this purpose, it has a department of statistics which collects, compiles and publishes the data regularly. It also conducts research on banking and other aspects relating to finance. This is a necessary activity which helps in the formulation and evaluation of the country's economic policies.

Promotional Functions of the RBI

Since India's independence in 1947, the RBI, in addition to its traditional functions has been involved in many other activities:

(i) It has been actively involved in the building and strengthening of India's financial infrastructure by building new financial institutions and the reorganization of the already existing institutions, keeping in mind the needs of a developing economy.
(ii) It has been formulating measures to influence the allocation of credit in the directions which are desirable for the development of the society.

Promotion of Commercial Banks: As per the Banking Regulation Act, 1949, the RBI has powers to exercise control over the functioning of the commercial banks. It has used these powers to

(i) Strengthen the structure of commercial banking in India by either liquidating the weak ones or by amalgamating them with stronger ones.
(ii) Extend the banking services everywhere in the country, especially in the rural areas of the country.
(iii) Improve the distribution of credit sector wise such that there is an allocation of credit in favour of the priority sector, including agriculture and the small scale sector.

Promotion of the Bill Market: In 1952, the RBI had introduced the bill market scheme. However, this scheme was not successful. In 1970, the new bill market scheme was introduced with the purpose of developing a bill market in India. However, from time to time changes have been made in this scheme.

Promotion of Rural Credit: Since its inception and also according to the Reserve Bank of India Act, 1934, the development of the rural sector was recognized as the responsibility of the RBI. To achieve this goal, a separate agricultural credit department was formed. Other important developments include the cooperative credit movement, setting up of the regional rural banks (RRB'S) and the National Bank for Agricultural and Rural Development (NABARD).

Promotion of Industrial Finance: To provide long-term and medium-term finance, the industrialized development banks were established, for example, the IDBI, IFCI, ICICI, SIDBI and others.

Promotion of Export Finance: To promote international trade, various steps have been taken from time to time. Attempts have been made to provide credit for exports at rates which are internationally competitive. In this direction, the export- import bank was also set up in 1981. For financing of international trade the export-import bank is the apex institution.

Commercial Banks

In any economy the commercial banks are one of the most significant sources which provide institutional credit. In India, the commercial banks are involved in all types of banking business and also in the financing of business and trade. In general, these banks are involved in advancing short-term loans. However, lately they are extending their areas of operation to include medium- and long-term loans also.

In India, banks can be classified into different categories according to the functions performed by them, their pattern of ownership and their operational coverage:

Scheduled Banks and Non-scheduled Banks

Scheduled banks are those banks which are listed in the second schedule of the Reserve Bank of India Act, 1934.

(i) They should be successful in convincing the RBI that their functioning is not detrimental to the interest of the depositors.
(ii) Their paid up capital and reserves should not be less than ₹5 lakhs.
(iii) They are statutorily required to maintain cash reserves(CRR) with the RBI. In turn they get facilities like remittance facilities from the RBI at concessional rates.

Scheduled banks can be classified as

(i) Cooperative banks
(ii) Commercial banks

Commercial banks can be further sub-classified as

(i) Foreign scheduled banks
(ii) Indian scheduled banks

Indian scheduled banks can be further sub-classified as

(i) Private sector scheduled banks
(ii) Public sector scheduled banks

Public sector scheduled banks can be further sub-classified as

(i) Nationalized banks
(ii) Regional rural banks

Non-scheduled banks are those banks which are not listed in the second schedule of the Reserve Bank of India Act, 1934. Over the years their number has declined.

Some of the scheduled banks in India in the private sector are ICICI Bank Ltd, Axis Bank Ltd, HDFC Bank Ltd, Indusind Bank Ltd, South Indian Bank and IDBI Bank Ltd.

Some of the scheduled foreign banks in India are Bank of Tokyo Ltd, Standard Chartered Bank, American Express Bank Ltd, and Hongkong and Shanghai Banking Corporation Ltd.

Commercial Banks and Cooperative Banks

Cooperative banks can be divided into two sub-groups:

(i) Rural cooperative groups whose primary aim is to cater to the financial requirements of the agriculture and allied activities. Thus, it aims at the rural areas.
(ii) Urban cooperative groups whose primary aim is to cater to the financial requirements of the small-sized trade and commerce. Thus, it aims at the urban areas. Since 1991 their licensing has become more liberal and there has been a deregulation of their lending and deposit rates.

A comparison of commercial banks and cooperative banks depicts that

(i) While the cooperative banks are regulated by the state government through the registrar of cooperatives, the commercial banks are regulated by the RBI through the Banking Regulation Act.
(ii) In the case of cooperative banks, the assets and liabilities are much smaller as compared to commercial banks.
(iii) While the principles of self-help and cooperation form the basis of cooperative banking, the same is not true for commercial banking.
(iv) While the functioning of cooperative banking is based on a 'no profit no loss' principle, commercial banking is based on the principle of profit.

Indian Banks and Foreign Banks

The Indian banks comprise of many branches which are spread throughout the country, encompassing both the rural and the urban sectors. They are involved in advancing loans to all the sectors in the economy including agriculture, industry, trade and others. They are governed by the RBI Act, 1934, and also the Banking Regulation Act, 1949. They are thus ruled by the guidelines of the RBI pertaining to liquidity requirements (CRR and SLR), priority sector advances and interest rates.

The foreign banks are those banks which have been incorporated abroad. However, they have license from the RBI to function in India through their branches, which are generally in the commercial areas and the metropolis. They use the latest technology and a wide range of products including credit cards, ATM and other electronic services. They also deal in foreign currencies that they provide for travel, trade and others.

A comparison of Indian banks and foreign banks depicts that

(i) While the Indian banks have been incorporated in India, the foreign banks have been incorporated abroad.
(ii) While the branches of the Indian banks are spread throughout the country, encompassing both the rural and the urban sectors, as far as the foreign banks are concerned, their branches are generally in the commercial areas and the metropolis.
(iii) Unlike the Indian banks, the foreign banks use the latest technology.

Private Sector Banks and Public Sector Banks

Private sector banks have been incorporated in India. They are governed by the RBI Act, 1934, and also the Banking Regulation Act, 1949. Some of the private sector banks are the old generation banks with their conventional style of functioning. Since 1994 there have emerged the new generation banks which use the latest technology with a functioning which is quite modern in outlook. Hence these banks are in a position to compete with the branches of the foreign banks in the country.

The public sector banks include the nationalized banks, the State Bank of India (SBI) and its subsidiaries. The first bank to be nationalized was the erstwhile Imperial Bank of India in 1955. Thus, the State Bank of India was born which is today the largest bank in India if one looks at in terms of its branches, capital, size of assets and profits. The regional banks of the erstwhile princely states were nationalized in 1959 to form the seven subsidiaries of the SBI. In 1969, 14 banks were nationalized, while later in 1980, six more banks were nationalized.

Nationalized Banks and Regional Rural Banks

The nationalized banks have already been discussed under the public sector banks.

The regional rural banks are scheduled commercial banks but their operations are localized and limited to the rural areas. They provide banking services and credit facilities to the small farmer, artisan, agricultural labour and small entrepreneur. They are jointly set up by the Central government, the state government and the sponsored public sector bank. They are governed by the Banking Regulation Act, 1949.

Development Banks

In the post-independence era, an important financial development took place in India in the form of the growth of development banks. They are unlike commercial banks, in that they do not accept deposits from the public, they specialize in medium-term and long-term finance, and most important they are involved in promoting the country's economic development through the promotion of business ventures and investment. The financial assistance may take the form of term loans and advances, underwriting of new issues, subscription to shares and guarantee for term loans.

As far as the structure of development banks is concerned, at the national level there are banks for industrial development, a bank for agricultural development and also a bank for the development of foreign trade; at the state level too there are banks for industrial development.

The Industrial Development Bank of India (IDBI): The Industrial Development Bank of India (IDBI) was set up in 1964 and was delinked from the RBI so that it could be made autonomous in 1976. Its independent board is represented by the government, financial institutions, commercial banks and the industry. Its role in providing finance to industry has gone up. As far as industrial development banking is concerned, it is the apex bank in India in the capital market and in industrial finance. It synchronizes, supplements and integrates the activities of the other development banks. It is involved in many activities:

(i) Providing the facility of refinance of loans advanced by banks, specialized financial institutions and others.

(ii) Rediscounting the eligible bills of exchange.

(iii) Grants of loans to industries.

(iv) Guaranteeing of loans.

(v) Underwriting of the debentures and shares in industry to the eligible banks and term financing institutions in three ways.
(vi) Subscribing to the bonds and the shares of the term financing institutions.
(vii) Provision of credit for exports.

The IDBI's role in the development of the industry is quite commendable. It has been giving special attention to the regional development and also activities encouraging innovations and promotion of industry. It has played a very crucial role in the development of the backward regions. It has directed its resources in a socially desirable direction.

The Industrial Finance Corporation of India (IFCI): At the time of independence, the industries were in dire need of funds. Commercial banks were not in a position to provide any long-term finance to the industries. The underdeveloped capital market of the country was unable to provide finance to the industries.

In 1948, the IFCI was established as the first industrial financing institution to cater to the long-term needs for finance of the industry. It is involved in many activities:

(i) Providing finance to the medium and large companies in both the public and private sector.
(ii) Granting loans (in rupees and foreign currency) to the industry.
(iii) Underwriting of the debentures and shares in industries.
(iv) Subscribing to the bonds and the shares of the term financing institutions.
(v) Organizing techno-economic surveys and setting up organizations for technical consultancy.
(vi) Promotion of export and import substitution.

Although the IFCI is empowered to provide all types of assistance to the industry, it has mainly concentrated on advancing rupee loans. Initially it lent largely to the sugar and cotton industries while later it widened its sphere to lend to the other industries as well. It often faced the problem of default on both, the interest and the principal. It has played a vital role in the modernizing of industries in India.

The Industrial Credit and Investment Corporation of India (ICICI): The Industrial Credit and Investment Corporation of India Limited (ICICI) was set up in 1955 with the initiative from the Government of India, the World Bank and representatives of the industries in India. The purpose was to create a development financial institution to provide for the medium- and the long-term needs of the industry.

Its activities include:

(i) Providing finance to medium and large companies.
(ii) Playing a major role in developing underwriting facilities in India.
(iii) Acting as a major source of loans in foreign currency to the industry in India.
(iv) Procuring its funds from the World Bank.

In a major corporate strategic move in 2002 through a reverse merger, ICICI integrated the group's financing and banking operations, both wholesale and retail, into a single entity, namely, ICICI Bank. The Industrial Credit and Investment Corporation of India Limited is thus now ICICI Bank. The ICICI bank is the largest private sector bank in India. By the size of its assets, it is the second largest bank and by market capitalization, it is the third largest bank in India. The ICICI has been a leader in using the latest technology in banking in India. It has also been responsible for pioneering Internet banking in India. It offers a variety of banking and financial services to its customers.

The Industrial Investment Bank of India (IIBI): The Industrial Reconstruction Corporation of India (IRCI) was set up in 1971. Earlier its main purpose was to restore and revitalize the sick industrial units in India. In 1985, it was renamed the Industrial Reconstruction Bank of India (IRBI). It was involved in many activities which included the provision of managerial and technical assistance to the industry and also securing guidance and assistance from other financial institutions for the industry.

In 1997, it became the Industrial Investment Bank of India (IIBI).It provides financial assistance, for example, term loans and underwriting and also provides merchant banking services.

State Level Industrial Development Banks: Similar to the national level, at the state level there are industrial developments which aim at the development of the small- and medium-industrial units.

The State Financial Corporations (SFCs) are mainly involved in the provision of financial assistance in the form of loans, underwriting and subscribing to debentures and shares. They are under the control of the IDBI and the state government.

The State Industrial Development Corporations (SIDCs) are mainly involved in the provision of financial assistance in the form of loans, underwriting and subscribing to debentures and shares. They also promote industrial units by making available to them power, land and licenses. They are set up by the state governments.

Export-Import (or Exim) Bank of India: The Export-Import (or Exim) Bank of India was established in 1982.It is the apex institution in India for financing of international trade. It not only provides financial assistance (for example, direct loans and refinance of loans), but also coordinates the functioning of those involved in the financing of international trade. Bonds, debentures, foreign deposits and the borrowings from the RBI are its major source of funds.

National Bank for Agricultural and Rural Development (NABARD): The National Bank for Agricultural and Rural Development (NABARD) was set up in1982 as an apex development bank for the development of rural credit in India. National rural credit – long-term operations, national rural credit – establishment fund, bonds and debentures, and the borrowings from the RBI are its major source of funds.

It provides credit facilities to agriculture, small and cottage industries. It does so by providing refinance to commercial banks, cooperative banks, regional rural banks and others. Not only does the NABARD coordinate the activities of the other financial institutions, it is also involved in the provision of training and research facilities. It is also involved in regulating the regional rural banks and cooperative banks through inspections.

RECAP

- In India, the banking system includes the central bank, commercial banks, and cooperative banks and developments banks.
- The RBI performs all traditional functions that are performed by a central bank. In addition, it performs some promotional functions also.
- In India, the commercial banks are involved in all types of banking activities and also in the financing of business and trade.
- Cooperative banks include the rural cooperative groups whose primary aim is to cater to the financial requirements of agriculture and allied activities; and the urban cooperative groups whose primary aim is to cater to the financial requirements of small-sized trade and commerce.
- Development banks are unlike commercial banks, in that they do not accept deposits from the public, they specialize in medium-term and long-term finance, and most important they are involved in promoting the country's economic development.

SUMMARY

INTRODUCTION

1. This chapter examines monetary policy and fiscal policy and their functioning.
2. An attempt has also been made at understanding the goals which these policies aim at achieving.

MEANING OF MONETARY POLICY

1. Monetary policy is an operation by the monetary authorities of the country to achieve certain well-defined macroeconomic objectives/goals.
2. It is generally the central bank of the country which undertakes the implementation of the monetary policy. It operates through changes in the quantity of money.

Instruments of Monetary Policy

1. The main objectives which the monetary policy aims at achieving include economic growth, a higher rate of employment and price stability.
2. To achieve the objectives of monetary policy there exist various instruments, which can be divided into two categories: quantitative or general measures and qualitative or selective measures.
3. Quantitative or general measures of monetary policy controls the total volume of credit and the cost of credit in the economy and thus the supply of money. They include open market operations, variations in reserve requirements, statutory liquidity requirement, bank rate policy, repo rate and reverse repo rate.
4. Open market operations refer to the sale and purchase of government securities and treasury bills by the central bank. It is an instrument of monetary control which is most powerful and which is most widely used by the central bank.
5. The advantages of open market operations are as follows: they are highly flexible, easily reversible in time and do not have any announcement effects.
6. Variations in reserve requirements can be divided under two heads: required reserves and excess reserves.
7. Required reserves are cash balances which banks hold to meet their statutory reserve requirements. The purpose of these reserves is to safeguard the interest of the depositors. It also enables the central bank to be able to control liquidity.
8. Excess reserves are reserves in excess of the required reserves. They are held by the banks for meeting currency drains and clearing drains.
9. It is often alleged that variations in reserve requirements are an inferior tool of monetary policy because they lead to lumpy and discontinuous changes in the deposits and also, in that they produce announcement effects.
10. Under the statutory liquidity requirement, banks are statutorily required to maintain a certain fixed proportion of their demand and time liabilities in the form of designated liquid assets.
11. In India, like the CRR, the SLR has not been very successful as an instrument of monetary policy.
12. Bank rate policy or the discount rate is the rate of interest at which the central bank rediscounts eligible bills of exchange or other commercial papers.
13. The limitation of the bank rate policy is that it is more sticky in comparison to the other rates and the changes in it are discontinuous and have announcement effects.
14. The repo rate is the rate at which the central bank infuses short-term liquidity into the system. In simpler terms, it is the rate at which the central bank lends to the banks. The reverse repo rate is the rate at which banks park their short-term excess liquidity with the central bank in exchange for government securities. It is the rate at which the central bank borrows from the banks.
15. Qualitative or selective measures of monetary policy control the direction and distribution of credit in the economy. They include rationing of credit, change in margin requirements, moral suasion and direct action.
16. Credit rationing is resorted to when there occurs a shortage of institutional credit.
17. Change in margin requirements works indirectly to influence lending and thus regulates the capital markets.

18. Moral suasion is a combination of persuasion and pressures which a central bank asserts to bring the erring banks in line so that they function in accordance with the central bank's directives.
19. Direct action refers to the coercive actions resorted to by the central bank against banks who do not function according to its directives.
20. Deficit financing refers to ways in which the deficit in the government's budget is financed. The central bank merely prints more currency and then puts them into circulation on behalf of the government.
21. One major problem that is associated with deficit financing is that it always results in inflation.

Limitations of Monetary Policy

The limitations of monetary policy are the existence of a time lag, presence of non-bank financial intermediaries reducing the impact of the monetary policy through an increase in the velocity of money and the underdeveloped nature of the money and capital markets.

MEANING OF FISCAL POLICY

1. Fiscal policy refers to the government's policy regarding government expenditure, taxation and public borrowing with the view to achieving certain well-defined macroeconomic objectives.
2. It was only with the coming of Keynes that fiscal policy gained importance.
3. The monetarists believed that, with the exception of some circumstances, in general, increases in government expenditures do not add to aggregate demand but in fact are responsible for crowding out private investment of an equal amount.

Instruments of Fiscal Policy

1. To implement fiscal policy, the government has at its behest several instruments which include taxation, government expenditure and public borrowing.
2. Taxation is one of the most important sources of revenue for the government in most countries. Taxes can be analysed under two headings: direct taxes which include corporate income taxes, personal income tax and taxes on wealth and property, and indirect taxes which include sales tax, excise duty and customs duty.
3. In developed countries, the direct taxes are a more important source of revenue for the government as compared to the developing countries where indirect taxes are more important.
4. Since the Great Depression, the government's role in economic activity is continuously on the increase. It was realized that government expenditure is imperative for an economy in the form of investments in capital goods industries, building of infrastructure, and payments of wages and salaries.
5. Though public borrowing is the second most important source of revenue, it is unlike taxes. All the borrowings from the public must be repaid back in the future. Public borrowing can take two forms: compulsory loans and voluntary loans where bills and securities are issued by the government.

Full Employment Budget Surplus

1. The full employment budget surplus measures the budget surplus at the full employment level of income.
2. It is a convenient way of analysing the impact of the budget and the effect of any fiscal plan on the economic activity.

Limitations of Fiscal Policy

1. The effective working of fiscal policy is hindered due to the existence of different obstacles.
2. The existence of a time lag includes inside lags and outside lags. In case of fiscal policy, inside lags are longer than the outside lags.
3. The underdeveloped nature of the less developed countries limits the effectiveness of the fiscal policy. It is difficult for the administrators to assess the taxes to be paid by agriculture sector. In most countries, the tax laws are highly complicated.
4. Often the resources which are generated through tax and other sources may prove to be insufficient and the authorities may have to resort to public debt.

Crowding Out and Its Importance

1. Crowding out is a situation which takes place when an expansionary fiscal policy causes an increase in the rate of interest leading to a decrease in private spending, especially the investment level.
2. An increase in government spending crowds out private investment spending. It is to be noted that the higher the increase in the rate of interest rate due to increase in government spending, the greater will be the crowding out effect.
3. The importance of crowding out can be analysed by considering three cases:
   (a) In an economy where there exist unemployed resources, a fiscal expansion may not lead to any crowding out.
   (b) In an economy where the level of output is below the full employment level, there will not be a full crowding out.
   (c) In an economy where the level of output is at the full employment level, there will be a full crowding out.

Banking Sector

1. The banking sector plays a very important role in a country.
2. In India, the banking system includes the central bank, commercial banks, and cooperative banks and developments banks.

Central Bank

1. The central bank of a country is the apex institution of the financial system.
2. The central bank of India, Reserve Bank of India (RBI), was established in 1935 under the Reserve Bank of India Act, 1934.
3. As far as the administration of the RBI is concerned, the governor is the executive head and is assisted by the deputy governors and other officers.
4. The RBI performs all traditional functions that are performed by a central bank. In addition, it also performs other promotional functions.

Traditional Functions of the RBI

RBI as a Currency Authority

1. In India, the RBI has the sole authority where it can not only issue and circulate but also withdraw and exchange the currency notes.
2. The RBI issues the currency in denominations of rupees 2, 5, 10, 20, 50, 100, 500 and 1000.
3. The RBI has two departments – the issue department and the banking department.
4. The issue department looks after the issue of the currency.
5. The banking department looks after the rest of the banking business of the RBI.

RBI as a Banker's Bank

1. As per the cash reserve ratio, all commercial and state cooperative banks, which are the scheduled banks, are required statutorily to deposit a stipulated ratio of their demand and time deposits as cash reserves with the RBI.
2. The RBI acts as a 'lender' of the last resort for the banks who can borrow funds from it in times of temporary need.
3. The RBI supervises, regulates and controls the commercial and cooperative banks.

RBI as a Banker to the Government

1. The RBI is a banker to the government, both central and state. It provides them with different banking services.
2. The government, in return for all these services, maintains its cash balances on current account with the RBI.
3. The RBI provides the government with short-term credit whenever the government is in dire need of funds.
4. The RBI imparts valuable guidance to the government on matters relating to banking and finance.

RBI's Function of Exchange Management and Control

1. Under this head, the RBI's tasks include acting as a custodian of the foreign exchange reserves of the country, managing the exchange control, maintaining the external value of the rupee and acting as the government's agent as far as India's membership of the IMF is concerned.
2. The RBI regulated the foreign exchange market through the Foreign Exchange Regulation (FERA) Act, 1947.
3. Later the FERA was replaced by the Foreign Exchange Management Act (FEMA), 1999.

RBI as a Controller of Credit and the Supply of Money

1. As the central bank of the country, the RBI performs the important task of controlling money supply, and also the volume and the cost of credit in the economy.
2. To exercise this control, the RBI has many instruments at its disposal which include open market operations, statutory liquidity ratio of banks and changes in the CRR.

RBI as a Source of Monetary Data

1. RBI acts as a source of banking and monetary data.
2. For this purpose, it has a department of statistics which collects compiles and publishes the data regularly.

Promotional Functions of the RBI

1. The RBI has been actively involved in building and strengthening of India's financial infrastructure.
2. It has been formulating measures to influence the allocation of credit in the directions which are desirable for the development of the society.

Promotion of Commercial Banks

1. The RBI has strengthened the structure of commercial banking in India by either liquidating the weak ones or by amalgamating them with the stronger ones.
2. It has extended the banking services everywhere in the country, especially in the rural areas of the country.

Promotion of the Bill Market

1. In 1970, the new bill market scheme was introduced with the purpose of developing a bill market in India.
2. From time to time changes have been made in this scheme.

Promotion of Rural Credit

1. The development of the rural sector was recognized as the responsibility of the RBI.
2. To achieve this goal, a separate agricultural credit department was formed.
3. Other important developments include the cooperative credit movement, setting up of the regional rural banks (RRB'S) and the NABARD.

Promotion of Industrial Finance

1. To provide long-term and medium-term finance, the industrialized development banks were established, for example, the IDBI, IFCI, ICICI, SIDBI and others.

Promotion of Export Finance

1. The Export-Import Bank was also set up in 1981.
2. For financing of the international trade, the Export-Import Bank is the apex institution.

Commercial Banks

1. In India, the commercial banks are involved in all types of banking business and also in the financing of business and trade.
2. In general, these banks are involved in advancing short-term loans.
3. Lately, they are extending their areas of operation to include medium- and long-term loans also.
4. In India, banks can be classified into different categories according to their functions, their pattern of ownership and the operational coverage.

Scheduled Banks and Non-scheduled Banks

1. Scheduled banks are those banks which are listed in the second schedule of the Reserve Bank of India Act, 1934.
2. Scheduled banks can be classified as cooperative banks and commercial banks.
3. Commercial banks can be further sub-classified as foreign scheduled banks and Indian scheduled banks.
4. Indian scheduled banks can be further sub-classified as private sector scheduled banks and public sector scheduled banks.
5. Public sector scheduled banks can be further sub-classified as nationalized banks and regional rural banks.
6. Non-scheduled banks are those banks which are not listed in the second schedule of the Reserve Bank of India Act, 1934.

Commercial Banks and Cooperative Banks

1. Cooperative banks can be divided into two subgroups.
2. Rural cooperative groups primary aim is to cater to the financial requirements of the agriculture and allied activities.
3. Urban cooperative groups primary aim is to cater to the financial requirements of the small-sized trade and commerce.
4. While the cooperative banks are regulated by the state government through the registrar of cooperatives, the commercial banks are regulated by the RBI through the Banking Regulation Act.
5. In the case of cooperative banks, the assets and liabilities are much smaller compared to commercial banks.
6. While the principles of self-help and cooperation form the basis of cooperative banking, the same is not true for commercial banking.
7. While the functioning of cooperative banking is based on a 'no profit no loss' principle, commercial banking is based on the principle of profit.

Indian Banks and Foreign Banks

1. The Indian banks comprise of many branches which are spread throughout the country encompassing both the rural and the urban sectors.
2. They are involved in advancing loans to all the sectors in the economy, including agriculture, industry, trade and others.
3. They are governed by the RBI Act, 1934, and also the Banking Regulation Act, 1949.
4. The foreign banks are those banks which have been incorporated abroad.
5. They have license from the RBI to function in India through their branches, which are generally in the commercial areas and the metropolis.
6. They use the latest technology and a wide range of products including credit cards, ATM and electronic services.
7. They also deal in foreign currencies that they provide for travel, trade and others.
8. While the Indian banks have been incorporated in India, the foreign banks have been incorporated abroad.
9. While the branches of the Indian banks are spread throughout the country encompassing both the rural and the urban sectors, as far as the foreign banks are concerned, their branches are generally in the commercial areas and the metropolis.
10. Unlike the Indian banks, the foreign banks use the latest technology.

Private Sector Banks and Public Sector Banks

1. Private sector banks have been incorporated in India.
2. They are governed by the RBI Act, 1934, and also the Banking Regulation Act, 1949.
3. These banks are in a position to compete with the branches of the foreign banks in the country.
4. The public sector banks include the nationalized banks, the State Bank of India (SBI) and its subsidiaries.
5. In 1969, 14 banks were nationalized, later in 1980, 6 more banks were nationalized.

Nationalized Banks and Regional Rural Banks

1. The regional rural banks are scheduled commercial banks but their operations are localized and limited to the rural areas.
2. They provide banking services and credit facilities to small farmers, artisans, agricultural labours and small entrepreneurs.

Development Banks

1. Development banks are unlike commercial banks, in that they do not accept deposits from the public and they specialize in medium-term and long-term finance.
2. Most important, they are involved in promoting the country's economic development through promotion of business ventures and investment.
3. Financial assistance may take the form of term loans and advances, underwriting of new issues, subscription to shares and guarantee for term loans.
4. There are banks for industrial development, banks for agricultural development and also banks for development of foreign trade.

The Industrial Development Bank of India (IDBI)

1. The Industrial Development Bank of India (IDBI) was set up in 1964 and was delinked from the RBI so that it could be made autonomous in 1976.
2. Its independent board is represented by the government, financial institutions, the commercial banks and the industries.
3. As far as industrial development banking is concerned, it is the apex bank in India in the capital market and in industrial finance.
4. The IDBI's role in the development of the industries is quite commendable. It has directed its resources in a socially desirable direction.

The Industrial Finance Corporation of India (IFCI)

1. In 1948, the IFCI was established as the first industrial financing institution to cater to the long-term financial needs of the industries.
2. Although the IFCI is empowered to provide all types of assistance to the industry, it has mainly concentrated on advancing rupee loans.

The Industrial Credit and Investment Corporation of India (ICICI)

1. The Industrial Credit and Investment Corporation of India Limited (ICICI) was set up in 1955 with the initiative from the Government of India, the World Bank and representatives of the industries in India.
2. The purpose was to create a financial institution to provide for the development of medium- and the long-term needs of the industry.
3. The Industrial Credit and Investment Corporation of India Limited is thus now ICICI Bank.
4. The ICICI bank is the largest private sector bank in India.
5. By the size of its assets, it is the second largest bank and by market capitalization, it is the third largest bank in India.
6. The ICICI has been the leader in using the latest technology in banking in India.
7. It has also been responsible for pioneering Internet banking in India.

The Industrial Investment Bank of India (IIBI)

1. The Industrial Reconstruction Corporation of India (IRCI) was set up in 1971.
2. In 1985, it was renamed the Industrial Reconstruction Bank of India (IRBI).
3. In 1997, it became the Industrial Investment Bank of India (IIBI).It provides financial assistance, for example, term loans and underwriting and also provides merchant banking services.

State Level Industrial Development Banks

1. Similar to the national level, at the state level there are industrial developments which aim at the development of small- and medium-industrial units.
2. The state financial corporations (SFCs) are mainly involved in the provision of financial assistance in the form of loans, underwriting and subscribing to debentures and shares.
3. The state industrial development corporations (SIDCs) are mainly involved in the provision of financial assistance in the form of loans, underwriting and subscribing to debentures and shares.

Export-Import (or Exim) Bank of India

1. The Export-Import (or Exim) Bank of India was established in 1982.
2. It is the apex institution in India for the financing of international trade.
3. It not only provides financial assistance but also coordinates the functioning of those involved in the financing of international trade.
4. Bonds, debentures, foreign deposits and the borrowings from the RBI are its major source of funds.

National Bank for Agricultural and Rural Development (NABARD)

1. The National Bank for Agricultural and Rural Development (NABARD) was set up in1982 as an apex development bank for development of rural credit in India.
2. National rural credit – Long-term operations, national rural credit – establishment fund, bonds and debentures, and the borrowings from the RBI are its major source of funds.
3. It provides credit facilities to agriculture, small and cottage industries.

REVIEW QUESTIONS

TRUE OR FALSE QUESTIONS

1. Monetary policy is an operation by the monetary authorities of the country.
2. The two categories of instruments of monetary policy at the disposal of the central bank are the quantitative or general measures and the qualitative or selective measures.
3. Required reserves are cash balances which the central bank holds to meet its statutory reserve requirements.
4. According to the statutory liquidity requirement, banks are required to maintain a certain fixed proportion of their liabilities in the form of designated liquid assets.
5. Reverse repo rate is the rate at which the central bank infuses short-term liquidity into the system.

SHORT ANSWER QUESTIONS

1. What is the meaning of monetary policy?
2. What is an open market operation?
3. What is fiscal policy? Discuss.
4. Why are variations in reserve requirements said to be an inferior tool of monetary policy as compared to open market operations?
5. Write a short note on the bank rate policy.

LONG ANSWER QUESTIONS

1. What are the instruments of monetary policy? How are the two categories different from each other?
2. 'Open market operation is an instrument of monetary control which is most powerful and which is most widely used by the central bank.' Discuss.
3. How can fiscal policy actions tackle the problem of stabilization in the economy?

4. 'To implement fiscal policy the government has at its behest several instruments which include taxation, government expenditure and public borrowing.' Comment.
5. What is crowding out? Why is it important?

ANSWERS

TRUE OR FALSE QUESTIONS

1. **True.** Monetary policy is an operation by the monetary authorities of the country to achieve certain well-defined macroeconomic objectives.
2. **True.** These instruments give the central bank the power to control the money supply and hence achieve the macroeconomic objectives.
3. **False.** Required reserves are cash balances which commercial banks hold to meet their statutory reserve requirements.
4. **True.** This is a statutory requirement where the banks are required to maintain a certain fixed proportion of their demand and time liabilities in the form of designated liquid assets.
5. **False.** Reverse repo rate is the rate at which banks park their short-term excess liquidity with the central bank in exchange for government securities.

Glossary

Accelerator Principle: The basic relationship which exists between the investment and the change in the output level is known as the accelerator principle.

Accommodating Transactions: Accommodating transactions are those transactions that take place for the specific purpose of equalizing the balance of payments from an accountant's view.

Accounting Profit: Accounting profit is the difference between revenue and explicit costs incurred.

Actual Costs: Actual Costs are the costs, which a firm incurs on raw materials, labour, machinery, advertising and other such expenses.

Advertisement Elasticity: Advertisement elasticity is a measure of the responsiveness of the quantity demanded of a particular good to a change in advertising, *ceteris paribus*.

Aggregate Demand: Aggregate demand is the total amount of goods demanded in an economy.

Arbitrage: Arbitrage is the simultaneous buying and selling of different foreign currencies in the different foreign exchange markets to take advantage of the difference in the prices.

Automatic Stabilizer: An automatic stabilizer is a built-in mechanism in any economy which automatically reduces the change in the output in response to a change in the level of the autonomous demand.

Autonomous Investment: Investment which does not change due to a change in income and the interest rate is called the autonomous investment.

Autonomous Transactions: Autonomous transactions are those transactions that take place independently of other items in the balance of payments. They take place for the satisfaction that they give or for the profit that they yield.

Average Product: The average product is the total product divided by the amount of variable factor employed to produce the output.

Average Propensity to Consume (A): The APC is defined as the ratio of consumption to income for different levels of income.

Average Revenue: Average revenue can be defined as the average proceeds earned by a firm from the sale of a certain amount of the output.

Balanced Budget: The budget is in balance when the government expenditures plus transfer payments equal the gross tax receipts, or in other words $G = T$.

'Balanced Budget' Multiplier: The 'balanced budget' multiplier is the increase in the output as a consequence of equal increases in the government expenditure and taxes. It is equal to 1.

Balance of Invisible Trade: The balance of invisible trade is the difference between the exports and imports of services.

Balance of Payments: The balance of payments is a summary statement of all the economic transactions between the residents of one country with the rest of the world during a particular time, which is usually a year.

Balance of Trade: The balance of trade is the difference between the exports and imports of goods.

Bank Rate: Bank rate or the discount rate is the rate of interest at which the central bank rediscounts eligible bills of exchange or other commercial papers.

Break-even Level of Output: The break-even level of output is that level of output at which a firm neither makes profits nor losses. It is the level of output at which total cost is equal to total revenue.

Break Even Point: Break even point is a point at which the firm makes zero profits.

Budget Line: The budget line represents the various combinations of the amounts of the goods, which the consumer can purchase given his money income and the price of the goods.

Budget Set: The budget set includes all the combinations on and within the budget line from which a consumer can choose any combination of goods x and y.

Budget Surplus: Budget surplus is the excess of government revenue over its total expenditures.

Calculable Risks: Calculable risks are those risks for which the probability of occurring can be calculated and thus they can be insured against, for example, risk of theft and fire.

Capital: Capital is the accumulated stock of plant and equipment, which is held by the business firms.

Capital Account of the Balance of Payments: The capital account of the balance of payments measures the outflow and inflow of capital into the economy.

Capital Budgeting: Capital budgeting is the process, which involves the planning of the capital expenditures in the various investment projects.

Cartel: A cartel is formed by a group of firms, which are producing a good and which may explicitly agree to coordinate their policies to set a price and to increase the profits of the member firms.

Certainty: Certainty is a situation, where there exists perfect knowledge about the conditions prevailing in the market. Under the state of certainty, there exists only one outcome to an investment decision and the investor is aware of that outcome.

Change in Demand: A change in demand or a change in the quantity demanded of the good is a movement, which occurs along the demand curve and is caused by a change in the price of the good, *ceteris paribus*.

Change in Supply: A change in supply or a change in the quantity supplied of the good is a movement, which occurs along the supply curve and is caused by a change in the price of the good, *ceteris paribus*.

Constant Returns to Scale: Constant returns to scale occur when all the factors of production are increased simultaneously in the same proportion and there is an increase in the output, which is in the same proportion.

Consumer Surplus: The consumer surplus is a measure of the benefit, which accrues to a consumer when the price that he is willing to pay for a good is more than the price he actually pays for it.

Consumer's Equilibrium: A consumer is in equilibrium when he is able to reach the highest indifference curve, given the budget constraint.

Consumption Function: The consumption function is a relationship between income and consumption expenditure.

Contraction of Demand: A contraction of demand is a fall in the demand for the good as a result of a rise in the price of the good.

Contraction of Supply: A contraction of supply is a decrease in the supply of the good as a result of a fall in the price of the good.

Contribution per Unit of Output: (P_x – AVC) is the contribution per unit of output. It measures the contribution made by each unit of output to cover the total fixed cost.

Cost Difference Variation: The cost difference variation in income is necessary to reduce the real income (equals the money income divided by the price of the good) of the consumer, which had gone up due to a decrease in the price of the good.

Cross Price Elasticity of Demand: Cross price elasticity of demand is a measure of the responsiveness of the quantity demanded of a particular good to a change in the price of another good, *ceteris paribus*.

Crowding Out: Crowding out is a situation which takes place when an expansionary fiscal policy causes an increase in the rate of interest leading to a decrease in private spending, especially the investment level.

Currency Board: Currency board is an arrangement under which the central bank of a country holds enough amount of a foreign currency to back, in a fixed ratio, each and every unit of the domestic currency.

Current Account of the Balance of Payments: The current account of the balance of payments measures the flow of goods, services and income, which occur across the national borders.

Decrease in Demand: A decrease in demand is a decrease in the demand for the good as a result of a change in any of the factors, which influence the demand other than the price of the good itself, for example, a decrease in the price of the substitute good or a decrease in the consumer's income.

Decrease in Supply: A decrease in supply is a decrease in the supply of the good as a result of a change in any of the factors, which influence the supply other than the price of the good itself.

Decreasing Returns to Scale: Decreasing returns to scale occur when all the factors of production are increased simultaneously in the same proportion and there is an increase in the output, which is less than proportionate.

Degree of Price Discrimination: The degree of price discrimination is the limit to which a firm can make a division of the markets and extract the surplus from the consumers.

Demand: The quantity demanded of a good is the amount of that good demanded at a particular price over a certain time.

Demand Curve: The demand curve is a graphical representation of the demand schedule.

Demand Forecasting: Demand forecasting involves predicting of the future demand for a good.

Demand Schedule: A demand schedule depicts the quantity of the good, which is demanded at each price, assuming that the price of the other goods, income of the consumer and tastes and preferences of the consumer remain the same (*ceteris paribus* assumption).

Devaluation: Devaluation refers to a conscious action by the monetary authorities to lower the value of a currency with respect to the price of gold.

Direct Action: Direct action refers to the coercive actions resorted to by the central bank against those banks who do not function according to its directives.

Direct Taxes: Direct taxes are levied directly and include personal income and corporate income taxes.

Discretionary Fiscal Policy: Discretionary fiscal policy refers to the deliberate changes in the government expenditure and the tax rates by the government in an economy in order to bring about stability in the economy.

Disposable Personal Income: Disposable personal income is the amount, which is actually available to the households and to the non-corporate business after they have fulfilled their tax obligations to the government.

Dollarization: Dollarization is a situation, where a country abandons its domestic currency and adopts a strong foreign currency like the dollar.

Dynamic Models: Dynamic models are those models that trace the changes that occur in the values of the different variables over time.

Economic Growth: Economic growth refers to an increase in the amount of goods and services, which are produced in an economy over time. Thus, it is an increase in the economy's capacity to produce goods and services in the long run.

Economic Profit: Economic profit is the difference between *TR* and *TC*, where costs include both the explicit cost and the implicit cost.

Economic Region of Production: Efficient range or the economic region of production is the range over which the marginal products of the factors, for example, labour and capital, are diminishing but greater than zero or positive.

Economic Rent: Economic rent can be defined as the payment to a factor of production, which is over and above the amount that the factor should earn if it has to remain in its present use. In other words, it is the excess of what a factor earns over its transfer earnings.

Economies of Scale: When a firm increases its output by changing its scale of operations, the benefits that it experiences are called the economies of scale.

Edgeworth Box Diagram: The Edgeworth box diagram has been named after F.Y. Edgeworth. It is a graphical technique to show the optimum allocation of given amounts of two factors between two goods and also the allocation of the (given amounts of) two goods between two consumers.

Elasticity of Price Expectations: The elasticity of price expectations is a measure of the responsiveness of the expected change in the future prices to the change in the current prices of a good.

Elasticity of Substitution: Elasticity of substitution between two factors is a measure of the degree to which one factor can substitute the other.

Elasticity of Supply: Elasticity of supply is a measure of the responsiveness of the quantity supplied of a good to a change in the price of the good.

Equilibrium: Equilibrium is a state of balance or a state, where there is no change.

Excess Capacity: Excess capacity is the difference between the ideal (the least cost) output and the profit-maximizing output of the firm.

Excess Reserves: Excess reserves are reserves in excess of the required reserves.

Exchange Rate: The exchange rate is the rate at which one country's currency exchanges for another country's currency.

Expansion of Demand: An expansion or extension of demand is a rise in the demand for the good as a result of a fall in the price of the good.

Expansion of Supply: An expansion or extension of supply is a rise in the supply of the good as a result of an increase in the price of the good.

Expansion Path: The expansion path is a locus of points of the producer's equilibrium represented by points of tangency of successive isoquants with the corresponding isocost lines.

Expected Value: Expected value is the sum of the different outcomes of an investment multiplied by the probability of their occurrence.

Expenditure-reducing Policies: Expenditure-reducing policies are aimed at bringing about a change in the aggregate expenditure in the country.

Expenditure-switching Policies: The expenditure-switching policies work mainly through changing the relative price of exports and imports.

Explicit Cost: Explicit costs are incurred by the firm when it buys or hires factors, which are required in the process of production. They include, for example, wages and insurance.

External Diseconomies: These diseconomies occur because of the growth of the industry as a whole leading to an increase in the per-unit costs.

External Economies: These economies occur because of the growth of the industry as a whole. They are generated from outside the firm and the benefit is shared by all the firms in the industry.

First Degree Price Discrimination: Under first degree price discrimination, the monopolist charges the maximum price that each consumer is willing to pay for every unit of the good. Thus, he is able to extract the whole of the surplus from the consumer.

Fiscal Policy: Fiscal policy refers to the government's policy regarding government expenditure, taxation and public borrowing with the view to achieving certain well-defined macroeconomic objectives.

Fixed Cost: Fixed cost is the cost, which does not vary with the level of output. It includes the cost of managerial and administrative staff, depreciation of building and machinery and others. It is also called the supplementary cost or overhead cost.

Fixed Factor: A fixed factor is one, where the supply is always inelastic in the short run.

Flow: Flow is a quantity, which is measured over time.

Foreign Exchange Market: The foreign exchange market is a market, where foreign currencies (or foreign exchange) are purchased and sold by individuals, firms, commercial banks and the central banks of the different countries.

Forward Transaction: A forward transaction is one, which involves an agreement between the buyer and the seller to purchase or sell a fixed amount of currency for a predetermined rate at a specified date in the future.

Full Employment Budget Surplus: The full employment budget surplus measures the budget surplus at the full employment level of income.

General Equilibrium: General equilibrium approach involves a state, where all the markets and the decision-making units in the economy are in a simultaneous equilibrium.

Grand Utility Possibility Curve: The grand utility possibility curve is a locus of points, which are Pareto optimum in production and consumption. This curve is an envelope of the utility possibility curves.

Gross Domestic Product: GDP is the total value of all the final goods and services produced by all the enterprises within the domestic territory of a country in a particular year.

Gross National Product: GNP is a measure of the value of goods and services, which the nationals or residents of the country produce regardless of where they are located.

Hedging: Hedging is an attempt at covering the risk involved in a foreign exchange transaction through a forward transaction.

Homogenous Production Function: A production function is homogenous if all the factors of production are increased proportionately and one can factor out the proportion.

Implicit Cost: Implicit cost is incurred by the firm when it uses the factors, which are owned by the firm in the process of production. They include, for example, rent and interest on building and capital owned by the firm.

Incalculable Risks: Incalculable risks are those risks for which the probability of occurring cannot be calculated and thus they cannot be insured against, for example, the effects of a recession on the profits of a firm. Thus, here there is an element of uncertainty involved.

Income Consumption Curve: The income consumption curve is the locus of points representing the consumer's equilibrium when there is change in the money income of the consumer, *ceteris paribus*.

Income Elasticity of Demand: Income elasticity of demand is a measure of the responsiveness of the quantity demanded of a good to a change in the income of the consumer, *ceteris paribus*.

Increase in Demand: An increase in demand is an increase in the demand for the good as a result of a change in any of the factors, which influence the demand other than the price of the good itself, for example, an increase in the price of the substitute good or a rise in the consumer's income.

Increase in Supply: An increase in supply is an increase in the supply of the good as a result of a change in any of the factors, which influence the supply other than the price of the good itself.

Increasing Returns to Scale: Increasing returns to scale occur when all the factors of production are increased simultaneously in the same proportion and there is an increase in the output, which is more than the proportionate.

Indifference Curve: An indifference curve depicts the various combinations of two goods, which give the same level of satisfaction or utility to the consumer.

Indifference Map: A set of indifference curves represents an indifference map.

Indirect Taxes: Indirect taxes are levied indirectly and include sales tax and excise tax. They are paid as a part of the price of the good.

Individual Demand: Individual demand is the quantity of a good that an individual is willing to purchase at a certain price over a given time.

Induced Investment: Investment which changes due to a change in income and the interest rate is called induced investment.

Input: An input is in the form of a service or a good that is used in the process of production.

Interest: Interest is a payment made for the services of capital. It is often defined as the price, which is paid for borrowed funds. Thus, it is the amount, which is paid by the borrowers to the lenders for using their funds.

Internal Diseconomies: These are diseconomies which are not in any way dependent on the actions of other firms.

Internal Economies: These are economies which are not dependent on the actions of other firms. An individual firm experiences them when it expands its production.

Internal Rate of Return: The internal rate of return is the rate of discount, which equates the net present value of the future net cash flows to the investment cost of the project.

International Monetary System: The International Monetary System refers to the institutions, rules, regulations and the policies, which are involved in determining the foreign exchange rates.

Investment: Investment can be defined as the value of that portion of an economy's output for any time that takes the form of new producer's durable equipment, new structures and the change in inventories.

IS Curve: The *IS* curve is a graphic representation of the goods market equilibrium showing the different combinations of the output levels and the interest rates at which saving equals the investment (or planned spending is equal to income).

Isocost Line: The isocost line represents the various combinations of the factors, for example, labour and capital, which the firm can purchase given the total outlay and the prices of the factors of production. It is also called the outlay line or factor price line.

Isoquant: An isoquant depicts the various combinations of two factors of production, for example, labour and capital, using which a firm can produce the same level of output.

Law of Demand: According to the law of demand, there exists a negative relationship between the quantity demanded of a good and the price of the good, assuming that the price of the other goods, income of the consumer and tastes and preferences of the consumer remain the same.

Law of Diminishing Marginal Utility: According to the law of diminishing marginal utility as the quantity consumed of any one good increases, while the consumption of all other goods consumed remains constant, the marginal utility from the good must eventually decrease.

Law of Equi-marginal Utility: The law of equi-marginal utility analyses the equilibrium of the consumer when he consumes more than one good.

Law of Returns to Scale: The law of returns to scale occurs in the long run where to increase production all the factors of production are increased.

Law of Supply: According to the law of supply, other things remaining the same, the quantity supplied of a good increases when the price of the good increases and decreases when the price decreases.

Law of Variable Proportions: The law of variable proportions occurs in the short run when to increase production only one of the factors of production is increased while the others are kept fixed.

LM Curve: The *LM* curve is a graphic representation of the money market equilibrium showing the different combinations of the output levels and the interest rates at which the demand for money is equal to the supply of money.

Long Run: The long run is that time in which the supply of most of the factors of production is elastic, though the production technology is assumed to remain unchanged.

Long-Run Costs: Long-run costs are those incurred over the long run, which is that time in which the supply of most of the factors of production is elastic. Thus, all the factors of production can be changed in the long run.

Macroeconomics: Macroeconomics is the study of how the national economy as a whole grows and the changes which occur over time.

Managerial Economics: Managerial economics is that discipline which requires the application of economics in the complex business decision-making process to formulate and achieve the rational managerial objectives.

Marginal Cost: *MC* is the addition to the *TC* as the output level is raised by one more unit. It is calculated as $\frac{\partial(TC)}{\partial Q}$.

Marginal Efficiency of Investment Schedule: The MEI schedule depicts the relationship between the economy's investment and rate of interest when the change in the price of capital goods is taken into consideration.

Marginal Physical Product (MPP): Marginal physical product is the change in the total product due to the employment of an additional unit of the variable factor, all other factors remaining the same.

Marginal Product: The marginal product is the change in the total product when additional amounts of the variable factor are employed.

Marginal Productivity Theory: According to the marginal productivity theory, the price of a factor like labour is determined by the marginal productivity of labour.

Marginal Propensity to Consume: The MPC is defined as the increase in the consumption per unit of increase in the income.

Marginal Propensity to Import: The marginal propensity to import is the fraction of any change in income that will be devoted to imports.

Marginal Rate of Technical Substitution: The marginal rate of technical substitution of labour for capital, $MRTS_{LK}$, is the quantity of capital that a firm is ready to give up for an additional unit of labour so that the level of output remains the same.

Marginal Revenue Product (MRP): Marginal revenue product is the change in the total revenue due to the employment of an additional unit of the variable factor, all other factors remaining the same. We can write $MRP = MPP \times MR$.

Marginal Revenue: Marginal Revenue is the change in the total revenue when the output changes by one unit. It is calculated as $\frac{\partial(TR)}{\partial Q}$.

Marginal Utility: Marginal utility of a good is the change in the total utility from consuming an additional unit of the good.

Market: A market is a place, where the buyers and the sellers of a good are in close contact with each other, where the contact may be direct or indirect.

Market Demand: Market demand is the total quantity of a good that is demanded by all the individuals in the market at certain price over a given time.

Market Supply Schedule: The market supply schedule shows the different quantities of good *x* supplied, per time period, by all the producers of good *x* in the market, at different prices, *ceteris paribus*. Hence, it is the aggregate of the supply of the entire producers of good *x* in the market.

Microeconomics: Microeconomics is a branch of economics, which analyses the market behaviour and the decision-making process of the individual consumer and firm and also the interactions between individual buyer and seller.

Monetary Policy: Monetary policy is an operation by the monetary authorities of the country to achieve certain well-defined macroeconomic objectives/goals.

Monopolistic Competition: Monopolistic competition is a market structure, where there are many firms in the market selling close substitutes (but not identical) for the good. Each firm has some discretion in fixing the price of its product.

Monopoly: Monopoly is a market structure, where there is a single seller of the good in the market with no close substitutes for the good. There is very little competition with the firm exercising a great deal of control over the price of the good.

Moral Suasion: Moral suasion is a combination of persuasion and pressures, which a central bank asserts to bring the erring banks in line so that they function in accordance with the central bank's directives.

Multiplier: The multiplier can be defined as the amount by which there occurs a change in the equilibrium level of income due to a change in autonomous aggregate expenditure by one unit.

Net Investment: Net investment is an accretion to the stock of capital.

Nominal GDP: Nominal GDP is the total of the value of the goods and services calculated at current prices.

Oligopoly: Oligopoly is a market structure, where there are a few sellers of the product, which may be homogenous or differentiated. Duopoly is a situation, where there are just two sellers of the product.

Open Economy: Open economy is an economy, which is engaged in trade with the rest of the world.

Open Market Operations: Open market operations are the sale and purchase of government securities and treasury bills by the central bank.

Opportunity Cost: Opportunity cost is the cost of the alternative option, which has been lost by putting the scarce resources in the present option.

Outcome: Outcome is the result, which appears due to the implementation of the strategy.

Output: An output is a service or a good that results from the process of production.

Overvaluation: Overvaluation of a currency is said to occur when the official value of a currency is fixed at a higher rate than would have been determined by the free market forces of demand and supply.

Partial Equilibrium Analysis: A partial equilibrium analysis is based on the assumption of *ceteris paribus*, that is we assume everything, other than the market we are analysing, to be constant.

Partial Equilibrium Approach: Partial equilibrium approach involves the determination of the equilibrium price and output in each market, *ceteris paribus*.

Payback Period Method: The payback period of a project is the number of years that it takes for the total net cash flows from the project to become equal to the total investment outlay involved in the project.

Perceived Demand Curve: The perceived demand curve of the firm depicts the demand for the good of one firm assuming that the other firms in the group do not change the price of their good.

Perfect Competition: Under perfect competition, there are a large number of buyers and sellers of the good. The price of a good is determined in the market by the demand and the supply. The firm does not have any discretion in fixing the price of the good.

Personal Income: Personal income is the income received by households and the non-corporate businesses.

Precautionary Demand for Money: The precautionary demand for money is the demand for cash by the public for contingencies, which may involve unexpected expenditures and opportunities.

Present Value of a Capital Asset: The present value of a capital asset is the sum obtained after discounting the expected future yields over its entire life at the market rate of interest.

Price Consumption Curve: The price consumption curve is the locus of points representing the consumer's equilibrium when there is change in the price of a good assuming that there is no change in the money income of the consumer, price of the other good and the tastes and preferences of the consumer.

Price Discrimination: Price discrimination is a situation when different prices are charged from different consumers for the sale of the same good at the same point in time.

Price Effect: The change in the demand for a good due to a change in its price, *ceteris paribus*, is called the price effect. The price effect can be split into two effects, substitution effect and income effect.

Price Elasticity of Demand: Price elasticity of demand is a measure of the responsiveness of the quantity demanded of a good to a change in the price of the good.

Private Cost: Private cost is the monetary cost, which a firm incurs in the production of a good.

Private Investment: Private investment refers to the investment in the private sector.

Probability: Probability is the possibility of the occurrence of a given outcome. The sum of probabilities of all possible outcomes of each strategy will be equal to one.

Production: In the simplest terms, production is a process where inputs (factors of production) are converted into an output.

Production Costs: Production costs include all the costs, which a firm incurs to manufacture the good and then to provide it to the consumer to meet his demand for the good.

Production Function: The production function is a technological relationship between the physical inputs and physical output in a particular time, given the technology.

Production Possibility Frontier: The production possibility frontier depicts the different combinations of the two goods x and y that an economy can produce by utilizing all of its resources of capital and labour given the techniques of production. Each point on the production possibility frontier is an efficient allocation of the inputs.

Profit: Profit is the residual that is left after all the costs of production have been covered.

Proportionate Demand Curve: The proportionate demand curve of the firm depicts the demand for the good of one firm when all the other firms in the group charge the same price and also change the price of their good simultaneously.

Public Investment: Public investment refers to the investment in the public sector.

Qualitative or Selective Measures of Monetary Policy: The qualitative measures control the direction and distribution of credit in the economy.

Quantitative Measures of Monetary Policy: The quantitative measures control the total volume of credit and the cost of credit in the economy and hence the expansion or contraction in the total amount of credit and thus the supply of money.

Reaction Curve: A reaction curve shows the profit-maximizing output that a firm will produce expressed as a function of what it thinks will be produced by the other firm.

Real GDP: Real GDP is the total of the value of goods and services calculated at constant prices.

Repo Rate: Repo rate is the rate at which the central bank infuses short-term liquidity into the system.

Required Reserves: Required reserves are cash balances which banks hold to meet their statutory reserve requirements.

Reverse Repo Rate: Reverse repo rate is the rate at which banks park their short-term excess liquidity with the central bank in exchange for government securities.

Ridge Lines: Ridge lines are the locus of points formed by the isoquants on which the marginal product of the factors is zero.

Risk: Risk is a situation, where there exists more than one outcome to an investment decision and the investor is aware of (or can calculate) the probability of each outcome. For example, as far as investment in a stock is concerned, there is more than one possible outcome of which the investor is aware of and can calculate the probability of each outcome on the basis of past experience.

Say's Law: The most famous tenet of Say's law is 'supply creates its own demand'.

Second Degree Price Discrimination: Under second degree price discrimination, the monopolist divides the different markets into sub-markets or blocks charging a different price from each block.

Selling Costs: Selling costs are costs, which a firm incurs to change not only the position, but also to change the shape of the demand curve for the good.

Shifts in Supply: A shift in supply curve is caused by a change in any of the factors, which influence the supply other than the price of the good itself. These factors include changes in technology and in government policies.

Short Run: The short run is that time in which the supply of some of the factors of production is inelastic or fixed.

Short-Run Cost: Short-run costs are those incurred over the short run, which is that time in which the supply of some of the factors of production is inelastic or fixed, for example, machinery.

Social Cost: Social cost is the real cost, which the society incurs in the production of a good, for example, pollution from a factory, which affects the health of people adversely.

Speculation: Speculation is an activity relating to the sale and purchase of foreign exchange in which risk is undertaken to take advantage of the fluctuations in the exchange rate.

Speculative Demand for Money: Often people hold money, which is in excess of their transactions and precautionary demand for money. This is money, which is held for purposes of speculation in the stock market. It is called the speculative demand for money and is inversely related to the rate of interest.

Spot Transaction: A spot transaction is one, where the seller of the foreign exchange has to deliver the exchange to the buyer on the spot, that is, within two days of the deal.

Stabilization: Stabilization means controlling the ups and downs of a business cycle without interfering in any way with the economic growth of the country.

States of Nature: States of Nature refers to the conditions, which exist in the long run and over which the investor does not have any control. These conditions influence the results of the strategy, for example, recession, boom, etc.

Static Models: Static Models are those models, where the relationship between the different variables relates to the same period in time.

Statutory Liquidity Requirement: The statutory liquidity requirement is a statutory requirement where the banks are required to maintain a certain fixed proportion of their demand and time liabilities in the form of designated liquid assets.

Stock: Stock is a quantity, which is measured at a point in time.

Strategy: Strategy is one of the various alternative actions that can be taken to achieve a desired goal.

Subsistence Level: Subsistence level is the minimum level, which is required for survival.

Supply Curve: The supply curve is a graphical representation of the supply schedule. It is upward sloping showing the inverse relationship between the price and the quantity supplied of a good.

Supply of a Good: The supply of a good is the total amount of a good, which the producer is willing to produce and supply at a particular price over a certain time.

Supply Price of a Capital Asset: The supply price of a capital asset is the cost of replacing the capital asset, which is under consideration, with a new one.

Supply Schedule: A supply schedule depicts the quantity of the good, which is supplied at each price, assuming that other things remain the same (*ceteris paribus* assumption).

Terms of Trade: Terms of trade is the rate at which the goods of one country are exchanged for the goods of another country.

Third Degree Price Discrimination: Under third degree price discrimination, the monopolist divides the consumers of the good into different sub-markets or different groups and charges a different price from each one of them.

Total Cost: *TC* is the total of all costs involved in producing a given output level. It is calculated as the sum of total fixed cost and total variable cost.

Total Product: The total product is the total output of a good, which is produced by a firm during a specific time. It can be increased by applying the additional amounts of the variable factor.

Total Revenue: Total revenue can be defined as the total proceeds earned by a firm from the sale of a certain amount of the output. It is calculated as price multiplied by the quantity sold or $TR = P \times Q$.

Total Utility: Total utility is the sum of the utility, which a consumer derives from the consumption of the different units of a good.

Transactions Demand for Money: The transactions demand for money is the demand for cash by the public for carrying on its various current transactions.

Transfer Earnings: Transfer earnings can be defined as the amount that a factor of production expects to earn if transferred to its next best use. Thus, it is the amount that the factor should earn if it has to remain in its present use. It is also called the reservation price or the opportunity cost.

Transfer Payments: Transfer payments are those government payments, which do not involve any direct services by the recipient, for example, welfare payments, unemployment insurance and others.

Uncertainty: Uncertainty is a situation, where there exists more than one outcome to an investment decision and the investor is not aware of (and cannot calculate) the probability of each outcome. For example, as far as the drilling of oil in a field is concerned, there is no past experience in that field.

Undervaluation: Undervaluation of a currency is said to occur when the official value of a currency is fixed at a lower rate than would have been determined by the free market forces of demand and supply.

Unilateral Transfers: Unilateral transfers (also called unrequited transfers) are one way transactions as there is no claim involved as far as repayment is concerned, either at present or in the future.

Utility: The utility of a good is the power of the good to satisfy a want.

Utility Possibility Frontier: The utility possibility frontier depicts the different combinations of utility of the two goods *x* and *y* that are received by the consumers when the economy is in a general equilibrium of exchange. It is also called the welfare frontier.

Value of the Marginal Product (VMP): Value of the marginal product is the value of the additional product due to the employment of an additional unit of the variable factor, all other factors remaining the same. We can write $VMP = MPP \times P_x$.

Variable Cost: Variable cost is the cost, which varies with the level of output. It includes cost of raw material, labour, fuel and others.

Variable Factor: A variable factor is one, where the supply is always elastic in the short run.

Wages Fund: Wages fund is the stock out of which the wages are paid.

Index

A

Adam Smith's theory of absolute advantage, 437–438
advertising elasticity
    defined, 54–55
    factors influencing, 55
    types, 55–56
aggregate demand–aggregate supply approach
    four-sector economy, 350, 351–353
    three-sector economy, 338–340
    two-sector economy, 312–315
aggregate demand for consumers' goods, 306
aggregate demand function, 306, 311–312
    shifts in, 317–318, 328–331
arc elasticity of demand, 46
autarky equilibrium, 442–443
automatic stabilizer, 427
autonomous consumption, 308
autonomous tax receipts, 344
average propensity to consume (APC), 308
average propensity to save (APS), 309

B

balanced budget multiplier, 346–347
balance of payment
    capital account, 468–469
    current account, 467–468
    disequilibrium, 473–474, 473–475
    double entry system of bookkeeping, 471–473
    foreign currencies, 469
    gold, 469
    loan repayments, 469
    long-term movements of capital, 468–469
    meaning and structure, 467–471
    process of adjustment, 476–482
    short-term movements of capital, 469
    special depository receipts (SDRs), 469–470
banking sector
    central bank, 512–515
    commercial bank, 515–517
    development bank, 517–519
barter economy, 294
break-even analysis, 161–163
break even points, 15
budget line, 95–96
    shifts in, 96–97
business cycles, 290
    bank rate policy and, 426
    cash reserve ratio (CRR), 425
    credit rationing, 426
    direct actions, 426
    discretionary fiscal policy and, 427–428
    factors influencing, 425–428
    fiscal policy and, 426
    government expenditure and, 426
    margin requirement, 426
    monetary overinvestment theory, 423
    monetary policies and, 425
    moral suasion, 426
    multiplier–accelerator interaction theory, 423–424
    open market operations, 425
    phases in, 421–422
    public borrowing and, 427
    pure monetary theory, 422
    qualitative measures control, 426
    repo rate, 426
    reverse repo rate, 426
    Schumpeter's innovation theory, 424
    stabilization policies, 424–425
    statutory liquidity ratio (SLR), 425
    variations in reserve requirements, 425
business economics, 6–7
business firm
    objectives, 10

C

capital, 392
    marginal efficiency of (MEC), 397–400
capital accumulation
    and rate of interests, 402–403
    and shift in MEC schedule, 403–405
capital budgeting
    cost of capital, 226
    decision to invest under certainty, 223–225
    decision to invest under risk and uncertainty, 226–229
    decision tree method, 228–229
    defined, 219–220
    determination of the optimum level of capital, 221–222
    internal rate of return, 224–225
    maximax regret criterion, 229
    maximin decision criterion, 229
    net discounted present value method, 223–224
    payback period, 223
    payoff matrix approach, 227–228
    probability theory approach, 228
    risk-adjusted discount rate approach, 228
    significance, 220
    sources of capital, 225–226
    steps, 220–221
cardinal utility, 77, 109–110
    limitations, 83–84
    marginal, 78
    total, 77–78
cartels, 210–211
Clark's profit theory, 12
classical economics, 300

Cobb Douglas production function, 126
consumer's equilibrium, 98–99
  and income consumption curve, 99–100
  and price consumption curve, 100–102
consumer surplus
  Hicks' concept, 108
  Marshall's concept, 107–108
consumption
  autonomous, 308
  function, 307
  linear form of function, 308
  non-linear form of function, 307
  spending, 306
corporate income tax, 344
cost
  average, 153
  average fixed, 153
  average variable, 153
  marginal, 153
  total, 151, 153
  total fixed, 151
  total variable, 152
cost function
  basic concepts, 149–150
  long-run, 150, 156–157
  short-run, 150–155
cost volume profit analysis. *see* break-even analysis
Cournot Duopoly model, 206–208
Cournot equilibrium, 208
cross price elasticity of demand
  defined, 53
  significance, 54
  types, 53–54

D

decision-making process, managerial, 6
  incremental principle, 20
  marginal principle, 19
  opportunity cost principle, 19–20
demand
  change in, 32
  and consumer's income, 30–31
  curve, derivation of, 105
  curve, downward sloping of, 28–29
  defined, 25
  elasticity of, 40–47
  for foreign exchange, 452–453
  function, 25
  income effect, 28, 104
  inferior good, case of, 31
  law of, 25–26
  law of diminishing marginal utility, 29
  market, 27
  normal good, case of, 30
  price effect, 29
  and price of other goods, 29–30
  schedule, 25–26
  shift in, 32–33
  substitution effect, 28, 104
  and tastes/preferences of consumer, 31–32
discounting process, 395–396
diseconomies of scale, 160
disposable personal income, 276
distribution, theory of
  wages, 235
dynamic theory of profit, 245–246

E

economic growth
  concept, 414
  factors determining, 414–415
  Harrod–Domar model, 416–418
  neo-classical growth theory, 418–420
  theories of, 415–420
economic objectives of a firm, 16–17
economic problems of scarcity, 1–2
economies of scale, 158–159
elasticity of demand, 40–47
elasticity of price expectations
  defined, 56
  types, 56–57
elasticity of substitution, 138–139
elasticity of supply
  defined, 57–58
  factors influencing, 58
  types, 58–59
entry, prevention of, 15
equilibrium, 38–39
  consumer's, 98–99
  with trade, 443–445
ex ante saving and investment, 313
exchange rate system, 450–460
  demand, 452–453
  disequilibrium, 455–456
  equilibrium, 455
  fixed, determination, 457–458
  fixed *vs* flexible, 458–460
  fluctuations in rates, 456–457
  rate determination, 451–458
  supply, 453–455
ex post saving and investment, 313
external economies of scale, 159

F

fiscal policy
  instruments, 504–509
  limitations, 509–512
  meaning, 504
forecasting of demand
  of aggregate demand, 69
  complete enumeration method, 70
  consumer survey method, 70–71
  defined, 68
  Delphi technique, 71
  direct interview method, 70
  expert opinion method, 71
  individual firm's demand, 69
  long-term, 69
  market experiments method, 71–72

sample survey method, 70
short-term, 69
time series analysis, 72
of total industry demand, 69
using survey of sales force, 71
foreign exchange market
arbitrage, 449
exchange rate system, 450–460
functions, 449
speculation, 449–450
transactions, 448–449
foreign trade multilplier, 354–355
four-sector economy, 348–349
aggregate demand, 349
aggregate demand–aggregate supply approach, 350–353
exports, 349
government transfer payments, 351–353
imports, 349
leakages equal injections approach, 350–351, 353
multilpliers, 354–355

G

game theory, 212–214
general equilibrium of production and exchange, 261–266
assumptions, 262
production possibility frontier, 263, 266
slope of the indifference curve, 266
Giffen goods, 106
government expenditure multiplier, 345–347
government transfer payments, 342–343
grand utility possibility curve, 268–269
Great Depression era, 300
gross domestic product (GDP), 274
and economic activity, 275
imputations, 274
intermediate goods, 274
inventories, 274
nominal, 274
and other measures of income, 275–276
real, 274, 275
gross national income (GNI), 279
gross national product (GNP), 273–275, 391

H

Hawley's profit theory, 13
Heckscher–Ohlin theory of trade, 441–445
autarky equilibrium, 442–443
equilibrium with trade, 443–445
Human Development Index, 280

I

income consumption curve, 99–100
income elasticity of demand
defined, 51
significance, 52
types, 51–52
income tax, 344
Indian economy
balance of payment, 483
foreign exchange reserves, 484
monetary policy, 501
performance of, 482
Indian economy, selected indicators of, 281–282
indifference curve analysis
appplications, 110
assumptions, 89–90
characteristics, 91–93
defined, 90–91
exceptional cases, 93–94
limitations, 108–109
slope of, 266
individual
demand curve, 26–27
demand schedule of an, 26
inferior goods, 106
innovation theory of profit, 247–248
interests
and capital accumulation, 402–403
classical theory, 248–249
Keynesian theory, 252–253
neo-classical theory, 249–252
rate determination, 251, 254
internal economies of scale, 158–159
internal rate of return, 224–225
international monetary system, 484–486
Bretton Woods system, 485–486
gold standard, 485
special drawing rights (SDRs), 486
investment
accelerator theory, 405–407
autonomous, 394
basic concepts, 392–394
capital, 392
decision to invest, 394
defined, 392
discounting process, 395–396
flexible accelerator theory, 407–408
gross, 392–393
induced, 393
marginal efficiency of (MEI), 400–401
net, 392–393
present value of a capital asset, 395–396
private, 393
public, 393
q theory, 408
investment expenditure, 392
investment multiplier, 318
IS-LM model
shift in, 378–381
two-sector economy, 366–367
isocost line, 134–135
isoproduct curve, 130
isoquants, 130–133

K

Keynesian economics, 288
Keynesian theory for interest rate, 252–253
Knight's profit theory, 12–13

L

labour
  aggregate demand schedule for, 296–297
  aggregate supply curve of, 298, 299
  demand for, 296–297
  determination of wage rate, 241
  firm's demand curve for, 237–239, 238–239
  individual firm's demand curve for, 240
  market in classical theory, 296
  profit maximising effect, 239–240
  short-run aggregate demand for, 297
  substitution effect, 239
  supply, 241, 297–299
law of demand, 80–82
law of diminishing marginal utility, 78–80
law of equi-marginal utility, 83
law of returns to scale
  constant, 142–143
  decreasing, 143–144
  increasing, 140–142
leakages equal injections approach
  four-sector economy, 350–351, 353
  three-sector economy, 338–341
linear consumption function, 308
liquidity, 17
loanable funds
  demand for, 250
  supply of, 250
long-run equilibrium of a firm, 175–176
long-run survival, 17

M

macroeconomics, 3–4
  classical school of thought, 288
  comparative statics, 292–293
  consumers' interest, 289–290
  disequilibrium, 291–292
  dynamic model, 292
  and economy's performance, 290
  equilibrium, 291–292
  firms' interest, 289–290
  general equilibrium analysis, 293
  governments' interest, 289–290
  Keynesian economics, 288
  Marshall's partial equilibrium analysis, 293
  need to study, 289–290
  partial equilibrium analysis, 293
  post-Keynesian economics, 288–289
  Say's law, 294–295
  static model, 292
  stocks and flows, 291
managerial economics
  application, 5
  and business economics, 6–7
  decision making, role in, 5
  defined, 1–3
  forecasting, role in, 5
  need to study, 4
manager's utility function, 15
marginal efficiency of capital (MEC), 397–400
marginal effi ciency of investment, 224–225
marginal efficiency of investment (MEI), 400–401
marginal productivity theory, 235
marginal propensity to consume (MPC), 308
marginal propensity to save (MPS), 309–310
marginal utility, 78
  law of diminishing, 78–80
  law of equi-, 83
market structures, types of, 169
microeconomics, 2–4
monetary policy
  deficit financing, 500
  instruments, 493
  limitations, 503
  meaning, 493
  measures, 494–500
money, demand for
  precautionary, 252–253
  speculative, 253
  transactions, 252
money economy, 294
monopolistic competition, 169
  characteristics, 192–193
  equilibrium of a firm, 193–194
  excess capacity, 196–197
  long-run equilibrium of a firm, 196
  selling costs, 198–199
  short-run equilibrium of a firm, 194–195
monopoly, 169
  average cost pricing, 191–192
  characteristics, 181–182
  control of, 191–192
  firm's revenue curves under, 182–185
  long-run equilibrium of a firm, 187–188
  lump sum tax, 191
  marginal cost pricing, 191–192
  price discrimination, 188–191
  relationship between average revenue, marginal revenue and elasticity of demand, 184–185
  short equilibrium of a firm, 185–186
  types, 182
multilplier
  foreign trade, 354–355
  four-sector economy, 354–355
multiplier
  alternative derivation of, 320–321
  applicability of, 322–323
  balanced budget, 346–347
  conditions necessary, 322–323
  government expenditure, 345–347
  investment, 318
  and paradox of thrift, 323–324
  shifts in, 328–331
  tax, 346, 347
  three-sector economy, 345–347
  uses and limitations, 321–322
  working of, 319–320

N

national income (NI), 276, 290
- expenditures, 278
- gross domestic product (GDP), 274–276
- gross national product (GNP), 273–274
- incomes, 278
- measurement of, 277–280
- net income from abroad, 278–280
- problems in measuerment, 280–283

net discounted present value method, 223–224
net national product (NNP), 276
non-economic objectives of a firm, 18
non-linear consumption function, 307

O

oligopoly, 169
- causes, 204–205
- characteristics, 205–206
- collusive models, 210–214
- Cournot Duopoly model, 206–208
- non-collusive, 206–208
- Sweezy's kinked demand curve model, 208–209

optimization process
- constrained, 20
- steps, 20
- unconstrained, 20

ordinal utility, 77, 109–110

P

payback period, 223
perfect competition, 169
- applications, 176–178
- characteristics, 170
- firm's revenue curves under, 171–172

personal income, 276
point elasticity of demand, 44–45
point of maximum social welfare, 269
post-Keynesian economics, 288–289
precautionary demand for money, 252–253
present value of a capital asset, 395–396
price consumption curve, 100–102
price discrimination, 188–191
- conditions necessary for, 188
- degrees of, 189–190
- meaning, 188

price elasticity of demand
- arc, 46
- defined, 40–41
- factors influencing, 41
- on a linear demand curve, 46–47
- outlay method of measurement, 43–44
- percentage method of measurement, 42–43
- point, 44–45

price leadership, 211–212
prisoner's dilemma, 212–214
production function, 295–296
- basic concepts, 125
- characteristics, 126
- Cobb Douglas, 126
- economic region of production, 139
- elasticity of substitution, 138–139
- equilibium of producer, 135–137
- expansion path, 138
- expression, 126
- general equilibrium of production, 262–263
- ineffi cient range of production, 139–140
- isocost line, 134–135
- isoquants, 130–133
- law of variable proportions, 127
- long-run, 129
- production possibility frontier, 263, 266
- short-run aggregate, 295–296
- stages of production, 127–129

profit
- as a control mechanism, 18
- dynamic theory, 245–246
- innovation theory, 247–248
- nature and measurement, 11–12
- risk theory, 246–247
- theories, 12–13
- uncertainty theory, 247

profit contribution analysis. *see* break-even analysis
profit maximization
- algebraic expression, 13–14
- graphical representation, 14–16
- managerial decentralization for, 18
- marginal approach, 15–16
- total approach, 14–15

Q

quasi-income effect, 120
quasi-substitution effect, 120

R

rent
- defined, 242
- modern theory of, 243–245
- Ricardo's theory, 242–243

revealed preference theory
- assumptions, 118–119
- contributions, 120–121
- defined, 117–118
- and law of demand, 119
- limitations, 121
- quasi-income effect, 120
- quasi-substitution effect, 120

revenue concepts
- average, 47–49
- marginal, 47–49
- relationship with price elasticity, 47–49, 50

Ricardian theory of comparative advantage, 439–440
Ricardo's theory of rent, 242–243
risk avoidance, 15
risk theory of profit, 246–247

S

sales revenue maximization, 15
satisfying behaviour, 16–17
saving
  aggregate demand function, 311–312
  average propensity to save (APS), 309
  function, 309
  marginal propensity to save (MPS), 309–310
  relationship between APC and APS, 310
  relationship between MPC and MPS, 310–311
saving–investment approach, 313–317, 367–369, 373
Say's law, 294–295, 300
Schumpeter's profit theory, 12
short-run aggregate production function, 295–296
short-run equilibrium of a firm, 172–175
social welfare function, 269
speculative demand for money, 253
stabilization in economy, 427
stationary equilibrium, 292
subsistence theory of wages, 235
supply
  change in, 36–37
  contraction of, 37
  curve, 34
  curve, upward slope of, 35
  defined, 34
  expansion of, 37
  for foreign exchange, 453–455
  function, 34
  market, 35
  schedule, 34
  shifts in, 37–38
  single producer and, 35
supply of labour, 297–299
  determination of employment, real wage rate and output, 299–300
Sweezy's kinked demand curve model, 208–209

T

taxes, 344
tax multiplier, 346–347
three-sector economy
  aggregate demand–aggregate supply approach, 338–340
  equilibrium income or output in a, 337
  government transfer payments, 342–343
  leakages equal injections approach, 338–341
  models of income determination, 338–341
  multipliers, 345–347
  taxes, 344
trade
  balance of, 467
  balance of invisible, 467–468
  gross barter terms, 445–446
  income terms, 446
  net barter terms, 445
  policy, 447–448
transactions demand for money, 252
two-sector economy
  aggregate demand–aggregate supply approach, 312–315, 367, 372–373
  equilibrium in markets, 372–377
  goods market equilibrium, 367–369
  goods market equilibrium condition, 372–375
  income determination, 323–328
  IS-LM model, 366–367
  money market equilibrium condition, 369–371
  multipler, 318–324
  process of adjustment, 377–378
  saving–investment approach, 313–317, 367–369, 373
  shifts in aggregate demand and multiplier, 328–331

U

uncertainty theory of profit, 247
unrequited/unilateral transfers, 468
utility
  cardinal, 77
  defined, 76–77
  ordinal, 77
utility possibility frontier, 267–268

W

wages
  determination under perfect competition, 235–240
wages fund theory, 235
Walker's profit theory, 12
welfare economics
  conditions, 267
  grand utility possibility curve, 268–269
  social welfare function, 269
  utility possibility frontier, 267–268